D0850116

FROM KNIGHTS
TO PIONEERS

ONE GERMAN FAMILY IN
WESTPHALIA AND MISSOURI

Anita M. Mallinckrodt

Southern Illinois University Press

Carbondale and Edwardsville

Designed by Chiquita Babb
Production supervised by Chiquita Babb

Library of Congress Cataloging-in-Publication Data

Mallinckrodt, Anita M.
    From knights to pioneers : one German family in Westphalia and
Missouri / Anita M. Mallinckrodt.
      p.   cm.
    Includes bibliographical references (p.) and index.
     1. German Americans—Missouri—Biography. 2. Mallinckrodt family.
3. Westphalia (Germany)—Biography.   I. Title.
F475.G3M34   1994
977.8′00431′00922—dc20
  [B]   93-16891
                                                        CIP

ISBN 0-8093-1917-9

A subvention from Mallinckrodt, Inc., helped make publication of this
volume possible.

The paper used in this publication meets the minimum requirements of
American National Standard for Information Sciences—Permanence of
Paper for Printed Library Materials, ANSI Z39.48-1984. ∞

For my dear brother
Hubert E. Mallinckrodt

and in memory of our parents
Hubert W. and Olga M. Mallinckrodt
who taught us to be proud of who we are

Contents

Contents

Contents

Contents

Plates

Figures

Figures

Preface

Many people today have great difficulty imagining the lives of their ancestors. Except among historians or history buffs, for example, there is little understanding of the Middle Ages' agriculturally based feudalism, that is, the manorial system of land ownership by lords, whose unfree serfs were tied to the land in exchange for the lord's protection, and knights that had its heyday in the ninth century. In Germany as elsewhere, feudalism was gradually replaced by the rise of urbanization and the founding of towns and guilds. The age of the Renaissance, which began in the fourteenth century, also seems remote, although it was a period made remarkable by the rejection of medieval values, the loosening of feudal and ecclesiastic restrictions, and the growth of nation states and commercial innovation. The age of the Enlightenment seems a little nearer because of the American War of Independence and the French Revolution, two events that introduced values and forms of government that subsequently triggered waves of European immigration to the New World.

For many people, these centuries take on meaning only through personalization, that is, when history is somehow linked to individuals, not only to dates and maps and lists of monarchs. And if one is especially fortunate, that personalization can be found in one's own family history, in one's own "roots."

Preparation of this book has been just such an effort, for the chronicles of the Mallinckrodt family mirror the history of Germany from the titled (*von*) land-owning nobility (*Landadel*) of the Middle Ages through the Enlightenment and then to the development and settlement of the American Midwest during the period of immigration in the 1800s: from knight Ludwig (c. 1241) and crusader Gerd (c. 1450–1504); to Dortmund mayors Heinrich (1687–c. 1748), Bertram (1708–48), and Heinrich Zacharias (1733–88); from publisher Arnold (1768–1825) and politician Hermann (1821–74); to Pauline, the founder of the Order of the Sisters of Christian Charity beatified in 1985 (1817–81), and to the American pioneers Julius (1806–88) and Emil (1806–92).

This book, therefore, is more than just one family's history. Rather, the experiences related on these pages reflect those of many German families who left their mark on centuries of history and of many midwestern families transplanted from the Old World to the New. Especially interesting for some is the continuity between the old and new ways of life—entries on genealogical tables need not end with the abrupt comment "immigrated to the USA," for immigrants often wrote notable chapters of family history that deserve recognition in their old homelands. Similarly, knowledge of pre-immigration history is essential for those Americans whose traditions surely did not begin, as oral history often suggests, with the mere fact that "great-grandfather arrived in the Midwest from Germany in 1831." The purpose of this book, thus, is to set a family's emigration chapter against its European background, without passing judgment on the cultural influence of outstanding individuals in the United States or of German immigration per se. Rather, I hope to illustrate the fascination of history found in the intertwining and extensive root systems that connect centuries and continents.

Fascinating, as well, is the possibility of unearthing such root systems. In the case of this Mallinckrodt story, doing so became a series of research adventures. For example, German historical societies and museums still hold many family documents that have survived hundreds of years and the conflagrations of World War II bombings that had destroyed up to 60 percent of archive materials. Words cannot adequately describe the emotional thrill of finding stacks of fragile, yellowed pages in dusty, unordered archive boxes—great-great-grandmother's girlish diary in elegant, flowery old German script, great-great-grandfather's careful record of the births and baptisms of great-grandfather and all the great-granduncles and great-grandaunts, and the letter written back to Germany on the very day the family's first emigrants set foot on the soil of the New World. It is such yellowed, sometimes badly deteriorated, old documents that give life to computer-generated printouts of the Mallinckrodt family tree; on the other hand, that lifeless computerized data now enable researchers to work with biographic information much more efficiently than previously when huge tables, often incorrect and almost always awkward, were the primary source of genealogical history.

A challenge in turning such research into a book was the matter of translating centuries-old German into readable English. Because the pre-twentieth-century letters and documents are in old German script, the handwriting first had to be deciphered and then transcribed into modern typed German. To retain the tone of that language, translation required unending consultation with antiquated dictionaries, for old German utilized a vocabulary and style as outdated and florid, by today's standards, as Victorian English is to modern English. The spelling of names was a challenge, too—over the centuries Everhard became Eberhard, Kracht changed to Cracht, and Krombach became Crombach. Then, too, immigration brought changes through bilingualism and subsequent inconsistent spellings—a baptized Gustavus at times is Gustav, or Adolphus is referred to as Adolph or Adolf. And, of course, a name such as Mallinckrodt was spelled a dozen different ways by document-writers. The solution here was to use whatever spelling appeared in the source being cited.

Beyond the mechanics of translation, genealogically oriented historical writing always presents the additional problem of how much—that is, whom—to include. In the case of the Mallinckrodt family, "all" would be an impossible answer, for the twenty-four generations from 1241 to the present have included more than one thousand direct descendants. Some of their biographies, in fact, are already known to German readers through the masterly two-volume collection of family documents from the years 1250 to 1650 (*Urkundenbuch der Familie von Mallinckrodt*), which Gustav von Mallinckrodt IV (1859–1939) published in 1911, or through numerous individual studies based on those and other records. All that, however, remained largely unknown to non-German readers. At the same time, there was almost no substantive material available in either German or English to shed light on the U.S. immigration experiences of the Mallinckrodts. Clearly, then, what was needed was a work focusing on that, but against a summarized historical backdrop and in a societal context—in short, the sociocultural biographic genre.

To highlight the family's history, stories of some its leading personalities were selected to illustrate their long-ago and unknown times—the 1451 and 1492 adventures of the mercenary knights Hermann and his son Wilhelm; the 1594 feuding of the noble brothers Dietrich and Hermann, which led to a double murder. Other personalities were included to represent intellectual legacies and traditions—the liberal Dortmund publisher Arnold's struggles in the early 1800s to establish freedom of the press and to free Westphalian farmers from serfdom; the rich, aristocratic Sister Pauline's remarkable efforts to bring care to poor and blind children of her day.

To tell the emigration story, the focus was confined to the first Dortmund pioneers—Julius and Emil (who immigrated to America in 1831) and Conrad, Hermann, August, Helene, Sophie, and Luise (who immigrated in 1838)—and their immediate families in Germany and in Missouri. Theirs is the story of the 1830s immigrants who cleared the forests, built the schools and churches, supported the German-language periodicals, and founded social and cultural groups—in short, those who blazed a trail from which the later, much larger waves of immigrants benefited. The story ends with the death of these early Mallinckrodt pioneers in the 1890s, at a time when the family was well established in the Midwest.

This book, therefore, clearly does not pretend to be comprehensive. It is, instead, primarily an effort to fill some immigration-history gaps with information from letters and documents currently available to me. That there is much more awaiting discovery is obvious—until now few letters have been found from some of the immigrants to America, and in the extensive files of others' correspondence there are long chronological gaps. It is hoped that this book will stimulate more family historians to dig for treasures in their boxes of old papers.

Even within the limitations of time and space, the Mallinckrodt source material nevertheless suggests some gripping themes that seem to run through centuries of this family's history. Each reader will find his or her own, but for me these themes are striking: the corruption of close family relationships through conflicts about ownership and profit; the subordination of women (unless they bear the family name beyond marriage, women do not figure in genealogical tables or public information); precarious health conditions (for example, the perils of childbirth, often resulting in the deaths of mothers and infants, and the many fatal epidemics that led to countless remarriages and numerous step-relations); a deep family loyalty and love of children; a dedication to intellectual learning, social justice, and moral responsibility; a fierce personal independence, including opposition to authority and the restrictions of class; and an adventurousness and industriousness.

With gratitude I offer this book to the many people who helped shed light on 750 years of European-American history, especially members of the Mallinckrodt family here and there: Kurt for his invaluable computerized *Sippendatei* and painstaking transcriptions, Hannah for generous permission to use the family archives in Köln, Horst-Gerhard for patient explanations and precious illustrations, Roland (now deceased) and Philip for background information on the St. Louis and western branches of the family, respectively, and above all Hubert for unending clues, follow-up errands, and constant moral support and draft-reading.

Thanks, too, to the home-town residents of Augusta, Missouri, who helped with their memories and records: especially the late Monika Schell Struckhoff, who shared the stories she had heard and the information she had gathered while growing up on Julius Mallinckrodt's former home place, and Dan Kemner, who with much effort made available a copy of the record book of the village, beginning with its 1855 incorporation.

As always, special recognition is due knowledgeable and patient archivists, especially those in Dortmund, Köln, and Bremen. I extend my deep appreciation foremost to Missourians Martha Clevenger of the Missouri Historical Society in St. Louis and Carol Wilkins at the St. Charles Historical Society—they efficiently and cheerfully dug through files, offered advice, answered correspondence, and photocopied stacks of documents. Their efforts were not only crucial to the research but a joy to the researcher.

Also appreciated are the friendly readers whose keen challenges to text and style saved the manuscript from untold errors and flaws. In this context, Professor Patricia Herminghouse, of the University of Rochester, and Professor Walter D. Kamphoefner, of Texas A&M University, are warmly thanked.

Very special appreciation, too, to Mallinckrodt, Inc., of St. Louis, specifically to its former president, Raymond F. Bentele, for providing partial financial support of the publication of this study. A German-American immigration history enthusiast himself, he found this story of his company's background and respected name worthy of public recognition.

Thanks also to Kurt von Mallinckrodt for permission to reprint Appendix A and to the Historisches Archiv der Stadt, Köln, for portions of letters archived in the Mallinckrodt Nachlaß.

To all named above, as well as to the many other unidentified helpers and moral supporters of this book, I offer my most sincere gratitude—and also apologies if any of the light they shed was not accurately transmitted.

Sources

Two preserved collections of Mallinckrodt family letters are central to this study. The first consists of the letters of Emil Mallinckrodt (1806–92), of St. Louis, to his brother Eduard (1804–59) in Dortmund, Germany. These letters were returned to Emil after Eduard's death, along with several letters from their father to their deceased brother Wilhelm. Via family members, the thirty-nine letters were placed in the Missouri Historical Society archives in St. Louis. They are found in its "Mallinckrodt Family Papers 1809–1852" file, along with an English-language summary of the letters' highlights and a transcription of the old German script into modern German, prepared by Kurt von Mallinckrodt, of Hünxe/Krudenburg, Germany.

The second collection is composed of letters to Gustav Mallinckrodt I (1799–1856), of Köln, from his cousin Emil Mallinckrodt in St. Louis, as well as from other family members. These letters are on file in the Historisches Archiv der Stadt Köln, Abt. 1068 (von Mallinckrodt Nachlaß), a closed collection of more than one hundred cartons of documents gathered by Gustav von Mallinckrodt IV (1859–1939). Gustav I's letters are an especially rich source of family history. Regarding many matters they are the only primary information available, since other similar collections were not made or did not survive the passage of time. For instance, Missouri letters from Julius, Conrad, and Hermann Mallinckrodt to their mother, Dorothea, have not been found. Therefore, the (preserved) perspective of family affairs is often not balanced—it reflects primarily Gustav I's role within the family, that is, who wrote or did not write him about what, and what correspondence he chose to save.

The entire collection of letters transcribed for this study—39 from St. Louis and 169 from Köln—is available to researchers in Kurt von Mallinckrodt's monograph *Die Auswanderer der Familie Mallinckrodt* on file with the Historisches Archiv der Stadt Köln (von Mallinckrodt Nachlaß). Its detailed index—Appendix A at the end of this study—includes the date the letter was written, by whom from where, to whom and where, and the source where the original German script letter is archived. Thus, letters cited in this book are referenced in the endnotes in this manner: Appendix A, no. 10. Readers can consult in Köln and in St. Louis the entire transcribed text as well as its original German script. The excerpts appearing in this study were translated by the author.

Another significant set of documents is a scrapbook collection of editorials written by Emil Mallinckrodt for the St. Louis *Westliche Post*, especially those editorials of the late 1870s. After Emil's death, his daughter Adele Schulenberg gave the scrapbook to Emil's granddaughter, Emmy Wiskott Engelhardt. Following Emmy's death in

1946, it was found by her son-in-law Kurt Müller von Blumencron, who, fascinated by its reflections of German thought on emigration, prepared an index to it. In 1989, both the index and the original scrapbook were generously given by Blumencron's son Albrecht, of Hamburg, to the author for deposit with the Missouri Historical Society in St. Louis. Thus, in addition to being extensively cited in this study, Emil Mallinckrodt's editorials have "come home" to St. Louis where they were written.

Also central to biographic information cited in the study is Kurt von Mallinckrodt's computerized *Sippendatei derer von Mallinckrodt*, or family tree, also deposited with the Missouri Historical Society, the Historisches Archiv der Stadt Köln, and the Dortmund Stadtarchiv. Incorporating the family's genealogical tables in the Dortmund Stadtarchiv and innumerable later corrective and supplementary sources, the *Sippendatei* covers twenty-three to twenty-four generations of the Mallinckrodt family and more than one thousand persons. The enumerated entries, including parents and children, enable a researcher to easily trace an individual's predecessors and successors, as well as contemporaries. The *Sippendatei* identification number for Mallinckrodts referred to in this study is included in the index in brackets—Arnold I [90] (1563–1610)—and on the Mallinckrodt family tree in Appendix B.

Part I

Old Stories Father Told

1810, June.

Dortmund, Kingdom of Westphalia

The six children gathered around the heavy wooden table turned pleased eyes toward Father. At supper he had said he would spend only a little time tonight at his writing bureau with the ledger books in which he entered the day's business affairs. Instead, it was to be an evening of telling them family stories, as he often did. Beginning with the knights and feudal lords fighting over land, Father always slowly wove hundreds of years of their family's exciting past into a thread that led right to their own front door at Westenhellweg.

Father's name was Johann Friedrich Theodor, but the family only called him Theodor. Mother had been baptized Sibylla Clara Juliane Theodore Feldmann—but people called her Dorothea. And then there were the six children. Gustav, now eleven, was the oldest and next came Ferdinand, who was nine. Sometimes they seemed a bit sad when Father told about the past. Maybe it was because of the loving stories about their mother, the gracious, sophisticated Sophie Fabricius who had died when Ferdinand was born and Gustav was just two. After Father married Mother eight years ago, the other four of them had been born. Leopold was now six, Julius four, Conrad two, and Hermann was only several months old.

Father often pointed out that most of them had been born after their home town of Dortmund had ceased, unfortunately, to be a proud *Reichsstadt*, or free imperial city. That had happened, he explained, because there had been a revolution in France in 1789 in which the people had overthrown the rule of the king and the privileged so there might be a republic, a government of the people. Since some of the French wanted so much to spread their liberating new ideas, they declared war on Austria where a king still ruled. That's when Germans became involved. To help Austria, the big state of Prussia—itself ruled by a king—decided to go to war against France. And so many young Germans were sent off to fight.

3

Meanwhile, France's successful military leader, Napoleon Bonaparte, took over the government in Paris. Because he, too, wanted to spread the revolutionary French ideas about liberty for and equality of peoples, he sent his armies marching off in all directions. War declarations involved most European countries.

One result came in 1803—Prussia ceded the left bank of the Rhine River to France. When Napoleon set up the Confederation of the Rhine it included Dortmund, and thus the city lost its position as a *Reichsstadt*. After a few more years, Napoleon seized more Prussian territory between the Rhine and the Elbe rivers and made his brother Jerome king of the territory to be ruled from the city of Kassel. In 1807, then, it was declared the Kingdom of Westphalia and, of course, included Dortmund.

All these changes were quite confusing at times. As Father said, the revolutionary ideas were exciting and good, but foreign rule was quite another thing, especially in Dortmund with the long tradition that its own "city air is freedom." To help understand all that, Father always went way back into history, to beginnings.

As he cleared his throat and pushed his maps into a neat stack, everyone sat up a bit more erect. The children knew he would not begin "Once upon a time . . ." That, he said, was how one began stories that were legends, that is, maybe not true. His old stories, Father said, were true because they were based on legal and family records covering centuries. Their family, the Mallinckrodts, had been part of German history since 1241. . . .

I

Early Times

Archaeologists say that the history of settlement around Dortmund began in the Bronze Age, probably around 1000 B.C. They base this date on items found in Dortmund excavations, for instance, a bowl filled with ashes and bits of bone which turned up near the location of an ancient cemetery.[1] The people who lived in this region, initially hunters and gatherers, were by this time simple farmers, residing in small villages or on individual plots with a house, animals, and cultivated fields. They were ancestors of Germanic tribes such as the Teutons or Cheruskas.[2] Skeletal remains indicate that the ancient people were, of course, relatively short, and historians believe the men probably had long hair and wore brief tunics over baggy trousers held up by a cord around the waist.[3]

While the northern European cultures of the time were simple, in present-day Italy civilization had developed further. In fact, the Romans had already founded their republic by around 510 B.C. and, beginning in about 264 B.C., expanded their rule westward. By 50 B.C. Roman legions occupied what is now Spain, France, and Britain. Twice they tried also to capture central Europe (Germania) but were resisted east of the Rhine River by the native tribes. To guard against the threat of these unsubdued tribes, the Romans built a fortified wall, called the *Limes*, running roughly parallel to the east bank of the Rhine. Behind the wall Rome built its colonies, including Köln (Cologne, established A.D. 50) and Xanten (A.D. 100), and in A.D. 300 made Trier the capital of the western Roman Empire.

After enmity had subsided, the Romans and the Germanic peoples took up trade with one another. Young Germanic men became legionnaires in the Roman army and even made careers in its service. Thus, Roman culture extended its influence into central Europe, in the region later to be called Germany. It is believed that around this time traders and merchants began settling in the area of present-day Dortmund, which was the linkage point to waterways running in four directions—the east-west trade route from the Rhine to the Weser rivers, called the *Hellweg* (bright way), and the north-south route from Köln over the Ruhr and Lippe rivers to the north. Logically, then, Dortmund grew up around the intersection of these two very important trade routes (plate 8).[4]

As Christianity became a force in Rome itself, it spread via the Roman armies to central Europe. Military settlements such as Köln then became powerful religious centers as well, and archbishops controlled much land. The church, in turn, used its enormous land wealth to benefit secular rulers, thereby acquiring loyalty, professional soldiers, and administrators for its provinces. This shared rule of church and state was to exist for many centuries under two sets of law, that of the worldly rulers and of the church fathers' canon law.

The indigenous tribes, however, did not always accept the rule of Rome. They fought with each other and raided Roman outposts. For instance, the Teutons were strong in A.D. 200–250 and even attacked Rome itself. The half-century A.D. 300–350 was the period of the Goths, with the Franks soon gaining power. It was they, allied with the Alemanni, who invaded the Roman province of Gaul (part of present-day Italy and France) in A.D. 350–400. That invasion began the breakup of the Roman Empire, hastened in 455 by the plundering of Rome by the Vandals.

The great Roman Empire, of course, did not end after a single event or rout. Rather, it fell gradually through defeats in the west by various tribes—Huns, Visigoths, Franks. With the demise of Rome's western empire, ancient history ended. Then began the Middle Ages, that long period of European history (roughly A.D. 500 to 1300) characterized by, among other things, power struggles between church and state—the Roman church and its representatives on the one hand and the kings and princes on the other.

In central Europe the church maintained its strong foothold, energetically converting the tribal peoples. Although the tribal leaders did not always follow their previous rulers' example of law, they had taken on some of the old Roman culture and titles. The secular hierarchy in Germany, for instance, had the Kaiser (from "Caesar") at the top as king or emperor. Attached to the king's court were *Grafen* (counts); next came the *Herzöge* (dukes), who were sovereign over large territories, and the *Markgraf* (margraves), who ruled border territories called *Mark*. In addition, there were *Fürsten* (princes), and at each level of the hierarchy the *Ritter* (knights), or mounted warriors who defended the rulers' territories and power. Together all these landowning leaders constituted the *Adel* (nobility).[5]

In 768, when the great leader Charlemagne (Carolus Magnus) was king of the Franks, he established numerous frontier districts, or marks, in western Europe. The rule over them was given to local leaders in return for their military support. Since that meant mounted warriors, the knights, too, received land. Such distribution of land and the power that went with it threatened the church's control, resulting in constant quarrels between local rulers and the papacy and its officials.

In 800 Charlemagne was crowned emperor of central Europe. His coronation was held in Rome to symbolize the restored empire of the Romans in the west, later called the Holy Roman Empire. Later, Charlemagne was known in Germany as Karl the Great. Part of his perceived greatness resided in his farsighted efforts to revive culture and learning. Karl was especially interested in educating leaders of the church, for it then was the channel through which cultural traditions were preserved and passed on to succeeding generations. At the same time, the emperor also established a palace school in Aachen (location of his *Pfalz*, or seat of imperial jurisdiction, since 794) and schools for children of all economic classes throughout his realm.[6]

Economic considerations were also central to the emperor's long-range plans. He recognized, for instance, the importance of the region around the intersection of the major German trade routes and declared that three villages in the area would constitute a new polity (naturally not yet a "city") called Dortmund. After its founding, it is variously reported that Charlemagne set up a court there for the Westphalian area and that he built a fortress nearby to control traffic on both the trade routes.[7] He did not, however, live at the fortress, for Aachen was the political center of the empire. Moreover, in those days the king usually had no permanent residence. Rather, he traveled about the empire, leaving local administration to the Grafen and Herzöge, who ultimately were responsible to him.[8] The political system which had gradually evolved meant that each level of leadership maintained its powers by making land grants (*Lehnen*) or fiefs to the level below it in return for pledges of military and political service.

The system of homage and mutual dependency in the Early Middle Ages is commonly called *vassalage*; this term derives from the word *vassal*, which had begun to appear in contemporary records by about the 730s.[9] At the very bottom of the system, of course, were the serfs, or peasants bound to the soil of landowners, for the economy of the time was agrarian. They worked for and were bound to the lords above them, producing the products which, in turn, were due to the next level up the ladder of rulership.

After the death of Charlemagne in 814, his empire became fragmented as successors divided up his lands, giving away many estates, offices, and rights to supporters. Such strengthened counts and other feudal lords (including bishops) were then clearly less dependent on a central power, and regional leaders became the focus of political developments.

In Germany King Konrad of Saxony ruled from 911 to 918. Northeast of the Hellweg intersection at Dortmund, he established a royal Pfalz, which served as a center for rulers of the northwest region of Germany for 150 years. Under Konrad's rule, the Hellweg was especially important as a tie between Saxony in the east and the Rhine. Under another German king and emperor, Otto the Great (936–973), Dortmund and additional cities flourished through an increase in trade with distant regions, especially Italy.[10]

Dortmund was not a large settlement on the Hellweg trade route, but it was well known. Designated as Trutmenni (A.D. 928) or Throtmennia (A.D. 947)—and then, as the *thr-* sound gradually changed to *dr-* or *dor-*, as Drodmannia (1016) or Drutmunni (1112)—it was the location for an annual trade fair held in the spring. It also was a center for the movement of ore and iron from the eastern Harz Mountains across to Flanders (Belgium) and on to England. In fact, Dortmund already had an association of tradesmen in the 900s.[11]

Some historians designate the period after A.D. 1000 as the High Middle Ages. It was a time when Europe was divided into the large kingdoms of Germany, France, and Italy. But in reality the Continent in the twelfth century was a mosaic of smaller principalities ruled by contentious lords bearing the titles of duke, count, and even viscount. As in earlier times, each had his own structure of subordinates, or vassals, providing military and political services. That medieval arrangement for maintaining mutual dependencies, based on fiefs (Lehnen), was then called the feudal system.

The church, too, had become feudalized over time, with its bishops, abbots, and other high clergy receiving Lehnen in return for military service to their archbishops, that is, providing knights to protect the church and its possessions. In addition, under the church's banner the knights were also making converts in "heathen lands." For example, Pope Urban II, who summoned the first crusade to Jerusalem in 1050, called on the nobles to "now become the knights of Christ, after you have so long been robbers."[12]

Thus, medieval society consisted primarily of three classes: the clergy, the armed knights, and the peasants. As it was said in those days, "The house of God is divided into three parts but is considered a whole. One part prays, another fights, and others work."[13] In practice, however, the knights and peasants obviously were not equal to landed nobility, and a more relevant definition of classes was the twofold division between the powerful and the poor. There was no such thing as legal equality.[14]

Education, too, was a matter of class and especially a clerical concern. German priests from "good families" went abroad to study in France and Italy and then returned to teach children (primarily the boys) of other "good families." Others had little access to learning. Since the schools were supported by the king and church, they taught law, administration, and other fields useful to the rulers.[15]

It is in this Middle Ages period of the 1100s that one finds the roots of the Mallinckrodt family. They left their footprints on the official history of the era when, for instance, family members quarreled over land rights before courts or held church commemorations for deceased parents. Such preserved Latin and Old German court and church documents of the Middle Ages contain fascinating accounts of Mallinckrodts in the rural areas near Dortmund and in that settlement itself. Their story, however, really begins at a castle called Volmestein and with people named Mesekenwerke.

2

1100

Burg Volmestein

At the end of the eleventh century, Archbishop Friedrich of Köln was a powerful force in Westphalia. He controlled the farming area of Gedern, on the right bank of the Ruhr River, between the settlements of Witten and Wetter. There in 1100 he made a *Burglehn*, or grant, to the Volmestein family to build a fortress (*Burg*).[1] This Burg Volmestein (or Volmarstein), along with Burg Wetter on the Ruhr, was to be the church's seat of power in Westphalia.

At the same time, the archbishopric in this Mark was in competition with the secular power, the *Grafschaft Mark* (regional count).[2] Perhaps, therefore, the archbishop hoped, as was often the case, that craftspersons and merchants would locate in the area protected by his Burg Volmestein and so gradually develop that vicinity's economic importance.[3] At the same time, the nobles tried to be as independent of the archbishop as possible, and there were many quarrels among them. One of the constant sore points concerned hunting rights, which the archbishop said belonged to him. This, of course, involved more than just sport, for hunting was a source of food. At Burg Volmestein the division of hunting rights was interesting—to the lords the right to hunt deer and wild boar, to the knights the right to hunt everything else.[4]

Despite all the power struggles of the time, the Volmesteins benefited from their position. Through the rule over land and people which they had been granted, they had became Adel, or more specifically *Landadel* (landed nobility). That rule of the noble class, in turn, was symbolized by the possession of a Burg, towering over the surrounding peasants living in their lowly houses with dirt

9

floors and thatched roofs.[5] The peasants supplied needed raw materials—wood, food, flax, grain, etc.—to the Burg, which was like a little city with many services.

Burg Volmestein's main fortress covered 100 by 80 meters (328 by 262 feet) and was supported by walls nearly 2.9 meters (9.5 feet) thick; it included a mighty tower of 11.7 by 11.2 meters (38 × 37 feet) whose walls also were more than 3.2 meters (10.5 feet) wide. To the north and south were small outpost fortresses (*Vorburg*) built to protect the major structure (plate 1).[6]

Life inside the Burg surely was not as romantic as many legends picture it. The castles were not always large, and they were usually dark and unheated with windows of oil paper or thinly shaved horn. Hygienic conditions were primitive, and there was no sound medical care. Food was not always healthy, and manners at the long rectangular table, flanked by benches not chairs, were probably coarse by later standards. Although there were knives to cut food, forks had not yet been invented, so to lift food from wooden or pewter bowls to their mouths people used their hands, knives, and later a kind of soup ladle.[7] Goblets and mugs completed the table setting.

In the castle life of the Middle Ages, women were clearly subordinated in the unmitigatedly patriarchal society.[8] Even their confining clothing suggested that role: necks and bosoms were covered with a cloth called a *wimple*, which also framed their faces,[9] or they wore a kind of scarf pulled low over the forehead and tied in back of the neck. Very little indeed is known about most of the women within the fortresses, except their names if they were the wives of noblemen. And usually those marriages were an instrument of dynastic politics, entered into in order to establish relationships with other ruling families and to produce children to carry on the family line. Barrenness was reason enough for a woman to be divorced.[10]

From such a castle, the Volmestein nobles, called *Burggrafen*, or "fortress counts," defended the surrounding territory within the Grafschaft Mark.[11] Their importance as a class rested on three basic rights. First, there was the right over land, including rents and goods from tenant farmsteads on *allodium* lands (that is, lands absolutely owned), as well as tenured land. Second, the nobles had some legal or police rights that were carried out through judges they hired.[12] And, third, while serving as professional warriors, the counts had peasants to till the fields. Increasingly, though, the nobles tried to extend their rights, for instance, that of inheritance: they wanted their land estates, or Lehnen, to be hereditary, that is, property they could pass on to sons (initially not to daughters).[13]

In return for the three rights, the nobles owed their political or clerical ruler three kinds of obligations. Most important, there was military service, which meant guarding the ruler's castle or fighting on his behalf. Then there were the political obligations, which included a kind of judicial service. In that context the nobles also offered counsel and judgment at Volmestein's *Lehnstagen* (meetings of all the landed where, for instance, their tenures were renewed or conflicts about them settled) and at its *Lehnskammer* (administrative sessions of tenure-holders).[14] Finally, there was the obligation of financial services, that is, rendering money and goods.[15]

To meet their obligations to the ruler above them, the Volmesteins, in turn, hired free soldiers to do the actual defending. These hired soldiers were called *Burgmänner* (men of the fortress) or, if they served specifically as tower guards, *Turm-Burgmänner*. A Burgmann could leave his job or even be fired. But as long as he and his compatriots were in the service of their lord, they lived at an outpost (*Vorburg*) of Volmestein, referred to as the *Burgmannsitz*, or soldiers' quarters.[16]

In those days war usually meant that the Burgmänner carried out arson or plunder for their lords, that is, burning or stealing the most valuable things an "enemy" had, his crops and buildings. Sometimes, too, hostages were taken. Such military service, of course, was a dangerous life and not very profitable. Usually after forty days of warring activity, the soldier's expenses might be paid by the lord, and because the soldiers' war-horses were very expensive, the lord sometimes promised to replace any lost in his service.[17]

Hostilities were often carried out as nobles exercised the *Fehderecht* (campaign right) against each other. For instance, after announcing his enmity (as in a challenge to a duel), a Graf would launch a major campaign of military revenge and retaliation against another count, somewhat in the manner of the blood feuds of other times. Always it was the Burgmänner who did the fighting, and always it was the rural people living on the plundered or burned estates who suffered. In general, farmers were not allowed to have weapons and were especially forbidden to carry swords or lances.[18]

The knights, of course, had not only lances (*Spiess*) and swords but also battle-axes.[19] Their chain mail armor was knee-length with half-sleeves, as well as an iron cowl over which they set a pointed helmet with nose band. An oval or pointed shield, almost as tall as the knight himself, completed the standard armament. When not riding about in such armor, the knights wore short tunics and ankle-length breeches fitted to their legs and drawn over knee-length hose. Their heads were usually covered with pointed or beretlike caps; for traveling they wore broad-brimmed hats fitted over hoods to protect them from the weather.[20]

Dortmund

Although the era was dominated by Westphalia's landowning nobles and 90 percent of its people were dependent on agriculture, the region's settlements also were growing.[21] Dortmund, for instance, not so far away from Wetter and Witten and Burg Volmestein, had become a trade center in the 1100s. Located on waterways or a juncture of roads, such medieval towns got woven cloth from Flanders, as well as grain, flax, fish, salt, wines, timber, hides, and other products their residents needed.

Dortmund merchants, for example, also traveled to the big fairs which were traditional in Europe at that time, especially in France. Sponsored by feudal lords who collected a tax on sales, the fairs sometimes lasted for weeks. There buyers could select from tradesmen's stalls every item made in Europe—copper pots, leather saddles, swords, armor, cutlery, anvils, wooden tubs, carts and cart wheels, clothing and shoes and gloves—as well as indigo and lacquer from the East, along with silver and other metals and silk, damask, and velvet cloth.[22]

Back from the fairs, the merchants then followed their usual routine. Business took them on early-morning rounds of the town—to the market to see to merchandise, probably to the guildhall or tavern to gossip about prices, home for meals, and early to bed. In Dortmund, many of those businessmen apparently dealt in textiles since the medieval town was known for its cloth.

Although records tell almost nothing about the volume of Dortmund's textile trade at that time,[23] it is known that the nobility used textiles generously in their homes for warmth as well as decorations, especially rugs on floors, walls, benches, and tables. They also sported attire of many colors, which meant they provided business for cloth dyers. By contrast, the peasants of the area could not have contributed much to the city's textile trade, for they usually made their own cloth and were required to wear only gray-blue or black clothing.[24]

Because Dortmund was a textile center, the economic power in the city clearly belonged to the *Tuchhändler*, or wholesale dealers in cloth, as well as the *Wandschneider*, or retailers who cut up the textile bolts for clothing and other goods. (The word *Wand* comes from the word *Gewand*, "costume, clothes"; *Schneider* means "tailor" or "cutter.") In fact, the wholesalers, referred to in the Dortmund histories as *Junkers* (lords) and as *Patrizier* (patricians), are said to have constituted the *Stadtsadel*, or urban nobility.[25]

This power of the textile dealers came from their monopoly economic position and their cooperative society, the *Wandschneider-Gesellschaft* (textile merchants society). Only its members could rent sales stands in the city's hall, and cloth could be sold only out of these stands. Thus, the Society had guildlike power: that is, it controlled every aspect of the business—prices, wages, amount of goods to be turned out, and the manner of their production. If the Wandschneider cut cloth for their own personal use, they could then sell from their homes remnants to friends.[26]

To protect flourishing trade centers such as Dortmund from the constant medieval conflicts, medieval businessmen persuaded the towns to build defensive walls around the settlements. In addition to stone ramparts and towers, the walls had gateways wide enough for carts to pass through. Despite such protective constructions, however, the settlement of Dortmund was destroyed and burned twice in the years 1113–1115 by the forces of Köln's archbishop and others.[27]

Rebuilt by the secular German ruler King Henry V, Dortmund was then given special privileges as a *Reichsstadt* (imperial city subject to the king but not to local princes, bishops, and so on). This new status was granted the city's leaders for supporting the king in regional conflicts at a time when his powers had become weakened. Royal privileges or freedoms of various kind were customary rewards for loyalty, service, or money.

In short, the 1100s were a time of growth for trade, guilds, and towns such as Dortmund. It was also the time of crusades; for instance, the Order of Teutonic Knights, founded in 1190, was becoming a force to reckon with in Eastern Europe and later in Prussia. (Some historians believe the order had a monastery on the Hellweg near Dortmund for knights in ecclesiastical service.)[28] Interestingly, some of the influences which the Crusaders brought back from the East were good for Dortmund's textile business—new demands for more rugs as floor coverings and for women's dresses with very long tunics and immensely long sleeves.[29]

In this period women not only enjoyed new fashions but also the relatively greater freedom provided by the developing cities. Although women were expected to marry very young and did not participate in city government, they nevertheless could take the citizenship oath and had more inheritance rights than previously.[30]

*W*hen we come to the 1200 and 1300s, Father said, we are talking about a period that historians call the High Middle Ages. The thirteenth century was a time of great vitality in Europe. Marco Polo of Italy was preparing to travel to China, and the German Order of Knights was establishing overseas missions, as in the Baltic area of Latvia. The University of Paris was becoming the philosophical center of Western culture. And here in Germany, where Gothic art was developing, as in France and England, the great cathedrals of Münster and Köln were being built.

In the Middle Ages, the German realms of the Holy Roman Empire were dominated by the so-called higher nobility, the princes, counts, dukes. They collected taxes, controlled the markets, and administered the king's territories. Beneath them was the "lower nobility," or rulers over the countryside where eighty to ninety percent of the people lived. These rural lords, or *Landadel*, lived at a central fortress, or manor house, surrounded by probably around three hundred to four hundred acres that they had inherited as land grants, or *Lehnen*. Their power extended not only over their personal servants but also the tenant farmers working parcels of the estate lands.

This is where our family has its roots—at Burg Volmestein on the Ruhr River, among its knights. Originally known as the Knights of Mesekenwerke, they began calling themselves *von Mallingrode* after they got their own estate, which included a woods clearing (*gerodete*) where the marker of an outdoor judgment seat (*Mal*) was found. Thus our name officially entered German history in 1348, and Knight Ludwig, first recorded in 1241, is the grandfather of us all.

At the same time, of course, not far from the rural estate of Mallingrode the settlement of Dortmund was developing, too. In later centuries, when, as it is said, the "country folk moved to town," it would become our home city. Thus we have both deep rural and urban roots.

There were only a few such settlements by the mid-1300s, home to ten to twenty percent of the people in the empire. Köln and Prague were the biggest cities, with Lübeck, Danzig, and Nürnberg next. In 1300 around thirty such large and small cities organized themselves into a trade association called the *Hanse League*. It extended some one thousand five hundred kilometers, from Köln to Tallin (Reval) in Estonia, that is, to German settlements established in the east as early as 1150. Some of the Hanse cities, like Dortmund, became important enough to be given the status of *free* or *imperial* cities with rights independent of local rulers.

Despite the general development, life in the Middle Ages was harsh. In the early 1300s a great plague, coming into central Europe from the Mediterranean, caused many deaths—whereas it is believed that fourteen to fifteen million people lived in the empire in 1340, by 1350 it was said to be only ten million.

Political life also was insecure. Everyone was subject to the rule of both the nobility and the church. However, here, too, changes were underway. For instance, in 1356 seven important German princes won the right to *elect* the German king. They were the *Kurfürsten*, or electoral princes. Thus the Pope no longer was a major influence in deciding political leadership, and understandably the competition between political and church leaders sharpened.

3

1200–1300

Knights von Mesekenwerke

At Burg Volmestein in the thirteenth century, knights going by the name of von Mesekenwerke had become the nobles' Burgmänner. As early as 1241, for instance, records show that knight Ludwig von Mesekenwerke was in the service of the Volmestein fortress near the settlement of Wetter on the Ruhr River. Where the Burgmänner originally came from, however, is not clear. During the Middle Ages, families often took the name of their birthplaces, but in this case the exact location of Mesekenwerke has not been established.[1]

What is known, however, is that in 1250 Ludwig was given *Burglehnen* (land grants) for his service to the Volmesteins. The most important was in the nearby area of Obergedern. That grant included a tract of cleared land where court was held, similar to the later U.S.-frontier practice of administering justice under a "Judgment Tree." By 1300 the Mesekenwerke family *Hof* (estate), included three *Hufs*, a land measure called *hide* in English and varying from 80 to 120 acres. According to a later survey, the Obergedern Hof comprised forests, arable fields, meadows, a fishery (with barbel, a kind of carp), and a weir in the Ruhr River (plate 2). A disadvantage of its riverside location was that the meadows were frequently flooded.[2]

Nature was not the only adversary of the Mesekenwerke knights. They were, after all, soldiers, and the ongoing political struggles of the time meant they were often at war. For example, during the Battle of Worringen in 1288, the Archbishop of Köln—despite the soldierly services of his many nobles and their knights, including the Volmesteins and Mesekenwerke—was defeated and taken prisoner by his regional opponent Graf Eberhard II von der Mark. In addition, the count destroyed Burg Volmestein and, even after a peace agreement, did not permit its reconstruction for some years. A second and especially decisive round in this struggle over Burg Volmestein came in 1324. This time the Graf von der Mark, now count Engelbert II, turned against Burg Volmestein, which his predecessor had permitted to be rebuilt. Engelbert captured and then destroyed the fortress, incorporating its land into his own territory.[3] That 1324 destruction of Burg Volmestein was a very important event in the life of the early Mesekenwerke knights: as Burgmänner, they no longer had residence responsibilities to the destroyed castle. Instead, the Mesekenwerke were free to move to their land grant in Obergedern. There they built their own modest Burg, which became the *Rittersitz* (knights' manor house) of the family.[4] From there they rode out to do their knightly duty for the count ruling the Mark. The frequent service of Herbord of Obergedern to Volmestein after it was rebuilt and to the ruler of the Mark, Graf Adolf V von Kleve, was often noted in the records of military campaigns and administrative matters.[5] Europe's roving warrior knights were on the way to becoming a settled rural aristocracy.

We do not know precisely what the Burg in Obergedern (plate 2) looked like, for there are no renderings of it. However, written descriptions do survive. According to one old document, until the 1300s, "The nobles on the land had small towers which they hardly could defend against their class peers. There were few castles and fortified places."[6] Although it seems that the Burg in Obergedern had no tower, or at best an ineffective one, the records do show that it was built mostly of wood, with some stone, and included several buildings.[7]

Having established the family home, the next step the Mesekenwerke knights took was very significant—naming it. They called their *Gut*, or estate of various parcels of land, *Mallingrode*, taking the name from the *Mal* (marker) of the outdoor judgment seat in the *gerodet*, or cleared area, referred to above. Since families by now were taking the name of their fortress or castle,[8] rather than just the locale of their birth, the descendants of Ludwig called themselves *von Mesekenwerke und Mallingrode* (first recorded in 1348). Knight Ludwig is thus the first officially recorded entry on the family tree bearing the name Mallinckrodt.[9]

Obergedern on the Ruhr was not, however, the only location of the family's members. Only about six hundred meters southeast of Haus Mallingrode (alternately called Gut Mallingrode or Hof zu Mallingrode), they also had a Burgmannsitz zu Wetter. It was a land grant, but from the Graf von der Mark himself. It might, in fact, have been where the Mesekenwerke/Mallingrode hired themselves out after the Graf destroyed Volmestein and consolidated his power over Köln's archbishop. Although no house was built on it, the Wetter land grant is referred to in documents as "old Mallinckrodt." Throughout history, it seems that records often confused these two nearby properties, and gradually they were considered as one.[10]

Records also show that the Mesekenwerke of Obergedern had close relations to the nearby cloister at Herdecke. That was logical, for the nobility of the time celebrated religious events at cloisters and often arranged for their daughters to serve them as *Stiftsdame* (canonesses). For this reason, it might be presumed that Mesekenwerke family members were also buried at Herdecke.[11] If so, they may have been buried under the name Mallinckrodt, for by 1367 Ludwig's descendants no longer used their earlier designation. Instead, they appear in the records only as Mallingrode (or Mallinckrode or Mallinckrodt), with land grants now also located at the Ruhr Valley settlements of Steinberg, Recklinghausen, and Dortmund. Thereby, as "Herr zu Mallinckrodt und Steinberg," Herbord (c.1330–c.1415), the prominent descendant of Ritter Ludwig, linked Haus Mallinckrodt in Obergedern to family members and property in Recklinghausen and then Dortmund (figure 5-1).[12]

Other Mallinckrodts apparently traveled far from the Ruhr River. They were involved, for instance, in trade with the north, in Lübeck and even Norway. That far away from the old family center, the wanderers sometimes called themselves "von Wetter" because that settlement was geographically better known than their estate Mallinckrodt.[13]

But wherever they were, as members of the landed nobility the Mallinckrodts were known by their *Wappen*, or coat of arms (figure 3-1). It consisted of three leaves surrounding a ball, with the usual helmet and shield. At the top of the symbol were two arms clad in what some believed were women's dress, their index fingers thrust through a gold ring. This, it is suggested, may have symbolized the family's roots in the period of knightly athletic competitions when women awarded the prize of a golden ring to tournament winners. Other scholars, however, say the ring represented an early marriage between two noble families. Initially such pictures and symbols on shields and armor identified knights in battle. Later the coats of arms distinguished whole families. Sometimes, too, the symbol was not just individual but collective. Historians have found that the Mallinckrodt Wappen was originally shared with other Volmestein Burgmann families.[14]

Although the knights' coats of arms did not change, over time their armor did. By the 1300s they were still using mailed armor, made of sewn-on or interwoven iron rings. The sleeves were now full-length, and armored gloves were added. Legs and feet were protected by mailed leggings and shoes. The cowl was lengthened so that a part could be pulled down over mouth and chin and fastened on the side.[15]

Over the years, the knights' major weapon, the sword, hardly changed its shape. But by the 1300s it had lost some of its importance to the longer lance, which was then the typical attack weapon of the knights, as shown in scenes on tapestries and memorialized in sculptures.[16] In fact, the use of weapons such as the eight-foot halberd changed the very nature of battle, for with lances the foot soldiers could stop the cavalry charges of knights on horseback. Other formidable new weapons were the crossbow, which could pierce armor at two hundred yards,

Figure 3-1. The Mallinckrodt family's coat of arms originated in the thirteenth century.

and the longbow, which was five times faster than the crossbow. The knights, meanwhile, continued to be weighed down by their heavy armor and were thus not very mobile.[17]

Dortmund

After its destruction in 1114, Dortmund made good progress under its new status as an imperial city, or Reichsstadt. Incorporating village settlements around it, Dortmund had grown to 81 hectares (about two hundred acres) inside its restored and strengthened city walls.[18] Four entrances—the East, West, Burg, and Wis-straße gates, which were bolted at night—led to the old street market in the Brückstraße, just south of Westenhellweg crossing the settlement.[19] Nearby was also the Marienkirche (St. Mary's Church), the three-nave Romanesque basilica built around 1225–1238, and the Rathaus (city hall) erected about 1232–1241.[20]

The wall around the city was more than three kilometers long. At its base it was made of earth up to 18 meters thick (59 feet) and reaching up 4 to 6 meters (13 to 20 feet). At that height was the 6-meter wide path along the ramparts where the guards stood. And reaching another 4 to 6 meters (13 to 20 feet) and sometimes up to 10 meters (33 feet) above them was a stone wall with notches (crenels) and firing slits. To add to the fortifications, a moat up to 35 meters (115 feet) wide ran along the wall; beyond the moat lay another lower wall and a dry trench.[21]

By the 1200s Dortmund was the trade center of a large continuous stretch of empire lands in Westphalia. Especially important to its growth and prestige was the addition in 1232 of a second trade fair, in autumn.[22] Additional political privileges were gained in 1240, when Dortmund was said to be a *freie Reichsstadt* (free, or exempted, imperial city). Although Dortmund was part of the empire and subject to the king, it could make some of its own laws and, indeed, had built a new Rathaus for its city council and court. The city had the power, for instance, to grant citizens landowning rights which could be freely inherited. (Of course, not everyone who lived within the city was a "citizen," for that designation often depended on property ownership.)[23]

The right to set some of its own norms sparked a lively respect for due process in general and for what later would be called the city's sense of freedom under law. A notable example of this spirit was Dortmund's provision for serfs: if serfs escaped into the city and remained within its walls for a year and a day, they were given their freedom from bondage.[24] Moreover, the guilds, or organizations of craft workers, were gaining rights too. Having organized gradually—first the tanners and shoemakers, then the bakers and butchers, followed by the smithies and grocers—by 1260 the six guilds were starting to take part in the selection of Dortmund's city council members.[25] Their guild house was located centrally, on the Westenhellweg, and as early as 1241 the shoemakers had their sales stands in what later came to be known as the Schuhof Street.[26]

The lives of women were also changing gradually. They could be involved in the textile trade, albeit with some limitations, and partnerlike personal relationships were developing between men and women in the patrician class. Life expectancy was still low for women—thirty years—because of many births and heavy work, but inheritance rights vis-á-vis husbands were improving. Although a husband still controlled his wife's property (to sell, loan, or give away), on his death she got back the money, rents, real estate, clothes, jewelry, and linen dowry brought into the marriage (*Brautschatz*), and she did not have to use it to make good his debts. Women, indeed, had gone to church courts to make that point when secular courts would not. A woman also inherited a half or a third of what she and her husband had mutually acquired in the marriage. By the 1300s, too, houses were set aside where women left alone with their children might live.[27]

In addition to the attraction of a favorable political climate, Dortmund had grown in the 1300s primarily because of a major economic advantage: it belonged to the German mercantile association of cities called the Hanse League (Hanseatic League). Close trade ties, therefore, existed with other member cities, especially northern German settlements such as Hamburg, Bremen, Lübeck, and branches in Russia, the Baltic, Flanders, Scandinavia, England, and elsewhere.[28]

As a result, Dortmund was already prominent and probably included in the list of two thousand settlements counted as "cities" during the 1200s, a time when numerous other cities were first being founded.[29] Its population was estimated at seventeen thousand at this time and its twelve-hundred-meter long (three-fourths of a mile) main street connecting the western and eastern city gates was referred to as the Westenhellweg and Ostenhellweg.[30]

The Hanse businessmen who created much of that economic growth in Dortmund became the city's *Patriziat*, or patricians—that is, they were its rulers, serving the free imperial city as judges and *Ratsherren* (councilmen).[31] Those were, however, not elected positions but inherited political seats reserved for upper-middle-class noncraftsmen who had wealth. As *Erbsassen* (inheritors), the well-to-do made public payments to the city in return for seats in the government; in case of an emergency, performance of military service with horses and servants was also required if the city ordered it. (Other citizens had to serve on foot.)[32] Not surprisingly, in Dortmund many of the Erbsassen were members of the prestigious textile society mentioned earlier, the Wandschneider-Gesellschaft. In fact, a family would often be in both bodies and would refer to its position in tandem, that is, *Erbsassen und Wandschneider-Gesellschaft*.

Many patricians were also members of the area's important Reinoldikirche, the thirteenth-century Gothic house of worship built just across from the older Marienkirche. It was known for its statues of the city's religious patron saint, Saint Reinold, and its political patron, Charlemagne, as well as for its school—

said to have existed already in 1268.[33] Here the city's sons, from craftsmen as well as patrician families, were educated in basic reading, writing, and arithmetic so they could go to universities. The instruction, of course, was in Latin, the international language of politics and economics at the time.[34]

Yet in this period of booming trade, Dortmund also had setbacks, such as the 1388–1389 *Fehde* (campaign) launched against it by both political powers in the region, the Archbishop of Köln and Graf Engelbert III von der Mark. It was a notable event at the time, entailing a twenty-one-month blockade of the city, involving some twelve hundred mounted soldiers. Once again Herbord von Mallinckrodt, by now a leading knight at rebuilt Volmestein, took part in the Fehde on the side of his ruler, the count, against Dortmund.[35]

Because of its political significance this was a historic struggle for the city: could Dortmund maintain its unique and progressive position as the only free imperial city (subject only to the king) within the surrounding area of Westphalia ruled by the king and his princes? At a time when Dortmund's status represented an important step forward in medieval political developments, the established religious force (Köln's archbishop) and the princely power in the area (Graf Engelbert, ruler of the surrounding Mark) had first isolated Dortmund economically and now tried to destroy it by seige.

That, however, was hard to do, although other Hanse cities did not come to Dortmund's aid. The city's walls were well fortified, and its citizens unified and spirited. Moreover, Dortmund had acquired the services of mercenaries—70 horsemen, 49 pikemen, 27 archers, and 4 noble "helpers" who fought for the city with their 79 horsemen. Thus the city was able to hold out, in part because of the large food supplies it had stored inside the city walls. *"So fest wie Dortmund"* ("as strong as Dortmund," or in the old German of the day, *"sau fest as Düopm"*) became a slogan of the time.[36]

The peace negotiations were long. When the Graf and his successors made a permanent peace treaty with the city of Dortmund in 1396, Herbord Mallinckrodt was a witness.[37] Dortmund had won, but it paid a severe economic price, including a large cash payment to the besiegers. In addition, the city's patrician leaders were presented with a political bill: in return for the guildmen's loyal defense of the city, they demanded more participation on the city council, that is, six of the eighteen seats.[38]

Another setback for Dortmund concerned health. Like many German settlements, it was racked in the last half of the 1300s by the Black Death which rampaged across Europe. And no wonder: medieval towns were "incubators of disease." Overcrowding was typical, with wooden houses built wall-to-wall along narrow alleys. Wells were polluted, sanitation primitive, streets swarming with rats and other animals, with their attendant fleas, which bred epidemics. During the Black Death, German towns such as Dortmund lost most of their population. It has been estimated, in fact, that a quarter of Europe's people died in seven years of the bubonic plague.[39] Paintings of the time show streams of people peering forlornly from somber hoods as they carry shallow caskets to be buried.

While there was death, beauty, too, was being created around Dortmund, as in the great Gothic cathedral being built in nearby Köln. It was a magnificent architectural undertaking—pointed arches, walls replaced by arcades, vaulted roofs offering breathtaking, heaven-directed vistas. There was color, too, for the art of stained glass, developed in the mid-1100s, could be used in the frequent openings of the cathedrals' outside wall; although the glass could be made only in small pieces, those could be joined together with lead strips. Overall, the impression of a Gothic cathedral was of space and light within a massive structure.

Perhaps the nobles and knights of Volmestein, Obergedern, and other houses were involved, too, in the construction of the mighty houses of religion. Men of means were naturally expected to support the financing and construction of the gigantic projects, not only by donating money but also by volunteering skilled craftsmen and peasant laborers. Especially sought were artisans who made stained glass.

At the same time, the brawn for the cathedral projects naturally came from the peasants, who quarried the stone and cut the timber, transported the materials to the construction site in carts, dug the foundations, and carried in baskets on their backs the slate and other heavy materials for the roof. The jumble of wind-lasses, hand winches, treadwheels, and other machines were intended to make the work easier, but cathedral building was still a feat of human labor.[40]

*O*n the one hand, Father continued, the Late Middle Ages—the 1400s—continued to be turbulent in Westphalia. In Dortmund, however, trade was expanding and the city prospered. The textile business, or *Tuchhandel*, had its place in a new *Rathaus*, that is, the city hall, and close relations were developing between Dortmunders and the merchant families of Köln, a major economic center.

Such businessmen lived well. They dressed stylishly—in the flat caps, pointed shoes, and doublet, or short jacket, with jerkin we know from old paintings—and surrounded themselves with fine Gothic-style furniture. We have seen many of the elaborately carved chests and cupboards with geometric floral designs, the great tall standing candlesticks of bronze or wrought iron for which Augsburg and Nürnberg were famous, and the tapestries with religious scenes from France, Italy, or the Netherlands. Books were available (at less cost since printing with movable type was invented in 1455), as well as copper etchings and relatively inexpensive paper.

Moreover, as a result of their prosperity, Dortmund's citizens were growing more self-confident. In fact, they increasingly demanded the administrative rights that ruling counts formerly carried out for the king. Thus, in 1400, the guilds (organizations of craftspeople and shopkeepers) for the first time won the lower six seats in the city council, while the patricians held the top twelve inherited, or *Erbsassen*, seats.

In addition, after 1471 imperial cities such as Dortmund could send representatives to a kind of parliament in Regensburg called the *Reichstag*, or imperial assembly. The princes and electoral-princes of the Holy Roman Empire of the German Nation also came there to express their interests to the emperor.

But the really intriguing chapters of our family history in this period are found in court documents concerning the lives of Mallinckrodt knights in the countryside. This was not an easy time for them, for power relationships were changing. Formerly, political power had been clearly shared by the church and landowners in the rural areas, and many knights represented the landowners. Now, growing towns and their developing bourgeoisie, or middle class, were challenging that power. For economic reasons, for instance, some landowners were founding towns and freeing their serfs to live there and develop the settlements. Seeking the same haven, other serfs were running away from landowner lords to the towns. Naturally, the knights and lords they served objected. The result was disruptive campaigns or feuds, *Fehde*, against cities, salespersons, and church territories, as well as among the duchies themselves.

Thus, the proud knight Hermann Mallinckrodt I was called before a secret kind of Westphalian court, with an infamous reputation, to answer charges of kidnapping a Dortmund citizen. A short time later Hermann's sister Elisabeth encountered Dortmund's famous 1332 "year and a day" rule of freedom for serfs, while Hermann's trouble-making son Wilhelm I rode around the region burning and kidnapping for his grateful lord. Their stories reveal a great deal about the law and customs of the Late Middle Ages' changing times, and the ancient court records have a flavor unfortunately rare in later history books.

4

1400

Mallinckrodt Knights

In 1445 the archbishop of Köln, this time together with the Dortmunders, carried out another particularly violent military offensive against Gerhard von Kleve, the count of the Wetter district of Westphalia. History books call the battle the *Soester Fehde*, named after the region where most of the campaign took place, that is, around Westphalia's important walled settlement of Soest on the Hellweg trade route. It was a massive assault, involving some fourteen hundred horses and five hundred citizens.

During the fighting Burg Mallinckrodt was destroyed, along with its three houses. Dietrich IV, then lord of the Mallinckrodt estate, was fighting for Soest and thus was not at home when his Burg was attacked. Despite pleas from Dietrich's wife, the archbishop ordered the nearly century-old manor house plundered and burned to the ground.[1] After the end of this enmity, the Mallinckrodts rebuilt their fortress, however modestly.[2] A later sketch shows various dwelling and work buildings erected close together, surrounded by a wall with firing slits, or portholes (figure 4-1). The structure reflected the old rule that one might "fortify a *Hof* with fences, palisades, or walls only high enough to deter a man sitting on a horse."[3] A tower, therefore, was not included in the rebuilding.[4]

Later, of course, moats were common. Castle walls, strengthened by towers and pinnacles, would be taller and stronger, and a rather fine residence was usually built next to the tower. An especially pleasant spot in the whole complex, of course, was the garden that was part of every Burg.[5] All of that, however, probably still did not make castle life very much more comfortable than in earlier times.

Neither, of course, was life very secure in the 1400s because of the incessant

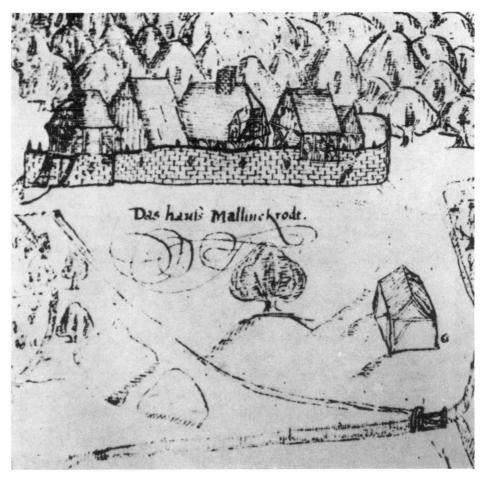

Figure 4-1. Haus Mallinckrodt as rebuilt after being burned in 1445, according to a 1612 sketch by Arthur Nauhaus. (*Courtesy Cologne Historical Archive.*)

power struggles between church and secular rulers and among the counts themselves. In such tumultuous times, knights naturally played a major role, and the name Mallinckrodt often made history. The chronicles of those adventures sometimes offer unusual insight into an entire era or way of life.

Knight Hermann

A unique perspective on the legal system of the Middle Ages is found in the 1452 account of the knight Hermann von Mallinckrodt. Born at Haus Mallinckrodt, Hermann I was the son of Dietrich IV, who had performed so bravely in the 1445 Soester Fehde as Burgmann to the estates of Wetter and Volmestein. At about the age of twenty, the younger Mallinckrodt came into conflict with the law and was summoned to appear before the regional *Fehmegericht*, often translated as "secret court." Its name is believed to have been derived from the verb *verfemen*, "to ban or to condemn." Whatever the derivation of its name, the Fehmegericht was notorious during the 1400s and was apparently feared by many.

Westphalia's court system, however, had not always been so frighteningly secretive. It included the church courts, which tried cases of heresy and witchcraft but were also involved in marital controversies and betrayal. The city council had a court dealing with business and trade disputes, and the ruling count's court heard civil and criminal cases.[6] After the thirteenth century, the *Freigerichte* (free courts) were founded by counts and princes who wanted to increase their own power during a time of legal confusion. The local Westphalian rulers saw that the old court system, dominated by bishops or kingly commissions, was deteriorating, and so they filled the power vacuum with institutions of their own. To make clear that their courts were new and independent of the weakened religious and monarchical system of justice, the Westphalians called their legal tribunals *free*.[7] The term also signified that these courts were concerned only with persons who were not serfs.[8]

The chairman of the free court was the regional count, the *Freigraf*. He in turn named jurors, or *Freischöffen*, from among the residents of his provinces and cities. They were said to number in the thousands. With so many members, the influence of the court was, of course, very broad. Furthermore, almost any one in Germany could come before it: a person who did not want to bring a complaint before the judge in his own province could go to Westphalia and seek redress at a *Freistuhl*.[9] These independent seats of judgment were said to have totaled around four hundred.[10]

By the 1400s Westphalia's Freigerichte had been organized into a network of secret courts, or *Fehmgerichte*, such as the one that summoned Herman von Mallinckrodt to appear before it in 1451–52. According to some historians, the jurors of these courts not only passed judgments but also carried them out. The jurors took their task very seriously; in fact, they swore an oath to place their loyalty to the court above even their loyalty to family members. The court sessions reportedly were held in secret, with the jurors meeting outdoors during daylight hours but also gathering at night in forests or underground locations. The Fehmgerichte dealt with both serious crimes and civil offenses, including heresy, witchcraft, assault, robbery, and murder. An oath by someone that such an act had been committed justified a juror to charge the defendant, even if no evidence had been presented. Then through a summons, secretly attached to the door of the accused's dwelling or nearby, the defendant was ordered to appear before the secret court. The summons did not include the name of the accuser.

Such a summons was posted up to three times. If the accused had not appeared after the third time, the court then met to "invite" him a fourth time. If he still did not appear, he could then be taken by the first juror, or *Freischöffe*, whom he encountered. A juror was free to capture the accused and hang him on a tree, not on a gallows, indicating that it was a juror who had carried out the consequences of four unanswered summons. If, however, the accused defended himself, then the juror had the right to kill him immediately, laying a knife next to the body to show that death had come not through murder but by the carrying out of a sentence.

Earlier historians often condemned the proceedings of the Fehmgerichte:

It is easy to imagine how many irresponsible legal murders were carried out in this way because of revenge, opportunism, or meanness. . . . With complete justification one can call these courts the most dreadful perversions of legal institutions. . . . What, after all, can be more dreadfully conceived than judges who never make the grounds for their judgments known, are never accountable for their use of power, and permit judgments to be carried out by assassin-like murder without having heard the accused.[11]

Later observers, though, have suggested that these Fehmgerichte were perhaps not so insidious as they are often assumed to have been. Rather, some have argued that the court proceeded honestly, although according to inflexible customs. "In those uncertain, often illegal times," the historian Gerrit Haren has written, "the Fehmgericht was surely frightening to many. But one has the feeling that it was a court where one could find justice." Haren also rejects the long-held view that Fehmgerichte were lay counterparts of the Inquisition, their masked members convening at night under torchlight:

The whole German attitude was that these courts should meet under open skies, in broad daylight, usually on a hillside. While the label "secret" contributed greatly to the false view of the court, that name was maintained to make clear that the court sessions were not public; only those with "knowledge" had entry. They were special courts in that only freemen (*Freie*) could judge freemen. The court's location was considered holy, that is, safeguarded from every incident by the king's protection.[12]

Such historical assessments were based in part on the study of Hermann von Mallinckrodt's famous encounter with the Fehmgericht system in the mid-1400s: "By fortunate coincidence," Haren wrote, "the records of these procedures have been almost completely preserved. They were found, along with other papers relating to the imperial court, in the false-bottom floor of the old Dortmund City Hall, preserved in an iron box."[13] The amazing preservation of the documents enabled historians and later the city of Wetter on the Ruhr to reconstruct the following story:

Without previously having declared a Fehde against the city, Hermann von Mallinckrodt in 1451 captured a Dortmund citizen, Steffan Kullart, who was traveling on one of the king's free roadways (*freie Königsstraße*). Robbing Kullert and taking him as prisoner to the nearby settlement of Unna, Hermann for good measure also set fire to Dortmund's grain fields. For unknown reasons, the city did not arm itself for a campaign of revenge but instead took the affair to the Dortmund Fehmgericht. There the captured man's friend, Reinhold Weselke, appeared as a juror before that seat of judgment to accuse Hermann.

The first summons to Hermann to appear before Dortmund's tribunal was from the court's chairman, Freigraf Wilhelm von der Sunghen (also spelled "Sungen" or "Zunger"). The paper was dated 27 July 1451. Addressing Hermann as *"synen guden Frund"* (Old German for "his good friend"), the count summoned the knight "through the power of the king and will of his judge, by which he has the right to judge over life and honor according to laws and rights decided by the Holy Empire." The charge said that Hermann had captured Steffen Kullart "on a free roadway of the empire and, without consideration, had damaged his honor, both vis-á-vis good custom and law."

Mallinckrodt, consequently, was being summoned to the secret court to answer "with his life and honor to the highest law." However, as historians point out, since Mallinckrodt himself was a member of the Fehmgericht organization, he was not obliged to answer the first summons delivered by two Freischöffen.[14]

At the same time, Dortmund also appealed to the city of Unna since Hermann had taken his prisoner there. In its answer, dated 30 August 1451, Unna said it recognized that Hermann and his brother Cracht had become Dortmund's enemies and that Hermann had seized a citizen without declaring a feud. However, Unna went on, it could do nothing about the matter: Mallinckrodt had not been in their city for a long time, and so Unna left it to Dortmund to proceed in the matter.

On 9 October, Dortmund's Count of Sunghen addressed a second communiqué to Hermann, this one delivered by four jurors. It said that court had been held on 5 October and the accusation had been repeated, but Hermann had not appeared despite proper initial legal summons by two jurors. The count pointed out as well that Hermann also had not sent anyone to represent him on this legal day of judgment and thereby had become "disobedient" toward the court. Consequently, through power of the 9 October letter and four jurors, the Count now officially ordered Hermann to appear "in person" on 23 November to defend himself. If Hermann did not appear, then, the communiqué continued, the count could not deny the plaintiff's demand that the court "might let the sword fall, that one might judge accordingly."

Hermann, however, did not appear at that second court session on 23 November. The document of the court's proceedings without him describes in some detail the theft, the summons, and Hermann's response. Concerning the last aspect, apparently the two jurors who delivered the first October summons had been made fearful by Hermann's angry response: in fact, his disobedience toward the court had deteriorated into "pain and broken bones." (He apparently assaulted the two jurors.) The second summons of November, the jurors testified, was taken to the residence of Hermann's father (that is, Haus Mallinckrodt), where Hermann lived with his parents. There the court emissaries posted the sealed communiqué on the gateway to the estate, thus making the summons "binding, valid, and legal." As Weintzek has reconstructed their story,

> The four entrusted jurors set out one day and tried to reach Burg Wetter via detours and rarely traveled paths through the woods and ravines. Near the fortress they waited until evening. Hans Wortmann, the smartest among them who knew the region best, volunteered to deliver the summons. The other three stood guard at the nearby slopes in order to warn him, through agreed upon signals, of approaching danger.
>
> Seen from the east side, the fortress seemed to rest on a high, jagged cliff. Between the fortress wall and the edge of the steep slope there was only a small edge, in places barely two feet wide. Since the jurors did not risk approaching the fortress over the usual paths, they tried to reach the entrance over the slope's narrow edge. The bold venture succeeded. Wortmann made his way unnoticed to the entrance gate, quietly and cautiously fastened the summons letter on the gateway lattice, cut three slivers out of the gate as evidence of his action, and returned to his companions by the same dangerous route.[15]

Since Hermann did not answer that second summons, a third, for 27 April, was delivered by six jurors. That summons, describing the substance of the pending case, closed with the words, "We must judge appropriately in order to protect the high court."

Apparently Hermann now realized that he had to answer. First he asked his lord, the Herzog of Cleve and Graf von der Mark, to mediate with the local chairman of the court, Freigraf Hermann Hackenberg of Volmestein. Then Hermann declared his willingness to appear before a court of judgment on 20 April, insisting that it not be in Dortmund (to which he felt he owed no allegiance). Instead, he said he would show up in Herdecke (where he did owe allegiance to the Count of Volmestein and, in turn, the Grafschaft Mark).

This position was stated in a letter that Hermann, together with his brothers Dietrich and Cracht, sent by ten men to Count von der Sunghen in Dortmund and the juror Renold Weselken, who had brought the charge. The same day the Count of Volmestein, taking up the cause of his knight, wrote a letter of his own to the Dortmund court, pointing out that the Grafschaft Mark also had forbidden the city of Dortmund to burden Hermann with its claims.

In the next round of correspondence, the Count of Dortmund refused, in turn, to appear in Herdecke; instead, he offered to be present at the king's court (*Königshof*) near Dortmund. Although a detailed record was not available for that date, analysts have deduced that the court session was postponed and further efforts made to bring Hermann to trial. Indeed, later research concluded (1) that Mallinckrodt also ignored that fourth summons, after which the *Verfemung*, or condemnation, was declared, and (2) that if the knight had answered any of the summons he would have been summarily hanged.[16]

According to Haren, the historian who studied Hermann's case, "We know nothing about the further developments of the trial. Nevertheless, a judgment of Hermann does not seem to have taken place." If there was a conviction, it must have been later dissolved, for it was clear from other documents that the city of Dortmund did not hold the affair against Hermann. This assumption was based on records showing that in 1456 Hermann's brother Cracht (Kracht) carried out a friendly debt-repayment transaction with Dortmund, that a letter of reconciliation was offered the city on behalf of the other brother Dietrich, and that Cracht and Hermann themselves became *Männer der Stadt Dortmund*, that is, soldiers in the city's pay.[17]

Hermann's brush with the Fehmgericht has interested more than historians concerned about the court's role in Prussian history. Painters, too, saw the case as dramatic subject matter, especially when old Westphalian records were available and figures as colorful as Hermann were ordered to appear before the problematic tribunal. Thus, although it is doubtful that Hermann ever presented himself to the court, a Düsseldorf artist, Professor L. Heupel-Siegen, later painted the scene as he imagined it (plate 3). *Hermann Mallinckrodt Before the Secret Court in 1450*, which hangs in the City Hall of Wetter, shows a rather fierce-looking knight clad in the plate armor customary to the time and facing his tunic-clad jurors.[18] The prize-winning picture, which Professor Heupel-Siegen painted in 1912 on commission from the Art Society of Düsseldorf, was described by Haren in this way:

> Jurors are gathered around a stone table on a wooded hillside. The site is surrounded by knights. Hermann Mallinckrodt, fully clad in armor, stands before them, obviously very agitated. He defends himself, and what he says is energetically contradicted by those present. The count who heads the stone table has jumped up from his seat. Two jurors exchange whispered views of what they have heard. The entire gathering follows the words with the most intense attention. Everything indicates great liveliness, and wonderfully realistic is the foreground figure of an old gnarled Westphalian with white beard. His thoughtful facial expression shows what a deep impression Hermann's actions make on him. The figure of Hermann is defiant and powerful: his right arm and armored fist is held high; the left is stretched out toward the court.
>
> The entire painting is a valuable historical document of that time. In this context, it is irrelevant whether, according to the records, Hermann really appeared before the court or not. The picture radiates the spirit of that time, reflecting the defiant stance of Hermann, who senses his power and refuses to subordinate himself.

Interestingly, Haren comments that "in response to a special wish, Professor Heupel-Siegen used the face of a living member of the von Mallinckrodt family as a model for his depiction of Hermann."[19] According to another explanation given by the city of Wetter, "The chairman took his place, laid his sword and willow twig on the table, called to his side the seven jurors who had to appear bareheaded, without weapons, and in short coats. The participants [*Umstand*] gathered around them (in Dortmund it had to be 30 persons). From here on total silence was a strict obligation."[20]

Elisabeth

As not only individual but also organized resistance against the Fehmgerichte grew, other old records tell us about another Mallinckrodt confrontation with the law. This time, about 1480, it concerned a servant of Hermann's sister Elisabeth. This case involved a Mallinckrodt serf's legal right to freedom if he resided within the city walls of Dortmund for a year and a day.

When Hermann's young sister Elisabeth I married the widowed knight Heinrich von Bergheim, he was lord of Hof Aprath in Westphalia and sovereign over some sixteen separate estates. (Meanwhile, brother Hermann through marriage had become lord of Haus Lüntenbeck near Elberfeld [plate 4].)[21] Heinrich was known as a stern lord who worked his servants very hard and did not deal justly with the farmers tilling his lands. To ease the homesickness Elisabeth might feel in that new environment, her father, Dietrich IV, had given her her own servant, Johann, whom she had long known at her home estate, Haus Mallinckrodt. Lord Heinrich did not approve, however, of Johann's special relationship to the mistress of Aprath, and the servant was assigned to fieldwork away from the manor house. Ill from that hard work, Johann after some time asked Elisabeth for permission to visit his parents and brothers and sisters, to go back just once more to the Ruhr Valley. Elisabeth, of course, could not grant the wish on her own. But when she asked her husband, Lord Heinrich agreed, and Johann set off happily.

On the day the servant was to return to Aprath from his visit, he was not seen. Weeks went by and he still did not return. He also was not to be found at Haus Mallinckrodt, his former home. He had disappeared without a trace.

About a year later another Aprath serf, Peter, who was steward and confidant to Lord Heinrich, visited the city of Dortmund, where he had gone to buy textiles for his lord. After he finished that transaction, Peter the steward went to a brewery to drink a glass of beer. As he sat down, he saw a man he thought he recognized. And know him he did: it was Johann, Elisabeth's servant who had been missing so long.

After they greeted each other, Johann proudly informed Peter that he no longer was a serf. Through the city he had escaped feudal servitude. In fact, Johann very soon would be a citizen of the freie Reichsstadt Dortmund, for he had lived there for a year and day. Explaining this to Peter with the Dortmund saying "The air of the city makes you free!" Johann related that at the next meeting of the city council he would get his certificate of citizenship. Moreover, Johann went on, he was now an apprentice in Hildebrand Sudermann's brewery, and maybe one day he would become a master brewer.

Returning to Aprath, Peter immediately informed his master of Johann's whereabouts. What Elisabeth said or felt is not known, but it was recorded that Heinrich at once began trying to get the serf back. Johann, however, did not answer the lord's letter demanding his return, nor did Dortmund's Mayor Kleppink or its city council.

When Lord Heinrich rode to Dortmund to see the mayor and personally demand Johann's return, his request was coolly heard. The mayor simply explained the city's laws about residency, adding that in Dortmund it was not a crime for a serf to escape bondage. Next Heinrich tried to play tricks with Johann's elapsed time of residence, that is, to make it shorter than the "year and a day" required for freedom. Again the mayor said only that the city council would check on it.

Now completely frustrated, Lord Heinrich began to plot to forcibly kidnap Johann. Brother-in-law Hermann von Mallinckrodt at Haus Lüntenbeck agreed to cooperate. And, of course, it was the loyal steward Peter who was sent back to Dortmund to lure the former serf into a trap. So, in fact, Johann was captured in Dortmund by Lord Heinrich's men, tied to a horse, taken back to Aprath, and locked in the tower.

When the Dortmund City Council members found out about the kidnapping of their soon-to-be-citizen, they were furious. This was simply an intervention in Dortmund's rights as a free imperial city! Immediately the council formulated a letter to Duke Wilhelm of Jülich-Berg, the ruler to whom the lords Heinrich and Hermann owed allegiance. Moreover, the mayor personally carried the letter to the duke's residence in Düsseldorf, asking him to bring pressure to bear on his subjects. The duke, however, pointed out to his mayoral visitor that in his duchy serfs were personal property and that not everyone shared Dortmund's liberal view of human freedom.

More than a year went by while Duke Wilhelm allegedly considered Dortmund's claim. Johann, meanwhile, was still being held in Aprath. Finally Dortmund's leaders lost their patience. They dispatched a letter of challenge, a *Fehdebrief*, to Aprath and Lüntenbeck and sent out an armed contingent of Dortmund soldiers led by Johann's brewery boss and city council member, Sudermann.

Arriving at Aprath where Johann was being held, the Dortmunders found neither their potential citizen nor the lord of the manor. Angered, they destroyed Heinrich's buildings and property. Then they rode on to Haus Lüntenbeck, the Hof of Elisabeth's brother Hermann, who supported Heinrich's efforts to get Johann back. Somewhere nearby they found Heinrich's loyal steward, Peter, who had been left in charge, and took him hostage.

Now there were two prisoners—Johann, still held somewhere by Lord Heinrich, and Peter, held by Dortmund. For four years the two parties argued, adamantly refusing to exchange their captives; mutual accusations, new attacks, new mediations by the Duke of Jülich-Berg followed.[22]

Unfortunately, how this story ended is not known: again the records are incomplete. Sadly, too, Elisabeth's personal views are not known, although she apparently was very fond of her servant and perhaps also no stranger to the idea of treating subordinates kindly. What was absolutely clear, however, was the attitude of Dortmund: its citizens took very seriously the saying that their "city air is equal to freedom" and were prepared to risk much to prove it. As would be seen, that tradition was passed on to many generations to come.[23]

Knight Wilhelm

About a decade later, in 1491, historical focus shifted to another Mallinckrodt, Hermann I's son Wilhelm I. The accounts of his activities in Westphalia once again illustrated the political power struggles of the time, as well as the legal ones involving feuds, serfs, and seemingly never-ending familial property quarrels. Especially interesting, too, are the records' insights into what life was like for the soldier knights of Germany toward the end of the fifteenth century as their military role in society was fading vis-á-vis the growing urban centers.[24] In fact, the irregular actions in which some knights were then involved would earn them history's label of "robber knights."

Like seven previous generations of Mallinckrodts who had been knights in the service of feudal lords, Wilhelm, too, was a free-lance soldier of his time. His father, Hermann Mallinckrodt of Haus Lüntenbeck (plate 4), had soldiered for the ruling princes and dukes of the day and come into conflict with Dortmund. So, too, did Wilhelm, who had his problems with the city as early as 1481.

Around that time the young von Mallinckrodt declared a feud against Dortmund because it was sheltering a runaway serf whom Wilhelm had inherited from his father. Once again (as in the case involving the servant of Wilhelm's aunt Elisabeth), Dortmund refused to deliver the serf who denied Wilhelm's ownership. And also again, like his father before him, Wilhelm captured the serf, destroyed crops, and carried on his feud against the city for all of the year 1482.

At the same time—and when not actively feuding—father Hermann and son Wilhelm were also involved, peacefully, with the bigger city of Köln on the Rhine River. In 1485, for instance, during a salt shortage, Köln opened its salt stores to meet the region's nutritional needs.[25] First stores at the *Schafentor*, or gate, were opened, and when they were not adequate, the city council decided to make those at the Hahnen gate available as well. There Hermann, as a salt dealer, was allowed to buy a certain amount on a specific day.

Throughout the next years, Wilhelm also frequently requested, and received, safe-conduct passage into the city on the Rhine to carry out his business and trade. Permission to enter the city was usually granted for a month, or shorter periods, provided Wilhelm gave a three-day advance notice and there were no "challenges from the citizens" (*exceptis civibus*). Sometimes the safe-conduct included Wilhelm's father Hermann or Wilhelm's servant. Interestingly, too, because of Wilhelm's regional feuds, Köln frequently wanted reassurance that he had not and would not trespass on its friendliness. In spring 1489, for instance, he wrote that his recent attack on his enemies had occurred three days after he had left Köln and, furthermore, that he had indeed released his captive.[26]

Over the years, in one action after another, Wilhelm contributed greatly to the enmity between two local dukes, the Duke of Kleve and the Duke of Jülich, the latter of whom Wilhelm favored as his father had. To reduce the tension, the Duke of Jülich even asked Wilhelm's father, Hermann, to try to influence his son. Interestingly, the old knight said he had no power over his offspring. And so the feuding went on, with the Duke of Kleve pronouncing Wilhelm his enemy, while the Duke of Jülich said he really had nothing to do with Mallinckrodt.

Not finding satisfaction or assistance anywhere for his charge that estate property had been taken from him, Wilhelm announced in 1491 that he would take matters into his own hands. And that he did: with the help of two servants, he rode into the Kleve area and captured a serf. Wilhelm justified his action by saying that he had become a poor man since his property was taken from him, and the capture of the Klevean serf was an act of revenge. He wanted ransom money for him. The whole affair did not, however, please his feudal lord, the Duke of Jülich, who wanted no new trouble with his opponent, the Duke of Kleve. But Wilhem refused to give in to his lord's demands or to appear at consultations between the two dukes. And so the matter went back and forth for some time, with threats being answered by counterthreats.

Meanwhile, in 1492–93 Wilhelm von Mallinckrodt turned a corner in his life: he joined forces with a young duke, Karl of Geldern, whom he would serve for twenty-five years. Wilhelm was hired as *Rittmeister*, or cavalry captain, of the soldiers Karl was recruiting for a campaign to regain areas he once controlled. From this position with Geldern, Wilhelm could continue to make life difficult for his old enemy, the Duke of Kleve, who was also the enemy of the young Duke Karl.

Wilhelm apparently exercised his enmity against Kleve with vigor: when the Archbishop of Köln tried to mediate the quarrel between Geldern and Kleve in 1496, he was given an impressive list of damages that Wilhelm von Mallinckrodt's war and plundering had cost Kleve. Included were 3,000 gulden in damage to its administrative headquarters, which Wilhelm had set on fire and robbed before taking prisoners. More attacks on Klevean towns followed. Repeatedly the Duke of Kleve had retaliated against Geldern towns, which were protecting Wilhelm.

Despite all the troubles between the duchies and towns, Wilhelm von Mallinckrodt remained a soldier in the service of Duke Karl of Geldern. Indeed, documents show that in recognition of his services and oath of allegiance, Wilhelm was given custody of Haus Lichtenborg, which Karl had bought to make into a fortress.

But apparently during his service to Duke Karl, the fortunes of war had also cost Mallinckrodt a great deal. For instance, the knight's settlement with his lord in 1501 showed how much Wilhelm had been paid over the years. Deducting that, his restitution demands then came to another 700 Rheinisch gulden—for time in prison, loss of horses and armor, outstanding pay, costs of fortifying Lichtenborg, plus his own armament and that of his servants. As payment, the duke gave Wilhelm the right to income from Lichtenborg and other estates in the duchy. (In turn, Wilhelm was to do service on the farms twice a year, once at hay harvesting time in spring and once at straw time in fall.) In addition, the duke promised to pay Wilhelm fifty gulden on the debt within the next quarter year and to pay thirty-nine gulden interest on the remainder.

Another recorded milestone in Wilhelm's life came shortly before 1513 when his father, Hermann I, died at the family estate Lüntenbeck. Wilhelm quickly left the Geldern area to take over his inheritance and to immediately install an administrator. But Wilhelm would have a long fight for this property: his half-sister Elisabeth II, demanding 50 percent of the parental inheritance, wanted Lüntenbeck for herself. Moreover, in pressing her claim against her brother, Elisabeth had powerful help: Wilhelm's old enemy, the Duke of Kleve, was on her side. To get back at Wilhelm and aid Elisabeth, the duke not surprisingly thought up some creative moves: the embargo of income from the contested Lüntenbeck estate and a trusteeship over its management until legal ownership was determined. Thus, when Wilhelm tried to enter his house in November 1513, he was denied access. Furthermore, the "trusty hands" into which the estate had been put were those of the magistrate in the city of Solingen, Johann Quade, who, not coincidentally, happened to be Elisabeth's husband!

While protesting these machinations and demanding a prompt judgment about the future ownership of Lüntenbeck, Wilhelm was dealt another blow. During his absence from Haus Lichtenborg, his antagonist the Duke of Kleve somehow managed to take it over. Thus, Wilhelm no longer had Lichtenborg nor yet had Lüntenbeck. Instead, he was staying at Haus Nyenbeck, which Duke Karl of Geldern had made available to him in custody.

Finally, apparently having had enough of all the quarrels and postponed hearings, the Duke of Geldern involved himself directly in his knight's dispute. Writing to the officials involved, Karl said that he had always appreciated the services of his dear and loyal Wilhelm von Mallinckrodt and, therefore, as Duke of Geldern, would like to see the property conflicts settled for all time.

This, unfortunately, was the last documentary evidence concerning Wilhelm von Mallinckrodt—a warm recognition of services rendered to the state of Geldern and also a high personal evaluation from the lord whom Wilhelm had served with all his strength for a quarter-century. Later documents showed that ultimately the controversy over the parental estate Lüntenbeck was settled in Wilhelm's favor: after his death at the end of 1521 or the beginning of 1522, the estate went to his only daughter, Agnes.

Church Officials

As the 1400s drew to an end, other Mallinckrodts, too, were leaving historical footprints. The Brunninghaus branch of the family near Dortmund, for instance, was making significant contributions through their service to the church. For example, Helmich became Bishop of Dorpat in 1459, and Everhard became *Domprobst* (cathedral provost, or head superintendent) in Dorpat in about 1468. Crusader Gerhard, who had gone to Riga and Reval and was Landmarschall there in 1462–1468, rose to the top of the Council of the German Order in Livland (an area in Latvia and Estonia) and was very active in church and state politics of the time.

By the 1500s, Father said, our family began to enter city life here in Dortmund. The landed nobility, moving to the city, served it as mercenaries. Not only Hermann and Cracht von Mallinckrodt, whom we met before, served Dortmund, but Eberhard VI, too. In fact, in 1515 he was the first Mallinckrodt to be listed as a Dortmund citizen; adjusting to city life and its growing middle class he stopped using the *von* in the family name. Other Mallinckrodts, starting with Arnold I in 1589, would make their way into the city's ruling circles through the powerful textile society, the *Wandschneider-Gesellschaft*.

This level of society naturally enjoyed the artistic and cultural achievements of the Renaissance, that period of European rebirth begun in Italy in the 1300s and ending the Middle Ages. In fact, the availability of more money and goods also stimulated formal contracts and public statements regulating finances between marriage partners. Interesting old documents disclose the arrangements, for instance, between Mallinckrodts at Haus Mallinckrodt in 1532, at Haus Küchen near Ahlen in 1540, and in Dortmund in 1562.

In this period the Peasants' War and Reformation also deeply touched the lives of family members. When Dortmund became Protestant, for instance, so did the Mallinckrodts living there. Elsewhere others remained Catholic for a while longer, for example, the Haus Küchen branch of the family. In fact, its son, Herman IV, possibly the first Köln Mallinckrodt, was buried in the city's St. Maria Ablass Catholic church in 1579.

Meanwhile at Haus Mallinckrodt on the Ruhr another family scene, typical of the so-called age of landownership, was being acted out— years of familial quarrels over who owned what. The story of the brothers Hermann III and Dietrich VIII is not only long but tragic, ending in murders that cast shadows on the proud old estate.

Incredibly, this, too, is another chapter of family history documented by court records preserved over hundreds of years. Time has not diminished the drama of the notary testimony, which I will read to you, taken after the 1594 death of Lord Dietrich von Mallinckrodt at the hand of his estranged brother's son, that is, his nephew. That testimony tells not only about greed and human weaknesses but also the nature of agriculture, military arms, the loyalty of serfs, and the language at that time. The lessons are as clear as the details are fascinating, a relevant footnote to the 1500s.

5

1500

Dortmund

Not only did Mallinckrodts contest with the city of Dortmund, as Herbord and Dietrich had, but they also served it. Indeed, the city nobility often used the landed nobility to defend their settlements—Hermann and Cracht von Mallinckrodt, for instance, in about 1456, and Eberhard VI in 1491.

Indeed, Eberhard is the first Mallinckrodt to be listed in Dortmund's records: he appears first as a taxpayer in 1497, followed by his son Goswin as a citizen in 1515; in 1524 he is recorded as selling property in the Stovengaße.[1] Through his later ties to Recklinghausen and in turn from there back to Steinberg and Haus Mallinckrodt, Eberhard thus links the Dortmund family members directly to Ludwig in the 1200s.[2] Eberhard exemplifies the Landadel moving to the city and serving it as mercenaries, or *famulus*. As the historian Joachim Bumke has said, "Almost everywhere they [city nobility] had close social and familial ties to the landed nobility and recruited . . . those to whom the city rulers wanted to give important posts."[3] These Mallinckrodts were not robber knights upsetting the countryside; rather, they were forerunners of an urban bourgeoisie whose rise signaled the coming of the modern era.

In this period, Dortmund citizenship was highly prized. Recorded on parchment sheets dating back to 1295, citizenship was granted after a number of rather strict requirements were met: the prospective citizen was required to own property, to pay a tax on that property, and then to swear fealty to the city, including an oath to serve in its defense. (As mentioned in chapter 4, serfs were required to reside in the city for a year and a day before being granted citizenship.) A citizen's "service" included helping to build and guard the city walls and standing watch

41

in stormy weather. In addition, he had to bring a good weapon to his watch and later also a leather water bucket (*Löscheimer*) for fighting fires. The service included as well the *Riet*, or obligation to ride after an enemy on horseback, as when the city bells rang and the call to arms and pursuit was heard.

In return for these obligations of citizenship, Dortmunders had the right to graze their cattle on the city's meadows and to cut wood in the city's forests. Those who could not or did not want to meet the requirements (for financial reasons) at first were called "half-citizens" (*Palbürger*) and later "residents" (*Einwohner*). The city council, of course, could withdraw citizenship for good cause, as from a Dortmund woman who married a noncitizen or from someone who served an outside lord considered to be an enemy of the city.[4]

In the 1500s Dortmund had fifty towers, four bastions, and triple-thick walls.[5] The bells of its thirteenth-century Marienkirche called the city council and the court into session. Before the council meeting, in fact, the *Erbsassen* (those holding inherited seats) met in the so-called mortuary (*Leichenhaus*) of the church and then went into the sanctuary for a sermon.[6]

In addition to four church schools, Dortmund also now had its *Archigymnasium* (academic high school), founded in 1543. After examination, children could transfer from the church schools to the gymnasium with its seven grades, which prepared pupils for academic vocations. It also was open to gifted sons of craftsmen families who were excused from paying the school fee or buying books.[7] Girls, however, were not allowed to attend this gymnasium, just as they were not allowed to join their middle-class brothers in attending Europe's growing universities.

From a business point of view, Dortmund was still a leader in textiles but also in the production of iron, hats, and beer. The city was also the staple market between Antwerp and Bremen where all goods in transit had to be offered for sale for three days.[8] In addition to their businesses, Dortmund's wealthy citizens now were earning income through land and real estate, too, and by loaning money.[9]

And, of course, with that wealth they bought new items of beauty and comfort, for it was the Renaissance, the rebirth of European artistic and cultural life. Typical purchases included stoneware, tiled stoves, and ivory carvings from Köln, tapestries from Brussels and Antwerp worked with mythological and historical scenes, gilt-bronze and brass clocks from Augsburg, as well as bronze lamps, candlesticks, and ink stands.[10] Other favorite furnishings were beautiful wooden chests decorated with details and ornaments, the new piece of furniture called the *dressoir*, with its several doors and drawers, beds with canopies, and cupboards with inlaid woods and ivory; by this time, too, the two-pronged fork had become common.[11]

Gradually this new monied, upper middle class, called the *Honoratioren* (perhaps best translated as "the honorable society"), gained the right to serve on the city council, a right that the Patriziat once had held alone. In 1585, for instance, the first nonpatrician Dortmunder to serve on the council in one of its first six seats took up his position.[12] Thus, the Patriziat, the *Honoratioren*, and the guilds each controlled six seats on the city council.

In this period, the role of the powerful Wandschneider-Gesellschaft was changing, too. As of about 1542 their textile stalls in the Rathaus apparently had been given up, and cloth could be cut only at open yearly trade fairs and midweek markets.[13] But business was good, especially with the demand for flat caps rather than hats and the new style overcoat, the *Schaube*. Shaped like a cassock without sleeves and often woven in bright colors and lined with fur, the Schaube was the fashion for well-to-do men.[14]

Marriage Contracts

The availability of more money and goods apparently also changed personal relationships. For instance, formal prenuptial contracts were signed between well-to-do partners and witnessed by their fathers and other relatives. According to the records, Mallinckrodts concluded such agreements at least as early as 1532: on 22 November of that year, Dietrich von Mallinckrodt VII, of Haus Mallinckrodt, and Elisabeth von Elverfelde, "legitimate daughter of Jasper of Elverfelde and tax-paying resident of Wetter province," signed a lengthy and detailed marriage agreement before witnesses.[15] Important in these contracts were the provisions made for women (now marrying later—that is, at age fifteen to eighteen) who at the time could not always inherit land in all jurisdictions. Especially interesting, also, are provisions made for the groom's father until his death.

Typical, for example, was the slightly later (1540) agreement between "Hinrick [Heinrich] Mallinckrodth [II], son of the couple Hermann Mallinckrodth and Elsa on the one hand, and Mechtelt von Oer, daughter of Berndt and Stine von Oer of Kakesbecke, on the other hand."[16] According to its provisions,

• Hinrick was to receive 1,000 Rheinisch gold gulden, 500 in cash, as the bridal dowry (*Brautschatz*).

• When the bride was brought to Hinrick's estate, Küchen, he would give her an honest *Morgengabe* [bridegroom's gift to his bride on the day after marriage, that is, his dowry]. Her father then would pay another 500 gold gulden to the mayor of Münster [to cover a debt incurred there by Hinrick's father, Hermann] and would have five promissory notes issued, each for 100 gulden. If Hinrick Mallinckrodt received those five notes, in addition to the 500 cash gulden, he would be very satisfied and write out a receipt.

• If Hinrick were to die after the wedding, Mechtelt might stay at Haus Küchen or Daellhuissen until Hinrick's next heir returned her bridal dowry, as well as 500 gold gulden, her clothing, and jewelry.

• If Mechelt died without offsprings, Hinrick within a year would pay her heirs 500 gulden, in addition to her clothing and jewelry.

• As was custom and law, Hinrick would also provide his wife with an annuity so that she would be cared for. Should Hinrick die before that was accomplished, his heirs should do so within a year. So long as it was not done [the annuity established], Mechelt would continue to enjoy the entire children's share of Hinrick's inheritance.

• If Hinrick were to die before his wife and leave offspring, Mechelt would assume the entire inheritance of her husband and take on the guardian rights over it for the children. If she remarried, she would keep, as long as she lived, only the annuity and the Morgengabe.

• Before her marriage, Berndt von Oer promised to provide his daughter, as was the custom of Münster, with clothing and jewels, in return for which she and Hinrick Mallinckrodt would waive all inheritance claims on the parents and parents-in-law.

• If the father, Hermann Mallinckrodt, could not live together with the young couple, then he would live in Daelhuissen. Then, however, the annual 50 gold gulden interest on the 1,000 gold gulden bridal dowry would stay at Haus Küchen and be saved for the father and mother's care. By contrast, if father and son lived in one house, then the annual interest should be invested to the benefit of Hinrick and Mechelt. "As long as the parents Mallinckrodth live, they retain unqualified ownership of Haus Küchen."

• If either the intended bride or groom die before marriage, this entire contract is void.

Witnesses on Hinrick's side: Melchior van Buren, cathedral servant; Hermann Mallinckrodt the father and his son Dirick; Johan von Schuren, citizen of Werden; Antonius von Laer; on the side of the bride, Berndt von Oer, the father; Rotger Smnisinck, cathedral dean and provost; Dirick Ketteler, cathedral sexton in Münster; Hermann von Oer, citizen of Delmenhorst; Johan von Aldenbockum; Bernt von Beverfoirde.[17]

Even among families who were less rich, fixed financial agreements apparently played a role in marriages. The legally binding arrangements were made public in the *Morgensprache*, or witnessed statements made the day after the wedding—that is, after the marriage was consummated. Mallinckrodts were often witnesses at the Morgensprache; Goswin, for instance, served in that capacity as early as 1559.[18]

The Morgensprache reflected Westphalia's gradually evolving property law, including property jointly acquired during marriage. One of the basic features of the Morgensprache was the provision that upon a spouse's death, his or her survivor would inherit half the estate and the children half; if there were no children, the deceased's relatives inherited half.

Care also was taken to include provisions that would avoid at least some inheritance quarrels among those relatives. Thus, the *Wederkar* was specified, that is, a certain sum to be inherited by a relative of the deceased if the deceased had no children; the relative was typically named in the Morgensprache. The Wederkar, which was to be paid within fourteen days of the person's death, was only a fraction, a token, of the deceased's total wealth. Later a *Godegift* was specified as well, that is, a gift for religious or other purposes. Although different for bride and groom, the two promises taken together were of equal value. In addition, it was customary in the Morgensprache to include the partners' "best clothes" as value brought into the marriage.[19] Thus, the following was recorded in 1562 in Dortmund:

> In the year 1562, on Monday the nineteenth day of October, a Morgensprache was held between the noble Heinrich Mallinckrott [III], on the one side, and the virtuous Anna, his legal wife, on the other side.
>
> Heinrich's Wedderkar is 50 Dortmund Taler; Anna's is 100 Dortmund Taler.
>
> Heinrich's Godegift is 100 Dortmund Taler and equally his best clothes; Anna's Godegift is 50 Dortmund Taler and equally her best dress.
>
> It was further said and promised at the Morgensprache that in case the bride would die without living heirs and the above agreed-to Wedderkar would be due, so the same Wedderkar shall go to the named bride's half-sister, named Nelleke van Raisfelt, or the legal heirs who would carry out the testament.

Along with the changes in economics, Dortmund's textile society had also evolved into a social-class association, as well as a professional one, and its procedures were becoming more democratic. The society was chaired by an alderman, decisions were made by majority rule, and disputes among members were settled autonomously.[21] The first Mallinckrodt to be registered as a member of the Wandschneider-Gesellschaft was Arnold I, whose name was first listed in 1589.[22] Like the first Mallinckrodt citizen in Dortmund, Arnold, too, dropped the *von* from the name while continuing to use the family coat of arms. This was seen as a gesture of accommodation to changing concepts of prestige emerging from the growing middle class in the cities.[23]

Reformation

News reached Dortmund slowly in the 1500s, but when it came it was exciting. Columbus had sailed for the Indies, Cortez had conquered the Aztecs in Mexico, and a man named Martin Luther was preaching reform in the Catholic church. It was the last news that dramatically changed life in Westphalia.

Some Dortmund leaders had advocated church reform early in the 1500s, but the City Council, wanting to keep peace among the citizens, persistently resisted change. However, after the Edict of Worms in 1521, unrest broke out anew within the city. More serious, though, was the great current of unrest in the countryside. Living in the shadow of a manor house or castle, the peasants felt themselves increasingly exploited. Their cottages—pictured so well in the paintings by Brueghel—were dim, dirty, and bitterly cold, and the peasants had to pay off their noble lord and the church before they could feed their own family. Moreover, mercenary bands roamed about the countryside attacking their villages.

The peasants' demands were then not primarily religious but rather economic and political, concerning even the right to wear red clothing as did the princes.[24] Nevertheless, Luther's Reformation sparked an explosion. What he said against the church's trafficking in indulgences was especially appealing to the oppressed; many unhesitatingly agreed that paying off one's sins only put more money into the church's already overflowing coffers and did little for one's soul.

The rural people, therefore, finally struck back, in the bloody Peasants' War of 1524. Beginning in the south, the rebellion spread over western Germany within a year. Although Luther condemned it, other religious leaders did not, and it went on for some time. It was a costly uprising: some 100,000 peasants were killed for their rebellion and countless others left homeless by the fighting. Their villages and fields destroyed, the peasants roamed the countryside, famine and disease erupting anew among them. Another cost was long-range: since Germany did not deal adequately with the needs of the peasants, it postponed a serious problem. In a later century it would boil up again and then involve a Mallinckrodt who became known as "the peasants' lawyer."

In the cities, by contrast, the call for church reformation brought different changes. In Dortmund, for instance, by 1527 four of the six guild members of the city council demanded new ministers. With growing news of changes in other parts of Germany, the pastor of Dortmund's Marienkirche by 1554 also preached openly against abuses within the church. In 1561 reform-minded citizens asked the city council to allow the churches to offer Holy Communion in the Protestant manner (serving of the wine to parishioners), as well as in the Catholic tradition (serving the bread only). The council now had to concede, for such citizens were already attending services in a nearby church where an Evangelical preacher was following the new communion practice. Then in 1563 German-language hymns were permitted, and the next year a book with Psalms and hymns by Luther appeared in Dortmund. Other prayer and communion reforms followed in the city's four churches.[25]

By 1577, then, Dortmund was considered a Protestant city. The venerable old Reinoldikirche and the Marienkirche were made Protestant. The latter, however, did not give up its Catholic name (Saint Mary's) or the Catholic artifacts decorating its Romanesque interior.

Other effects of the Reformation were also felt and heard in Dortmund. For instance, the city's oath of citizenship changed, from "so help me God and all saints" to "so help me God and his holy gospel" (*und syn hillige evangelium*). In addition, a Dortmund citizen now swore not to be "obligated to a religion forbidden in the Roman Empire."[26] New goals for education also were being discussed. Reformation leaders demanded schools for the common people where boys and girls would have at least two hours of instruction daily in reading and writing; in this way they would learn to read the Bible and also learn the Ten Commandments, the Lord's Prayer, and the Confession of Faith.[27]

From the early 1600s on, the Dortmund Mallinckrodts were members of the Lutheran congregations of the Marienkirche and the Reinoldikirche. (The later Catholic line of the family came through conversion or confessional differences in marriage.)[28] Outside of Dortmund, however, other Mallinckrodts remained Catholic for a while longer—for instance, the family of Heinrich II of Haus Küchen near Ahlen. Heinrich's son Herman IV, possibly the first Mallinckrodt to establish himself in Köln, was buried in 1579 in its Saint Maria Ablass (Saint Mary of Indulgences), one of many magnificent Roman Catholic churches in a city hardly touched by the Reformation. An old parish church, it was referred to in records dating to A.D. 927 as the Church of Mary and was probably constructed in Köln's great church-building period around 900.[29]

Here in Saint Maria Ablass, Hermann IV was buried in 1579. Several years later a family grave was bought in the church and forty Reichstaler paid to adorn Hermann's tombstone with the family's engraved coat of arms.[30] In 1608 Heinrich IV and Eberhard VII, Hermann's brothers, and other noble relatives complained to the city of Köln that Hermann's grave had been desecrated. The casket had been opened and the coat of arms chiseled out of the stone. Promising to restore the tombstone, the city council also said it would punish the guilty parties.[31]

Not many of the church's old graves and their inscriptions from the 1500s survived in readable form, and Hermann von Mallinckrodt's inscription was not among those preserved. It may have been lost when the church was closed in 1804 and the structure removed in 1808. Nevertheless, the Chapel of Our Lady— where Hermann and his family probably lit votive candles—survived five centuries. Under old protective trees, the little white chapel is intact, and Mary still smiles in its venerated fresco. Seated on a throne, she shows the child Jesus, standing on her knees, a flower in her right hand, which he apparently rejects in favor of the small book in her left hand.[32]

Haus Mallinckrodt

Outside Dortmund, Mallinckrodt family members continued to be involved in the legal struggles for ownership that marked this period of land division through inheritance. In 1575, for instance, the brothers Hermann III and Dietrich VIII divided the original family estate. According to knightly rules of the time, older brother Hermann received the Gut Mallinckrodt, consisting primarily of meadows, cleared land, and a mill, while younger brother Dietrich received the land grants to Burg Wetter and Burg Volmestein and some other property, including Hof

Steinberg. The forests were to be shared. Each brother was also to furnish two of the four sisters with a dowry. Dietrich, however, felt he had been shortchanged, and years of court quarrels between the brothers followed, from 1586 through 1592. The conflict ended tragically in 1594 with a double murder: Hermann's son Henske stabbed his uncle Dietrich with a lance; Dietrich shot his nephew with a long gun (*Büchse*).[33] Both Mallinckrodts soon died of their wounds[34] (plate 5, figure 5-1).

The deaths led to more legal difficulties among the heirs, especially when the reading of Dietrich's 1588 will revealed that he had left only one Reichstaler to his brother Hermann and his considerable property to his sisters.[35] All this was reflected in the following testimony, recorded by the notary public in July–August 1594 at Hof Steinberg:[36]

1594 22 July 22–29 August
Witness testimony before notary Konrad Pankuch regarding the challenging behavior to Junker Dietrich von Mallingkrot by his brother Hermann von Mallingkrot and his sons Bernd and Hensken:

On 22 July 1594 Adrian Pijrschutte declared that several years ago, on order of his Lord, the late Dietrich Mallingkrot, he had driven a number of oxen which had grazed in Dietrich's meadows from there over Hermann's meadows because the Ruhr River had flooded Dietrich's meadows and he had no other possibility to save the life of the animals. Now when Hermann Mallingkrot saw this, Adrian was

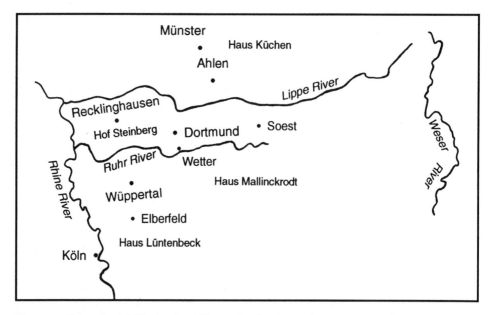

Figure 5-1. The major Mallinckrodt residences in the sixteenth century were located in the Rhine-Ruhr area.

attacked by four men, suffering five head wounds and two on his arm, which caused him to lie dangerously ill in Dortmund.

In God's name, Amen. Declared 8 August 1594. At eight o'clock A.M. the noble, honorable, and virtuous Misses Cathrin, Anna, and Elisabeth von Mallingkrot, sisters, appeared before me, as notary. They implored to file a declaration and made the following public:

> Unfortunately after their pious, dear brother Dietrich von Mallingkrot—God have mercy—was recently miserably and wretchedly slain and killed because of their brother Hermann's instigation and incitement (and that of his son called Hensken, born of the peasant serf Cathrin Storck), the sisters now consider it their duty to witness, along with numerous others who had knowledge, and prove that the named brother Hermann caused and instigated this death. Therefore, they demanded that I, professionally, under oath, and duty-bound, thoroughly investigate and hear their dear late brother's long-time servant Cathrin Blanckebeill of Börck and his former servant Hanss of Luningkhaussen, in addition to others they would yet name, recording the testimony and also sending them [the sisters] one or more notarized copies therefore.

Since I could not consider this request as improper and therefore had to grant it, the named Cathrin Blanckebeill personally appeared before me, at my request, between seven and eight A.M. on the tenth of the above-named month of August in the above-named year, in the presence of the hereafter named witnesses who were individually invited and asked to appear. After she was requested by me to report on the above-mentioned situation and was also reminded not to testify anything untruthful and not to take sides out of love or pain, rather to state only the pure and open truth according to her best knowledge, and after it was pointed out to her that, if necessary, she also could later be put under oath, she promised to certainly comply with all this. Thus, she testified as follows, as stated above:

> About four years ago in summer, Hermann von Mallingkrot and both his sons Bernd and Hensken forcefully took from the late lord, the blessed Dietrich von Mallingkrot, from his own property close to his house Gedern, his treasured herd of pigs and then attacked them with spears [*Spießen*] and guns [*Büchsen*] and killed those that could not escape. Then they cut the buttons out of Dietrich's jacket and scolded him as a scoundrel. It also happened that he, Hermann, with his son Bernd, had approached and wanted to take from the late, blessed lord his cows which grazed near the estate called Middeldrop which belongs to Lord Dietrich's residence and his manor and belongs to Gedern. Hermann had then attacked his brother Dietrich with a gun and if she—the witness—had not intervened and implored that it stop, it would not have taken much before one of them would have been killed. Moreover, Hermann's sons now and then took the path behind the above-named residence of Lord Dietrich von Mallingkrot and then had often fired their guns out of defiance or pure maliciousness, indeed had even shot through the gates, intending to bring the lord out of his house.

In addition, the named Cathrin said that the above-named Hermann von Malling-krot and his sons had for many years made attempts against her late, blessed lord's life, limb, honor, and possessions and before and after dealt him endless violence, defiance, ridicule, insults, and damages, indeed had attacked his noble honor and his good name with damaging invective, screamed at him and insulted him, and had also often seriously threatened his life and limb. Throughout the long years she had served her lord, she had daily seen, heard, and experienced this—and in part she had been present or very nearby. And that this all had been as she said and not otherwise. She testified so because of legal necessity—out of inner pressure to have to honor the truth and to underline these statements with her personal oath, for otherwise all would not be notarial and legally adequate. Now with the misdeed—God have mercy—this situation had been abundantly testified to.

On 10 August (about seven o'clock A.M.) in the year 1594, in the same affair, in the presence of Hermannus Dene and Dietrich Walrafe in the village of Herdicke. Taking place in the village of Herdicke, in the house and living room of Herman Dene in the year, etc., in the presence of N. N. as witness.

Thereafter in the same year, on Thursday, the eleventh of the above-named month of August, ordered by the power of the foregoing request, personally appeared before me, the notary, and the named witnesses the above-named former servant of Dietrich von Mallingkrot, called Hanß von Luningkhaußen. After he was asked by me in the same manner as the previous witness and warned to be truthful and avoid untruths, he swore to make public the simple truth and by his love for God and justice not to add or suppress anything. Thus he testified, as is noted in detail in the following:

First, about three weeks before the next Martini [Saint Martin's Day] of this ninety-fourth year it would be seven years ago that it had happened that he with his blessed late lord Dietrich von Mallingkrot had gone from this house and residence at Gedern to the cattle enclosure on the Ruhr and in fact through the big meadow because it had been very muddy on the road. At that time, Hermann Mallingkrot and his son Hensken had gone on another meadow, and when he saw his brother Hermann had said to his son, "Look there, there comes the riff-raff!" Now when the blessed Dietrich heard this, he answered, "You will take that back!" Thereupon Hermann defiantly uttered insults and invectives, and among other things he said, "Look, here I have one"—and he meant Hensken, whom he simultaneously clapped on the shoulder—"and, indeed, some more. He will kill you. Look out that what happened to Brembt with Staill does not happen to you, that is, to be knifed on the spot!" When lord Dietrich heard this, he had said to him [the witness]: "Listen carefully, Hanß—you will later witness these words for me!" and to his brother Hermann that he should not forget what he had said nor add to it. Thereupon Hermann said, "Oh, my good one, what do I care about you! You've been a scoundrel from the womb on!" Dietrich in turn answered that if he were a scoundrel was not Hermann also one, since he had been inside the same mother? Thereafter they went their own ways.

Further, Hanß testified, it had happened in the same winter, about fourteen days before Shrove Tuesday, that the late lord and he had gone to the lord's cattle enclosure and had checked their piers along the Ruhr. Now as Hensken Mallingkrot also was walking around the piers, Dietrich Mallingkrot asked Hensken what he was doing there on Dietrich's property. Thereupon Hensken answered that it was their property, and they would walk on it as often as they pleased. In contrast, lord Dietrich von Mallingkrot said it wasn't that way because he and the Countess of Sayn, his sister, had received this property legally. Thereupon Hensken said his shoes were still a bit too small, but when they had become larger, he [Dietrich] would soon see what he had to do with him [Hensken].

In addition Hanß testified: Thereafter his named lord and he had gone from the stone quarry via a village of the Eije to the cattle enclosure. Now when they met his brother Hermann and his son Hensken, Hensken had begun to ask Dietrich insolently where he was going. Dietrich asked what business it was of Hermann's, that he, Dietrich, was on his land, that which he and his sister owned by law and judgment. Thereupon Hermann said that was a lie. The countess had taken the land from him [Hermann] illegally; our honorable prince and all those who recognized that as legal had acted like scoundrels and thieves. Thereupon Dietrich said that was not so. Hermann answered that he wanted yet to see the day when this land would again belong to his house, because all that had happened had not happened with the will of the feudal lords. In reply, Dietrich said he should be satisfied with that which he had received legally. And then they again went their own way.

Hanß testified the following: He had heard and had been present when his blessed lord had come out of the briars along the stone quarry to his meadow and had already been at the cattle enclosure, when Hensken Mallingkrot had come to him and had asked why he was going through their cattle enclosure. He should stay out! And if he [Dietrich] would set foot once again on it, he Hensken would deal with Dietrich in such a way that they would have to carry him out, and Dietrich would see what else Hensken had in mind for him.

Hanß further testified: After his blessed lord had learned that his brother Hermann was fishing in that part of the water which in his opinion his sister, the Countess of Sayen, had been legally given as her property by judgment and law, the lord and he [the witness] had gone there. And as the lord approached them and asked who had permitted them to fish, Hensken Mallingkrot answered that his father had. Thereupon lord Dietrich said his father had no legal right to this part of the water, for it was the legal property of the countess. Hensken countered by saying that Dietrich lied like a scoundrel. Subsequently Berndt Mallingkrot, Hensken's brother, and four other persons approached the above-named Dietrich and held a sharp-edged swine lance [*Schweinespieß*] against his chest. Hensken had come from behind with a long gun and would have shot lord Dietrich if not prevented by Johan Blanckenarm. Now as lord Dietrich went to Wetter to file a claim with the authorities against these acts of violence, Hermann saw him. He ran after Dietrich with a long swine lance and called to his sons to beat his brother. This would also have happened and great disaster would have resulted if Gerhardt von Scheuren, with the help of God, had not prevented it. Rather, Hermann and his sons and a caretaker called Hagebelle had then gone after the lord with implements and broken his arm.

Hanß further testified that, among other things he had seen, just the previous year in summer Hensken Mallingkrot had come up and driven his late lord's cows, which were grazing on the meadow called Little Hair, through the Ruhr River to Hermann's ground. It should appear as if they had gone there on their own, so that one could round them up and claim them.

The following was stated by Hanß: In the past summer, the year ninety-three, his blessed lord had fished with two rods in a quarry—located up in his pasture near the river [*Spiek*] in the cattle enclosure; Hermann Mallingkrot with his two sons Berndt and Hensken and two other persons—his servant Jaspar and Duppen Jurgen, a soldier—had approached with three long-barreled guns and two swine lances and forcefully took from the above-mentioned his two rods. But they didn't stop with that, but rather at once chased after his lord. Next Hensken Mallingkrot had held his gun to Dietrich's chest, but the witness had shoved it aside. Hensken Mallingkrot then grabbed a javelin with his hand and wanted to hit lord Dietrich over the head. As he drew back to strike, Hanßen [the witness] was able to block the blow. At that time Hermann Mallingkrot also held a lance against his brother Dietrich's chest and his other son Berndt came running up with a long-barreled gun: it was obvious that they wanted to murder Dietrich themselves. This event took place not far from the place where his blessed lord recently was killed by the aforementioned Hensken.

In addition Hanß testified: He had seen that on the just-past Saint Stephen's Day in the year ninety-three, as his late lord Dietrich together with his wife went to Ennede to their church for services, the lord wanted to stand in his usual place before an altar which his forefathers before this time had bequeathed. The brothers Berndt and Hensken Mallingkrot had also stood there and had laid three long, cocked guns and two sidearms on the altar in front of them. They did not want to tolerate him and started such a quarrel with Dietrich and created such a tumult during the service that the pastor was disrupted in his sermon and the entire people were excited and restless. But they did not leave it at that. Rather, Berndt and Hensken left the church during the service and stood in the churchyard with their cocked guns and long sidearms to wait for lord Dietrich. They said, "Now where is that riff-raff? Now he is much too stupid to come out here to us!" The witness saw how Hensken rode back several times, in the opinion that he would encounter the aforementioned lord Dietrich. Moreover, he had heard that Hensken Mallingkrot had said to the late lord's servant Henrich that he should go and tell the lord to come out to them, they awaited him.

Finally, the frequently mentioned Hanß stated and testified that during the time he had been in his blessed lord's service the aforenamed Hermann Mallingkrot and his sons had previously, later, and endlessly created and dealt his lord many more acts of violence, outrage, and maliciousness. They had often taken his animals away, kept them and let them hunger, ruined them. They had robbed his meadowlands, fishing waters, and shelters, for which he and his sister were legally recorded owners. They had secretly or openly cast off, sunk, taken by force, destroyed, or stolen his boats, rods, fish tanks, and fish. They had threatened his dear person and insulted him with many coarse, unnecessarily slanderous invectives. Daily they passed in front of and alongside his lord's house and over his property and inherited land with cocked long and short guns, swine lances, sidearms, javelins, and other axes, with weapons and arms. They had shot and carried out all kinds of wantonness so that it was a wonder that they had not already killed the lord earlier. In equal measure, the aforementioned Hermann and his son Berndt carried out their mischief against the lord's widow and her servants and farmhands: they appeared now and again with the same weapons and the same arms and threatened to strike her with them. Only recently they had done that when he, the witness, and others wanted to turn and dry hay as the widow ordered. At that time the above-mentioned Hermann von Mallingkrot, in the presence of his son Berndt and numerous other persons, had spoken to them threateningly: they should quickly get out of the meadow or they would fix them so that they longer could walk away, rather one would have to carry them off. At that time Hermann and his people had two long, sharp swine lances, long sidearms, two long-barreled guns, and six iron hay forks.

What other mischief and violence had been previously or later all undertaken against the life of his blessed lord he [the witness] could not remember in a hurry, but should he recall anything else, he would report it.

But what he previously had testified, was the whole truth, for he wanted to live and die with the truth and also swears to it by oath. Therefore, resolved and read.

Anno 94, Thursday, the eleventh of August about eight A.M. the above-named Hanß of Leuninckhaußen acknowledged the above-mentioned points as true and was prepared upon request to affirm them with his oath. Recorded in the city of Hatneggen in my, the notary's, house, in the living room, in the presence of the honorable and devout Messers Henrich Kopmann and John Trapman.

Further, in the above-mentioned year on the twenty-ninth of August at about three P.M., there appeared Hilbrandt Sluick and voluntarily stated and testified that Hermann Mallingkrot on one of the next days after the death of his brother Dietrich von Mallingkrot had openly said to others in Sluick's courtyard that now he had again brought the Mallingkrot property together in one basket. Thereupon Peter Vost answered him that if that were the case, either the Mallingkrot property had become very small or the basket was very large. The above statements were openly witnessed by the noble and honorable Caspar Wandhoff zum Ruwendaell on behalf of his wife (Elisabeth von Mallingkrot) and her siblings and for them asked that one or more public copies [of this protocol] be sent them.

Thus, issued and read at Hof Steinberg, Superior District [*Oberamt*] Buchum, in the foyer of the house in the year, month, day, and hour as noted above, in the presence of the worthy and noble Messers Johann Smidt, pastor at Wenigern, and Hilbrandt Aellermann, especially invited and requested to witness.

Now since all and each of the above-mentioned appearances, statements, examinations, questions, answers, testimonies, and protests, in addition to all other above-named matters, were made in the presence of my person, Konrad Pankuch, as notary, and the named witnesses also saw and heard everything and I at once noted everything in writing and so produced this protocol written in my hand and signed by me—and have witnessed it with my first and middle names and my notary seal—it is especially requested and prayed that all the above-mentioned matters be believed.

The quarrel about Haus Mallinckrodt went on for years more among the heirs before Hermann finally won out.[37] For a time, then, he could contemplate with pleasure the rents he collected. One court document of the time, for instance, inventoried nearly two dozen different parts of the estate, including meadows, pastures, fisheries, and hunting areas. Some twelve parcels of land (worked by tenant farmers) produced for the owner, among other goods, some sixty chickens per year, eleven swine, a few sheep and geese, and the service of fifteen horses, as well as quantities of rye, hay, oats, barley, and cereal grains.[38]

*F*rom your history lessons, Father went on, you may think of the 1600s as the era of William Shakespeare in England, the devastating religious Thirty Year Wars in Europe after the Reformation, the great sculptor Bernini and scientist Galileo in Italy, and across the Atlantic the French explorations of North America. And the early 1700s may be seen as the period of Peter the Great in Russia and of the brilliant literature and philosophy in France from the pens of Marivaux, Rousseau, Voltaire, and others. Known as the Age of Kings, it is not surprising, then, that card-playing became newly popular, with the high cards called kings and queens.

While Europe thus was changing, very important family events, too, were setting a tone for the future. At Haus Mallinckrodt, for instance, there were troubles that darkened the horizon. First the Ruhr River changed its course, damaging the Mallinckrodt property. Then, in 1619, the house burned down and had to be rebuilt.

Here in Dortmund, however, the family's roots were strengthened. Johann Christoph I acquired this house at Westenhellweg 451 where we now live, called *Der Rehfuß*, and so founded our line of the family. In 1732 Rötger bought the Betenstraße 20 house that came to be known as *Mallinckrodtshof*. And in 1747 Johann Christoph II enlarged *Hof Sonnenschein*. In the fashion of the times, the houses were decorated to reflect the court style of the French palaces at Fontainebleau and Versailles.

Also becoming prominent was another Dortmund family, with which we would have very close business and family ties for a long time— the *Feldmanns*. They entered the textile society, the *Wandschneider-Gesellschaft*, and served on the city council along with many Mallinckrodts. Over the years men and women from these two families often intermarried: the first time in 1732 and the second time in 1758, when a brother of my great-grandfather married a Feldmann girl. And, as you know, the marriage between your mother and me was another union of the two families—but that is a later story. There were also many times when Mallinckrodts married other Mallinckrodts, that is, one of their numerous cousins. In this period, for instance, Bertram, who was mayor of Dortmund from 1746 to 1748, did just that.

In public affairs, family members were very active from 1600 to 1750—active in religious and political life, as well as in business. In fact, your great-grandfather Johann Dietrich Friedrich I's textile business was quite successful, and he, too, was a member of the textile society and *Konvokans*, or chairman, of the *Erbsassen* representation on the city council. In general, there was great hope throughout the region that the recovery from thirty years of war would continue and times would remain good, especially because young Fredrich II—later called Frederick the Great—became King of Prussia in 1740.

6

1600–1750

Haus Mallinckrodt

The seventeenth century was not to be a quiet time at the old castle on the Ruhr River. First there was the problem of the river itself. New breakwaters built on both sides of the Elbe at Wengen had changed the flow of the stream so that around 1612 the Mallinckrodt family went to court to sue for damages. The western banks of their property had been washed away, meadowland flooded, and an island formed (figure 6-1).[1] (In 1579 there already had been similar problems when the river took four to six acres of land.[2])

When contrasted with the map of the earlier Mallinckrodt property (plate 2), the 1612 surveyor's drawing (figure 6-1) shows how the land across the river from the Burg had disappeared when the Ruhr changed its course. At the same time, this survey included a very detailed listing of the estate's extensive remaining properties—Haus Mallinckrodt and garden, cultivated acreage, meadows, woods, and areas worked by tenants.[3]

A second round of trouble for Haus Mallinckrodt came a few years later, in 1619. On 28 September the structure again burned down (cause unknown), as did at least five additional smaller buildings. The next year the Burg was gradually and modestly rebuilt on the original foundations and enclosed by a bastionlike wall.[4] Owner Bernhard von Mallinckrodt I may have thought that additional fortification would ensure Haus Mallinckrodt's peace, at least for a while.

Dortmund

Meanwhile, with the growth in business and trade, the active chapters of Mallinckrodt family history in the seventeenth century focused on cities rather than the

Figure 6-1. A 1755 survey of the Mallinckrodt estate showed a listing of the traditional properties shown in plate 2—properties (*lower left*), Haus Mallinckrodt and garden (*dotted area in the center*), cultivated acreage (*white areas north and east of house*), and meadows, woods, and tenant-worked fields (*dark shaded areas*)—and the changed course of the Ruhr River. (*Courtesy Cologne Historical Archive.*)

countryside. The urban Mallinckrodts, for instance, were beginning to attend universities, especially sons from Haus Küchen near Ahlen, now also a Protestant family.[5] From there brothers Heinrich IV and Eberhard VII (sons of Heinrich II and Mechtelt) entered the University of Rostock in 1576.[6] In turn, Heinrich's son Bernhard matriculated at the University of Helmstedt in 1607, transferred to the University of Marburg in 1609, and in 1615 transferred again, this time to the University of Köln, where he converted to Catholicism in 1616.[7] Another brother of Bernhard, Rembert, enrolled at the University of Marburg in 1612.[8] Their sisters, naturally, were still not permitted to attend universities.

And in Dortmund, Mallinckrodts were entering public service. From 1589 through 1677, five Mallinckrodts, who were all members of the influential textile society, served on the city council. They filled inherited (*Erbsassen*) seats held by the Honoratioren, which naturally included businessmen in the city's important cloth trade. Dortmund's textile business, in fact, was doing well. By 1610, for instance, its society, the Wandschneider-Gesellschaft, controlled the dyeing of cloth, a very important economic sector within the textile business. In addition, the city's *Laken* (sheets, or pieces of cloth representing the normal production of one loom) were cheaper than those woven elsewhere. Thus sales were good, and ties with the big, traditional textile centers of Amsterdam and Antwerp were increasing.[9]

Finally, because there was less tension between the wholesale and retail branches of the cloth business, the garment trade flourished as well, introducing new styles and making luxury attire fashionable among people enjoying the higher standards of living of the early 1600s.[10] Elegant women wore two skirts, petticoats, and a bodice; for men the doublet and jerkin were still stylish, but now they adorned themselves with shorter cloaks and wide-brimmed hats turned up rakishly in front or back.[11]

Important changes were underway in the textile society as well. The original professional guild character of the Wandschneider-Gesellschaft was giving way to that of an upper-middle-class family affair. Though not in the cloth business, academic and scholarly sons claimed a "right" to membership. They wanted the backing of the society's influence in obtaining city jobs, rather than in entering city government service, as had been their fathers' tradition.[12]

Along with economic developments, the government's make-up obviously had evolved, too. The "honorable society" had its six inherited seats, and the craft guilds still held their six seats, now representing tanners/shoemakers, bakers, butchers, smiths, shopkeepers, and chandlers (candlemakers). In 1632 the first nonpatrician Dortmund citizen began to serve the city as mayor, just as nonpatricians several decades earlier had gained council seats.[13] Over time the council evolved until it consisted of two *Bürgermeister* (mayors), two *Rittmeister* (military officers), and two *Kämmerer* (financial officers). In addition, because it was a Reichsstadt, Dortmund sent a representative to the *Reichstag*, or Imperial Assembly, in Regensburg.

Over the decades Dortmund's textile society families and those in the city government came to know each other well and were often related, as in the case of the Mallinckrodts and the Feldmanns. The old noble Mallinckrodt family had first entered Dortmund's Textile Society in 1589 (through Arnold I) and the city's government in 1605, whereas the Feldmanns came out of a guild background. About a half-century later the Feldmanns also entered the city council (1656) and the Wandschneider-Gesellschaft (1671). Not surprisingly, then, they frequently intermarried—the first time in 1732. (Apparently, however, the families had had contact since 1625, for records show that at that time they mutually participated in a baptism.)[14]

In cities other than Dortmund, Mallinckrodts left their marks as well, especially through church service. With the official religion of the area now Protestant, Everhard VII, of Haus Küchen near Ahlen, became rector (*Domdechant*) of the Protestant cathedral in Minden in 1594. Some three centuries after Eberhard's death in 1617, the restored stone monument sculpted in his memory was remounted on the north wall of the cathedral. The top half of the memorial consists of religious scenes, beneath which is a carved representation of the deceased's head and the following inscription:

> His Reverence Mr. Eberhard von Mallinckrodt, illustrious rector of this basilica and simultaneously provost of Levern, honorable, distinguished cleric, luminary light of truly noble conviction, confessor of a unique religion, model of rare intelligence, guarantor of justice, protector of peace.
>
> In this year of the Lord 1617, on 18 January, in appropriate devout honor, [from] your friends, who keep you in honorable memory.[15]

Eberhard's nephew Bernhard, the scholar and political activist who had (as mentioned above) converted back to Catholicism, was named rector of Münster Cathedral in 1625. Deeply and uncompromisingly involved in church politics, he so angered his bishop after years of contention that in 1657 he was put under house arrest for the remainder of his life (until 1664 or 1667). Being deprived of his library (more than five thousand volumes) is said to have been Bernhard's greatest punishment.[16]

Regardless of where they lived or what faith they practiced, Mallinckrodts were deeply affected by the devastating religious strife that followed the Reformation, the Thirty Years' War, which ground on from 1618 until 1648. Sparked in Bohemia, then joined by Denmark, Sweden, France, and Germany, the fighting never seemed to end. For many years Dortmund had troops of the defenders of the Holy Roman Emperor or those of attacking Protestant Gustavus Adolphus II of Sweden camped before the city walls.[17] In addition, great mercenary armies marauded across the countryside, plundering, killing, spreading disease.

As the historian Carl Schulze Henne wrote about Haus Küchen near Ahlen,

> The Thirty Years' War was also a time of trouble for the family von Mallinckrodt. . . . Warring troops—the Hessians and surely also others—caused great losses to the Münsterland and its residents. The von Mallinckrodts were often without horses and wagons, for everything was requisitioned by the Hessian troops. The Mallinckrodts suffered from the death of numerous family members through battle deaths and illness—the plague. In their affairs they were so limited through greatly reduced income that they could hardly meet current obligations. Repeatedly their Lehn lords demanded that they be armed for the fatherland and that they report the quantity of their arms.[18]

Although the 1649 Peace of Westphalia eventually affirmed the Protestant orientation of Dortmund's churches and schools, it is reported that only a third of the city's citizens survived that long conflict and that Germany as a whole had lost a third of its population.[19] The losses in rural areas were estimated at 50 percent.[20] Moreover, the church cleavage was clear, and the wars had not brought religious unification; Germany would remain a land of both Protestants and Catholics, with the ruling princes deciding which prevailed in a given area. Recovery from three decades of war would be slow.

Under the Peace of Westphalia, which emphasized the rights of Germany's princes and reduced those of the emperor, Elector (*Kurfürst*) Friedrich Wilhelm became the strongest ruler in north Germany. Many of the steps he took in Brandenburg-Prussia set the pattern for later German developments—founding a large army (eighty thousand troops) and a strong civil service to serve the state and centralize its administration. Thrift, simplicity, and order were the rules of the day. With the strengthened institutions of the military and civil service, the upper class once again lost some of its power.[21]

In Dortmund itself as the 1700s began, the citizens faced not only the postwar challenges of religious disunity and economic dislocation but also a unique and thorny problem—Dortmund's geographic isolation from a natural hinterland and trade with the rest of Germany. This had come about because the imperial free city (Reichsstadt) of Dortmund, subject only to the emperor or king, was surrounded by a Prussian duchy, the Grafschaft Mark, under a regional leader. On a map of that time, the city looked like an island.

Although Dortmunders longed to change the situation, there seemed to be little hope for success as long as Frederick William I was the king of Prussia. He had come to the throne in 1713, succeeding his father, Kurfürst Friedrich Wilhelm, who later had been named King Friedrich I in Prussia. Like his father, Friedrich Wilhelm I also followed the pattern of building up the military and civil service institutions. The military, however, clearly had priority, with a budget two to three times that of the civilian administration. In fact, Friedrich Wilhelm I, known as the "soldier king," wore a military uniform and recruited an army double the size of his father's. Its officer corps consisted largely of the old nobility, which had lost much of its power through the rise of cities and their middle classes.[22]

While many Dortmunders were concerned about their future under such leadership, other citizens made a good living from the city's business and trade. In fact, the businessmen did so well that they could invest half their wealth in land while maintaining in-town businesses and residences usually located near the central marketplace, on named streets paved with stones.[23]

One such residence was the Mallinckrodt's Rehfuß Haus. It was located very near the center of the city (see *R* on figure 6-2) on Westenhellweg, the main street which extended to the western gate in the city wall. Johann Christoph I had bought it in 1694 and thereby founded the so-called Rehfuß line of the family.[24]

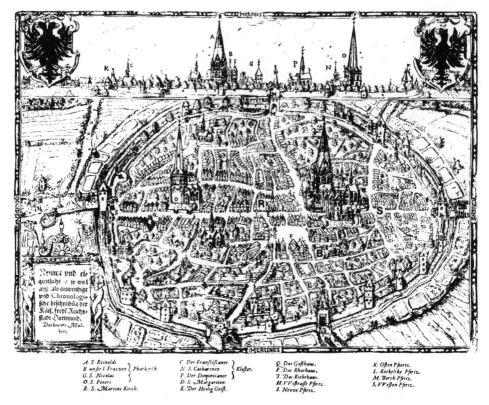

Figure 6-2. As can be seen in this drawing by Detmar Mulher, three of the prominent Mallinckrodt family homes in Dortmund in 1610 were Haus Rehfuß (*R*), Haus Sonnenschein (*S*), and Mallinckrodtshof on Betenstraße 20 (*B*). (*Courtesy Dortmund City Archive.*)

But the history of the famous old house, located at Westenhellweg 451 on 6.8 are (about one-sixth of an acre) of land, went back much further, to 1473.

At that time the Dortmund city council decided to make the wine business public and so established two city wine houses. One was called *Rehfuß* (deer's foot) and appropriately pictured the animal on its sign (*Hausschild*). Said originally to have been the nickname ("fleet-footed") of wine merchant Heinrich who operated the Westenhellweg house, Rehfuß remained the name of the building for nearly four hundred years. Records say it served as an inn from the early 1500s, attracting important guests until 1604. Anna Mallinckrodt, daughter of Arnold who owned the old wine house Krone on the marketplace, and her husband von Diest then purchased Rehfuß. In 1694 the von Diests in turn sold it to businessman Johann Christoph Mallinckrodt I, who now also owned the famous brewery/pub property Krone. After Johann Christoph's death in 1715, Rehfuß passed on to son Johann Dietrich Friedrich I, then in 1763 to son Johann Dietrich Friedrich II, and in 1797 to the next son, Johann Friedrich Theodor, in the seventeenth generation of Mallinckrodts.[25]

Another famous Mallinckrodt home was Hof Sonnenschein, in the Rosenthal section of Dortmund (*S* on figure 6-2). It came into the family in 1721, through Judge Johann Christoph II, who enlarged it significantly until it included nearly two acres, with barns and vegetable and fruit gardens. After his death in 1751, the estate passed on to son Heinrich Zacharias Hermann and then for a time to both his prominent sons, Christian Detmar Carl and Franz Heinrich Zacharias.[26]

Meanwhile, another Dortmund residence became associated with the Mallinckrodt family—the Hof at Betenstraße 20, one of Dortmund's oldest streets, probably named in the Old German of the time as an abbreviation of the name Elisabeth or Bette.[27] Built in 1610, the famous old house was bought in 1732 by the physician Dr. W. Rötger Mallinckrodt. Located on the south side of the city, near the central marketplace and the Neutor (New Gate) in the city wall (see *B* on figure 6-2), it was about one-third acre (12.8 are) with barns and garden. (Part of it burned in 1778.)[28]

According to the artist's sketch (figure 6-3), Rötger's house was a two-story structure with an attic third floor. The entrance was on the south side, from

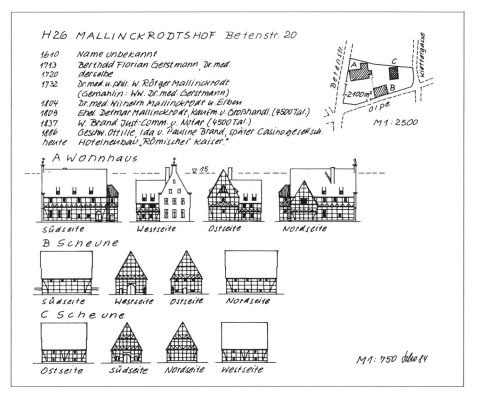

Figure 6-3. In this reconstruction drawing by Heinrich Scholle, Betenstraße 20 in Dortmund, known as Mallinckrodtshof in the 1700s, included a residence (*Wohnhaus*) and two barns or sheds (*Scheune*). (*Courtesy Dortmund Historical Society.*)

63

Betenstraße.[29] The Hof also included two smaller outbuildings referred to as *Scheune*, or barns. All were constructed in the *Fachwerk* style of the time, that is, an initial wooden latticework structure with the openings walled in with clay. (Sometimes, too, reeds were woven into the openings between the wooden strips; sometimes stones were later set in place and then smeared over with clay until a sufficiently thick wall was created.)

Another house associated with Mallinckrodts was the small Haus zum Spiegel at Markt 12, in the family from 1634 until 1704 (including ownership by Heinrich VI). The nearby Krone brewery and pub, which sat on only about one-fifth acre of land (8.10 are), was owned by Mallinckrodts for 117 years, passing from father to son. Bought by Arnold I in 1598, it then went to his son William II, then to son Arnold II, and finally to son Johann Christoph, who also owned Rehfuß.[30]

At Wisstraße 14 was another big home, also called Mallinckrodt Hof. Set on about one-fourth acre (10.2 are), in the 1500s it was known as Wallrabe Hof; in 1700 it was bought by Dr. Arnold Mallinckrodt III. From 1726 until 1752 it belonged to Dr. jur. Heinrich Mallinckrodt II, who died in the house in 1748. Inherited in turn by Johann Dietrich's widow, it passed to her grandson Johann Friedrich Theodor and was sold in 1818, shortly before his death.[31]

From such homes the Mallinckrodts of Dortmund went forth to serve their city and businesses.[32] They strode through the streets dressed much like their contemporaries in colonial America—coat, waistcoat, breeches buttoned below the knees, white wigs, and three-cornered hats. Later they would also wear shoes with enormous buckles. The women's fashions are also familiar from paintings— powdered hair and hoop skirts up to fifteen feet wide.[33] Historians say that women of this upper class had to be accompanied by a male when going to church or theater. And for girls, education remained the same old problem; sometimes they and their brothers were instructed by a private tutor who came to their home (*Hauslehrer*).

When the Mallinckrodts entertained at home, it was amidst highly polished walnut-veneer furniture with mirrorlike surfaces. The tables, cupboards, and commodes placed against papered walls had tops of colored marble. Chandeliers fashioned of gilded wood or decorated with porcelain flowers reflected candlelight off carved wood ceilings; bronze wall sconces added warmth to the atmosphere. Especially popular were new furniture designs and decorations—cupboards for books (which formerly had been shelved in closets), writing bureaus, and widely popular Meissen porcelain figures. The traditional harpsichord, too, would soon be replaced by the newly popular piano.[34] Silhouettes were fashionable and framed as wall decorations.

Mallinckrodts continued to be active in the city's affairs. Four Mallinckrodt names graced a large 1732 trophy glass of the Wandschneider-Gesellschaft, used at festive occasions.[35] Another quite different symbol of the family's prominence in the city was in the Marienkirche. Its big wooden baptismal font, bearing the family coat of arms, had been donated to the church in 1687 by businessman Johann Hermann Mallinckrodt.[36] Other members of the family were and would be honored through burial near the front of the side naves, their graves covered by tables bearing their old and proud Dortmund name.[37]

In counting up such politically active Mallinckrodts in Dortmund from 1605 until 1802 (when the city came under French control), one historian reckoned that at least 16 members of the family had held a total of 150 city council seats (seventh most for a single family in the period 1600–1700 and third most from 1700 to 1802).[38] Other historians counted up four Mallinckrodts who also served as judges and two as mayors in that period.[39] Including home ownership, the list of Dortmund's prominent Mallinckrodts reads as follows for the years 1605–1832:[40]

Name	Born/Died	Public Service		Textile Society Entry	House
		(Imperial City)			
1. Arnold	1563–1610	Councilman	1605–1610	1589	Krone (1598)
2. William II (son of 1)	1589–1646	Councilman	1627–1646	1611	Krone
3. Heinrich VI (son of 1)	1597–1655	Councilman	1647–1655	1618	Spiegel
4. Arnold II (son 2)	1612–1679	Councilman	1650–1677	1641	Krone
5. Arnold III, Dr. jur. (son of 4)	1645–1718	Councilman Judge	1690–1691 1690–1691	1687	Wißtr. (1700)
6. Johann Christoph I (son of 4)	1656–1715	Businessman		1687	Krone/Rehfuß (1694)
7. Johann Hermann I (son of 4)	1646–1700	Councilman	1700	1672	
8. Johann Dietrich (son of 4)	1652–1730	Businessman		1677	Rehfuß (1726)
9. Heinrich XII (son of 7)	1675–1725	Councilman	1722–1725	1699	
10. Heinrich II, Dr. jur. (son of 5)	1687–1748	Judge Councilman Mayor	1718–1721 1722–1746 1742–1747		Wißtr. (1726–1752)
11. Johann Dietrich Fr. I (son of 6)	1698–1762	Councilman	1745–1762	1726	Rehfuß (1718)
12. Heinrich Andreas, Dr.med. (son of 6)	1694–1768	Mayor	1730	1730	
13. Wennemar Florenz Petrus (son of 9)	1702–1775	Councilman	1740–1775	1730	
14. Johann Christoph II (son of 5)	1698–1751	Judge	1730–1733 1742–1745	1732	Sonnenschein (1721)

(Continued)

Name	Born/Died	Public Service		Textile Society Entry	House
15. Arnold William, Dr.jur.	1706–1739	Councilman Judge	1734–1737		
16. Wilhelm Christoph (son of 7)	1685–1756	Councilman	1744–1753 1755–1756		
17. Bertram Wennemar (brother of 15)	1708–1748	Councilman	1746–1748		
18. Wilhelm Rötger, Dr. med. (son of 13)	1732–1804			1759	Betenstr. 20 (1732)
19. Johann Dietrich Fr. II (son of 11)	1734–1814	Councilman	1764–1788	1761	Rehfuß (1763)
20. Christoph Kaspar (son of 13)	1737–1777	Councilman	1773–1777	1764	
21. Heinrich Zach. Hermann (son of 14)	1733–1788	Councilman Mayor	1761–1788 1784–1788	1765	Sonnenschein
22. Christian Detmar (son of 21)	1769–1842	Privy councillor*			Sonnenschein; Böddeken
23. Arnold Andreas Fr., Dr. jur. (son of 19)	1768–1825	Councilman	1795–1802	1794	
24. Wilhelm, Dr.med. (grandson by marriage of 18)	1783–1841				Betenstr. 20 (1804)
25. Johann Fr. Theodor (son of 19)	1774–1822			1797	Rehfuß (1797) Wißtr.
26. Johann Christoph (son of 19)	1773–1815	Privy councillor*		1807	
27. Detmar (grandson of 11)	1777–1841	Businessman		1807	Betenstr. 20 (1809)
28. Franz Heinrich Zacharias (son of 21)	1760–1841	Councilman	1801–1802		Sonnenschein
		(French Rule)			
		Councilman Mayor Deputy Mayor	1803–1805 1806–1808 1809–1813		
		(Kingdom of Prussia)			
		Mayor	1814–1832		

* Oberregierungsrat
**Hofrat

*T*he late 1700s and first decade of the 1800s are, of course, a time about which you have heard a great deal in this house. Your great-grandfather, Johann Dietrich Friedrich I was a prominent Dortmund citizen. He became a member of the *Wandschneider-Gesellschaft* in 1726, served on the city council in 1745 as *Konvokans* (chairman) of those holding inherited seats (*Erbassenstand*), and was in the textile business all his life. In 1758 his tax declaration described his property as "50 Morgen land [about 105 acres], 21 parcels of garden land (*einfache Gartenstücke*), my residence [Rehfuß Haus inherited in 1718], and capital."

Your grandfather, named after his father, married your grandmother—his cousin Christine Margaretha Dorothea Mallinckrodt—in 1761 in the *Marienkirche* where her father Dietrich Wilhelm was the pastor. In 1763 they inherited Haus Rehfuß. Bearing his name, your grandfather's textile and wool business—the firm of Johann Dietrich Friedrich Mallinckrodt (II)—was operated by him and his son-in-law Ernst Wiskott. It thrived and grandfather, too, was considered a wealthy citizen of Dortmund. As many Mallinckrodts before him, he also was a member of the *Wandschneider-Gesellschaft* and served the city council in one of the inherited seats.

In the next generation came my oldest brother, also a Johann Friedrich, followed by the now-famous uncle Arnold Andreas Friedrich, born in 1768, and my next brother, Johann Christoph in 1772. And the next year, which you know is the year of my birth, was also when the third Mallinckrodt/Feldmann marriage took place—your grandfather's sister Anna Dorothea married Friedrich Zacharias Feldmann. Your mother was their daughter. But enough now of the family background.

It was the political events of 1750 to 1810 that are so very important to all of us now. In 1786 our intellectual and decisive leader Friedrich the Great, by then called "Old Fritz," died after ruling nearly half a century; unfortunately he was succeeded by his extravagant nephew Friedrich William II, who depleted the treasury. Then came the French Revolution in 1789, eventually sweeping Napoleon Bonaparte to power and bringing a massive extension of individual political rights as millions more now could go to the polls to choose their rulers. It also brought turbulent property changes, for the church lost much of its great wealth, the hereditary nobility was ended, and subsequent wars swept across Europe. In 1795, for example, French control was established along the left bank of the Rhine River.

We hoped for better days after 1797 when Friedrich William III came to power but were disappointed. Instead, as Napoleon's troops entered Germany, Dortmund lost its free city status in 1803; in 1806 it was made part of the Rheinisch Confederation; and since 1807 we have been part of the Kingdom of Westphalia under Napoleon's rule. Many members of our family already have been deeply affected by these events, as I will tell you. And surely there will be more hard years ahead.

7

1750–1810

Prussia

As the eighteenth century approached its midpoint, Prussia was a powerful military state. Its ruler since 1740, Friedrich II (better known as Frederick the Great), like his father before him, believed the army was the key to Prussian power. His officers (sons of the nobility) and soldiers (conscripted peasant sons) seemed never to be without a war somewhere. From 1756 to 1763, for instance, Friedrich conducted the Seven Years' War against Austria, Russia, France, and Sweden.[1]

Friedrich's vaunted army continued to consume much of Prussia's public revenue. The military likewise dominated the political life of the country, with officers active, for instance, in city governments. In a sense they were even above the law, for along with their families and servants, Friedrich's army officers were exempt from municipal court actions.[2] In this period, then, the word "Prussian" became synonymous with military dominance, precision, and drill, and with elitist arrogance exercised by a nobility that still strictly controlled the peasants working their land.

Friedrich II, however, was not just a militarist but also an intellectual. He was very different, in fact, from his coarse and tyrannical father. Caring deeply about the quality of life inside Prussia, Friedrich thought that if the country's security was assured abroad, the conditions of everyday life at home could and should be improved. Legal and penal reforms were therefore undertaken, trade and education supported, roads and canals built, and new towns founded. Despite his "enlightened absolutism," Friedrich's powerful German state nevertheless remained a society divided by strict economic and social class lines. At the top were the owners of territory, for in largely agrarian areas land naturally was wealth, as it had been since the Middle Ages. Land wealth, in turn, meant influence, which equaled power—the right to the most prestigious military and diplomatic positions in the empire, tax exemptions on landholdings, and control over peasants. Such was the position of the Prussian landowning nobility, with its inherited titles. At the same time, a new bourgeoisie was growing. With an increasingly sophisticated and differentiated civil service, more academically trained people were needed. In fact, Reichsstädte were becoming centers of intellectual life and the arts as well as of trade and business.[3]

At the bottom of Prussian society were the tillers of the soil, who still lived in harsh conditions. Some were so-called freed peasants, while others were serfs (*Leibeigene*) who belonged to the soil on which they lived, much as slaves in the United States and elsewhere belonged to individual persons. Although liberal Prussians felt that the serfs must be emancipated before their country could really call itself modern, that liberation was a long time coming.[4]

Meanwhile, between the top and bottom layers of Prussian society was a middle group—craftspersons, small manufacturers, shopkeepers, minor officials, and professional people. They were constantly fearful that economic hard times might come and push them back down into the serving class. Such Prussians were always anxious about losing their middle-class status.

Many of these people were concerned also about their children's education. The promise of the Reformation to make education accessible to all classes had progressed slowly. The fees for attending church schools were still significant. Consequently, by about 1750 some private schools (called *Klippschulen* or *Winkelschulen*) had been established to compete with Dortmund's church institutions. Because the private schools reduced the potential income of city-supervised schools, they were officially forbidden. Nevertheless, because they were cheaper, such learning centers continued to attract pupils.[5]

In Dortmund, a free imperial city within the Prussian empire, Johann Dietrich Friedrich Mallinckrodt II was representative of the Westphalian upper class. He owned the profitable textile firm bearing his name and Haus zum Rehfuß on Westenhellweg, was a member of the Wandschneider-Gesellschaft, and held one of the inherited seats on the city council. In 1761 he married his cousin, Christine Margaretha Dorothea, the daughter of the Reverend Dietrich Mallinckrodt, who served the city's Marienkirche. (Their first son, Johann Friedrich, was born in 1762; there followed Arnold Andreas Friedrich in 1768, Johann Christoph in 1772, and in 1774 the third son, Johann Friedrich Theodor, who would carry on the family business. Daughter Sibilla Katharina Dorothea was born in 1764 and Dorothea Judith Friederika in 1775.)

Other Mallinckrodt cousins served Dortmund as mayor—Heinrich II from 1742 to 1747 and Bertram from 1746 to 1748. It was Heinrich Zacharias Hermann's turn from 1774 on. Educated as a lawyer, as his father and grandfather had been, he served thirteen years on the city council before becoming mayor. In addition, Heinrich Zacharias had inherited the Mallinckrodt residence Sonnenschein, was involved in coal mining as well as public life, and was a first lieutenant in Dortmund's citizen cavalry.

Politically, Heinrich Zacharias was very concerned about Dortmund's geographic isolation: its islandlike encirclement by the Prussian Grafschaft Mark meant that the city lacked an adequate economic hinterland. When Friedrich II visited the region in 1768, councilman Heinrich Zacharias called on him to begin negotiations for connections between the Prussian area and that of Dortmund. After that contact was ratified in 1777, Dortmund began to bloom anew economically and intellectually. Heinrich Zacharias's next mission, then, as mayor, was to revise Dortmund's outdated city constitution and to introduce efficient bookkeeping procedures and accountability into city government.[6]

While there were more than enough such challenges for improving life at the local level, Prussians at the same time continued to long for a less autocratic national government. In the late 1700s two events, taking place in foreign countries, greatly intensified that yearning for a freer political system in Prussia. First of all, across the Atlantic the American colonies in 1776 declared their independence from England and its king and set up a democratic government of the people; then in 1789 the revolution in France overthrew the monarchy so that a republican form of government might be set up there, too.

The American Declaration of Independence and the French Declaration of Human Rights sent bolts of lightning across Prussia. Ideas such as "all men are created equal," the "inalienable rights of individuals," the rights to "liberty, property, security, and resistance to oppression," as well as guarantees of the right to freedom of speech and press, were electrifying.

The American and French concepts, and the philosophies out of which they had grown, were widely discussed in Germany, and those inquiries in turn set off the influential new studies and works of the Age of Enlightenment. At the University of Königsberg, Immanuel Kant, professor of logic and metaphysics, taught, among other things, that humankind must be treated as an end, not a means. From there his innovative school of thought spread quickly. The University of Jena, for instance, became a center for Kantian studies: there Friedrich Schiller, a dramatist and poet known for artistic attacks on political tyranny, held forth on Kantian thought as professor of history (1789); Friedrich Wilhelm Joseph von Schelling, contributor to the romantic movement in philosophy, become a Jena professor in 1798; in 1792 the philosopher and law professor Ludwig Feuerbach joined the Jena faculty.

The ideas the great professors taught would be sorely tried in the next years when Prussia was ruled, after the death of Friedrich II, by Frederick William II. During his reign (1786–1797), there was little reflection in Prussian public life of the emancipatory ideas heard at German universities. Moreover, Frederick William

II was extravagant and depleted the treasury. No wonder, then, that many people felt that Napoleon was the kind of strong figure Prussia needed if it ever was to know freedom.

One of the many young Germans concerned about Prussia's future was Arnold Andreas Friedrich Mallinckrodt of Dortmund. After he finished his gymnasium study there, he went to the University of Halle in 1788 and then on to Jena. There young Arnold, too, absorbed the Kantian concept of freedom. But he was not quite sure where his intended study of law would take him. His younger brother Johann Christoph was prospering in his career as a civil servant, but that course did not appeal to Arnold; nor was he eager to imitate another younger brother, J. F. Theodor, who was running the family business. Arnold thought he would like to serve the people, as his mother, the pastor's daughter, had taught him and as so many in the family had done. Arnold had been very impressed, for instance, at Mayor Heinrich Zacharias Mallinckrodt's death just a short time ago, for Dortmund had shown great affection for one who had served the city well. Before the late mayor was buried in a vault in the Marienkirche, music tolled from the Reinoldikirche tower for half an hour, followed by a sevenfold tolling of all the city's bells.

With that honor in mind and contemplating his own possible future as a lawyer, Arnold found it interesting to recall the famous mayor's biography. He had studied law at Göttingen, and his son Detmar had done the same, at Marburg and Erlangen. Heinrich Zacharias's other son, Franz, would now study law at Jena.[7] It therefore seemed a good choice to Arnold, especially since his gymnasium school director had recommended him so highly to the Jena law professors, referring to young Mallinckrodt as "the flower of the best youth."[8] Following that family tradition, Arnold thus studied law and earned his doctoral degree at Jena.

Returning to Dortmund, Arnold began to practice law and serve the city as chairman of the Erbsassen representatives on the city council. There was, of course, much in public life to challenge him, for Frederick William II had done little to ease the causes of unrest in Prussia. Instead, the king chose to strengthen the military more, even decreeing compulsory military service for Westphalia, where it had not previously existed. When the people protested, they were offered a compromise: potential conscripts could pay to be exempted. In 1792 the king made another problematic move: he went to war against revolutionary France. Its military leader, Napoleon, had gone to war against Austria, and Friedrich wanted to help the latter. His Prussian army, however, was no match for Napoleon's zealous troops, and the Prussians were forced to withdraw. Apparently the vaunted Prussian officer corps was not as effective as had been thought.

Seeing so much that needed addressing, Arnold Mallinckrodt began writing about the problems around him. In his first publication, for example, he called for constitutional reform for Dortmund, just as Mayor Heinrich Zacharias had.

But Arnold went a step further: he also appealed for a citizens' newspaper. If it would emphasize national and public well-being, Arnold thought, it could further the spirit of community and patriotism.[9] The idea for a newspaper was already a clear sign that the trained lawyer would find his future calling in political journalism. After all, he felt, the time was right since new and growing audiences, responding to the offers of subscriptions, had created a favorable new climate for journalism. But before such a paper came into being, Arnold married his cousin— Wilhelmina Mallinckrodt—in 1794, and their first son, Wilhelm, was born in 1795.

It was in that same year that Napoleon's troops moved into Prussian areas west of the Rhine. Now French revolutionary ideas and practices were much closer, and Arnold felt the need to intensify his writing. In 1796, therefore, he made good his earlier call for a publication close to "the people": he launched a quarterly, *Magazin für Dortmund*, and soon modified the title somewhat to *Magazin von und für Dortmund*. The new Mallinckrodt publication concentrated on historical articles and public issues concerning the city.[10]

At about the same time there was great excitement at Westenhellweg 45I: J. F. Theodor had met the enchanting Sophie Fabricius, daughter of an old and well-situated cloth manufacturing and trading family in Burdtscheid. Apparently Sophie was as enchanted by young Mallinckrodt as she was enchanting to him. In keeping with the customs of the time, Sophie had to have her father's permission to marry. When he did not quickly answer her request for that blessing, Sophie wrote her father a follow-up letter. Composed in her beautiful, calligraphic handwriting, the letter was dated 9 February 1796 and sent from the Feldmann home, where Sophie was staying in Dortmund:

My dear Papa!
For many days now we futilely await an answer to our good Feldmann's last letter. But the slowness of the mail must be responsible, for it is impossible that my good father would be so cruel and leave us in uncertainty for so long concerning a matter that will determine my entire future happiness. Yes, my dear Father, I love the young man who has asked you for my hand. I believe to discover in him characteristics that I wish for my future husband, with whose helping hand I think I could wander happily through life. Also my good Feldmanns agree with my choice and esteem Mallinckrott highly. Yet without your agreement, my best Papa, without your complete agreement I will never risk such a step, never be content without it. You will consider the well-being of your Sophie, will without partisanship think it over coolly, as I will, and then tell me your opinion. I will follow it promptly, even if it should hurt my heart. I hope I have cultivated such a frame of mind that although I would be deeply sad about a negative answer from you, I nevertheless would not become unhappy.

Oh, my best Papa, I sense the full significance of the step that I will perhaps take. I see all the responsibilities that I then will have to fulfill. How important your fatherly blessing and counsel will be! Dear Papa, why must we be separated by a distance of thirty hours? A hundred times a day I wish myself with you, to ask you about this or that which is impossible to write about. My good Feldmann is often a great support to me and always shares with me his loving council as if I were a daughter. Should the fates have destined me for Dortmund, so his presence certainly would add much to my happiness.

Again on 27 February Sophie wrote, this time from Essen, where she was visiting because "the Dortmunders ordered this trip as a prescription against the homesickness that struck me so often that I myself feared I would become ill":

For six weeks we have daily awaited a letter from you. Our anticipation is very high, and still no line from you can be seen. I do not know how to explain this except that you disapprove of Mallinkrot's [*sic*] intentions toward me and it hurts you to have to tell me. Even if that should be, certainty is still always better than the uncertainty in which we now float.

I indeed treasure M. very much but I have not so attached myself to him that I could not be happy without him. I believe he combines the characteristics that I wish for my future husband and that he would use them to make me happy. Yet when I think that through my marriage to him I would, so to say, give up all my dear relatives and friends who are so very dear to me, my heart is too heavy and I cannot entertain happily any thoughts other than to quickly see the other side of the Rhein shore and all the dear ones whom I have there. O, if M. could follow me there forever, what happy prospects I then would have! But the dear Lord, who until now has always cared for me so paternally, will also guide this for my good, better than I as a shortsighted creature ever could wish to do.[11]

Finally Sophie's dear Papa, Father Fabricius, answered J. F. Theodor's father, Johann D. F. Mallinckrodt. In flowery language, he explained that he was taking his time to consider the marriage wish because of the youth of his daughter and her intended. Finally, in mid-March 1796, he gave his final permission, provided that Sophie would wait until she reached her twentieth birthday.[12] That occurred on 5 May 1797, and the wedding took place on 9 July 1797. The young couple made its home at Haus Rehfuß, which Father Mallinckrodt had given to his son.

The year of Sophie and Theodor's marriage was also the coronation year for another king of Prussia, Friedrich Wilhelm III. Though he was well intentioned, he was weak and indecisive. Although some reforms were indeed undertaken, deep disappointment came when the king reneged on the constitution he had promised.[13]

Arnold, of course, was especially displeased and told Dortmunders so in print. About the same time, in 1797, he signaled to his readers that he intended to communicate with an area larger than the city; he changed the name of his publication to *Magazin für Westfalen*. (In 1799 the name of his publishing firm changed as well, to Mallinckrodt Brothers [Gebrüder Mallinckrodt], when he took his younger brother Christoph into the firm.)[14] The paper's content also

Plate 1. Right: Ruins of Burg Volmestein near Wetter. *Bottom*: An artist's concept of Burg Volmestein (Volmarstein), which Mallinckrodt knights served in the thirteenth century. (*Courtesy Wetter City Government.*)

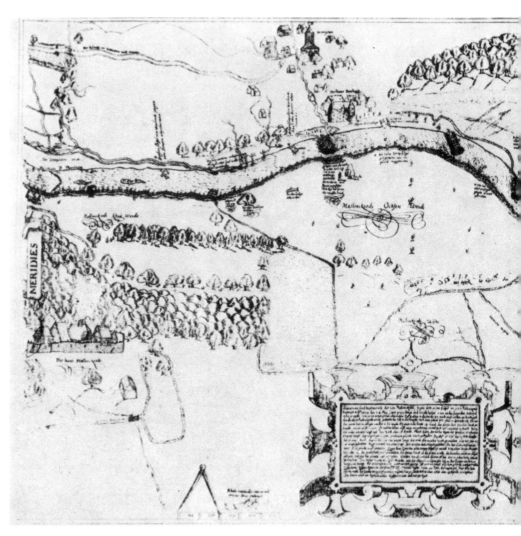

Plate 2. A 1612 survey of Mallinckrodt estate properties on the Ruhr. (*Courtesy Cologne Historical Archive.*)

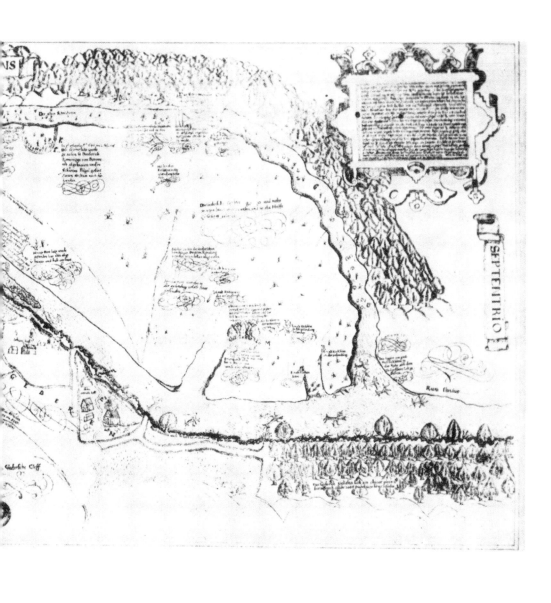

Hermann von Mallinckrodt vor dem Vehmgericht, 1450. Wandgemälde im Rathaus zu Wetter von Prof. Heupel-Siegen

Plate 3. Artist Heupel-Siegen's painting *Hermann von Mallinckrodt Before the Secret Court in 1450* hangs in the city hall of Wetter, Germany. (*Courtesy Wetter City Government.*)

Plate 4. Haus Lüntenbeck, near Elberfeld, was home to knight Hermann and his son knight Wilhelm von Mallinckrodt in the fifteenth century. (*Courtesy Cologne Historical Archive.*)

Plate 5. One of the victims of a dramatic family double murder in 1594 near Haus Mallinck-rodt was Dietrich von Mallinckrodt, whose tombstone is shown here. (*Courtesy Cologne Historical Archive.*)

Plate 6. Arnold Mallinckrodt, Dortmund publicist and lawyer, in 1815. (*Courtesy Dortmund City Archive.*)

Plate 7. Gustav Mallinckrodt, Cologne industrialist (c. 1830). (*Courtesy Cologne Historical Archive.*)

was broadened, for according to its subtitle, it was a publication "to further proper education and morality."[15] During the next year Arnold again changed his paper's name, this time to *Westfälischer Anzeiger*; under this title the twice-weekly newspaper would become famous.

Westphalia's new *Anzeiger* set a high priority by declaring itself "a fatherland archive for the fastest possible dissemination of all worthwhile and useful knowledge for human well-being, for domestic and bourgeois happiness from a political and moral point of view." A secondary purpose of Arnold's newspaper was no less far-reaching: "to awaken, nourish, enliven a spirit of community in Westphalia, increasingly to kindle love of the fatherland, to bring and disseminate useful information to wider circles, to support every virtue when an opportunity presents itself, to give substance and nourishment to the noble meaning of goodness, religion, and virtues, to test and encourage that which eases and beautifies social and bourgeois life."[16]

Because of such high goals and values, Arnold Mallinckrodt was able to gain written contributions for his publication from many prominent political and intellectual Westphalian leaders. About a fifth of them were active in justice and administration, around a tenth were doctors, and twenty-five were scholars at universities and other institutions of higher learning. Educators, economists, businessmen, and representatives of many other fields also found their way into print in the *Anzeiger*. Such articles won circulation for the newspaper throughout a large geographic area. Education was a favorite theme—for example, Arnold's 1798 call for reforms at his old school, Dortmund's famous gymnasium.[17]

Inspired by the ideas of the French Revolution, Arnold Mallinckrodt and his friends wanted to eliminate privileges of the nobility and general social inequities so that ordinary people might have more rights. At the same time, such reform-minded Germans wanted to retain private property, free enterprise, and a free press. In short, they wanted a constitutionally restricted monarchy, not a revolutionary republic as in France.[18] Their goal was a kind of middle way between deteriorating monarchical absolutism and its leftover feudal ideas, on the one hand, and the emerging radical democratic ideas of a popularly ruled republic, on the other hand.

In short, the turn of the century in Europe was an exciting time, especially for intellectuals. It was the Age of the Enlightenment, a new period in European writing, thinking, and creativity. Emphasis was on logic instead of revelation and so on philosophy rather than religion. Human goodness was stressed over selfishness, the joy of living instead of repression, and above all liberty instead of absolutism. In the next years the greatest German writer of all times, Johann Wolfgang Goethe, celebrated such dimensions of the human spirit, and the philosopher G. W. F. Hegel went to the University of Jena (1803), where he set another milestone in German philosophy.

By the beginning of the 1800s, however, the great German state of Prussia clearly was still not "enlightened." Its nobility was frightened by ideas of equality, the middle class afraid of hard times, and peasants stirred by hopes for the kind of French freedoms they had heard of. The need for change, reflected in Arnold Mallinckrodt's newspaper, was seen throughout the land, but not by its ruler, Friedrich Wilhelm III.

Meanwhile, as the nineteenth century dawned, the Mallinckrodts in Dortmund counted up the pluses and minuses common to big families of the time. For instance, at the family home on Westenhellweg, generations changed. Theodor's parents moved out in February 1798 (to Ostenhellweg), and his mother died shortly thereafter, in July—deeply mourned, as Theodor wrote, for "she taught me and my siblings to love and respect virtue." A year later, in 1799, Theodor and Sophie's first son, Gustav, was born. Both grandfathers were sponsors at the baby's baptism, giving their blessings to another generation of Mallinckrodt heirs, the eighteenth.

Very soon, however, the family gathered at Westenhellweg to mourn rather than celebrate. Incredible as it seemed to father Theodor and his two-year-old son, Gustav, the beautiful young wife and mother Sophie Fabricius was dead at age twenty-four. She died in 1801, giving birth to a son, Ferdinand. The young widower Theodor, his pain still raw, recorded what had happened, sorrowful testimony to the dangers of childbirth for women in the 1800s:

On 23 March 1801 I greeted the dawn's light with such happiness. My Sophie, my tender and honored wife, after three hours of suffering, gave me the second pledge of our love [their second son]. Already I lifted my heart gratefully to the righteous Father, already I breathed easier and belonged to the happiest of mortals when shortly thereafter it pleased the master over life and death to destroy my happiness through the most rending pain and to take her, she the mother who was so dear to my heart, to him through enervation caused by too great a loss of blood. She died, my pale one, two hours after her delivery, in my arms and those of my sister.

Her excellent heart, her noble feelings, the greatness of her spirit, the denial of self flowing from contemplation—and moral principles! Beautiful, noble soul, who now lives transfigured in higher regions, through your tender, natural, and honorable behavior you infused me with respect for you and contemplation about myself.

It is you whom I thank for the good that I now possess, and therefore your image will be unforgettable to me. It will accompany me on all the ways of life and be my leader or walking stick across uncultivated, rough ways until it pleases Providence also to call me to a better life and to again unify my self forever with you!! God our Father give me the strength to do good and preserve me for the pledges of our love [the two children]. I recognize the double burden that I now have toward them. Just give me courage, perseverance, and *proper knowledge* to carry them out. . . .

On 3 April the new arrival was baptized by Pastor Kuithan Jr. He was given the name Ferdinand Heinrich. His sponsors are Herr Carl v. Curmonz, Herr W. Feldmann, Sr., Herr Dr. Arnold Mallinckrodt, Mme. Henryette Fabricius, and Frau Dorothe Hülsemann.[19]

Two years later Theodor remarried. His new wife, and the little boys' new mother, was someone they had long known—Sibylla Clara Juliana Theodore Feldmann, called Dorothea. She was of the Feldmann family with whom the young Sophie Fabricius had lived before her marriage into the Mallinckrodt family. Moreover, it was Dorothea's father and mother (Anna Dorothea Mallinckrodt and Friedrich Zacharias) who had contracted the third Mallinckrodt-Feldmann union; she and Theodor were the fourth.

The new couple's first daughter, Sophie, was born in 1803 and the first son, Arnold Leopold, in 1804. The boy's baptismal sponsors included his prominent Mallinckrodt uncles, Arnold the publisher and Johann Christoph the Prussian government official. Also acting as Leopold's sponsors were two members of his mother's family, the Feldmanns, as well as a sister of the late Sophie Fabricius Mallinckrodt, for ties with that family would remain close.[20] Thus, life settled into new patterns at Westenhellweg. Outside in the political world, however, great changes were taking place. The spread of the French Revolution was transforming the map of Germany. By decrees of secularization and partition, here and there principalities were merged and counts and petty princes were absorbed by territorial princes, as were imperial cities, imperial knights, imperial constitutional law, and so on. In short, the king's empire was cut down to size.[21] So, too, was the church, as its lands were absorbed by the states. In several years even the possessions of the powerful Order of Teutonic Knights were secularized.

For Dortmund the changes were dramatic. In 1803 it lost its old status as an imperial city and instead was made part of the enlarged nearby entity of Nassau, now French-governed Orange-Nassau. The old free city government, of course, was dissolved, and its administration allocated to Napoleonic rulers, the prince of Orange and a governing council. Public servants of Dortmund then faced the question of loyalty. Should they continue to serve their city and the region of Westphalia although the rulers now were foreign? For the Mallinckrodts the answer was to remain loyal to Dortmund.

Arnold, therefore, worked on as the city's legal counsel (*Regierungsrat*),[22] and his cousin Franz was on the Dortmund city council from 1803 to 1806. In 1806 some sixteen south and western German princes, under Napoleon's protectorate, established the Rheinisch Confederation, including Dortmund. Franz Mallinckrodt served as its police mayor from 1806 to 1809, and then as deputy mayor from 1809 to 1813; Franz's brother Christian Detmar, a high-ranking Prussian public servant, became tax director for the new French-ruled government in 1808.[23] Perhaps not coincidentally, the property they jointly owned at the time, Hof Sonnenschein, was used by the French as a government office in 1808.[24] While Franz was a Dortmund deputy mayor, so was W. Feldmann, of the family closely interrelated with the Mallinckrodts. At home at Betenstraße 2 since 1721, the Feldmanns had often also served on the city council (1656–1680, 1690–1701, and 1784–1800), and one of them later would serve as mayor.[25]

Under French influence, Dortmund's economic life naturally changed along with its government. The new rulers, bent on establishing more equality, dissolved the monopoly position of the guilds. Instead, four trade associations were permitted: the textile society, blacksmiths, iron masters, and general shopkeepers.[26] And among the craft societies, those of the shoemakers, butchers, smiths, tailors, weavers, carpenters, and bookbinders were sanctioned. Citizens also felt keenly Napoleon's demands for heavy taxes and more and more soldiers from the former Prussian territories, which were now organized by the French into the confederation.[27]

Military concerns were, in fact, Napoleon's first priority. Overseas, for instance, he feared he could not hold French territory in the pending war with the great naval power England. For this reason he sold the immense American heartland to the United States, its 1803 Louisiana Purchase. Perhaps sensing that area's future immigration opportunities, a leading German scholarly journal reported promptly and with wonder that the "almost immeasurable territory" of the United States had now become "sixteen to seventeen times greater than that of Great Britain and Ireland," with only six million persons living "in that enormous region."[28]

In Europe, Napoleon, now emperor of France, was hungry for even more power. In 1805 his forces conquered Austria and Russia in the famous battle of Austerlitz. By the next year he occupied the largest part of the monarchy of Prussia and marched into Berlin. Vacillating, Friedrich Wilhelm III could not bring himself to order a strong counterattack. Once again it was clear that more territorial rearrangements were on the way, along with economic hard times for businessmen. Since it was an age of nautical transportation, when Britain became involved in war with France, both maritime powers carried out the conflict on the high seas. Their blockades and confiscation of ships, the order of the day, were heavy blows to trade.[29]

In 1807, after a treaty with Napoleon, Prussia was left only with its provinces in the north and east. French troops then occupied Dortmund, and the Kingdom of Westphalia was established on the French model, extending all the way east to the Elbe River. It was ruled from the city of Kassel by Jerome, Napoleon's brother whom he had made king, and administered by the Grand Duke of Berg; Dortmund was the major city of what the French then called the Department of the Ruhr.

In many ways the Kingdom of Westphalia thrived under the new rule. The French Revolution had cleared away the feudal system and its stultifying privileges, destroyed antiquated forms of rulership, and quickened the desire for intellectual independence and a chance for economic development. Freedom of trade, equality before the law, good roads, religious tolerance, and other progressive measures were seen as positive by the people, despite stern censorship of the press. Westphalia had become a modern state in terms of its new legal system (based on the Napoleonic Code), careful public administration, and a constitution that permitted popular representative bodies.

In this time Dortmund's academic high school, the gymnasium, bloomed. In part through Arnold Mallinckrodt's political influence, Professor Johann Wilhelm Kuithan was named director in 1807. Related to the Mallinckrodts through marriage, Professor Kuithan was widely known as a progressive educator. Mathematics was to be central to his plan of humanistic study, and Arnold's publishing house printed the textbook for the field. The study plan itself, also published in Arnold's newspaper, was astonishingly varied for the times. There was, of course, the traditional focus on Greek, Latin, and French, but students could also choose private instruction in Italian, Spanish, Portuguese, and English. In the study of mathematics, arithmetic, geometry, trigonometry, and technical drawing were offered, as well as summer exercises in land surveying. The natural sciences were emphasized, and even psychology was included.[30]

Another indication of Professor Kuithan's progressive approach was his concept of having several schools in one building, taught by the same teachers. There was not only the academic high school (gymnasium) but also the middle and higher common school (*Bürgerschule*), with practical training classes also open to gymnasium pupils. Thus, children could go to church or private schools for their first four years and then transfer at the age of ten—either to the higher common school (for some four to five years of training for the business world and other vocations, that is, to the age of fourteen or fifteen), or to the gymnasium (for about nine to ten years of study, culminating at the age of eighteen or nineteen with the *Abitur* diploma, which entitled the holder to enter the university).

Influenced by the French Revolution, even European clothing had become more "free." Men no longer wore wigs but brushed their hair in a "wild mop" over the forehead; boots replaced shoes, and long-tailed coats came into fashion; women put aside their bustles, corsets, and hoop skirts.[31] Furniture styles also lightened, from the intricately ornamented dark mahogany to golden satinwood devoid of curves.[32]

For Westphalians, however, the French occupation also meant foreign rule and, to some, repression. There was no German state, no German realm to reflect the intellectual and creative developments of recent years. Instead, Germany remained "a collection of dynastic states under French protectorate."[33] Most disturbingly, the French Revolution surely had not brought peace to Europe. And the people were growing increasingly weary of it all.

The Mallinckrodts had meanwhile adapted somewhat to the new times. As always, family life went on, with children born and couples married. Three sons, for instance, were added to the family tree—in 1804 Eduard, Arnold and Wilhelmina's second son, in 1806 Emil, their third son, and also in 1806 Julius, Theodor and Dorothea's second son (with aunts Lisette Feldmann and Wilhelmina Mallinckrodt as sponsors, as well as uncles H. A. Meininghaus and Ernst Wiskott).[34] Clearly their childhoods would be marked by the turbulence of the times into which they had been born. Similarly, Johann Christoph, now privy counselor (*Hofrat*), chose 1807, the year the Kingdom of Westphalia was established, to marry his cousin

Katherina Helena Friederike Mallinckrodt; in the same year another set of Feld-mann-Mallinckrodt partners married, Lisetta Feldmann (sister to Theodor's wife Dorothea) and Essen businessman Ludwig Mallinckrodt.

Perhaps seeing the economic handwriting on the wall, in 1808 Theodor, together with his brother-in-law Hermann A. Meininghaus, took his wool trade into a newly founded firm.[35] Arnold, too, was especially active, since once again the poor leadership of King Friedrich Wilhelm III had created a new "cause" for the lawyer-publisher to pursue, that of rights for peasants.

Having missed so many opportunities to move his region forward, the king finally tried to stimulate at least what was left of Prussia. He permitted one of his councilors, Baron von Stein, a knight of the old nobility, to draw up plans for improved justice, efficiency, and participation in public life. Taking a cue from the French Revolution, Stein's first measure dealt with the old, unsolved problem of the peasants: an act emancipating them was put on the books in 1807. With the abolition of serfdom, Germany's peasants were free to move from one class to another and no longer bound by heredity to stay in the position to which they had been born. They were free to leave the land, marry whom they wished, and learn a trade. For the peasants who stayed on the land, however, the reform did not alter their obligation to work for and make payments to their lord. Neither did it allow a peasant to become the owner of his little holding without paying an immense price, giving up one-half to one-third of it to the already wealthy lord of the land.

In this issue Arnold Mallinckrodt found a calling. He became, so to speak, the "peasants' lawyer" in a long struggle that took on hateful forms and embittered years of his life. Court case followed court case, with the farmers losing out in their effort to extend the rights of the 1807 reform. To help them, Mallinckrodt used his influence as a high-ranking civil servant wherever he could. In addition, Dortmund's liberal journalist obviously used the press, in which he believed so strongly, to educate and organize resistance. Untiringly he conveyed his views through newspapers, fliers, farmers' calendars, and whatever forum he could find. Judges who decided against the serfs were criticized as partisan perverters of the law, and they in turn defamed Arnold as a servant of the French and as a corrupt peasants' lawyer. His reputation as a political-moral publicist spread far beyond Dortmund.

Not surprisingly, the French wanted to censor the troublemaking newspaper, the *Westfälischer Anzeiger*. Equally unsurprisingly, Arnold Mallinckrodt preferred to cease its publication in 1809 rather than bow to censorship.[36] His sense of defeat was keen. Although bitter about the reception of his work, Arnold nevertheless did not permit that to show up in a touching letter he wrote the same year to his eldest son, Wilhelm, who was away at school.

Seated at his beloved secretary, surrounded by numerous tall book cupboards and facing the big rectangular table piled high with paper, Arnold wrote Wilhelm on the boy's fourteenth birthday in November 1809. Greeting his maturing son as a "youthful friend" rather than a child to be led through obedience, Arnold gave his son six guidelines for the coming years of young adulthood. That birthday letter clearly reflected Arnold Mallinckrodt's own philosophy:

- Do not weaken your own strength and spirit but live modestly.
- Believe in God and pray for strength to do what is right.
- Be a good and noble person by respecting responsibility; it will always determine what is right.
- Be a rational intellectual person, not believing blindly but asking always for reasons.
- Prepare now for a life that will benefit society; without public activity we are of little use to the world and therefore cannot be happy. ("Make efforts now toward progress in learning, for I could die early and then, as my oldest son, you would have to be the support of the family, caring for the life of your mother and siblings.")
- "For a happy social life acquire for yourself the social virtues of friendliness, sociability, loving thoughtfulness for others. Try to master the contrariness that previously existed in your life. Be especially and exemplarily tender, mild, loving in your familial relationship toward your siblings, servants, and above all show your mother love and obedience."

The letter was signed, "From my heart, your loving father and friend, Arn. Mallinckrodt."[37]

As the first decade of the nineteenth century finally closed, one more economic measure of far-reaching consequence for the Mallinckrodt family went into force. Dortmund's guilds and trade associations were dissolved in 1810 by the French-controlled government. Those vocational groups, of course, had been central to the textile business around which generations of Mallinckrodts had built their lives. The move was not, however, a total surprise, for in 1803 the scope of the guilds and trade associations had already been narrowed. Now they were replaced altogether with a new "patent system" through which every citizen with a business certificate could be admitted to a guild job.[38] As a result, the traditional monopolies of skilled workers, on which the textile business had depended, seemed past, or at least significantly changed.

Part II

Father's Newer
and Last Stories

1815, Christmas.
Dortmund, Prussia

*T*he children gathered at the round wooden table turned pleased eyes toward Father at the head. Once again he had promised an evening of family stories and historical explanations. So much had happened over the past five years that the Mallinckrodt children were very excited about the special story hour. Father had said it would be special not only because it was the holiday season but because they could be very thankful that the war with France was over and their Westphalian homeland had become part of the Kingdom of Prussia in early June.

The children had changed, as had their times. Gustav, now sixteen, Leopold at fourteen, Julius at nine, and Conrad at seven were all in school. Five-year-old Hermann had to wait a while longer. The two littlest ones were Albert, now three, and the only girl in the family, Dorothea, just a year old. Missing was dear Ferdinand, who had died three years ago when he was twelve. His death was especially tragic, as if he had been somehow marked by fate—first his birth had caused his mother's death and then his own death came in childhood. That left Gustav with no brothers but five stepbrothers and a stepsister. No wonder he was more thoughtful than ever during the story hours when Father told about the family's tradition and responsibility to each other and society.

The years had put pressure especially on the adults in the family. Father, having had to liquidate his century-old textile firm, now was concentrating on his wool business. Uncle Arnold, the journalistic voice of the family's liberalism, could finally start up his newspaper again after years of Napoleonic censorship. Father's cousin Detmar, briefly arrested by the French at Paderborn, hoped now to get on with his career in public service; in Dortmund, his brother Franz Heinrich Zacharias had become mayor in 1814, like father Hermann Heinrich Zacharias before him. And Uncle Johann Christoph, who had held so many high positions—justice commissioner, privy councillor (*Hofrat*), and municipal councillor (*Munizipalitätsrat*)—had died just a week ago, at forty-three. Widowed Aunt Helene was left with seven-year-old Ernst and one-year-old Sophie, fatherless this Christmas at Ostenhellweg 56.

Friedrich Wilhelm III was still king of Prussia. And despite all his good intentions, he remained weak and indecisive; many of the reforms that he had begun to make were not carried out. A very good step, nevertheless, had been taken in the Military Service Reform of 1814. Through it the nobility's monopoly over the officer corps had been broken and there was general conscription.

As Father cleared his throat and pushed aside the plate of Christmas *Stollen* Mother had set out on the table, everyone sat up a bit more erect. The children knew he would not begin "Once upon a time . . ." Rather, he would explain their own times, for their family was, as always, part of German history.

8

1815–1819

Dortmund

The spring of 1812 marked a turning point in the Napoleonic conquest of Europe that had created the Kingdom of Westphalia.[1] Gradual resistance was emerging in many of the regions under French rule. Key was a signal from the Russian czar that restoration of the large German state of Prussia should be the most important goal in liberating Europe; indeed, a kind of Prussian nationalism had been growing since the reformation of the state's discredited army. The old officers who had not performed well had been replaced. In addition, soldier morale was up because of reduced officer brutality, and many thought the combination of a professional Prussian army and a national militia was a good idea. It was hoped that the new army of regular troops could liberate the area from Napoleon.[2]

King Friedrich Wilhelm III nevertheless put off as long as possible the challenge to Napoleon that the czar encouraged. When it came, slowly, it was through an alliance between Prussia and Russia. Thereafter the king issued a famous "call to my people," made the Iron Cross a popular military symbol, and called for volunteers. Those outside Prussia, in areas still under French rule, were organized into special free corps. In the Rheinisch Confederation that included Westphalia, the German princes nevertheless still trusted Napoleon and provided the troops he requested.[3] The confederation administrators were not yet prepared to throw in their lot with Prussia, even if it had the backing of Russia.

This lack of German unity between the confederation and Prussia created a strong mood of political uncertainty and fragmentation in Westphalia. It was reflected openly in Dortmund and in the Mallinckrodt family in 1812. On the one hand, Franz Heinrich Zacharias agreed to continue his service to French-controlled

Dortmund as mayor; on the other hand, his cousin, the famous journalist Arnold, decided to leave the city's public service after many years. The equally uncertain economic situation was seen in the family, too. J. F. Theodor, for example, had to give up the large textile firm that had been in Mallinckrodt hands for a century and focus instead on the wool company he had set up several years earlier with his brother-in-law.

The mood of uncertainty changed in June 1812, when Napoleon made his fateful mistake. He invaded Russia and marched his troops to Moscow by September. Then, however, they were defeated by the formidable Russian winter, it was said. The result was the rout of the greatest army ever assembled in Europe, some 500,000 men. Withdrawing from Russian soil, Napoleon's retreating Grand Army suffered its decisive loss in October 1813 at the Battle of Leipzig, fought against Russia, Austria, and Prussia. That was Napoleon's last battle on German soil. His Rheinisch Confederation collapsed, and the French-controlled Kingdom of Westphalia ended. The crucial question then was how the German territories would be reconstituted. Also important was whether Britain's war with Napoleon, as well as with the United States, would end and free trade on the high seas could be resumed.

Once again the times affected the Mallinckrodt family very personally. For instance, in the turmoil after the October 1813 defeat of Napoleon, Detmar, director of the tax office in Paderborn, was arrested on suspicion of having acted against the French. Apparently only the arrival of Russian troops in the former Kingdom of Westphalia and the flight of Napoleon's brother, King Jerome, saved Detmar's life and the lives of other officials.[4]

With the departure of the French and a new European era in sight, Arnold, the previously censored publisher, was contemplating the future—not only politically, as he constantly did, but personally as well. Physically unwell (he complained of constant dizziness, light-headedness, and circulatory irregularities, "which may be signals of an attack or fever of the nerves"), Arnold in 1813 wrote his eighteen-year-old son Wilhelm a letter that he "should consider a Testament." Perhaps he was remembering how quickly death sometimes comes—as it had two years before, when brother Theodor and Dorothea lost their firstborn, Sophie, eight, and then a year later, when they lost Ferdinand, twelve. (Theodor recorded the death "of this good and promising boy" as resulting from an "infectious clot [*Rinsal*].")[5]

Arnold's "Testament" was a remarkable reflection of the thoughts of a prominent public figure in troubled times. First, Wilhelm was counseled to give up his bookstore business, because it was too uncertain, and always to turn to his uncles for advice and help. Next, Arnold listed five specific business principles worthy of following:

1. Do not start a business that you do not understand precisely.
2. Undertake only one business activity at a time.
3. Do not strive for great things; "little and pure" brings a contented life.

4. Above all avoid speculations (see Engels's *Philosophy for the World*, part 2, and remember the Bible verse "Take no thought for the morrow").

5. Avoid business deals; it is better to be completely your own master.

Next came Arnold's general fatherly advice about marriage: "Above all," Arnold said, Theodor should not "marry too young," but rather wait until he was twenty-six to thirty years old and had a secure income. He then offered two specific admonitions: (1) "Do not marry within our family. For too long we have married too closely within the family and thereby family illnesses, family weaknesses, and one-sidednesses are repeatedly created. It is better if new, healthy blood comes into the family. (2) In order to make a happy choice, one does not first have to fall in love."

In following paragraphs Arnold bequeathed his philosophy of family relations:

Children can never make good to their mothers the great effort and care invested in their childhood. You brothers should always be loyal to one another, helpful, and supportive in advice and deed. . . . All of you try to be good, understanding, and useful people to the world. . . . Your father will not leave you much wealth, but blessings he leaves you. In his life he has worked a great deal for others and tried to support that which was good according to his best knowledge and conscience and as much as he was able, but too often he thereby neglected his own well-being, which basically was not quite right. . . .

The experiences and observations that I have made in life, and my principles, you will find in my little book, "Observations and Experiences, Small Contributions for Practical Living." I have given you, dear boy, one; two other well-bound copies are there for Eduard and Emil. Give them to them when they enter young adulthood. And something else: I do not wish that any of my children study [that is, attend a university]. Nevertheless, should Eduard in the future show special ability and wish to do so, so he may, if our future financial situation would allow that. He would probably be happier, and especially more peaceful and more contented, in another field. But if he devotes his life to public service, then he must devote himself entirely to others. God let him then be happier than I have become. Emil will probably be most suited for economics and probably will be the happiest.

I have frequently been unjustly judged by the world, misunderstood, and unfortunately have many enemies. It is dreadful to be in a situation where, by following principles conscientiously, one collides with the interests of others. It is then essential that children know that their father has not earned many such derogatory judgments. My letters and papers will not leave you in doubt about that. You will find these mostly in my cabinets above the writing bureau of the *comptoir* [secretary]. To you, my dear boy, I give these things. Preserve them carefully, order them, in all cases fasten them [clip together]. These papers will give you, and in the future your brothers, certain information about my character, my thought, and my behavior. If many then judge me falsely even after my death this will not lame you, my children, in your courage and your efforts toward good. And your loving remembrance of me will be my forgiveness. After all, God knows me, too!

And now once again, children, always strive for good, believe warmly in God, in religion, in virtue. God will be with you and the good you will do in the world will please me.[6]

In addition to that statement of his personal philosophy, Arnold meanwhile had summarized his political principles. In part already published in the *Anzeiger*, the new 1814 work was entitled "What Should Germany Do at Europe's Rebirth?" Looking forward to political developments in the next years, Arnold's advice was that of a reformer: introduce new, unfamiliar institutions only gradually and without bloody harshness, for "rapid, complete changes of law are a kind of revolution, and every revolution results in evil for many."[7]

Another caution concerned him: "One should take the religious persuasions and dynastic feelings—yes, even the prejudices of residents—into consideration in order not to plant hate and bitterness against the new government in all hearts for many generations." And finally there was the voice of the rationalist in this two-volume challenge. What reason demands must be prepared by education, Arnold wrote, for "according to its nature, reason develops slowly; to try to force it is against nature."[8]

One hopeful sign of what Arnold wanted for the future came in the same year his work was published—a major reform of the Prussian military service in 1814. No longer was lifetime or twenty-year service required, nor could men buy their way out of military obligation through a substitute. Instead, three years of active duty followed by two years of reserve duty were compulsory, via general conscription. Moreover, with proof of education and provision of one's own equipment, a young man could volunteer for a very advantageous one-year tour of duty.[9]

Then in 1815 came the development for which so many Dortmunders had hoped for so long—Westphalia's incorporation into the Kingdom of Prussia. In June that year the international Congress of Vienna restored Westphalia and other territories the French had ruled to German provinces. Thus ended the era of the Napoleonic Empire. Now Franz Mallinckrodt, the mayor of Dortmund, would serve a Prussian city. (Indeed, he served in that capacity until his death in 1832, completing 225 years of the family's public service to Dortmund.)

Arnold Mallinckrodt, of course, was delighted. As a lawyer and inspired supporter of constitutionalism, he was especially encouraged, too, by the Vienna Congress's promised constitution for Prussia. With its guaranteed rights for the masses and restrictions on the monarchy, it would be "an age of new creativity." And, happily, Arnold could reestablish his newspaper, the *Anzeiger*, at the very time his home region needed new ideas and concepts for restructuring its future. Thus, he worked late into the nights, composing suggested constitutional provisions for dealing with governmental and financial questions. He was also pleased by the new progress at Dortmund's gymnasium, where in 1816 his sons Emil (ten) and Eduard (twelve) were among the seventy or so full-paying students, along with mayor Franz's son Christian (eleven).[10]

While the Mallinckrodts rejoiced at Arnold's return to his newspaper and public influence, they mourned the death of Johann Christoph. The loss was especially bitter because, having risen to high governmental rank, Johann Christoph had not lived to see the new chapter in Prussian and Westphalian history. He died on 18 December 1815, at the age of only forty-three, a victim of "nerve fever" (later identified as a kind of typhus). He left his widow, Helene, alone with their seven-year-old son Ernst and one-year-old daughter Sophie in the house Auf dem Trissel at Ostenhellweg 56.[11] (In medieval Dortmund the *Trissel* was a rotating cage for public imprisonment of merchants who had cheated customers; the rotation caused an appropriately punishing illness.)[12] Arnold also deeply felt Christoph's loss, for he had been a partner in Arnold's publishing business and now would be replaced by Arnold's eldest son, Wilhelm.[13]

Trouble was also brewing for the family's other famous public servant. In 1816 Christian Detmar Karl intended to marry a Catholic woman in a Catholic church. Since the empire required its civil servants to be Protestant, Detmar was inviting censure from his Prussian superiors. Liberal Detmar, nevertheless, had promised Bernhardine von Hartmann that she might raise their children Catholic, regardless of Prussia's civil service rules.

1820, June.
Dortmund, Prussia

*F*ather, leaning heavily on his elbows, said that at times it seemed as if life just could not again settle down for the Mallinckrodt family. In fact, he had such a sense of foreboding that he had recently completed the personal entries in his big record book—his marriages and the children's births—and made sure that everyone knew where the book was kept in his writing bureau.

Despite such rejoicing at the end of the Napoleonic Wars, Father said, troubles continued. He was especially worried about Uncle Arnold and Aunt Wilhelmina, whose eldest son Wilhelm had died in 1817. And then in 1818 Arnold's newspaper was closed down again, this time by the Prussians. In resignation he had withdrawn from public life and bought the *Topps-Hof* estate at Schwefe near Soest. He wanted to live there quietly, to farm and to continue his writing. The boys, Eduard and Emil, were in good apprenticeships nearby. In his civil service job Cousin Detmar was still facing trouble, too, Father said. Detmar had married in a Catholic church and had permitted his daughter Pauline, born in 1817, to be baptized in that faith. His actions spelled trouble because Prussian civil servants were supposed to be Protestant.

Moreover, throughout Prussia there was great intellectual unrest and even student protest. Workers were being replaced by machines, and many German craftsmen were immigrating to America. Demands for constitutional government grew louder, Father reported, and there was some talk about poems of freedom being written in Bonn by the university student Heinrich Heine.

And to everything the king of Prussia, as usual, was reacting with harshness. Not only was Uncle Arnold censored, but it was said that the death penalty or life imprisonment had been the fate of some of the student dissenters. The hope for reform that had burned so brightly was being snuffed out, Father feared.

9

1820–1825

Dortmund

For the Mallinckrodts in Westphalia, the first years following the end of the Napoleonic wars were anything but peaceful, either politically or personally. In 1817, for instance, the religious trouble brewing with his superiors in the Prussian civil service surfaced for Christian Detmar Karl: he had permitted his baby daughter, Pauline, to be baptized Catholic.[1] While family members were concerned about the consequences of that baptism for Detmar, they also had reason to be happy and sad about promising young Mallinckrodt adults. At Westenhellweg, Theodor and Dorothea were especially proud of seventeen-year-old Gustav's achievements. He had completed six years of study at the gymnasium plus a two-year apprenticeship as a salesman in Lippstadt, worked as a clerk (*Commis*) in the Lübeck trading firm of his uncle (Feldmann & Behn) after the summer of 1816, and planned to travel a while in France.[2]

At Arnold and Wilhelmina's, by contrast, it was a time of deep mourning. In February 1817 their eldest son Wilhelm, to whom the father had so lovingly written when the young man came of age, died at the age of twenty-two. The cause of his death is unknown. In the *Westfälischer Anzeiger* Arnold wrote simply that his son, "a friend in every sense of the word," had "died during my absence; I return home and stand at his grave."[3]

Moreover, Arnold (plate 6) was upset and angry about yet another loss—his treasured freedom of expression as a political journalist. Just as the French rulers in Westphalia from 1809 to 1815 had been frightened by his political ideas, so now the Prussians, too, were censoring them. In fact, the government had sentenced

Mallinckrodt to two months' imprisonment for publishing in his *Rheinisch-West-fälischer Anzeiger* an article criticizing the behavior of Prussian troops.

This was an interesting case for several reasons. First was Arnold's specific criticism of the military; he wrote that the music accompanying its drills disrupted the public peace and quiet of Sundays and holidays. Second, Arnold's defense against the government's charge was a journalistic landmark: he refused to reveal the name of an informant in Münster, saying instead that he had witnessed the disruptive military action himself in Dortmund. And, third, the authoritarianism implicit in the judgment was troublesome: Mallinckrodt had "done serious verbal injury to the royal military," it was said, and so would go to jail and also pay court costs.

Arnold refused, however, to go to prison and fought for his right to free speech in one Prussian court after another. The Prussia-wide campaign of support for his cause was heartening, and he indeed won his appeals, first from the prison sentence and then from payment of court costs.[4] But the atmosphere was discouraging since obviously the postrevolutionary Prussian rule had not brought Westphalia the "new age of creativity" in which Arnold and other public leaders had believed.[5] Probably, too, Arnold was being paid back for his energetic stand against landowners during his campaign to end serfdom.

Though deeply disappointed, liberal Westphalians were perhaps not surprised at the turn of events. After all, Arnold had warned about the repercussions that revolutions might produce. It was also true that while Westphalians had gained lasting ideals of liberty and working models of law and administration from the French, the wars had left Prussia exhausted, and it suffered now from famine and epidemics. No wonder, then, that the progressive element to which Arnold belonged was only one of the social movements of the time. Whereas the progressives called for measures of a representative government and a constitutionally limited monarchy, a reactionary movement wanted an even stronger and more authoritarian monarchy that would restore order, by force if necessary. These were people who beat especially loudly on the drums of nationalism.

And it was those drummers whom King Friedrich Wilhelm III heard. In 1817, for example, he was frightened by a sizable student festival in Thuringen at which students burned symbols of military authority; such an action, the king felt, was clearly revolutionary and had to be countered. Obviously in such a political situation, he thought, reforms had to be postponed. Past practices were safer.

Not surprisingly, then, Arnold Mallinckrodt lost the struggle for press freedom, and in 1818 his paper was forbidden in Dortmund, at that time a city of nearly 4,300.[6] He even had to give up the already published four-part *Newest Magazine of Geography, History, Statistics about Westphalia*.[7] Selling his bookstore and printing equipment, the former publisher decided also to sell his house at Ostenhellweg 35–37, which had been in the family since 1703.[8] He would pack up the family and try to find a new profession in the world of teaching, at his old university in Jena. There, Arnold thought, he might play a role in the current intellectual debate. On one side were those calling for evolutionary, or gradual, political change, such as Mallinckrodt and his friends advocated; on the other side were the deeply disappointed who had lost faith in that mild approach and instead demanded radical, revolutionary turnabouts in Prussia. In Jena he could teach law and publish, as a kind of "public meeting hall" for all of Germany, the *Neuer Rheinischer Merkur*, which the Prussians had forbidden on their territory.[9]

Both attempts failed, however. Bitterly disappointed and now also physically ill, Arnold decided to retreat into a more private life. He would realize his old dream of becoming a farmer. After all, Arnold had been concerned with farming for twenty-five years: not only had he intensively studied the subject and written much about it, but he also had carried out various experimental farming practices on lands he owned around Dortmund. Returning to Westphalia, he bought the estate Topps-Hof at Schwefe near the historic town of Soest in 1819. Since his son Emil was also interested in agriculture, the estate was bought with the boy's inheritance of it in mind.[10]

A year after purchasing the estate, Arnold reported on his new life in a letter to his sons, sixteen-year-old Eduard, then apprenticed in Soest, and fourteen-year-old Emil, an agricultural apprentice in Schwelm: "The freezing weather has certainly hindered our work. About twenty-four morgen (50.4 acres) of land are still unplowed, and in the garden beets, turnips, and potatoes are still in the ground. So we have cleaned up a bit around the buildings, cut wood, and today or tomorrow a manure bed [*Miststatte*] will be completed. Three head of cattle are in the old horsebarn; one is 1½ years old, which I bought for 9½ Thaler."[11]

At the same time, of course, the journalist spent time at his writing desk. With that letter to Emil, for instance, Arnold included four manuscript notebooks that the boy was to deliver to his father's colleague in Schwelm. And always the teacher, Arnold also wrote both his sons lengthy paragraphs of advice about their studies—especially Emil's handwriting! Mother Wilhelmina wrote, too, including a list of clothing she was sending the schoolboys—handkerchiefs, vests, scarves, collars, bed linens, and so on. Interestingly, both parents praised and encouraged the brotherly love between the two: "Yes, be brothers! In the future you will be closer to each other than to anyone in the whole world and can find much happiness and joy in life through constant and active brotherly contacts."[12]

About the same time that Arnold and Wilhelmina found joy in their sons' development, Theodor and Dorothea also had reason to be pleased. Gustav had completed his one-year voluntary military service with the Fifteenth Infantry Regiment in Münster, where he also found time to attend lectures in chemistry, a subject he had learned to appreciate during his studies at the gymnasium. In 1820 he had cofounded a business in St. Petersburg, Russia, a leading European trading center.[13] Gustav's future looked very promising. The course of that future, however, was determined by "strange decrees of heaven," as brother Leopold would put it.[14]

In late summer 1822, "nerve fever" again coursed through Dortmund. Young

Leopold, planning European travel in September and the beginning of his one-year stint in the military, was struck by the infectious illness and bedridden for a time. Characterized by a high fever affecting the nervous system, the sickness included dizziness, a sense of lameness, and mild delirium. Very worried about Leopold's condition, father Theodor set off on a longer business trip to Leipzig and was delighted on his return to find his son recovering.[15]

Hermann Meininghaus noted that on 8 September his brother-in-law Theodor Mallinckrodt enjoyed a good visit with him, and the next day they went hunting together. But on the tenth, when the men were taking leave of each other, something seemed to trouble Theodor. "He almost did not want to let me go and was very different than otherwise," Meininghaus wrote.[16] Perhaps Theodor then already did not feel well and had caught the fever from Leopold. On 4 October, Johann Friedrich Theodor Mallinckrodt, almost forty-nine years old, unexpectedly died of nerve fever.

The shock to the family of his sudden death was enormous. His eldest son, Gustav, then age twenty-three, was in St. Petersburg, and with him was sixteen-year-old Julius, who was to learn about the business world from his older brother. Being so far from home, they heard about their loss through comforting letters from the family. Cousin Wilhelm Feldmann, for instance, wrote them, "You have lost a good, loyal, loving father whose untiring activity was for the well-being of his children." Uncle Hermann Meininghaus wrote them not to worry about the family business. Several years before, their father had made a testament naming Meininghaus and Gustav trustees with the children's mother, Dorothea, thus preventing intervention by chancery and any disruption of the business.

Meininghaus also used this letter to assess for Gustav all the siblings who now would be under his care:

> I hear with pleasure that Julius makes efforts to progress, and I hope he will become a good man. You, dear Gustav, will have to assume the father role for him. Leopold [age eighteen] is a very good person who makes great effort to progress in all that is good. He has been with us in the office for a whole year, and father and I were pleased with him. He should have done his voluntary one-year military service, but now he must stay with us and I hope that as eldest son at home his widowed mother will be pleased. Conrad [age fourteen] was determined by his blessed father to become a jurist, and he learns well. Herr Professor Smittmann already previously took a great interest in him and told me recently that he would give him very special attention. Hermann [age twelve], a good boy, enjoys instruction with Mr. Klöpper [a teacher at the Reinoldikirche school] and Albert [age ten], as well.[17] My blessed brother-in-law determined them both for the business world if no interest in another field showed itself. Both are boys with good abilities and can become good people. Dorchen [age eight], as a girl, will grow up under the blessed hand of her mother and is a good girl. So God will.[18]

One of the most touching letters to Gustav and Julius in far-off St. Petersburg was from their brother Leopold, now at age eighteen head of the family at

Westenhellweg. He wrote how he had always longed to get out into the world to travel. "The strange decrees of heaven," he felt, "have always been against my deepest wish to soon leave the family home and try out the world": apprenticeship problems, illness, and now "the shocking and irreplaceable loss also of our dear father robs me of the possibility to ever get out of here." But, he assured his brothers, he would stay home, try to adapt, and support their mother, for surely they could not interrupt their careers in St. Petersburg. "Please you, too, help me, dear Gustav," Leopold wrote, "and let's all stick together more!"[19]

The four-page letter from Dorothea to her sons in Russia, written on the same day, was naturally one of deepest mourning:

> How my hopeful sons must have felt about the terrible news "Father is dead"!— so your voices echoed from afar in my ears, and I saw your tears. I saw how you, dear Gustav, who was so close to his [Theodor's] heart, could not conceive the dreadful finality. How you, my deep-feeling Julius, deeply moved and beside yourself, threw your arms around your older brother's neck, saying "Father is dead! Dead, we will never see him again in this life!" God! I could not write you during the first pain.

Turning to the future, as the other letter writers had, mother Dorothea counseled,

> You, dear Gustav, are so mature that you also can support me. Our Julius's training is now entirely in your hands. I thank heaven that he is with you. . . . You, Julius, your father's voice calls to you from the grave: "Continue to be good and upright; try to train yourself to be a useful member of human society and to some day also be a support to your mother!" [Marginal notation:] Dear Julius, try hard to become a very good businessman but do not lose sight of your higher calling as a human being. And, both of you, think also about how to enjoy life wisely and how to be happy with our existence.

Interestingly, too, Dorothea wrote Gustav and Julius about a fantasy their brother Leopold had had during the feverish hours of his illness:

> How shocking Leopold's fantasy still is to me: "Father is dead! Mother, Mother, that is terrible!" This is what he called out. "Mother, I cannot stay with you! Shall I give up my dearest hopes of travel? Can you demand that of me? But now, yes, it must be!" he said with tears. Then he added, "Klöpper [the teacher], you and I must not leave our mother. Come here, dear brothers and little sister, I will now take care of you!"

"These were the omens for me of the dark future," Dorothea reported. Yet when their father returned from his travels, she told her sons, they had laughed about Leopold's fantasy. Father Theodor had even said, "Good that we see in it that Leopold would take care of you after all!"[20]

Although the mourning mother viewed Leopold's words as a feverish "fantasy," a kind of omen, Leopold himself wrote the same thoughts to his brothers in St.

Petersburg after he was well and their father was indeed dead. The brothers may have wondered together if the deep sorrow Leopold now expressed at being tied down reflected his mother's report of his so-called fantasy, or no fantasy at all but rather rational thinking, both during his illness and after—that is, a very intense and real yearning, albeit combined during his fever with uncanny foresight.

During its time of mourning the family apparently found comfort in the rationalist Christianity that was its tradition. It was a belief which rejected an emphasis on institutionalized churches and ecclesiastical organizations, which stifle and coerce the true spirit of religion, and stressed instead individual knowledge (reason), spiritualism, and self-determination. In this belief system there was a Supreme Being, the creator, as well as hope of an immortal life for the soul and human perfectibility. At the time of their father's death, Gustav, writing from Russia for himself and Julius, assured their uncle Meininghaus that their belief in life hereafter "makes it possible for me and my brother to be comforted over the loss of the best and dearest father." In Gustav's words, their belief was "the Christian religion's hope, which has been an assured expectation, that death does not eternally separate us from our loved ones, that it does not destroy us—that an early death is an early departure for a better land where we, too, sooner or later, will follow."[21]

The death of Theodor Mallinckrodt was also the occasion for a cousin to remind Julius and Gustav of the rational component of their religious belief. In their time of mourning, wrote cousin Wilhelm Feldmann, the bereaved sons should not forget that "it is the obligation of reason-endowed humans—and even more that of Christians—to keep even their most noble feelings within the limits of reason. Forget not that time, after all, heals pain and that it is irrational not to permit this comforter to come to one's aid through reason."[22]

Family loyalty was another source of strength. For instance, reacting to all the new responsibility thrust upon him, Gustav, now as head of the family, wrote Uncle Meininghaus, "The image of our blessed father, the totally self-sacrificing family father, will never disappear from his children's memories. Even in later years it will remain the ideal for what we will try to become with our own families."[23]

It was clear, too, that after winding up some details in St. Petersburg, Gustav would return home at once to assume his new role. Young Julius, by contrast, knew enough about the business to carry on for a time with Gustav's business associate, Voigt, in the Russian port city. The fates had indeed played them all strange cards. And more were yet to fall.

After Gustav returned to Dortmund, life moved forward quickly. Having assumed the role of family head determined by his guardianship over his siblings,[24] Gustav started his own family as well. He married Henrietta Strohn, daughter of a well-to-do industrial family, at the end of 1823. Meanwhile, Leopold, the next oldest, was living at home with mother Dorothea and the rest of the children, while Julius was still in St. Petersburg.

The family's contact with Uncle Arnold Mallinckrodt at Schwefe were very close after Theodor's death. Arnold counseled his nephews in legal matters (addressing Gustav as "Friend"), and they tried to help him with his farming business.[25] Economic times were not good for agriculture, and Arnold was depressed. As he wrote Gustav, "Won't the grain prices ever stop being so low?" Complaining that he could not pay his debt to Gustav, which was approaching its term, Arnold added, "In the hands of you businessmen such [future market speculations] do better. I have such little luck." Arnold apparently had even bought a lottery chance to try to gain funds. "Heaven will decide" about his winning, he wrote. "Good luck would do me good, for I owe 3,000 Courant by November."[26] Businessman Gustav answered sympathetically:

Unfortunately I can't tell you anything comforting about the assumed developments in the grain trade. Unlike all other sectors, this one obviously still remains stagnant. . . . The grain stores are still very significant, and if there is a good harvest again this year, then it may be a long time before prices go up. . . .

If one looks at the price changes over the past ten years, for many traded goods one finds that often, *perhaps usually*, the rises and falls were so extraordinarily irregular that . . . all speculations were pure games of chance.

Regarding a big lottery then going on for the estate Engelthal (Valley of the Angels), Gustav wrote, undoubtedly with a touch of irony, "If heaven would decide that I should win Engelthal, then according to our agreement you would not have to ask much more about grain prices. But to contemplate that is to build castles in the air."[27]

Not only economics troubled Arnold, but his health, too. In May 1825 he wrote Gustav,

If there are presentiments, then I have them that I will not be here much longer. That moves me to ask if I may have the joy that you will care for my wife and children. In the hope that you will not reject the request, together with my wife I have named you, in place of your good father, as guardian of my children, together with Meininghaus and Vollmann senior. They, in addition to your father, had already previously taken on the foster care of my loved ones.[28]

Gustav, of course, agreed, but he assured Uncle Arnold that he and Aunt Wilhelmina would yet hold numerous grandchildren on their laps.[29]

In early June 1825, Julius set out from St. Petersburg for home. His three-week sea route, he wrote, would take him from Petersburg to Kronstadt, then to Copenhagen, Lübeck, Hamburg, and Dortmund.[30] A fragmentary letter to his mother expressed clearly his spontaneous and adventure-loving spirit: "Oh, you know, I am itching until the sail fills. I could wish that a real storm would overtake us on the voyage so that I could tell a bit about the sea—as one hears described what a storm is like. How the ship is up and down, how the waves crash over it, how the table and chairs fly about the cabin, first here, then there."[31]

Julius had not yet arrived when the next blow fell on the family: Arnold Mallinckrodt died in Dortmund on 12 July 1825 and was buried at Schwefe. Though he had been ill for some time, his death was nevertheless unexpected. As Leopold wrote, "Last Sunday we were still so hopeful for the recovery of our good and noble uncle. But we hoped in vain. It pleased the Lord yesterday afternoon to call him from this vale of tears to a better, eternal life! His long-time wish is now fulfilled, and he is at peace!"[32]

Closely involved with his Uncle Arnold's illness, Leopold had many worries: "Aunt Meininghaus [Arnold's sister] is now bedridden. . . . I must admit I am very uneasy about her. . . . I don't know where my brother Gustav is. . . . Julius is still not here, and I am becoming concerned about him, too."[33] Making Aunt Dorothea Meininghaus's condition worse was the fact that her brother Arnold had died at her home.[34] (The home was probably located at Kampstrasse 13–15, where in 1800 the Meininghauses built their family home on the land of the former Katharine Cloister, the only home for Catholic nuns in old Dortmund.)[35] Cryptically, Leopold added another concern: he apparently did not get along very well with his mother, Dorothea, who was, he said, "still grumbling."[36]

By late September, Julius was back in Dortmund, helping Leopold with the business. In fact, Leopold and he together signed business letters to Gustav.[37] But Julius's stay was brief: he was off within the first days of October to begin his year of conscripted military training in Münster, where Gustav also had served. Apparently it was not very hard duty, for the officers were not required to live in barracks. Julius, in fact, found a very pleasant two-room apartment in the heart of the city and took his meals with the family.

About the military duty, he wrote his mother, "The drilling [*Exerziren*] still continues, probably another fourteen days until we enter the company. After that we have to drill much less, and so I will also have more time for myself." Already Julius had invited friends to tea and wine and, reporting that the guests had enjoyed themselves, said about himself, "That's just my nature, that I have the greatest pleasure if I have brought others joy." In that letter from Münster, Julius' relationship to his mother was also expressed in interesting fashion. Both conceding and challenging points of direct concern to her, Julius wrote in his usual candid, open manner that

> if you wish it, I will be glad to eat again with my right hand. [Perhaps he was left-handed.] I am glad you told me, for as far as it concerns my good mother, I surely want to live as she wishes.
>
> I know very well that you wish to get along better with brother Leopold. But in my opinion, to a great extent you yourself are responsible for the absence of a friendly relationship between you. When you talk to him about marriage, which does not yet suit him, what should he then answer you? There is so much other useful material for conversation.[38]

For Conrad and the other young Mallinckrodt sons attending the gymnasium, these years were exciting. Their three-story school in the center of the city was being renovated, with no little pressure on Mayor Franz Zacharias Mallinckrodt from its director, Professor Kuithan. By September 1825 the work was completed. Even more satisfying, however, may have been the growth of the school's library. Prussian restrictions on the public lending library had been severe (for instance, pupils had only restricted access to books considered "too democratic"), and so the school library had been built up instead. From some fifty-seven meager volumes in 1825, Professor Kuithan increased the collection to about seven hundred over the next years.[39]

Part III

In Immigration

1826, August.
Dortmund, Prussia

No more story hours with Father. He died four years ago, and we miss him so much. As Mother says, he really was too young to die, only forty-eight. And then in 1825 Uncle Arnold also died, and he was not old either, only fifty-seven, and Aunt Wilhelmina died about the same time, too. That left our cousins Eduard and Emil orphans and us with only Mother.

But it seems Gustav is going to watch over all of us, including Mother. Last month he and Uncle Hermann Meininghaus signed a joint "Tutorium," or guardianship. So now at twenty-seven Gustav is responsible for five stepbothers and a stepsister—Leopold, twenty-two; Julius, twenty; Conrad, eighteen; Hermann, sixteen; Albert, fourteen; Dorothea, twelve—and our two older cousins, Eduard, twenty-two, and Emil, twenty. At the same time, poor Gustav has his own problems. The wife he married in 1823 died prematurely and next year he intends to remarry.

As Gustav reminded us the last time we all sat together around the big table, the old clock ticking away in its big case in the hall, "There are no more stories, children, of what was. It is now. It is our turn to live out what others some day will call 'their family stories,' that is, our stories. Whatever we do, we must try to help one another and continue to bring honor to the name Mallinckrodt. Through what our father told us over the years about our family, we know what that honor means."

And so we went out to write our paragraphs for history. . . .

IO

1826–1830:
New Roles

After the death of J. F. Theodor Mallinckrodt in 1822 and his brother Arnold in 1825—as well as Arnold's wife Wilhelmina in 1827—the lives of their children took on new dimensions and greater responsibilities. Gustav, for example, as Theodor's oldest son, was not only to carry on the family business but also to be legal guardian (*Vormund*) for his siblings and Arnold's sons as well.

That was not always easy, for Gustav had his own losses and stress. His first wife, Henrietta Strohn, died only a year after their wedding, and Gustav married her sister Emilie several years later, in 1827. Through these marriages, Gustav became ever more active in the business world, for he was made co-owner of the Strohn tannery and leather business and its trade in hides. According to a summary of Gustav's intricate business dealings, the Strohn tannery in 1825

> was merged with the firm "Mallinckrodt & Co." which he [Gustav] and Heinrich Vollmann had founded in Krombach to produce shoe-sole leather. A year later Gustav opened a firm in Dortmund to carry on trade in English and German manufactured goods, as well as a business to manufacture textiles from cotton and flax. By November 1826 he could already point with pride to the fact that his tannery in Krombach was among the most important in Prussia and that his Dortmund factory already employed four hundred people.[1]

In 1826 brother Julius, having returned from St. Petersburg in 1825 and served his year in the military, began helping Gustav in these businesses. Traveling by horseback, Julius traded in wool, leather, hides, and textiles, sometimes living at home in Dortmund and sometimes at Gustav's in Krombach. There he took care of Gustav's horses, exercising them, building barns, and buying hay. He also established Gustav's gardens, selecting grape plants, potatoes, and other items.[2]

Gustav's oldest stepbrother, Leopold (age twenty-six), had also been in the family business for about ten years and was at this time involved especially in its Antwerp branch.[3] In 1827 seventeen-year-old Hermann, too, went there to be trained, and Albert followed.[4] Conrad, the student in the family, was at the university in Munich.

The guardianship Gustav held for his stepbrothers and stepsister was shared by their uncle Hermann Meininghaus, who had married Dorothea Judith, their father's sister. Away from home, the young Mallinckrodts often wrote Uncle Hermann, expressing deep gratitude for his help to them but also giving an accounting of themselves. For instance, when Conrad completed his gymnasium studies in Dortmund in October 1828, his gymnasium listed him as nineteen-and-three-quarters years old and planning to go to Munich to study philology.[5] From there, then, he wrote his uncle the next year:

> The first year of my academic life is quickly coming to an end and therefore I often ask myself if I have achieved the goal for which I went to Munich. Since there is still so much to be desired, so much of importance for me to learn here, I would very much like to remain until Michaeli [Michaelmas Day in September]. I have gotten permission to do so from Professor Kuithan [director of the Dortmund gymnasium and one of Conrad's baptismal sponsors]. How very much I love and honor him I surely do not have to tell you. . . .
>
> My selected field of study [pedagogy, and not legal studies, as his father had desired] pleases me more every day. Years ago I was prejudiced against the field because I imagined only its unpleasant and bad side, which may have had much to do with the way the teachers instructed the beginning classes in our gymnasium. Now it is just the opposite—I almost believe that I picture a teacher's effectiveness as more exciting than it in reality can be. Otherwise how could it be that so few people feel called to this field?
>
> But what can be more wonderful than to adapt to the hearts of a whole future generation? It is, after all, pleasant to see how a tree grows that one has grafted, and how much more pleasant it must then be to see a person out of one's school enter life ennobled. You can not imagine how such observations spur me on to not disappoint the expectations of those close to me when I finish my studies.[6]

By late 1829 or early 1830, Julius had joined Leopold, Albert, and Hermann in Antwerp. From his job as clerk in the family's business office, twenty-four-year-old Julius wrote his Uncle Hermann in July 1830:

> I remain grateful to you for your recommendation to me, via brother Leopold, to Mr. Depouhon & Co. I am especially obligated to you because the recommendation, combined with a personal one from your brother here to the deputy chief of the house, Mr. Seybold, contributed to the fact that I have found a job in this firm, as you probably know from brother Leopold. I am especially pleased herewith to express my pleasure and thankfulness for your intercession. Although for now I have only a small unpaid position, I will surely progress.

In our correspondence with Nerviers & Co. I find my assumptions confirmed that the *failliten* [troubles] that have broken out there have lamed all businesses. I can imagine how negative these events are for our wool business there. Thank goodness, as I hear from your brother, *we* do *not suffer much* through the failliten. For that we thank your activities and caution!

I see your brother daily in the house where I live with my two brothers [Julius and Albert] because there is also a chess club there which he often visits. Not rarely have I the pleasure of playing a game of billiards or whist with him.[7]

(The failliten to which Julius referred may have been the rebellion that broke out that year in Brussels against the Kingdom of the Netherlands, which acquired dominion over Belgium at the 1815 Conference of Vienna.)

Albert, too, wrote Uncle Hermann. In a very excited letter (undated, but probably written in 1830), he told his uncle about a bombardment of Antwerp. The action probably took place when the Dutch invaded Belgium after it declared itself free.

In the very moment that I was sealing a letter to my brother Leopold and wanted to take it to the post office, a strong bombardment on the city began from the citadel and from the warships. We began at once to pack our things to carry into the cellar. Julius and I were still in our room when a 36er [artillery shell] fell on the house, smashed the roof, broke through three walls, and gently fell at our feet. We fled to the cellar.—It was four o'clock in the afternoon yesterday when the bombardment started and it continued until twelve or twelve-thirty. We experienced the most dreadful night; the entrance [to the harbor and] fort St. Michel and the surroundings went up in flames. Your brother's house is undamaged.

This morning a convention was held with General Chassee, who gave his word not to bombard the city again. . . .

We are out of danger and that is all I can report to you now. . . . Please be so good as to pass along this news in whatever way you think best. Tomorrow the mail will leave again, so more then.[8]

In a letter to brother Gustav, Hermann also mentioned the Antwerp bombardment, which he had experienced along with Julius and Albert. But Hermann's real news was economic:

The reason why I left Antwerp was to look for a different position, for after working two and a half years for the Messers. Dtripe nothing really took place in this business which could contribute to my future existence. I intend to spend the winter here [in Dortmund] because trade generally is rather stagnant and businessmen are reducing their activities as much as possible. Therefore it probably would be wasted effort if I wanted to find a job at once. Furthermore, I can surely find something to do in our head office since cousin August is presently doing his military service.

Brothers Julius and Albert stayed in Antwerp because they did not want to give up their jobs, with which they are more content than I. But today brother Albert wrote that Messers. Depouhon & Co. had curtailed their payments and brother Julius will probably lose his position and so also return to Dortmund.[9]

Other letters to stepbrother and guardian Gustav (plate 7) concerned financial or family matters for which Gustav's advice as guardian was essential. In particular, twenty-four-year-old Emil, Arnold's son, was in frequent correspondence in 1830 with his cousin Gustav about all the burdensome problems at his Schwefe estate. Emil seemed most troubled (1) by his dire economic situation, (2) by his brother Eduard's ill health (among other things, a visual impairment), and (3) by gossip among the Dortmund family about his personal life. Apparently Emil's offer of marriage to a young woman named Lina had been refused, and he was enraged by his family's suggestions that he solve his money problems by marrying someone wealthy, regardless of whether he loved her.

In explaining his financial situation, Emil first asked Gustav not to believe "that I shy away from strenuous efforts. I am used to that since my youth and I never worked unwillingly."[10] Later in 1830 he wrote, "You know, dear cousin, that my good father, through the purchase of this estate, immediately brought himself into difficult circumstances that have not become better through the bad economic times of the last decade. In this context I have experienced a hard time. The situation has deprived me of the joy of youth to which every person is entitled. And now I do not want to remain in circumstances that would turn me gray with thirty years."[11]

This combination of problems called for a decision, and Emil thought out the matter carefully before writing Gustav:

Dear Cousin!

I now am forced to tell you that I cannot over time meet the obligations I have to you. Therefore I have one way out. I have carried the following idea around for half a year and am firmly resolved to implement it:

I want to formally convey this estate and everything on it to you, even including the linen, also the little estate in Hanover, in short everything that I until now have owned as property. But the land which we still own near Dortmund, along with the library, I want to transfer to M. & M. [the firm Mallinckrodt & Meininghaus] to pay the Zichner debts.

In return, I would have to ask you to promise me that if my brother Eduard should no longer be able to earn his daily bread, for example, if he had the misfortune to lose his eyesight, that you would take care of his modest income. Sadly enough he already also suffers from a rupture. . . .

You have done everything for me that only a brother could do for the other. But I therefore have obligations to you, and I want to resolve them *now* while I am still a free man.[12]

In a letter a few weeks later, Emil's anger over family gossip about his marriage intentions again found expression, as did his idea of leaving Dortmund permanently: "What would my father say to that—to poison the until now affirmed propriety of his son for the noble price of gossip. I have to force myself not to become bitter. I will gladly forget it, but I will no longer stay. . . . In addition I earnestly ask you, in case you can see your way clear, not to sell the estate. There is a lot of perspiration connected to this inheritance."[13]

Several months later Emil elaborated the idea of emigration, which he obviously already had discussed with Gustav:

> I cannot yet give up the thought of seeking a new fatherland, that is, should my situation not have changed significantly until spring. Then I would, according to your advice, sell everything, pay my debts, and then in God's name go. You call "Courage" to me! Of that I have enough. To eat my own bread during a hard life. If I cannot do that as an honest man, then I have enough courage to *leave* the world. But it will not come to that as long as I have healthy arms and legs. I will consequently follow this my disposition because I believe it is right.[14]

Gustav probably understood well Emil's political reasons for wanting to emigrate, for Prussia at the time was hard indeed on free spirits and thinkers. All the books Gustav was reading on politics, law, and history convinced him that political and social change had to come—and quickly—or there would be revolution, and that he did not favor any more than his uncle Arnold had a decade earlier.[15] Furthermore, now that the Napoleonic conflicts and the British–U.S. War of 1812 were over, sailing ships were again crossing the Atlantic, and the waterway to America was open to restless European souls such as Emil Mallinckrodt.

II

1831: Taking the Risk

Not discouraged by guardian Gustav, Emil began to formulate plans for emigrating. As he would later write, "It was as if I was constantly *driven away* from there by an irresistible force. . . . *Nothing*, not even the subsequent *shame* [financial], could have hindered my leaving. I was too hurt by numerous situations and needed sea air to heal. Had I stayed, I would have had to die."[1]

It is not clear when Emil first began to discuss his plans with cousin Julius and how they reached the decision to emigrate together. Undoubtedly they were influenced, as were many other young Germans, by a book published in 1829 by Gottfried Duden.[2] In his *Report on a Journey to the Western States of North America*, Duden, who was born in Remscheid and had earned a degree in jurisprudence in Göttingen, reported on his 1824–1827 visit to the state of Missouri.[3] The *Report*, consisting of letters to a friend, contained Duden's carefully recorded observations of everything from Missouri's rivers, soils, plants, and animals to its frontier customs and way of life.

The author—the first university-educated German to settle in Missouri—was very enthusiastic about that area, which had been admitted into the union of American states in 1821. The state constituted the country's frontier and had space for millions, he wrote, especially farmers and craftsmen (figure II-1). But Duden cautioned, "Without any funds, emigration is a risk to which only the greatest need should drive one." Moreover, he wrote,

> I must advise against moving here by oneself and without careful consideration.
> . . . If a person has successfully survived the first two years, he is safe. But that is
> a difficult condition to meet. The initial effects of the new climate, the lack of
> domestic stability and service, attacks of homesickness . . . produce disturbances
> in the healthiest body, which even if they do not endanger life, usually decrease

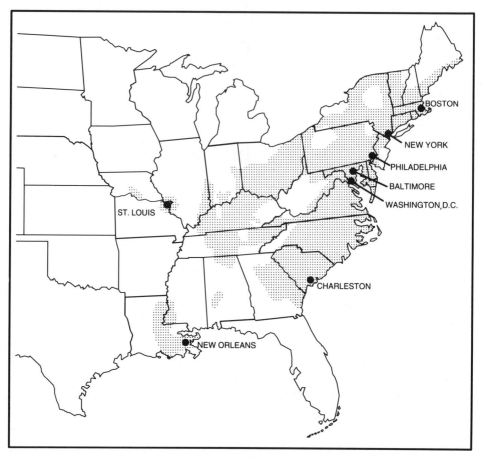

Figure II-I. The settled area of the United States in 1820 extended only about seven hundred miles west of the capital in Washington, D.C. St. Louis was a frontier settlement. (*Map by Shelly Price McCaskill.*)

one's means considerably and cause one to lose the courage to use properly what remains.[4]

Despite the warnings, Duden's description of frontier Missouri appealed to Emil and Julius.[5] Because of the family's foreign business connections, they had heard and read quite a bit about American frontier developments, which had, after all, involved Europeans. For instance, around 1673 the French explorers Marquette and Joliet discovered the upper Mississippi River, and in 1682 the French explorer La Salle, making his way from the Great Lakes down the Mississippi to its mouth, claimed the whole valley for France and called it Louisiana. The name New Orleans was given to the 1718 French settlement established there where the Mississippi entered the Gulf of Mexico. News of the lucrative French fur trade with the Native Americans had, of course, spread through Europe. The fur-trading center of St. Louis, founded in 1764 at the confluence of the Missouri and Mississippi Rivers by the trappers Pierre Laclede and René Chouteau, was widely known in Europe. (In the period 1770–1803 the town was under Spanish control.) In 1764 St. Louis was a city of about fifty families—gentlemen, hunters, merchants, boatmen, former soldiers, and Indians.

European intellectuals were excited, too, by reports of President Thomas Jefferson's $15 million purchase in 1803 of the Louisiana area from France and the subsequent 1803–1806 Lewis and Clark expedition to open the upper Missouri River. The origin and course of that stream had mystified French explorers for decades.[6] Jefferson's purchase, first referred to as the Indian Territory, was renamed the Territory of Louisiana in 1805. In 1812 it was subdivided, with the Missouri Territory (with an area of 70,000 square miles and a population of about 10,000) put under the governorship of Captain William Clark of the famous Lewis and Clark expedition.[7]

Wars with Native Americans had, of course, characterized the early history of Missouri. Like all other struggles with indigenous peoples, those in Missouri represented the increasingly futile attempt of America's natives to remain on their ancestral lands and avoid being driven west. The settlers pushing them out, mostly of Anglo-Saxon background, came from Kentucky, Tennessee, Virginia, and North Carolina, an area then plagued by the American War of 1812 with the British. Their emigration to the newly created Missouri Territory brought the population of its five counties up to 25,000 by 1814.[8] In November 1819, for instance, a St. Louis newspaper reported that for some time an average of 120 settlers' vehicles (wagons and carts) per week, with about eighteen persons each, had passed through nearby St. Charles. The settlers "came almost exclusively from the States south of the Potomac and the Ohio bringing slaves and large herds of cattle."[9] At the same time, forts were built, settlements started, steamboat traffic introduced, and more courts and counties organized. Thus, in 1820 the territorial government of Missouri applied for admission to the American union (figure 11-2). After furious debate about the extension of slavery into new territories, the U.S. Congress agreed on the historic Missouri Compromise, admitting Maine as a free state and Missouri as a slave state. One argument for Missouri's status was that many of its early settlers were Southerners with proslavery sentiments. In fact, population figures of the time showed 10,000 slaves and 375 freed blacks, plus 56,000 whites and 6,000 Native Americans (Osage, Sac, Fox, Shawnee).[10] After all the discussion, Missouri was proclaimed a state in August 1821.

In that Missouri of few people and much fertile land, Emil and Julius Mallinckrodt decided to seek a new homeland—indeed, in the very area where Gottfried Duden lived. They also determined to become farmers, as Duden had advised. The cousins believed that with Emil's extensive knowledge of farming and with what Julius had learned from Gustav plus Julius's business experience, they could surely succeed in their venture. They both had the advantage, moreover, of know-

Figure 11-2. Missouri was the westernmost state for about thirty years after coming into the Union in 1821. (*Map by Shelly Price McCaskill.*)

ing school English and being fluent in French. Still another positive point was Gustav's surprising offer to extend them credit as soon as they arrived in the New World and had good prospects.[11]

They might not become rich, they thought, but at least they would be rid of the strictures of German society, which at times weighed heavily on their free spirits and political liberalism. They were not, therefore, like some 300,000 earlier Germans who emigrated to colonial America in the 1600s and 1700s to escape religious repression or the economic destitution of landless farmers and rural laborers. They also differed from the roughly 5,750 who in the past decade (1820–1829) had left Germany, especially the southwestern regions, because of the disastrous harvest and economic dislocations after the Napoleonic War. Nor had they yet endured the kind of severe political coercion that would double the emigration stream in the 1840s.

It seemed instead that Emil and Julius, along with nearly 125,000 German emigrants to America from 1830 through 1839,[12] sought not only social and political but also individual freedom. They wanted the opportunity to try something different, to develop interests and abilities other than those that old Europe allowed men of their tradition and status. As a Dortmund historian would later suggest, it was the mentality of the times. Dortmund no longer had the élan of an international Hanseatic city, and its old spirit as a free Reichsstadt was gone. Behind Dortmund's walls a middle-class way of life had set in, a life of quietness and contemplation. "No wonder," concluded Haase-Faulenorth, "that fiery spirits were suffocating."[13]

And precisely because of their free spirits, Julius and Emil decided to strike out completely on their own rather than relying on one of the numerous associations being formed to advise and direct emigration. Knowing they wanted to go to Missouri, they would decide themselves how to get there by sailing ship. That meant first of all selecting the U.S. port of entry most advantageous for travelers wanting to go to the western frontier of America.

After some discussion, Julius and Emil excluded Baltimore, which Duden had used, and chose instead the southern port of New Orleans. The voyage there was a bit longer and thus about 10 to 15 percent more expensive than passage to northeast U.S. coastal ports. However, it was less costly to reach St. Louis from New Orleans via the Mississippi than to travel overland to Missouri from Maryland. Then, too, sailings to the American South were increasingly available because more and more ships were voyaging to New Orleans to pick up the freight Europe wanted—tobacco, cotton, and sugar.[14]

Next the Dortmund adventurers had to choose a European port at which they could find one of those ships sailing to New Orleans. Their choice of departure points, however, was quite limited. The only way to get to European coastal cities in those pre-railroad days was by expensive mail coaches or less costly riverboats. The choice usually fell among one of Europe's four major western European ports—Amsterdam and Rotterdam in Holland, Antwerp in Belgium, and Le Havre in France (figure 11-3). All of these ports could be reached by early emigrants from the central Rhine area of Prussia via the Rhine River and its connecting streams, plus overland coach routes.[15]

Because of the family business connections in Belgium and the help they could get there with legal and financial arrangements, Emil and Julius decided to go first to Antwerp. Then they would go on to Le Havre, where they felt the choice of ships for New Orleans was greater than from other ports. For instance, many ships plying the transatlantic route at that time were freighters, which offered emigrants miserable steerage passage on bunks between decks. From Le Havre, however, voyagers could book small so-called staterooms on packet ships, vessels that carried mail as well as freight and passengers and sailed during all seasons. American packets dominated the transatlantic trade because nautical technology developed during the war with England gave the United States a lead in fast,

Figure 11-3. The major European ports of departure in the 1830s for emigrants seeking passage to America were located along the coast of France and Holland. (*Map by Anita M. Mallinckrodt.*)

seaworthy vessels. Gottfried Duden, for instance, had sailed on an American ship, the *Henry Clay*.

With the major emigration decisions made—to travel from Le Havre to New Orleans to Missouri—the final task for the Mallinckrodts then was the sale or transfer of Emil's estate at Schwefe near Soest. That happened on 8 September 1831, when cousin Gustav's mother-in-law, Frau Anna Maria Strohn, bought it for 10,000 Prussian Thaler. Gustav, however, was apparently not pleased with the whole Schwefe transaction, telling Julius and Emil that his first letter to them in the New World would be one of complaint. Especially troublesome was a bankruptcy declaration prerequisite to the sale of Schwefe but unpublicized to avoid embarrassment for Emil; later it would lead Frau Strohn to accuse Gustav of false speculations.[16]

Although members of the family generally believed that the Schwefe money went to finance Emil's emigration, his letters suggested otherwise. At one point, for instance, he wrote his brother Eduard, "You believe, dear brother, that I took money from home? Dear God, are you in error. Not one red cent that was not borrowed."[17] It seemed instead that the funds were in fact not available to Emil for some time, nor was income from sale of the estate's furnishings and harvests.[18] Rather, much of that money went to pay father Arnold's debts. Yet at the same time Emil promised to share whatever little he had with Eduard, reflecting their father's early teaching about brotherly love and loyalty. As Emil wrote Eduard, "Do not be oppressively concerned about your future existence because the good Lord will care for us together. As long as I live, I will share the last morsel with you."[19]

Le Havre

Regardless of how amiable or confused the final financial arrangements were, or how much cash Emil and Julius had or could borrow, they did not wait long after the September sale of Schwefe to get underway. By 22 October 1831 they were in Le Havre, waiting for a ship to carry them to the New World. From there Emil wrote cousin Gustav:

> From Antwerp we had to travel here via Paris and Rouen because that is the postal route. Unfortunately we have to remain at anchor until the twenty-fifth. Then we will travel with the *Bolivar*, Capt. August Welch, to New Orleans. We were not able to get the passage cheaper than eight hundred francs per person. But then that covers everything.
>
> I hope with the bill of sale you were able to bring everything in order with your mother-in-law. May I please request seriously once again, dear Mr. Cousin, to somewhat supervise the sale of my furnishings and the harvest. . . . One had best wait until spring to sell the straw and hay.

In that last letter from Europe to his brother, Julius added more business details:

> I received a credit of £150 from Lemme & Co. to Schmidt & Co. in New York, in addition to several very good letters of recommendation to New York and New Orleans and here [Le Havre]. Because the journey until now cost us rather much— because of the heavy baggage and the high trans-Atlantic price—in New Orleans I must at once get money on the basis of this [letter of] credit. I will think about how I can best do that.
>
> Moreover, it appears to me rather certain that even before we have seen and become acquainted with the state where we want to buy, our cash will be rather melted away. Therefore we both wish that the Schwefe matter will soon be realized,

which surely will result in yet several thousand Taler for us. In the private statement between Emil and you we forgot to include six Thaler Emil paid for the transport of the two cows. I ask you to please enter this amount.[20]

These first emigrant-communiqués from Emil and Julius contained themes they would repeat over and over throughout the years—the unsettled disposal of Emil's estate, the economic difficulties caused by distance, and the need for credit and help to get started in America. (Indeed, the initial £150 credit Julius referred to would cause a serious family dispute in the future.)

In style, the first letters also set a pattern: Emil addressed Gustav as "Dear Cousin" or "Dear Mr. Cousin" and used the formal *Sie* (you), while Julius wrote "Dear Brother" and used the informal *Du* (you); both usually signed their letters "Your faithful [*treuer*]" brother or cousin and frequently closed with the touching phrase "Keep us in love" [*behalte uns lieb*].

The *Bolivar* on which the emigrants booked their passage from Le Havre was an American ship owned by a New Orleans merchant. On Emil and Julius's 1831 voyage it carried 28 cabin passengers: 9 single men, 4 single women, 4 servants, 4 children, 2 married couples ("Mr. F, Lady, servant"), and 3 additional males (accompanied by children or servants). Twenty-two additional passengers were in steerage, including a group of 17 adult Swiss and 5 children. In the cargo area the ship carried for the owner, among other merchandise, tiles, liquor, china, and clocks, while the captain logged in for himself 4 boxes of vases, 1 organ, 2 cages with four birds, and 2 boxes of harps. For other consigners the ship contained wearing apparel, cheese, cordials, and endless boxes, packages, cases, bales, and so on. Ship's stores included beef, champagne, claret, wine, brandied fruits, bread, chocolate, potatoes, flour, and other goods—surely intended for the cabin, not steerage, passengers.

Indeed, the cabin passengers checked in not only a plethora of trunks (averaging one to five each) but other interesting items as well. For instance, women passengers often had "boxes of bonnets" or "wearing apparel," while many of the male passengers had "pistols" and "guns." For Emil and Julius Mallinckrodt together, the "heavy baggage" Julius had written about included "5 trunks, 5 guns, 1 pair pistols, 1 guitar."[21] (The guitar, popular in Europe since the 1700s, probably was Julius's, for Emil later said he had developed an "extraordinary love for music" and "regret that my youth passed without it.")[22]

Even as cabin passengers, Emil and Julius did not particularly enjoy the fifty-nine-day voyage to New Orleans. Arriving on 26 December 1831, Emil, taking on the role of family reporter that he would assume over many years, immediately wrote to Gustav: "Brother Julius and I are now very well and happy. I suffered much from sea sickness and he not at all. Moreover, we found life at sea extraordinarily boring. If one sees nothing but water for five weeks and is shut up in a box for eight, then when one is released one hops about with happiness like a bird."

The difficulties of the voyage that Emil described in their first letter from

America were of course customary for sailing vessels: storms and capricious winds often delayed progress. Nevertheless, there were real delights to central Europeans: "On the first island [between Cuba and Domingo] we saw the palm trees which a passenger, a born Domingan, said grew ninety feet tall. Here the ocean wriggled with fish. We once saw more than twelve whales circling our ship, in front of which the flying fish ascended in a herd. One flew on board. We also caught a porpoise and four dolphins."

New Orleans

Also impressive, especially to an experienced farmer's eyes, were the Mississippi Delta and Louisiana in December. As Emil wrote:

> On 23 December we lowered anchor at the mouth of the Mississippi. On the twenty-fourth a steamboat towed us and three other ships to the city [New Orleans], where we arrived this morning [26 December]. One thousand vessels from all nations are at anchor. On the lower Mississippi everything is green and in bloom. Plane trees [sycamores], trees of life, a curious kind of oak, azaries [azaleas?], and a mixture of the most various foliage form a forest which does not yet have an owner. Farther up we found sugar plantations and rice fields, which flourish extraordinarily here. The most beautiful orange groves surround the country houses. . . . There are a tremendous number of waterfowl here. This morning the market was full of fat wild ducks, geese, woodcocks, squirrels, and also one rabbit. . . . There is a beautiful race of horses here. They are medium large, have fine feet, cylindrically formed bodies, a nice back, and fine neck. Poorly built and heavy horses are not seen.

New Orleans's population seemed astonishing to Emil and Julius as well:

> The black population is clearly the majority. These women are very ugly—they smoke bits of tobacco from short clay pipes. This morning we also saw four wild Indians wandering about—they had a wonderful appearance which contrasted with animals only in their upright position. They came out of curiosity, or perhaps hunger also drove them to the city. We met many German emigrants here, some of whom are working during the winter. . . . One sees little villages of Negro huts around the plantations where they work as slaves. We saw numerous persons who wore leg chains while working very hard. We were told they had stolen something.[23]

In closing their letter, the newly arrived immigrants again brought up the subject of money. Somehow they had turned the £150 letter of credit to New York, which Julius had gotten in Amsterdam, into $750 in New Orleans, with the understanding that the New York firm would get the balance from the Amsterdam company. At the same time Emil wrote that "we still have money for the first needs," but "just the same it would be very good for us to have $2,000 as soon as possible."

Referring to his Schwefe estate transactions, Emil added, "If that much is not left over for us, would you be willing to loan us the remainder? If this does not suit you, forget it. Surely something will be left over for me. In any case, we will get by."[24]

And so the next day—having changed money, bought provisions, and sent their baggage up river—they set off on foot along the Mississippi, the "Mother of Waters" or "Fish River," as the Native Americans called it.[25] Although the steamboat passage to St. Louis would not have cost much, they wanted to get to know the countryside and were prepared for a difficult journey. With the guns they had brought along they would hunt the rabbits, turkeys, deer, and squirrels along the trail. They hoped to reach Natchez after one hundred hours of hiking. From Natchez they would take a steamboat upstream to the Ohio and on to Missouri, where they planned to arrive in April.[26]

In addition to the flatboats, rafts, and keelboats on the Mississippi, Emil and Julius saw some steamboats, which struck the Europeans as astonishingly elaborate. "They do not resemble ours in any way," a German wrote, adding that the vessels looked "like an ordinary boat with a rather big house built on top."[27] Another traveler of the time described them in more detail:

> These steamers have three decks and 20 to 80 staterooms. Down below in the hold is the merchandise, then comes the engine, exposed in the middle of the ship; the remainder of the space is for passengers. On the second deck are the staterooms for ladies and gentlemen, the ship's offices, and various storage compartments. On the third or top deck is the Captain's bridge. The first and second decks are surrounded by railings, but not the third deck, which serves as a promenade in good weather.[28]

On such rivercraft deck passengers paid only about eight dollars from New Orleans to St. Louis, whereas those with a cabin were charged thirty dollars.[29]

Clearly Julius and Emil enjoyed the trek from New Orleans to Natchez on foot and then the Mississippi steamboat travel on to St. Louis. "There is no riverway in the world that can equal the Mississippi and Ohio," Emil enthusiastically wrote home:

> Try to imagine when I say that from New Orleans to St. Louis we came twelve hundred miles and along the long way saw not one square mile of cleared land. Everything is still covered with forests and here and there among them a plantation. Nothing causes more astonishment than the unbelievable vine growth in these forests—stems of three-quarters to one-foot thickness often grow up freely to ninety feet and then form like a roof over a tall tree. In Louisiana and Mississippi we found more than half of the cotton and sugar cane still in the fields [in January], which interested us greatly.
>
> In these states there are ten blacks to every white. That won't continue much longer. Therefore projects are being undertaken to send at least the freed Negroes

back to Africa. Unusual that the French, who at home talk so much about equality, are known throughout America as those who treat their slaves the worst. And truthfully: in Louisiana we saw examples of this.[30]

St. Louis

In mid-February 1832, Emil and Julius reached St. Louis. Obviously they had made the journey up the Mississippi in much less time than they estimated when they first arrived in New Orleans. As their steamboat pulled up to the western bank of the Mississippi River, they saw why St. Louis had a promising future. Built on a limestone bluff sloping gradually down to the river, St. Louis's waterfront was excellent for picking up or depositing cargo from ships that could tie up at the water's very edge.[31] In addition to St. Louis's favorable terrain, Emil and Julius saw, too, the advantage of the city's midway location on the mighty Father of Waters. At the city's wharfs, for instance, southern cargo was being unloaded from a New Orleans ship while goods for the upper Mississippi were being packed onto a different steamboat. In fact, St. Louis was a river terminal, a point for reloading cargoes from the shallower-draft boats used on the upper river onto the larger steamers plying the deeper waters of the lower Mississippi.[32]

Other vessels, however, were taking on pioneers and products headed in another direction, westward into the interior of the American continent via the intersecting waterway, the Missouri River. Navigated by steamboat since 1819,[33] the now increasingly traveled Missouri was giving new meaning to St. Louis's name "Gateway to the West." In the 1830s the city was gradually cultivating that new western orientation as a second geographic asset, supplementing its older north-south advantage on the Mississippi. Long dividing the settled eastern United States from its yet largely unknown western half, the Mississippi now was a transit route to the Missouri and the country's unexplored wildernesses.

Before thoroughly scouting the Mississippi settlement of five thousand people,[34] Emil and Julius first had to take care of their finances. In the letter they wrote home from St. Louis (their third to cousin Gustav since leaving Dortmund), Julius again requested money from his brother. Probably reacting to stories heard on St. Louis streets, the new Missouri immigrants made their repeated request sound reasonable by also reporting how cheaply land could be bought: "For $1.25 [per acre]," they wrote, "we have the best prospects of acquiring the best land from among the millions of acres here which are only sparsely settled by planters who have become very well-off through their knowledge but also the ease of earning their living."[35]

By this time Emil and Julius also had learned about the intricacies of international money transfers: they had had to pay a 2.5 percent commission to the New Orleans firm that gave them money, and Gustav would have to pay another commission to the New York firm that made good the transaction. "We would not like to experience such irritating losses a second time," they wrote Gustav. "Please, therefore, instruct the New York firm where you have accredited us to send the amount as a certificate of transfer to the Bank of the United States in St. Louis. As soon as we have an address, we will report it to the New York firm since they have to forward our letters to Germany."[36]

After their visit to the bank, it was undoubtedly life on St. Louis's streets that most fascinated the new arrivals from Germany. As a countryman at that time wrote about the city,

> No European can imagine the human hustle and bustle on Main Street and up and down Water Street, where people of all races and colors can be seen: Americans from the eastern states; Frenchmen from New Orleans (or born here); Negroes of all shades; Germans who have lived here for several years and who look quite Americanized; German peasants, newly arrived, who still run around in their native dress; Indians of all the different tribes, at whom the peasants stare in open curiosity.[37]

The Native Americans, however, were not numerous, for they had been pushed westward by the tide of Anglo-American settlers. According to a later view, "With the encroachment of whites came disease, violence, and illicit traffic in whiskey, to say nothing of broken pledges."[38] For instance, even before Missouri officially became a state, its spokespersons had asked the U.S. Congress to halt all Indian immigration into Missouri, "to remove all tribes recently pushed into the state from the east, and to nullify all claims to land by the Indians." Thus, the Osage, Sac, Fox, and Iowa tribes were removed, then the Shawnee, Delaware, and Kansas. Missouri's white population demanded even the land along the Platte River that President Andrew Jackson wanted to save for Indians, and so in 1830 the protective Treaty of Prairie du Chien was abrogated.[39]

When Emil and Julius Mallinckrodt arrived in St. Louis, America's natives no longer had permanent dwelling places in Missouri. Small groups still came to hunt, and sometimes Indian canoes with piles of skins were seen drifting down the Missouri River. Usually, however, the new European settlers were reminded of the Indians only when they found their burial mounds in the forests.[40]

It was on St. Louis's colorful streets that the new arrivals had their first experience with language difficulties. It happened to Julius, and later he relished telling the story on himself. He met a man on the street and, wanting to ask something, spoke what he thought was English. The man could not understand him. Neither could the St. Louisan understand the German and Latin that Julius tried next. Finally, excited and angry, Julius exclaimed in French, "Parlez-vous Francais, Monsieur?" Instantly the man threw his arms around Julius's neck and embraced him, tears of joy running down his cheeks: he was a Frenchman who could not find anyone with whom he could converse. Since Julius spoke French almost as fluently as German, especially after his Antwerp days, a warm friendship, which lasted for years, sprang up between two strangers who had met in a strange land.[41]

Having seen a bit of St. Louis, Julius and Emil traveled on to Duden country, some sixty miles west. How they traversed the distance is not known. There were two possibilities at the time. One was by steamboat, first a short distance up the Mississippi north from St. Louis and then west into the Missouri (an Indian word meaning "Muddy").[42] The confluence of these mighty rivers would have impressed them, as it had explorers over the centuries. Père Marquette, for instance, wrote that he and Joliet in 1673 had heard such a great roaring where the two rivers came together that it frightened them.

Even if Emil and Julius did not hear roaring, since the rivers then were not at flood stage, they would have been awed by that distinct, rippling dividing line where the Missouri River, flowing from the west, meets the Mississippi. Such a meeting of waters they had never seen. In fact, these Western rivers were quite strange, for they were rivers of sand as well as water. As Emil and Julius and other pioneers would learn, both streams washed away their own banks, and with that material then built great sandbars in their own paths. One pioneer described the mingling of waters this way: "Where the broad Missouri mingles its yellow, slimy waters with those of the Mississippi, the color of the stream changes. At first the water of the latter is clearly distinguishable from that of the former, one side of the stream being dark brown, the other pale yellow. Soon, however, the Missouri with its tremendous water mass overwhelms the Mississippi, and then the entire stream becomes clay-colored."[43]

Turning into the Missouri, their steamboat would have headed for one of the riverfront landings close to the Duden plantation they first wanted to visit. That probably would have been at Marthasville, about sixty miles upstream, the principal landing place for the entire area later comprising Warren County.[44]

If the Mallinckrodts took this river route, the landscape would have reminded them somewhat of the Rhine River area of their homeland, for there the wide Missouri flows between limestone bluffs. The travelers would not, of course, have seen ancient castles looking down on the river from the high hills on either side, as in Europe, but rather miles and miles of wooded rolling hills. As another German underway at the time saw it,

> So far the only difference between the Missouri and the Mississippi is a more rapid current and more frequent bends. There is a great navigational hazard from the snags, and therefore the boat has to anchor at night until the moon rises. . . .
>
> The farther one travels up the Missouri, the higher and more wooded the banks become. The scenery changes frequently from bluffs to bottom land. Also there are a few towering rocks. Such a phenomenon would attract little attention in Europe, but on these American rivers, where the scenery is usually very monotonous, each change is noticeable. The river-banks are sparsely inhabited. The eye sees nothing but dense forest and fast-moving, muddy water; now and then a sand

bar on which driftwood has accumulated; otherwise the same picture for 300 miles.[45]

Julius and Emil may, however, have traveled by wagon trail from St. Louis to Duden country, the St. Charles and Warren County areas surrounding Duden's original property and later the Dutzow settlement (figure 24-1) founded by Baron von Bock. This second transportation possibility first meant going from St. Louis to St. Charles, about twenty miles west on the Missouri, either by an overnight steamboat or one of the thrice-weekly stagecoaches covering that distance by land. A traveler described that twenty-mile trip by road this way:

> We made the trip in four hours in a rented wagon. The road to the Missouri runs partly over flat land and partly through hills covered by forests. Before reaching the banks of the Missouri, one must cross the so-called bottom land, a black, muddy soil that is completely covered by water at flood stage. The wagon is brought to a halt on a steam ferry that crosses the river. At this time of the year [October] the Missouri is not nearly so wide as the Mississippi, but the current is much stronger. St. Charles is located on a bluff and has one street and a few scattered houses. The town is one of the oldest in the state of Missouri, inhabited by Frenchmen and Germans. . . . The banks of the Missouri are thinly populated, the land being mostly a virgin wilderness.[46]

St. Charles, founded in 1769 by Louis Blanchette as a military outpost for the Spanish controlling the territory, had grown slowly.[47] When the area was organized into a county within the Missouri Territory in 1812, St. Charles became the county seat, its name reflecting its French and Spanish past. The settlement's population then stood at around thirty-five hundred people.[48] The elected officials were early settlers of English background; the few businesses included a tavern, billiard hall, and wine and liquor stores.[49]

After Missouri became a state in 1821, its first legislature met in St. Charles in a row of three brick buildings. One of the assembly's initial decisions was to build a permanent state capital in an entirely new city but meanwhile to continue meeting in St. Charles. To keep its temporary distinction, St. Charles offered free meeting rooms for both branches of the general assembly and committee rooms, plus cut-rate boarding for the legislators and their horses.

That offer cost the town a great deal. In fact, if Emil and Julius on their way upriver that winter of 1832 stopped off in a St. Charles saloon, they probably heard its patrons still complaining about what it had cost them to host those "temporary" legislators. The state government had lingered for five years because the move to the new capital, Jefferson City in the center of the state, had not been made until 1826. Meanwhile, local tales about those first assembly members had become part of St. Charles's lore:

> All the members were dressed in primitive style, either in homespun or homemade clothes and buckskin moccasins. Some had slouched hats, but the greater portion

wore caps made of the skins of wild cats or raccoons. Governor McNair was the only man who had a fine cloth coat and that was cut in the old "pigeon-tail" style. He also wore a beaver hat and endeavored to carry himself with the dignity becoming a man finding himself in that situation.[50]

Although no longer the state capital, St. Charles, a town of more than forty-three hundred by the 1830s,[51] was known as the starting point for a famous wagon trail westward, the Boone's Lick Road (figure 11-4). An extension of the National Road beginning at Baltimore in the east, the road passed from St. Charles through Missouri's new areas of settlements, initially to the town of Franklin and later to Fort Osage, 275 miles west of St. Louis. At the end of Boone's Lick Road began another trail that would become almost legendary in the next decades, the Santa Fe Trail; forty miles further on, the equally famous Oregon Trail branched off to the northwest.

Boone's Lick Road, named for the famous pioneer Daniel Boone, was surveyed by his son in 1820. The elder Boone had come to Missouri from Kentucky at the invitation of the Spanish when they briefly ruled the Louisiana Territory in the late 1780s. The frontiersman and colonel of the Kentucky Militia was offered large land grants in the Femme Osage District of Missouri, near St. Charles, if he would lead pioneer settlers there. In financial difficulties and feeling crowded, Daniel Boone accepted and set out in 1795, saying, "I want more elbowroom!"

Figure 11-4. In the 1800s Boone's Lick Road reached from St. Charles to Franklin, Missouri. (*Map by Shelly Price McCaskill.*)

Boone's earlier passage through a gap in the Appalachian mountains on his way to the West was immortalized in 1851–52 by George Caleb Bingham, known as the "Missouri artist." Generations would come to think of Boone as Bingham's tall, buckskin-clad frontiersman leading a white horse ridden by his wife, Rebecca. Behind them march their daughter and men carrying rifles and axes, symbolizing both hunters and settlers; far behind them shines a brightly lit sky, said to symbolize the settled East from which they have come.[52]

Arriving in Missouri, Boone was named district magistrate, in charge of Spanish military and civil administration in a large area. It was said that Boone "was doctor, nurse, judge and advisor to hundreds of pioneer families. He was seen everywhere skillfully treating the sick, holding court under the famed 'Judgment Tree,' riding down the river in his huge canoe loaded with the skins of a winter's trapping, aiding the settlers and carrying on his own business and legal affairs until his death at the age of 84."[53]

By the 1830s the road named for Boone and its stageline ran from St. Charles through Missouri's rolling farmland, a terrain broken by hills, dales, and gentle slopes. At first the stagecoach through that countryside left St. Charles weekly for points west. Soon there were two and three trips a week over Boone's Lick Road, and finally the stage line ran four to five coaches a day from St. Charles. The Road was also the route for hundreds of individual wagons and four- and two-wheeled carriages heading west each month. It was said that many times one could stand on the road and not be out of sight of an emigrant wagon.

It is quite possible, therefore, that Julius and Emil, along with their five trunks, also traveled over that route by stage. If they did, then about twenty miles west they reached the Marthasville Road; following it some fifteen miles southwest they would have come to their first destination—the Duden farm.[54]

12

1832: Putting Down Roots in Missouri

However Emil and Julius arrived, their two-week visit to Duden's plantation was encouraging even though Duden himself was not there. (He had returned to Germany because of his mother's illness.) The Mallinckrodts therefore visited with Duden's friend Ludwig (Louis) Eversmann. "We stayed there fourteen days so that we could convince ourselves on the spot that Duden, thank goodness, reported the situation so truthfully," Emil wrote.[1] The new arrivals' primary concern, of course, was verification of the area's productiveness, for they already had seen its natural beauty. They wanted to know how fruitful the land was, what crops grew best, how farm produce could be marketed, where one could buy land, and so on. And what was the climate really like? That Duden had written about mild winters and hot summers seemed too good to be true to Germans from the Ruhr.

At their initial stop at Duden's property, Emil and Julius asked Eversmann, the area's first permanent German settler,[2] about buying land. He advised them to go to nearby Mount Pleasant, about six miles southeast. There were acres of uncleared woods to be had around that small St. Charles County settlement on bluffland hugging the Missouri River's northern bank.

Aptly named for its spectacular view, Mount Pleasant was located on very hilly, broken terrain, among numerous little creeks pouring down from stony, steep hills and narrow hollows into the Missouri. From these northern bluffs one could look across the wide river to its valley on the south side, the fertile Darst Bottom, and beyond to the parallel range of limestone bluffs.

A Virginian, Leonard Harold, had bought the Mount Pleasant land in 1812. By 1830 the few scattered families there were settlers who had followed the path blazed by Daniel Boone from Kentucky to the new Missouri Territory. Their names included Bryan, Bigelow, Coshow, and Darst.[3] As yet no Germans were recorded in Mount Pleasant.

When Julius and Emil arrived in the area about 1 March 1832, they found lodging with a Scottish farmer, Z. McClenny, who had come to Missouri from Kentucky. He took them around on horseback, pointing out available tracts of land. Much of it was U.S. government public land, surveyed and divided into sections and available at $1.25 per acre. McClenny explained that a purchaser paying the land office was given a certificate certifying the sale; a duplicate sent to Washington brought the purchaser, in turn, a land patent bearing the signature of the president of the United States.[4]

Buying Land

After a week of scouting the countryside, the Dortmund emigrants bought their first piece of America by about 10 March—230 acres of Missouri land, just a few miles west of Mount Pleasant, for $475. Emil described it enthusiastically:

> We bought 150 acres at $2.50 from a private party with the condition that we pay this fall, and 80 acres of public land for $1.25, which we paid in cash. This land is in one piece on the bank of the Missouri, fifty English miles above its outlet into the Mississippi [at St. Louis].
>
> It lies 100 feet above the river level and has soil that even Americans call rich, i.e., will need no fertilizer for the first fifty years. All of the land is covered with woods, consisting of hickory, sassafras, walnut, mulberry, eight kinds of oaks, redbud, foxwood, poplars, ash, lindens, and covered over with wild grapes. . . .
>
> You cannot believe how satisfied we are with our situation until now. We now own a place that we could hardly have imagined. Because we are sixty feet higher than our entire surroundings, we not only have a healthy location but at the same time enjoy a marvelous view. Steamboats pass up and down before our door, and thereby we have a constant market where we can sell everything.[5]

Years later such land purchases would be criticized because the acreage was hill ground, not meadowland. However, at a time of water transportation the choice of bluffland on the Missouri was eminently logical. The terrain back from the river was rolling hills, with rich soil and slopes good for the crops—corn, fruits, and vegetables—the Mallinckrodts planned to raise. After all, they were not going into cattle and grain farming, which required prairie land. Instead, as Emil wrote, "An almost passionate inclination for agriculture and horticulture has driven me since youth,"[6] and Julius wanted especially to apply what he had learned when establishing stepbrother Gustav's gardens in Westphalia.

So, not pausing long to celebrate their extraordinary luck at finding such a location, Emil and Julius immediately rented a wagon and went to work clearing the woods they had bought. In two weeks they had enough space for a garden and building site. Another goal was a twenty-acre clearing for planting corn, which, they said, "flourishes unbelievably here—in one ear nine hundred nice kernels!"

According to early settlers, the work of clearing land was hard labor:

The first farms were opened up in the timber. The timber was all cut down. That which would make rails or fencing was so utilized. The rest was piled and rolled together and burned. The stumps of the saplings were grubbed up, and then the land was plowed.

The plow used was a very simple affair, with sometimes an iron point and sometimes without, and always a wooden mold-board. It is said that some farmers used a plow made from the fork of a tree. . . . There was, of course, the usual difficulty in plowing regarding the stumps, and as most of the pioneers were not profane men, their sufferings at times were intense![7]

Cutting down the trees caused special problems for Europeans. As a German settler, raised on the land and knowing how to use many tools, wrote: "The way of cutting down trees here first had to be learned. Since we did not know the kinds of trees—and one of course has to know for what each one is good, which ones split, which ones are durable and which ones are not—a lot of mistakes were naturally made and a lot of useless effort expended."[8]

Next came the building of a small house. It cost only about sixty dollars, for the materials were at hand—logs and stone—and neighbors helped. After three months of boarding with the McClennys, Emil and Julius moved into their own log house in May 1832.[9] Old Missouri accounts describe what it may have been like:

These [houses] were of round logs, notched together at the corners, ribbed with poles and covered with boards split from a tree. A puncheon floor was then laid down, a hole cut in the end and a stick chimney run up. A clapboard door is made, a window is opened by cutting out a hole in the side or end two feet square and finished without glass or transparency. The house is then "chinked" or "daubed" with mud. . . .

The one-legged bedstead . . . was made by cutting a stick the proper length, boring holes at one end one and a half inches in diameter, at right angles, and the same sized holes corresponding with those in the logs of the cabin the length and breadth desired for the bed, in which are inserted poles. Upon these poles the clapboards are laid, or linn bark is interwoven consecutively from pole to pole. Upon this primitive structure the bed is laid.

The convenience of a cook stove was not thought of, but instead, the cooking was done by the faithful housewife in pots, kettles or skillets, on and about the big fire-place.[10]

With so much achieved so soon, it was no wonder that Emil and Julius then thought of sharing their good fortune with the family in Dortmund. As Julius wrote Gustav about their brothers,

> The conditions here are so favorable for every kind of undertaking and as easy as is possible only in a new land. . . . We think therefore about Albert and Hermann coming over after we have checked everything out carefully. I bring this up already now so that they do not undertake their year of [military] service. With the money that would cost them [to meet the prerequisite of buying their own equipment if they chose to serve only one rather than three years] they could create good and independent situations here.
>
> I advise Albert to stick to learning the tannery business—skins are cheap here, tanning bark and wood is there for the peeling, traps and leather are expensive. It would be good if he could learn to make upper leather [for shoes] and harness leather.[11]

That first letter from St. Charles County, Missouri, closed with perhaps a touch of homesickness after about five months' absence: "We also ask you to write us soon and in detail about our family—we wait with longing for news from home." In addition, an explanation was given for using the old practice of *cross-writing*, in which horizontal lines were written down the page in the usual way and then, with the page turned sideways, another set of lines written at right angles to the first: "I have cross-written because to save postage we may not use more than one folio [a sheet of paper folded once] or have enclosures," Emil said (figure 12-1).[12] Then the letter was sent from the Missouri State/Marthasville Post Office to a New York firm, from there forwarded by ship to Le Havre, and finally transported to Prussia, all of which took two months.

The family news that came back to Julius and Emil bit by bit in 1832 was unlike their own optimistic progress reports home. Gustav was dissatisfied with Leopold; Leopold was concerned that the business did not go well; Mother was worried and restless. Albert had been with Gustav in Krombach for a time learning the tanning business but had to give up that physical work and return to the Antwerp office. From Conrad in Munich, on the other hand, the news was good: he was preparing to take his exams after four years of study and might be home by the end of the year.[13]

Hermann seemed to pose the greatest problem. After returning from Antwerp, he had taken a volunteer job in Elberfeld until he could begin his one-year military service. He was unsure, however, just when and where that would be.[14] The military was not accepting recruits at the moment but filling its vacancies with reservists. In light of a possible war with France, however, a substitute infantry company was being formed to be stationed in Dortmund. That appealed to Hermann, who said he had "always had a special interest to serve in the infantry."[15] Meanwhile, since he "had not yet fully decided to go to America," he wanted to bridge the months by working for Gustav.[16] Gustav, however, apparently had

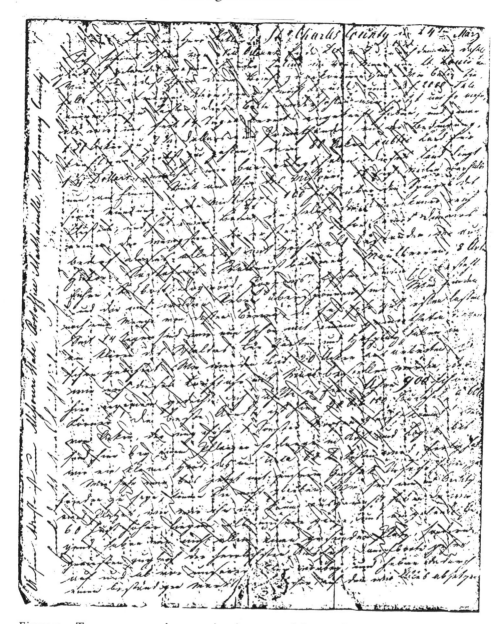

Figure 12-1. To save paper and postage immigrants used the practice of "cross-writing" their letters home to Europe. (*Courtesy Cologne Historical Archive.*)

misgivings: Hermann could work for him only if he "promised to *always be busy*, even if I am not there. . . . Albert earned my unqualified praise because he always found work on his own, and if there was nothing to do for the business, he worked for himself."[17] Moreover, Gustav warned Hermann to be very thrifty and not to tell anyone how poorly the family business was going.[18]

By July 1832 Emil and Julius were beginning literally to realize the first fruits of their efforts, for their garden now flourished: "On our cleared land corn, tobacco, potatoes, cabbage, and melons grow in such abundance that it is impossible for you to imagine," Emil reported. And Julius added, "It is astonishing to me that we now have grapes which will ripen on the short-rooted grape plants that we covered over with soil last spring. Already the berries are as big as a cherry! We have melons in the garden with vines eighteen feet long! Also corn sixteen feet high!"[19] Perhaps even then Julius was thinking ahead to what Duden had written: "for emigrants from the Rhineland nothing is more important than viniculture" because the Americans "have not the slightest knowledge or experience in its production."[20]

The Mallinckrodts' list of first garden produce also naturally reflected the foods of the area, for the settlers lived off the land (as did their descendants for generations to come). They concentrated on raising animals for slaughter, primarily hogs and cattle; the meat was preserved by salting and smoking and was then stored in a smokehouse. Most of the settlers raised chickens, and they hunted game in the thickly wooded countryside—rabbit, squirrel, deer, turkey, pheasant, quail. The transplanted Dortmunders also learned to enjoy catfish, eel, pike, and buffalo fish from the Missouri and ducks and geese shot in flight or while resting on the river.

In addition to meat, bread was a staple food. It included the kinds Europeans knew, made from rye and wheat flour, but also from oats. Baking such breads, however, was difficult, for it was a daily task carried out at the fireplace with big iron pots, not with pans in an oven. More astonishing, however, was the corn bread, which Emil and Julius discovered was a main food in frontier homes. Exactly as Duden had written, corn was "a main product of agriculture. One could call it the wet nurse of a growing population."[21] Accustomed to thinking of it only as food for animals, the German settlers were surprised that it was equally nourishing for humans. As one wrote at the time, "It can be eaten as a vegetable with butter when it is yet in a green stage. Excellent bread and even cakes are made from its meal. It is also used in different ways for soup. Corn is to the American what the potato is to the German."[22]

Other surprises for the German settlers included sweet potatoes, pumpkins, and sweet syrups, made from the sap of maple trees or corn or the heavy, dark molasses cooked down during the sugar-making process. Along with such syrups, preserves, and marmalades which were put on breads, there was apple butter, too. Probably introduced into the area by Pennsylvania Dutch settlers, this spread, thicker and darker than applesauce, was made by cooking cut-up apples outdoors in a big open iron kettle. Seasoned with sugar, cinnamon, and other spices, the apples were "cooked down" during an all-day simmering and stirring process; by afternoon the apples' liquid content was reduced and a buttery, sweet, dark substance remained. Poured into crocks, the apple butter was stored for year-round enjoyment.

Central to food preparation were, of course, eggs and dairy products. The eggs were daily gathered from the chicken house that every settler had, and from their dairy cattle the farm family gained the needed butter and milk. These dairy products were often kept in a "springhouse" built over the source of a well or spring; there foods were placed in, say, a tin trough and kept cool by the running water. Puddings could be offered as special desserts, along with custard fruit pies made from the orchard's peaches, apples, and berries. Cooked cheese was made from soured milk. At Christmas traditional German foods were brought to the table, including fruit breads and cookies such as *Anise, Pfeffernüße, Lebkuchen, Zucker-plätzchen,* and *Zimtsterne.* Some of the baked goods were made with butter, but many also with the lard rendered from pork at butchering time.

The list of vegetables grown in the gardens along the Missouri River was endless: peas, beans, lettuce, cucumbers, carrots, spinach, turnips, beets, tomatoes, and cabbage. Potatoes, of course, were plentiful, including the sweet potato unknown in Germany. The settlers' orchards provided not only fruits but also the liquors that cheered frontier social life—cider, brandies, cordials, and *Schnapps,* made from apples, peaches, and berries of all kinds. In addition, the grain fields offered ingredients for making the favorite American liquor, whiskey.

The first months on their land were thus a time of discovery for Emil and Julius—new foods to be made from their garden and orchard produce, three valuable springs ("one eighty paces from our house, in the cliffs along the Missouri, which we use as a well"), and proficiency in the English language. "We use it without difficulty," Julius wrote, perhaps laughingly remembering his linguistic adventure in St. Louis.[23]

With pride, then, they sketched, as best they could, their 230-acre home on the river, consisting of "three hills and two valleys" (figure 12-2). According to the drawing, the Mallinckrodts' house stood atop the center hill; a field stretched

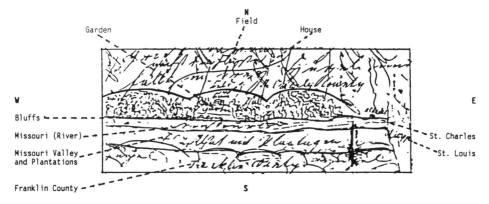

Figure 12-2. In a letter to Germany, Emil and Julius Mallinckrodt sketched their new 230-acre home in Missouri as consisting of "three hills and two valleys." (*Courtesy Cologne Historical Archive.*)

out behind it, and in front the garden ran down to the bluffs and the Missouri. Beyond the river, to the south, was the river valley (Darst Bottom, Hancock Bottom, etc.) and its big farms or "plantations."[24]

Even though they did not include a boat in their drawing, Emil and Julius were fascinated by the parade of steamboats up and down the river in front of their door. They watched especially for the *Yellow Stone*, built for Pierre Chouteau, Jr., western agent of the American Fur Company owned by John Jacob Astor. In spring it passed their place, a big American flag flying from the bow, headed for fur-trading posts on the upper Missouri. It was a famous steamboat and often carried prominent passengers: Julius and Emil later heard that when they had seen the *Yellow Stone* that spring (1832), it was carrying George Catlin, the well-known painter of Indian life. Months later the steamboat passed downstream again, carried rapidly along by the Missouri's fast current. In winter it was not seen, for in those months it traveled the Mississippi south to New Orleans. The *Yellow Stone* was a river beauty—120 feet long, 20 feet wide, with a 6-foot hold, as well as paddlewheels on each side 18 feet in diameter and 6 to 8 feet broad. Along the way the boat stopped while its crew cut firewood for its steam boilers or bought the fuel from settlers who piled it up on the riverbanks.[25]

In July 1832 the Mallinckrodts had two important events to celebrate as new immigrants. One was their first Fourth of July in America, marking the country's independence. Finding it a "wonderful celebration," Emil used considerable detail to tell Gustav about it:

One of the local farmers held a wonderful speech before he read the Declaration [of Independence], a true masterpiece. Unfortunately I cannot send you the entire speech. We six Germans were present.[26] The speaker once turned to us, asking, "Why do noble men leave the hearths of their homes in old nations, why have the respectable Germans now among us left their fatherland, their brothers, their people and language, their ways and customs, the ashes of their ancestors? Was it not your love of justice and freedom, the recognition of humankind's worth without disadvantages of birth, equal opportunity to all the advantages which our political society offers, which brought you to us? So you are welcome, new citizens, friends."

The speaker said, "Europe already has long said that our state, with our present republican constitution, could not long endure. That the entire nation would spiritually and morally fall so deep that we would become dependent children; that through the bonds of prejudice and ignorance and physical and spiritual decay we would sink so far that one or more persons would have to oversee the entire nation, dealing with us with arbitrariness, as oxen by their driver.

"Therefore, my brothers, it is intelligence which preserves us, which will permit us to exist like a powerful giant for a thousand years. Preserve it, plant it in your children—never stand still, broaden your insights, follow the arts and sciences, nourish honorable freedom, justice, and the people's well-being in your breasts. For then after one thousand years our people will, as today, still gladly take leave of king and emperor, prince and pope, priests and prejudices. And then, as today, America will still be the haven, or better the homeland, of the persecuted noble people of the whole earth."[27]

Julius Marries

The second big July celebration was Julius's marriage on the fifteenth to Mary McClenny. She was a daughter of the farmer with whom they had first stayed, on the plantation now located behind their own. "Julius could not have made a better choice," Emil wrote about the Scottish frontier lass who had become his cousin by marriage. "The family is one of the most respected in the state, characterized by a sense of justice, industriousness, and freedom of spirit."[28]

Julius added his own report: "I am very happy and believe I have made as good a match, concerning character, education, and intellectual abilities, as I could have in Europe." Thinking perhaps of the trauma Emil had suffered when the Dortmund family insisted on a marriage for wealth, Julius added for Gustav's contemplation, "Rich matches can't be made here, even through self-sacrifice and investment of everything which otherwise could motivate marriage. Even if there is great wealth, there are always so many children (often fifteen to twenty) that when the inheritance is divided each portion is small. Therefore, I had no reservations about taking as a wife the first best one (character, family, behavior) I liked." In addition, Emil wrote, "Economically we, also with Mary, have made our house as pleasant and nice as we could wish."[29] Perhaps that was recognition that the experienced frontier woman had taught them not only about innovating and "making do" in their unaccustomed simple environment but also about adding taste and comfort.

Julius obviously was happy in a compatible partnership that would be long-lasting. Contracting a marriage on, or for, the frontier, was, however, not always unproblematic. Although many young couples were among the immigrants, most of them were single men. Consequently, marriageable young American women had many potential suitors, but some young German men hesitated to marry the local girls because they often did not speak German. Then, too, as one observer put it, many of the German men "had not yet shaken off the views and pretensions of the so-called refined classes in the old country."[30]

In such cases, they sometimes chose to bring a wife over from the old homeland and that, in turn, posed other problems. German women, especially from cultured backgrounds, frequently found it very difficult to adjust to frontier conditions. Others, of course, were able to adapt to the modest (in some cases primitive) living conditions and hard work and to enjoy the sense of equality that the new world offered.

On the whole, however, the frontier life of women, American- or German-born, was not easy, either physically or psychologically. It was strictly a man's world, with women present to keep hearth and home going and to produce all the children nature would possibly allow, many of whom were stillborn or died in infancy.

Women's work included not only cooking with the simplest of equipment but also making clothing. Using small hand carders, along with a small spinning wheel for flax and a much larger one for wool and cotton, the frontier women wove the cloth, called "homespun," for the family's coats, shirts, trousers, skirts, and blouses. The dyes used to color Missouri's flax, hemp, and wool were indigo for blue and the bark of forest trees for black, browns, or grays. That left the hats to buy—broad-brimmed and low-crowned—and an occasional pair of shoes, usually a kind of half-boot.[31] Some fathers, however, made the shoes for everyone in the family, all according to the same pattern.[32]

The women were skilled, too, at other crafts. For instance, they made brooms from the broomstraw that grew well in Missouri; this straw is a kind of corn that "has the seed in the tassels but no ears."[33] And if they had any time left, the women also made candles, although the family usually relied on the light of the fireplace plus a small oil-burning lamp.

While the work was hard and seemingly unending, at the same time there was a sense that somehow frontier women were "free." Germans, for instance, noted that American women usually did not work in the fields as European women did, were seldom brutally treated, and went to school whenever one was available. Moreover, following English common law, daughters could inherit as well as sons.[34] Even Gottfried Duden had seen women riding horseback as a symbol of extraordinary freedom: "Women and girls, old and young, ride (sidesaddle in the English manner) at a rapid or slow pace without difficulty, and they last in the saddle as long as the men."[35] There was, then, a kind of equality in many frontier marriages, a partnership of couples struggling hard to carve a home out of the wilderness. It was told with pride in Duden country, for instance, that Rebecca Boone, the beloved wife of the old explorer Daniel, even accompanied him on his hunting trips.[36]

Then, too, there was companionship among women on the frontier—an early kind of "sisterhood" that undoubtedly gave them strength and pleasure when they came together to help one another. For instance, bringing along their own favorite paring knives, women gathered at someone's home to spend hours peeling and cutting up apples for the next day's apple-butter cooking or, with their favorite thimbles in their pockets, they came together to quilt. At butchering time the menfolk did the heavier work of cutting up and trimming the meat while the farm women neighbors made the sausage (*Bratwurst, Leberwurst, Blutwurst, Kopfkäse*).

Unfortunately, what the women talked about during their gatherings, what they *thought* about all this work and their life in general, is not widely known. As in Europe during the preceding centuries, diaries and accounts of everyday life in frontier Missouri were written by men and therefore were about men's activities. As a later historian would write about immigrant women, "Our view of them has almost always been through the eyes of their husbands, sons, or other male observers, who tended to see them as one-dimensional stereotypes, heroic in many cases, but silent and stoic figures in the background of the drama of immigration."[37]

Moreover, there are no records from meetings of emancipation and women's suffrage groups, for those concepts, which were being discussed on the U.S. East Coast and in larger cities, found little echo on the American frontier of the 1830s and 1840s. (It would be more than a century before an autobiography and preserved collection of letters from a Missouri immigrant woman of that time was published, describing in her own words the loneliness and hardship of the frontier experience.)[38]

After Julius's marriage, the little house he and Emil had built obviously was not roomy enough, so they built a second dwelling for Julius and Mary on the bluff east of the first. It was finished several months later, by October 1832, when the German Heinrich Martels, scouting the Duden area for land to buy, visited Emil and Julius. His report, later published in Germany, was very complimentary of the Dortmund immigrants' efforts:

> 31 October. Today we made the acquaintance of two stout-hearted countrymen, the Messrs. Malinckrodt [*sic*] from Dortmund who bought property here a year ago. Their farm has a wonderful location on the Missouri, and they can look up and down the river for ten miles. With astonishing industry these active people have made a large field cultivatable, and with the help of a carpenter and a helper they have built two rather nice houses. The older Mr. Mallinckrodt [Julius] is married to the daughter of the neighboring farmer who is also judge for St. Charles County. Since they are very acquainted with the area, they offered to accompany us on our excursions.[39]

Toward the end of 1832 Emil and Julius finally received their first news from Gustav, written some nine months after they had left Dortmund.[40] Apparently addressed to Julius, the reprimanding communiqué written in July was a shock to the new Missourians, in part because they did not know what family difficulties Gustav had had on their behalf. Perhaps also Emil had forgotten how quick the family was to judge its members' affairs even, as in this case, when they did not understand conditions on the Missouri frontier.[41]

As Julius replied to his brother, "Your epistle, with which you pursue us even across the ocean, was very unexpected. . . . We certainly did not expect to be so censured, for neither you nor anyone has a right or reason for that. We are of age and completely independent of you, even if it was friendly of you to take on the ordering of Emil's affairs and to promise to help us with your means to make good and rapid progress."[42]

Julius rejected not only Gustav's right to criticize but also his demand for a

promissory note for £250, or $1,200, which had been sent instead of their re-
quested $2,000. Julius also offered a spirited and loyal defense of Emil, whom
Gustav had characterized as "an inexperienced young man whom Julius had
influenced to a questionable undertaking." Always the businessman, Julius also
defended them both against the accusation that they "intended to make a lot with
a little":

> One can make money here from cattle, but how can one make much if one does
> not have many cattle? Initially this costs money. Land costs money. It costs money
> to build buildings. To build a house and plant fields costs money. Negroes, which
> one has to buy because one cannot work a farm alone, cost money. All of these
> things cost money, and that is what we wanted to make clear with our reports,
> for it was what we expected. . . .
>
> As desirable as the money would be, so little are we inclined to accept your
> conditions, especially if it then occurs to you to lecture us. We'll get along also
> without that, and so release you from your promise to give us appropriate credit.
> But if you think the $1,200—or £250—already sent us gives you that right, then
> just write us and you shall have it returned.

(This sum, too, would later become a bone of contention between Julius and
Gustav.)

Emil, also answering Gustav, defended Julius ("if I caused a friend problems,
that doesn't belong on his bill") as well as himself: "I have the pleasure to tell
you that it goes unusually well with us, better than we would have dared to guess.
Our wealth lies in our wonderful places. . . . Especially important for me, who
lay under the yoke of difficult conditions, is to breathe so freely here when minimal
work is so richly rewarded and where one lives in peace and friendship."

On the progress of the area itself, Emil had many positive developments to report
to Gustav. For instance, at the end of 1832 the Mallinckrodts no longer were novel
as "first German emigrants"; instead, the six Germans at the Fourth of July celebration had increased to nearly fifty Duden-followers: "In the last six months forty
Germans, mostly people from the upper class, have settled with their families near
us. At least two-thirds of them are as content as we. All of them are trying to persuade
their relatives and friends to come here. Thus, it is certain that we will have a German
school in two years. Duden's book brings almost all countrymen here now, and their
property ownership has increased 50 percent."

The farming was going very well, too, Emil wrote, and "until now [late Decem-
ber] we have had weather such as one has in Germany in the nicest days of May."

> The bees are constantly in flight. The honey harvest this year has been especially rich.
> Many wagons, full of honey found in the forests, go to St. Louis fifty miles away.
>
> Recently I was twice in St. Louis for several days, which is becoming the largest
> and most important city in Western America. It already has almost as much trade
> as Antwerp. By boat we travel from our door one and a half days to get there and

then have a market for everything. You can imagine how important the direct location on the river and the nearness of St. Louis is for us.

After some additional comments on American politics, Emil added the personal and political fact that "Brother Julius is expecting a young Republican the beginning of May."[43] This reference, of course, was to the fact that most German immigrants to Missouri were supporters of Thomas Jefferson's liberal Republican party (later called the Democratic Republican party). At that time they could not foresee that their support would change over the problem of slavery when it exploded into the national issue of civil war.

Slavery in Missouri

In fact, slavery was an issue confronting German immigrants arriving in Missouri. Although the slave trade had been outlawed by Britain in 1807 and declared to be piracy by U.S. law in 1820, slavery remained legal in the United States, and Africans were still being kidnapped and brought there. In 1830, for instance, Missouri had 25,091 slaves and 569 freed African Americans among its white population of 115,364. Most of the big slaveholders were in the western counties, near the Kansas Territory, where hemp cultivation made slave labor profitable.

For the most part, though, Missouri was a state of small slaveholdings where the slaves served as fieldhands, cooks, or personal servants.[44] Immigrants needing help in their fields or businesses, for instance, often turned to blacks when they could not find white hired hands in the sparsely populated areas where they were putting down roots. Freed or runaway slaves could be hired for around $100 a year plus board (lodging and food) and clothing. Of course, slaves could be bought outright since Missouri was a slave state. The cost for a good field hand in the 1830s was around $450.[45]

Although Missouri had laws requiring slave owners to be humane, including a ban on Sunday field work, such laws were often ignored. Legally, slaves were personal property and could therefore be bought, sold, or inherited. Slaves could not, among other things, own property, make contracts, testify against whites, or meet in groups.[46] They had no rights of citizenship since the First Congress of the United States had made citizenship available only to free whites, and the Second Congress said only they might be members of state militias. (Thus, even the five thousand freed African Americans who had served in the American Revolution were noncitizens.)

The situation of *freed* blacks in Missouri was precarious, too, especially if they had been released from slavery by a verbal promise or somehow managed to buy their freedom. Without a legal document to prove that status, free blacks were usually assumed to be runaways. If they were caught twenty miles from home without a pass, they were regarded as fugitive slaves who should be captured and returned to their owners, a law that was strictly enforced. Only rarely was it possible for slaves to sue for their freedom, that is, to demonstrate that they were being illegally held.[47]

In Duden country it was well known that Warren County had organized patrols to keep a constant lookout for escaping blacks and "to disperse all gatherings of the colored people . . . the patrolmen were ordered to arrest and prosecute any and all strangers conversing with slaves." At the same time, however, slave owners were occasionally harassed by neighbors who opposed their traffic in human beings.[48] In fact, opposition to slavery in Missouri was growing, especially as churches actively took up the moral issue.[49] Sentiments were forming that would make Missouri a crucible in the pre–Civil War decades.

Meanwhile, German emigrants to Missouri in the 1830s dealt with the economic and moral dilemma of slavery in different ways. Louis Eversmann, Duden's traveling companion, chose to become one of the first German slaveholders in Duden country. Owning a male and female slave and a child, Eversmann supported slave ownership until the end of his life. His example outraged many of his fellow Germans.

One well-respected observer of the Missouri scene reported that Eversmann "was very wealthy, but was not well liked among his German countrymen." Furthermore, "to the honor of the Germans, be it said that he [Eversmann] found but very few who followed his example."[50] Another observer delivered an ostensibly harsher assessment. First expressing the racist view that most slaves "are not worth much, being deceptive, lazy and thieving," that immigrant nevertheless wrote, "I cannot see how freedom-loving Germans can subscribe to the principles of slavery, and it certainly must require a great deal of Americanization in order to start a negro factory, if I may express myself that way, as Eversmann for example has done."[51]

Thus, Eversmann clearly represented a minority among the German settlers in Missouri. According to many historians then and since, the majority held moral principles that prevented them from becoming slave owners. Yet there was a third group of Germans—men who initially felt pressured by their economic situation to buy a slave but who later became supporters of the emancipation cause.[52] Julius Mallinckrodt seems to have been in this last group, as suggested in his comment to Gustav about "Negroes which one has to buy." However, it might be presumed that Julius's position was not shared by Emil at this time. He, after all, was the son of a man who had fought long and hard for the freedom of Germany's serfs.

Emil Marries

In 1833, as the area around Mount Pleasant continued to grow, so did Emil and Julius's families. On 10 February Emil married "a pretty young American named

Eleanore Luckey [Luckie]," commenting only that "for a long time my deepest wish was for a marital relationship, which I think I deserve after so many troubles in my life."[53] (Where he met her is not clear, but it was probably in St. Louis.)

Perhaps Emil did not at first share much information about his sixteen-year-old wife's background because he vividly remembered the earlier Dortmund family gossip concerning his personal relationships there. Later, however, and precisely because of a new round of such gossip, Emil was compelled to tell the family more about his wife, even her race. "My dear wife is not only white," he assured Gustav, "but because of her beauty is praised by people of all tastes, young and old. Really, she is beautiful as few are." Caustically, Emil pointed out that "marriages between white and colored do not exist, for they are not recognized in the states."[54]

Only later would Emil tell the family that Elly, as he sometimes called her, came from one of "Kentucky's first and richest families. . . . At least in her childhood [she] was reared in abundance and well-being." Later, though, the family's fortunes declined when Eleanore's father, "who had a banking business in addition to a tannery, lost the greatest part of his wealth through the emerging United States Bank."[55]

In addition to Emil and Eleanore's marriage, another big event for the new Missourians in 1833 came when Julius and Mary's first child, a daughter named Mathilde, was born on 28 April. Summing up their general sense of married well-being, Emil wrote, "Brother Julius and I now reside next to each other in two little houses and live happily in the free air of North America, where wiser laws and better relationships prevail than in poor Germany. Until now we bless the hour, God be praised, when we left it and now wish our friends here so that they might enjoy with us a better homeland."[56]

A nagging concern nevertheless continued to trouble the transplanted Dortmunders—their lack of news from Gustav. Since they left in October 1831, they had received only the July 1832 letter whose sharp criticism had so shocked them both.[57] However, by late summer 1834 Emil had finally received a first letter from his brother Eduard, and they also had had news from Julius's brother Albert as well.[58] The problem of correspondence with Gustav, therefore, was clearly not a matter of faulty mail forwarding.

Thus, in August 1834 Emil wrote Gustav with some pique: "Although I have not had an answer from you to any of my letters, I nevertheless have to again ask about you. I would so much like to hear that life goes well for all of you, and that you are content and happy." Having gotten that off his chest, Emil quickly went on to report positively about the Missouri Mallinckrodts: he and his wife, Eleanore, were happy but had lost their first child at birth, a daughter; Julius and Mary's second daughter, Caroline Dorothea, had just been born; their first brought joy to everyone. Out of his deep love for children, Emil tenderly described fourteen-month-old Mathilde, saying she "is healthy, pretty, and lively and already speaks mostly English. Her little mouth seems formed for everything but German—she speaks not one word of it, although she hears it just as often as English."

In addition, Emil had astonishingly good progress to report about their material success after just one and a half years in Missouri:

> Julius and I live in houses which we built 150 paces apart. Julius already has good buildings, consisting of a good and comfortable house with cellar, cook house, Negro house, smokehouse, and corn crib, as well as a barn. One builds almost everything oneself, with the help of neighbors, for building materials are available. Stonemasons and carpenter work are expensive, as, indeed, are all kinds of daily labor.
>
> Around us we have 2.5 acres in cultivation on which corn is now in wonderfully luxuriant growth. Our present animal herd consists of 100 hogs, 5 horses, a pair of oxen, 11 cows and calves, and 12 sheep, along with a lot of poultry and also bees. . . . Between our houses is our nice garden, running down to the river where vineyards, fruit, melons, and garden fruits of all kinds thrive.
>
> Steam and keel boats of all kinds pass by us going up- or downstream, often stopping and loading and unloading. This location really is unique and is justifiably considered the most beautiful along the entire river.[59]

Despite all that had been achieved, Emil and Eleanore nevertheless were thinking of striking out on their own. As Emil wrote, "I intend next fall or spring to settle near St. Louis, a booming city of 9,000 residents. I sold Julius my part of our present place. Thus he now has a nice property of 310 acres in one piece on the Missouri, all of which is covered with the most wonderfully high forest."

The reasons Emil gave at that time for his planned move were economic: "All our products find their uniquely advantageous market in St. Louis. Transportation from here to there is expensive and time consuming. To find the right moment to sell is difficult from far away. Because of the distances, one cannot ship fresh products, and when the river is frozen we cannot travel there at all, and that is precisely the best market. In addition, our place is not appropriate for two businesses."[60] Later Emil would tell Gustav that personal reasons, too, had played a role in his decision: "Over the long haul we [Emil and Julius] could not get along, and for that one as well as the other was probably responsible. It was not our wives."[61]

By moving to a city said to have fifteen or so German families in 1833,[62] Emil was to become part of a constant ebb and flow of emigrants, a situation that fascinated him:

> It is astonishing how the emigration of Germans to America, and especially to this part of the state of Missouri, is progressively increasing. One family draws after it another ten, and these again hundred families. Recently the largest part of the 400-member Gießen Society arrived here under the leadership of Valenius [Follenius]. Some settled very near us, and Valenius himself five English miles away. Conse-

quently, land values here have risen three- and fourfold in two years. Thus, almost all Americans in this area have sold and are moving farther toward the south and west.

Counts, middle-class persons, and farmers come here every day from all regions of Germany. Already we have German preachers, teachers, and doctors among us—the first of these do not, however, necessarily bring much joy here. Money is very much in demand, especially now. . . . Ten percent is the average [interest], but since the continuation of the present United States Bank looks uncertain, it is possible to get 15 percent for a lot of money and, in fact, with double security.[63]

Emil's concerns about his brother and his unsettled financial affairs continued, too. At the end of his August 1834 report to Gustav, he "dared to ask another favor"—that his brother Eduard "be given the remaining linen of our mother in Dortmund," apparently a very valuable possession within the Mallinckrodt textile family. At the same time, Emil reassured Gustav that "the merciful Heavenly Father will bless my efforts here so that after a time I will be in a position to support my poor brother."[64]

The reference to a personal God was clearly not in contradiction to Emil's previous cutting remark about German preachers whose arrivals on the frontier did not "necessarily bring much joy." Rather, the comment reflected the clash of beliefs on the frontier. On the one hand, there were the "rational Christian" convictions of Emil and Julius Mallinckrodt and other early German emigrants, described by contemporary historians who knew them this way: "They discard all miracles and the doctrine of atonement through the blood of Christ, believing that we make our own future condition by the life we live here, receiving punishment for our evil deeds and rewards for our good ones. They accept Christ as a good man and a great teacher, but do not believe that he was divine."[65]

On the other hand, there were "pietists" with overly sentimental or emotional devotion to religion. Since the Reverend Hermann Garlichs, who arrived in Duden country in 1833, was described this way, he may have been among the preachers Emil had in mind as not bringing "much joy" to the frontier.[66] From Bremen, Germany, Garlichs in about 1834 began the first Evangelical German church west of the Mississippi, in a log cabin near Femme Osage, and another at Friedens, near St. Charles, around the same time. At the former, Garlichs soon encountered trouble with those in his congregation who opposed the idea of eventually joining a synod, a form of religious affiliation and organization they vigorously rejected.[67]

In the next years these differences in belief would cause serious conflicts in Duden country as more and more of the "German preachers" Emil referred to arrived. Leading the rational Christians would be Friedrich Münch, with Julius Mallinckrodt a strong supporter.

13

1834: Emil to St. Louis

Going their own way at the end of 1834, Emil and Eleanor Mallinckrodt left Duden country on the Missouri River for St. Louis on the Mississippi. There they found a two-hundred-acre farm to rent for three years at two dollars an acre. It lay six miles north of St. Louis and just two miles from the west bank of the river. The land, Emil wrote, belonged to an "honorable" and "very kind" man, a General Clark—undoubtedly the coleader of the famous Lewis and Clark expedition of three decades earlier, former governor of the Missouri Territory, and brigadier general in the Missouri Militia.[1]

Emil at once planted some of his favorite crops on his new farm—potatoes and six acres of vegetables. He also hoped to harvest much hay from the surrounding prairie. Although counting on an income of only five hundred dollars that year and desperately wishing for his own, rather than rented, land, Emil was happy: "I live here alone with my wife and with a female Negro rented [that is, hired] some time ago," he wrote, "am pleased and, taking into account the situation, making progress."[2]

The departure from Julius, he said, had "hurt bitterly"; they often wrote each other, and Emil felt they "both will still be sad for a long time." Julius nevertheless was very well, "with two of the dearest little girls who are pretty and extremely lively." His plans for the future were exciting, too, since he had staked out a new town that he would build on his land adjoining the river. "The site has a healthy and wonderful location," Emil reported, "and for years the community there [that is, Mount Pleasant] has waited for a town."[3]

To add to his own happiness, Emil finally received the long-awaited letter from cousin Gustav—an "honored communiqué" for which he was "very grateful," Emil said. (The letter had been underway from 22 January until early July 1835.)

Apparently conciliatory and not continuing the earlier criticism, Gustav's letter prompted Emil to answer within two weeks. In that lengthy response he unburdened his soul about financial affairs.[4]

Most troublesome, Emil wrote, was his conclusion that Uncle Meininghaus in Dortmund was not dealing fairly with his unresolved estate problems. This sad judgment, arrived at in mid-1835, in fact echoed Julius's earlier assessment; he had warned his brother Gustav several years before that some members of their family "seek their own advantages by creating disunity. In this way Mghsn. [Meininghaus] brought much irritation into our family and will continue to do so as long as we permit it."[5] Evidently now also resigned to this view, Emil wrote Gustav, "Sell the books and land, get the money from M & M, pay the last heller of debts. If you then want to send me what is left, so I am forever helped."

Although Emil's money affairs in the old homeland were troubling, the economic well-being of his new hometown, St. Louis, was a delight. It was, indeed, becoming "the Mother of the West," connected to the South by the Mississippi River and to the expanding West by the Missouri, which carried settlers inland along the river valleys:

> Fifteen years ago St. Louis was a spot hardly worth mentioning, and now it has ten thousand residents and a very flourishing trade. Here are the yards of more than one hundred steamboats, which carry on the eastern trade down the Ohio, the southern trade from New Orleans upstream, and the western trade with Missouri, as well as the northern and western trade down the Mississippi. All of that meets in St. Louis, where they load and unload. Life there is like an ocean city and increases daily. Whoever has a bit of land around here has it good.[6]

A year later Emil was, if possible, even more enthusiastic about his choice of S. Louis as a place to live and work:

> St. Louis is caught up in an expansion that one in Europe cannot imagine and is on the way to becoming the most important city in the American interior. It already is the second, with Cincinnati the first, and I doubt whether Bremen now has more trade than St. Louis. Trade is increasing so that one hardly believes one's eyes.
>
> Last week public land from two to five English miles away, which five years ago was not worth $40, was sold up to $337 an acre. The house and garden of H. Chouteau [the famous old French trapper of the late 1700s] on Main Street in St. Louis was sold this winter for $225,000. A stretch of land on the hill bordering on St. Louis, sold twenty years ago for two gallons of whiskey, now is a property estimated at several million dollars. . . .
>
> "The unparalleled prosperity and welfare of our country," as the people here so frequently recite in words and writing, is indeed no exaggeration, but rather fact. The able and industrious craftsman has better wages here than the top bureaucrats

in Germany, not excepting the governmental president. In addition to that, he is a completely free man, which one surely cannot say about them.[7]

Weather and Epidemics

By 1835 Emil's letters also included his first complaints about Missouri's weather. Reacting to his own three years of experience, Emil said Duden was wrong about the climate, "for it is much more raw than he pictured it." The last two winters (1833–34)] "we had down to thirty degrees under zero."[8] Several years later, Emil also would react to a particularly harsh Missouri summer—"a real tropical heat and drought from the beginning of June until mid-September."[9] Emil was not the only German settler ready to rewrite Duden's climatic assessment. Another pioneer of the time was equally critical: "The climate here is by no means such as one might expect from the geographical location and from the report of Duden. The weather is very inconstant and is subject to the most extreme changes."[10] That, of course, was Missouri's real climate as experienced over a period of time rather than just during one or two years—as Duden had said, basically mild winters and hot summers, but with dramatic changes that could create frigid winters and scorching summers.

Emil's complaint about Missouri's weather was accompanied by his first mention of illness: "Last fall [1834]," he wrote, "I had a bad diarrhea and for four weeks this spring a fever. Otherwise I have never been sick here. Neither have Julius and his family."[11] A few months later, however, Emil reported Julius ill: "Brother Julius visited me [in St. Louis] and became ill here. He suffered very much for fourteen days with the ague."[12] With its alternating chills and fever, the "ague"—malaria—was one of the most prevalent frontier diseases. Carried by mosquitoes breeding in swampy prairies and bottoms, ague usually was treated with quinine.[13] Other types of malarial diseases also took their toll, and there were epidemics of typhoid.[14]

Most terrible, however, were the cholera epidemics, first brought to Missouri in 1832 by European immigrants. Fortunately the Mallinckrodts and their families were spared this terrifying disease, which could kill in twenty-four hours.[15] As a historian of frontier experiences described it, "First came diarrhea and painful cramps, violent vomiting and resulting dehydration. The victims' faces became blue and pinched, their arms and legs cold, the skin of their hands and feet puckered from loss of body fluids. . . . Recommended cures were many. . . . Doctors were helpless, too."[16]

The words of a German immigrant who arrived in St. Louis on 2 July 1834 were much more graphic:

> The heat had for some days been extremely great. In the cities along the Ohio sporadic cases of cholera had been reported, also a sort of fever which the natives

called bilious fever. In St. Louis also some persons were afflicted with the ailment. But we were still all well, perfectly well.

[6 July] At six o'clock [daughter] Auguste died, and half an hour later little Ernst was a corpse. [7 July] My dear wife, with whom I had lived so very happily began to complain of great weariness. She went to bed, slept almost continuously, and died on Wednesday morning, the ninth of July. On the evening before, my youngest child, Lebrecht, died of the terrible cholera also.

Thus, the newcomer had lost his wife and three children within four days, and the fourth and last child died two weeks later. "Almost everybody," he wrote, "suffered from abdominal troubles." Asking rhetorically, "How could it be otherwise under the circumstances?" the bereaved man answered:

Such frightful heat, clouds of dust in the streets, stench everywhere in the city, arising from animals which had died in the streets, or from swamps near the city that were drying out, or from tanneries, slaughterhouses, and similar sources, for boundless is the filth in the American cities, and nowhere a trace of rules of sanitation. No wonder that one sees the hearse almost continuously on the streets during the hot months.[17]

The dreaded cholera, as gradually became clear, was indeed caused by infectious organisms in the human digestive tract, spread by contaminated sewage to drinking water or by unclean hands to foodstuffs.[18] The pioneers tried the few frontier medicines known to them—quinine, calomel, castor oil, laudanum, and camphor dissolved in alcohol[19]—but all to no avail, and worse epidemics were yet to come.

Despite such brief health scares, Emil's own situation on his rented farm was good. His first year had been successful, and he thought he would be able to pay back Gustav within three years for "greatly helping." Emil had earned more than $350 cash in 1835 from his vegetables, and he was now plowing twenty acres of prairie. For that work he had hired six big oxen, a Negro for the time of the work, and another friend (for $120 a year) who would daily go to market to sell their produce. The remaining concern, one that would long plague Emil, was his wife's fragile health and their childlessness.[20]

14

1835: Julius's Dream—
New Dortmund

The year 1834 was an important one for Julius, too. On 15 January he and Emil filed first papers for U.S. citizenship in the St. Charles County Circuit Court. As a "free white alien," each testified to his dates of birth and arrival in the United States and swore to "forever renounce all allegiance and fidelity to every foreign prince, power and potentate, state and sovereignty whatever and particularly to the King of Prussia of whom he was formerly a subject."[1]

In addition, Julius was preoccupied by his idea of founding a new town in the Mount Pleasant area. It seemed like a financially sound plan, for more and more German immigrants were coming into the region. They included not only farmers but also craftspersons and tradespeople who needed a town in which to set up shop and offer needed services.

In 1832, for instance, following Emil and Julius Mallinckrodt's arrival in Duden country in February, new immigrants included the Martels in the fall and another forty additional families toward the end of the year.[2] In 1832–33 the Berlin Society, including estate owners and nobility, bankers, merchants, and doctors, came to the Mount Pleasant area.[3] In 1833 a group of Westphalians showed up, along with the Reverend Hermann Garlichs from Bremen, who would become the first German Evangelical clergyman west of the Mississippi.[4] Several more groups appeared in 1834: the Solingen Emigration Society of 153 persons, led by Frederick Steines, a teacher;[5] the first section of the Gießen Society, led by Paul Follenius;[6] some settlers from Osnabrück; and the second section of the Gießen Society, led by Follenius's brother-in-law Friedrich Münch, who would become a leading German-American intellectual.[7] Although these societies made current headlines and later histories, most immigrants by then had and would continue to come alone or in family groups.[8] Those in Duden country would be described by later historians as "a formidable colony of mostly highly educated immigrants."[9]

By mid-1835, therefore, Julius felt there were enough potential buyers for him to stake out his new town on the river.[10] Located just east of his blufftop home on roughly 20 of the 151 acres of land he had bought from Louis Eversmann in 1834,[11] it would be called new Dortmund. This seemed like a good time, Julius thought, to put down roots that would publicly reflect his own background. He had begun to make his mark in the community, and since the name of Mallinckrodt had been linked to the name of Dortmund, Westphalia, for centuries, why not also here in America?

This was not, however, an effort to re-create Germany in America, as some emigrants and emigrant societies back home wanted to do. After all, Julius reasoned, he had left to find and found something different. Yet neither he at age twenty-five nor any other immigrant had been transformed into a new person simply by setting foot on American soil. They brought with them their backgrounds, especially memories of family and home, and often they desperately missed what they had left behind. Many felt lonely because their fresh roots were still shallow. Perhaps having a new settlement named after one in the old homeland would help bring the two worlds together. New Dortmund seemed like an idea whose time had come, for the community as well as for Julius.

Such thoughts about his role as preserver of family tradition in a new homeland were further sharpened for Julius on 6 October, when Mary gave birth to their son. He was not the first American-born Mallinckrodt, but he was the first who could carry on the family name in the New World: little Mathilde and Caroline Dorothea would proudly sign their names Mallinckrodt for years, but that would end when they married. The new baby's name was therefore very important. Following the family's tradition of passing on male names, Julius called his first son Conrad Theodor, honoring his younger brother in old Dortmund (who must have been especially close to Julius, or an older brother's name probably would have been chosen) and their late father.

According to cousin Emil's report, the baby "came into the world weightily, namely with twelve pounds. Julius is very happy, for in addition he has two girls—in the state of Missouri there are none prettier or healthier. He seems to confirm his Uncle Feldmann's statement that 'one only has to send half a dozen Mallinckrödter into America's wilderness to populate it.'"[12]

Perhaps in recalling that quote Emil was also remembering with some amusement Julius's own observation shortly after they got to Missouri: "It is surprising for a European when he first arrives here to find all the houses full to the top with children. That's because without other great concerns, one can concentrate on making children. . . . Many farmers whom I know have become rich or well-off through their children, or better said, by making children."[13]

Not surprisingly, then, Emil found when he visited Julius over New Year's 1836 that "only blessings rest on his family." In addition to being full of plans, Julius "has three children who are healthy, lively, and pretty. He lives very happily and contentedly on his beautiful place, which pays off a hundredfold."[14] Moreover,

Julius's new town called Dortmund "is located more beautifully and fertilely than the European one."[15]

And so the town was registered, in St. Charles County, Missouri, on 28 May 1836:

> Be it remembered that on this 28th day of May A.D. 1836 before me John Smith, a justice of the peace with and for the county afore said personally came Julius Mallinckrodt the proprietor of the Town of Dortmund of which the within is a plat and acknowledged that he had had the said town laid out and the within plat therefore made for the purpose of being filed in the clerk's office of said county in compliance with the law in such cases made and provided.[16]

Interestingly, about two months before Julius filed his original plan for Dortmund (figure 14-1), Leonard Harold also appeared (on 31 March 1836) before the St. Charles Circuit Court to file a town plan—for Mount Pleasant.[17] The people of the area were clearly in the business of "settling in" along the river.

In July, Julius filed a revision to his original town plan: three alleys, or roads, were added, reducing the size of the lots from 125 to 120 feet in depth.[18] Then, in addition to selling such lots to individuals, Julius decided to hold public auctions as well. For that purpose he needed plenty of sale bills printed. He and Mary both liked these bills, which featured their names in large type along with that of Dortmund and provided space for the lot descriptions, their signatures, and, at the bottom, the notarization of the justice of the peace.

Public Auction of Lots

At two of the public auctions in summer 1836, according to Emil, Julius "sold $3,000 worth of building lots."[19] A German traveler's eyewitness account of one of those auctions, on 8 August, provided a fascinating picture of Julius in his Missouri environment (as well as revealing the aristocratic, class-critical views of the traveler):

> For a long time it has been my desire to witness an auction in a newly developing town. Dortmund was of particular interest to me because it was [being] founded by a German. If one does not have a horse in this part of the country he is just as badly off as a human being without legs. . . . All my efforts to rent a horse [in Washington, Missouri] were in vain, so I decided to go on foot. . . .
>
> We crossed the river by ferryboat, then along a road through wet bottomland and dense woods. The trees were covered by creepers and wild grape vines. [Duden had said they were twelve inches thick.] . . . The road was not clearly defined, and it was necessary to pick our way through tangled brush and swamps. We crossed a rain-swollen creek on a fallen tree and climbed several high fences. My guide finally led me to our destination, the farm of Mr. [Julius] Malingrott [*sic*]. . . .

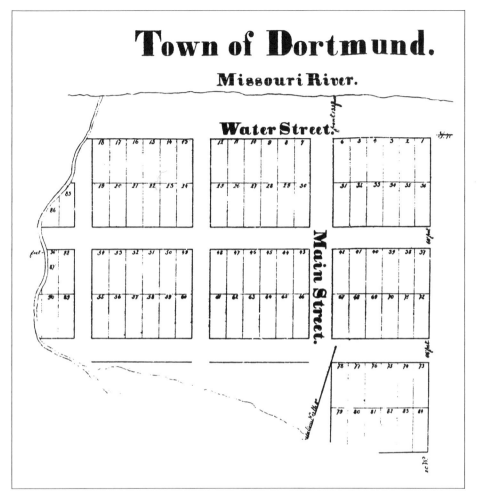

Figure 14-1. Julius Mallinckrodt's plan for Dortmund, Missouri, was registered with St. Charles County in 1836. (*Courtesy St. Charles County Recorder of Deeds.*)

Toward noon we reached our objective, at the foot of a steep hill. We climbed the hill to the home of the founder of the new town. Forty to fifty riding horses were tethered in front of the house . . . on the top of a hill, with a majestic view of the Missouri River. The eye can follow the river for a great distance as it bends and winds through the forest. On the other side of the river there is a farm in the bottomland, the buildings looking very picturesque. . . .

Mr. Malingrott, a tall, thin man and a true busybody in his manner, approached us. He looked over all the people, then said; "Gentlemen, let us start the sale of the lots." We all moved to the rear of the house, then to the woods where the sale was to take place. The area was full of people, most of them Germans, only a few well dressed, and many of them in rags.

At a table on which lay the town plan and other papers, sat a fat fellow, presumably the squire; next to him the clerk, the constable, and another official. Beside the table were two barrels, one filled with whiskey and the other with brandy. On another table, surrounded by benches, there were two or three glasses and a bucket of water. A Negro slave belonging to M. Malingrott sat beside the barrels and kept the glasses filled; everyone had plenty to drink. The cultured people were enjoying themselves by telling jokes, but a group of peasants from Osnabrück, dressed in red striped jackets and blue overalls, began telling obscene stories. Osnabrücker are known here as Ossagen.

A few more serious-minded people were discussing past and future events. Among them was a Mr. [George] Münich [Muench]. Suddenly the American auctioneer, standing on a chair, cried: "Silence, gentlemen!" He then started to read the conditions of the sale; then Mr. Münich stood on a chair and began to interpret what the auctioneer was saying, but he had difficulty, and so another German took over as interpreter. "How much is bid for a first-rate lot, number 54?" The afore-mentioned Ossagen, now thoroughly intoxicated from the whiskey, roared: "Ten, twenty, thirty dollars" until all the lots were sold. With one exception, all the buyers were Ossagen. They were overjoyed to learn that they had a year to pay for the lots and could sell them for a profit.

Mr. Malingrott, himself, was very busy with the sale, and it was amusing to hear him say that we were standing in the market place when actually we were surrounded by heavy woods. After the sale was over, we all went to the house where two hams, a big basket of bread, and whiskey were offered to the buyers and guests.

In his pessimistic manner, the traveler continued his account:

The terrain of this embryo town is not of the best, and some say it is not in the least suitable for a town. Between two hills is a deep ravine in which the main part of the town is supposed to be.

Since the sale of lots, other difficulties have developed that will be to the town's disadvantage. . . . There can be no ferry in Dortmund because there already is one in the neighboring town of Mount Pleasant. Also . . . the founder of Dortmund has had an argument with his neighbors regarding the direction of the road between the towns. And the Americans already have a store in their town, which is a great advantage; and a grocery is being built. [Apparently the visitor saw Mount Pleasant as an "American" town while Dortmund was obviously "German."][20]

Among the bills of sale signed that day was the one on lot 70 for $24[21] (figure 14-2). In addition, some twenty land sales from Julius to persons in the community were recorded with St. Charles County officials between 1836 and 1847.[22]

Know all Men by these Presents, That we, **JULIUS MALLINCKRODT** and **MARY,** his wife, in consideration of *Twenty four* dollars to us paid, DO GRANT, BARGAIN AND SELL to *Herrmann Heinrich Mette* one Lot in the Town of **DORTMUND**, in St. Charles County, in Missouri; being Lot No. *70* on the Plat of said Town. Said Lot is *laid off fifty* feet front, on *Ridge Street* Street, and extending back *one hundred & twenty* feet to an Alley, ten feet wide, bounded on the north by *Ridge Street* on the east by *Lot No 6 9* on the south by *an alley* and on the west by *Lot No 71*

And we do warrant the title of said Lot to said *Herrmann Heinrich Mette his* — heirs and assigns forever, free from all claims of all persons whatever.

IN TESTIMONY WHEREOF, we hereunto set our hands and seals, this *Eighth* day of *August* — in the year eighteen hundred and thirty-six.

Attest,

Julius Mallinckrodt ◇ SEAL ◇

Mary E Mallinckrodt ◇ SEAL ◇

STATE OF MISSOURI,
COUNTY OF ST. CHARLES.

On this *twenty secondth* day of *March* in the year eighteen hundred and thirty-*7*, before me, a Justice of the Peace for said county, personally came *Julius Mallinckrodt* and *Mary* his wife, who are both personally known to me to be the persons whose names are subscribed to the foregoing instrument of writing, as having executed the same, and severally acknowledged the same to be their act and deed, for the purposes therein mentioned. She, the said *Mary,* being by me, first made acquainted with the contents thereof, and examined separate and apart from her husband, acknowledged and declared that she executed said deed, and relinquishes her dower in said lands and tenements therein mentioned, voluntarily, freely and without compulsion, or undue influence of her said husband.

Taken and certified the day and year aforesaid.

Moses Bigelow
Justice of the peace

Figure 14-2. Bills of sale for lots in Julius Mallinckrodt's planned town of Dortmund sold at public auction in 1836 were registered with St. Charles County the following spring. (St. Charles [Mo.] Collection, *Missouri Historical Society Archives, St. Louis.*)

15

1836: Conrad's Visit

Not only was Julius happy about the prospects of building a new Dortmund in Missouri, he was also looking forward to a visit from his younger brother, Conrad, of the old Dortmund. Missing his cousin Emil's companionship after they had shared so much, Julius was especially glad that Conrad would soon be there to talk with. Two years older and physically bigger, Julius had always felt quite protective of Conrad and genuinely liked him as a brother, although their temperaments were different.

Conrad was the bookworm in the family, and Father had early determined that he should study law while the other boys went into the business world. Even as a youngster Conrad had digested the series Reise Beschreibungen für die Jugend (Travel Descriptions for Youth), edited by Joachim H. Campe. He had been especially interested by the third volume, *Neue Reise in die Vereinten Staaten von Nordamerika, Gemacht im Jahre 1781 von dem Französischen Bürger J. P. Brossot* (New Travels in the United States of North America Made in 1781 by the French Citizen J.-P. Brissot). Other favorites were English translations, especially the adventure stories of James Fenimore Cooper, of which Conrad had collected at least seven volumes by the time Julius left home.

Although loving the quiet world of books and ideas, Conrad was also the temperamental one among the children, given to impetuous, even tactless outrage over matters of principle, as he saw them. One day their seventy-four-year-old mother, reminiscing over a long life, would sum it up for Conrad: the year of his birth was especially memorable to her, but he had been a "very touchy child" (*sehr kritisches Kind*).[1]

Now Conrad was coming to visit the country about which he had read so much. Although cousin Emil and brother Julius had already been in America for five years, Conrad had wanted to acquire some years of teaching experience before visiting them. After completing his liberal arts studies in Munich, he had taught German, Latin, French, history, and geography at the Dortmund gymnasium since 1833 as assistant teacher (on probation).[2] He had done well, for in 1835 the school director wrote a very positive recommendation about Conrad's teaching: he had "shown exceptional interest in the institution" and had "also interested himself in delinquent scholars, energetically bringing them back to the straight path [of learning]."[3]

Another Dortmunder—Carl Wencker—decided to make the voyage with Conrad. Just as Emil and Julius in 1831 had deliberated about the best ports of departure and entry, so Conrad and Carl also studied the situation in 1836. By now Bremen was popular with immigrants from the Rhine/Ruhr area. It offered frequent sailings since its newly built port for oceangoing vessels attracted more and more transatlantic ships, especially from the United States; the new port had also stimulated more local shipbuilding. To avoid long delays for passengers, the port had also regularized sailing schedules. Attracted by such advantages, 12,581 persons had sailed from Bremen in 1834,[4] and so it was the choice of Conrad Mallinckrodt and Carl Wencker for their 1836 voyage.

It also seemed logical to them at that time to choose Baltimore as their port of entry, since it was a leading harbor for ships sailing from Bremen to the New World. It was a favorite with German vessels because in Baltimore they could load valuable cargoes of tobacco and flour, which came from the farming regions of Maryland to the city via the state's chain of turnpike roads. Perhaps most important, however, was the fact that from Baltimore immigrants could travel directly into the American heartland via the National Road, a turnpike that by then ran from Maryland into Indiana in the west.[5]

Conrad and Wencker therefore booked passage on the Baltimore-bound *Ulysses*, a brig owned by the Kuhlenkamp Brothers in Bremen. Their fare as cabin passengers was forty-five Thaler each. By early May 1836 the two-master, underway from America, was announced for a July departure, along with a list of twenty-four persons who would occupy cabin quarters. Now they needed to get the rest of their money together, especially at least another 100 Thaler to take them from Baltimore to Missouri.[6] And they had to obtain passports.

In the absence of modern photographic identification, documents of the time described travelers in words, as seen on the left side of Conrad Mallinckrodt's travel pass (figure 15-1): "Religion (Evangelical), Age (28), Height (5' 5"), Hair (brown), Forehead (covered), Eyebrows (brown), Eyes (gray), Nose (large), Mouth (usual), Beard (brown), Chin (pointed), Face (oval), Face Color (healthy), Stature (medium), Identifying Marks (none)." Conrad's pass was issued on 30 June 1836 for a trip to America "to visit his brother."[7]

Traveling to Bremen, probably by overland wagon, around 10 July, Conrad and Carl went by riverboat from there to the nearby harbor of Bremerhaven,

Figure 15-1. Conrad Mallinckrodt's 1836 travel pass, or passport, was issued by Prussian officials in Arnsberg for a "visit to his brother." (*Courtesy Earl Mallinckrodt*.)

where the *Ulysses* was anchored. Along with some of the other cabin passengers, they stayed at the Bremerhaven house of "the master shipbuilder Cornelius" until their vessel was loaded and ready to sail.[8]

It was on 12 July 1836 that the *Ulysses* got underway with the two young Dortmunders on board.[9] Not long thereafter, on 23 July, their families and friends read the "Farewell Notice" from them on the first page of the local weekly, the *Dortmunder Wochenblatt* (figure 15-2): "At our departure for America, we bid our relatives and friends a sincere farewell and ask for their continued friendly remembrance."[10]

Dortmunder
Wochenblatt.

N°. 30. Sonnabend, am 23. Juli 1836.

Abschieds-Anzeige.

Bei unserer Abreise nach Amerika sagen wir unseren Verwandten und Freunden ein herzliches Lebewohl, und bitten um die Fortdauer ihrer freundschaftlichen Gesinnungen.

Bremerhafen, den 14. Juli 1836.

Conrad Mallinckrodt.
Carl Wencker.

Figure 15-2. When setting out from Dortmund for America and Missouri in 1836, Conrad Mallinckrodt and Carl Wencker used a newspaper advertisement as a "farewell notice" to Dortmund family members and friends. (*Courtesy Dortmund Institute for Newspaper Research.*)

Among Conrad and Carl's thirty fellow cabin passengers was a physician's wife who wrote, "We were allowed to do our own cooking if we did not like the food for the steerage class. All in all it was a good group." About their voyage, captained by H. Spilcker, she reported:

> The wind was adverse from the very first evening and remained so for almost three weeks; we did not pass the English Channel until 2 August and had to cope with very heavy stormy weather in the North Sea. On the open sea things went fine in the beginning; later we sailed southward and experienced a calm and great heat. The longing to reach land as soon as possible became greater and greater. The water was very bad and the food was not very appetizing; how good that we had ham and sufficient wine with us. But there were lots of other things lacking.[11]

Baltimore

Baltimore harbor officials recorded the *Ulysses* as having arrived on 19 September, showing both Conrad and Wencker on the passenger manifest as "Farmers." (In fact, there were 51 male "farmers" among the 130 passengers, along with some physicians and merchants.)[12] According to fellow passenger Jette Bruns, however, they arrived earlier: on "Saturday, the 17th, after the doctor had left the *Ulysses*," cabin passengers, including "Wenker and Mallinckrodt," were put ashore. Hurrying to the William Tell Hotel in Baltimore where they were staying, *Ulysses* passengers "immediately went and bought fruit and everything tasted magnificent."

The joy of being on land after two months at sea was great, despite Maryland's hot July temperatures.[13] The young German men strode energetically about the Baltimore harbor, admiring the sailing ships from South America, the Orient, as well as Europe anchored there.[14] People excitedly pointed out to them the speedy little Baltimore clippers, which were setting new speed records; for instance, in 1832 the *John Gilpin* achieved the then-incredible rate of 183 miles a day.[15]

In the shipbuilding harbor, the air was filled with the smell of tar and paint and the sound of hammers and saws, the creak of ropes and rattle of chains.[16] There was also constant movement. Teams of horses strained up the wharfs, pulling big wagons heavily laden with tobacco, whiskey, grain, and especially flour from the Susquehanna Valley and the west. On the wharfs, the goods were stowed in sailing ships headed for Europe. At the same time, stages loaded passengers and mail to be carried from Baltimore over the Frederick Turnpike to connect with the famous Cumberland Road and its stations in the west.[17] And casting its shadows over the whole harbor was Fort McHenry. The fort was considered majestic by Baltimorians because during the War of 1812 it had withstood a twenty-five-hour bombardment and saved the city from occupation.

In the city itself the new arrivals heard much German spoken, especially in the little shops where meat, bread, saddles, shoes, and other items were sold, for these businesses had been started by early German immigrants to Baltimore in the 1700s. At some of the shops the newly arrived Germans, asked where they were going, were assured that if they chose to stay in Baltimore, the German Society of Maryland, founded in 1817, was there to help them. They also heard French on Baltimore's streets, for the city had attracted its share of immigrants after the French Revolution. And then there were the black residents of the city, both free and enslaved African Americans, for Baltimore was a major slave market at the time.[18]

Overland

After the weekend in Baltimore, Conrad Mallinckrodt and Carl Wencker explored the various arrangements for the journey inland. Like other immigrants in the past, they had to use a combination of horse and wagon transportation over the Cumberland Road and National Road and then riverboats to St. Louis (figure 15-3). Built with U.S. taxes and the sale of public lands, the road had stretched from Cumberland, Maryland, to Wheeling, Virginia, by 1818, and then to Columbus, Ohio, in 1833; work then began in both directions from Indianapolis, Indiana, and by 1835 grading had been started to Vandalia, Illinois.[19] In the next years the road was to push on to St. Louis. It would then stretch more than eight hundred miles "as the crow flies" across the new nation.

All along the way Conrad and Carl knew they would encounter, as had others before them, the discomforts of long days of travel in all kinds of weather. But this was autumn, and the elements therefore should not be too unfavorable. The travelers, of course, also anticipated the awe of the open, unsettled expanses stretching ahead and around them as far as they could see.[20]

In all, it would probably be a three- to four-week trip to Missouri. Although stagecoaches could generally make forty miles a day in good weather, travel over the Allegheny Mountains was difficult. In past years immigrants had reported traveling as long as two weeks just to get from Baltimore to Wheeling, Virginia,[21] whereas faster mail coaches were expected to reach the Virginia stop from Washington, D.C. (an additional forty miles from Baltimore), in only thirty hours.[22]

Nevertheless, the Cumberland Road, or the National Road as it was also called, was an engineering feat of the 1800s. With a roadbed originally eighty feet wide, it was said after "leaping the Ohio at Wheeling" to "throw itself across Ohio and Indiana, straight as an arrow." It was seen as "one of the great strands which bound the nation together in early days when there was much to excite animosity and provoke disunion."[23]

As Conrad and Carl were told, transportation along the entire road was provided

Figure 15-3. In the 1830s immigrants and other settlers often followed the National (Cumberland) Road, a major route to the American West. (*Map by Shelly Price McCaskill.*)

by a vast network of stage lines. These lines competed with each other by offering faster horses, more comfortable coaches, well-known drivers, and favorable connections. Moreover, some stages carried mail and so had to maintain faster schedules; other stages and wagons carried both passengers and freight and traveled at about half the speed. For instance, the mail coaches reached Columbus, Ohio, in 45½ hours, whereas the freight wagons took 88 hours.[24]

Tolls were charged according to wear on the road system; for instance, wagons with wider wheels paid less than those with narrow wheels, which cut more deeply into the roadbed, and heavier cattle were charged twice as much as sheep or hogs. A horse and rider paid 6¼ cents per mile in 1836, but fares for all users averaged about 4 cents a mile. Schoolchildren, clergymen, U.S. mail vehicles, and vehicles carrying U.S. military property traveled toll-free.[25]

The parade along the way constituted what a later fan, Archer Hulbert, described as "the real life of the road":

Coaches numbering as many as twenty traveling in a single line; wagonhouse yards where a hundred tired horses rested overnight beside their great loads; hotels where seventy transient guests have been served breakfast in a single morning; a life made cheery by the echoing horns of hurrying stages; blinded by the dust of droves of cattle numbering into the thousands; a life noisy with the satisfactory creak and crunch of the wheels of great wagons carrying six to eight thousands pounds of freight east or west.[26]

The actors in this early American pageant were stage- and mail-coach drivers, express "wagoners," and hundreds of thousands of passengers and immigrants. The hardy teamsters, with particular routes between two towns and always under time pressure, were expected in favorable weather to make ten miles per day with their four- to six-horse teams, earning for their labors around twelve dollars a day. Often they drove at night, a dangerous undertaking on the mountain routes.[27]

The stagecoaches, called "mountain ships" because of their shape, differed from those known in Europe. The bed of the vehicle was low and deep, bending upward at both front and back. At either end was the driver's boot and baggage boot, and a white canvas top was drawn over broad wooden bows. Thick, wide leather straps served as springs, protecting passengers from at least some jolts. One or more passengers on the Concord-type coach could sit next to the driver, on his high outer seat, while others sat inside, three on each of the three seats.[28]

Because of the strenuous travel, frequent stops were made along the way. Simple frame wagonhouses stood every mile or so, and there the weary horses could rest in barns and drink from troughs while their drivers slept on the floor or out in the open. Both urgently needed the rest, for the loaded wagons were heavy and the work of guiding them hard. Seven-horse teams were reported pulling a 9,000-pound load, and six-horse teams pulled up to 11 hogsheads (or 11,000 pounds) of tobacco. Furthermore, the harness used on the road "was of giant proportions"—fifteen-inch backbands, ten-inch hipbands, and heavy traces made of chains with short, thick links.[29]

Frequent taverns, "the hearts of the Cumberland Road," dotted the route and became famous as food and overnight lodging stops for weary stage passengers. Each stage line had its own favorite taverns, which were ordinary wilderness cabins of one or two rooms. They offered a fireplace, bar, and fare such as hunters had (wild game, fish, potatoes, and common cereals).[30]

Some of the *Ulysses* passengers headed straight west from Baltimore along the Cumberland Road. Others, including Conrad Mallinckrodt and Carl Wencker, first journeyed north from Baltimore, on Wednesday, 21 September, by wagon to Philadelphia. The women and children rode with the baggage on the heavy wagons, while the men "roamed around with their guns and inspected the country and the people." From Philadelphia they continued west by roads and canal boats over the Alleghenies to Pittsburgh and then down the Ohio River to Wheeling. Writing about that trek, shared with "the gentlemen, Professor Conrad Mallinckrodt [and] Carl Wenker," Mrs. Bruns described it as "a wonderful trip, back on firm ground, traveling through beautiful country in a free nation."[31]

In Wheeling the travelers had to wait a week for the wagons bringing their freight from Baltimore over the Cumberland Road. Then they took passage on the overcrowded little steamer *Cavalier* and proceeded "to St. Louis without any trouble."[32]

St. Louis

After the sixty-six-day transatlantic voyage and six-week inland journey, Conrad Mallinckrodt and Carl Wencker set foot on the St. Louis waterfront at the beginning of November 1836. The view at first was dreary, for it was raining.[33] But when the sun came out, the traveling friends found a bustling city of about twenty thousand people.[34] Thanks to its river location, it had become a marketing center, a great receiving and distributing depot for the upper Mississippi area.[35]

Not only was St. Louis's waterfront booming, but the stories told there fascinated the newly arrived Germans. It was said, for instance, that because of the hazards of the "Big Muddy," Missouri River pilots were among the most skilled in the country and their boats of the sturdiest design. The stream's shallow water and swift current constantly changed the riverbed, so that sandbars, snags, and logjams, along with fierce storms and grinding ice, took a heavy toll on the vessels, usually limiting their service to five years.[36]

The explanations of the snags in the Mississippi and Missouri especially intrigued the travelers. They were told that when banks washed away or the streams overflowed, trees fell from the heavily wooded shores into the river. Although the branches tore away, the roots of the trees often sank, anchoring themselves in the bed of the stream. Those below the water were, of course, invisible to the ship's pilots, while those closer to the surface could be detected by the break they caused in the water flow. At night or in fog, therefore, pilots could not see the snags. When a boat ran onto one, a hole might be torn in the hull and the boat sunk.[37]

Some of the stories Conrad and Carl heard in St. Louis were also about imminent changes. There was talk of the coming railroads, which would offer severe competition to the steamboat companies. The first railroad convention had been held in St. Louis in April and resolutions passed for the construction of several lines, including one on the route of the Boone's Lick Road.[38] Conrad and Carl also heard the growing talk in St. Louis of abolition of slavery and the fact that more and more of the city's slaves were being freed (twenty-eight in 1836–37). At the same time they saw, too, the thriving slave market at the eastern door of the city's courthouse.[39]

New Dortmund

Making their way west from St. Louis to new Dortmund, probably by boat, Carl and Conrad arrived at Julius's place. The brothers' greetings after five years' separation were very excited, as was Conrad's meeting with Julius's family, especially the children. After all settled down, Conrad brought his brother up to date on family affairs back home. There was, for instance, the news of their cousin Detmar, the high-ranking public servant: he had sold his family's old Dortmund home, Sonnenschein, in 1831 and in 1834 had been honored for his long service to Prussia through a grant (or restoration) of the "von" title which the family had so long carried.[40] Moreover, Conrad reported, Detmar now was on visiting terms with two promising young Prussian civil servants, Otto von Bismarck and Franz von Savigny; perhaps he would not suffer after all for having married a Catholic wife and baptized his children in her church.[41]

In after-supper conversations, with their heavy boots pulled off and stocking feet stretched toward the fireplace of Julius's frontier home, the Mallinckrodt brothers must have found some amusement in the turn of events within their family. Raised in comfort and education and taught to respect centuries of family tradition, they now sat in a rustic cabin thousands of miles from Germany, talking about past and present titles of nobility that seemed infinitely remote.

In Germany the honorific *von* was inherited or earned through public service, but in America, as Julius explained, the frontier was the great equalizer of social classes, at least for now. Not many frontier settlers could take time out from making a living to become involved in political life and earn the prestige which that naturally brought to a family name. Furthermore, foreign-born citizens could not yet hold public office.[42] Instead, the American equivalent of noble titles was the community's respect, earned through neighborliness, hard work, and honesty. And that is the way, Julius and Conrad thought, the Mallinckrodts would make their mark in Missouri.

They and other immigrants of the 1830s were often laughingly called "Latin farmers" because of their excellent education, which had included classical as well as modern languages, and were seen as doomed to failure on the agricultural frontier. Often overlooked, however, was the fact that many of them had had experience on family lands in the old country; in addition, their excellent intellectual training, which had included a great deal of science, helped them to understand and adapt to their new circumstance. Julius, for instance, with some farming and considerable business experience back home, plus the advantages of early Missouri land purchases, was doing very well. Emil, the trained and very experienced Westphalian farmer, would perhaps make some initial entrepreneurial mistakes, but he, too, was learning quickly how to turn his high-quality work and agricultural sense into profitable undertakings. And if Conrad stayed, he could use his higher education to make important intellectual contributions.

Such fireplace discussions occupied Conrad's thinking during the winter of 1836 as he became acquainted with the life led by his brother Julius and by his fellow German emigrants in the St. Charles County area of Missouri. He was awed, for instance, by the beauty of nature he had so enjoyed reading about over the years and could now experience for himself.

There were the gentle sunrises and sunsets reflecting on the river, which reached like an endless beige avenue toward the horizon, with no hills or peaks to suddenly eclipse the sun. The peace of the early morning woods when they hunted was interrupted only by the rustle of small, scurrying animals or the raucous caws of blackbirds and crows startled from their perches in the high trees. At midday redbirds flitted in bright bursts of color around the outbuildings, and at dusk big bullfrogs sang their bass chorus from the creek banks. In warm weather the hypnotic buzz from the bee hives was heard all day long, and after dusk the cicadas, or "katydids" as Missourians called them, filled the night with their chirping. Sometimes, too, in the cold dark they could hear the howl of wolves traveling in packs across the countryside.

Conrad also discovered trees that he had not known in Germany. He appreciated most of all the soft-wooded cottonwoods, which sometimes grew to six feet in diameter and sent their fiber-coated seeds drifting gently to earth like cottonballs.[43] The hard brown seedballs of the tough-wooded sycamore swayed with the breezes high above the gray-and-white-splotched trunk until, when ripe, they too separated into tufts of soft down.

Life on the frontier, of course, was not just communion with a nature that was awesome and yet at times gentle. Conrad looked as well for the intellectual fruits of the life about him. He was pleased, for instance, to read the weekly St. Louis newspapers that Julius received, an American paper, and the well-known *Anzeiger des Westens*, edited by Wilhelm Weber, an immigrant who had studied law and economics at Jena and Leipzig.[44] Both newspapers carried news about Europe, so Conrad did not feel out of touch.[45]

In fact, a later historian of the St. Louis German-language press, Steven Rowan, would see Weber as setting its tone. He "did not spare the acid," Rowan said, when he wrote about what he saw as "backward elements within the German community." That at first meant conservative religious groups and later the institution of slavery. Consequently, St. Louis's press, supported by the city's business community, raised Missouri Germans "above parochialism and provided a complete—and distinct—perception of both American and German realities."[46]

Conrad was fascinated, too, by the religious controversy that had broken into the open among Missouri's German immigrants. In 1836 a missionary report to a Reformed church synodical meeting in Pennsylvania had criticized Duden country's former Protestant minister and intellectual leader, Friedrich Münch, for unwillingness to form a congregation in his area.[47] Münch, in turn, replied on 25 March 1837 in the pages of the *Anzeiger*, known for its anticlericalism. Not yet rejecting synods per se, Münch wrote that in the past they had not prevented the "unworthy from seducing the guileless through deception and folly."[48] Thus, as historians later saw it, this frontier conflict reflected the oppressive conditions in the old homeland, where princes governed state churches.[49]

Münch, meanwhile, was doing his part as a "teacher of religion" in his own free congregation at Dutzow where he lived. In fact, "Over the years, Münch served several independent congregations, . . . among them Charette Township, Marthasville, Femme Osage and Dutzow, apparently on an irregular basis and partially competing with Garlichs of Femme Osage."[50]

As a teacher, Conrad also found accounts of the growth of education in Missouri especially interesting. For instance, in late 1836 St. Charles College opened in the county seat, and in November of that year the first German-English public school was founded in St. Louis.[51] Maybe Conrad could do something like that; it certainly would not earn the kind of money Julius was making, but it would be a chance to work for future generations.

Conrad was told, for instance, that since many of the German parents in St. Louis had had a good education in their home country, they wanted suitable instruction for their children and had approached Frederick Steines to be their teacher. Among other things, they wanted a school that would exclude religious instruction (leaving that to parents and the churches), would teach English as well as German, and would offer arithmetic, geography, and natural sciences, "the subjects which, after the language of the country, are of greatest importance."[52]

Such education in America was one of the reasons a German convention had been called for October 1837 in Pittsburgh. Delegates from various parts of the country—including St. Louis newspaper editor Wilhelm Weber—would come together to share ideas not only about education but also about the relations of Germans to Americans (naturalization, the opportunity to hold public office, etc.), treatment of poor immigrants at seaports, prevention of the influx of European criminals, and so on.[53]

Conrad was also impressed with Julius's farming, which was going well. Julius had founded a horticulture nursery the year before and planned to grow fruit for sale, especially apples; this would be the first orchard in the county designed exclusively for market production rather than home use.[54] The hillside running down to the river in front of where Julius and Emil had built their first house was optimal for fruit trees.

Naturally, Conrad was also excited about the future potential of Julius's new town. The building of a steam sawmill had begun, and Julius had opened a store. Moreover, Conrad's travel companion Carl Wencker had so impressed people with his competence that he was starting a tannery on Julius's property, where he would make good use of the fine springs.[55] (It was probably located on the central hill where Emil had lived.) In fact, things were going so well by January 1837 that Carl had taken on a traveling companion from the *Ulysses*, Bernhard

Geisberg, to help him. Finding Wencker "a magnificent man," Geisberg spoke "of him and the Mallinckrodts with the greatest sympathy."[56]

There was talk, too, of flour mills, breweries, distilleries, and other businesses to process the richness of the land. Grist mills, for instance, were especially needed for grinding wheat and corn since the settlers now bought such flour from passing steamboats or spent laborious hours crushing it by hand.[57] Everywhere there seemed to be opportunities that appealed to Conrad, and both Julius and Emil encouraged him to stay in Missouri, among the thirty thousand Germans who had made it their home by 1837.[58]

Conrad, however, did plan to return briefly to Dortmund. While Wencker was toying with the idea of going back within the year to find a wife, Conrad would return to get his younger brother Hermann, who had finished the military training he had begun in 1832.[59] Shortly before Conrad's May 1837 departure for Dortmund, he and Julius visited Emil to discuss their plans at length. Subsequently Emil wrote Gustav that he wanted to take cousin Hermann on "as a partner, if that suits him." Adding that Conrad liked it at new Dortmund "and plans to be here again by New Year," Emil enthusiastically wrote, "Now it seems very probable to me that one by one our entire family will come over, and you [Gustav] hopefully will be no exception."[60]

During his last days in Missouri, Conrad received Julius's final instructions regarding new Dortmund in writing: "According to our agreement, take this map of my town of Dortmund along to Germany and try to sell as many of the odd-numbered lots as possible. Half of the price is your commission. From here on you will have to cover all costs which you thereby incur. If the brothers want lots, then give one to each; otherwise the price is accordingly $100, $175, $200. God be with you. Your Julius Mallinckrodt."[61]

Old Dortmund

Back home Conrad obviously carried out his assignment well, as a Dortmund chronicle compiled for the 1830s reported:

> Several Dortmunder who previously emigrated to America have returned and assure us that they were well pleased with what they found. Among them is Conradt [*sic*] Mallinckrodt, candidate for a top-level teaching appointment, who formerly taught for several years at the gymnasium here. He visited his brother Julius, who lives on the Missouri not far from St. Louis. Julius has bought considerable acreage and is occupied with the founding of a new town which will have the name New Dortmund. The town is staked off and has received an official license. Its main streets, markets, and gateways shall have the same names as in our city. In the coming spring several young Dortmund men and women want to travel there to settle in this newly planted town, among others a third brother Hermann Mallinckrodt, a cousin August Mallinckrodt, and numerous craftsmen.[62]

Clearly, then, Conrad had persuaded his younger brother Hermann, then twenty-eight, to come to America. In addition, among the "young Dortmund women" going with them was the wife Hermann would take along, his twenty-two-year-old second cousin Luise Mallinckrodt; she, in turn, would be accompanied by her older brother August, age thirty, the "cousin" referred to in the report. They lived at the well-known family home on Betenstraße which their businessman father Detmar had bought or inherited from the physician William Mallinckrodt.[63]

Also among the "young Dortmund women" going to America with Conrad would be twenty-four-year-old Sophie Mallinckrodt, a teacher. She was going as Mrs. Conrad Mallinckrodt, for apparently Conrad had decided to follow his friend Wencker's idea of finding a German wife. Sophie was Conrad's first cousin—his late uncle Christoph's daughter—who had grown up on the other end of Dortmund's historic main street, at Ostenhellweg 56.[64] She was unusual in the family because, unlike most young women of her age, Sophie was educated and had a profession.

After the death of Sophie's father, her mother and other adult relatives had insisted that her good mind be trained. Because she was not allowed to attend the gymnasium or university as her brother had done, Sophie was probably educated at home by a tutor or at a private girls' school. Such education usually included German and French, geography, drawing, and music (especially piano, although some women also played the guitar).[65] She could plan to become a teacher, for that was a profession she as a woman might enter, if not at the gymnasium then at a church elementary school or a private school for girls.[66]

Sophie's mother Helene, age fifty and a widow for two decades, would join her only living child on the trek across the Atlantic. (Sophie's brother, Ernst, who had completed his gymnasium studies in October 1827 and gone to the University of Halle to study theology,[67] had died in 1834.) That meant in all six more Dortmund Mallinckrodts for Missouri.

Such groups were not, however, uncommon in the late 1830s, when more and more family members were emigrating together. And clearly it was not unusual for Luise and Sophie to have been Mallinckrodts before and after marriage: marrying cousins had long been a tradition in their large family. In fact, Luise's parents (Detmar and Christine) had been second cousins, and so had Sophie's parents (Christoph and Helene).

Conrad Clashes with Gustav

Not all Conrad's efforts after his return from America were as successful, however, as his marriage plans and the publicity for Julius's new Dortmund. Conrad, for instance, clashed vigorously with the family's mentor, stepbrother Gustav.

It seemed, in fact, to be a second round in their antagonism. A first bout had occurred in 1835, when Conrad was still teaching in Dortmund and before his first journey to America. At that time Conrad apparently had heard from his brother Albert that Gustav wanted to buy back a watch that he had given Conrad eight years earlier; Gustav even wanted to purchase it from Conrad at its original price of fifty Thaler. In a sarcastic letter dated 2 January 1835, the young teacher first asked his stepbrother Gustav if the watch should be sent to him or be deposited somewhere in Dortmund. Second, he let loose an economic arrow: since the watch was now worth no more than twenty-five Thaler, for usage one should calculate interest on the original sales price, as well as the fifty Thaler in repairs he had paid over the years.

Gustav's reply of 9 February was equally brusque. He chastised Conrad for not having perceived that Gustav's intention in purchasing the watch from Conrad for its original fifty Thaler price was to render Conrad a favor (perhaps to make money available to him). That gap in logic, Gustav added cuttingly, might have come because Conrad, in his eager study of philology, had neglected the humanities (*Humanoria*); moreover, his mathematical calculations had been flawed.

Conrad immediately replied to the criticisms of his intellect. Regarding the math, he wrote Gustav on 12 February, "Above all, my thanks for the correction of my calculations," adding in the margin, "which I still do not quite understand." Then in an exercise of philosophical logic, probably intended to provoke pragmatic businessman Gustav, Conrad continued, "Since I now find myself in the same situation you were in 1827, when you said the watch had cost you too much in repair, I do not know how I can [morally] as a favor return it to you." The letter closed, "In that he acknowledges with guilt an obligation for the favor, Conrad Mallinckrodt sends greeting." And in a final postscript, Conrad jabbed back at nonacademic Gustav's knowledge of the world of study: "Since humanities (*Humanoria*) and philology are one and the same, I do not know how one can be neglected in favor of the other."[68]

What lay behind this exchange—beyond Gustav's clear lack of enthusiasm for Conrad's studies—is unknown. It may have been, however, that Theodor Mallinckrodt's teenage children, especially one as temperamental as fourteen-year-old Conrad, resented their stepbrother Gustav's taking over when their father died, especially if Gustav did not approve of what they wanted to do (for instance, study rather than become a businessman). Similarly, it was probably difficult for Theodor's older sons Leopold (eighteen) and Julius (sixteen), who were working in the Antwerp branch of the family enterprise, to accept stepbrother Gustav's new business role. Problems with Leopold, for instance, clearly existed. Soon after their arrival in Missouri, Julius wrote Gustav that, while "we do not want to defend Leopold's behavior toward you," it might be understood that "the dear boy seems so confused and destroyed through the interference of so many that he does not know how to behave in order to reconcile himself with you."[69] It may, in fact, have been Gustav's management of the family business that motivated Julius to leave his position with the firm and the future that implied.

By contrast, Cousin Emil's relations to family mentor Gustav were clearly different from those of Conrad and his siblings. Aware that he was not a brother ("Dear Mr. Cousin"), Emil appeared more cautious. Furthermore, without parents and only a handicapped brother, Emil needed a friend: "You valued friend," he wrote Gustav, "you know me better than anyone in Europe."[70] Probably equally important in Emil's attitude was his complicated debt situation and Gustav's management of it: that is, Emil was very financially dependent on Gustav and would remain so for some years. Gustav, in turn, may have found in Emil the thankful, intellectually compatible family member not present among the step-brothers.

All these differing relationships and roles in the family seemed reasonable in the mid-1830s. None of the Mallinckrodts then could know that in several years the feelings would explode, leading to a quarrel that would split the family for generations. Yet signals of trouble were clearly in the wind.

Perhaps Emil sensed something, or perhaps he only recalled the prior encounter when he cautiously wrote Gustav shortly before Conrad's return to Dortmund from Missouri in May 1837: "I have asked Conrad to visit you. He can tell you much that is interesting. I wish that you would see each other." In closing the letter, Emil again said about Conrad, "Please see him," and added a thought that may have been intended to promote peace: "If I were one of your brothers, they would all be a joy to me." And in a final request, motivated by real financial need, Emil wrote, "I want to ask you, dear Gustav, please have the linen sent to Conrad [to bring along on his return trip to Missouri] that is at his mother's; it has little value there but very much for me."[71]

The meeting between Conrad and Gustav that Emil encouraged was not, however, to take place. Gustav explained to Emil what had happened:

> Your friendly wish "that you should see Conrad," which was my wish also, for I would so gladly have heard in detail about your and Julius's doings, remained unfulfilled because of Conrad's, to put it mildly, ugly, clumsy [*ungeschicktes*], and insulting behavior. Without enclosing a syllable to indicate to me that he had returned, which I did not know, Conrad sent your letter to me in Crombach, although he must have known from his brothers that I no longer live there.
>
> Later he wrote me a letter here [Köln] that even more obviously documented and proved his total lack of tact and rearing and showed that the great amount of money spent on his study had been used, at least to a large extent, *without benefit*. I copy that letter for you word for word, as well as my answer. To this letter, dear Emil, I have had no answer, and I do not think I will receive one, regardless of how unjust it would be of Conrad if he did not send me a receipt regarding the linen received for you.[72]

The exchange of letters Gustav included for Emil was indeed strange.[73] First, soon after returning to Dortmund, Conrad had confronted Gustav by letter, apparently out of loyalty to Emil but perhaps also motivated by his own old antagonism toward Gustav. Either way, Conrad's use of a formal, rather than familiar, form of address to his stepbrother made his hostility clear:

28 August 1837

Mr. G. Mallinckrodt

At the moment I am motivated by a story Mrs. Meininghaus told the Mallinckrodts in the Betenstraße. She contends, namely, that she knows through a letter from Emil to you that Emil's wife is black and a slave who is banned by the white community from church as well as society.—Although I certainly know how to judge such gossip, nevertheless, the maliciously mean intent of this woman in telling something like that precisely in that house moves me to immediately ask you to explain to me whether you possess such news from Emil himself. If I were not still lacking a receipt for the letter which I brought you from America from cousin Emil, I would at the same time ask you to furnish me with a disposition concerning the linen.

With respect, Conrad Mallinckrodt.[74]

The letter did not make clear why Conrad was raising the issue of family gossip at this time. It actually was an old affair, going back to a year after Emil's marriage in America in autumn 1833. In response to a January 1835 letter from Gustav, probably reporting the stories making the rounds, Emil had written, "Happily, negative gossip does not bother me. . . . My wife is white."[75] Many other sources also had informed Emil about how "the entire Meininghaus family said he 'lived in misery, had married a Negro, etc.' "[76] Since Conrad lived in Dortmund, he surely had also heard those rumors and then discussed them with Emil while in America. While not, therefore, based on anything new, Conrad's letter to Gustav, immediately after returning from Missouri, may have been the impulsive response to a new belief that Gustav had been involved in spreading the earlier rumors.

That that does not seem to have been the case was suggested by Gustav's prompt response challenging Conrad to find out who really started the story. At the same time, Gustav's coolness toward Conrad was unmistakable, especially in his avoidance of any form of greeting such as "Dear Conrad":

4 September 1837

I don't understand you, Conrad, neither regarding the form nor the content of your letter of 28 August!

You speak in your letter . . . about a notice of receipt for a letter that you brought along for me from Emil. I did indeed receive a letter from Emil in Crombach, where you *probably* sent it. But since you wrote nothing accompanying it, can you rationally expect a receipt which I clearly owe no one other than Emil?!

Your question "whether Emil wrote me that his wife is black and a slave" appears, if possible, even more strange, for you met Emil's wife and *so are convinced* that Emil could not possibly have written such a thing. On the other hand, I find praiseworthy your wish to uncover the source of such malicious gossip and hopefully also to shame the mean originator!—You would, however, if you will be so good as to permit me to express my view, achieve your goal more quickly if you brought together and confronted the people in the Betenstraße who told you this with Mrs. Meininghaus, from whom they said they heard it. Hopefully you will yet do that?! I would be very pleased if you want to use the enclosed certificate to receive Emil's linen that is there and deliver it to him, but do send me a notice that it has been taken along.[77]

No wonder, then, that Gustav, while informing Emil about what a cad Conrad was, also went on record about the whole Mallinckrodt family for whom he had inherited responsibility after his father's death.[78]

In general, my stepmother and her children, among whom I nevertheless whole-heartedly except Hermann and Dorchen, have to a great extent behaved so disdain-fully and in part thanklessly to me that they have thereby totally alienated themselves from me. That has hurt me a great deal, for I have loved them all as my own children and have done much for them, everything in my power.

But I have gotten over it and have found my peace in the fact that I certainly never gave cause to demands—so excellently traced to Leopold's and Albert's indecent greed—that I should (1) give up on your demands of M & M, and (2) support the demands which they make of Mghs., and perhaps yet will make in the name of all the heirs, but which I declare as unfounded according to my conscience and against my own interest.[79]

16

1837: Emil to Pike County

Although Gustav did not meet with Conrad after his return from Missouri, he was nevertheless informed about Emil's doings in America. And the news was not all good. As Emil himself put it the beginning of 1837, "I have had much unhappiness." During her second pregnancy Elly had been so ill that Emil had to leave the rented farm outside St. Louis and move into the city to have help for his wife. Despite the move, several weeks thereafter the baby was born prematurely and died:

> My wife is still so weak that she often stays in bed. Doctors and the expensive cost of living here [in the city] cost us a great deal. The weakness of my wife does not allow us to pursue agriculture again.
>
> Therefore, I will start a store at the beginning of March and probably in the town of Lousiana, which is on the right bank of the Mississippi 100 English miles from here and from where a railroad to Columbia on the Missouri has been begun. Businesses of all kinds go extraordinarily well inland. In all directions flourishing towns grow up as quickly as corn out of the earth.[1]

Emil was also distressed about his business matters at home, saying that Uncle Meininghaus must know that "he *deliberately* presented the matter falsely." Philosophically, though, Emil added, "But why more about this? It involves only a small amount. . . . It hurts me less to lose the last bit of property than to see a relative, whom one was taught to respect from youth on, behave in this way." The next year his conclusion would be much harsher, and identical with Julius's of six years ago: "I have much reason to believe that you [Gustav] have been betrayed by Meininghaus as the rest of us, especially also as it concerns your father's children."[2]

Aside from such family business matters, the letter-writing cousins engaged in an unusually interesting exchange of ideas in early 1837. After Emil's five years of enthusiastic "New World reports," Gustav in Köln finally composed an "Old World reply." Beginning with a description of his city's position as a European trade center and the building of railroads, Gustav then summarized,

> Thus you see that the old world is not lagging so far behind the new. But it certainly remains true that one is not in a position to obtain riches here as there. With the *best* business one earns at the most an average of 10 percent here, while there one gets 10–15, even 20 percent interest.
>
> That is indeed very pleasant for a businessman, but, on the other hand, what advantages does Germany offer us? We live in a context that is in every case still more civilized and sincere than one can hope to find in America. That lies in the nature of the situation and in the cold, egotistic character of North Americans. It cannot be different where large settlements of Americans form.
>
> Now as to child rearing and school education, how very advanced that is here and how backward there.—Finally with the exception of mechanics, in what childhood phase do the arts and sciences find themselves there?—What are music and painting other than tooting (*Gedudel*) and scrawling (*Gesudel*)?—What finally are medicine and theology other than quackery and mysticism, the latter which we unfortunately also suffer here. . . . Nevertheless, I am not giving up the plan to make a trip there [to the United States] and would be happy if I could gain a more positive conviction.[3]

Despite that thoughtful and quintessentially European challenge to Emil's assessment of America's advantages, the new Missourian responded with unabated optimism: "America is by a long shot not as far behind as you believe in your letter. In every respect culture is making good and fast progress. This country offers everything that could make a reasonable person happy."

Storekeeping

Even Emil's move to Louisiana, Missouri, and his entry into the storekeeping business seemed to go well at the moment. Then a busy Mississippi River town, Louisiana lies about a hundred miles upstream from St. Louis, not far from Hannibal, the town that Mark Twain would make famous. For his rented store on the Louisiana waterfront in the middle of the settlement, Emil had bought a $3,000 supply of liquor, groceries, porcelain, and hardware, which was selling for an average 50 percent profit. "In addition, the turnover is very fast," he reported. "Every day we have the steamboats in front of our door to whom we can sell everything." Within eighteen months, Emil thought, he would be in a position to repay Gustav "your advance and other sums."[4]

Gustav's subsequent reaction to Emil's news of a change in vocations was unconcealed astonishment: "So, my friend, you have become a storekeeper in Louisiana? I would sooner have anticipated the collapse of the heavens than this decision by you, for you previously seemed to have absolutely no taste for business." Despite Gustav's surprise, he nevertheless found Emil's decision very good: with "insightful leadership and punctuality, combined with *very essential* caution regarding expansion, a sales business will pay off better with much less effort than farming!"

After sharing his own principle of limited business expansion, Gustav then reacted to Emil's plan to take cousin Hermann Mallinckrodt into the business after he arrived within the year from Dortmund with Conrad: "Don't go into partnership *with anyone*," Gustav warned, just as Emil's father had warned long ago, "regardless of who he is!"[5]

17

1838: Second Emigrant Contingent

After returning to Dortmund in late summer 1837 and quarreling with Gustav, Conrad was busy arranging his emigration to America. Originally he had planned to sail again by the first of the year or even sooner, that is, within a few months.[1] That, however, became an unrealistic date when he and his brother, Hermann, decided to marry and to emigrate not only with wives but additional family members. Organizing that many persons and their belongings was a time-consuming task. In addition, all looked to Conrad, who had been to America, for advice as to what they needed to take along for their new lives in Missouri and what living conditions they would find there.

With some expertise, he could advise the women to leave behind their bulky hats, which were no longer fashionable anyway, as well as their fans and parasols, which would serve no purpose on the frontier. Their jewelry collections, however, might be financially useful even if not fashionably appropriate: the lockets, gold bracelets, mosaic and cameo brooches, even the gold chains supporting little bottles of perfume, which European women had found so sensational until just recently—all could be turned into hard cash. Conrad and Hermann naturally would not take along the canes they had sported in years past.[2]

At the same time, Conrad and Sophie also spent many hours working out ideas for the school they wanted to start together near new Dortmund. It was exciting for the young teachers to plan an educational institute from the ground up. There they could put into practice many of the pedagogic ideas that had been stored at the back of their heads during the years they taught in Dortmund's old school system, with its traditional and established ways of doing things (Conrad at the gymnasium and Sophie possibly at a private school for girls).[3]

After the death of Professor Kuithan in December 1831, the study plan at the gymnasium had become rigid,[4] and Conrad's teaching there (1833–1835) may not have been as innovative as he wished. Sophie—who would later say, "I had been teaching school for eight years, and my establishment had improved with every year"[5]—may have wished for better schools in Dortmund, too. The city's education for girls was not very progressive. Professor Kuithan's planned higher school for girls had not come about.[6] In 1835, as a temporary solution until the new higher school could be opened, girls who completed the top classes at the city school (*Stadtschule*) were offered two grades of private education, with emphasis on language and sciences. (In fact, the promised "Higher School for Girls" would not be started for another three decades!)[7]

If the Mallinckrodt teachers could now complete the plans for their new Missouri school—for girls as well as boys—when they reached St Louis, they could at once arrange publicity and try to launch it by spring 1839. It would, of course, reflect the pedagogical philosophy of Conrad's mentor, Professor Kuithan, including emphasis on recreation, physical education, and ethics, as well as order and industriousness.[8]

With the school in mind, as well as his own love of books, Conrad spent hours sorting through his bookcases. Deciding what to take along was not easy. There were, of course, his dog-eared old favorites, the Campe series Travel Descriptions for Youth, which had first fired an interest in faraway places, including North America. As another German immigrant teacher would write, "Our much deserving Mr. Campe doubtlessly little dreamed that his *Robinson Crusoe* gave the impulse to more emigration than Duden's books and publications of that nature. For conceptions so beautifully formed in a boy's mind are never blotted out, and the hope of their realization is never entirely given up."[9]

Then there were the collected works of James Fenimore Cooper, that fascinating American author who had fed Conrad's interest in the American West. He had been collecting the compact little volumes from publisher Sauerländer for a decade and bought four new editions just published in German in 1838—the frontier novels *Notions of the Americans* and *The Pioneers*, the nature story *The Water-Witch*, and the political novel *The Bravo*. Inscribing his name carefully onto the bottom of many of the title pages, he took special delight in writing it precisely above the title of one of the older volumes so that it read "Conrad Mallinckrodt/ *The Last of the Mohicans*." Those sixteen brown-backed Cooper books (published 1827–1838) made quite a stack, but since they were small they would definitely all go to Missouri. The Bulwer series consisted of little books, too, including translations of English favorites such as *The Last Days of Pompeii*, works by the English philologist Eugene Aram, and others.

The collection of Latin books and Shakespeare volumes, of course, had to be included for later teaching use. And for general reference there was the 1830 edition of the Brockhaus encyclopedia. Its twelve huge volumes were heavy, but they clearly belonged in the library of any German intellectual: even its title proclaimed it to be the *German Encyclopedia of General Information for the Educated Classes.*[10]

Although excited and happy about his future, Conrad also had misgivings as he sorted his books into stacks on the drop flap of his writing bureau and then carefully fitted them into the trunks. Quite simply, he would miss all the comfort of such a warm German home: the light of a chandelier reflecting into the big mirror over the fireplace; old Flemish tapestries that had hung in the family home for generations; the worn pedestal of a dining table where children too often had rested their shoes; handsome wooden chests and cupboards carved long ago; writing bureaus of golden yellow wood with pigeonholes and little drawers that had always fascinated him because of the order they provided; the warm shades of a rose-colored marble top on a clothing commode. Such things, he knew, he would not at first have in his new life.

Mother Dorothea's Concerns

But Conrad was worried about his mother, too. She came to his room frequently and sat quietly watching him pack. Since he had been living at home for years while teaching in Dortmund, she would miss him very much. But she was concerned by more than just his imminent departure: Julius was already gone; Leopold and Albert flitted in and out from their jobs in Antwerp; and now Conrad and Hermann would both leave. Their departure meant that only twenty-six-year-old Dorothea, named for her mother but called Dorchen, would still be in Germany, that is, "at home." That would be hard for mother Dorothea, Conrad thought. She had been a widow for about fifteen years, and with most of the children gone, she would be more lonely than ever, as lonely as Sophie's mother, Helene. And at sixty-one Dorothea was not able to trek along with her children to America as Helene had decided to do.

Thus, when Dorothea asked her son Conrad the ageless question of widows, "What do you suppose your *father* would think?" she was referring to more than their own children leaving Germany. Rather, it seemed that her late husband's whole family was dissolving. Those left in brother Christoph's family after his untimely death, Helene and Sophie, were going; brother Arnold's son Emil was already gone, leaving only Eduard in Dortmund; two of cousin Detmar's children, August and Luise, were packing, and there was talk of two more following later; and three of her and Theodor's seven children would soon be in America.

Quite simply, the Mallinckrodt family was losing many of the members of its eighteenth generation. Perhaps their fathers, Christoph, Arnold, and her own Theodor, would have approved, but she was not certain. Even when Conrad promised that they would write often and would return for visits, his mother was not reassured. America was so far away, and so much could happen so quickly.

The big family in which they had grown up would not be there to help them through rough times. Moreover, the Mallinckrodts' two-century-long record of public service to the city of Dortmund—from 1605 to 1832, from the days of the Freie Reichsstadt through French control and then incorporation into Prussia—was over. The sons who might have continued the tradition were leaving.

It was so hard to be a mother, Dorothea thought as she pondered her future. Indeed, it was difficult to be a woman. In addition to the sorrow over husbands who died young, there were the emotional scars left by so many miscarriages and stillbirths, the long-remembered pain of carrying to the cemetery the many Mallinckrodt babies who had died in infancy or youth. Theodor's mother, for instance, had buried two infants and a seven-year-old, and then she and Theodor had lost four children, aged eight, eleven, six, and one. Brother Arnold and Wilhelmina had mourned two infants and twenty-one-year-old Wilhelm. Christoph and Helene lost three babies and then, in 1834, Sophie's twenty-six-year-old brother, Ernst, who had been studying theology. Luise's parents had seen the deaths of two or three babies. And now the children who had lived were leaving the country.

Marriage and Farewell

Mother Dorothea was happy, however, when she saw her sons and new daughters-in-law, Conrad and Sophie, Hermann and Luise, marry on 19 February in the family church in Dortmund, the Reinoldikirche. All the children had been baptized by its pastors,[11] and even if some were now going far away, it was good that they would take with them a marriage blessing from the family church. Their father would have liked that, for it was an old, old family tradition to go to the Reinoldikirche to fulfill the state's requirement for a church marriage.[12]

Besides, she was proud of them and their appearance, for they were all young, attractive people. Luise, twenty-two, and Sophie, twenty-four, were pretty: the bonnets and shawls now so stylish in Europe, with hair worn in ringlets around the face, were becoming to women, as were the modest dresses of subdued colors falling gracefully around their ankles. Hermann, twenty-eight, and Conrad, thirty, were handsome in their top hats, cutaway coats, and plain, unruffled shirts. When she and Theodor had married, ruffled shirts were still in vogue, and the short, square-cut waistcoats with the high collars were rarely buttoned so the shirts would show. The waistcoat was of a different color than the tight-fitting breeches tucked into boots, but the top hat had been about the same as now. In addition, corseting had been the custom, so that one could scarcely breathe, and a shawl was worn over the very low-cut dresses.[13]

In addition to the good wishes and farewells at the wedding, one more act of leave-taking from Dortmund was traditional for emigrating Mallinckrodts—an announcement in the newspaper. As Conrad had publicized his first departure in 1836 in the *Dortmunder Wochenblatt*, so Sophie and her mother now also placed a small notice among the classified advertisements (figure 17-1).[14]

Transatlantic

And so it was off to Bremen, where the ship *Copernicus* had arrived on 16 April.[15] The *Copernicus*, captained by H. Haesloop, was a relatively large three-masted frigate (plate 8): it displaced 250 Lasts (or about 440 tons) and was more than one hundred feet long and thirty feet wide.[16]

Among the 176 passengers boarding the *Copernicus* in Bremen, the Mallinckrodts were recorded first on the passenger list (figure 17-2). That preserved but scarcely legible document describes itself as "List or Manifest of all the passengers taken on board the Bremen Ship Copernicus whereof H. Haesloop is Master, from Bremen to Baltimore—Burthen 440 Tons."[17] Below were columns giving each passenger's name, age, sex, occupation, country of origin, and the country which he or she intended to become an inhabitant of, and finally a column listing anyone who died on the voyage. The columns at the top of the first page read:

1. Widow Mallinckrodt	51	Female	—	Dortmund	Missouri
2. Conrad Mallinckrodt	30	Male	Teacher	Dortmund	Missouri
3. Hermann Mallinckrodt	28	Male	Merchant	Dortmund	Missouri
4. August Mallinckrodt	30	Male	Merchant	Dortmund	Missouri
5. Gott. C. Brockhaus	30	Male	Physician	Dortmund	Missouri
6. Sophie Mallinckrodt	24	Female	—	Dortmund	Missouri
7. Luise Mallinckrodt	21	Female	—	Dortmund	Missouri

Interestingly, Sophie's mother, Helene, the oldest in the group, was signed up first (as "Widow" rather than with a first name), the three males next (Conrad this time as "teacher" rather than "farmer" as in 1836 or "philologist" as the church marriage record said), followed last by Sophie (no profession) and Luise (listed as being a year younger than on the marriage records).[18]

In addition to the physician Brockhaus, who somehow penetrated the parade of Mallinckrodts, the manifest also lists quite a number of other Dortmunders heading for Missouri—for instance, Rud. and Luise Velthaus and Wm. Schulte (nos. 9–11). Emigrant professions listed on the three-page manifest often read "farmer," but coopers, tailors, shoemakers, millers, joiners, smiths, masons, linen weavers, soap boilers, and butchers also appear. Their destinations were Missouri, Illinois, Ohio, Baltimore, and sometimes Virginia or Pennsylvania.

On 17 May 1838 the *Copernicus* got underway. Whether the crossing was stormy is unknown, but it must have been relatively smooth, for within about five weeks

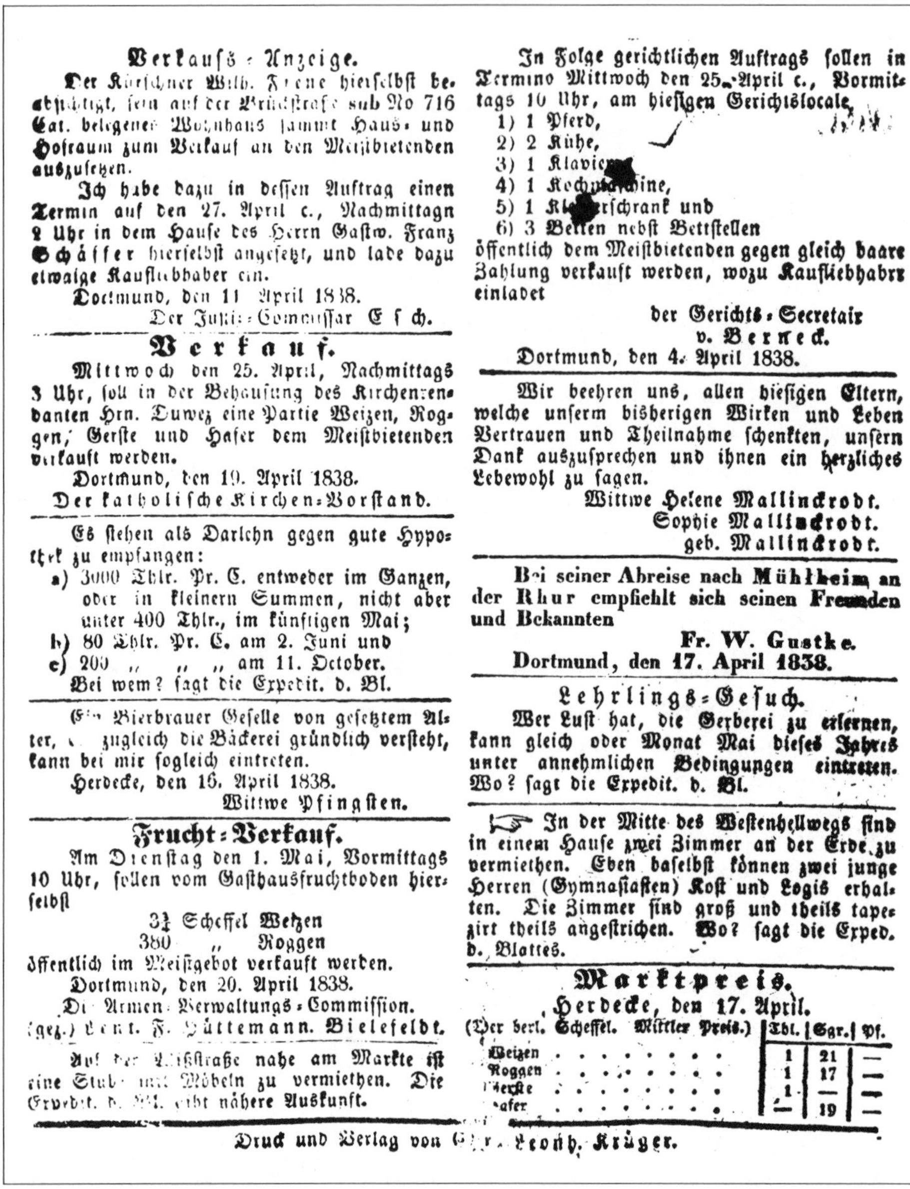

Verkaufs-Anzeige.

Der Kürschner Wilh. Frene hierselbst beabsichtigt, sein auf der Brückstraße sub No 716 Cat. belegenes Wohnhaus sammt Haus- und Hofraum zum Verkauf an den Meistbietenden auszusetzen.

Ich habe dazu in dessen Auftrag einen Termin auf den 27. April c., Nachmittagn 2 Uhr in dem Hause des Herrn Gastw. Franz Schäffer hierselbst angesetzt, und lade dazu etwaige Kaufliebhaber ein.

Dortmund, den 11 April 1838.

Der Justiz-Commissar Esch.

Verkauf.

Mittwoch den 25. April, Nachmittags 3 Uhr, soll in der Behausung des Kirchenrendanten Hrn. Duwez eine Partie Weizen, Roggen, Gerste und Hafer dem Meistbietenden verkauft werden.

Dortmund, den 19. April 1838.

Der katholische Kirchen-Vorstand.

Es stehen als Darlehn gegen gute Hypothek zu empfangen:

a) 3000 Thlr. Pr. C. entweder im Ganzen, oder in kleinern Summen, nicht aber unter 400 Thlr., im künftigen Mai;
b) 80 Thlr. Pr. C. am 2. Juni und
c) 200 „ „ „ am 11. October.

Bei wem? sagt die Expedit. d. Bl.

Ein Bierbrauer Geselle von gesetztem Alter, [illegible] zugleich die Bäckerei gründlich versteht, kann bei mir sogleich eintreten.

Herdecke, den 16. April 1838.

Wittwe Pfingsten.

Frucht-Verkauf.

Am Dienstag den 1. Mai, Vormittags 10 Uhr, sollen vom Gasthausfruchtboden hierselbst

3¼ Scheffel Weizen
380 „ Roggen

öffentlich im Meistgebot verkauft werden.

Dortmund, den 20. April 1838.

Die Armen-Verwaltungs-Commission.
(gez.) Rent. F. Hüttemann. Bielefeldt.

Auf der [illegible]straße nahe am Markte ist eine Stube mit Möbeln zu vermiethen. Die Expedit. d. Bl. giebt nähere Auskunft.

In Folge gerichtlichen Auftrags sollen in Termino Mittwoch den 25. April c., Vormittags 10 Uhr, am hiesigen Gerichtslocale,

1) 1 Pferd,
2) 2 Kühe,
3) 1 Klavier,
4) 1 Ko[illegible]ine,
5) 1 Kl[illegible]rschrank und
6) 3 Betten nebst Bettstellen

öffentlich dem Meistbietenden gegen gleich baare Zahlung verkauft werden, wozu Kaufliebhaber einladet

der Gerichts-Secretair
v. Berneck.

Dortmund, den 4. April 1838.

Wir beehren uns, allen hiesigen Eltern, welche unserm bisherigen Wirken und Leben Vertrauen und Theilnahme schenkten, unsern Dank auszusprechen und ihnen ein herzliches Lebewohl zu sagen.

Wittwe Helene Mallinckrodt.
Sophie Mallinckrodt.
geb. Mallinckrodt.

Bei seiner Abreise nach Mühlheim an der Rhur empfiehlt sich seinen Freunden und Bekannten

Fr. W. Gustke.

Dortmund, den 17. April 1838.

Lehrlings-Gesuch.

Wer Lust hat, die Gerberei zu erlernen, kann gleich oder Monat Mai dieses Jahres unter annehmlichen Bedingungen eintreten. Wo? sagt die Expedit. d. Bl.

☞ In der Mitte des Westenhellwegs sind in einem Hause zwei Zimmer an der Erde zu vermiethen. Eben daselbst können zwei junge Herren (Gymnasiasten) Kost und Logis erhalten. Die Zimmer sind groß und theils tapezirt theils angestrichen. Wo? sagt die Exped. d. Blattes.

Marktpreis.

Herdecke, den 17. April.

(Der berl. Scheffel. Mittler Preis.)	Thl.	Sgr.	Pf.
Weizen	1	21	—
Roggen	1	17	—
Gerste	1	—	—
Hafer	—	19	—

Druck und Verlag von Gebr. Leonh. Krüger.

Figure 17-1. In 1838 Helene and Sophie Mallinckrodt followed the family practice of saying "farewell" to Dortmund in a newspaper advertisement (*second entry, right column*). (*Courtesy Dortmund Institute for Newspaper Research.*)

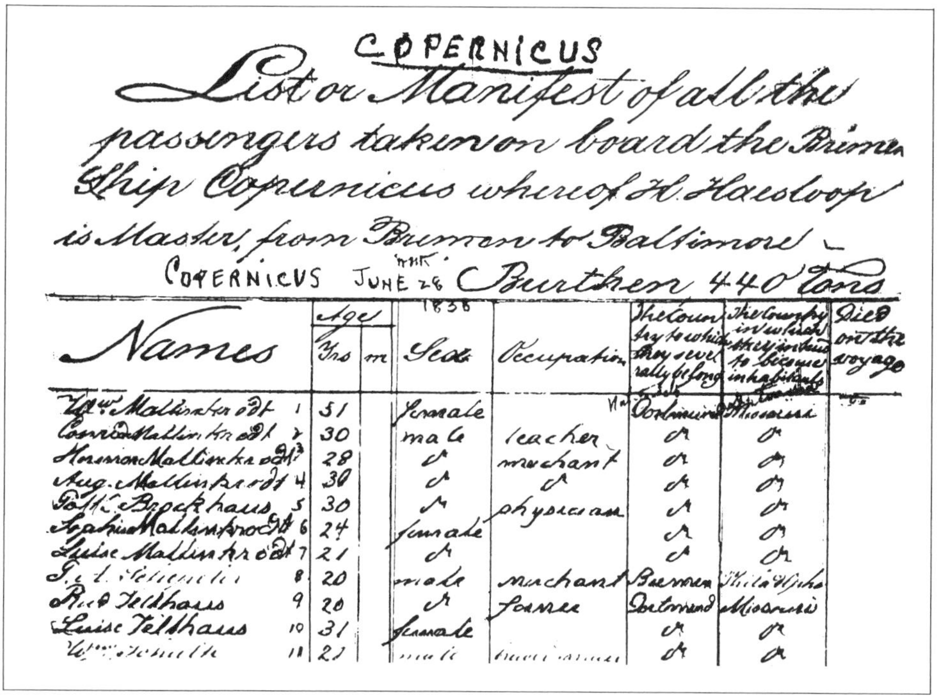

Figure 17-2. The passenger manifest of the *Copernicus*, sailing from Bremen to Baltimore in 1838, listed six Mallinckrodts. (*Courtesy U.S. National Archives.*)

it was completed.[19] Without any notations in the "Died" column, the *Copernicus* arrived in Baltimore on 28 June 1838.

New Dortmund

The month-long overland journey to Missouri, however, was not pleasant. As Emil reported: "Our friends now finally arrived very well the beginning of last month [August] at Julius's and are now all well. That earns a lot of happiness and respect since they arrived at the most unfavorable time for foreigners and made the long overland trip from Baltimore to here in the hottest period. Moreover, we had a real tropical heat and drought from the beginning of June until mid-September."

Although letters recording the impressions of the new Missourians were not preserved, Emil's correspondence told how they had settled in:

• Mother Helene stayed at Julius's and was paying $100 a year for room and board. (Emil referred to her with her German title *Hofrätin*, that is, "the wife of a Hofrat," the high political rank her late husband had held.)

• Conrad and Sophie moved into Wencker's nearby house, built over his tannery, probably on the center hill where Emil had lived.
• Hermann and Luise went to Emil's home in Louisiana, Pike County, where Hermann was helping with the store, now called E. & H. Mallinckrodt.[20]
• August apparently stayed at new Dortmund, hoping to find work.[21]

Meanwhile, the established Missourian, Julius, was helping the newcomers and exuding optimism about his and their futures: "without much money [Julius] has everything that one can wish for a peaceful and pleasant life—a good wife, four healthy children, a fifth soon expected, a healthy place on a wonderful location with very rich soil." At the home of the other "old-timers," Emil and Eleanor, the welcome in Lousiana for Hermann and Luise was very warm. Emil and Eleanor themselves, however, were alternately hopeful and fearful: they had lost a third child at birth and were expecting again.[22]

Conrad and Sophie's School Plan

Conrad and Sophie awaited responses to the announcement of their school: Conrad had arranged the publicity in St. Louis, and the notice that they had formulated in Dortmund appeared in the *Anzeiger des Westens* on 15 September 1838 (figure 17-3). In translation the text read,

German Educational Institute for Boys and Girls
on the Missouri at Dortmund, St. Charles Co.

In one of the most healthful regions of the hill land on the Missouri's northern bank, 30 miles above St. Charles, the undersigned founded a German Educational Institute for Boys and Girls. To parents and guardians who want to entrust their children to us, both my wife and I can document, through good recommendations, our theoretical training and numerous years of educational activity in Germany. However, we hope to recommend ourselves to the German public more through the success of our efforts.

During a lengthy visit I became convinced that my enterprise would not be superfluous among numerous institutes of this kind in Missouri and neighboring states. Many parents, concerned about the well-being of their children, complain about instruction that is inadequate, incorrect, or more ostentatious than useful. In addition, bookkeeping methods not customary for such institutes in Germany are used, whereby food, lodging, heating, light, laundry, and every branch of instruction are calculated separately. Taken together, one can then usually add up a rather considerable sum.

So that the reader can convince himself that, and how, I intend to avoid these deficiencies, I request that the following plan be considered carefully.

General Plan

The Institute intends to give children the moral, intellectual, and physical education essential to later life.

How frequently is a sickly life in later years the result of neglected care of the body. Free use of the limbs, enjoyment of open, clean, country air, useful exercise and clothing, and above all extreme cleanliness are means for protecting our charges from this danger.

To the practical American people, intellectual training often appears superfluous, especially when the pure practitioner so often encounters European education that is useless for everyday life. But if such education is not abstract, but rather is specifically designed for life here and reflects the best experiences, then failure to acknowledge its essentiality can result only from a lack of understanding of its usefulness. It will be our task to teach the children what they need for their future life and, indeed, not deny them, as in Germany, the application [of their learning].

All of life's activities would, however, be reduced merely to a training of certain abilities if moral ennoblement were not the basis and the major goal [of education]. As now increasingly also generally recognized, that does not mean dependence on a confession or belief system, for each human, whatever his belief, can also be a good and noble person. Therefore, we will do everything to awaken good convictions and true religious perceptions in our charges, namely using Sunday morning for instruction in basic Christian teaching.

Instruction Plan

I. For Boys
1. Languages
   German: Reading and writing, according to general grammar and practice. Weekly 4 hours.
   English: Reading and writing according to Lloyd's Grammar. Weekly 4 hours.
   French: Writing and conversation. Weekly 2 hours.
   Italian, French, and Greek, if desired, privately.
2. Natural Sciences
   A. Mathematics: (a) Arithmetic (where necessary). Weekly 4 hours.
   (b) Algebra. Weekly 1 hour.
   (c) Geometry, Solid Geometry, Trigonometry. Weekly 3 hours.
   B. Physics: (a) Chemistry, Mechanics (basics with vocational-oriented practice). Weekly 2 hours.
   (b) Nature (gathering/ordering of minerals, plants, animals). Weekly 2 hours.
   (c) Geography and Astronomy (according to Ritter). Weekly 2 hours.
   History to be learned in the German readings.
3. Arts
   A. Drawing: Freehand drawing, according to Peter Schmidt method, of still-life landscapes and objects from everyday life and imagination. Weekly 2 hours.

B. Music: Choral. Basic instruction in piano and guitar. Weekly 2 hours.

C. Calligraphy: Practiced by giving special attention to the form of written works.

D. Gymnastics: Gymnastic exercises according to age and physical condition of the children.

II. For Girls

1. Languages

German   2 hours weekly

English   2 hours weekly

2. Natural Sciences

A. Nature   4 hours weekly

B. Geography and Astronomy

3. History

Readings from the best German and English historical works. Weekly 6 hours.

4. Arts (simultaneously)

A. Drawing from nature, flowers, landscapes.

B. Knitting, sewing, and fine handwork. Weekly 6 hours.

C. Embroidery and preparation of artificial flowers. Weekly 2 hours.

D. Music: Choral and basic instruction in piano or guitar. Weekly 3 hours.

E. As physical exercise, instruction in the art of gardening.

The class hours for the boys as well as girls serve to guide their own elaboration and study, which then will be carried out under supervision in the remaining time.

Price

For instruction.

For food.

For lodging.

For heat.

For light.

For laundry.

Total 150 dollars, with four prepayments for every child.

Konrad Mallinckrodt

With Conrad and Sophie eagerly awaiting responses to the announcement of their visionary school, all seemed well with the Missouri Mallinckrodts, except Emil. He wrote the Dortmund family in fall 1838 that doctors had recommended a long sea voyage for Ellen, who had long been ill; they therefore planned to travel to Europe in spring. Hermann would take care of the business in Missouri while they were away.[23]

After arriving in Bremerhaven in July 1839, Emil informed cousin Gustav and brother Eduard that he and Ellen were going to a spa on the North Sea for four or five weeks and then would visit Dortmund and Köln. Their anticipated joy at the forthcoming reunions with family after eight years was, of course, tremendous. At the same time, Emil's concern about his wife was equally intense:

Deutscher
Anzeiger des Westens.

Herausgegeben von Wilhelm Weber.
Pine Street.

Motto:	Motto:
1. Dies ist einer von uns. Dies ist ein Fremder: So sprechen niedere Seelen. Die Welt ist ein einiges Haus.	2. Wer die Sache des Menschengeschlechts als seine betrachtet, nimmt an der Götter Geschäft, nimmt am Verhängnisse Theil.

Jahrgang III. St. Louis, Mo., 15. September 1838. No. 47.

(Für den Anzeiger des Westens.)

Sentenzen.

That virtue which requires to be forever guarded is scarce worth the sentinel. — *Goldsmith.*

Die Tugend, die stets Huth begehrt, ist kaum des Schilderhauses werth.

To neglect at any time preparation for death is to sleep on our post at a siege; but to omit it in old age is to sleep at an attack.— *Johnson.*

Gar nicht des Todes gedenken, ist auf gefährlichem Posten, wo du zur Wache gestellt, schlafend statt wachend zu sein; aber im Alter noch immer dich auf den Tod nicht bereiten, ist als schließt du ein, wenn schon der Angriff begann. —

H. W.

Deutsche Knaben- und Mädchen-Erziehungs-Anstalt,

am Missouri, zu Dortmund, St. Charles Co.

In einer der gesundesten Gegenden auf dem Hügellande des nördlichen Missouri Ufers, 30 Meilen oberhalb St. Charles, errichtete der Unterzeichnete eine deutsche Erziehungs-Anstalt für Knaben und Mädchen.

Sowohl ich als meine Frau können uns durch gute Zeugnisse über unsere theoretische Ausbildung und mehrjährige Wirksamkeit im Lehrfache in Deutschland bei Eltern und Vormündern, die uns Kinder anvertrauen wollen, ausweisen, hoffen jedoch uns mehr noch durch den Erfolg unserer Bemühungen, namentlich dem deutschen Publikum

zu empfehlen. Denn davon daß bei vielen derartigen Anstalten in Missouri und den Nachbarstaaten mein Unternehmen nicht überflüssig sei, habe ich mich bei längerem Aufenthalt, woselbst durch viele Klagen von Eltern, denen das Wohl ihrer Kinder am Herzen lag, über mangelhaften, verkehrten, mehr prunkenden als nothwendigen Unterricht überzeugt. Dazu kommt dann noch das in Deutschland nicht gebräuchliche Rechnungswesen jener Anstalten, wodurch man Kost, Logis, Feuerung, Licht, Wäsche, jeden Zweig des Unterrichts, was alles besonders berechnet wird, zusammennimmt, und meistens recht erkleckliche Summen heraus addiren kann.

Damit der Leser sich überzeuge, daß und wie ich diese Mängel vermeide, bitte ich nachstehenden Plan mit Aufmerksamkeit durchzugehen.

Allgemeiner Plan.

Die Anstalt bezweckt den Kindern im späteren Leben die nothwendige sittliche, geistige und körperliche Bildung zu geben.

Wie häufig ist in späteren Jahren ein sieches Leben Folge von Nachlässigkeit in Sorge für den Körper. Freier Gebrauch der Glieder, hinlänglicher Genuß freier, schöner Landluft, zweckmäßige Uebung und Kleidung, und vor Allem die äußerste Reinlichkeit sind die Mittel deren

Anwendung diese Gefahr von unsern Zöglingen abwenden sollen.

Eine geistige Ausbildung erscheint dem praktischen Volk der Amerikaner häufig als überflüssig zumal wenn der reine Praktiker so häufig europäische Schulung in seiner Rathlosigkeit fürs Leben begegnet. Ist aber solche Ausbildung nicht abstract, sondern konkret mit diesem Leben, und für dasselbe nach den besten Erfahrungen berechnet, so wird wohl nur der Unverstand ihren Nutzen, ihre Nothwendigkeit verkennen. Es wird demnach unsere Aufgabe sein, den Kindern das zu lehren was sie im späteren Leben brauchen und zwar ihnen stets, wo Gelegenheit ist, die Anwendung in Deutschland, deren Anwendung vorzuhalten.

Alle Thätigkeit des Lebens aber würde auf ein bloßes Abrichten zu gewisse Fähigkeiten hinauslaufen, wenn nicht sittliche Veredelung ihre Grundlage wäre und ihr Hauptaugenmerk bliebe. Es macht deshalb auch nicht, wie heutzutage ja auch immer allgemeiner anerkannt wird, von irgend einer Confession oder Glaubensform abhängig, da ja jeder Mensch, weß Glaubens er auch sei, auch ein guter und edler Mensch sein kann. Wir werden deshalb alles thun, um gute Gesinnungen und wahrhaft religiösen Sinn in den Zöglingen zu wecken, und namentlich den Sonntag Morgen zum Unterricht in der reinen christlichen Lehre verwenden.

Unterrichtsplan.

I. Für Knaben.

1. Sprachen.

Deutsch: Lesen und Schreiben, nach der allgemeinen Sprachlehre, und deren Anwendung — Wöchentlich 4 Stunden.

Englisch: Lesen und Schreiben nach Lloyd's Grammatik. — Wöchentlich 4 Stunden.

Französisch: Lesen, Schreiben und Sprechen. — Wöchentlich 2 Stunden.

Italienisch: Latein und Griechisch, wenn gewünscht, privatim.

2. Naturwissenschaft.

A. Mathematik: a. Rechnen (wo es nöthig ist). — Wöchentlich 4 Stunden. b. Algebra. — Wöchentlich eine Stunde. c. Geometrie Stereometrie und Trigonometrie. Wöchentlich 2 Stunden.

B. Physik: a. Chemie, Mechanik, (erste Anfangsgründe. mit Anwendung auf Gewerbe). — Wöchentlich 2 Stunden. b. Naturbeschreibung (Sammeln und Ordnen von Mineralien, Pflanzen und Thieren.) — Wöchentlich 2 Stunden. c. Erdbeschreibung und Himmelskunde (nach Ritter). — Wöchentlich 2 Stunden. Geschichte soll durch die deutsche Lektüre erlernt werden.

3. Künste.

A. Zeichnen: Freihandzeichnen. nach der Peter Schneidt'schen Methode, Gegenstände aus dem Leben, Landschatten und Köpfe. — Wöchentlich 2 Stunden.

B. Musik: Singen. — Anfangsgründe auf Piano und Guitarre. Wöchentlich 2 Stunden

C. Kalligraphie: Wird durch Aufmerksamkeit auf die Ausführung schriftlicher Arbeiten geübt werden.

D. Gymnastische Uebungen, nach Maßgabe des Alters und physischen Anlage der Kinder.

II. Für Mädchen.

1. Sprachen.

Deutsch 2 Stunden und englisch 2 Stunden wöchentlich.

2. Naturwissenschaft.

A. Naturbeschreibung. — Wöchentlich 4 Stunden.

B. Erdbeschreibung und Himmelskunde.

3. Geschichte.

Lektüre der besten deutschen und englischen Geschichtswerke. — Wöchentlich 6 Stunden.

4. Künste.

(Zu gleicher Zeit.)

A. Zeichnen nach der Natur, Blumen und Landschaften.

B. Stricken, Nähen und feine Handarbeiten. — Wöchentlich 6 Stunden.

C. Sticken und Verfertigen von künstlichen Blumen — Wöchentlich 2 Stunden.

D. Musik: Singen und die Anfangsgründe auf dem Piano und der Guitarre. — Wöchentlich 3 Stunden.

E. Als Leibesübung: Anleitung in der Gartenkunst.

Die Lehrstunden dienen den Knaben sowohl wie den Mädchen zur Anleitung zu eigenen Ausarbeitungen und Studien. die in der übrigen Zeit unter beständiger Aufsicht ausgeführt werden.

Preis:
Für Unterricht.
Für Kost.
Für Logis.
Für Feuerung.
Für Licht.
Für Wäsche.

Summa 150 Dollars. mit 4 Vorausbezahlungen für jedes Kind.

Konrad Mallinckrodt.

Figure 17-3. Conrad Mallinckrodt's school plan was advertised in St. Louis's *Anzeiger des Westens* in 1838. (*Author collection.*)

The great deal of hard work I did in clearing three farms, the confined manner of living as a storekeeper that damaged my health very much, my three moves, which caused big losses—all that is child's play and even produced some good results. But the endless sorrow of a beautiful and beloved wife is almost more than I can quietly bear. We are now in our seventh year of marriage and have lost four children, one after another, all in those moments just before they were born. And that isn't even all: the reasonable fear of repeated cases of this kind constantly tortures me. How is this to end? We cannot separate—to live the rest of our lives as brother and sister does not work! To a large extent, my only remaining hope is based on this trip.

As for the rest of the family in Missouri, he reported, "Our dear ones in America were all well when we left there in March."[24] To brother Eduard, however, Emil added an additional thought about their American family: "The *Hofrätin* is adjusting there better than one would have thought and is really a fine woman, worthy of respect."[25] Emil did not say, however, when and how often he had seen Aunt Helene during her first six months in the new environment, nor did he mention what she was doing.

Perhaps what Emil had feared were reactions such as another German observer described: "Imagine people from the finest German classes living in miserable huts! Previously they had lived in comfortable houses, and now they have to eat the plainest of food, . . . surrounded by black forests and cut off from society and all the conveniences of life. They live in memory of the sweet past, in contrast with the miserable present, and in contemplation of a sad future, one illusion after another."[26]

While Helene's reactions probably were not that negative, Sophie would later say that the adjustment to Missouri had been much less smooth for her and her mother than Emil thought: "When we arrived at last in the so-distant city of Dortmund [Missouri], we saw at the first glance that Mr. Mall. [Conrad] had deceived us in all the descriptions he before had made to us over the future place of residence."[27]

Ironically, just at this time Jette Bruns, who had traveled with Conrad and Carl Wencker in 1836, was planning to visit them to inquire about how intellectual German women around new Dortmund were adjusting to frontier life. Because her sister contemplated emigration, Mrs. Bruns was tormented by the advice she had to give the younger woman about coming to Westphalia, Missouri: "So as not to deceive myself, I have resolved to accept the invitation of the Mallinckrodts, who have many educated German neighbors, in order to become acquainted with their wives and their views. If this visit should turn out as desired, then I would continue to think about it [her sister's emigration]."[28]

It is not clear whether Mrs. Bruns indeed visited new Dortmund in early spring 1839 and, if she did, what she observed. Perhaps Conrad in fact had told her during his earlier visit to the Bruns that problems were brewing in his family.[29]

However, Mrs. Bruns and probably many others did not yet know that a terrible storm was hovering over the Mallinckrodts in Missouri. The family in Germany was especially in the dark, for it was, after all, just the time that Emil was reporting in Westphalia that all was well back in America. Yet in spring to late summer 1839 the brewing storm began to whirl.

The troubles were not a tragedy of human life and death but rather of precisely the family loyalty and honor about which so many talked so much. And as in the Shakespearian tragedy they loved on stage and paper, many of the family members would take on roles from *Julius Caesar*. They would act out in everyday life the parts of characters whose perceptions of their own nobility numbed their intelligence so completely that they could not see the consequences beyond their principles. Had that not been so, the drama could have taught much.

The trouble in Missouri, among other things, involved basically good people with fine values who had not quite made the cultural adjustment to emigration. Watching the clash of these transplanted Europeans, old-time Missourians were astonished by the vindictiveness of public quarreling within a prominent settler family, and old Dortmunders back home were simply scandalized by the combatants. As on Shakespeare's stage, those farthest from direct knowledge would pass the harshest judgments. That, perhaps, would be the real and lasting tragedy.

18

1839: Mallinckrodts in Missouri Courts

The crisis that would initiate generation-long alienations within the Mallinckrodt family exploded in autumn 1839, in St. Charles County, Missouri: Sophie Mallinck-rodt brought suit for divorce from her husband, Conrad, after a marriage of only seventeen months.

Sophie Versus Conrad: Divorce

The shock was profound in both Missouri and Germany. In the family's long history there had been few, if any, divorces. That the suit was initiated by a Mallinckrodt wife, after only a very short marriage, was especially hard to understand. Since both Sophie, twenty-five, and Conrad, thirty-one, were highly educated persons, it was thought that they should have been able to work out their problems without dragging the family name into court. During only a year on the frontier, they could not have forgotten all they had been taught about family loyalty and tradition. To some in Germany the reports from Missouri must have seemed like other bizarre stories they had read about the raw American West, where old values and ways of life were easily set aside.

To Missourians, too, the case probably seemed strange, and for some of the same reasons. Many neighbors, for instance, would have disapproved of publicizing a family quarrel and advocated quieter channels for divorce, especially at a time when divorce law was changing. Furthermore, pragmatic acquaintances of the Mallinckrodts no doubt wondered whether lawyers were putting the legally naive immigrant Sophie up to these measures; while she did not understand the legal system and the court dramatics she was initiating around her name, the publicity clearly would benefit the lawyers' reputations. And even if her lawyers were scrupulous, probably not too many people believed that Sophie really appreciated the difference between divorce procedures in her old homeland and on the frontier. Later students of emancipation, fascinated by Sophie Mallinckrodt's case in its historical context, would also wonder how much she really understood.

To others, however, surrounding conditions such as the frontier context were not central to the drama. Rather, the character flaws of the immigrants themselves were key. This view was dominant among family members in Germany, and surely some Missourians who knew the Mallinckrodts must have thought that "the uppity Germans" had caused their own problems. Then, too, almost everyone in the family wondered what would happen to Sophie, divorced and alone on the frontier with only her widowed mother as a companion. Men could manage there, but what would the women do?

Such questions, and even some of the early judgments, were not unreasonable. Clearly Sophie and Conrad were not uncomplicated personalities, reacting to and in a foreign environment. Their story unfolded slowly across distance and time, and only a few family members preserved the reports. Now, after many letters and documents have disappeared, the family controversy can at best be only partially reconstructed and understood in its personal and legal context.

The marriage between Sophie and Conrad apparently had not been compatible from almost the beginning. Emil would describe it as a "marriage that was and remained a dreadful misfortune."[1] Only as long as they were still in Germany, Sophie told her lawyer, was Conrad's behavior to her and her mother proper. Although he then impressed her as "a young man of good sense and agreeable manners," friction surfaced during their transatlantic voyage on the *Copernicus*. "We had not yet touched America," she said, "when Mr. Mallinckrodt became so morose and so mean in his behavior toward both myself and my mother that we began bitterly to regret our folly in following him." The "mean behavior," according to Sophie, was motivated by Conrad's jealousy, for he "upbraided me with having entered into a collusion of the meanest sort with *everybody* in the ship." This, she felt, was not justified, for that had never been her pattern, and Conrad had known her all her life. "Moreover," she added, "I was so sea-sick during the whole passage that I hardly was able to speak a word."[2]

Once in Missouri, where Sophie and her mother saw that Conrad had "deceived" them "in all the descriptions he before had made to us about our future place of residence," he "grew every day more intolerable." Jealousy, described by Sophie in pathological terms, continued to be the major difficulty. It was directed against Sophie's alleged behavior toward the two young men living in their house, Wencker (Conrad's 1836 traveling companion) and Velthaus (their 1838 co-emigrant from Dortmund).[3]

Conrad found fault with Sophie's behavior as well, but he did not deny that he was sometimes intemperate. Although his entire side of the story is not known, it is not impossible to imagine at least some of it. For instance, he now was not a "visitor" on the frontier, as he had been the last time, but a real immigrant, responsible for a wife and mother-in-law. And their adjustment was not what he had hoped, although Julius and Mary did all they could to help. In fact, at first they took in mother Helene as a boarder. Sophie and her mother, however, complained much about their living conditions—privately, of course, speaking only to each other and not in front of "Americans" such as Mary, for their manners were too good for that. Although it was understandable that they found frontier life primitive, they also made Conrad feel that it was his fault.

Besides, there was little privacy in Conrad and Sophie's crowded living quarters. They lived in Carl Wencker's house, above his tannery, and he lived there, too, along with Velthaus, who had come over with Conrad's group.[4] While they and others were busy with the hides, Conrad was engrossed in work for his school. Launching it properly required a great deal of thought, writing, and reading. But when he was so engaged, or when he wandered along the river, lost in thought or even quietly depressed, the others often complained that he was lazy and should work off his bad moods by cutting down trees. He loved nature, but "taming" it was not his profession.

Sophie's pregnancy, it seemed, inflamed that unhappy atmosphere. In a statement to her lawyer, she said that Conrad had expressed early misgivings about the child's paternity. In fact, at the time of its difficult birth in spring 1839, he bluntly charged that it was not his child. "Such scenes occurred almost every day," Sophie reported, "and hindered my recovery to such a degree that our physician found it necessary of keeping him [Conrad] absent from home for some time . . . to take a little trip up the country wherein he [Conrad] spent some weeks." The continuing verbal clashes caused Sophie one day to faint and her mother, now living with them, to carry her to bed. At this point Sophie concluded "the necessity of a divorce," especially since Conrad "threatened in full earnest" to whip her. Furthermore, she charged that while she was ill with the bilious fever, he "almost had murdered me," and she described a scene in which she was awakened from sleep by a rude hand pressing down on her and a rude voice cursing her.[5]

After that confrontation, Sophie said she had "found a refuge" at a neighbor, Mr. Hospes, and "my mother with my child followed me thither." When the Hospeses also became ill, she moved to the home of Dr. William Koch, her physician. (According to the doctor's medical bill, that stay began around 13 August 1839.)[6] On 6 September 1839, while living at Dr. Koch's, Sophie notarized her divorce bill of complaint against Conrad before the justice of the peace, and it was filed by her lawyer, John D. Coalter, before the St. Charles County Circuit Court.[7]

Coalter, the twenty-one-year-old son of a Southern family, had been educated at South Carolina College and started his law practice in St. Charles. Sophie may have been one of his first clients. Later, according to historians, Coalter "became one of the most successful lawyers at the bar." He "was a forcible, clear and lucid speaker, and impressed a jury most favorably."[8] Through someone's advice and influence Sophie apparently had made a good choice—that is, if she indeed intended to dramatize her family quarrel in public.

And she would receive a fair hearing, for the St. Charles County court had a very good reputation. As early as 1803 the governor of what was then the Indian Territory had appointed five men, any three of whom could set up a court of common pleas for the St. Charles district. They, like the first grand jurors, were all Anglo-Americans, and for many years they would meet in "crowded rooms in homes, tavern, and churches." Historians suggest that many would have been shocked by "the informal dress of the lawyers, the democratic and offhand manner of administering justice, the loquaciousness and youth of the bar" and "roughly dressed farmers and villagers" who served as jurors. Despite this informality, the courts nevertheless were generally respected.[9]

After St. Charles became a county in 1812, its legal system was organized on a county and township basis. A governor's commission appointed a clerk and three justices of the county circuit court, admitted four men to practice as attorneys and counselors at law, and named five township constables as well as seven constables and two justices of the peace.[10] All were of Anglo-American background.

The justices of the peace, usually appointed (later elected) for four years, one or more per township, had considerable power. As the *St. Charles Demokrat* would write a few years later, "The justice of the peace is closest to the people—the peace and tranquility of the citizens are more dependent on him than any other officials." Moreover, "the office is especially important to Germans, for they are accustomed to consider the justice of the peace (*Friedensrichter*) as a legally knowledgeable official and therefore they often consult him in legal questions."[11] Conceivably, then, Sophie could have taken her quarrel with Conrad there rather than to a lawyer.

Initially justices of the peace had jurisdiction in all civil suits, considering themselves arbitrators who frequently could settle cases without using juries, which cost money.[12] In fact, they represented county law and order among settlements that had not yet organized themselves as political entities. The justices of the peace maintained the peace, performed marriages, wrote wills and testaments, and confirmed the transfer of property. In breaches of the law, the justice could order arrests, call witnesses and juries, or in serious crimes put an accused under bond until the next term of the circuit court.[13]

The lawyers, too, were important in the early legal system. Historians would say that "some of the first lawyers of the State" came from St. Charles County.[14] While those who had come to the frontier from the South usually had studied law, there also was a tendency around 1830 to let young men who knew a few legal fundamentals practice and learn by doing. These frontier attorneys were not located in only one jurisdiction; rather, they traveled on horseback from circuit court to circuit court in various counties to present their clients' cases.[15] In St. Charles the circuit court continued to meet in a prestigious private home until 1849, moving then to a small wooden building on county land.[16]

Although that court was considered competent and St. Charles County's lawyers above average, the laws of frontier Missouri in the first decade after its statehood were still evolving. Much of the old British common law, widely taken over in the United States, needed reconsideration and adaptation, as the Mallinckrodts would discover in Missouri courts. Changes were especially required in dealing with the age-old problem of dissolving marriage—the problem that Sophie and Conrad faced in autumn 1839.

Although the day was nearly gone when men could exchange wives almost at will, women were still frequently discriminated against through laws determining what and how proceedings might be brought against them or initiated by them. The general trend, therefore, was to broaden and specify the grounds for divorce for both parties.

In many countries reasons for ending marriage had generally come to include adultery, cruelty, and desertion. As early as 1643 poet John Milton pleaded in England for recognition of "incompatibility" as an additional ground, but English law remained conservative. In the United States, after its War of Independence from England, attempts were made to relax some of the old British strictures, and various states added impotence, bigamy, and cruelty as acceptable reasons for ending marriage. Nevertheless, grounds for divorce remained a problem for each state to resolve. By contrast, throughout the Germany that Sophie knew, the liberalizing influence of the Napoleonic Code made not only impotence and insanity but even irreconcilable hatred grounds for divorce.

In addition to the issue of acceptable causes for divorce, another ongoing and related debate in the American states was about who should grant divorce: should marriage be dissolved by legislative action, as in England, or by the courts? The practical problem was obvious: if a legislature had thirty to forty divorce petitions to consider each session, it either spent an inordinate amount of time considering them individually or, to be done with the unhappy matter, lumped all of the cases into one indistinct heap.

In Missouri that problem had been acute in the early 1830s. The governor in 1833 had sharply vetoed an accumulation of divorce petitions, saying that divorce was a judicial task. The lawmakers, however, passed the divorces over the governor's veto; during the next session he again rejected another box full of such petitions, and again they were passed.[17]

In 1835, then, new legislation was enacted stating that "the circuit court, sitting as a court of chancery, shall have jurisdiction in all cases of divorce and alimony or maintenance." The grounds for divorce in Missouri were also broadened. They included not only impotence, bigamy, adultery, desertion, conviction of crime, and habitual drunkenness but also cruelty, permitting divorce when a marriage partner "shall be guilty of such cruel and barbarous treatment as to endanger the life of the other, or shall offer such indignities to the person of the other, as shall render his or her condition intolerable." The 1835 reform, furthermore, prohibited the guilty party in the divorce from remarrying for five years.[18] According to at least one legal historian, for a time longer private legislative divorce bills were still possible, and several years later the taboo on remarriage was reduced to two years.[19]

Although divorce was not uncommon on the frontier,[20] Sophie Mallinckrodt's case was somewhat unusual because it came before the St. Charles County court at a time of changing law. In that context, (1) she appealed to a circuit court whose power had been strengthened rather than using the more private but longer legislative approach;[21] (2) because older divorce grounds did not apply to her case, she chose the newly permitted "cruel and barbarous treatment" charge. The first factor made her case highly public; the second made it very inflammatory.

Since the new cruelty clause was not specifically defined, lawyer Coalter and plaintiff Sophie not only used the exact language of the law (quoted below in italics) but also structured their charge to allege primarily "verbal" cruelty or abuse. In the bill of complaint, therefore, they said that Conrad

> has not behaved to her with the friendship and affection of a husband but on the contrary has abused and insulted her, has accused her of offenses shocking to the feelings of an innocent and virtuous woman, has accused her of infidelty to the marriage bed, and asserted that the child of which she was pregnant was not his. . . . [He] has not confined himself to words, but has used violence to her person, he has been *guilty of such cruel and barbarous treatment* to her, as *to endanger her life* and has *offered such indignities to her person* as to render her *condition intolerable.* . . . This treatment of her has been without any cause given of her, that she is entirely innocent of the foul charges made against her, which she is ready and offers to prove to the satisfaction of this honorable court, as far as a negative proposition can be proven, that she has always conducted herself towards her husband as a dutiful and affectionate wife. (Emphasis added)

Without spelling out in detail the background of the principal charge of alleged verbal "abuse and insult" and the secondary charge of "violence to her person," on 6 September 1839 Sophie requested that the court grant her "alimony and maintenance" as well as "a divorce from the bonds of matrimony." No request was made for child support.[22]

Sophie's personal situation shortly worsened, for while she was living at Dr. Koch's, the baby died. The death occurred around 25 September, as indicated by the doctor's later bill for the baby's care.[23] Thereafter, Sophie and her mother moved back to their former residence to arrange their affairs, mother Helene renting the dwelling in her own name from Wencker as of 1 September 1838.[24] Whether Conrad continued to live there, or next door at Julius's, is not known.

Interestingly, nowhere does Sophie's detailed account of the events of 1839, or any other preserved legal document, mention the gender of the child, its name, or exact birth and death dates. (Neither is there a baptismal record or a gravestone.) At the same time, relatives in Dortmund, Germany, somehow heard that the baby was a boy, for "son" was later entered on the city's genealogical tables. Emil, however, wrote his brother Eduard in March 1839 that "a daughter has arrived at cousin Conrad's whom they call Ellen."[25]

While Emil's report of a girl baby was probably correct, it is highly unlikely that the name Ellen was entirely accurate. Given the family's tradition, the child would have been the namesake of an immediate member—for instance, grandmother Helene, who was helping to care for it—rather than of Emil's wife Eleanor or Julius's wife Mary Eleanor.

The news of Sophie's September divorce action stunned the family in Dortmund, although who wrote what to whom and when is not known. Evidently, however, the word had gotten around by mid-October 1839. Emil, in Germany because of his wife's health, visited cousin Gustav in Köln and then on November 17 reported to him the opinions prevailing within the Dortmund family:

We found, as I expected, the mother in Westenhellweg [Conrad's mother] deeply troubled. In four weeks she aged four years. In her opinion, Conrad took on the sicknesses of both the Feldmanns [mother Dorothea's family] and Mallinckrodts. I am happy about her view, because in it she finds comfort and excuse for her favorite. In contrast, public opinion is very opposed to Conrad, who already was previously known as terribly eccentric [*verschroben*] and passionate.

On the other hand, Sophie and her mother enjoy the empathy and respect of their relatives here. From Essen her relatives are supposed to have written her and tried to get her to come back; they wanted to keep a residence for her and help her to set up a school. Here one intends to do the same; they say they will meet her and lead her back with jubilation.

I have to acknowledge opposition, for I would be very sad if she returned. It would give cause to much bitterness and quarreling, which would be especially painful for Conrad's old mother. I hope that August [Mallinckrodt] or Wenker can still thoroughly dissolve the knot of embarrassments and mistakes. But enough of this sad story.[26]

Not surprisingly, Gustav's response about his stepbrother a week later was in the same tone:

If Conrad is considered by his mother to be half, even if not completely, crazy, then I declare myself in total agreement. If he were not, he could not have behaved that way. That he has incurred the most intensive indignation of the Dortmund public I find as understandable as the fact that the most active empathy is expressed for Sophie and her mother. But in both matters, after several weeks the fervor will cool, if unexpected news does not feed the fire anew. There is nothing more inconsistent than public interest.

I am in entire agreement with you that it probably would be best for the family and also for the women if neither one party or the other would ever wish to return to Germany. But I do not credit little August with too much ability and almost dread to hear that the women have tied their fate to his.—Wenker would appear to us much better and reassuring.

In another sentence to Emil, Gustav added a thought that would become a leitmotif in the whole controversy: "Possibly because of the name Mallinckrodt, I hope to God that you and I will in every respect bring it honor, you in America as I here!"[27] Clearly, that was the aristocratic view of family roles and propriety: males were responsible for maintaining family unity no matter what happened (including marital problems); if something did go wrong, the men were not to blame the women. As legal "head of the clan," Gustav took the male responsibility very seriously.

At new Dortmund, meanwhile, Conrad of course had prepared a reply to Sophie's divorce bill of complaint. His response was filed with the St. Charles court on 10 December 1839. In it he rejected his wife's accusations point by point, adding that he was "saving to myself all advantage of the numerous insufficiences and defects of said bill." In addition, he also denied that Sophie always behaved as a dutiful and affection wife. On the contrary, "she often conducted herself in such a manner as to fill my mind with the deepest sorrow and mortification. Many of her acts occurred in private and the knowledge of which was confined to ourselves, but which were exceedingly painful to me, and through the efficient agency of other persons she was induced to commit acts of indiscretion and impropriety that gave me great unhappiness."

Somewhat acknowledging his lifelong pattern of intemperate statements, Conrad went on to say,

I state these occurrences did at times cause me to express some dissatisfaction with her condition and to ask of her an explanation of some matters respecting which I had my suspicions, but it was always done from the best of motives and with a desire to be satisfied on the subject. Anything that I ever said on the subject was in spirit of sorrow, and in the nature of inquiry and not for the purpose of injuring her or wounding her feelings.

Finally, repeating that Sophie was not without responsibility for their troubles, Conrad also asserted that she had been subjected to influences outside the marriage:

I state that I . . . have always treated her well, and at many times with a greater degree of indulgence than she merited. I state it as my belief that she has been instigated by other persons to treat me in such a manner as an affectionate wife ought not to treat her husband, and afterwards to desert me and to bring this suit for divorce. I deny all the charges made against me by her in her bill of complaint and pray that said bill of complaint may be dismissed.[28]

The lawyer who helped Conrad with his response was William M. Campbell, a thirty-four-year-old native Virginian. Graduating there from Washington and Lee University, Campbell had come to Missouri in 1829 and opened a law office in St. Charles. As historians wrote, "His ability soon became known, and from that time he was able to command any practice he wished. . . . He was a fine classical scholar, and spoke both French and Spanish. His style of speaking was bold, logical and fluent, and before a jury was almost invincible."[29] Although politically conservative (Whig) in a strongly liberal county, Campbell was "logical and studied in his arguments, and invariably carried the reason of his hearers along with him, as he did their feelings."[30] Not only popular with St. Charles juries, Campbell was appreciated by his clients because he never asked for his fee and by his colleagues because he possessed prodigious writing skills and a phenomenal memory.[31]

The frontier lawyers thus were well matched in what may have been a unique case at a time when verbal cruelty was not a frequent grounds for divorce. As historians assessed the young lawyers, Coalter "was a man of finer mental culture" than Campbell and had "something of the genius of the orator." Nevertheless, while Coalter's speeches read better than those of Campbell, "they by no means had the electrifying effect that Campbell's speeches invariably produced. Both were men of temperate habits and strictly honorable, upright lives."[32]

It was these two men, then, who drew up a summary of the four points in the case of *Mallinckrodt v. Mallinckrodt*: (1) the plaintiff's two charges of verbal insult (i.e., Conrad's statements about infidelity and the questionable parentage of the child); (2) one charge of "violence to her person by the infliction of blows"; (3) one charge "cruel conduct" on Conrad's part; and (4) the defendant's denial of all allegations.[33] Now it remained for the court to set a trial date, summon witnesses, and call a jury to meet at Dr. Reynal's house, the court's home.[34]

Back in Germany feelings were heightened by continual reports of the events in Missouri. Emil, still visiting in Dortmund, wrote cousin Gustav on 16 December, for instance, that "Wenker wrote confirming as true facts all the previous troubling news from America [about Conrad and Sophie]." Then Emil concluded, "That Julius took an active part is dreadful for me. Our friendly relationship is eternally disturbed. I would have expected better insights from him and would not have considered him capable of such blindness."[35] Given that Emil himself had often been the victim of secondhand reporting and that he was far from the Missouri situation, this definitive statement is astonishing.

What Julius had specifically done was not discussed. Also left unstated were Emil's motivations for abruptly and "eternally" writing off his friendship with Julius. Reasons also were not given for the accusation of "blindness," although Emil had not talked with Julius personally and Julius obviously was the most direct witness to what happened next door at Conrad's. Perhaps, however, Emil had received a letter from Julius, offering explanations that were unacceptable.

However, Emil may have been influenced by discussions in Köln with Gustav, who clearly disliked Conrad and was not overly fond of Julius. In fact, Emil may have adjusted his reactions at a time when he was asking Gustav to help him financially in America. Emil desperately wanted to return to farming, on purchased rather than rented land. He had already collected young Westphalian fruit trees to take back to Missouri, which he thought of as "a golden treasure" for his future plans.[36]

Although the family reunions had been wonderful, Ellen's health was improved and Emil wanted "to go home" to America, to "my new Fatherland."[37] In Europe he again had had the opportunity to consider the advantages of the New World vis-à-vis the Old. He felt that only Prussia, among all the German principalities, was a "distinguished" state: "I wish that all of Germany with its thirty-eight princes and princesses would fall under its [Prussia's] scepter. Then Germany would be a free and powerful country." His home city, too, he found as stagnant as when he left eight years before: "Dortmund and its residents all bear the symptoms of unchangeability. The rural towns have no movement, but the people in them squander the time in a quiet life and become old. Here I again see people who were already gray in my youth, and now they are the same as they were twenty-five years ago."[38]

Emil had been pleased, though, by the dynamic good news within cousin Detmar's family. After receiving the king's permission to retire from his distinguished public service career, Detmar in June had moved from Aachen to his estate in Boeddeken, near Paderborn. Pauline, his older daughter, would go with him, while his two sons, George and Hermann, were at the university in Berlin, and younger daughter Bertha would stay at boarding school in Aachen.

The Dortmund Mallinckrodts gladly accepted invitations to Boeddeken: Detmar was charming company and Pauline the same fascinating individualist as ever. As in Aachen, Pauline soon became involved in working with the poor around Paderborn. And there were many. It often did not go well for people who came to the cities looking for work after losing their spinning and weaving jobs in north Germany to machines. First Pauline had organized a group of women who recruited households to take turns delivering meals to patients at the hospital. Then, too, poor sick mothers concerned her, as well as day care for their children. Pauline said they needed a nursery school.[39] And as family members knew, "If anyone can arrange that, Pauline will."

Having thus caught up with family news in Germany, and dreading what they might hear in Missouri, in February 1840 Emil and Ellen set off for home. Taking a boat down the Rhine to Rotterdam, they hoped to board a steamboat there or at Le Havre. In a touching thank-you to brother Eduard, his wife, and her sister, Emil wrote,

> How great was the friendship and love with which you took us in. How you beautified our days and made us happy. We now bless the time we spent with you. It will be remembered all our lives. With how much goodness you all take care of

my brother, and how I am comforted about him through your love. My father often invoked a blessing upon him—certainly his prayers could not have been answered more fully than through the comforting, protective goodness of your hearts to his physically and spiritually burdened son.[40]

The stormy transatlantic voyage was one of illness for Ellen, but after arriving in New York on 27 March Emil wrote, "I jumped onto the American shore at 12 o'clock, with a never-experienced joy. I was like newly born." After giving Ellen several days to recover, they set off inland and arrived back in Missouri on 14 April.[41]

In addition to immediately buying land near St. Louis where he could carry out his new farming plans, Emil seems to have become involved in the ongoing family controversy. He planned to go to cousin Sophie's divorce hearing in the St. Charles Circuit Court on 14 May. Soon thereafter she would live next door to Emil in St. Louis, where she had gotten a job as governess (*Erzieher*) for the children of his rich German neighbors, the Angelrodts,[42] a position that Emil probably helped her to obtain. (Where Sophie and mother Helene lived in the months after the divorce suit was filed was not discussed.)

Emil's opinion of Conrad was by now poisonous. Interestingly, Emil's outrage against him focused on a characteristic Sophie had emphasized in her report to her lawyer, that is, Conrad's alleged laziness.[43] As Emil wrote his brother Eduard, "This miserable wretch [*schreckliches Rindvieh*] Conrad! Sophie would be able to feed a dozen no-goods like him here. But what good luck that she will be rid of him—the sooner, the better. The time will come when he has to beg for his bread!"[44]

It is unclear whether Emil witnessed the family trial in St. Charles, as he intended, and if so whether he spoke to Julius and Conrad. That, however, would probably have been hard to avoid in the small room at 119 South Main where the court met. What is documented, however, is that Sophie's physician, Dr. William Koch, appeared as her witness. He probably testified, as Sophie had stated,[45] that because of Conrad's mistreatment of her, the doctor discontinued house calls to treat his patient. Having made that point in support of Sophie's "abuse" charges against Conrad, Koch may have been cross-examined, as he later would be in another case. Then, for instance, he was asked whether it was not also true that Conrad had shown great care for Sophie during her delivery, in fact demanding that Koch stop his attempted cesarean operation on her.[46] Summonses had also been issued to Charles Wencker, Rudolph Velthaus, Louise Velthaus, Matilda Poppelmann, Matilda Nasse, and August Mallinckrodt to appear as witnesses for Sophie, and to Moses Bigelow and Hermann and Julius Mallinckrodt to appear for Conrad.[47] How they testified is not known, for the court records of the divorce proceedings in which Sophie's allegations were heard are not available. It is also not known whether she was granted maintenance and alimony, although later evidence clearly shows that she was divorced.

The jury's verdict in Sophie's favor might have ended the matter. But her May 1840 divorce judgment was far from the last act of the family's court dramas. Nor, indeed, had all its resulting tragedies played themselves out. There was, for instance, Conrad's professional future. His plan to start a school was obviously a destroyed dream, at least for now. Parents with German cultural values would not entrust children to a divorced teacher accused of the abuse that Sophie had claimed. And such news spread, especially when the case involved prominent lawyers and clients.

Maybe he could still teach in American schools, Conrad thought, but Missouri's educational system was making slow progress. Although in 1821 the new state had set public lands aside in each township for the use of schools,[48] by 1839 just 114 public school districts had been organized. They offered a total of only 163 months of school to about five thousand of Missouri's one hundred thousand eligible children. In addition to the short terms, the schoolhouses and equipment were usually poor. And, of course, there were no public high schools, for education at that level was available only at private academies, such as those many settlers had known in the Southern states.[49]

However, the new 1839 legislation to give Missouri a complete school system was promising.[50] It reflected Thomas Jefferson's belief that public education should be provided for all children. The new law also provided for permanent township school funds. But if the public school system was really to progress, it would need local taxes and have to be able to compete with the existing privately supported academies, subscriber schools organized by small groups of families, governess-led schools in single households, and parochial schools.[51]

Then, too, even if Conrad could qualify for the public school challenge, there was the problem of teaching in the English language. Moreover, the curriculum of Missouri's schools probably would not include his field of European languages. It might therefore be better to try to find private students to tutor. And then still another professional future, Conrad mused, might be found in learning a new vocation somehow suitable both to the frontier and to his intellectual bent.

For now, though, all that remained problematic. He needed time to think. But at least one positive thing had been accomplished: on 10 December 1839, in the St. Charles County Circuit Court, Conrad had filed his intention of acquiring American citizenship, as was possible a year after entering the country.[52]

Helene's Death

While Conrad contemplated ways to repair his humiliation, the next sad family chapter played itself out. Sometime during the months around the May 1840 divorce, mother Helene died at age fifty-three. As Sophie would later write,

My poor mother survived all this misery but a short time. Mr. Mall. [Conrad] wrote such insulting letters to her [where she lived that he might write her is unclear] that she, full of horror and grief to have fallen into such hands, fell severely sick and after three days' suffering changed this vale of sorrow for a better home, leaving her only daughter in so desolate a situation that I cannot but long after the day that will put my misery to an end.[53]

Neither Helene Mallinckrodt's death nor burial is recorded in St. Charles County, nor is either mentioned in any preserved correspondence. However, genealogical tables in Germany noted Helene's death as occurring in "St. Louis,"[54] suggesting that she lived with or near Sophie after Sophie went to work for the Angelrodts, next door to Emil.

What is on record with the St. Charles County Court, however, are four short legal documents reflecting the sadness of Helene Mallinckrodt's brief life in Missouri, which very likely ended in late spring 1840:

- An authorization dated 6 July 1840 by the Clerk of the St. Charles County Court for Moses Bigelow, Justice of the Peace, and Dr. William Koch to accompany Sophie Mallinckrodt "in opening and exploring the books, money, and papers of Helene Mallinckrodt and making an inventory of the same."
- The 20 July 1840 inventory, signed by Bigelow and Koch, who "did accompany Charles Wenker attorney in part for Sophie Mallinckrodt to the late residency of the deceased and that we found no money or books and no papers except the above described bond," that is, "a bond for fifteen hundred dollars acted 1st Sept. 1838 [soon after Helene's arrival in Missouri] drawing interest at 10 per cent—from date to be paid per yearly and signed by Julius Mallinckrodt as principle and Conrad Mallinckrodt, Hermann Mallinckrodt, and Carl Wenker, interest appearing due this day is $284.35."
- The 20 July 1840 appraisal of the estate of Helene Mallinckrodt by Moses Bigelow and Conrad Hospes: "1 clothes press [chest of drawers], 1 wash stand, 1 table, 1 bed stead, 1 skreen. Total value—$32.75."
- The 20 July notarization of Bigelow and Hospes's appraisal by Justice of the Peace E. Bryan.[55]

Helene's tragic path thus had led from a position as widowed *Hofrätin* in the lovely Ostenhellweg home to maternal petitioner of her only daughter, asking that she not marry the America-bound cousin Conrad Mallinckrodt.[56] Having lost that plea, Helene next began an odyssey as a reluctant immigrant companion to the daughter. Probably feeling very out of place on the frontier, she tried to pay her own way (even loaning what money she had) and thereby to gain her own acceptance. Her final role, then, was as sorrowful witness to her only child's misery and as resolute companion in their effort to see it through together.

Helene's relatively youthful death with total possessions worth only $32.75 in one room in the new Dortmund area was perhaps not the final scene. If Helene

Mallinckrodt indeed died in St. Louis, as German records said, it was possible that she and Sophie had most of their possessions with them and that the older woman did not die in near poverty. Perhaps, then, the grieving mother had been reassured before her death that the daughter could support herself with work and would overcome her trauma with strength of spirit. Possibly, too, Emil somewhere arranged a burial befitting the first death of an immigrant Mallinckrodt, following her short and turbulent encounter with the New World.

Although her mother would not see the justice they sought, Sophie and her supporters planned another round of court actions against the brothers Mallinckrodt at the new Dortmund. First, Dr. William Koch, Sophie's physician, would sue Conrad for an unpaid bill of $15 owed for Koch's medical care: $5 as "ballance on former bill at the time I attended on your wife and child at Hospes" and $10 "for medical services rendered to your wife and child from the 13th August 1839 to the 25th September of the same year, this service rendered at my residence [after Sophie had left Conrad]."[57] This lawsuit was brought on 25 September 1840.

Soon thereafter, on 3 October, Conrad was summoned to answer the charges before the justice of the peace on 7 November, and William Hospes and Christian A. Miller were called as witnesses for the plaintiff. Julius, too, was summoned by the township constable at almost the last minute, on 2 November, to appear as a defense witness before the justice of the peace in Augusta. Lawyers were not involved in this case, only the justice of the peace, who had authority to deal with such a relatively minor dispute. Instructions were sent out to the township constable to have six lawful men appear for jury duty, and a jury venire was drawn up.[58] Again, minutes of the 7 November proceedings are not available.

It is recorded, however, that the jury, which apparently was gathered at the office of Justice of the Peace Fariss, decided for Dr. Koch within "about half an hour." They may have thought that $15 was $15, no matter what principles the defendant had about not paying someone he did not like for services he did not consider adequate. In addition to the $15, Conrad was charged the $4.875 court costs. He immediately requested an appeal of the verdict, and about a week later, on 13 November, he and Julius "entered into recognizance," claiming their debt of $46 to Dr. Koch void if Conrad won his appeal.[59] (The documents did not make clear the nature of Julius's debt to Dr. Koch.)

Sophie Versus Julius: Slander

While Conrad's appeal was under consideration by the Circuit Court, another dramatic Mallinckrodt versus Mallinckrodt prosecution was initiated on 12 November 1840—Sophie versus Julius! Again the family name was central: plaintiff Sophie, "always reputed and esteemed by and amongst all her neighbors [in St.

Charles County] and other good and worthy inhabitants of the state," accused Julius of slandering her by calling her a liar. That, she contended, was worth $10,000 in damages.

Specifically, Sophie charged, Julius had said she committed perjury in her divorce testimony. That statement, meaning she was a liar, was intended to injure her "in her good name, fame, and character and bring her into public scandal, infamy and disgrace." Moreover, Julius had caused "a foul report of her to be carried back to Germany, her native land."[60]

Interestingly, Sophie described herself as a citizen of St. Charles County although she now lived in St. Louis. Indeed, it may have been through her contacts there (and obviously also Emil's) that she acquired the counsel of a famous and rich forty-three-year-old St. Louis lawyer, Edward Bates, for her case against Julius. However, Bates's wife was a sister of Sophie's former divorce lawyer, Coalter, so that may have been her channel to Bates.[61]

In addition to practicing law, the native Virginian Bates was a Whig (conservative) member of the Missouri state legislature at the time.[62] Contemporary historians, in fact, rated Bates as "the most distinguished citizen of St. Charles County in the early history of the State" who was, "nevertheless, more of a lawyer than a politician." And as a circuit lawyer, it seems Bates found this Mallinckrodt versus Mallinckrodt slander case so unusual, or so precedent setting, that he later would preserve Sophie's passionate background statement about it in his files.[63]

Opposing Bates to defend Julius was the lesser-known Thomas W. Cunningham, a prominent Warren County attorney. (Although rarely mentioned by legal historians, he apparently later became a St. Charles resident, serving that city as councilman in the late 1840s and mayor in 1855; for a time he was also a law partner of Arnold Krekel.)[64] Perhaps Julius hoped they would be a match in court, in substance if not in prominence, for much was at stake.

Sophie's charges could hardly destroy his vocational future, as they had Conrad's, nor could they besmirch Julius's name; he had been around too long and was too well known for a newcomer—especially a woman—to harm him. But her absurdly high claim of $10,000 damages would be hard to pay, although in Germany the word had spread that "Julius has become very rich." At least a jury of his peers would know, if others did not, that Missouri land values were not cash, and $10,000 could not quickly be picked off his fruit trees.

But what upset Julius as much as the money were all the principles involved. He cared just as deeply about family loyalty and unity as did Emil and Gustav, those "honorable men," as Conrad might have quoted the cynical lines from *Julius Caesar*. But honor and dishonor were not as one-sided as they seemed to think. For instance, from Julius's point of view, it was logical to see Sophie's behavior as very divisive; she had gone dramatically public with the family's difficulties and then had not told the truth in her sworn statements.

The situation had been difficult for everyone involved. At first Julius and Mary had daily tried to help Sophie and Aunt Helene, but it had not worked. The newcomers could not get over their shock that the frontier was not what they had imagined: unable in the old country to visualize accurately what Conrad described to them, they became angry with him for their own false images. Besides, Sophie was constantly torn between giving priority to her husband and giving it to her mother. Such division could not bring harmony. It was completely understandable, of course, that Sophie would be especially solicitous of Helene, whose adjustment surely was the hardest because of her age and background. Finally there was the matter of frontier housekeeping; despite Mary's patient teaching, Helene and Sophie did not easily get the hang of it. How could they, when many tasks of their former daily life at Ostenhellweg had been performed by servants?

But perhaps most crucial was Sophie's emancipation: she was educated and a professional teacher, a rare position indeed for a woman in the early 1800s! When she thought of the many generations of Mallinckrodt women who had not been permitted to go to school as she had, she was hardly willing, or able, to follow all the male admonitions that she now "become a Missouri frontier housewife." No, Julius probably mused, the problem had not been only Sophie's ignorance of U.S. law and the lawyers who may have taken advantage of her; rather, her own independent spirit, not yet adapted to frontier life, may also have driven her to take the public stand, whatever the price.

And then there was Conrad. He had always been a bookworm, and such people often had difficulty settling into daily frontier life. Over the years Julius had known many such persons. They needed time and help. In fact, Mary and Julius had often counseled Conrad to temper his tongue, not to permit his frustrations with daily life to drive him to words he would regret. They had asked Sophie, too, to have more patience with her husband until he got used to all his new responsibilities. And if she could not do that, they even told her that she should come to stay with them for a while until things settled down. Moreover, after the stormy birth of the child, it was Julius who convinced Conrad to go upriver on a business trip (possibly to visit his travel companions, the Burnses) so that Sophie could recover. She had even put all this in writing to her lawyer, Bates.[65]

But then when Sophie left Conrad's house, she had first chosen to go to the neighbors, the Hospeses, and then to Dr. Koch, about whom Julius had deep misgivings because he knew how the physician had behaved at Sophie's delivery. Furthermore, it was while Sophie was at Koch's that she contacted John Coalter, the St. Charles lawyer, and started the divorce litigation.

When Sophie came back from Koch's she reacted very negatively to the deal Julius presumably offered her if she would modify her divorce action. Naturally she did not discuss the specific contents of the offer in written statements to her lawyer but only referred disdainfully to it as "the paper."[66] Probably she hoped to get a bigger maintenance settlement from the jury, playing on its sympathy for women.

When Sophie would not discuss Julius's offer, he and Conrad had simply gotten a cart and yoke of oxen and loaded up the furnishings out of Sophie's room to take to Julius's.[67] Admittedly that had not been very honorable either, and perhaps it was the act that had so outraged Emil. But Julius and Conrad were angry, too, having tried everything possible to prevent the family court confrontation.

But what angered Julius most of all was that Sophie had publicly charged Conrad with "violence" to her person. That the younger brother had an intemperate, perhaps even at times "violent," mouth and pen had been known in the family for years. But he did not hit women! Julius knew that, for he not only loved and understood his younger brother but had lived shoulder-to-shoulder with him during all the difficult months. Yet Sophie had included that charge, probably on the advice of her lawyer, to impress a local jury familiar with the notion of physical violence but not with that of so-called verbal cruelty. That had been the zenith of her unfairness, in Julius's view, and was "proved" at the May proceedings only by lies.

On top of all that had happened in the past half-year, Julius now faced the fact that Sophie in November had hired a famous lawyer to prosecute him for saying she had lied. Julius, of course, could hardly be blamed if he wondered how much influence Emil, living next door to Sophie in St. Louis for the past seven months, had had on that decision. After all, the city cousin and former partner had made clear not only his disdain of Conrad but also his "eternal" rejection of Julius. As Emil had written to Dortmund in October, "The more I see of her [Sophie], the harsher must be my judgment of Conrad and Julius. I have broken off all and every contact to them and could do no other! Their mother may say whatever passion motivates— I admit freely that the boys have behaved most terribly against our late aunt and Sophie and continue to defame both."[68]

Sometimes Julius could almost laugh over Emil's judgments, which sounded so self-righteous. Such moments came when Julius recalled Gustav's verbal attack on them soon after their arrival in Missouri; Emil had been grateful when Julius stood up for them, challenging Gustav, "Are you a judge? Who is the accuser? Above all why don't I get time for a defense?"[69] To all appearances, though, Emil no longer felt that questions about judging and accusing were appropriate—nor, for that matter, was any discussion at all required.

Julius also enjoyed other moments of ironic humor about their situation when Conrad got out his beloved Shakespeare volumes and vigorously read aloud, from act 3, scene 2, Antony's cynical observation about the "honorable men" who had killed Caesar:

> They that have done this deed are honorable,
> What private griefs they have, alas, I know not,
> That made them do it: they are wise and honorable,
> And will, no doubt, with reasons answer you.

Even better, Julius found, was the passage in the next act where Brutus tells Cassius, "I do not like your faults," and Cassius quietly replies, "A friendly eye could never see such faults." The family bookworm was right: in times of trouble, literature could be a solace.

Julius, however, found little to laugh at in the specific slander charges Sophie filed against him on 12 November in the circuit court. First, the accusation that *he* had made "a foul report to Germany" about her was simply beside the point. It was known, after all, that when the times of trouble started in Missouri, numerous people from Dortmund, Missouri, had evidently written "reports" to people in Dortmund, Germany. What, for instance, had Sophie written about Julius, not to mention about Conrad?

And then there was the charge that on 10 July—in front of cousin August Mallinckrodt, friends C. A. Muller, C. Wencker, and others—Julius had said that Sophie and Koch committed perjury in their divorce testimony, that they had sworn a false oath against Conrad (*"einen Meineid begangen"* or *"Sie hat einen falschen Eid geschworen"*).[70] For having said that, she now charged that his "truth" was slander!

Julius did not always understand the fine differences in British common and American law between moral truth (in this case his personal, factual truth) and legal slander. According to the third volume of Conrad's always useful encyclope- dias, slander (*Diffamation*) seemed not to be so grave, at least not back home: a defendant either proved his contention or was ordered to remain quiet on the subject; if material harm had been done, the plaintiff could file an injury suit for damages.[71]

Anglo-Saxon law, however, was clearly quite different: defaming "words spo- ken" were treated as seriously as "words printed," that is, libel. And the burden of proving that the alleged slander was true—that Sophie had, in fact, lied—lay with Julius, that is, in the defense of "justification."[72] In other words, Julius would have to prove that Conrad had *not* mistreated Sophie as she had charged under oath. Unfortunately, "mitigating circumstances," such as the Mallinckrodt family quarrel, could not be considered part of that defense.[73]

Clearly, it would not be an easy trial. On the one hand, Sophie would have a hard time proving that damage actually resulted from Julius's "speaking the words." But on the other hand, he had accused her of an indictable offense, that is, perjury before the courts. In the Anglo-Saxon law of precedent, his lawyer told him, there were many past cases illustrating how serious his precise Germans words had been because they charged perjury in a specific legal proceeding.[74]

Probably equally clear to Julius was the fact that if he needed a great deal of legal help to understand all the complexities of U.S. slander law, then so did Sophie. Thus, he again and again wondered who had influenced her to bring that particular suit. He also wondered why she was so concerned about her perceived image in an area of the country where she no longer lived. And why was she suddenly so worried about her "good name," which she would change if she ever married again but which Conrad would carry as long as he lived? This, after all, was not Dortmund, Germany.

But precisely that, Julius could have thought, had been the problem from the beginning. Missouri was not a totally "new" region into which they as Germans could simply insert themselves and carry on their accustomed ways of life. Rather, it was the frontier of an existing society, where a basically Anglo-American culture was already firmly in place, especially in the legal system. Back home they would have known the laws and not become involved in scandals arising out of their ignorance of consequences. But here newcomers first had to take time to learn and to adapt, or they would do themselves and others great harm. Immigration was a much longer process than just leaving one country, getting on a ship, and sailing to another.

While pondering such aspects and doing his legal homework, Julius's lawyer Cunningham succeeded in delaying the case from the court's 1840 winter term (it was originally scheduled to be heard in November) to the 1841 spring session.[75] Julius first had to concentrate on helping Conrad with his plans for what to do next. It would take a bit more time to change course, but as sure as their name was Mallinckrodt, Emil would eat his words about Conrad having to beg for his bread.

Meanwhile, there was good news about the case *Koch v. Conrad Mallinckrodt* regarding the unpaid bill. The court recorded on 11 December 1840 that, on appeal from Justice Fariss, the case had been dismissed "for want of cause of action."[76] Perhaps Conrad, wanting to be finished with the business, simply gave Koch the $15 out of court.

In all likelihood, it was around this time that Conrad got his first vocational break—a private student to tutor. The young man was Arnold Krekel, who had come to Missouri at about age sixteen with his father Francis, one of the 1832 German immigrants to Duden country. During his 1836 visit to Missouri, Conrad may have met Arnold and encouraged the young man, then working as a farmhand, to study at the new St. Charles College, which was opening at the time. Arnold did just that later on and may have studied with Conrad for a time to prepare for a career in law.[77] Conrad's later great pride in "his tuition and careful instruction" of Arnold Krekel, contributing to a distinguished legal and civic career,[78] may have reflected Conrad's own need at the time for intellectual activity and challenge.

On 11 May 1841 Cunningham filed Julius's denial of Sophie's slander charges and asked for their dismissal. Repeating his deep conviction that Sophie had falsely sworn about Conrad's violence to her person, Julius vigorously countercharged, "Whereas in truth and in fact the said Conrad Mallinckrodt before the time the said plaintiff took her said oath and made her affidavit as aforesaid had not used violence to the person of the said plaintiff and the said plaintiff . . . well knew that her said husband had not used violence to her person."[79] Thus, Julius's basic defense was "truth," or justification, and in spring 1841 Cunningham began a series of complicated legal maneuvers to get some of the individual charges dismissed, continuing the case at defendant Julius's costs.[80]

Julius Versus Emil: Debts

At the same time, however, Julius was soliciting additional legal counsel concerning Sophie's slander suit against him with its huge claim for damages. And perhaps not astonishingly, given his anger at and suspicion about Emil's behavior, Julius was also preparing to sue his former partner for unpaid debts going back to the time of their immigration.

For this litigation Julius chose Hamilton R. Gamble, a great student of jurisprudence. Like many of his legal colleagues, Gamble was a native Virginian who came to Missouri prior to statehood; before he was twenty-one, he had been admitted to practice law in three states.[81] As irony would have it, Gamble's wife was a sister to Coalter, who had defended Sophie in her divorce trial, and Gamble was also a brother-in-law to Edward Bates, Sophie's present lawyer in the slander case against Julius.[82]

Why Julius engaged a lawyer with possible familial conflicts of interest concerning his two ongoing cases is not clear. Perhaps, however, Julius thought Gamble could "use" precisely those sources of information within the family to Julius's benefit. Whatever his assumptions, on 28 July 1841 Julius impatiently wrote to Gamble:

> According to our verbal agreement, I wrote to you in May last by mail, concerning the suit for slander of Sophia Mallinckrodt against me, pending in the Circuit Court of St. Charles, which letter ought to have reached you, according to my calculation, before you left St. Louis for the East. I have not received the expected answer from you to that letter. Please, tell me if this mentioned message has come to hand.
>
> Further let me know by mail, if you please, what you have done relative to the notes of Emil Mallinckrodt of $431—and of $32 or about that amount, handed to you for bringing suit. Is my term set for this matter which I ought to attend to.
>
> I remain respectfully, Sir, your most obedient servant, Julius Mallinckrodt, postoffice Missouriton, Mo.[83]

Over the next months Julius repeatedly tried to make clear to Gamble the financial arrangements that he, Emil, and Gustav had had at the time of immigration. They were complicated because agreements had been made on the basis of trust rather than formal papers. Out of the Mallinckrodts' confused finances, Gamble was able to formulate five precise questions ("Interrogations"), which were conveyed to Gustav in Köln. Included were the following:

> Do you know of any transaction of a business or pecuniary nature between Gustav, Julius and Emil Mallinckrodt in the years 1831 and 1832? If yes, state the nature of such transactions fully—and also state, if you know, whether there was a balance of indebtedness arising from such transactions in favor of Emil Mallinckrodt against

Julius Mallinckrodt, or in favor of Julius against Emil? If so, state in favor of which of them such balance existed and the amount of the same.

Other questions concerned the loan of £150, the amount of indebtedness on December 1840, and any correspondence Gustav had had about it.[84]

As defendant, Emil had his lawyer, T. Polk, send Gustav almost identical interrogations. The few variations, however, reflected Emil's significantly different recollections and assumptions about his financial arrangements with Julius. For instance, in addition to Julius's request that Gustav tell what he knew about actual "transactions," Emil wanted Gustav also to testify "whether any and what *promise or promises* [emphasis added] have been made to pay . . . by the party owing the balance." Regarding the communications involved, Emil wanted Gustav to testify not only about his own correspondence but also about letters relevant to the debt with "any other person or persons." And, interestingly, Emil's lawyer added a question in the interrogations to Gustav that was not included in those from Julius's lawyer: "State any other pecuniary transactions, or any other transactions of a business nature that you know to have taken place between Julius and Emil Mallinckrodt either in company with other persons, or between themselves alone." This question may have referred to Emil and Julius's Duden country partnership, which Emil later would say had been dissolved unfairly, that is, to his disadvantage.[85]

Also noteworthy, at the bottom of the questions from Emil's lawyer in St. Louis to Gustav in Köln, Julius's lawyer penned supplementary questions referring to the £150 loan, queries not included in the initial interrogations.[86] These additions clearly reflected Julius's doubts about Gustav's bookkeeping, as expressed by Julius in a letter to his lawyer:

> My brother Gustav Mallinckrodt as a merchant kept book in 1831 and 32. Let him prove by his prime notes how he booked the transaction of £150 at the start. I strongly believe that his books will show that he booked the transactions arbitrarily at a later date. . . . Methinks that when I started from Germany with the order of my brother to F. L. Lemme Co. in Antwerp to give me a credit letter of £150, it was agreed upon that my brother after the transactions were made and that he had paid for the credit letter to Lemme Co. he should make up an account of the principal and cost in Prussian money, deduct the proceeds of my payments and charge the residue if any to Emil Mallinckrodt. Gustav has never given this account to me. I think that I requested him in one of my letters from here to give me this account which was as apt to come out in my favor as in his.
>
> Have my brother Gustav asked if I requested him when I started to this county to give me an account . . . and if he ever gave me this account?[87]

Koch Versus Julius: Slander

For Julius, trouble seemed to draw even more trouble. In July 1841 a *second* slander suit was filed against him, this time by Dr. William Koch, who demanded $5,000 damages! Represented by the same lawyer who handled Sophie's divorce case, John Coalter, Koch, too, now wanted his "good name" restored—accompanied, of course, by some of Julius's alleged wealth. His charges were the same as Sophie's had been. In fact, Coalter filed for Koch almost word for word what Bates had charged for Sophie, that is, Julius's statements that Sophie and Koch had committed perjury in their divorce testimony. Two of the persons before whom the anti-Koch statements allegedly had been made were the same as in Sophie's lawsuit—August Mallinckrodt and Christian Miller—but Koch also added Hermann Garlichs.[88] And Julius probably expanded, vehemently, his list of "honorable men"!

That Coalter should take on Koch's case was interesting. By now Coalter was so well off that it was said he avoided rather than sought legal practice. Contemporaries said, "He only went into the courts when urged by his friends, or when called upon by some old clients."[89] Sophie may have been such an "old client" with influence, or the brothers-in-law Coalter and Bates might have found it legally interesting to be simultaneously prosecuting slander cases against Julius Mallinckrodt, Coalter for Koch and Bates for Sophie. If nothing else, they could share their legal research.

Again Cunningham, still Julius's defending attorney, used the argument of "justification" on his clients' behalf.[90] Now he would have to prove what Koch had really done, that is, prove that he had lied about his actions in court. Thus, Cunningham argued in Julius's defense statement that at Sophie's divorce trial, in which Koch appeared as witness for the plaintiff,

> it then and there became and was a material question on the cross examination whether he the said Koch acting as accoucheur [obstetrician] and physician in attendance on the said Sophie Mallinckrodt . . . did not want to perform upon the body of the said Sophie Mallinckrodt . . . a surgical operation thereby meaning the performing of the Caesarian operation.
>
> . . . [T]he said Koch . . . not knowing the fear of God . . . but contriving and intending to prevent the due course of law and justice and to aggrieve the said Conrad Mallinckrodt . . . and subject him to the payment of sundry heavy costs, charges and expenses then and there on the trial of the said issues upon his oath aforesaid falsely, corruptly, knowingly, willfully, and maliciously . . . did depose and swear . . . that "I," meaning himself the witness, *"never thought of performing a surgical operation upon her."* . . . Whereas in truth and fact the said Koch . . . did want to perform the Caesarian operation and . . . was only and solely prevented from the performance of the said operation by the timely interference of the then tender and affectionate husband of the said Sophie.[91]

While Cunningham sparred with Coalter during fall 1841 regarding the various counts of Koch's charges,[92] Julius petitioned the same court for a second postponement of Sophie's lawsuit against him until the next term. (This petition may have reflected the advice of both Gamble in St. Louis as well as Cunningham.) The reason given in Julius's 1 November petition was that his key witness, Hermann

Mallinckrodt of Pike County, had not received the subpoena sent him and so had been unable to testify but surely would be able to do so within the court's next term. Without Hermann's testimony, Julius argued, he could not "go safely to trial," for he knew of "no other witness by whom he can prove the same facts which he expects to prove by said witness."[93]

Concerning Julius's second pending case, the old immigration debt, it seems that Emil counterfiled. As Julius candidly wrote Gamble in late November, "I do not mean that his [Emil's] *demand* [emphasis added], if he should prove it afterwards, should be barred. No Sir! But let him first pay this note, and I know he never will try to prove his pretended former demand."[94] The two debts Julius referred to probably concerned first the initial £150 emigration fund Julius was trying to collect and then some demand from Emil for settlement of their land deals in Duden country.

Emil apparently won one case, probably the land settlement demand, for three years later he would write his brother Eduard, "After Julius saw that he couldn't win against me with his judgments [*Sprüche*], he paid the costs and gave me a complete receipt. I have already told you a number of times that I left Julius with nothing and that is the absolute truth. He *alone* has enjoyed the advantage of our first mutual settlement, which is known to people here."[95] How the question of the £150 was resolved is not clear.

Sophie Remarries

As if all this were not upsetting enough for the Mallinckrodt family, another startling legal event took place in late 1841: on 17 November Sophie Mallinckrodt married Christian Koch, the brother of her former physician William Koch and a wine grower in the area.[96] (Christian Koch, a thirty-year-old native of Cur Hessen, had applied for citizenship the previous year.)[97] Emil, of course, had known about the plans and written his brother Eduard some weeks before the marriage that "Sophie will probably marry soon and, in fact, an honorable man by the name of Koch, a brother of Dr. William Koch. He has a brewery located three miles (an hour) from Julius M. Since he knows the whole previous situation, one need not fear that he would ever reproach her or entertain any kind of unworthy suspicion about her. Since the matter is not yet public, for the time being do not tell anyone about it."[98]

And Julius, just as naturally, had heard about the marriage. He may, in fact, finally have found in it the answer to his question about why Sophie had been so intensely concerned about her "esteem" in the area: apparently she had planned for some time to renew her life in St. Charles County. That, in turn, raised a new question about how long her romance had been going on: had it possibly influenced her decision to seek a divorce and later to bring suit against Julius by "joining forces," as it were, with her future brother-in-law, Dr. William Koch?

While Julius did not have those answers, he did know that there was a legal problem with Sophie's marriage and wrote his St. Louis lawyer about it on 23 November:

> I have not yet been able to ascertain the report about Sophie Mallinckrodt except the part that she was married to the cooper Koch, brother of Dr. W. Koch; it is publically said that she was married in this county [St. Charles] last Thursday by a justice of the peace from Warren County; many people think that the justice was not authorized by law to do so [that is, perform a marriage in a county other than the one in which he had his commission].[99]

Julius's information was correct, for the Warren County justice of the peace in question recorded,

> I have joined in matrimony on the 17th day of November 1841, Christian Koch and Sophia Mallinckrodt, both of the county of Saint Charles in the State of Missouri, this matrimony being solemnized in the County of St. Charles and doubts being entertained whether it was legal or not the parties appeared before me on the 14th day of February A.D. 1842 at my office in the County of Warren and at their request were joined in matrimony this 14th day of February A.D. 1842. Frederick C. Rasmus.[100]

Thus Sophie was doubly married, a year and a half after her divorce from Conrad. Indeed, her marriage was reported to the court at its next term (March 1842) as a factor in the ongoing slander case.[101]

The next move in the family's series of legal quarrels came in the slander litigation of *Koch v. Julius Mallinckrodt*. At its spring 1842 term, after rejecting Koch's demurrers to Julius's pleas, the court ruled the case continued.[102] That same court session, however, had another Julius Mallinckrodt case on its docket. All the stress apparently took its toll on Julius's mood, and in July 1842 he became involved in a serious confrontation with his neighbor, Hermann Struckhoff, that led to a charge of assault and battery. Justice of the Peace Fariss brought the case to the circuit court, which heard it on 26 July. Unable to agree on a verdict, the jury was discharged and the case continued. On 2 August, Julius again appeared in court, withdrew his not guilty plea to the assault and battery charge, and was fined $5.00 and court costs to be paid in thirty days.[103]

On the same day, Julius again requested that the Koch slander case against him be continued at his costs and that the court summon as a material witness the other doctor present at Sophie's delivery, Dr. William Krug.[104] Wanting thereby to discredit Koch and his charges, Julius argued that without Krug's testimony the defendant "cannot go safely to trial [in] that he knows of no other witness by whom he can prove the same facts which he expects to prove by Doctor

Krug." Julius also asked that the case be continued into the next term, when Dr. Krug would be free from business pressures and able to attend. Moreover, Julius petitioned the court to pay Dr. Krug's costs for participating in the proceedings.[105]

Although medical testimony by Dr. Krug, if given, is not available in preserved records, there is the testimony of Anna Catharina Struckhoff. She was Sophie and Conrad's neighbor who acted as midwife at Sophie's delivery. On 26 October 1842 she appeared before Justice of the Peace Arnold Krekel (Conrad's tutorial student, who was now studying law) to answer questions put to her first by Julius and then by Dr. Koch:

> Mrs. Struckhoff testified that when she went to Sophie's home the day before the delivery, Dr. Koch was present but the birth pangs were few and weak. Mrs. Struckhoff said that during some of the severest pangs the doctor had used instruments without success, that is, the child's birth was not facilitated. According to the midwife, Sophie several times "asked Dr. Koch to let her alone." At one point the doctor had said "that the child could not possibly be born under the existing circumstances." Mrs. Struckhoff also testified that Conrad had said to his wife that he could save her but not the child.
>
> When the second doctor, Dr. Krug, arrived the midwife described the birth pangs to him, and he had said, "these were no pangs at all." Moreover, according to the midwife's testimony, "I heard Dr. Krug say to Dr. Koch that the child was in the right position, the only obstacle that the child could not be born were cramps. Then Dr. Koch said, I thought so, too, as she has been often afflicted with cramps during my former attendance to her."
>
> As Mrs. Struckhoff testified, when the child was born it was "a sound child" but had spots on both sides of the head allegedly from the use of instruments, but she had not seen them used at the moment of birth. In the questioning by Dr. Koch, the midwife was not able to say how often he had used instruments, but that the first time had been about 15 minutes. Some point also was made about Koch having gotten additional medicines from his saddle bags before Dr. Krug arrived.[106]

This testimony clearly underlined Julius's need for Dr. Krug's witness: Was Dr. Koch competent or not? Why was a cesarean delivery discussed and instruments used if cramps were the problem, not the position of the baby in the womb? Clearly not only Koch's veracity—and thus his fitness to charge slander—but also standards of frontier medicine seemed at stake.

Perhaps as a legal maneuver, Julius withdrew his plea of not guilty to the Koch slander charge the same day the above testimony was given and the case was scheduled to come before a jury. On the following day, then, the court recorded that the jurors "cannot agree upon a verdict" and so were discharged and the case continued. Next the court ruled, on 28 October, that the plaintiff Koch "give a bond and sufficient security for the costs of this cause at least 30 days before the next term of this court."[107] And so the matter continued.

But rather than Dr. Krug's testimony, or that of anyone else, the next preserved court document relating to *Koch v. Julius Mallinckrodt* is a highly unusual one. Writing in flawed immigrant-English, William Koch asked the clerk of the circuit court during its 1843 spring session not to have his case go into the next term because he, Koch, intended to go public to find his satisfaction. Included for the court's consideration was Koch's announcement to the public, referring to a lawsuit involving Conrad as well as Julius:

Dear Sir!

I inform you by this presents, that the law suit depending between myself and Julius Mallinckrodt shall not be brought again before the Court at the next term, being willing to finish this affair in an other way to my fully satisfaction. At the same time I wish you send me an account of the costs of the last term, which I have to pay.

The manner in which I am going to finish this lawsuit you will see by the following notice.

St. Charles Co. Respectfully, Your most obedient

Dr. Will Koch

19 June 1843

To the Public.

Next Monday on the 26th June afternoon shall the lawsuit now existing between the Mr.s Julius and Conrad Mallinckrodt and myself be on my part publically discussed in the following manner in the German language.

1. The evidence which Mr. Conrad Mallinckrodt gave against me at the last court shall be confirmed [*sic*] *by oath by 3 witnesses*, Mr. Garlichs, Mr. Chr. A. Muller and August Mallinckrodt.

2. I will by *six evidences, given under oath* by Mr. R. Velthaus, Mistress Sophie Koch, Miss Mathilde Pöppelmann, Chr. A. Muller, August Mallinckrodt, and Charles Wenker confute, partly direct partly indirect, the evidence of Mr. Conrad Mallinckrodt so plainly that the most partial man shall doubt no longer.

3. I will read to the public a writing wherein I have explained clearly the whole secret net of malice and vengence of the Mr.s Mallinckrodt and wherein I have enumerated facts which shall after this be handed to the Public in the German and English language. The discussion shall be in the presence of the Justice of the Peace, who will take the depositions of the witnesses.

St. Charles Co. 19 June 1843
Dr. Will. Koch[108]

At its 17 July session, the court ruled that since Koch had "failed to give a bond with security for costs according to the order of this court at the last term, it is considered by the court that the said action [slander charges] be dismissed." The court also ruled that Julius recover his costs.[109]

Unfortunately, it is not known whether Dr. Koch did indeed hold his extraordinary "public event" announced for 26 July, and if so, whether his new sister-in-law, Sophie Mallinckrodt Koch, was present to testify against her Dortmund relatives. The last evidence of the Koch versus Julius controversy was a court notation of 13 November 1843 that a "motion to relax costs" had been filed.[110] Also unknown is the outcome of Sophie's slander case against Julius, that is, whether Hermann Mallinckrodt or anyone else ever testified and, if so, how Sophie's case against her former brother-in-law Julius, who was still her cousin, turned out. Again, the frontier court records are incomplete but nevertheless suggestive of the flavor of "law and order" in the early 1800s.

Thus, of the five interrelated court cases involving Mallinckrodts in Missouri in the period 1839–1843, the results of four prosecutions are known:

1. Sophie was granted a divorce from Conrad.
2. Dr. Koch's charge against Conrad for debt payment was dismissed.
3. Dr. Koch's slander case against Julius was dropped by the plaintiff.
4. Julius lost one financial claim against Emil.

The outcome of the fifth case, the major slander litigation of Sophie versus Julius, is not known.

However, even from the fragmentary documentation available, a picture of the actions and their tragic consequences becomes clear—irreparable damage to family unity. After these cases the family was split. Emil represented the so-called St. Louis branch, including Sophie and contacts to Hermann; Julius and Conrad constituted the Dortmund, Missouri, branch, including August and also contacts to Hermann and Luise.

Emil's views of his Missouri relatives, probably passed on to his own children and to Germany via his correspondence with Gustav, are a matter of record:

Julius: "May he answer to God how he treated me and others. I left him empty-handed. Not only that, he in addition loaded me with debts. Nevertheless I concede him all that is good, especially because of his children. I feel sorry for them because he is ruining himself through his obstinancy [*Halsstarrigkeit*], conceit [*Eigendünkel*], and stubbornness [*Trotz*]."[111]

Conrad: After a devastating epidemic of fever, "Julius lost his main support, his so precious wife, and she left him with seven children. . . . Conrad also lay deathly ill—had he but died instead of the dear mother."[112]

Hermann: "Hermann and Luise are happy, because they want to be: they mutually make life as pleasant as possible. Hermann is really a dear person, and he surely has no enemy in the world".[113]

Sophie: "The present Mrs. Koch is well. Her husband is practical, and she ceremoniously honors him. I am happy that she now shows the world that she can live happily with a man. Thereby she is a competent housewife. But by the way, according to my humble opinion, she is a silly goose [*alberne Gans*]. God bless her."[114]

Unfortunately, again, a good record of the views of the other family faction in Missouri, that is, Conrad and Julius's, is not available to balance out the legacy. A few bits, however, are known:

1. Years after the bitter court fights, there was touching evidence that Julius continued to care very deeply about Emil: when there was a railroad disaster near St. Louis, Julius rode horseback all night to get there, for he firmly believed that Emil had been on the train and that his family would need consolation.[115] After the 1849 cholera epidemic that hit St. Louis so hard, Julius also took the initiative to look up Emil and his family.[116]

2. Hermann and Luise and their children kept up family contacts with both sides. In fact, it was their oldest son, James Ferdinand, who had Conrad's visionary school plan reprinted for posterity. It was also he who collected a great deal of information about the family and sent it to Germany.

3. According to oral history, Conrad's second son also tried to reestablish family ties to the St. Louis relatives but allegedly was rejected at the front door because of his "country" clothing. Whether or not the story was true, its telling perpetuated alienation. When that son's grandchildren asked in turn, "Why don't the Mallinckrodts in St. Louis have anything to do with us?" they were told the rejection story, with the added summary, "You see, they are rich, and since we are farmers we are not good enough for them." That negative class-consciousness would be a painful legacy, especially for the four of those inquiring seven grandsons and seven of the eight granddaughters who would work their way through higher education despite their parents' modest, indeed poor, means.

Obviously the family, in both Germany and Missouri, would have been better served by a more factual account of the bitter quarrels of the 1840s. There was much to learn from the experiences of honorable men and women caught between their Old World backgrounds and New World contexts. Those lessons of immigration, however, could not become clear until much later, after the entire and inspiring legacy had been recorded, both in the city and the country.

19

1840: Emil's New Beginning

While in Europe in 1839 because of his wife Eleanor's health, Emil had much time to think about their future in the United States. One thing he resolved was to return to farming rather than continuing the life of a shopkeeper in Louisiana, Missouri. This was such a major decision that Emil wrote cousin Gustav to explain himself:

> Daily it becomes clearer to me that I must return to agriculture. Nature has fashioned me to belong to the happiest profession in the world. . . . The great sacrifice I made for my wife [to leave farming and try an easier way of life] has been my resaddling. However much I afterwards devoted myself to an unaccustomed business [storekeeping], so my thoughts nevertheless turned only toward rural work and quiet domestic happiness. My body was just as unable to become accustomed to the new, inactive situation. Now I daily wonder whether Hermann could cope [with the store] alone. I would really like to buy ten acres close to St. Louis and next spring already plant the unique and valuable precious fruit on my own soil.[1]

To make that important new start, Emil wrote that he needed $1,000 for ten acres of land, $200 to build a house and barn, $70 for a horse and a good milk cow, and $60 for a plow, harness, and wagon. Then he would put two acres into a nursery, use three acres for an orchard and vineyard, and allocate five acres to vegetables. He felt a location near St. Louis was best because of the market it offered for a good nursery and vegetable farm. Moreover, "in my case it is necessary with few resources to produce much and do that quickly. . . . I have a lot of obligations to settle, and as an honest person would like to do that soon."[2]

Westphalian Fruit Trees

The "precious fruit" Emil referred to were the "200 two-year-old plum plants grown from stones, along with improved pears, apples, and cherry stems, about 60 of the best kinds" he had collected during his visit in Westphalia.[3] But before he got those and more trees to Missouri, they would be central to an amusing yet serious adventure. Later, when his German trees became an orchard that was a key to Emil's prosperity, he may have seen their journey as symbolic of his own life—troubled beginnings turning into success.

The adventure of the trees began in February 1840, when Emil and Ellen set off with them from Dortmund to return to Missouri. They would take a boat down the Rhine to Rotterdam, where they hoped to board a steamship for New York. Near Arnheim, however, their Rhine steamer was rammed and within eight minutes had sunk in the middle of the river, trees and all. Emil dramatically recounted the mishap for brother Eduard:

> It was dark and we screamed for help. Soon boats arrived to rescue us; so many jumped into the first two that I did not risk putting Ellen into them. As the third one came up, I carried Ellen into it and pushed off with mighty force so that our boat would not be overfilled. We arrived safely on shore and all were rescued. . . .
>
> That trunk from you, our traveling bag, and my trees lie under at least ten feet of water. I will try to see today what can be done, but we were glad to escape with our lives. . . . Do not be frightened; we are well and cheerful. Ellen has a heroic nature.[4]

Emil's next letter, from Liverpool, carried on the story of the trees:

> On the second day I had the big case and my trees fished out of the river. So we lost nothing save the traveling bag with my new boots and many other pieces of clothing. . . .
>
> When we arrived at Rotterdam, we unfortunately found no opportunity to embark—unhappily, the steamer for Le Havre left almost at the moment we arrived. So there was nothing to be done except to hasten on, since the steamer left every ten days. [From the steamboat to England] I found a little conveyance for London, and we arrived there on the twenty-fourth, after we had been very seasick. . . . We traveled here [Liverpool] by train in nine hours. . . . This trip has cost me terribly. Today we take the ship *Europa* for New York. We have stateroom passage for 6½ pounds sterling per person. We furnish our own meals. . . . I am terribly worried about Ellen as she is pregnant since January. . . . God help us through. There are 223 deck passengers—all wild Irish people—on our ship. This is very unpleasant.[5]

Arriving safely in New York, Emil reported, "My trees are well preserved only they are sprouting too much, having lain in the Rhine under water for three days."[6] The plants were still healthy when, after an overland trip of about two weeks, Emil and Ellen arrived back in St. Louis on 14 April: "The trees have maintained themselves wonderfully, and I will probably lose no more than 10 of the 600. Their freight cost a dreadful price because I had to transport them with all the Rhine water. But I do not regret that, since perhaps they therefore kept so well."[7]

A New Farm

The trees had to be planted at once, and Emil lost no time putting his new plans into action. First he bought land, about thirty-nine acres on Bellefontaine Road on the north side of St. Louis, for $11,700—about ten times more than he had initially figured. Because he could not pay the fifth of the principal that was due by mid-September (the rest in eight years at 8 percent interest), Emil offered Gustav one-third interest in the new property in return for cash to make the first payment.

Next Emil thought of building a house, for there was only a log cabin on the new land. But it was more important to get his vegetables into the warm spring earth quickly. He would therefore board with a neighbor for fifteen dollars a month, and Ellen, pregnant for the fifth time, would stay temporarily in Louisiana with Hermann and Luise. Although Luise had been ill, she was well again, and Hermann had taken good care of Emil's store while he was in Europe.

During the next three weeks Emil planted three acres in melons, onions, carrots, cabbages, beets, and potatoes. Next on the planting schedule were fifteen acres of corn, as well as a beginning fruit tree nursery, an acre of strawberries and asparagus, and another acre of grapes. The harvest from these crops would easily pay for his land in the next years; only this autumn's payment was a problem. The Westphalian fruit trees meanwhile "continued to thrive well," and in spring Emil wanted to plant another three hundred.[8] In addition, he had bought twenty feeder swine, four ewes, two work oxen, and two good milk cows (which he was feeding with corn and pumpkins).

Next Emil built a house on his new property. It obviously was not just a modest cabin, for it cost $1,400. The house—built of brick, like most St. Louis houses because of the nearby clay deposits—had four rooms, a broad central hallway, and a kitchen in the basement.[9] Although the house was located on the edge of the city, all around it St. Louis was expanding. At the city's flourishing markets, Emil sold his vegetables and fruits. "I have been very busy," he wrote, "and almost have too much to do."[10]

A First Son

In fall 1840 Emil had a tremendous joy to report home: after the deaths of four infants, on 27 September "a healthy, strong boy was born" to him and his wife.

As Emil put it, this was their "fifth child, the third son!" (Sophie Mallinckrodt, living next door at the Anglerodts, helped during the delivery.) The little boy "belonged in part" to the Dortmund family, Emil wrote his brother, because Ellen had become pregnant during their visit there: "Our visit to you was our good fortune, and we hourly bless that time. Ellen says that the careful, sincere, and friendly care that she enjoyed from our beloved sisters gave the little boy his life.[11]

Despite the touching words to his Dortmund brother, Emil named his first son for his cousin and financial mentor, Gustav. (Interestingly, Emil later wrote brother Eduard that it was Ellen who "insisted that, God willing, our next son will be named after you.")[12] Little Gustav showed the physical characteristics of their own immediate family, Emil told his brother:

My fat son with his big blue eyes and little hawk nose [a Mallinckrodt facial feature] is sitting on a pillow next to me playing. He has given me three kisses for his dear and only uncle in the world, and three kisses for each of his dear aunts. Pass them on, my brother, with thoughts of the only grandson which our dear parents now have. May the boy grow up to honor his grandparents, love you, and be a joy to all people.[13]

By the time the little fellow was eighteen months old, Emil felt that he greatly resembled the portrait that Eduard had "of our Wilhelm [their deceased brother] as a little boy."[14]

Hermann's Farm

Perhaps seeing how well Emil and Eleanor were doing on their own land, Hermann and Luise took the same step in November 1840, when they moved to a small farm near Louisiana, Missouri. This, of course, was the pattern of early immigration years: after working for others or renting property for a time, one could buy one's own land. There is some indication that Hermann's land had been purchased with help from home, for on his visit in Dortmund Emil had asked mother Dorothea for the money her son Hermann had not yet received from his brothers Leopold and Albert.[15]

Although they liked the life of farmers, Hermann wrote Gustav that "the farm is indeed in a neglected condition, and our two houses leave much to be desired." Hermann was nevertheless optimistic:

With time and my own eforts I will correct both these negative conditions. Meanwhile we have to adjust to timing and situations, and we can do that for we both are meant for America. Rather that than give up our independence.

We have a farm suitable for raising cattle and no debts that we could not at once cover in case of need. All that is left for us to wish is continued good health. My Louise, one of the most lovable and best women, completes my happiness.[16]

Before long Hermann, like Emil, was planning changes. In the next winter, 1842, he would begin farming together with another Mallinckrodt cousin—another Hermann, from Elberfeld—who had come to Missouri in February 1838.[17] To-gether they could be more productive. Economics also took a new turn for Luise's brother August, who had emigrated with them. He was still working with Carl Wencker, but now in addition to tanning they were making cigars out of the tobacco being intensively cultivated in Duden country.[18]

Hard Times and Election Time

By contrast, the economic situation in the United States was not as good as Emil and Hermann's land purchases and plans for bigger farming operations suggested. Prices for agricultural products were very low, and there was a serious shortage of capital in the whole country. In addition, many working men were either out of a job entirely or receiving very low wages.[19] For those with money, though, it was an excellent time to invest, as Emil repeatedly wrote.

The atmosphere of general discontent made the presidential election of 1840 an important one for Missouri, and the campaign was conducted with great enthusiasm. In fact, much later it would be seen as the "jolliest and most idiotic" campaign in U.S. history.[20] On the liberal side, the Democratic candidate was the incumbent president, Martin Van Buren. He was considered a good successor to the former president, Andrew Jackson, who had been a friend of the expanding West and states' rights. His challenger from the conservative, or Whig, side was a military hero, General William Henry Harrison, and his running mate, John Tyler. In the War of 1812 against the British, Harrison had made a name for himself at the Battle of Tippecanoe, fought in Indiana. The Whigs touted their colorful candidate and his running mate in the famous slogan "Tippecanoe and Tyler Too!" Another Whig slogan, "Log Cabin and Hard Cider," referred to a newspaper report that had depicted Harrison as a backwoodsman who, given a barrel of hard cider and a sizable annual pension, would be glad to sit out the rest of his days in a log cabin rather than in the White House. The insult backfired, and Harrison was praised for appreciating the simplicity of the log cabin. Van Buren's supporters meanwhile reminded the public that their candidate was heart-ily endorsed by "Old Hickory," former president Andrew Jackson.

The waving of hickory boughs and cardboard cutouts of log cabins therefore dominated the big political rallies during the autumn of 1840, probably to the great astonishment of many European immigrants. There were log cabin floats at state conventions, log cabin buttons and banners, lyrics about the virtues of log cabins set to the music of "Auld Lang Syne" and "La Marseillaise," and even whiskey bottles shaped like log cabins.[21]

Despite the slogans and country fair atmosphere, economics was the principal issue of the campaign. As the incumbent, Van Buren was harshly blamed for the economic hard times. During his administration, the Whigs charged, he had done little to stop the economic tailspin his predecessor, Andrew Jackson, had begun by permitting the federal Bank of the United States to die. In fact, however, the unsettled bank issue had divided voters ever since the country was founded.

In 1791, when the bank was first chartered by President Washington on the recommendation of Alexander Hamilton, many had argued that the Constitution prohibited the federal government from setting up a bank; that was instead the right of the individual states. Supporting that view, Andrew Jackson had not renewed the bank's charter in 1836 and had withdrawn federal deposits from it, precipitating the so-called Panic of 1837. Farmers especially had suffered and were angry, as a German settler made clear in a letter home:

> The bank humbug in the United States has made the times harder and harder, so that at the present time scarcely any good money is in circulation. If . . . the Democrats are victorious and re-elect Van Buren, things will soon be better again. The paper money swindle will then be buried, business will be put on a sound basis once more and take a regulated course. Now it is very bad. The merchants and the rich speculators allow everything to go topsy-turvy. . . . The wicked Whigs cry out "These are the fruits of the present administration, the Bank of the United States ought not to have been abolished, then we would not have such distressing times." . . . However, there is scarcely a doubt but what the Democrats will be victorious again, and the aristocracy of the rich will be abolished for a long time.[22]

But the settler was wrong: Harrison won. Most people did believe that Van Buren was responsible for the economic hard times, so they voted against him, especially in the western states. Missouri, however, was one of two frontier states that stuck with the Democrat Van Buren; indeed, in Missouri he received a majority of nearly seven thousand votes.[23] Part of that support clearly came from Germans, who were staunchly Democratic.

The German immigrants were enthusiastic voters, in part because in the early years local laws barred foreign-born persons from running for office; thus, their influence was limited to voting after they became citizens. At that time their fellow Americans welcomed the active German participation and voting, especially, as was cynically said, since "the Germans did not aspire to offices" and "had no numerical preponderance."[24] In the next trying decades on the frontier, however, that acceptance of immigrants would change, as did many other sentiments.

President Harrison, whom the German settlers had generally opposed, lived to govern only a month before he died of pneumonia. It was then left to President Tyler to solve the banking crisis that so troubled the economy of Missouri and other farming states. But Tyler's administration was turbulent, including a mass resignation of the Cabinet. The banking and tariff questions were not dealt with adequately.

The Tyler administration also largely ignored the issue of slavery, although abolition was becoming an increasingly popular cause among many Americans. For instance, in 1839 the first so-called civil rights case heard and judged by the U.S. Supreme Court had become a cause célèbre. The case involved a slave, Cinque, kidnapped from Sierre Leone, Africa. During his transportation on the Spanish ship *Amistad*, Cinque led a mutiny and killed the ship's captain. Spain demanded that Cinque be extradited to be tried for piracy, but Van Buren, then president, refused. Abolitionists took over Cinque's case, which finally reached the U.S. Supreme Court. The African's famous defense attorney was the aged former U.S. president John Quincy Adams, appearing in his last trial. He argued that the slave trade was illegal, both by American and Spanish law, and that all people had a natural right to freedom. Adam's presentation was so impressive that even the majority of Southerners on the Court voted to free the *Amistad*'s blacks and return them to Africa.[25]

Cases opposing slavery were coming before American courts in increasing numbers and educating public opinion. At the federal level, petitions flooded the U.S. Congress, demanding the abolition of slavery and the slave trade in the nation's capital, the District of Columbia. Many were incensed when they learned that from the windows of the Capitol building congressmen could see coffles of chained slaves marching by, guarded by armed men, and that the slave market where auctions were held was not far from where the representatives worked and lived.

In Missouri, too, voices protesting slavery were growing louder, especially in the German press. For example, in 1840 one-third of the fifteen thousand citizens of St. Louis were German, and their principal newspaper was the abolitionist *Anzeiger des Westens*.[26] Anticipating and fearing the growing antislavery mood in the state, the Missouri General Assembly in 1837 had passed legislation against exciting slaves or other colored persons to rebellion or murder. In addition, some abolitionists had been sent to the penitentiary for stealing slaves, and the preacher and newspaper editor Elijah P. Lovejoy had been driven out of St. Louis and then murdered because of his antislavery publications.[27] It was clear to many that if the issue of slavery in Missouri had initially been primarily economic, by the early 1840s it was rapidly becoming political.

St. Louis Grows

Throughout the economic ups and downs and political unrest, Missouri's business center, Emil's beloved St. Louis, grew and grew. (With increased immigration from Ireland, as well as Germany, the city's population doubled from 1840 to 1845 and doubled again during the period 1845–1850 to reach a population of nearly 78,000.)[28] As Emil noted with astonishment in spring 1841, despite the general lack of money and rising land values, one thousand new buildings would go up that year. The city had in fact spread to within five miles of his farm. It was difficult, he reported, to get through the crowded business section. "You would be astonished," he wrote, "to see the mass of goods piled up that two hundred steamboats load and unload."[29]

One reason for Emil's astonishment was that he in fact could see all the waterfront commerce spread out in front of him. The city did not have warehouses near the river, and so the levee, with its paved slope up to the first row of buildings, was used for storage space. Of this waterfront, which was said to be the "busiest scene in the Mississippi Valley," the historian Wyatt Belcher has written, "A mile or so of steamboats unloaded and received sacks, bales, boxes, and barrels of produce and merchandise as far as the eye could see. Hundreds of drays, wagons, and carriages rushed to and fro, and thousands of men jostled each other in handling the trade."[30]

Regarding his own property, Emil thought that "in less than ten years my purchased place will have a tremendous value."[31] Cousin Gustav, far away in Köln, was also profiting handsomely from his investment in Emil's new undertakings north of St. Louis. After Gustav presumably sent money, Emil began to speak of that property as "the beautiful place I bought together with cousin Gustav" and referred to Gustav's business dealings with him as "fatherly." At the same time, the St. Louis farmer and partner said he also "had the joy that Gustav's advantage in our purchase will be furthered for one of his children, who thereby will become rich."[32]

In fact, only a year later Emil reported:

Cousin Gustav and I will have a quick fortune from our place. . . . This summer I sold a building lot for $300. . . . In five years we can sell all the land for bulding lots. It already is being built up around us. Our property won four big buildings this year: (1) Schulenburg's big starch factory plus mill, (2) a two-story brick building on the sold lot, (3) and (4) two brick houses that cousin Gustav had built to rent.[33]

By spring 1842 seven families, totaling thirty-six people, were living on Emil's land, most of them tenants. Gradually becoming a real estate developer, Emil Mallinckrodt now felt that "if cousin Gustav continues to support our undertaking, we will soon have solid wealth."[34]

For Gustav, however, prospects may not have been that rosy. Economic conditions in Germany were bleak: an industrial crisis in 1840 had brought unemployment, with a fourth to a third of the workers on relief. Consequently, the embryonic trade union movement was growing, and students and intellectuals were agitating for change.[35] The object of their opposition was the absolutist rule of the Prussian king Friedrich Wilhelm III, who died in 1840, and then of his successor, Friedrich Wilhelm IV. Although the latter hated regimented bureaucracy, he nevertheless believed in paternalistic government and censorship of printed ideas he did not like. The king also favored conservative laws, for instance, making divorce a matter for churches to decide, not secular courts.

Gustav's Politics

The king's attitudes, of course, clashed with those of intellectual Germans who had been deeply impressed by French ideas of liberty. Such progressive thinkers were found especially in the Rhineland, among young men who had grown up there when the area was under French rule from 1795 until 1814. Köln was the center of their activities, and Gustav Mallinckrodt was intensely involved. Like other businessmen of the city he was very socially conscious, feeling that the state had far-reaching duties toward society.

To discuss and publish their ideas of reform, some of the men of the city formed the Köln Club. Among the members were young lawyers, doctors, social philosophers, financiers, and industrialists such as Gustav Mallinckrodt.[36] Gustav was one of the stockholders in a company the club formed in September 1841 to found the *Rheinische Zeitung-for Politics, Commerce, and Industry*. Its goal was to defend interests of the Rhineland's middle class—safeguarding the Napoleonic Civil Code and its principles of equality for all citizens before the law, ultimate political reunification of Germany, and economic expansion of industry and commerce, for example, by accelerating railroad building.

Because the Köln Club saw poverty as a social and not merely political question, it attracted thinkers who belonged to the new school of thought called "socialism." Among them were Moses Hess, who believed in action, not just talk to free people from oppression; Georg Jung, a prosperous young Köln lawyer who supported the radical movement; and Arnold Ruge, the editor of a publication that had to be printed in Dresden because King Friedrich Wilhelm IV forbade its appearance in Prussia.[37]

Among their friends was the young Karl Marx, a journalist who had received his doctoral degree from the University of Jena in spring 1841. On Marx's visits from Trier or Bonn to Köln, he came to know the Köln Club, and in 1842 he wrote many articles for the *Rheinische Zeitung*. The articles reflected the club's concerns, calling for a constitutional government, for civil equality, and for freedom of law, the press, and religion. Marx became chief editor of the paper in October 1842, and its circulation soon doubled. By the end of the year the *Rheinische Zeitung*, with a circulation of 3,500, had gained a reputation throughout Germany.

The critical articles, of course, did not please King Friedrich Wilhlem IV, and government pressure on the newspaper increased. In January 1843 Marx published an article about the poverty of grape farmers on the Mosel River; this would be his last piece for the Köln paper, which was banned by the king in 1843. Gustav Mallinckrodt was one of the Köln Club members who not only protested locally but also traveled to Berlin with a delegation hoping to persuade the king to lift the ban—to no avail.[38] The affair must have seemed to Gustav like a replay of the banning of his Uncle Arnold's Dortmund newspaper in 1818.

But the struggle for reform would continue. As a leader of the liberal political movement in Köln, Gustav Mallinckrodt (together with his confidant and co-worker Gustav Mevissen) would see what could be done about achieving social change.[39] He did not have to withdraw from public life as Uncle Arnold had, for his financial base was relatively secure. And emigration certainly was not an option, since Gustav felt deeply about the future of his own country. He wanted to work actively, though not radically, for social reform, and emigrants almost always had to avoid that. They had to adapt, to fit into their new chosen environment, because if they were dissidents they usually would not be accepted by those already established. Gustav would therefore carry on in Westphalia, as Mallinckrodts before him had. He would not become a member of the communist movement, which his acquaintance Karl Marx went on to found, but later historians would perhaps see him as an early social democrat.

In St. Louis, Emil was doing something quite different for Westphalia: he was making its horticulture known. The plants from there remained his favorite possession, and they were doing very well. Since the rapid expansion of the city made him "frightened for my nice German trees," he resolved to "transplant them somewhere else after several years."[40] Meanwhile, Emil's detailed accounts to his brother of the Mallinckrodt orchard and vineyards in St. Louis reflected an interesting chapter in frontier agriculture:

> The cherries, pears, Renes de clouds [possibly a variety of peaches], raspberries, and roses are especially luxuriant. So are the improved plums, as well as an apricot von Coert, which also has bloomed. The apple trees are not thriving as well; neither are the walnuts and gooseberries which first must adapt to the climate. It is too hot here for early improved wines; therefore I planted them on the north side of the house. Those which flourish best are the Isabelle and Catawba grapes, which grow wild in North Carolina. The vineyards at Cincinnati on the Ohio and those in South Carolina grow almost only the Catawba. I saw these wonderful grapes last fall, excelled by nothing on the Rhine. Since these American varieties of grapes suffer from neither cold nor heat, they fit our climate; therefore I planted mostly these sorts. Now they are blooming, and I hope this year to harvest ripe fruit already.[41]

Emil was especially enthusiastic about the improved Catawba grapes. He described them as "dark red, when very ripe almost black, spicy, juicy, and thick of berry, very full bearing and large grapes. In Cincinnati the vineyards are only of this kind. They make a fiery wine of a highly yellow color." Summing up his horticultural joys, Emil put it briefly: "The trees we brought from Germany are our favorites."[42]

Emil also beautifully described his entire property:

Imagine a neat country house on an Indian mound in the middle of the property— on the eastern side the great Mississippi, south of it the spread-out city, on the west Bellefontaine Street, to the north the suburbs. We are in the middle, on all sides the most lively activity of human endeavor! Imagine in addition two morgen of land around our dwelling, planted with hundreds of fruit trees of all kinds, already in full bloom since the twentieth of last month [March], especially peaches, cherries and apples—and then finally my house entirely entwined with grape vines that already show blooms, as well as the roses.[43]

A First Daughter

In addition to the farmer's joy of thriving plants and animals, Emil had another happiness to report in 1842—the birth of his first daughter on 16 December. "In honor of our blessed mother," Emil wrote his brother, the little girl was named Gertrude Wilhelmine Dorothea, later shortened to Minna.[44] It may have been during this period of happiness that Emil had his portrait painted by the St. Louis artist Adele Gleason (plate 9).

By the end of 1842, however, Emil's optimism about his economic future had been shaken despite his thriving gardens and orchards. The year, he said, had been "the most worrisome" of his life, and later he would call the period from 1836 to 1842 "the great trade crisis" for the country and frontier.[45] Many banks in western America had failed. St. Louis alone had lost $3 million, financially ruining a third of the inhabitants. Emil, too, had lost a great deal on his properties in Louisiana, Missouri: he could not sell them and received only low rents.[46] In fact, he had been forced again to ask Gustav for help—at 10 percent interest. As Emil wrote Eduard,

Before I came to Germany, I had paid only about $1,900 on my property. By last summer the remainder had grown to $2,500 because of the high 10 percent interest current here. I should then have paid the whole debt, and I could not. In my emergency I turned to Gustav, . . . but I have not yet caught my breath. . . . May God help us for one or two years until the terrible crisis, which began in 1836 in New York and New Orleans and which only now shows its effects in the Mississippi Valley, is over. Then I shall be so far that I can thank Gustav very well in deeds and be free forever from all my embarrassments.[47]

St. Louis newspaper reports reflected the situation: By 1842–43 wheat had fallen to 35 cents a bushel, potatoes and corn were 18 cents, well-cured hams 5 cents per pound, and tobacco $3.10 a hundredweight. On the positive side, groceries were also cheap: coffee was 10½ cents a pound, sugar was 7 cents a pound, and both molasses and whiskey sold for 25 cents a gallon.[48]

Emil's health was also becoming a more frequent theme of complaint in his correspondence: "In the past year I had the fever for seven months. It hit me very hard. At the beginning of this month [April 1841] it recurred twice, but I broke it easily with a homeopathic powder. For six months now I have used this homeopathic cure with much success against my old stomach problem."[49]

Health, of course, was always a problem on the frontier, and sickness struck at Hermann and Luise's, too. That most dreaded of immigrant experiences— infant diseases and death—had come to them in spring 1841, when they lost their only child, a two-week-old daughter, probably to jaundice. (In the correspondence the illness was described as "the brown one.") Despite that sorrow, Emil observed, Hermann and Luise were happy, for their marriage was based on "unusual mutual love."[50]

Neither in Louisiana, nor in St. Louis, nor elsewhere in Missouri could the family know that their "time of troubles" was not over. Although they had had their bruising encounters with frontier law and cyclical economics, soon Nature itself would turn against them. Its unexpected vengeance would take both income and human life.

20

1844: Flood, Disease, Death

Sixty miles west of growing St. Louis, whose population had reached nearly forty thousand by the mid-1840s, the Mallinckrodts at new Dortmund enjoyed the quieter life they had chosen to lead. As farmers, however, they had their problems, too. Depression and low prices had hit them hard in the early 1840s, and Julius's plans for new Dortmund had lagged. After the mid-1840s his sale of lots recorded at the county seat decreased significantly.[1]

At the same time that they worried about customary crop prices, Julius and his fellow settlers in Duden country had discovered that the wine industry could nevertheless be profitable. Systematic trials were underway to see which grapes were best suited to the soil.[2] If settlers could adapt this traditional German undertaking to Missouri, it could become a profitable new business.

Missouri's population had jumped from 350,000 in 1840 to 500,000 by the end of 1844. In the winter of 1843 alone, a thousand Germans arrived in St. Louis. Although many craftsmen remained in the Mississippi River city, others pushed farther west, toward the Kansas border. More and more pioneers also were heading through Missouri to take either the Oregon Trail to the Columbia River on the West Coast or the Santa Fe Trail to the Pacific Ocean. The expansion in the past two decades had been striking (figure 11-1). By 1840 America's settled areas had pushed about a thousand miles inland from Washington, D.C., to the territories west of Missouri. In fact, the new settlers and settlements were increasing so rapidly that another "Mount Pleasant" had been founded in Missouri. To avoid confusion, especially for the postal service, the General Assembly of the State of Missouri resolved on February 22, 1843, that "Mount Pleasant, in the county of St. Charles, shall hereafter be called Augusta." Why the name Augusta was substituted is not clear.[3]

Institutions on the frontier were evolving, too. By 1840, for instance, Missouri had six colleges with a total of nearly five hundred students enrolled. And although the University of Missouri struggled with restricted funding, it would nevertheless graduate its first two students by 1843.[4] There was a crucial shortage of high schools, but more public grade schools had been established—642 elementary schools by 1840, with a total of 16,788 students.[5]

Churches

More churches were also appearing. By 1840 the Femme Osage congregation, with the Reverend Garlichs conducting services, had laid the cornerstone of a new church.[6] Garlichs also served five additional preaching stations in the area (New Melle, Schluersburg, Warrenton, Washington, and Holstein) and held services every other Sunday afternoon in a private home in Augusta from 1843 to 1845.[7]

In addition, Garlichs was a delegate to the meeting held on 15 October 1840 near St. Louis that led to the founding of the German Evangelical Synod of North America, the Kirchenverein.[8] By 1841 an annual conference of the Association of German Evangelical Churches of the West was held at his church at Femme Osage; although the association had only eight pastors, the number of churches they served was many more.[9] Catholic churches, too, were being founded throughout Duden country, with one of the first established at Dutzow in 1837.[10]

Two organizational events within the German Evangelical community triggered a second round of religious controversy on the Missouri frontier. In the *Anzeiger des Westens* of December 1841, Friedrich Münch, speaking for many concerned citizens, publicly explained the opposition to a synod. As the historian Gerd Petermann later summarized, Münch felt that the religious and political consequences of forming of a synod in the West

> threatened the spiritual freedom and independence of that region, so far spared from any "priestly assumptions." . . . To state that the entire Bible were the word of God is, in Münch's eyes, sheer madness. How could one confuse the most imperfect beginnings of religious ideas (in which the Mosaic God is concerned about the mode of the weaving of a robe or the clipping of a beard) with the most perfect state of development (in which Christ taught to revere God in spirit and truth)![11]

Münch had other problems that found their way into the press in 1842. When Garlichs indirectly accused Münch of trying to take over his congregation, Münch replied in the *Anzeiger*, rejecting the accusation and reminding Garlichs and others that so far he had earned his living with his own hands and would continue to do so.[12]

Julius Mallinckrodt, too, was very upset by religious developments in the area. He is credited with a spirited letter that appeared in the *Anzeiger* on 21 January 1843 under the byline "Observer on the Femme Osage."[13] Criticizing ministers at work in the area and citing a specific case of alleged immorality among them, Julius fervently concluded:

> I would like to ask you, Mr. Editor, how long Germans in the West should tolerate the depraved pietistic rabble trimmed at German mission factories and Eastern synodal schools who, in the garb of piety, sneak in as religion teachers and like blowflies carry the worms of depravity and lewdness into the intimacy of families?— how long the Germans want to trust the instruction of their children to miserable hypocrites capable of poisoning the core of their charges' virtue; and whether it is not finally time, as previously suggested by Friedrich Münch, for the friends of enlightenment and reason to come together to form a strong dam against the machinations of obscurantists [*Finsterlinge*] and hypocrites who degrade religion to a farce and to a procurer for their animal desires and infamous acts?[14]

Troubled by the alliance between church and state in Germany, which many immigrants vividly remembered, others, too, began to write. In 1843 Eduard Mühl, editor of the twice-monthly publication *Licht-Freund*, moved it from Cincinnati to Hermann, Missouri, where it became a major voice of the rationalist religious cause. (It took its name from the movement Lichtfreunde, or Friends of Light, in Germany.) In the first Missouri issue (August 1843), Mühl proposed founding a "Friends of Light" association, which Julius had mentioned in his letter. Münch, whose idea it had been and who later became coeditor of the Hermann publication, endorsed the association, as did Follenius.[15]

In April 1844 thirty-eight charter members of the Friends of Religious Enlightenment gathered in Augusta to found the *Verein vernunft-gläubiger Christen* (Association of Rational Christians). Friedrich Münch was elected chairman and Julius Mallinckrodt secretary. As directors, Arnold Krekel was named for St. Charles County, Dr. Ruge for Franklin County, and Friedrich Münch for Warren County. The association's program, which was presented to the public in Mühl's *Licht-Freund* three weeks later, reflected fear not only of synodal encroachment but also of the wave of revivalism sweeping the area after the economic crisis of the 1830s and 1840s. The association warned against "irrationality," "superstition," and things "specifically miraculous."[16]

Mallinckrodts and Schools

The school system, meanwhile, had been improving, if only slightly. It was probably during this period, in fact, that Conrad Mallinckrodt, having charted a new course after his divorce, began to tutor students. It is known, for example, from local historians' interview with Conrad when he was an old man that he had tutored Arnold Krekel, who went on to a distinguished legal career. Conrad must have done that teaching in the early 1840s since Krekel was already a justice of the peace by 1842 (he took the testimony of Anne Catherina Struckhoff in Julius's defense against William Koch's slander charges) and began his law practice by 1844.[17]

In all likelihood it was also during this time that Conrad Mallinckrodt began his work as a Missouri teacher. After their interview with him, the historians wrote that Conrad "taught the first public school ever opened in St. Charles County. The school was in Augusta."[18] Astonishingly, however, no official records are available to supply exact dates.

The available evidence, however, suggests that Conrad's reported teaching in Mount Pleasant began in the early 1840s. First, in late 1842 Emil wrote home that "Conrad is teaching the children of the community their ABCs."[19] Second, by that time more elementary schools needed teachers. Third, it is reported that "as early as 1843 there was a number of good public schools in St. Charles county";[20] thus, if Augusta's was the first, as noted above, then it probably had been founded in 1841 or 1842. Finally, in 1841 the founder of Mount Pleasant, Leonard Harold, had transferred to the County Board of Trustees for Schools a block of his settlement to be used as a site for a school.[21]

Julius Mallinckrodt was also involved in school efforts, apparently outside of the settlement. As was written at his death, Julius "involved all his energy and strength at the time [1839–1840] the federal government gave the state an area of forest for the purpose of establishing a first school."[22] The reference seems to be to a school in the New Hope district west of Augusta, only several miles through the woods from Julius's property.

Perhaps the former student Arnold Krekel and the teacher Conrad consulted each other about positions in the field of public education, for Arnold was on the board of directors of the forty-pupil school in St. Charles, the county seat.[23] At that time, elected County Commissioners for Education chose the teachers, who were required to have either state or county certification. The state certificate, valid throughout Missouri, was granted to applicants who passed a personal written examination in the common fields of education plus the natural sciences and higher mathematics. The county certificate, requiring less knowledge and valid only in the county, included various pay levels based on the teacher's qualifications.[24]

Conrad Becomes a Surveyor

At the same time, Conrad apparently was busy learning new skills he found interesting and suitable to the rapidly growing frontier—land surveying and notary public work. Preparation for the latter position was relatively easy: study, an examination, certification by the county, and then purchase of the long-handled seal that impressed one's name and title on legal documents.[25]

The land-surveying skills, of course, were more difficult to master, and it is not known how Conrad obtained them. It is possible that he had studied technical drawing and land surveying while he was a student in Dortmund and adapted that basic knowledge in Missouri to the given system of measurements. In any case, the leather-bound notebook in which he recorded his surveying notes shows county township surveys for 1847, and the 1850 U.S. Census (unlike the 1840 census) records Conrad's profession as "surveyor";[26] thus, he apparently began his study in the early 1840s. In a letter to Conrad, mother Dorothea commented on her son's serious illness (in 1844), apologized for not having written sooner because she had an impaired hand, and then said, "That you became notary and surveyor made me happy. I think this is your field." This remark suggests that Conrad's new vocation and his illness had been earlier reported to his mother as somewhat concurrent events.[27]

A second clue to Conrad's preparation for and beginning work as a surveyor in the early 1840s may again be found in his relationship to Arnold Krekel. Krekel had studied surveying and was county surveyor before he began his law practice in 1844;[28] in the early 1840s, therefore, he might have learned surveying from Conrad as part of the tutoring mentioned above. By contrast, if Krekel had already learned the surveying before becoming Conrad's student, perhaps he interested his teacher in taking up surveying as an additional vocation.

Aside from who motivated whom to study surveying, Julius and Conrad were proud of Arnold Krekel, the local boy who had made good with Conrad's help. They knew Arnold would go far in whatever he undertook. Beyond the practice of law, he might, for instance, become involved in politics or the newspaper business, which interested him very much. As with so many other immigrants, Krekel's positions reflected his background. Historians would say that although Arnold Krekel's father was a devout Catholic, the son was known for liberal, rationalist religious views as well as liberal Democratic political positions common to Duden country Germans.[29] However, in his autobiographical essay (written in 1874), Krekel reports that his father came from a Huguenot (that is, Protestant) family, that as a boy he himself went to a Protestant school from about the age of ten to fifteen, and that he married a young woman raised without family religion and little formal education except from Protestant pastors.[30]

By the 1840s Julius and Conrad Mallinckrodt's circle of friends and acquaintances in Duden country included other examples of German immigrants who had felt it essential to master Anglo-Saxon law and had done so successfully enough to be certified as lawyers. For example, Christian Kribben, after spending some years working in his father's grocery store in St. Charles, had studied law with Thomas W. Cunningham.[31] Kribben then was his co-defense attorney on

Julius's behalf in Koch's prosecution of slander charges.[32] Indeed, it was Kribben and Julius who witnessed the St. Charles's court's granting of Conrad's citizenship on 30 March 1842, just as Arnold Krekel would be a witness at the citizenship proceedings for August Mallinckrodt on 7 May 1844.[33]

The career of still another Missouri lawyer interested Conrad and Julius, but not because he was either a German or a friend. Indeed, Edward Bates was their antagonist, prosecutor of Sophie's slander charges against Julius. His cases, however, were often political, and some signaled the explosion over slavery that was sure to come to Missouri. In 1842, for instance, in a celebrated Missouri case, Bates had secured a slave girl's freedom in a case concerning whether or not a verbal promise of manumission, or freedom, was binding.[34] That case, along with many others being talked about, showed that slaves' rights were gaining ground, although the process was very difficult. In 1844 Massachusetts Congressman John Quincy Adams even won repeal of the U.S. House of Representatives' so-called gag rule against the people's antislavery petitions, which he had fought so long.[35]

Mississippi and Missouri River Floods

Just as the U.S. economic climate had begun to improve, Missouri was dealt another and very different setback. Nature turned against the settlers with a stunning vengeance as the great flood of 1844 roared down both the Mississippi and Missouri Rivers. Some frontier ministers, who had long warned about the speculative greed of the time, now intoned, "God punishes those who reach too far for wealth."

The catastrophic chain of weather events actually began in the winter of 1842–1843—a terribly long and cold winter in which "from the beginning of November until the third of April the earth was continually like a lump of ice," Emil wrote. Snow in the Rocky Mountains lay twenty-four feet deep. When it melted in spring 1843, almost all streams were flooded, including the Mississippi. Most of the lowlands of the West, including five acres of Emil's land at St. Louis, were partly underwater for as long as two months.[36] There was also illness. As Emil reported,

> Fever laid low half the population. It was greatest among the children. Our dear Minna became ill in May, and her condition increasingly became worse until mid-September, when she passed a crisis for the better. The poor little thing screamed uninterruptedly for four months and hardly had any rest or sleep. In August I took Ellen farther into the country, into a hilly area away from the river, where they improved very much.[37]

Although the winter of 1843–1844 was mild with little snow, there was "endless, cloudburst-like rain."[38] By mid-June 1844, then, the highest flood in a hundred years rolled over the Mississippi and Missouri River valleys.[39] Land along some five thousand miles was under incredible water levels. Many people lost their lives, millions of domestic animals died, and more than twenty thousand houses were carried away. And again Missourians feared that a hot, dry summer would also bring death and disease in the wake of the floods.[40]

Even settlers who had endured much hardship were unprepared for the fury of a Mississippi/Missouri River flood. Although there were tales of a big flood in the mid-1700s, no living Missourian had seen it, and none could warn settlers about the ugly side of life along the rivers.

Over the years, of course, the settlers had learned quite a lot about their famous river, especially from the stories of steamboat captains. The settlers knew, for instance, that there were violent descents in the upper reaches of the Missouri, including a ninety-foot drop at Great Falls in Montana. They also knew that farther downstream the river first picked up the black clay soil known as gumbo and the rich, powdery, light-yellow soil called loess, which dissolved in the river as sediment; next it collected from the Yellowstone tributary the silt which gave the river its Indian name, the Big Muddy. And, of course, they knew well that in the Midwest, from Sioux City, Iowa, to St. Charles, the river flowed between sandy banks and over a sandy bed. That bed, the captains had said often enough, was freakishly unstable.[41]

Over time the settlers along the Missouri had also come to know about high water. In spring it was caused by snow and ice melt coming from the west; at other times it was caused by heavy rains in the plains or farther downstream. But what they had never experienced, or even imagined, was the coming together of those two flood crests. Yet that is what happened in 1844, producing the highest flood on record.[42]

The flood was especially astonishing to the settlers, for the streams had been the pioneers' friend, carrying them to the untouched wealth and space of the Midwest and then serving as channels of contact to both East and West. Now the waters turned on the valley people as if to drive them back to wherever it was they had come from. Their awe before nature's enormous strength was well expressed by a German settler of the time:

> The Missouri afforded a frightful and at the same time imposing aspect, when it had attained the highest stage. Multitudes of people gazed at it with awe for hours, witnessing the uninterrupted and incessant changes and alterations on the surface of the stream.
>
> As far as the eye could reach nothing could be seen but tree tops and water. Far away among the tree trunks the water was glistening in the sunlight. The gaps among the trees indicated that the fields had been submerged. A roof or a chimney projecting out of the water showed where the homes had been.
>
> The stream proper presented the most manifold entertainment. Even at some distance there could be heard the splashing and roaring of the mighty river. Large

flakes of thick, dirty foam, embracing an area of acres, rolled down the stream. Bursting bubbles dispersed these large fields of scum into many small ones. Dense masses of driftwood were seen amid the foam. Fence rails, cord wood, furniture and occasionally whole log houses drifted by. The large giants of the forest glided down stream easily as if they had been matches. Drowned livestock floated by, and occasionally a live animal was seen struggling with the waves.

The settlers in the bottoms had not been surprised by the overflow. The people had been informed of the unusual amount of snow in the mountains by the fur-trading firms in St. Louis . . . also by the remotest military posts and finally by the little steamers which ran toward the source of the river. . . . The old experienced settlers in the bottoms removed their families, their stock and a good deal of their personal property to the hills. The inexperienced and the negligent succeeded in saving their lives but lost nearly all of their property.[43]

Looking down from the Mallinckrodts' hills onto their valleys and beyond, Julius was dazed. The river at his feet was no longer a mere mile wide, stretching to the bottomland against the far-off southern bluffs. There now was no bottom. The river seethed from bluff to bluff, three miles wide.

The stream, whose sounds started and ended his days, no longer murmured and sang as it carried produce and brought customers, its treacherous currents deeply hidden. The river now roared and foamed, ferocious anger riding its surface waves. It not only charged forward downstream but struck sideways, too, lashing against its confining limestone bluffs—pushing, slapping, drawing back, each time heaving forward again a few inches higher than before.

When the water had finally gathered enough height and force, it swept past the bluffs to reach into the ravines between them. In the lowland west of Conrad's central hill, the waters found new space in one of the Mallinckrodts' valleys. To the east of Julius and Mary's house, the muddy water poured into another valley, onto Julius's new Dortmund dream (figure 20-1), helplessly asleep in the Missouri spring.

Day after day the waters came. Upstream at the German settlement of Hermann, as well as downstream at St. Charles, the river stood nearly fifteen feet above flood stage.[44] At St. Louis, the swollen Missouri flowed into the equally bloated Mississippi, pushing the water level up to thirty-nine feet, or nine feet above flood stage.[45] Once again the rivers roared when they met, as they had when La Salle first saw them. In the city itself, the three lower streets were under water, and in First Street the flood reached the second story of the houses.[46]

Finally the water began to fall, then withdraw, almost discreetly, to its former channels. But it would be a while before anyone knew if the channels were really the same. When boats traveled up and down again, captains would learn what this mysterious river of water, silt, and sediment had wrought: even under normal conditions it was not unusual for the Missouri to change its position between banks within a day. For now, though, Julius could look across to the river bottoms

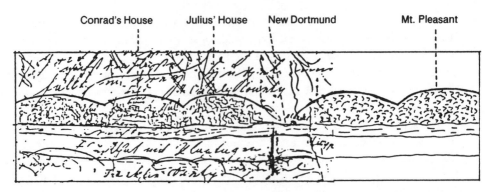

Figure 20-1. An adaptation of figure 12-2 showing Julius Mallinckrodt's "new Dortmund" property, on low land between hills, which was flooded in 1844 when the Missouri River surged high and wide over its customary banks. (*Courtesy Cologne Historical Archive.*)

on the other side and see the sandbars and new piles of sediment drifted up on the fields.[47]

As the waters withdrew, the stench of rotting vegetation floated up the bluff to Conrad, Julius, Mary, and the children. Their mood was as sad as the incessant song of the river frogs. Had the Missouri told them it would never allow another settlement to be built in the lowlands along its northern banks? By showing that it could reach and overflow new Dortmund, had the river killed Julius's dream? Or had it only tried to remind people that despite all their pride in taming nature, they had not and could not? The Missouri would return. People had short lives and limited powers; the river, though, was twenty-five thousand years old and mighty. It would become even older.[48]

Illness and Death

If the flood had given a warning "message" about human life, it again became cruelly real very soon. Despite relatively low summer temperatures, serious fevers raged through the river valleys, although they did not develop into epidemics. Many people were very ill; some died.

On the Mississippi at St. Louis, Eleanor Mallinckrodt was ill for two months with bilious fever, but Emil and the children remained well.[49] Hermann and his family also suffered much from fever, but the illness spared their children: two-year-old James Ferdinand (named after Hermann's brother, who had died at the age of twelve) and baby Cecilia, born in December 1844.[50] As Emil wrote, "Eight months of the year western America is the healthiest land on earth—but oh, from July until the end of October! St. Louis has 120 doctors who have eight-month vacations but then there are hardly enough for forty thousand people."[51]

On the Missouri at new Dortmund, even more deadly fevers raged. August

Mallinckrodt, and the Wenckers with whom he still lived, "suffered much illness."[52] Conrad, too, "lay deathly ill." But the real tragedy occurred at Julius's: Mary died while Julius, too, was ill, leaving him with seven sick children, including an infant. In Emil's report to Gustav, he wrote, "Julius lost his main support, his so precious wife. He himself was deathly ill, as were almost all his children when neighbors buried the mother. . . . Had [Conrad] but died instead of the dear mother."[53]

As was routine on the frontier, during their illness the Mallinckrodts were no doubt tended by those neighbors who remained well, friends who quietly nursed them all, applying cold cloths to soothe fever and spooning quinine into burning throats. And when Mary died, no one used the phrase of the next century, "How terrible when they die so young." So very many did. On the frontier, wonder was reserved instead for those fortunate enough to grow old.

Quietly, then, the women prepared the body of thirty-five-year-old Mary Mallinckrodt for burial and continued to look after her widowed husband and motherless children. There were no undertakers in those days, and the dead were usually buried within twenty-four hours. Since Julius was not able, his neighbors made a simple casket and dug a grave on the family cemetery behind the house where Conrad lived. If the body remained in the house overnight, it is likely that the same neighbors kept watch over it.

Although Julius could not leave his bed to be present at the burial, everyone knew the routine. Two pieces of wood were laid crosswise at the bottom of the grave, so the casket would not rest directly on the soil. After the casket was lowered, boards were laid on top of it, and noiselessly covered over with earth, as well as the grave filled. A mound was thrown up over the grave, with two small, upright boards marking its ends.[54]

So it was that Mary was buried, facing the east as was custom. Later a simple stone marker, inscribed with German words, was erected at the head of the casket:

HIER RUHT

MARIA ELLEONORE

MALLINCKRODT

Geborene McClenny

GEB.

1. April 1809

GES.

22. September 1844

The weathered gravestone still stands behind the remains of Conrad's house, shaded by overgrown trees. A small square of Missouri earth containing Mary's tombstone is protected by a fence (plate 10).

No diaries report what Julius and Conrad thought, did, or said when they regained their health. It is almost certain, however, that as soon as they were strong enough to walk, they went together to Mary's grave and may have covered it with the customary evergreen boughs. As people do at gravesides, they probably spoke of others whom they had lost. Julius may have recalled, with new understanding, the pain his father recorded in his testament when he described the death of his young wife.

Whether they said it aloud or not, Julius and Conrad Mallinckrodt must have felt deeply their aloneness at new Dortmund. As Mother had warned Conrad, they did not now have the larger family to support them in times of trouble. When Conrad first visited Missouri, they were three—he, Julius, and Mary. For a short time then they were four, with Sophie. Then again they were three, all of whom in the last months had gone to the edge of death. When Mary crossed over, that left them as a family of just two brothers and Julius's seven children— Mathilde, 11; Caroline Dorothea, 10; Conrad Theodore, 8; Emilie, 7; Herman Adolph, 5; Luise 4; and Lydia Anna, 9 months. To care for the children, Julius obviously would have to ask one of the neighbor women for help.

Another thought surely hung in the air between Julius and Conrad as they stood at Mary's grave. They were brothers, more than ever. Father had taught them what that meant in the years when Uncle Arnold was repeatedly in political difficulties; Mother had reminded them a thousand times of their responsibilities to each other after Father was gone. Now when Conrad looked up at his older brother, he knew it was his turn. As Julius had been there to help Conrad over the past years of divorce and humiliation, so Conrad now would stand by Julius until he found his way. They were "the brothers Mallinckrodt," as historians would repeatedly later describe them.

Gradually the land ceased to reek of the flood's decay. The river sang again. It was winter 1844, and it was mild. The quiet in Julius's house was still deep, but occasionally there was laughter from the children. And then spring would come, always a time of rebirth in Missouri, when the new green would spread slowly and featherlike across hills and valleys and riverbanks.

21

1845: Boom Times for the Nation and Cities

The air on the Missouri frontier in the late 1840s was filled with full-throated hurrahs for expansion. In the Northwest, the United States, despite Britain's counterdemands, claimed the Oregon Territory and encouraged American immigration to it. In the Southwest, moves to annex Texas clashed with abolitionist fears that several more slave states would be carved out of the territory and that Mexico would declare war to keep Texas under its control. In the presidential election of 1844, the Democratic party ran its winning candidate, James K. Polk, on an expansionist platform, claiming both Oregon and Texas for the United States.

Reflecting the "Oregon fever" of the time, Emil Mallinckrodt in early 1844 wrote his brother Eduard in Dortmund, "Many Americans are now wandering to the Columbia River on the west coast of America on the Pacific Ocean. From here [St. Louis] it is a distance of four thousand miles through a continuous wilderness."[1] Viewing the territorial disputes, Emil was full of confidence—and an immigrant's nationalism:

> Texas is as good as incorporated, and England has to give in about Oregon, if not peacefully then surely through war. North America will and may risk a war, even against England; there could be no doubt about the final success. For the third time America would end up victorious, more so than ever, and England's power must fall before the young but inexhaustible giant of the new world. England should think it over well before it enters the lists against us. . . . In this century North America will yet achieve world rule, hopefully for the happiness of all people on earth since they can only expect something better from our institutions.[2]

Mexican War

That belief in America's obligation to spread over the entire continent would be called the doctrine of "manifest destiny." It was behind Congress's resolution to annex Texas, which resulted in Mexico's angry termination of diplomatic relations with the United States, and General Zachary Taylor's alert to U.S. military forces in the Southwest. His subsequent reports of "skirmishes" led to the American declaration of war against Mexico in May 1846.

For two years "the dirty little war" would rage, prompting later historians to call it the "rape of Mexico." Essentially splitting Mexico in half, the United States devoured the territory that would make up the later states of California, Arizona, New Mexico, Utah, Nevada, and parts of Colorado and Wyoming.[3]

Nowhere, wrote the historians in the 1800s, "did the fires of patriotism burn more intensely than in Missouri."[4] Although the white population of Missouri accounted for only 1/45th of that of the whole country, the state furnished 1/11th of the nation's volunteers to the Mexican War.[5] German settlers were no exception. In fact, as one wrote about a younger friend who had volunteered, "He has the honor and good fortune to be a free citizen of the free United States, and has the added and greater honor to be permitted to defend his adopted fatherland. . . . I regard this war absolutely just on our part."[6]

About ninety volunteers from St. Charles County were organized to fight against Mexico. After drilling in the county seat, they "were presented with a handsome silk flag made by the ladies of St. Charles . . . and the brave-hearted volunteers then marched off to the war, buoyant with hope, nobly enthusiastic for the cause of their country, and ambitious to distinguish themselves on the field of action." However, on reaching Fort Leavenworth, Kansas, they did not go on to Mexico as they hoped but were first detailed to prevent the Sioux from going on the warpath. Next they were sent to Nebraska to help build Fort Kearney. By the time that assignment was completed, peace had been declared, and the St. Charles County men returned to Missouri without ever having seen Mexico.[7]

While the Texas question was being resolved through military actions, Emil gave thought to Oregon and California, which would, in his words, "be our next inheritance." He described for his brother in Germany the emigration then underway from St. Louis westward over the Santa Fe Trail. California, he wrote,

is the most beautiful land in North America. Winter and summer are the same, for eternal spring prevails with the healthiest climate on earth. This year ten thousand people emigrated there from other states. They travel three thousand English miles west of here over land and mountains through uninterrupted wilderness, in wagons drawn by oxen or mules. The trip usually takes five months. The emigrants go in caravans to protect themselves from continual attack from Indians. They drive along herds of cattle by which they are nourished.

A colony of Germans already exists in California. They made a wonderful settlement on the Sacramento River in 1837. Captain Sutter, from Switzerland, chief owner, is a friendly acquaintance of mine. He has recently sent us an invitation to settle there. Oranges, olives, grapes, and all northern fruits bloom and bear there almost constantly, and the government gives every settler a German square mile of land.[8]

Emil was excited by the emigration, for he believed that "a person should not remain stuck on that soil where his mother coincidentaly bore him. . . . The person who never leaves his own walls remains a commonplace fellow as long as he lives." In fact, Emil thought that his "children will probably go there [California], as I first followed the Mississippi."[9]

With Texas annexed, 1845 was clearly a very good year in America. The Oregon and Minnesota Territories were also established, and those in Utah, New Mexico, and Washington would soon be proclaimed. In addition, Wisconsin and California were admitted into the Union.

For Emil personally, times were also good. For instance, 1845 started off with the birth, on 21 January, of Emil and Eleanor's second son, Eduard.[10] To the uncle for whom he was named, the baby was described as "another real Mallinckrodt with a hawk's nose."[11] Already Emil was thinking about going to Germany for some years so the children could have better schools—in five years, he thought, when his financial plans had ripened.[12]

North St. Louis Booms

In his business life, Emil was very pleased with "Bremen," the new settlement on St. Louis's north side that he and his neighbors had formed and incorporated. They had eight hundred sales contracts printed for the business they anticipated, especially following favorable publicity in a St. Louis newspaper.[13] The inauguration of a horse-drawn bus line past the property, with buses traveling every twenty minutes, made it an unusually attractive location. The prospects of big real estate profits were good. Emil seemed equally pleased, however, by his tremendous fruit harvest, including peaches weighing a half-pound each![14]

In October 1845 Emil sent cousin Gustav a draft for $23,000,[15] perhaps to repay the emergency money he had had to borrow several years earlier. To cover that loan, Emil apparently had offered the Köln Mallinckrodts a mortgage on his property. On 25 September 1847 Gustav and his wife, having received the $23,000, signed a deed in Köln giving Emil sole ownership of thirty-nine arpents (an old French land measure equaling 0.84 acres) on Bellefontaine Road—land they had "held as tenants in common with said Emil Mallinckrodt and which was acquired of him by the deed recorded . . . 21 April 1841."[16] At the end of 1848 Emil would then report to his brother,

> The mortage on my property is paid off—$17,000 with interest. Now I have to pay Cousin Gustav $30,000. I already have half of this, and before I come to you [on a visit to Germany], I must pay off the rest, which I can easily do. Then I shall have enough of my own fortune to give my children a splendid education, which is the best capital and which must secure them against any changes in life.[17]

In all likelihood, Emil was able to pay off his debt to Gustav thanks to the land boom in north St. Louis. Around six hundred new buildings were erected there in 1844. In addition to the bus line, another attraction of north St. Louis was that the main road, running through Emil's property, had been macadamized by fall 1846. Not surprisingly, Emil sold fifteen building lots that year. The profit must have been considerable, for lot prices had gone up 50–100 percent in the past several years.[18]

The starch factory on Emil's property was going well, and a porcelain firm with fifteen workers had located there, too. In addition, the property featured a sawmill, two cabinet makers, two carpenters, a shoemaker, a blacksmith, a wagonmaker, a saddler, and a butcher. Later a meat and vegetable market was built across from Emil's house.[19] Ellen had won the prize at the St. Louis Garden Club for her red and white wine, and Emil won a prize for "the best fifteen varieties of pears from the little Dortmund trees."[20]

In fact, all Emil's enterprises did so well that he and Eleanor could afford to add a second story to their house. "Now we live healthily," he said, "and enjoy a charming view on the river town and surrounding countryside. Really there are few locations as good as mine, and the best thing of all is the success that is bound up with this property. My finest expectations are long surpassed."[21] (Of course, Emil could not yet know that the property's real "success" would be as the future site of a big chemical plant.)

Everyday life was indeed pleasant for the Emil Mallinckrodts:

> Our dwelling surrounded by six hundred fruit trees is a little paradise. We also have bath water on the second floor through a force pump. After using, one pulls a cork out of the bottom of the bathtub, whereupon the water runs out to the outside through another lead pipe. We would live here in the greatest comfort if we could only get servants. Although I pay eight dollars a month for a kitchen maid, I can hardly obtain one. Everyone works for himself. Only slaves hire out and are expensive and good ones hard to get. So Ellen must overwork terribly to get through with the housework, for the children cause much work and trouble.[22]

He continued his description in a later letter: "We live with the greatest convenience. We have a well with the finest water before our kitchen door, also a cistern for rainwater, with a pump on it that pumps the water to the second floor. I also have a horse and carriage and can go driving with my family whenever I wish."[23] Having enumerated his comforts in a city where the gracious "Southern way of life" prevailed,[24] Emil added, "How could I mention all these good things that we enjoy without constantly thinking of my noble friend, Cousin Gustav, whom I have to thank for everything. He has dealt with me like a good father toward his own son. And what a pleasure and satisfaction it is, that I have the means to express my gratitude."[25]

Along with the land boom in north St. Louis, which had brought such personal gain, Emil was also pleased with the city's general development. "St. Louis has nearly 60,000 inhabitants," he wrote in mid-1847, "and when I came in 1832 it barely had 5,000."[26] Symbolic of its material growth were the 42 million bricks used in St. Louis from January to November 1845 and the gas lamps installed to light the streets.[27]

Then, too, there was the boat-building industry, which Emil estimated to be worth half a million dollars. By 1844, he wrote, the city owned a hundred boats, and in the first five months of 1845 another seven were built. One was the *Missouri*, which Emil described as "the biggest freshwater boat that ever existed on earth. I have forgotten the dimensions, but surely by contrast Noah's Ark was a skiff."[28]

Indeed, St. Louis was a booming river city in the mid-1840s. The upper Mississippi was the chief feeder into the St. Louis market, and the lower river was the outlet for its trade. Quite simply, the Mississippi River system had no competitor as a means of travel and transportation between the vast interior and the Gulf of Mexico. Thus, St. Louis remained closely linked to New Orleans; as a later observer wrote, "The two river cities had to stand or fall together."[29]

The romance and greatness not only of the Mississippi but also of the Missouri were widely known to Americans in the mid-1840s through the paintings of George Caleb Bingham, "the Missouri artist." His *Fur Traders Descending the Missouri*, *Boatmen on the Missouri*, *The Jolly Flatboatmen*, and other oils depicted the sturdy flatboats and honorable raftsmen gradually being replaced by steamboats.[30]

Railroad Fever

Although the decade of the 1850s would be the "golden age of steamboating in the river history of St. Louis,"[31] by the late 1840s Emil Mallinckrodt and other farsighted St. Louisans were already excited by visions of a future including railroads. In ten more years, Emil thought, "St. Louis would be connected with the big railroad from Baltimore," for by 1845 the line was already finished to Wheeling on the Ohio, under construction from Cincinnati, and planned for St. Louis.[32]

At the same time, however, that the eastern railroads were expanding, Missouri itself had funded none of the eighteen railroad corporations it had chartered within the state as early as 1836–1837. The state's major city, St. Louis, showed no symptoms of "railroad fever" but instead left its money tied up in steamboats. A conservative business center, the city considered the new railways secondary in importance to existing waterways. In fact, it was later said that "while St. Louis worshipped the rivers, Chicago used the iron horse to draw the trade from the valleys."[33]

Indeed, with the coming of railroads, St. Louis would face some significant competitive disadvantages. For example, whereas both Chicago and New York had built elevators and warehouses right next to their waterfronts, St. Louis had not. Thus, in St. Louis, storage meant that "grain had to be handled six times and hauled in drays twice to receive warehousing before being forwarded. . . . The total expense of handling grain at St. Louis, including charges for dockage, tarpaulin hire, drayage, and storage, was estimated to be from six to eight cents a bushel. Losses from exposure to the weather and rough handling also added [to the costs]."[34] Geography, too, made Chicago a formidable rival for St. Louis. Located on Lake Michigan, Chicago was a major port of the Great Lakes and so a center for northwest trade. Moreover, the Erie Canal, completed in 1825, connected Chicago to the East.

At stake, then, in the competition between St. Louis and Chicago was commercial dominance of the Mississippi Valley, constituting about half of the country's total area. The question was whether the growing trade of the great Midwest would go south to New Orleans via St. Louis or east to Atlantic coastal cities via Chicago.[35]

That rivalry had manifested itself clearly in October 1849, when St. Louis hosted the first National Railroad Convention. Now that the westward expansion was underway, both Chicago and St. Louis were bent on obtaining special advantages for construction of a railroad to the Pacific. As Gateway to the West, St. Louis naturally thought it should be the eastern terminus for such a rail line. However, because of the slavery issue, the U.S. government was reluctant to allocate monies that would give an advantage either to the North, represented by Chicago and Illinois, or the South, including St. Louis and Missouri.[36]

Thus, the two states began carrying out their own railroad construction, but with strikingly different results. Chicago continued to expand steadily the first five miles of the Galena and Chicago Union Railroad, completed in 1848, and other lines. Missouri chartered the North Missouri Railroad in 1851, but its exact route northward from St. Louis to the Iowa boundary was not decided for years, and construction was begun only in 1854.

In 1851 Missouri also granted aid to the Hannibal and St. Joseph Railroad, but again construction was not begun until spring 1853.

With huge fanfare and fireworks, St. Louis broke ground for the Pacific Railroad on 4 July 1851. On 1 December 1852 the first locomotive west of the Mississippi River was put on the tracks of the Pacific Railroad at St. Louis, and by mid-1853 some thirty-seven miles of rails had been laid, extending to Pacific, Missouri. Lack of adequate capital, however, meant slow progress: it took fourteen years to build 283 miles. Thus, by the time of the Civil War, Chicago would have 11 railroad lines, 4,915 miles of track, and the reputation of "railroad center of America"; by contrast, Missouri would have 7 lines, with a total of only 796 miles.[37]

Looking forward to more rail transportation and other tools of progress, Emil sometimes seemed almost amused that so much of the St. Louis growth he applauded was stimulated by the German immigrants, who in 1850 accounted for one-third of the city's population:[38] "One hears almost as much Low German on the streets and markets as English. Almost all Germans are, without exception, well off. They own one-third of St. Louis. . . . We live here almost as if in Germany, wholly surrounded by Germans. Missouri is now becoming New Germany for America, and the name of Mallinckrodt will spread from here to the Pacific Ocean, for this the present Mallinckrodts are good witnesses."[39]

Nativism

Throughout history such immigrant groups faced the dual problems of their "fitting in," or feeling comfortable in their new context, and of being accepted by other ethnic groups. In St. Louis the Germans apparently had a generally positive image among the population as a whole; they were seen, for instance, as "one of the most law-abiding groups among the immigrants." However, some people also saw the Germans as clannish and "the most quarrelsome, contentious, and annoying group."[40]

By the 1840s Emil and other Germans were aware of increasingly negative feelings among the public toward the flood of new immigrants arriving in the city. The most serious criticism came from the National American party, which organized itself in St. Louis by 1840 as an opponent of immigrant participation in politics generally and of Roman Catholic immigrants specifically.[41] Germans, of course, were in both camps.

In the 1845 elections these so-called nativists won every city office in St. Louis except mayor, and in 1846 they won that, too. As an obvious jab at the big German community, the city council then passed an ordinance forbidding public transportation after 2:00 P.M. on Sunday, thus restricting the German custom of using Sundays as a day of recreation rather than Puritanical restraint, worship, and meditation.[42]

Moreover, the language used against Germans in the nativists' newspaper, the *St. Louis American*, was vituperative. In 1846 it called them a "moral and political pestilence," and in the next year it demoted them to "offscourings of Europe" and the "most filthy and inferior beings." A later historian summed up the nativist picture of German immigrants:

When the Nativists had finished dissecting the immigrant, there was little good left about him. He was impoverished, worked for less, drove down wages, and lowered the standard of living. He came from the lowest class of society; he was a jailbird. He continued to speak "Dutch" and was clannish. Still worse, however, he sometimes voted illegally; and when he voted, legally or otherwise, he somehow seemed to vote the wrong way, that is, against the "Natives," with surprising regularity. In fact, he was an undemocratic individual, unsuited for absorption into the United States, incapable of understanding American politics, and certainly unfit to hold public office. For, according to Nativist dogma, "An European education, in a great measure, disqualifies a man for the proper discharge of his duties as an American citizen." As likely as not the German was not merely German, but a combination of the twin evils: German *and* Roman Catholic.[43]

Despite all the local turmoil, Emil nevertheless was generally optimistic at the moment. As 1847 ended, he wrote, "No year of life was so favorable," and he felt that his economic "circumstances give brilliant promise within a few years." In addition, Ellen was fairly well, and a third healthy son, Otto, was born in August. In fact, all four children were a joy: Gustav, seven, was going to English-language school; Minna at five was a bright little girl; Eduard, two, was a beautiful child, as alert and merry as a little squirrel; and infant Otto looked just like his brother Eduard. About the rest of the adult Mallinckrodts, Emil reported, he did not hear much, and although he had recently seen Conrad by accident, the cousins had not even spoken.[44]

Although Emil was pleased with national politics, St. Louis economics, and his family life, he nevertheless was very concerned about his own health. In fact, he wondered how he might legalize the bequeathing of his property to Gustav. At that time in Missouri, he wrote Gustav, as a foreigner "you cannot have a deed, cannot even inherit. Therefore, my will and testament in your favor is really not valid according to the law."[45] Emil was troubled by his chronic ill health:

> Although not ill, in truth for the last eight years I have rarely been healthy. I have suffered a thousand deaths because of my completely disturbed digestive system. I am strong and vigorous and *less ill than most of my neighbors, but I swear to you that I do not enjoy a single healthy hour.* . . . If no change occurs *I will not grow old.* I do not enjoy real rest, for sleep also does not bring me refreshment. I have inherited a predisposition to abdominal illness, and the terrible diarrhea that almost cost me my life ten years ago, plus a hot climate, may be causes, for I have always lived correctly.[46]

The digestive system problem, Emil felt, "was probably inherited from Father, who suffered [from it] his entire life."[47] Toward the end of 1847 Emil even doubted he would live much longer and begged his brother to take care of his children should he die. Some time later, however, Emil would begin taking sulphur baths in St. Louis, and that seemed to help him.[48]

Hermann and Luise

Emil was also concerned about cousins Hermann and Luise, upriver from St. Louis at Louisiana. Their plan to farm with Hermann Mallinckrodt of Elberfeld had not worked out, and by mid-1845 the Elberfelders had moved to St. Charles, where Hermann was earning twenty dollars a month as a storekeeper.[49] (By 1852 he was serving on the city council.)[50] Emil thought the property was "a bad choice," and he believed that Hermann "is no farmer although he is active and ambitious to do everything he can";[51] nevertheless, the Dortmunders stayed on their farm a while longer.

But they needed help. In turning to stepbrother Gustav for a $500 loan, Hermann shared many insights about his way of life on the frontier:

> I intend to buy a Negro woman since one apparently never has the possibility of hiring good household help. . . . Furthermore, the wages are so enormously expensive that one hardly can get the money together; five to six years of wages almost pay for a Negro woman. Last year for several months I had hired one who took such advantage of us that I lost all interest in trying that again this year. With my help Luise can do her work when she is well—but that is not the case at the moment—and that, plus the fact that I lose too much time that I should spend on my work, is the reason why I so want some good female help.
>
> For four years now I have been farming, struggling with the most frightening difficulties. I so tested myself that I am able to find my way through even the most crooked situations of life. Naturally I paid a big price for the learning. But I now have the advantage of farming with a profit and can fill certain roles in life determined by my nature but withheld for so long through bad luck.
>
> Since the death of our Delia, my dear Luise gave me our James Ferdinand and last 6 December our Cecilia. The first will be three years on 20 July—he is a stout-hearted boy. . . .
>
> My farm is free of debt and worth $1,000. I would send you the interest promptly every time.[52]

Gustav responded rather quickly, and by December 1845 Hermann traveled to St. Louis to exchange 757.17 Thaler for dollars. The unfavorable exchange rate gave Hermann $500, for which he sent Gustav a promissory note at 6 percent interest. In an accompanying letter, Hermann reported on his slave purchase:

> For four weeks now we have had a young Negro girl, fifteen years old, named Tiller (nickname for Mathilde). I already had her in mind for a long time, and we all have reason to be pleased. Her owner, an old widow who would not consider selling as long as she lived, accommodatingly died just as I received your money. The girl cost $350, a price which five other interested bidders also offered. But the heirs gave me priority because the girl preferred to come to us. She is a well-reared maid, and we are happy she belongs to us. Tiller is almost grown, black as the

night, a full-blooded Negro, industrious, willing, quick, and modest. In addition to the housework, she is able to help me in the fields. That will save me the wages of one hired hand next year. Except for a burn injury on her right foot—which Bartlett, my doctor, assures me does not hinder her—she is very healthy.[53]

By early 1847 Hermann had additional problems and again asked Gustav for money: "Despite my experience, my ability to work, and my ambition, I lack good help, a loyal Negro, and about $900 working capital in order to achieve something in a short time." To back up his request, Hermann offered Gustav a very interesting and detailed explanation of farming possibilities in his area of Missouri:

> Most farmers grow tobacco, hemp, and wheat, and therefore the prices for those products are so low that they guarantee only a moderate wage. Cattle raising, which requires capital, is pursued by few, and not many raise mules, which bring profitable prices. Young mules can be bought at weaning time in autumn for 15 to 20 dollars, and after two to three years of modest feeding they bring 45 to 50 dollars here but 75 dollars in the South. Since mules, despite their toughness, cannot tolerate the hot climate, they are finished in a short time. Cotton and sugar farmers therefore are forced to renew their stock of mules every two years, and that is why they are so sought. Cows and pigs produce a modest but usually a nice profit.
>
> Two years ago I fenced in thirty-five acres of the best bottomland and have ten acres of it in cultivation. With the help of a Negro I could easily clear the rest and count on a harvest of at least 1,200 bushels of corn. I have two good prairies nearby so that my cattle would cost nothing from spring to fall.

In closing, Hermann offered a deed of trust to his farm in return for $1,500 for six years at low interest, as well as the optimistic assessment, "Our situation certainly is different from our previous life, but I and my Louise are happy and content, which is proof to me that I have a 'diamond' of a wife. Ferdinand and Cäcilie [*sic*] bloom like roses, grow up happy, and are naturally talented."[54]

This time, however, Gustav could not help Hermann because he had no liquid capital. "The money market," Gustav wrote, "not only in Germany but in all of Europe is so deplorable that general distress and great distrust prevail, so much so that money is almost not available at any price." Encouraging Hermann to rely only on his own energy and to have no illusions about eventual inheritances, Gustav added the thought, "You are lucky with your Louise and your children— perhaps by far the happiest of your siblings."[55] If Hermann and Luise had hoped to inherit from Luise's grandmother, they surely were disappointed in May 1847: the total inheritance was 320 Thaler.[56]

Germany's 1848 Revolution

Whereas 1847 had been a favorable year for Emil, in several respects 1848 was an especially dramatic one. First, he was able to pay off all his local debts and so "owe not one dollar to anyone in America."[57] Second, the political news from Germany was exciting—the attempted revolution there against the rule of Emperor Friedrich Wilhelm IV. (News was traveling much faster by now; a letter sent via steamship from England reached St. Louis in four to five weeks.)[58] As Emil wrote his brother on 26 April 1848, "While we live here in deepest peace, the European news frightens me, concerning you. . . . We had a great festival on Monday in honor of the French and German revolutions. From New York reportedly a thousand armed Germans have already gone to help the patriots against the reigning princes. Here in St. Louis we collect money and people for the same purpose."[59]

Many other German settlers in Missouri shared Emil's enthusiasm for constitutional government in the old country. One contemporary wrote that, although newspaper reports in St. Louis were uncertain and often contradictory,

> we have heard of the June Revolution in Paris, and were not a little rejoiced to see that the good cause has won, and that the new republic has stood the trial of fire.
>
> In Germany too, blood will flow, but what is that compared with the freedom of the whole people. I am sure that you would share my point of view, if you had been a citizen of our fortunate free America for thirteen years, as I now have.[60]

Emil, too, was concerned, writing his brother, "Since I recall all too well how our parents suffered during the war years, I am very worried about you now."[61]

But the attempt to change the government by action at the bottom of society, by the German people, failed to chase the Prussian king from his throne. He sat tight, punishing those who had tried to unseat him. When the political refugees of the failed 1848 Revolution began arriving in the United States, German settlers in St. Louis and elsewhere seemed more impatient than ever with their former homeland. One wrote, "The German people were on the right track, but they allowed themselves to be diverted from it by vain promises. I fear they do not want to become free. We pity them with our whole heart."[62] Almost in the same tone Emil had written Gustav a bit earlier:

> I wonder whether the railroad will kill philistinism in Germany. We are very correctly informed about your current circumstances, much more exactly than the Germans themselves: therefore our newspapers in German are prudently forbidden. [As mentioned above, King Wilhelm IV of Prussia censored publications.] From there an American writes to our government newspaper that "German loyalty is subservience, as is always the case with little children who would justify themselves vis-à-vis a father. But in a nation of adult and educated people such a canine subservience is contemptible."[63]

That harsh description did not, of course, apply to Gustav Mallinckrodt, Köln's progressive liberal. In fact, a biographer of his economic career later would write:

During the revolutionary days of March 1848 we find Gustav Mallinckrodt in the camp of the liberal property owners who sought free political development, constitutional government, and national unification under Prussian leadership, but not any further-reaching democratic republican moves. As with most compatriots of his economic class, he was clearly concerned about revolution, "mob rule and communists." To avoid that, he hoped the government would make necessary concessions quickly. But he was disappointed.[64]

Although the attempted political changes of 1848 failed, Gustav continued his activity among constitutionally oriented liberals in Köln and the surrounding area. But, as the biographer would write, in the years 1848–1849 Gustav's "hopes for the realization of national unity within a constitutional state waned more and more." He felt that the liberal middle class, to which he belonged, had not met the challenges of the attempted revolution. In fact, he criticized it sharply for cowardice and lack of unity.[65]

Those political developments in the old country disappointed Emil, but at the same time family news from Germany pleased him and other Mallinckrodts in Missouri. After their cousin Detmar died in Paderborn in 1842, his extraordinary older daughter, Pauline, incorporated her nursery school and learned Braille to teach several blind children who were enrolled. In 1847 Pauline Mallinckrodt had founded the Institute for the Blind in Paderborn and in the following year was thinking of establishing a new religious order of Catholic sisters to care for blind and poor children.[66] It was to be called the Sisters of Christian Charity. On 21 August 1849 Mother Pauline became its superior.

Gold Rush

Around the same time that Germans, after their failed revolution, were wondering what course their country would take, a new excitement, also involving direction, gripped America: "Go West!" was the trumpeted slogan, for gold had been discovered! It was found precisely on the property of Emil's friend Captain Sutter, who had gone to California and asked Emil to come, too. Arriving in America in 1834, Johann Augustus Sutter had spent that winter in St. Charles, visited the Duden settlement the next year, and then gone to St. Louis. There the German settlers were quite interested "in Sutter's trade ventures to Santa Fe, mounted with borrowed money that he invested in pistols, trinkets, and German student jackets bought in a St. Louis pawn shop for trade with the Indians."[67]

Settling in California, the adventurer, who claimed that he had been an officer in the Swiss Guard, built Sutter's Fort. He was already rich and powerful when his partner in a sawmill venture found gold on the lower Sacramento Valley property on 24 January 1848. The news of the gold find spread like wildfire, and the gold rush that followed brought adventurers from all parts of the United States and such distant countries as China and Australia.[68]

The news had reached Missouri by summer 1848, and parties at once were organized to seek the wealth of the West.[69] During the warm months, Boone's Lick Road from St. Charles across Missouri was crowded with gold seekers whose covered wagons dotted the road. According to historians, a county official at the time

> counted the emigrant wagons going West, and they numbered from the time he came to his office in the morning, about seven o'clock, until he left at six in the evening, 142, an average of one wagon every five minutes during the day. The California emigration was of much benefit to the farmers living on the line of the Boone's Lick road. The gold hunters bought feed for their teams and supplies for themselves from all who had it to sell, and paid good prices too.[70]

Sutter, however, was appalled by the rush. The crowds killed his cattle, swarmed over his land, and left him a ruined man who later returned to the East.[71]

Slavery Question

As always, beneath the surface of expansionism and easy wealth long-existent currents of unrest and change also continued to flow. In the late 1840s these currents included constantly intensifying clashes between supporters of slavery and abolitionists. Reacting fearfully to the growing antislavery movement, the Missouri State Assembly in 1847 once again passed a regressive law: "No person shall keep or teach any school for the instruction of any negroes or mulattoes, in reading or writing in this State." The obvious goal was to prevent blacks from reading the abolition literature of the day. Despite the penalty for disobeying that new law—a $500 fine or up to six months imprisonment—some church people nevertheless went on teaching African-American members.[72]

By 1847 another controversial step was taken: free blacks were explicitly forbidden from entering the slave state of Missouri. As the historian Paul C. Nagel would later write:

> Controversy in Missouri over the Negro deepened as the state's population grew more complex. Missouri had welcomed southerners with their black servants, but had also greeted other groups of new citizens whose views sharply differed from those of slaveowners. These newcomers, mostly from Germany and New England, were outraged not only that Missouri permitted black bondage, but that northern states could accuse Missouri of being a breeding place for slaves to be shipped farther south. However, it was not easy in Missouri to oppose slavery openly.[73]

In 1849 the slavery question "came directly before the people of Missouri," as German historian Gert Goebel wrote.[74] Legislator C. F. Jackson amended an old resolution to read "that it be declared to be the duty of Missouri to join the South in case the southern states should consider it expedient to secede from the northern states." Historically known as the "Jackson Resolution," the proposal was given to Senator Thomas H. Benton to introduce into the legislature. He refused, denouncing it as "a concoction of the slaveholders, and by no means the opinion of the loyal citizens of Missouri."[75] Thus, despite great public debate and outcry, the issue which most frightened the approximately forty-five thousand German settlers in Missouri around 1850—the breakup of the American Union—was suppressed for the moment.[76] Germany might continue fragmented, but America was whole.

The issue, however, would surface again and again. In 1850 many Americans were upset by five new legal measures concerning slavery, together called the Compromise of 1850. The Fugitive Slave Act, one of the five laws, especially outraged antislavery citizens, for under its terms fugitive slave cases were placed exclusively under federal law, "fugitives" claiming to be freemen were denied the right to a jury trial, and their testimony was made inadmissible as court evidence.[77]

Exactly how the Mallinckrodts in Missouri felt about the slavery issue is not known. Although increasing numbers of slaves were being freed in St. Louis,[78] Emil never included that theme in his detailed reports home. Nor did he mention slavery per se when, in summer 1848, he wrote to brother Eduard that he and Ellen "at last [had] excellent help in the house since I bought a good Negro woman for $450. She does all the work well, and Ellen therefore has easy days."[79]

Cholera Epidemic

Despite purchasing a slave, Emil and Eleanor were still not leading a completely joyful life in their north St. Louis home. Before the decade turned, the city once again would endure an especially devastating cholera epidemic. Perhaps recalling Europe's plagues, Emil apprehensively wrote in December 1848 that "we will have the cholera next week, for it has broken out among German immigrants on three steamships on their way here from New Orleans."[80] In mid-1849 Emil reported:

> Never have I experienced such circumstances, for the cholera epidemic has taken thousands of lives, depopulating city and county. One-third of the inhabitants are dead or fleeing from here. Many families died out entirely, and the death rate does not diminish. Care for my dear ones does not allow me to be happy; still, I cannot leave and go . . . where? One encounters the illness everywhere. . . .
>
> Even the markets have been closed since there is a fine of $100 for bringing in fruits, vegetables, fish, pigs, veal, or sausage meat. Last week 960 people died, whereas the deaths previously numbered 90 for this period.[81]

Later he wrote: "We have all been ill. Ellen, Minna, and I had the fever, Gustav and Eduard the cholera, and Otto still suffers with diarrhea. During June and July five thousand people died of the cholera, and suffering and misery were endless."[82]

Another German immigrant in St. Louis at the time reported the 1849 horror in slightly different statistics: "20 to 30 persons die daily" and "yesterday there were 85 funerals, 65 of which were victims of the cholera." He provided more details in late July:

> The greatest number of deaths that occurred during a period of twenty-four hours was 192. I do not think that there are 20 families in St. Louis that did not lose at least one member by this dread disease. In most of the families several deaths occurred. Some families have died out entirely. The road to one of the 10 cemeteries of the city leads past our house. On many days we saw more than 20 funerals go by. During the worst time of the epidemic nothing but funeral processions could be seen on the streets. All business was paralyzed. Many business houses were entirely closed.[83]

This experience frightened Emil so much that he resolved to take the family to Europe in the following spring: "I would be lacking in my holy duty to my children," he wrote, "if I ever again spent a summer here." The plans were to sell house and garden but keep most of the property and give its management over to a lawyer.[84]

Perhaps the fearful illnesses also stimulated spiritual reactions. Emil, for instance, wrote home that cousin Julius Mallinckrodt had been to visit him,[85] perhaps to see how the family had fared during the epidemic. Although the motivation is not known, it is clear that they were speaking again; perhaps they were reconciled. Then, too, Emil had all the children baptized together. It was a "grand" and "very festive" occasion on 18 November 1849, attended by fifty guests who were "nearest friends and godparents": "The three oldest children stood hand in hand in a circle. Ellen, the children's grandmother [Mrs. Luckie], and I with Otto on my arm, formed the second circle around them. They were beautifully dressed and wreathed in flowers. The minister read the speech composed by me." In the speech that Emil wrote for the minister, Emil's father, Arnold, would have heard many of the rationalist ideas he had sought to pass on to his sons: Emil urged rearing children to be "good and useful citizens of the world," and he used, among others, the phrase "in the name of virtue, reason, and freedom, and universal love of humanity."[86]

Before leaving for Europe, Emil and Eleanor welcomed to St. Louis two more members of the family from Dortmund—Luise's sister, thirty-one-year-old Wilhelmina Karoline (called Lina), and Sophia Christine, thirty-six. Although Dortmund genealogical records say the sisters arrived in America in 1850 and married there (Sophie to Wilhelm Amend and Lina to Louis Ruetz), Emil reported that Lina arrived in 1848 and that Sophie was in Milwaukee by summer of that year.[87]

Having failed to obtain help from Gustav, Hermann and Luise decided in 1849 to go with sister Lina to join Sophie in Milwaukee. There the sisters, Luise and Sophie, opened a business, and Hermann operated a *Weinhaus*.[88] While in Milwaukee, Hermann's family was recorded on a daguerreotype in December 1850 (plate 11). Present were Ceilia Henriette (five), Hermann (thirty-nine), John Frederick (two), James Ferdinand (seven), and Luise (thirty-three). Hermann and Luise's fourth child, Delia Louise, was born about the time the photo was made.

By April 1850 Sophie was back in St. Louis, writing to relatives in Köln about business matters and reporting that later in the day she would go up the Missouri to visit her brother August and the others at Augusta.[89] Her visit there was lengthy or she visited again, for she was counted there with August by the 1850 U.S. census takers who appeared at his door on 7 September. August was recorded as a forty-one-year-old male "tobacconist" (that is, a tobacco farmer), and Sophie was listed simply as a thirty-six-year-old female.[90]

Emil Goes to Europe

In spring 1850 Emil, Eleanor, and the children set off for Europe, to seek cures for Emil's illness and to avoid another unhealthy St. Louis summer. Their first visits were with cousin Gustav in Köln and brother Eduard in Dortmund at Westenhellweg 45 (the house that his wife, Dorothea, had inherited).[91] Emil did not enjoy his old hometown at all, although with the coming of the railroad in 1847 its population had grown to more than 10,500.[92] As he later wrote his good friend F. Schulenberg in St. Louis,

> I did not like it. The surroundings are not pretty, and the business life as well as way of thought of the Westphalian rural townsmen moves in such narrow limits that we no longer find accord with them and they not with us, especially if one is without activity. Their pedantry and fearful envy is really absurd. . . . The Dortmunders were irritated that I no longer would be impressed with their progress. They could not understand how one could overlook it.[93]

Traveling with a maid for the children, Emil reported that the next stop for the family was Bonn, where Emil took some health cures. To make better use of his time, during fall 1850 he also took a semester of courses at the university—in chemistry, physics, and geology, reflecting the interest in science that all the Mallinckrodt sons had learned at the Dortmund gymnasium.

In early 1851 Emil apparently traveled alone to Italy for some months. During this time he was occupied, too, with the planned trip of his Köln cousin, Gustav

II, to the United States. In St. Louis, Gustav was to look after a whole list of Emil's real estate business matters and also to inquire about Hermann Mallinckrodt. Writing about the best time of year to visit and routes to follow, Emil's long letter from Nizza to Köln was an abbreviated travel guide to America.

Enthusiastically he wrote young Gustav that New Englanders were "the most intelligent, adaptable, ingenious, and entrepreneurial race in the whole world!" However, he warned that ship travel on the Great Lakes was so very dangerous that one should remain near the stern of the steamer to avoid being injured when the boilers blew up. "Follow this *advice rigorously*," he added, for it is *very important.*" Emil also had another warning for his "Dear friend Gustav junior":

> Take as little luggage as possible. Nowhere in the world can one travel cheaper, faster, and better than on American steam-boats, but one is easily robbed. Take very little cash along and avoid exchanging words with Americans. Generally they are intelligent and accommodating, but also passionate. They can tolerate *no* insults, not even *presumed* ones, and instead immediately draw their knife.

Despite the warnings, Emil was as optimistic about America as ever. During your lifetime, Emil wrote to Gustav, the country "will exert a tremendous influence on Europe. . . . What England formerly was, the U.S. will be in ten years, namely the mightiest nation on earth—and more powerful than the world has ever seen."[94]

Toward the end of March 1851, Emil began two months of water cures, "after having been fed all of Bonn's medication for ten months," without positive results. In June the Mallinckrodts moved to Switzerland, where Emil again took a lengthy cure—cold-water baths. There the doctors diagnosed the problem as liver impairment.[95]

In August it was on to Italy, to Nizza, to enjoy the favorable weather during the winter months. With a cook for the family, a tutor for the children, and a routine of saltwater baths, Emil had time for writing and thought. The cures were not helping, he wrote Schulenberg, "and my joy in life is still crimped." Nor was travel of this kind easy, Emil concluded: "We are enjoying our stay in Europe, although traveling around with a family of little children causes a lot of discomfort: weariness, a changed way of life, the disadvantage of setting up housekeeping in foreign cities without knowledge, providing education for the older children, and of course the great expenses, all this directs a family back toward a permanent place of residence." The birth of another daughter, in Nizza in October 1851, was nevertheless a joy: she was referred to as the "unnamed one," for she was not to be baptized until the family returned to Dortmund in May 1852.[96]

Always the horticulturist, Emil found delight in Italy's southern vegetation— its olive trees, figs, oranges, and other fruits. In Sardinia the farmer in him also discovered something interesting—mules and donkeys. The latter impressed Emil especially, and he wrote Schulenberg, "They are ideal in beauty and *size*. The best cost 200 francs. I would like to send twenty to the U.S. and myself take up their breeding. What do they cost there, and how would I ship them? The donkey is such a useful and contented animal that humankind shames itself to compare its own nonuseful species with him!"[97]

Meanwhile, the news from Hermann and Luise was not good. Writing together to "Dear Emil and dear Gustav," Hermann reported in July 1851 that his Milwaukee business did not go well, and the raw northern climate did not agree with Luise's health. They therefore planned to relocate in St. Louis, and this time, Hermann wrote, he was going to look for office work. By October 1851 he and his family were back on the Mississippi, but months went by without his finding a suitable job. As Hermann wrote Emil and Gustav, "Several times I got close to being hired, but then again my unlucky star surfaced and my deep wish came to naught!"[98] Meanwhile, Luise and the children were living with Julius in Duden country and with cousin Hermann in St. Charles.[99]

While Emil and his family were still in Italy, Hermann wrote to Gustav in March 1852.[100] With no office job in sight, Hermann said, he was thinking of renting a little store in St. Louis close to the bakery that his brothers-in-law Ruetz and Amend were operating. A fruit market also was a possibility, Hermann thought, or a cigar business. He even considered purchasing either a shoe shop or a grocery store and house. For such a purchase, he needed $1,500 capital.[101]

Gustav's response to Hermann was a firm but friendly no:

> I do not see as practical your suggestion that I give you the means to establish some kind of store. You have enough experience to see that that [running a business] is not suitable for you. If you now expect better success, I am sorry that I cannot share that view but believe you are creating illusions for yourself.
>
> I, and also Emil, would be glad to help you if this could take place with the guarantee that you would be permanently helped, that the future were *secured* for you and your family. At the same time, however, we are not inclined to do something if we must tell ourselves that sooner or later the same situation will prevail.
>
> If you do not yet have a job, which I hope, you will have to continue your efforts in this direction. And, indeed, with even more energy, for you surely have to tell yourself that it cannot be pleasant to live for a longer time from subsidies that you perhaps will never be able to repay us.[102]

By spring 1852 Emil apparently was back in St. Louis, having left his family in Dortmund. Catching up with business was time-consuming, and his health was not much better. Emil thus must have laughed when he read the lines written by his elderly Aunt Dorothea in Dortmund in October: "With sorrow I heard from Eduard that your old suffering has set in again. Now I remember that I once heard of a man who cured himself with only warm, freshly milked cow's milk; as often as the patient has appetite, he drinks a glass of milk, every time freshly milked, and nothing else. Do you want to try this? You can have the milk so easily—you only have to sacrifice the best cow, you dear economist."[103]

Emil was greatly missed by his family in Dortmund. His twelve-year-old son Gustav wrote from Dortmund to his Uncle Gustav in Köln in December 1852:

We had also a letter from father on Thursday, we were overjoyed to hear from him. . . . He writes he was very much fatiquet [fatigued] with the last of his trips, and thinks that he will not return before June, a long time for him and us, much can happen in that time but we must trust to the Almighty hand of providence whom we hope will guard and protect him. . . . We are all well excepting mother who still has a cough. She would have written herself but her being not's [*sic*] well and thinking at the same time it better for me to keep in practice. I would have written in German but it won't go uncle. . . . With respect your Gustav Mallinckrodt III.[104]

Meanwhile, Gustav II was underway in the United States, more or less following the travel plans Emil had outlined for him. When he wrote home to Köln in late February 1853 from Havana, Cuba, he reported none of the wild adventures Emil had warned against. His steamer, however, had indeed run aground on a sandbar, where it stayed for five days. He found the view of Havana from the sea *wunderschön* and visited numerous plantations inland.[105] One was owned by a German from Saxony who, after political difficulties at the university, had immigrated to the island in the 1830s. Gustav's impressions of Dr. Doring's sugar plantation and slavery were reported with some cynicism. Mr. Doring, Gustav wrote,

is the absolute master, living alone in a wonderful house and leading as quiet, comfortable a bachelor life as possible. His rooms are for the most part decorated with trophies of his student years and memories of previous dreams of freedom. Among them are several strong riding whips and familiar utensils to keep his Negroes in order.

He has about two hundred of them who are locked up each evening in a courtyard surrounded by high walls and fences. During the day they have to work as much as possible in the courtyard. They are divided into various groups—every five to ten have a black overseer and every fifty a white one who swings the whips around their ears during work.

The contrast between the former and present efforts of Mr. Doring is not insignificant! But he nevertheless seems to view himself positively. He is always in a good mood, drinks very good red wine, smokes good cigars, and receives his guests in the most remarkable manner![106]

Traveling on to St. Louis in late March, Gustav II wrote from there—with some irritation—that Emil had departed the city ten days earlier to return to his family in Dortmund, leaving business matters quite confused. Moreover, Emil was involved in a serious court case involving some real estate transactions.[107]

"Emil is an extraordinary person," young Gustav wrote his father. "Despite his best intentions, his illusions permit him to see the fact of various matters in a different light at a different time, thereby creating the most noticeable contradictions in his judgments." About the rest of the Missouri family, Gustav had nothing to report. Instead, he closed the account of his American adventures with an interesting footnote on the country's railroad progress:

> The railroad route from Wheeling to Baltimore was tiring and dangerous. The railroad had been open only for several months and in many places was still provisional. Most of the bridges were incomplete, and at most of the dangerous places the rails had not been carefully joined. . . . The Americans' driving ability knows no limits—despite the sharpest curves and many dangerous spots, they drove [the locomotive] twenty miles an hour, including stops![108]

22

1845: Growth in
the Countryside

W hile the late 1840s was a time of economic boom for America's cities, it was a period of renewal for Duden country. After its convulsive flooding, the Missouri River again flowed peacefully past Julius Mallinckrodt's property. Although "Oregon fever" was not high among settlers living along the river, they saw its symptoms daily—the many steamboats headed upstream with immigrants bound for Oregon and California via the Missouri's tributaries and the Platte River.

While others sought their luck in the West, the German farmers in the Missouri River valley found enough new opportunities at their own front door as they diversified and expanded with their area. St. Charles County, for instance, was growing rapidly. Whereas the population was only 4,320 in 1830, it had risen to 7,911 by 1840, and would go to almost 11,500 by 1850.[1]

Churches

Religious life, too, was expanding and intensifying as the settlements grew. In 1845, a majority of the Association of Rationalist Christians, which was founded in Augusta, voted to have not only lectures on religious subjects but also "services with prayer, singing, and sermon." The Union Church in Augusta was selected as the site for these services, which would be held before the Association's regular meetings.[2] Throughout the area, in fact, the demand for ministers was growing so rapidly that in 1849 the Association of German Evangelical Churches of the West resolved to open a theological seminary the next year. It was to be built on a sixty-acre tract of land between Femme Osage and Marthasville.[3]

Orchards and Vineyards

While the population was increasing, agriculture, too, was spreading over the land. More and more acres were becoming fruit orchards since Julius and his neighbors found that the few apple, peach, and pear trees they had planted initially were flourishing. In fact, people now generally recognized that the soil and climate of their hill properties above the Missouri River were especially suited to horti-culture.[4]

After the discovery early in the 1840s that the industry of winemaking could be lucrative, vineyards appeared on the hillsides, as well. But still more experimen-tation was necessary to learn which varieties of grapes would grow best in Duden country. European vines had proved complete failures. Some domestic varieties grew better, but one kind of grape after another was given up when it was found not to thrive. Moreover, the wines the settlers did try to make were not especially good. At the German settlement of Hermann, Missouri, for instance, the Isabella grape had been introduced by 1843. "Wine lots" were then sold by the town to citizens who would pursue the new venture. In 1847, for example, Michael Poeschel started a small vineyard.[5] Gradually, however, it was found that the Catawba variety of Ohio grape adapted well, and the settlers also had learned a thing or two about wine-making. By fall 1848, then, Hermann could hold a wine fair to celebrate its new successes with grape culture. As a visitor to the wine festival later wrote,

> I can still remember very well the first Weinfest in Hermann in the fall of 1848 . . . as we arrived there towards evening a six-pounder thundered its greeting and welcome over the hills and valleys. The reports of this [wine] success had penetrated into all parts of Missouri where German was spoken at that time, and even visitors from St. Louis, ladies and gentlemen, had come on steamboats.
>
> The next morning an entire cavalcade made its way to the vineyard of Mr. Michael Poeschel, and as a matter of fact, I didn't regret having traveled the long distance of 20 miles, when I beheld the splendid grapes there with my own eyes. His bearing vineyard covered hardly the area of a single acre, but the rows of posts seemed to constitute a wall of nothing but grapes and among them not a single rotten berry was to be found. The income from the vintage of this small vineyard was very large, for good Catawba, which when handled properly, resembles Rhine wine very closely, and was then in great demand and brought a good price.[6]

For Hermann this was an important success since its beginning as a settlement had been difficult. Founded as a colony by the German Settlement Society of Philadelphia, Hermann's first settlers arrived in the winter of 1837. By 1839 there were 450 people trying to establish a foothold on the hills above the Missouri River. Poor soil and disease caused the Society to collapse, but its members struggled on, building their brick homes and maintaining the German culture that would not fade for generations. The river, of course, was the village's tie to the West as well as to St. Louis downstream, and Hermann was therefore known for its riverboat captains—as well as for the 1843 explosion of the steamer *Big Hatchie* right at the wharf.

In the seasons after the Hermann festival, the Concord grape was also successfully fermented into a good table wine.[7] Step by step the farmers were becoming vintners, and by 1850 regularly staked vineyards were seen here and there.[8] As contemporary chroniclers wrote about the Germans around new Dortmund,

> They caused barren hillsides to blossom with grape vines and fruit trees, and opened large farms in the midst of dense forests. Swamps and marshes were drained, and fertile fields took the place of stagnant ponds that for years sent out their miasmas to poison the atmosphere of the surrounding country and breed fevers, chills, and pestilence. Villages and towns sprang up where soltitude had previously reigned, and the liberal arts began to flourish.[9]

Julius Mallinckrodt was one of the settlers experimenting with vineyards. He later would be one of the first to establish an Augusta winery, building a brick wine cellar on the northwest corner of his new Dortmund property. Julius's fruit orchards had in fact grown so well that he was thinking of going into legal partnership with his eldest son, Conrad Theodor. The teenager who was learning the business seemed also to "have a green thumb." Referred to as the area's "celebrated nurseryman" in the 21 February 1852 issue of the county's German-language newspaper, the *St. Charles Demokrat*, Julius was asked sometimes to write educational articles for the newspaper, such as the lengthy, detailed piece published in 10 January of that year entitled "Citizens, Plant Fruit Trees."

The big event in Julius' life, however, was his remarriage. After Mary's death in 1844, Julius had gotten along quite well with the help of neighbors. But it had not been easy, and it was not the best situation for the children. The three teenagers—Mathilde (sixteen), Caroline (fifteen), Conrad (fourteen)—and even twelve-year-old Emilie could care for themselves and were a great help around the house. But then there were the three youngest who needed more looking after—Hermann Adolph (almost eleven), Luise (nine), and Lydia (nearly six).

In 1849, after five years as a widower, Julius then decided to form a second partnership with Marie E. Böhmer Rothert. A widow with one child (Regina), Marie Böhmer, like Julius, was an immigrant; her family had come to Warren County from Westerode near Fürstenau, northwest of Osnabrück, in Hanover, Germany. Julius and Marie Böhmer were married in the Evangelical Church in Femme Osage in September 1849. Possibly Julius went to church for his second marriage because Marie was from an actively religious German family or because the Reverend Mr. Garlichs had left Femme Osage in 1845, and the new minister, the Reverend Mr. Bode, was more acceptable to Julius. When Julius and Mary's first child, Christian Albert, was born in 1850 he, too, was taken to the Femme Osage church to be baptized.[10]

Frederick Wachs Is Murdered

Before long, however, Julius's new family was involved in a kinfolk drama such as even he probably had not imagined. In early October 1852 his daughter Emilie, age fifteen, perhaps partly in rebellion against her new stepmother, married the significantly older Frederick Wachs, twenty-six, of Sontra, Curhessen, near Kassel. Two and a half months later he was dead—stabbed in an Augusta saloon on Tuesday night, 28 December 1852.

The death was, of course, a family tragedy. But it was an example, too, to the community (and to history) of how "law and order" was maintained on the frontier via justices of the peace.

For instance, according to the records of the Wachs case,[11] it was before the county justices of the peace in the small settlement of Augusta that Philipp Wachs filed a charge of murder against Gustavus Schäffer who had stabbed his brother, "from which said wound Frederick Wachs died immediately." At the time each township in the county had four elected justices of the peace, with Fariss and Bigelow serving the Augusta area.

Hearing Wachs's charge and exercising their authority, the next day they first ordered the Femme Osage Township constable to arrest the accused and then to subpoena witnesses—Philipp Wachs, August Mallinckrodt, Charles Thon, Charles Lachenmeyer, Charles Blumenstengel, George Meyers, August Staudinger, Hermann H. Holtmann, and Joseph A. Weidner. This was done and the accused put under guard. The prosecutor, defendant, and witnesses then appeared before the justices on 30 December at the scene of the alleged murder in Augusta.

The state's witnesses were heard first. The testimony they gave told a bizarre story of newcomer German men (ages and professions unknown in this period of transient immigrants) exchanging seemingly harmless though inane insults that provoked hot-headed reactions ending in death in an Augusta waterfront pub. According to the record (including the awkward translation and recorder's errors in spelling), witness August Mallinckrodt gave the following account:

> In consequences of a house raising me and some other friends were invited by Phillipp Wachs night before last night to take a glass of beer with him at Mr. George Meyers.
>
> There arose between Mr. Thon and Schäffer about some trifling matter a dispute. Some provoking words were exchanged between them when Mr. Fr. Wachs jumped up and attacked Mr. Schäffer who was sitting quietly on a chair, by seizing him

by the collar and chake [shake] him. Schäffer told Wachs to let him alone. They were separated, but Wachs repeated his attacks and Schäffer told him every time to let him alone. Then I saw Mr. George Meyers taking hold of Wachs and heard him say that he would not suffer any fight in his house, when Wachs told Schäffer to go with him out doors and to fight with him. Schäffer refused and said to Wachs that the next morning was the more proper time to settle this matter and that he was then at his service.

When Wachs left Meyers he was standing near the counter and close where I was sitting in a much excited state so that I could not help asking him, "Wachs, are you acting reasonable;" he answered me as far as I recollect, "No, I am not." Almost in the same moment I saw Fr. Wachs attacking Schäffer again . . . taking hold of him by the collar he shook him.

I saw then Wachs suddenly stepping back and sinking on a chair. I had no idea of what had happened until I heard Mr. Lachenmeyer say, my lord he dies. When somebody else examined his brest, I saw the blood. Then I saw Schäffer advancing towards Wachs, but he was pushed bak by P. Wachs, and Schäffer left the scene.

Thon's testimony added other facts about the nature of the insult—ethnic and economic class—that had triggered the confrontation:

Shortly before the beginning of the conflict he and Philipp Wachs had gone to Tiemann & Wenckers [waterfront] store to fech a trunk from there. When returned he cald upon Frederic and Ph. Wachs his brothers-in-law to go home with him. Where upon Schäffer asked him if the blind Hessians had already lost their currage to drink beer. This he took for an insult and he replied, perhaps as much currage as a dismissed officer of the army. Thereupon Schäffer cald him a *Knote*. Thereupon Fr. Wachs took his part and seized Schäffer by his collar. Then Fr. Wachs was kept back by several, to finnish the affair. Himself [witness] believed the matter settled and then addressed himself to Blumenstengel and Fr. Wachs.

Prosecutor Philipp Wachs's testimony, though muddled by the clerk switching from "I" to "he" in the record, added details of his own peacekeeping efforts and emotional reaction to the stabbing death of his brother:

Until then Schäffer had remained quietly at his place, Schäffer at the same time did not appear excited, rather selfpossessed and deliberate. I [witness] stood at the side of Schäffer tring to appease him, telling that I was near him [and] never they should hurt him. Silmultianously the rest of the company was endeavering to keep Wachs from doing any rash act. I then stepped aside, participating in a discussion with Blumenstengel and Thon.

During that time, while my back was turned towards Schäffer, Wachs stept again toward the latter but the deponent [witness] could not observe what was farther going on. On this occassion he concludes that Wachs had been wounded, for when he turned round he saw his brother sink down on his chair. He first believed his brother were in a state of apoplexie or fainting. He recieved him in his arms as well to support as to defend him against all sorts of assaults, creiing now let my brother alone. At the same time one of the company exclaimed o lord there is blood, and on examining his breast a wound going to his heart was discovered. An other one exclaimed, o lord he dies, he is dead. Then Schäffer rose up, run towards Wachs but with what intention he [witness] cannot state. He thrust Schäffer [away] who then has [?turned] towards the door creing [crying], I go for the doctor.

Details of what Schäffer then did were provided in the testimony of Hermann Holtmann, that is, first going to the doctor, who was not home, and then coming to Holtmann to accompany him to the justice of the peace: "between 11 and 12 o'clock Mr. Schäfer came to my house and asked me to go along with him to squire Faris [justice of the peace], he had stuck Fr. Wachs with a knife and did not know if he was dead or alive and he wanted to give himself up to law." In cross-examination Holtman added that Schäffer had been in "sorry excitement about what has happened" when he arrived at his house to get help in finding where the justice of the peace lived.

The cross-examinations concentrated on additional aspects of the accused's behavior. One was the nature of his personal insult—*Knote*—to which the dead man had reacted; this apparently was a crucial point among immigrants trying to establish and maintain their credibility within a new, shifting society. According to witness Philipp Wachs' "own understanding of the word [*Knote*], it always signifies an uneducated rude and vulgar person," that is, both a social and personal slur. (Similarly, the translator had said "a mean fellow of a mecanical trade.") A second behavioral point of the cross-examination was whether the alleged murderer was quiet or excited, had the knife been open or closed. The dead man's behavior was cross-examined, too, that is, was he known as a drinker or not. According to the justice of the peace record, the defendant, speaking through an attorney (identity unknown), and defense witnesses were next heard. (These records are not available.)

After all the evidence was recorded, the justice of the peace decided to bind Schäffer over for appearance before the next Circuit Court session, to be held on 9 May 1853, or five months hence. Thus, after being under local guard three days and two nights, Schäffer was taken to St. Charles, the county seat, under a "warrant of committment" issued by the township justices of the peace to the county sheriff or constable and to the "keeper of the common jail of the County of St. Charles." The transcript of the proceedings (including depositions translated by Friedrich Münch) was then filed with the Circuit Court.

After nearly a month of imprisonment, Schäffer filed a petition of habeas corpus, citing irregularities in bail and charging procedures. This petition was sworn to on 29 January 1853, before St. Charles Justice of the Peace Hermann Mallinckrodt, of Elberfeld. Whether or not the writ was granted is unclear from the records, but such an appeal could be made if the bond was too high or the crime had not been intentional.[12]

Schäffer came to trial, as scheduled, on 18 May 1853, and the grand jury returned a bill of indictment.[13] In it the grand jury found that Schäffer "feloniously, wilfully, deliberately, premeditatedly and of his malice and forethought did kill and murder, against the peace and dignity of the State." The jury found that Schäffer, "with a certain knife, of the value of one dollar," which he held in his right hand, did strike and thrust it into the left side of Frederick Wachs, giving "one mortal wound of the breadth of one inch, and the depth of three inches" of which Wachs "then and there instantly did die."[14]

The following day, 19 May, the defendant and his attorney petitioned the court "to grant a commission to take the depositions of a witness [for the defense] who is about to remove from the State of Missouri." The commission was issued, and, in addition, Hermann Mallinckrodt (the local justice of the peace) and Leopold Schäffer posted bond for the accused until the autumn term of court in September 1853.[15]

The next entry in the court records, however, is in the following spring, 18 May 1854. Apparently, the jury was instructed that under Missouri's laws at that time justifiable circumstances in the case of murder included (a) self-defense and (b) provoked combat without dangerous weapon. In addition, (c) third-degree manslaughter was defined as killing "in the heat of passion, without the design to effect death by a dangerous weapon" and not excused by "a" or "b." The judge also said (d) that third-degree manslaughter was applicable if the defendant killed "while the deceased was engaged in the commission of a trespass upon him, or in an attempt to commit such trespass."[16]

Within these instructions, however, the jurors could not reach a decision. According to the record, they "appear and say they cannot agree upon a verdict in this case, and therefore by consent of parties said jurors are discharged."[17] "Mistrial" was noted on the court docket.

It seems that the attorney and judge then worked out a solution. Two days after the mistrial, on 20 May 1854, the defendant Schäffer pleaded guilty of manslaughter in the fourth degree and was sentenced to a $100 fine and three months in the county jail. (The *fourth-degree* charge had not been included in the jury's initial instructions.) Clearly, then, at the same time that frontier German tempers were short, legal processes were long but could be mild, with justices of the peace playing a key role.[18]

At the Mallinckrodts meanwhile, Julius had buried his murdered son-in-law in the small family cemetery, near Julius's first wife Mary. The weathered tombstone (plate 10) still standing gives Frederick Wachs's name, Hessian birthplace, date of death, and adds "26 years old." (Mary Mallinckrodt's tombstone is shown in the background.) For Wachs's young widow, Emilie Mallinckrodt Wachs, the drama, of course, was not over. She gave birth to their child the next year, 26 May 1853, naming the little girl Frederika.

At the same time that Julius was involved in those problems of his first family, his second was growing. In 1853, he and Marie had a daughter Wilhelmina.

Conrad Surveys and Farms

Living quietly on his hill next door to brother Julius, Conrad apparently was not yet ready for a second try at wedded bliss. He was very busy professionally. Through assignments here and there he sharpened his surveying skills and prepared to become a farmer, too. Having accumulated some money, Conrad bought what seems to have been his first piece of land in 1848 or 1849.[19]

Also wanting to get into the orchard business, Conrad acquired more acreage in 1850.[20] He now bought the land on which he had been living—that originally owned by Emil in 1832 and sold back to Julius when Emil moved to St. Louis. It was roughly the western half of the Mallinckrodts' "three hills and two valleys" (figure 12-2) totaling around 100 acres and leaving Julius with 240 acres remaining.[21] Interestingly, Conrad paid Julius in two currencies, "1700 Prussian Dollars and 278 American Dollars and 76 cents." The sale was notarized 9 July 1850 (Julius's wife signing her name Mary, not Marie), and the deed filed 17 May 1854.[22]

According to oral history, Conrad's newly purchased hilltop was the spot on Julius's property where Carl Wencker, Conrad's travel companion, had built his 1836 tannery and the house where Sophie and Conrad lived when they arrived in 1838. It seems likely that Conrad continued to live there after his divorce, perhaps for a time with Wencker since the Mallinckrodt and Wencker families had close ties.[23] Conrad, thus, stayed on the family property, making his "home place" the house just across the hill from his brother, which he bought from Julius in 1850 (figure 20-1). The 1850 U.S. Census recorded this separate dwelling for Conrad, whereas a decade earlier he had not been listed as a head of household, but rather probably was counted as one of the two thirty- to forty-year-old males Julius reported then as belonging to his household.[24]

As agriculture and population expanded, more roads were needed to serve the area. Conrad surveyed many of them. As the historians wrote, he was "an accomplished civil engineer and surveyor, and through his efforts many of the best turnpike roads in the county were laid out and completed."[25]

On 20 January 1851, for instance, Conrad surveyed the road from the west end of the Main Street of Julius' new Dortmund to where it should connect with the Tugue Prairie Road. Conrad's survey report said he had family help. Julius and his sixteen-year-old son Conrad Theodor were chain carriers, and thirteen-year-old son Hermann Adolph acted as forevaneman, or flagman. According to the surveying guide book of the time, which Conrad and other Mallinckrodts used, the chains which the surveyors carried were composed of one hundred pieces of iron wire, or links, and every tenth link marked by a piece of brass.[26] Thus measurements were written down in chains and links which then were converted into feet.

Chain carriers Julius and young Conrad, thus, had to make sure that the chains were not tangled, or kinked, and that the same force was always applied when stretched across distances. They worked as a pair. Forward chainman Conrad Theodor drew out the chain and inserted pins along the way; more skilled Julius, as hind chainman, checked that the chain was not twisted or bent and then sighted and instructed his son to lift or lower it ("lined up") until the chain was properly stretched out. At that point, surveyor Conrad tallied and recorded the measurements.[27]

The brothers Mallinckrodt shared not only practical work such as surveying but also intellectual interests, including politics. In March 1852, Conrad attended the St. Charles County convention of the liberal Democratic Party and was elected as a delegate to the party's state convention.[28] In addition, Conrad had his railroad interest: in November 1852, for example, he was a delegate to the North Missouri Railroad convention intended to start the building of that line, chartered the previous year and now seen as urgently necessary.[29] He also wrote frequent editorials on current political issues for the *St. Charles Demokrat*, signing them "*M.*"[30]

Later the same year it was Julius's turn to go on record politically, again in writing as frequently was his custom. This time he called for the state legislature to deal with "the infamous Jackson Resolution" that gave Missouri the image of a rebel state.[31] For Julius, education was a continuing interest, and as an Augusta school trustee he publicly, "in the name of the children of our district," expressed appreciation for county support.[32]

With all the activity around new Dortmund and Augusta, life was also going well for August Mallinckrodt. He apparently was still working for Carl Wencker raising tobacco and making cigars. According to account books, in 1847 August was boarding with Friedrich Münch, pastor-turned-farmer, who would become one of the area's authorities on grape culture. Although later historians would write that Münch planted his first vineyard in 1860, it may be that his interest in growing grapes began earlier. For instance, by summer 1847, during the time that Hermann, Missouri, was advancing in its grape culture, August Mallinckrodt and Münch traveled there. Account books showed that Münch paid his companion's 25-cent fare on a Missouri River ferry to reach that settlement; there August laid out 37.5 cents for Münch for a tin kettle, perhaps for wine fermenting.

The relationship between Münch and his boarder must have been very friendly, for the former often paid out money for August, which he entered as "Debt" in their account books, along with the $1.25 per week for room and board. For instance, Münch paid for August the $16.50 still owed C. Wencker for fourteen weeks of boarding there before August changed residences, $1.64 for a "school fund" (probably school tax), 5 cents to mail a letter to St. Louis and 17.5 cents for one to Germany, $2.00 for a "pastor's fee" (possibly for a special service such as baptism, burial, or Holy Communion), $9.00 for 114 pounds of tobacco, 75 cents for taxes, and so on. In addition, August owed 6 percent interest on the balance of his account. On the other hand, August sometimes advanced money for Münch that was later refunded—the tin kettle in Hermann, items bought at an auction sale, or tobacco and cigars.[33]

Very important, of course, to all the Mallinckrodts around new Dortmund in Duden country was the growth of the nearby settlement of Augusta. In 1851, for example, a congregation of the German Evangelical Church was organized there under the leadership of seminarian Rev. George Maul.[34] Now people wishing religious services no longer had to ride eight miles on horseback through the hills to the Femme Osage church. Apparently Maul was not a supporter of rationalist Christianity, for his March 1853 missionary report said the church in Augusta still had to be shared with the Rationalists.[35]

Within the next years, however, some of the Rationalists, such as Julius and Conrad Mallinckrodt, apparently made their peace with organized religion and counted on pastors to marry them, baptize their children, and bury their dead.

Augusta (Mount Pleasant) Incorporates

In 1855 the settlement on the bluffs overlooking the Missouri River was incorporated as a town on 1 March. On page one of their new leather-bound ledger book, the town fathers wrote, on 3 March 1855,

be it enacted by the General Assembly of the State of Missouri, as follows:

1. That all the districts of country, at present known as the town of Augusta, formerly known as Mount Pleasant, in St. Charles County, state of Missoury, as laid down on the original plat of said town . . . shall be, and continue a body politic and corporate by the name and style of the town of Augusta. . . .

2. The corporate powers of said town shall be vested in a board of trustees to consist of five members: Joseph A. Weidner, Diedrich Baare, Philipp Benner, Charles Thiemann and Georg Meyer, shall be, and they are hereby constituted the first board of trustees; hereafter said board is to be chosen by the qualified voters of said town.[36]

Especially interesting was the new board of trustees' power to pass by-laws and ordinances

- to prevent and remove nuisances,
- to prohibit gambling and gaming houses,
- to license and regulate theatrical or other amusements and exhibitions or shows of any kind,
- to prevent or restrain the meeting of slaves,
- to regulate and establish markets,
- to prevent the firing of firearms,

- to prevent the furius and unnecessary running, galloping, riding or driving of any horse or mule within said town, or such part therefore, as they think proper,
  - to establish night watches and patrols,
  - to prevent and suppress bawdy houses and such other disorderly houses within the limits of said town.[37]

Most amazingly, the town fathers, from the first day on, kept that record book entirely in English although it is almost certain that their meeting discussions were in German. Most, if not all of them, had after all been born and educated in the old country. That language background, however, was not visible in the words the clerk used to describe the board's affairs, but rather in the German style penmanship and the use of some German-script letters in the English words, especially *d*, *t*, and *s*.

The trustees' names of course also indicated their language background. In addition to the first five members named in the Act of Incorporation, the appointed clerk was B. E. Hoffman, assessor and treasurer was William Sehrt, and collector and constable was William Dubbert.[38] The first publicly *elected* board (April 1856) then included Fr. Wencker, Louis Gerling, William Sehrt, Heinrich Dammann, Phil. Benner, and Alex. Schrader acting as clerk.[39]

Since they lived some two miles outside the newly incorporated town's limits, Conrad and Julius Mallinckrodt were not residents and could not serve on its board of trustees or hold other town offices. They, nevertheless, watched the settlement's growth with great interest, for it affected the life of the entire area. And many interesting steps were indeed taken to launch the new town.

Originally it had consisted of Leonard Harold's nine blocks registered on 31 March 1836 and a fifteen-block addition registered about a month later, on 18 June 1836.[40] Soon thereafter two areas of land were added on the north side of the town limits—known as Knoernschild's first addition (blocks 25 to 34) and Knoernschild's second addition (blocks 35 to 40). Conrad Mallinckrodt was the surveyor who registered these plats (figure 22-1) with the county a month after incorporation, that is, 18 April 1855.[41]

It is interesting to note that within the original settlement, the land given by Leonard Harold for a school constituted an entire block, no. 23, and for the church, half of block 21. Down at the waterfront, the Mindrup hotel and Wencker-Tiemann store shared block 7, with Wencker's house behind them. Up from the river, on the relatively developed east side of the settlement, would be Limburg's well-known hotel and saloon, on block 25. Also prominent were blocks 4 and 9, almost entirely owned by Charles McLee Farris who came from Virginia in 1826 and served the area as justice of the peace until his death in 1853. (Undocumented oral history says that a big sugar maple tree near Farris's property was the "Hanging Tree" or the "Slave Tree." The former is not likely, for justices of the peace took capital cases to the county seat in St. Charles for judgment; the latter is quite possible, for Missouri was a slave state and many of the early Southern settlers

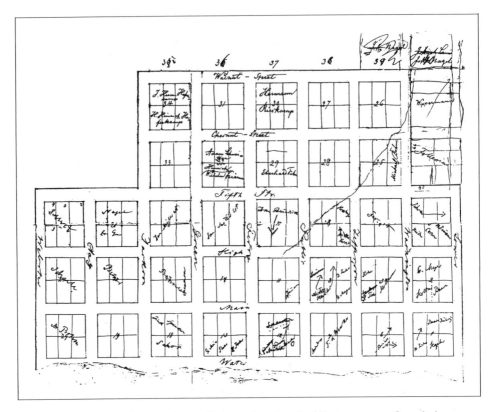

Figure 22-1. Conrad Mallinckrodt's preliminary drawing for his 1855 survey of newly incorporated Augusta, Missouri. (*Courtesy Hubert E. Mallinckrodt.*)

in the area, such as Farris himself, were slave owners and could have held slave auctions under the tree.) In a later addition to Harold's original settlement, block 31 was then designated as the "Market" place, and it was on this higher ground (then called "the plateau") that business relocated after the Missouri River abandoned the waterfront at the foot of the bluffs.

During the first year of its incorporation, to raise money Augusta's Board of Trustees passed a poll tax of fifty cents on all free males age one through fifty-five, set a fee of two to ten dollars for peddlers of goods and those "holding a public show, or exhibition, or theaterical amusements," and fixed a five-dollar license fee for stores and groceries.[42]

Other resolutions of the first months called for

- repair of the public spring
- removal of debris from the streets
- fencing off a well "so there is no danger for any person to fall in"
- banning the sale of brandy and whiskey on election days
- moving "the burying ground from the school property to another location" on notice from school trustees

- fencing of toilets ("all privats have to be fenced and made in such a way, so that no nuissance [*sic*] can run out of it to the streets. Fine from one to five dollars.")
- killing all dogs running free
- making Main Street "a good wagonroad"[43]

Especially significant was the town's relationship to the Missouri River flowing at its feet. Not only was "bathing at daytime alongside the limits of the town" forbidden,[44] but a Street and Wharf Inspector was appointed in January 1856 to be responsible for the town's lucrative waterfront.[45] Since townspeople sold wood to steamboats passing by, it was resolved, "That all persons who put on the levee any lumber, wood, etc. will be charged 5 cents for every 32 square feet of ground. Every time, if the lumber, etc. will be remufed or sold, the payment shall be renewed and also shall the payment be renewed if said lumber etc. is not sold or remufed in the time of four months for every following four months."[46]

Other waterfront concerns were keeping the steamboat landing repaired, as well as the warehouse on the wharf.[47] Sometimes, too, unused boats were tied up at the wharf and stayed there without paying usage fees. For instance, it was resolved that "the proprietors of the Ferry Boat at Augusta be informed that from and after the 14th of this month they would be charged wharfage at the rate of $1.00 per week by the Board unless they remove their boat from the wharf or commence to run it again as formerly."[48]

Collecting such fees and taxes was a very difficult problem for Augusta. Time and time again lists of delinquent property taxes were posted; after thus being advertised for ninety days the lots were sold. At one such sale of tax-delinquent property, the town itself bought a lot—which had belonged to founder Harold— for twenty cents![49]

Interesting, then, was the 1858 ordinance passed by the town concerning its revenue. It required "every holder of property, within the corporate limits of the town, to *deliver to the assessor, upon oath if required* [emphasis added] a list of their property made taxable by law." Taxes then would be levied on the following items that reflect the frontier life style:

All free male persons over the age of 21 and under 60 years of age;
all lands and town lots, all pieces and parcels of land including the improvements thereon;
all slaves;
gold and silver plate,
all piano fortes,
household property over the value of 100 Dollars;
pleasure carriages of all kinds; all carriages, hacks, wagons, buggies, and other articles of every kind and description;
all horses, mares, mules and work oxen, all cows, all hogs kept up,
all clocks and watches with their chains;

all shares of stock in banks, all money on hand or deposited with banks or other
    incorporated companies, brokers or other persons,

all money loaned at interest, all notes due and drawing interest; all State and County
    bonds, shares of stock and all other interest held in steamboats or ferry boats,

all printing presses, type and machinery therewith connected;

all grist mills, saw mills, woolcarding machines and buildings containing the same;

all distilleries, breweries and tanneries;

all goods wares and merchandize;

all drugs and medicines;

all jewelry kept for sale.

All of the foregoing property to be taxed at the rate of one half of one per cent
    of its cash values.

All dogs and bitches at the following rate:—each dog 50 cents, each bitch 1 Dollar.[50]

Although Conrad, now an elected justice of the peace as well as authorized
notary public, did not always witness the affairs of the little neighboring town,
he often did. For instance, there were marriages to perform—in his register of
marriages solemnized, the earliest date recorded was 1856, the marriage of Julius
Mallinckrodt's stepdaughter Regina Rothert to Hermann Haferkamp.[51] After
town elections, Conrad legitimized the swearing in of new trustees, and throughout the following decades he frequently performed other justice of the peace and
notary services for the town. His signature and seal became well known (figure
22-2).

Culture, Newspapers, Schools

Life in Augusta, however, was not limited to business and law. There was culture,
too, and thereby hangs an interesting tale. According to colorful local history
accounts, temperance laws were being enforced in Missouri in the late 1850s. The
German residents of Augusta objected because they could not enjoy themselves
without interruption around the wine table, as they were accustomed to do.
Taking advantage of an ice blockade in the Missouri River in January 1856, they
went out onto it, erected a tent on the ice, and organized the Augusta Harmonie-
Verein. For many years thereafter they were compelled to use a flat boat on the
river as a meeting place for their musical and social society and to exist without
a charter.[52] As a historian later would write, "Whoever has a sense for meaningful
and *gemütlich* entertainment, will feel very well in this little Augusta, for in contrast
to its limited population one finds residing there disproportionately many very
intelligent and alert men."[53]

Life in the outlying regions of the county was changing, too. German settlers
in Duden country were very pleased by an event in the county seat. Arnold Krekel,

State of Missouri
County of St. Charles. We Philipp Benner, Frederick Woncker Wm Sehrt. Henry Dammann and Henry Mindrup elected Trustee for the Town of Augusta in said County on an election of the qualified voters of said Town held Monday April 4th 1859 make oath that we will faithfully demean in office according to law and that we will support the constitution of the U.S. and of this State.

Philipp Benner
Henry Dammann.
William Sehrt
F. Woncker
Henry Mindrup

Subscribed and sworn to before me this 11th Day of April 1859.

Conrad Mallinckrodt
Justice of the Peace

Figure 22-2. As justice of the peace and notary public, Conrad Mallinckrodt witnessed many official acts recorded in the Town Board records of Augusta, Missouri. (*Courtesy Hubert E. Mallinckrodt.*)

now a respected attorney, founded a German-language newspaper, the *St. Charles Demokrat*. Its first issue appeared on 1 January 1852. There was great excitement among the many German-speaking/reading citizens of the county who appreciated a local newspaper in their native language. The paper, of course, reflected Krekel's liberal Democratic party principles and, therefore, would play a central role in the imminent struggles leading to the Civil War.[54]

Developments in the state's education system were also encouraging. Major school legislation passed in 1853 thoroughly revised the management of education. Obviously the need was great, for "less than half the children in Missouri were going to school . . . and hardly a school was doing more than elementary work."[55] After 1853 a state superintendent of schools was to be elected rather than appointed, county commissioners were to examine teachers and visit the schools, and the traditional township school districts would have trustees to employ teachers, levy taxes, and so on. (As noted above, Julius Mallinckrodt became one such elected trustee.) Money to pay the teachers was to come in part from the proceeds of swamp- and overflowed-land sales. Notably, the Act of 1853 also had something to say about the content of education—namely, curriculum and textbooks were recommended and teachers were counseled to discontinue pupils' oral recitation of their lessons to increase retention of knowledge.[56]

Railroads

The "iron horse" also was coming, slowly, to Missouri. By 1855 the first division of the *North Missouri Railroad* reached St. Charles, and four years later it reached St. Joseph. On the *Pacific Railroad*, across the Missouri River from Duden country, one could get from St. Louis to Pacific by mid-1853, to Hermann by 1855, and to Jefferson City by 1856.[57] And by the end of the decade travelers could reach St. Joseph and Hannibal on their connecting line.[58]

Though considered modern and essential, the railroad was not always regarded as safe. The shocking Missouri railroad accident in 1855 caused Julius to fear for Emil's life. The accident seemed especially terrible to many; since mass movement of people over rails was still relatively unfamiliar, so too was mass death along the rails.

In St. Louis, on Thursday, 1 November 1855, some six hundred persons boarded the twelve cars of the Pacific Railroad train making the inaugural run of the line to its brand new station at Jefferson City. Two military companies in "gay uniforms" contributed "stirring music" to the occasion. At 8:30 A.M. the train started. All along the way people had gathered to cheer, shout, and wave their hats and handkerchiefs. In Hermann, a cannon "pealed forth the glad greetings of the hearty citizens."

About nine miles beyond Hermann the train engineer and passengers saw the bridge across the Gasconade River. Approached by an embankment terminating in a massive stone abutment, the thirty-foot-high bridge was held up by four stone pillars above the 250-yard-wide river. Then, as newspaper accounts reported, the train slowly moved along the embankment and came onto the bridge. The weight of the locomotive, baggage car, and two heavily loaded passenger cars "was too much for the long, slender timbers which supported the rails and the enormous load above." Suddenly, "we heard a horrid crash," it was reported, and "then there came crash, crash, crash, as each car came to the abutment and took the fatal plunge." In all, "six cars fell in one mass, each on the other, and were shivered into fragments. The seventh fell with its forward end to the ground; but the other end rested on top of the abutment. . . . The eighth and ninth cars tumbled down the embankment before they reached the abutment. Such a wreck we never saw, and hope never again to see."

According to a passenger's letter hastily written to his wife from the scene of the accident, "nearly all the cars are torn to atoms. The one on which I was is . . . literally shattered into little strips and splinters. How I escaped seems a miracle." In the first hours it was believed that thirty persons had been killed and equally as many wounded.[59]

In St. Charles, the *Demokrat* newspaper wrote that eyewitnesses reached the county seat with news of the accident Friday evening, that is, about a day and a half after it happened.[60] Somehow Julius Mallinckrodt, too, heard the news—most likely from a horseback rider or steamboat passing by his farm—and set out for St. Louis to be with Emil's family if he had been on the train. Riding all night on horseback to assure himself that Emil was well, Julius was glad to learn that Emil had not been among the passengers. (Brother Hermann in St. Louis, to whom Julius had close ties, reported this act of concern home to Dortmund.[61])

Despite such failures of vaunted technology, the 1850s had brought growth and many changes to the Mallinckrodts and to Missouri's countryside. Julius and Conrad now owned around three hundred fifty acres of land along the Missouri River, as shown in the center of a township map (figure 22-3), which gravely misspelled their names and those of other German settlers around Augusta.[62]

The map showed the extensive uncultivated, forested areas existing back from the river at that time, the squarely laid-out town of Augusta, and the Roman Catholic church northwest of the town. Another church shown just to the north had been founded by a conservative faction of the German Evangelical Church in Augusta (which had split off from that denomination, later to affiliate with the Lutheran Church of Missouri).

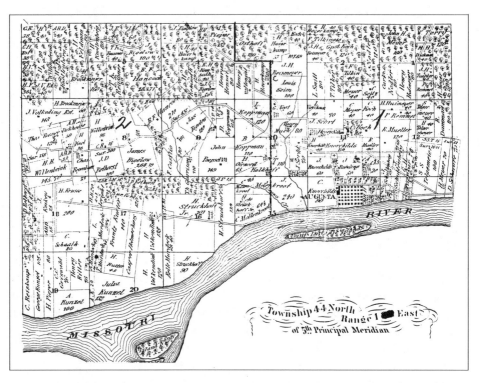

Figure 22-3. A Femme Osage Township map showing Conrad and Julius Mallinckrodt's property on the Missouri River in the 1850s also shows the square layout of the nearby town of Augusta to the east. (St. Charles Co. Atlas, *1875*.)

23

1850: A State and Nation Divided

Under and around all the positive events marking the lives of the Missouri Mallinckrodts in the mid-1800s flowed currents of the gathering storm over slavery. As German immigrants, they deeply feared that a breakup of the American union of states would leave fragmented and weakened political entities such as they had known in the old homeland.

When Julius and Conrad Mallinckrodt in Duden country sat together and tried to sum up what had happened and where it all was going, it was a bleak overview. In St. Louis, their brother Hermann's and cousin Emil's talks with each other and with their friends were equally disquieting. Then, too, prominent Missourians the Mallinckrodts had come to know—lawyers, politicians, newspaper publishers—were saying more and more openly that it was time to take a clear stand on the side of preserving the union and abolishing slavery.

In the border state of Missouri those two issues were painfully intertwined, and its residents used both economic and legal arguments to make their case. As St. Charles County historians summed up the sentiments of the time,

> In the days of the Colonies and in the early years of the Republic negro slavery was an institution generally recognized, and the present constitution was formed with that as one of the property interests of the country . . . when the agitation arose for its [slavery's] abolition they bitterly opposed the threatened revolution in their labor system, and exerted themselves to their utmost for the protection of their slave property.
>
> They held that the Union was instituted for the protection of the rights and property of the people of all the States forming it, and that when those of one section sought to destroy the property interests of another section, they were working to defeat one of the principal objects for which the government was

established; that the North had no more right to interfere with slavery in the South than the South had to prohibit manufactures in New England, or the working of white employes at starving rates of wages; that all knew that slavery was one of the recognized institutions of most of the States when the Union was formed, and that if any had conscientious scruples against it, they ought not to have entered into association with slave States, much less afterwards have attempted to abolish it in other States.

The North, however, disclaimed any intention to interfere with slavery in the States where it was already established, but asserted that it ought to be prohibited in the territories and not allowed in any of the new States to be formed. Still, there was no mistaking the tendency of the anti-slave movement—that it would ultimately result in abolition of slavery throughout the Union.[1]

The Mallinckrodts heard and saw many expressions of these views. For instance, editorials calling for outright abolition were the stock in trade of both the German-language newspapers they read—St. Louis's *Anzeiger des Westens* and St. Charles's *Demokrat*. The St. Louis editorials were written by editor Heinrich Börnstein (a "Forty-eighter" immigrant) and those in St. Charles by the Mallinckrodts' publisher friend Arnold Krekel (a "Thirty-er" immigrant).

The two editors thus represented major streams of thought among Missouri's Germans—the militant liberalism (or radicalism) of the Forty-eighters, who hoped to realize in America the political goals they had not achieved in Germany, and the less militant Thirty-ers, who had been around long enough to adjust somewhat to American life. Both groups, on the other hand, shared a clear sense of egalitarianism and rejection of political authoritarianism.[2]

Under Börnstein's editorship, then, the *Anzeiger* "grew even more biting and aggresive" than it had been. Embodying the Forty-eighters' militant platform of antislavery, anti-Prohibition, and anti-Catholicism, the *Anzeiger* for many represented the incivility of the German-language press in St. Louis. That perception was not entirely unfounded, for in the view of a later historian, "Throughout much of its history, the German-language press of St. Louis tended to represent extremes rather than moderation," albeit during a time when the press per se was unrestrained.[3] Moreover, slavery was a real and deep-felt issue for many Germans, including the Forty-eighters. "As the most visible contradiction in a nation of free institutions," it frequently was the object of their editorial fire.[4]

The message was similar from politicians the Germans trusted. Senator Thomas H. Benton, moderate leader of Missouri's Democrat party (which the Germans supported), believed in preserving the Union at any price and did not want slavery extended.[5] St. Louis's more radical Democrat leader, Frank Blair, a German favorite, vigorously opposed slavery; for a time he also saw a possible solution in so-called colonization—a plan to procure territory in Central or South America on which to found a colony of freed slaves.[6]

Lawyer and politician acquaintances of the Mallinckrodts also were heard from.

For example, St. Louis's famous lawyer and political activist Edward Bates, whom the Mallinckrodts had gotten to know when he represented Sophie in her divorce trial, supported the American Colonization Society and its efforts. Julius's lawyer, H. R. Gamble, was on the front lines of the controversy, as well, championing gradual emancipation and calling for a toning down of public agitation.[7]

1850s: Escalation

To many people it seemed that an escalation in the conflict between proslavery and abolitionist forces had begun around 1850. The passing that year of the Fugitive Slave Law—legalizing, among other things, the hunting down of runaway blacks in the cities and countryside of the North—was a watershed. In the debate over the "soul of the nation," that measure was seen in the North as an outrage.[8] The Fugitive Slave Law, for instance, moved the minister's daughter Harriet Beecher Stowe, of Connecticut, to write the novel *Uncle Tom's Cabin*. And it, in turn, set Northern feelings even more on edge through its description of slavery's brutality and injustice. First serialized in 1851–52 in an abolitionist newspaper, the novel then was published in March 1852 as the book which stormed the nation. Some 300,000 copies were sold in the first year, and 1.2 million by mid-1853.[9] Missourians read it.

Antislavery feelings also were crystallized by increasingly numerous acts of violence. There had been mob actions against a school for black children in Maine, the burning of blacks' homes in Philadelphia, and harassment of the Boston emancipator William Lloyd Garrison and the staff of the antislavery journal *The Emancipator*. Starting with the American Anti-Slavery Society, organized in 1833, abolition and antislavery groups in the North had grown. By the 1840s their membership exceeded 150,000. Prominent writers and poets joined the cause, and court cases were frequent. In St. Louis, Edward Bates was often emancipation's defender. In short, as a historian would later write, "Abolition was an irresistible power in a world awakening to new concepts of humanity."[10] The so-called Underground Railroad was also significant to the sharpening mood. This secret network of people helped runaway slaves or free blacks avoid capture or kidnapping by "conducting" them from "station to station" until they reached free areas in the North. In Missouri, the Underground's helpers and "safe houses" aided African Americans on their way to non-slave Illinois and Iowa or on their way, via Kansas, to Canada.[11]

Central to the growing abolition movement in Missouri and elsewhere was anger about the fact that slaving was increasing, not decreasing. True, the slave trade was illegal and ship captains transporting slaves were therefore considered pirates and subject to death. But slavery, that is the owning of humans as property, was protected by law in the United States. Consequently, as long as there was a profitable market, the demand was met by kidnapping Africans and smuggling them to America's legal slave markets. There a prime field hand brought $2,000 in the late 1850s. Profits of 60 percent per voyage were reported, despite the untold numbers of kidnapped Africans who died in slaveship holds unfit even for animals.[12]

Concerned citizens thus read in the 1850s that the slave trade was larger than it had been half a century earlier when the commerce was still legal. Especially discouraging, many in the American South were calling for even more sales—they wanted to relegalize the African slave trade (reasoning that smugglers then no longer would demand such high prices) and extend slavery into new territories.[13]

Americans were upset, too, to think that because the United States did not enforce its own antislavery trade laws, their flag in essence protected the traffic in human flesh on the high seas. The British navy, in fact, was the only force seriously trying to suppress the inhumane business. And that, of course, was an ironic turn of history—more than half of the some 10 million slaves brought to the New World had been carried in English ships to English colonies, and now it was H. M. Queen Victoria's African Squadron which pursued the pirate slave ships.[14] Although the British naval force was small, it had made 600 ship seizures from 1843 until 1857, of which 562 were condemned; the U.S. Navy in the same period had captured nineteen slave ships and only six ships were condemned.[15]

Missouri's Tormented Position

In this whole context, Missourians agonized over the geography and politics of their slave state. A later scholar would describe the tormented region this way:

> The exposed position of Missouri—"a slave-holding peninsula jutting up into a sea of free-soil"—was primarily the cause of her continued unrest. This peninsula, unnaturally formed for political reasons to reconcile irreconcilable sections, was exposed still more by the two great rivers. The Missouri, coming out of free territory, flowed past free Kansas for a hundred miles and then swerved off through the heart of Missouri's great slave counties. The Mississippi for hundreds of miles alone separated Missouri from an ever-watchful abolitionist minority in Illinois. The great interstate shipping along the Mississippi offered a chance of freedom to any plucky black who might be hired as a boat hand or stowed away by a sympathetic or a venal crew till a free port was reached. The Underground Railroad was busy on three borders of the State . . . Missouri was from its very inception in a state of unrest and feverish apprehension.[16]

The discovery of gold and the opening of the far West had underlined Missouri's geographic dilemma. On the one hand, being the Gateway to the West brought great economic advantages. On the other hand, needed communication and transportation ties, such as post offices and railroads, now stretched to the Pacific Ocean. That, in turn, created a need for political, or state structures, in the area west of Missouri, the Indian Territory. Organizing it as a state brought up anew the old question of "slave or free."

For Missourians the prospects were alarming. If a new state to its west became non-slave, Missouri would then have three legally "free" borders (west, north, east) over which its own slaves would increasingly flee. Moreover, the few areas where slavery thrived in Missouri were precisely along its western border with the new state to be called Kansas. Should it be free, there would be border conflicts. "Geography and politics," wrote an historian, "began once more to torment Missouri."[17]

St. Louis's Fears

On the east side of the state, in St. Louis, Emil Mallinckrodt and other intellectuals were especially apprehensive about Missouri's future. They feared its slavery-oriented geography and politics would drive it into secession from the Union. On the other hand, their home town of St. Louis—Missouri's largest and booming city of 160,000 people—included only about 1,300 to 1,500 slaves by 1860 and around 1,700 freed blacks.[18] (Emil may have found it interesting that many of those blacks belonged to a large Baptist congregation whose well-educated [and self-educated] minister, Richard Anderson, was a slave freed by E. Bates, Sophie's lawyer.)[19]

Although St. Louis's sentiments may have been generally status quo, or proslavery, its many foreign-born residents often thought differently. And at least half of them were the Germans who were known for their vigorous opposition to slavery.[20] Only a few were slave holders—nineteen, judging by who paid taxes on slaves in 1860.[21] The arrival of so many immigrants in the 1850s had provided such a large work force that slave labor was not necessary. As a historian somewhat cynically put it, "the decline of slavery reflected economic realities rather than humanitarian sentiment. With Irish and German labor available at $200 a year, only those with a sentimental attachment to the institution [of slavery] or to individual servants could resist the temptation to sell their slaves at high prices to Southern planters."[22]

Conservative though they were, many of St. Louis's leading businessmen were nevertheless opposed to slavery. It was a drag on the commercial interests of the city, as well as a moral wrong. Simply put, staying in or seceding from the Union was a matter of life and death for the Gateway to the West; its four thousand steamers plied the Mississippi River down to the slave-holding South as well as up the Missouri into the free West.[23]

Furthermore, the businessmen knew that the rivers would remain crucial for some time, although clearly the eastern railways were coming—by 1857, for example, the railroad from Baltimore reached St. Louis if one changed cars five times, crossed rivers twice on ferries, and added two short steamboat trips.[24] Ultimately railways indeed would tie Missouri to the East and the North, as rivers did to the South and West. And even within the city itself there was a new sign of the importance of rail transportation, a railroad-type car drawn by horses along a track laid on city streets. On its first run in 1859, horses pulled St. Louis's streetcar about six blocks; unhitched then rehitched to the other end of the car, they pulled it back along the track on the so-called return trip.[25]

Secession's threat to the city's essential river traffic was only one reason for St. Louisans' fear of the future—another was city violence between proslavery and antislavery groups of which they already had had their share. Additional clashes were sure to break out in the heated atmosphere. The memory of what had happened in 1836 was still fresh. That year St. Louis newspaper publisher Elijah Lovejoy was driven out of the city for his abolitionist views, specifically for criticizing the killing of a black man, Francis McIntosh, who allegedly had stabbed a white officer. Some historians said simply that McIntosh was a "mulatto . . . burned by a St. Louis mob."[26] Others later spelled out that he had been a slave "burned to death over a slow fire in a public square."[27] Lovejoy's office was pillaged by a mob; that of Wilhelm Weber, editor of the *Anzeiger des Westens*, was threatened for he, too, had denounced the murder of McIntosh.[28]

Anti-Germanism and Politics

Another current of social unrest greatly troubled Missouri's German immigrants, both in St. Louis and the countryside—reappearance in the mid-1850s of the so-called nativism, or anti-foreigner, movement. In 1852 a German tavern in St. Louis had been burned down in a clash with "native" Americans during city elections, and the conflicts had continued.[29] Not by accident, then, in 1853 the political party known as Native Americans, or "Know-Nothings," became active precisely around Duden country where so many Germans had settled. In 1854 it established its first lodge in Montgomery County.[30] As historians of the day wrote,

> The party was a strange one, as it was a secret political order whose members were oath-bound, and which had its lodges, its signs, grips and passwords, and worked secretly to accomplish its openly professed objects. It was composed chiefly of old Whigs (conservatives), although there were many ex-Democrats in its ranks. The cornerstone of its platform was the principle that "Americans must rule America," in other words, that none but native-born citizens of the United States and non-Catholics ought to hold office, and it also favored a radical change in the naturalization laws (21-year residency for naturalized citizenship instead of 5 years).[31]

The party got its name because members answered "I know nothing" when asked about their secret activities; other historians would say that "I don't know" was the password used by members of the secret lodges.[32]

Be that as it may, by 1854 the party had become an important political force.[33] Attacking specifically Roman Catholics and groups of foreigners (Irish and German immigrants), as well as liquor laws, the Know-Nothings challenged existing political parties and frightened citizens. By 1855 there had been open attacks on Germans and riots in Cincinnati and Chicago.[34]

The Mallinckrodts and others knew their history well enough to recall that whenever times were troubled, frightened people looked for scapegoats. Now with civil war just around the corner, Missourians were doing exactly that. In fact, years later, looking back over German immigrants' disappointments, Emil Mallinckrodt would publicly write in the *Westliche Post* that it was the "nativist persecution of the 50s" which taught Germans that they had not "become part of the democracy" in America.[35] Instead, nativists saw the Germans, with their solid, unwavering opposition to secession, bringing war to Missouri.

In addition, immigrants no longer were trickling into Missouri but rather flooding it. About 88,487 Germans had come by 1860.[36] Some insecure groups therefore felt the foreigners were "taking over" politics as well as economics. Then, too, some of the 1848 Germans, immigrants from Europe's failed revolutions, advocated radical ideas which stirred up the public.[37] Finally, the rather moralistic Know-Nothings did not approve of German fondness for beer and wine! And the German immigrants began to fear the growing prohibition movement.[38]

Concerned citizens looking to the major U.S. political parties for help in opposing the Know-Nothings were disappointed. The established parties were unable to deal with the issues behind the movement—anti-foreign nationalism, anti-Catholicism, anti-abolitionism, and pro-temperance—because they lacked clear policies of their own at the time. Whigs and Democrats alike were so internally divided on the issues of abolition and secession that they split into numerous pro and con factions, or wings. Thus left with an impression of confusion, many Missourians supported the protesting Know-Nothings.

Bloody Kansas

Into this troubled scene came new turmoil when the U.S. Congress began to take up seriously the question of how to organize the territory west of Missouri. One bill proposed two territories, Kansas and Nebraska, another just a single Nebraska territory. Either way, when the Kansas-Nebraska Bill became law on 30 May 1854, it permitted the settlers themselves, not the federal government, to decide whether their future state should be slave or free. Thus the Kansas-Nebraska Bill killed the old 1820 Missouri Compromise principle that all areas north of thirty-six degrees thirty minutes should be free. As a historian wrote, with that act "the fat was in the fire."[39] The bloody struggle for political control of Missouri's bordering territories began.

Already, in April 1854, the New England Emigrant Aid Company had begun to promote settlement of antislavery groups in Kansas—the goal was to have people there who would vote for a free state when the time came. The company thus brought in some two thousand settlers who founded Lawrence, Kansas, and other free state communities. As the respected antislavery voice of St. Louis's Germans, *Anzeiger des Westens*, wrote,

> We must oppose the extension of slavery over the new Territories. . . . Slavery is a real pestilence to the State of Missouri. No one denies it, but one also cannot doubt that the establishment of new slave States on our western borders will make the abolition of slavery in our own State still more difficult, if not entirely impossible. We are for the abolition of slavery in Missouri, but of course only constitutionally . . . in our own interests we demand of the Northern States that they from now on constitutionally fight for every foot of land that has not yet been conquered for slavery![40]

The passing of the controversial Kansas-Nebraska Bill brought an important development in the confused political party scene, too. In July 1854, a new outrightly antislavery party was founded in Michigan, naming itself "Republican." It impressed Missouri's German immigrants very much with its call for repeal of the Kansas-Nebraska Bill and the Fugitive Slave Law, as well as abolition of slavery in the nation's capital, the District of Columbia. The new Republicans came from the antislavery wings of both the Democrat and Whig parties, as well as Free Soilers; the leaders were also diverse, for example, Edward Bates, the conservative but antislavery Whig of St. Louis, and the radical Massachusetts senator and lawyer Charles Sumner.[41]

On the proslavery side of the conflict there were momentous developments, as well. In response to the antislavery settlements in Kansas secret societies began to form in Missouri for the opposite purpose, that is, to establish slavery across the border.[42] Even before Indian titles had been extinguished, proslavery Missourians flocked into Kansas to stake out claims.[43] The stage was being set for a long and ugly drama.

Meanwhile, the violence that St. Louisans had feared broke out. Pitched battles between "native" Americans and Irish Catholics took place during city elections in August 1854. Although the Germans were able to stay out of the fight, other lives were lost as police and militia helplessly tried to restore order. It came only when Edward Bates organized a force of seven hundred armed citizens to frighten away the rival mobs.[44]

Although elections were democracy's device for peaceful leadership changes, they again brought violence in November 1854. In Kansas the question of how settlers would vote triggered the foreseen armed conflict between proslavery and antislavery forces in that region. In the area's first elections—for Kansas's territorial delegate to the U.S. Congress—more than half the votes were cast by Missourians from across the border! Indeed, most of that election's fraud and violence was the work of about seventeen hundred armed men from Missouri's western counties.[45] Their numbers grew, especially when their proslavery candidate in Kansas won.

Even the great respecter of democratic procedures, Missouri painter George Caleb Bingham, who himself was a politician, subtly included elements of the state's 1850s election violence and chicanery in his big canvases of that time. For instance, his painting *The County Election 1* included a man with head wound and bandage in the far right foreground, while a drunken man attracted attention to the left side of the painting; in *The Verdict of the People* the drunken citizen is prominently placed in the foreground of the painting.[46]

By the time the Kansas Territory chose its first legislature in March 1855, it was reported that "nearly 5,000 Missourians, including students from the university, marched into the area to vote with flags, firearms, knives, and whiskey . . . more than 6,000 votes were cast in a territory boasting barely 2,000 eligible voters." The election results were repudiated, legally contested, and forcibly fought over. Gradually two new terms entered America's political vocabulary—border ruffians, for the some 5,000 Missourians who consistently interfered in their neighbors' politics, and Bloody Kansas (or Bleeding Kansas), after the consequences of their deeds.[47] Kansas had truly been converted "into a cockpit of civil war."[48] Missouri's proslavery forces, contributing to the violence and disorder in the territory, helped prepare for that war.

Kansas, in fact, seemed by now to have become an obsession in Missouri conversations, newspaper columns, and political activities. In July 1855, for instance, representatives of twenty-six Missouri counties traveled to the western town of Lexington to hold a proslavery convention. There they passed resolutions and issued heated statements highlighting the danger to western Missouri's slave property and condemning the Emigrant Aid Society. The convention, however, changed nothing, and northern settlers continued to arrive in Kansas.[49]

In fact, rumor had it that the northern settlers were flooding Kansas. And many Missourians, it was later said, "came to the conclusion that these 'pioneers' were traveling on Eastern emigrant society complimentary tickets."[50] Perhaps to put the Kansas settlements in perspective, Arnold Krekel reprinted in his St. Charles German-language newspaper an eyewitness account of Lawrence, Kansas, from a sister newspaper, the *Missouri Demokrat*. Its reporter had written from Lawrence that

> a traveler first sees this place from about 2 miles away. It is surrounded by hills on the south and west and on the north by forest, located in a rich, beautiful almost level prairie at the foot of a gentle hill and not far from the river hidden behind foliage. Known throughout the entire Union, it naturally excites the expectation

and curiosity of a traveler. But the first feeling one has from afar is disappointment and doubt.

Yet when one enters the square, and especially when one sees the resolute, serious and religious character of its residents, one stops entertaining doubt or feeling disappointment. It is a village of working people. There are no thieves and no loafers.

Less than a year ago there was not a single cabin there where Lawrence now stands. Now there are 120 log cabins and farm houses, 3 or 4 big stone houses and a big hotel of stone, 3 saw mills doing considerable business, from 20 to 30 stone and wooden houses abuilding and an industrious, energetic and selected population of from 800 to 900 souls.

The town borders enclose ¼ mile. The streets from east and west are named after the heros and scholars of the Revolution; the parallel streets running north to south are named for the states laying north and south of the Mason-Dixon line.

In a recent census it was found that ⅙ of the adult male population of Lawrence had attended colleges and universities and that the majority of them are active members of Christian churches. Not more than ¼ of the population belong to the fair sex.

There are five slaves in Lawrence, recently brought here by a family. And it is a fact, as strange as it may seem, that no inclination to upset their possessions or their person is shown. There are about 10 pro-slavery people in Lawrence, who all appear to live as peacefully and comfortably as anyone else in the population. They indeed entertain the intention to make Kansas a slave state. They speak openly and freely but nevertheless have friendly and uninhibited relations with other residents. I am told that there isn't a person in Lawrence whose travel here was paid by someone else. The 'Emigrant Aid' Society only sold tickets to native-born Americans.[51]

Against this chaotic background, a locally known Illinois politician and lawyer in October 1855 condemned the Kansas-Nebraska Act and denounced slavery.[52] His name was Abraham Lincoln.

In St. Charles County, Missouri, the German settlers' concern about the growing Know-Nothing movement was so great by March 1856 that they called a protest meeting. Julius Mallinckrodt was one of the Democrats so outraged by the Know-Nothings' anti-German and other policies that he rode to Cottleville near St. Charles (twenty-five miles or five to eight hours by horseback) on 29 March to express his concern. Chaired by Arnold Krekel, the Saturday meeting defined the Democrats' dissatisfaction and intentions in a series of resolutions drawn up by a committee of which Julius was a member, representing Femme Osage Township. They very clearly said that those who called for an "America ruled by Americans"—and for making the coincidence of one's birthplace and religious views the basis of "Americanism" and a prerequisite for holding office— were anti-Constitutionalists. Underlying the entire meeting, however, was another theme—the sense of regionalism. Politically, it was said, the interests of "the West" had been neglected and the area had been drawn into North-South quarrels; thus a "Party of the West" was needed to reflect the new spirit sweeping through the people of the area.[53]

By May 1856, "Bleeding Kansas" was considered to be in a state of civil war. The taking of towns and attacks back and forth constituted a state of guerrilla warfare throughout the territory. On 21 May the free settlement of Lawrence, Kansas, was taken and sacked by Missouri "border ruffians" who burned and pillaged the little village the St. Charles newspaper had described. Additional fuel was added to the fire of inflamed Northern antislavery sentiment when, in retaliation for the Lawrence affair, the abolitionist leader John Brown carried out a massacre of proslavery colonists.[54]

Not all violence, however, happened on the frontier. In Washington, D.C., in May 1856, seated at his desk in the Senate of the United States of America, Charles Sumner, a leader of the Republicans, was beaten senseless by a Southerner. The beating, "chastisement" for a vituperative speech on "The Crime Against Kansas," left Sumner able to return to his desk only now and then.[55]

The bitter divisions of the American nation were clearly reflected in its November 1856 presidential election—"Bleeding Kansas" was the central campaign issue. The Democrats, supporting the Kansas-Nebraska Act, chose James Buchanan as their candidate; the new Republicans, favoring congressional authority to control slavery in the territory and admission of Kansas as a free state, ran Colonel John C. Frémont as their leader; the Know-Nothings (now called the American Party), running on their nativist platform, nominated Millard Fillmore for President.

The Democrats and Buchanan won, with the electoral votes of fourteen slave and five free states. The Republican candidate, Frémont, took the North, however, and came close to uniting it and the West against the South. The Know-Nothings also showed surprising strength. In Montgomery County, Missouri, for instance, they swept the ticket, and across the nation the party polled nearly 875,000 votes, or roughly one-fifth of the total.[56] America's sectional divisions were now clearer than ever.

Meanwhile, America's politics continued inexorably discordant. Two days after President Buchanan's inauguration, the next highlight in the slavery struggle occurred, and it directly concerned Missouri—the Dred Scott Decision. Scott, a slave taken from St. Louis to the free state of Illinois and then to the free territory of Wisconsin, sued for his liberty in Missouri courts in 1846. His grounds: he had become free because of his stay on free soil. A lower Missouri court decided in Scott's favor. But when the case went to the Missouri Supreme Court (1852) the ruling was overturned (that is, decided against Scott). Judge H. R. Gamble (Julius Mallinckrodt's lawyer), president of the court, was the only judge who dissented from the decision.[57]

On appeal the case went to the next and highest court in the land. There, in

1857, the U.S. Supreme Court decision also went against Scott, ruling that blacks, indeed, had no legal rights. Another part of the decision seemed to mean that the Missouri Compromise principle of not extending slavery to Territories was dead. Again antislavery Americans were shocked at the political trend this decision reflected.

Trouble in Augusta

The tumult raging from Washington, D.C., to Kansas in the mid-1800s did not leave even small settlements such as Augusta untouched. There Conrad and Julius Mallinckrodt needed only to look out onto the Missouri River below their hills to read the currents of the time. Boats loaded with slaves were moving downstream to safer areas; slaveowners wanted to avoid the kidnapping or freeing of their property by abolitionists.[58]

Apparently, "nativism" had hit the countryside, too. On 3 August 1857, when town elections were held, violence broke out between American and German immigrant settlers. According to the *St. Charles Demokrat*'s first report (headlined "Shooting Affair in Augusta"), "As we learned today, on election day in Augusta there was a bloody clash between an American by the name of P. Fulkerson and several Germans. A number were wounded. Since we are not exactly informed about the facts, we will wait for a better report from the pen of our friend 'Sch' who certainly is sufficiently interested in the truth and the honor of the Germans to send us a complete report."[59]

A week later, then, the *Demokrat* further reported that "an investigation into the incident in Augusta during the election will take place on 24 August. The previously set date had been postponed. Since we ourselves [lawyer Krekel, also the newspaper publisher] are involved, we prefer to wait until later to fully report the facts as they will be presented by the witnesses to be heard."[60]

The Augusta Town Board, meanwhile, meeting the day after the election, resolved that

> whereas acts of violence against the laws of Missouri have been committed and the peace of the citizens of this town has been disturbed, be it ordained . . . that 50 dollars be appropriated out of the treasury of this town for the employment of competent attorneys to prosecute the rioters and disturbers of the peace at the proper courts. That A. Krekel of St. Charles be solicited to take charge of this matter.[61]

Although the outcome of that hearing, at which Arnold Krekel represented the town of Augusta, is not known, clearly the town had been shattered by the violence. A year later, when a newly elected Board of Trustees took office, it passed a series of new ordinances (perhaps adapted from revised state statues) which included three dealing with "law and order." One was to elect a town attorney who would attend to all the Board's legal duties. In addition to a salary, unspecified, the town attorney was to receive two dollars "for every conviction for any offence against the ordinances of the town to be taxed against and recovered of the defendant as other costs."[62]

The second ordinance passed by the Board of Trustees at the same meeting prescribed the duties of the town constable. Among other responsibilities, the constable had "the special duty . . . to visit all parts of the town, to make diligent inquiry after all breaches of the ordinances of the town . . . and to report all offenses to the town attorney whose duty it shall be to prosecute therefor."

Another "special duty" was "to arrest, without warrant, all persons who may be found in the streets of the town in a state of intoxication, and convey them to some safe place of confinement, there to remain until they shall have become perfectly sobered."

Apparently also hoping to take preventive action before violence occurred, the town fathers resolved that the constable should

> visit all suspicious and disorderly houses and neighborhoods, and all parts of the town, where disorder and breach of the law are most likely to be committed and to arrest and take into custody, without warrant, all and every person who may be found in the commission of any offence against the ordinances of the town, and cause such offenders to be dealt with according to the existing ordinances and the laws of the State of Missouri.[63]

In a continuation of the meeting several days later, the Town Board added yet another law-and-order ordinance. Mirroring the turmoil of the late 1850s, this one was entitled "To Suppress Routs, Riots, and Unlawful Assemblies." Specifically forbidden were assemblies of three or more persons with the intent of "any unlawful act, with force or violence, against the person or property of another or against the peace or to the terror of people." Individuals were forbidden to "disturb the peace and quiet of any street or alley, or any neighborhood" by "any unusual noise, by profane swearing or obscene language or conversation, or by tumultuous or offensive language or carriage, by threatening, scolding, challenging or fighting."

The ordinance's instructions to the town constable and deputies about what to do with offenders reflect not only the dominant role of the justice of the peace, but also the necessity of taking into account possibly long travel time by horseback. Specifically, following the arrest the peace officials were to

> forthwith carry such offender before a justice of the peace within Femme Osage township, if said offender shall have been arrested by said constable or deputy in the daytime, there to be dealt with according to the provisions of this ordinance; but if said offender shall have been arrested after six o' clock p.m. the constable

shall commit said offender to some safe place of confinement in said town, where said offender shall remain until an early hour on the ensuing day, when it shall be the duty of the constable to carry said offender before a justice of the peace within Femme Osage township.

Finally, it also was resolved that "all free white male inhabitants" older than eighteen might be asked by the Town Board chairman to assist the constable and if refusing could be fined up to twenty dollars.[64] It may be that Conrad Mallinckrodt was Augusta's justice of the peace during these difficulties for he had been elected to that post for Femme Osage Township in 1856. As one of the few elected officials with a German name, his selection may have reflected an earlier appeal from the German community for a justice of the peace who would serve the specific needs of immigrants.[65]

All was not violent, of course, in the little settlement of Germans. It was in fact described as a quite pleasant place in the first of a series about towns in the county, published in the *St. Charles Demokrat* in fall 1857. About the Augusta settlement of four hundred to five hundred people, the newspaper wrote,

> There are 3 stores in Augusta with a great variety of goods, 1 well-supplied pharmacy, 2 guest houses [pubs], and a steam saw- and flour mill. The buildings for a second steam mill, whose owner is Mr. Schaaf, are already constructed and it will not be long until the mill is running. A great number of craftsmen of all kinds have settled in the little town and from here supply the surrounding area with necessary manufactures.
>
> Previously a good school already had been provided, and great attention is given to the children's education. The school building is also used as a church by various denominations, and despite the very divergent religious views they nevertheless get along very well. Better social life is also provided here than in many a larger town. Augusta has a musical choir under the direction of Mr. Fuhr which is not excelled by any in the west. Numerous concerts are given weekly which the citizens of the town can attend free.
>
> The location of the town is extraordinary, with a beautiful view onto the Missouri and the bottom on the other side. Meanwhile, the good landing eases transportation with St. Louis, which buys most of the products of the area from Augusta's merchants who ship them on steamboats. The ties to the Pacific Railroad, which has a depot exactly opposite from Augusta on the other side on the river only 2 miles away, are excellently served by a ferry run by competent people. This way the town gets its mail three times a week, and that soon will be increased via a northern and southern delivery route.
>
> The hill land around Augusta is among the best in the state, and the industrious and intelligent people living there are mostly well-off. The great bottoms just below, above, and across from the town are entirely under cultivation and produce a lot of products, most of which are sold in Augusta.
>
> Vineyards and orchards are especially stressed in the Augusta area, and the grapes of Mr. Meyer, as well as the finished products of his vineyards, enjoy a well-

deserved reputation. A half mile from town is Mr. Koch's brewery which delivers an excellent beer. Mr. Mallinckrodt's widely-known nursery, which has won and maintained public confidence and yearly ships thousands of young plants [seedlings] to all parts of the state, is located just above Augusta on the river.

The pending completion of a road being built along the bluffs to connect the lower and upper bottoms will be as beneficial to Augusta as the surrounding area. Influenced by this situation, Augusta's trade and population will increase and through its own citizens much also can be undertaken to further this result. Through timely ordinances the city fathers themselves can prevent many noticeable disadvantages and they will not neglect to do so.[66]

At the same time, of course, the growth of the village continued. In 1856 it had bought an acre of land to give the town a proper cemetery and another acre would be added in 1859.[67]

Conrad Remarries

The year 1858 was an important one for Conrad Mallinckrodt—in April, eighteen years after his divorce from Sophie, he married again. The new Mrs. Mallinckrodt was Wilhelmina Caroline Böhmer, a sister to Julius's second wife, and also an immigrant from Westerode near Fürstenau, Germany. Conrad was then fifty and Wilhelmina thirty-six. She was widowed and had seven children, aged four to fifteen years old.[68] The U.S. census two years later showed five of the children resident in Conrad and Wilhelmina's household—one daughter (Christine) had meanwhile died, and eldest son Christian, seventeen, lived away from home as an apprentice.[69]

It was probably around this time that Conrad decided to enlarge his home. Some years ago he had replaced the initial little wooden house on the central hill he owned with a modest one-and-a-half-story brick structure facing the river. Consisting primarily of office space for his notary, surveying, and justice of the peace work, the house was built over a deep wine cellar made of rock and with an outside entrance. Above the eighteen-by-eighteen-foot study there was attic storage space.

Now Conrad designed and had built a parallel one-and-a-half-story western wing, for the dining room and kitchen areas with sleeping space above, and an approximately twenty-by-eighteen-foot, two-story center wing for the downstairs living room and upstairs bedrooms (plate 12). Five chimneys for the fireplaces topped the house, and three front doors on the south side provided separate entrances for each wing. To the back, toward the woods, where the family cemetery was located, were the smokehouse and various outbuildings serving the kitchen and other family needs.

While a brick residence was grand for its time, it was the separate study room, or wing, which made the house especially impressive to generations of neighbors and family. The very fact that it was elevated above the living room, that one had to go up two steps to enter, made it a world unto itself.[70] On the south side of that doorway was Conrad's dark walnut desk, certainly of his own design and Dortmund memories—drawers at the bottom, in the middle a locking dropleaf secretarial section with pigeon holes that tilted forward when the desk was opened, and above it, behind their own doors, bookshelves reaching to the ceiling. On the other side of the entrance door was another built-in walnut wooden wall unit of bookshelves with doors reaching from the ceiling to about five feet above floor level, leaving space possibly for a worktable. Two windows to the south provided a view of two stately cedar trees in the yard and the river valley in the distance; the two to the east looked out onto Julius's home. It, too, faced south toward the river, but was a one-and-a-half-story, with white weatherboard covering the original log sections. Like Conrad's home, Julius's kitchen had a fireplace.

While Conrad concentrated for a time on establishing his new family, Julius carried on their political activism, for in the view of many German immigrants the political situation in Missouri was quite serious by July 1858. In fact, fearing for the Union, about one hundred St. Charles county residents, from every township, gathered on a very hot Saturday in the midst of wheat harvest time to further a new political party; a Union Party might be the way to deal with the crisis. Julius Mallinckrodt and his son-in-law Heinrich Nahm were among those who rode the many horseback-hours to Cottleville, near St. Charles, to nominate pro-Union candidates for the state legislature. Both, in fact, were named to the twelve-person nominating committee.

A long list of grievances troubled those Missouri Unionists gathered in Cottleville on 3 July—the resolutions they passed called for Western unity, an indivisible Union, noninterference in the Kansas territory, a sound national economy, support for public schools and mass education, end of slavery agitation, encouragement of immigration, honesty and ability as prerequisites for holding public office rather than political or religious views, and so on. After a midday break because of the July heat, the audience reassembled to hear Arnold Krekel and other Unionists speak.

President Buchanan's Democratic party, which many German immigrants had favored for years, was sharply criticized as one which Missourians no longer could/ should support. Instead, as later reported, "Today's meeting was called so everyone who loves the Union and supports positive change in domestic politics can join the new Union Party being formed."[71] Not reflected in the report, of course, was the dismay, and uncertainty, among Germans once again about to give up one set of failing political beliefs for another.

Death of the New Dortmund Dream

At Julius's in the late 1850s the mood was mixed. His orchards were doing so well that he hired several field hands and nursery laborers, and the value of his real estate reached $7,000.[72] But apparently he had to bury his dream of new Dortmund.

It is not possible to know just exactly when the dream began to die; diaries and letters are not available, and dreams, after all, die slowly, bit by bit. There was, however, a published explanation from Julius himself toward the end of his life. In the early 1880s, St. Charles County historians evidently interviewed him, and based on that personal information wrote in their subsequent publication (1885) that the death of the Dortmund dream came in the early 1840s: "The place was killed in its infancy; in fact, soon after Mr. Mallinckrodt had sold many of the town lots, and before building operations began, the ever changing waters of the Missouri swept around to the opposite side of the broad bottom lands and left the village without a river front. This unfortunate circumstance nipped the embryo city in the bud, and the property again came into the possession of its original owner."[73]

What happened is not impossible to imagine . . . Julius and Conrad and everyone else along the Missouri River had become sensitive over the years to its vagaries. As they watched the Big Muddy they saw sandbars near its north side growing larger with additional accumulations of soil and debris coming downstream; they noticed how the clogged-up channel then sought space farther south, cutting away at the river bottoms on the other side. It was clear that the main channel was gradually drawing back from its northern shoreline fronting their property.

Julius and those who had bought his new Dortmund lots grew skeptical about the area's future. And when the 1844 flood swept over the Dortmund property—something that had never happened before—they had serious doubts about the wisdom of building there. Besides, finances had become a real problem. Local historians wrote that "times were very hard upon the people of the county in 1842–43. Money was scarce and very hard to get, and produce and wages ridiculously low."[74] In fact, in May 1844, even before the great flood, Julius had mortgaged almost his entire property, including the Dortmund lots, for five hundred urgently needed dollars. Not surprisingly, then, after the mid-1840s Julius's lot sales recorded at the county seat dropped off significantly.[75]

Under the circumstances, Dortmund's founder and his lot buyers may have had to agree, probably around the mid-1840s, to just give up the plan. If ledger books were available one would see to whom and when Julius refunded the money. Although such evidence was not preserved, it is clear from the settlement of Julius's estate after his death that he refunded; he did not give up the land. The records show that the mortgage above was paid off on July 1857. It is also clear that the new Dortmund repossession transactions were informal, among men who knew and trusted each other and did not feel they had to go to court. Before the court which probated Julius's estate, his children testified about the Dortmund property: "Second:—This town site was afterwards abandoned with the consent of all the owners of the lots, and Julius Mallinckrodt. A verbal understanding only. The purchasers of said lots never took possession of the lots so purchased, except J. Y. Graif, the owner of Lots 3 & 34, who built on one of the lots and afterwards gave up possession to Julius Mallinckrodt. All of this happened a few years after the dedication [1836]."[76]

Clearly then, a much later, occasionally quoted version of how and when Julius's new Dortmund dream died is highly doubtful. In a personal observation written and printed in 1870 in *Der deutsche Pionier* published in Cincinnati, Friedrich Münch of Warren County, near the original Duden property at Dutzow, reported that "the big city of Dortmund planned on the banks of the Missouri by Julius M., or more correctly the ground on which it should be built, has recently again been degraded to a corn field. The speculation was sound—thousands of dollars flowed into M's pockets—and for a trifle, the amount of remaining unpaid taxes, he took everything back (*zog das Ganze wieder an sich*)."

Though "recently" (that is, late 1860s to early 1870s) is not a tenable date, alleged delinquent taxes do not seem like a credible explanation for the dissolution of new Dortmund.[77] There was in fact a tax angle to the story about the planned town, which Münch may have heard, but it related to the purchase of land for new Dortmund, not its demise. As the witnesses testified at Julius's estate settlement in June 1902:

> To Whom It May Concern:—
>
> This is a statement of facts concerning the irregularities and deficiencies in the title of Julius Mallinckrodt's, deceased, legal representatives to a part of the North-East fractional ¼ of Section 15, Township 44, Range 1 East, situated in St. Charles County, Mo.
>
> First:—The town of Dortmund which is not definitely located in the original dedication in Book "K", pages 223 & 224, was located in the South-West ¼ of, and the South-East ¼ of the North-East ¼ of said Section 15, and North of the present Railroad track. . . .
>
> As shown in a deed dated Nov. 18, 1865, recorded in Book "V" No. 2 page 237, Julius Mallinckrodt purchased 18 acres in the North-East fractional ¼ of Section 15, Township 44, Range 1 East at a tax sale. This 18 acres was supposed and intended to embrace the entire town site of Dortmund. The said Julius Mallinckrodt and his present legal representatives have had actual, notorious, adverse and continuous possession of the town site of Dortmund for over 50 years.[78]

Clear and central to the story of Julius (plate 13) and his dream are two undisputed facts: (a) the Dortmund land never left Julius's possession as long as he lived; (b) the Missouri River, too, never really gave up its original location—whenever it flooded dramatically in the century to come it always renewed its pre-1844 claim, that is, stretching from bluff to bluff across all the channels or beds where it had ever rested.

Conrad apparently held onto his brother's dream somewhat longer than the mid-1840s. In 1851, for instance, he still used the location "Dortmund" when surveying a road in the area. And in 1853 he was still listed as the county newspaper's sales agent from "Dortmund."[79] By 1857, however, Julius seems to have given up the idea entirely. By then the river landing had moved several miles downsteam, to Augusta, and that now-incorporated settlement was growing. The country also was experiencing another serious financial panic and inflated prices, and there was no hope for reviving the Dortmund plan, even without a waterfront.[80]

And so Julius Mallinckrodt began to use *Augusta* as the designation for his location, rather than Dortmund, on his sale bill and advertisements (figure 23-1).[81] Julius's orchard, in fact, was well on the way to becoming the second largest in the county, and he entered into partnership with his son Conrad Theodor in 1857.[82] The varieties and numbers of fruit trees which Julius had for sale were impressive. Advertisements for his root-grafted fruit trees appeared regularly in the St. Charles newspaper owned by the family's friend Arnold Krekel (figure 23-1). One noted at the bottom that,

- In addition to fruit trees, "Cedar trees . . . and some Catalpa two years old" were also available.
- "Orders from the upper part of the Missouri will be promptly executed by the return of the Packet Steamers from St. Louis."
- "My stock ready for sale this season consists of about 50,000 Apple Trees of 2 and 3 years standing, and 1,500 grafted Peach Trees."[83]

Here, too, as on the bill of sale, Julius used the *Augusta* designation, for the little settlement had become quite widely known. In fact, by the end of the decade it was included on a list of notable Missouri towns and described as "entirely German, appears to be favorably located for the wine industry."[84]

Emil's Time of Troubles

Across the Atlantic, Emil, having spent more than two years in Europe with his family, was very troubled. Ellen was quite ill; in fact, she was not sure that she could survive the transatlantic voyage home. Wrote Emil, "I think of the need and abandonment I and my small children would face if during the voyage we had the misfortune of losing their mother."[85]

Emil's other deep concern was the break in his relations with cousin Gustav, perhaps resulting from the business situation Gustav II had found during his visit to St. Louis. Writing Gustav I in Köln shortly before departing for America, Emil thanked him for all kindness and said, "I would have thought it *impossible* that this friendly relationship would be disrupted, and until my last breath I will be unhappy about the misfortune. But that does not in the least detract from your former love for us."[86] This letter was signed *"Für ewig Lebewohl!"* (For ever farewell!).

Returning to St. Louis in late September 1855, Emil was not greeted with good

CATALOGUE

of

ROOT-GRAFTED FRUIT TREES

CULTIVATED

BY

Julius Mallinckrodt

Near Augusta, St. Charles County, Mo.

THIS EXCELLENT ASSORTMENT OF VIGOROUS AND HEALTHY TREES WILL FULLY ENABLE ME TO MERIT THE CONFIDENCE THE PUBLIC MAY CHOOSE TO HONOR ME WITH.

Winter Apples.

Jenetons	Spitzenberg
Newark - Pippin	Renette of Berlin
Yellow Newton - Pippin	Winesap
Spitzenburg	Holland Pippin
Boston - Russet	Renette of Normandy
Mñam	Dodson apple
22 ounce Pippin	Golden Renette
Missouri red	Father Abraham
Long green Pippin	Gravenstein
Golden Russet	Pryor's red
Sweet Jeneton	Imperial Pippin

Fall Apples.

Fall Pippin	Colliers fall
Rambo	Hughes'crab
Calville	Harrison cider
Maidens blush	Rhode Island Greening

Summer Apples.

Matsen	Summer - rose
Smith summer	Yellow harvest
Darst early July	Early red Margaret
Preserve apples	Early June eating
Summer bellflower	Summer redstreak
Red bellflower	

PEACH-TREES.

Sugar rareripe	Grants large Yellow
Hancocks large freestone	Heath Peach
Blood Peach	Morrison white cling
Longworth large freestone	Early rareripe
Early York freestone	October Peach
Early July id	Apricot
Silverskin	Early Ann
George the IV	Teton de Venus
Apricot	Early Cling
Washington cling	Great mashree
Hills Madera	Snow Peach
Poplar Peach	Albert Galatin

☞ Cedar-Trees at 10 cts. and some Catalpa two years old.

☞ According to the opinion of practical and experienced men, Fruit Trees may be safely transplanted in the fall after the 1st day of November.

Orders received from the upper part of the Missouri will be promptly executed by the return of the Packet Steamers from St. Louis.

☞ My stock, ready for sale this season consists of about 50,000 Apple Trees of 2 and 3 years standing, and 1,500 grafted Peach Trees.

Price of Apple Trees 3 years standing	20. cts.
„ „ 2 „ „	15 cts.
„ Peach Trees	20 cts.

"ST. CHARLES DEMOCRAT OFFICE."

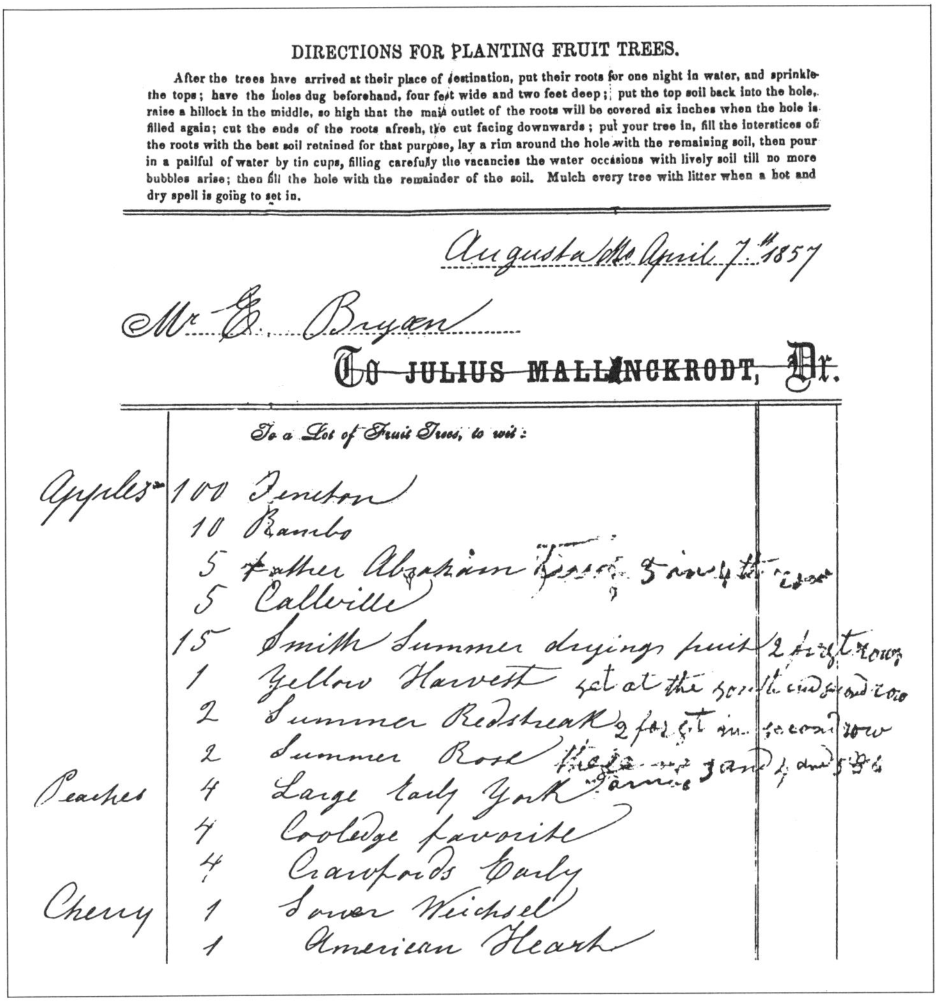

DIRECTIONS FOR PLANTING FRUIT TREES.

After the trees have arrived at their place of destination, put their roots for one night in water, and sprinkle the tops; have the holes dug beforehand, four feet wide and two feet deep; put the top soil back into the hole, raise a hillock in the middle, so high that the main outlet of the roots will be covered six inches when the hole is filled again; cut the ends of the roots afresh, the cut facing downwards; put your tree in, fill the interstices of the roots with the best soil retained for that purpose, lay a rim around the hole with the remaining soil, then pour in a pailful of water by tin cups, filling carefully the vacancies the water occasions with lively soil till no more bubbles arise; then fill the hole with the remainder of the soil. Mulch every tree with litter when a hot and dry spell is going to set in.

Augusta Mo April 7th 1857

Mr E. Bryan

To JULIUS MALLINCKRODT, Dr.

To a Lot of Fruit Trees, to wit:

Apples	100	Peneton
	10	Rambo
	5	Father Abraham
	5	Calleville
	15	Smith Summer drying fruit 2 first rows
	1	Yellow Harvest set at the south end of 2nd row
	2	Summer Redstreak 2 forget in second row
	2	Summer Rose
Peaches	4	Large Early York
	4	Cooledge favorite
	4	Crawfords Early
Cherry	1	Sower Weichsel
	1	American Heart

Figure 23-1. Julius Mallinckrodt's 1857 bill of sale (*above*) and newspaper advertisement (*left*) for fruit trees from his widely known orchards and nursery. (Emil Mallinckrodt Papers and William S. Bryan Papers, *Missouri Historical Society Archives, St. Louis.*)

family news. Cholera had struck and struck hard. Luise's sister Lina had died 19 June 1854, followed by her husband Louis Ruetz on 7 July, leaving a little son John (then probably about four years old) for sister Sophie Amend to raise. At the same time, the Amends, themselves very ill, lost their own son Wilhelm Jr., then probably about three years old, in August.[87] When Sophie Christine wrote her Köln cousin Gustav from St. Louis in September 1854 to tell him the news of the family deaths, she also asked him for two hundred to three hundred dollars to bridge the income loss their bakery business had sustained during her family's illnesses. Emil had helped her, too, she wrote.[88]

Hermann and Luise meanwhile were making another new start in St. Louis— by October 1855 they had opened a fruit store.[89] Julius was supplying Hermann with fruit and nursery trees from Duden country, but Emil felt the business was not going very well.[90]

Emil himself was also making another new start. Probably because of Eleanor's failing health, Emil and his family left St. Louis in March 1856 to settle down on a small farm he had bought ten miles west of St. Louis. He intended to spend the rest of his life there.[91] The property included fields and gardens, woods and meadows, as well as an excellent water supply. Emil worked the fields and gardens to improve his health, while Ellen enjoyed the sunshine and the children the physical outdoor activities. Indeed, Emil said, to complete their readjustment they were to be kept out of school that fall.

Twice a week, then, Emil went into the city to look after his real estate business in north St. Louis in the suburb of Bremen. But those affairs did not go well either—as Emil said, they had "become disarranged during my long absence." Therefore, in addition to such property, one "has to do something which feeds one, as for instance the farm."[92]

Emil continued to be plagued, too, by the misunderstandings between him and cousin Gustav, which had left painful wounds. As he wrote Gustav, "I often wonder whether they could not and should not have been avoided. The matter was not worth the sorrow which it gave me and still does. My soul is no longer free of bitter feelings as it once was, but I gladly try to recall the many friendlinesses which you so good-heartedly showed us. I remain thankful to you and your dear wife for all my life."[93] From Gustav there was no mention of the quarrel in his polite responses to Emil's letters.[94]

Before long it was too late for either of them to apologize. Gustav died suddenly on 17 November 1856, at the age of fifty-seven. The stress of the revolutionary years in Germany and rheumatic illness had taken their toll.[95] Liberal government had lost a strong supporter, and Gustav was fittingly buried prominently among its early leaders in Köln's Melaten Cemetery, in fact near his colleague Mevissen. Emil, in America, on the other hand, had lost his best friend. When he wrote Gustav II, Emil referred to the younger Mallinckrodt's late father as "always a true brother," "the friend of my life," and the friend "whom I loved so sincerely since youth and to whom I owe so much."[96]

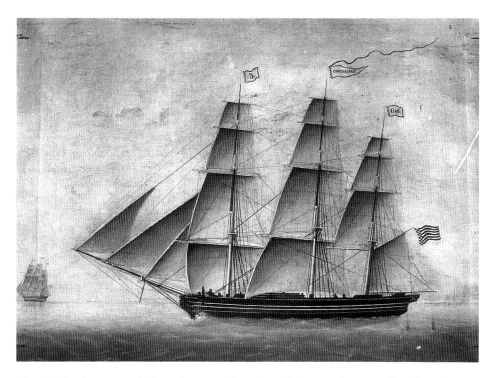

Plate 8. The three-masted *Copernicus* was a favorite with 1830s emigrants sailing from Bremen to Baltimore. (*Photo: Hermann Kippenberg. Courtesy Bremen City Archive.*)

Plate 9. Emil Mallinckrodt, St. Louis farmer and real estate developer, as painted by Adele Gleason, c. 1845. (*Courtesy Missouri Historical Society, St. Louis.*)

Plate 10. The tombstone of Frederick Wachs, who was buried in the small Mallinckrodt family cemetery then located behind Conrad Mallinckrodt's house near Augusta, Missouri, 1852. Mary Mallinckrodt's tombstone can be seen in the upper lefthand corner. (*Courtesy Karl Roe.*)

Plate 11. The Hermann Mallinckrodt family in 1850. *Left to right*: Cecilia Henriette (age five), Hermann (age thirty-nine), John Frederick (age two), James Ferdinand (age seven), and Luise (age thirty-three). (*Courtesy Philip A. Mallinckrodt.*)

Plate 12. Conrad Mallinckrodt's initial brick house was the eastern wing (*above*), which he expanded to include a central and western wing (*below*) probably in the late 1850s. (*Courtesy Karl Roe.*)

Plate 13. Julius Mallinckrodt, St. Charles County, Missouri, horticulturist (c. 1850s). (*Courtesy Wayne Heger.*)

Plate 14. Julius Mallinckrodt's c. 1869 wine cellar was unusual—it was made of brick and was three stories tall. (*Author collection.*)

Plate 15. Conrad Theodor (1835–1910), the son of Julius and Mary McClenny Mallinckrodt of Augusta, Missouri, was the first Mallinckrodt son to be born in America. (*Courtesy Roland Mallinckrodt.*)

Plate 16. Conrad Mallinckrodt, educator, surveyor, justice of the peace, c. 1877, at Augusta, Missouri. (*Author collection.*)

By 1858 Emil would mourn again. In June 1858 he wrote his cousin Gustav II that his wife Eleanor, "who had struggled against physical suffering since early youth," was "visibly sinking; we all suffer with her without hope."[97] On 30 September 1858, some months after they celebrated their twenty-fifth wedding anniversary, Eleanor died at the age of forty-two. Emil was left with their three sons (Gustav III eighteen, Eduard thirteen, and Otto eleven) and two daughters (Minna sixteen and Adele nearly seven). Only Gustav was "on his own," so to speak—interested in going into the drug industry with his brothers in the future; he had been working at Richardson Drug Company since September 1857 to gain experience.[98]

As Emil wrote Köln, "my poor wife went to sleep after years of painful suffering from tuberculosis (*Lungenschwindsucht*), which I had long feared . . . loving daughter Minna had constantly cared for her mother for one and a half years and scarcely left her side." (Before that, she had been in school in St. Louis.[99]) Now unable to carry on the household alone, Emil planned to leave his farm and board for a time with a family in St. Louis. Someone would care for the farm to which he hoped to return in spring.[100]

Perhaps because of his own sorrows at this time, Emil's letters to Köln did not mention the other St. Louis deaths, mourned especially by Hermann and Luise. In October, 1858 it was their six-year-old nephew, John, who had survived the death of his parents Louis and Lina Mallinckrodt Ruetz four years earlier, who died, and a month later, in November, their brother-in-law and the boy's adoptive father, Wilhelm Amend. That left the widow Sophie Mallinckrodt Amend with her brother-in-law Hermann and sister Luise, and their brother August.

The next spring, in March 1859, however, the little family unit from Dortmund would also lose August. Apparently he had moved to St. Louis from Augusta sometime after 1852 to join his sisters, and died there. His name was included on the cremation urn of the Ruetz and Amend families.

While those deaths may suggest that St. Louis may once again have been visited by an epidemic in 1858–59, the city's economics, nevertheless, had picked up a bit since 1857. Emil was somewhat encouraged. He again had made several good real estate sales (for example, to build a foundry), six new banks had been accredited in Missouri, and farm land was increasing in value.[101] Emil apparently did not yet see the coming conflict.

Abraham Lincoln: *1860 Election*

By the late 1850s warning signals were clearly being heard. For instance, the Mallinckrodts at Augusta and other Missourians were increasingly reading speeches by the still largely unknown Abraham Lincoln of Illinois. Putting the country's turmoil into perspective, Lincoln, in an address to the Republican Party state convention at Springfield, Illinois, on 16 June 1858, for example, "struck the keynote of American history for the seven years to come":

> We are now far into the *fifth* year, since a policy was initiated, with the *avowed* object, and *confident* promise of putting an end to slavery agitation.
> Under the operation of that policy, that agitation has not only, not *ceased*, but has *constantly augmented*.
> In my opinion, it *will* not cease until a crisis shall have been reached, and passed. A house divided against itself cannot stand.
> I believe this government cannot endure permanently half *slave* and half *free*.
> I do not expect the Union to be *dissolved*; I do not expect the house to fall— but I *do* expect it will cease to be divided.
> It will become *all* one thing, or *all* the other.[102]

Over the following summer and autumn months of 1858, Missourians heard a lot more about Lincoln. In a campaign for Illinois's U.S. senatorial seat, Lincoln engaged in a historical series of seven debates with his opponent Stephen A. Douglas. In them, Lincoln spelled out clearly his rejection of slavery, though he avoided a radical position. Slavery, he said, was "a moral, a social, and a political wrong." Although Abraham Lincoln lost that senatorial race, he emerged from the Lincoln-Douglas Debates as a national figure. Many in the nation had followed his words and thoughts carefully, seeking to understand the disaster they foresaw.[103]

The atmosphere of hate and fear that Lincoln said was spreading indeed intensified once again in October 1859. The abolitionist John Brown, of the earlier Kansas massacre, seized a federal arsenal at Harper's Ferry, Virginia, with a vague plan of setting up a republic of fugitive slaves in the Appalachian Mountains. People were killed and taken prisoner at Harper's Ferry. Captured, Brown was put on trial and convicted of murder. His speedy hanging fed the smoldering revenge and shock on both sides of the slavery question. In addition, rumors of slave insurrection made the rounds, terrifying the South.[104]

With the fires of unrest so well stoked by events of recent years, the presidential election of 1860 obviously would be momentous. In addition, it would be confusing because the political party landscape had changed, or at least names had.[105]

On the liberal side of the political spectrum was the old tradition of Thomas Jefferson's Republican party (later called Democratic Republicans and then just Democrats) with a new label.[106] Under the tension of the slavery issue, part of that tradition had reorganized itself in 1854 into a new Republican party opposed to slavery. Splitting the existing Whig and Democratic parties, the group had done quite well in the previous election and now was the Republican party of Abraham Lincoln—and increasingly of Missouri's Germans who saw it as the defender of the Union.

This was logical because ever since their arrival on the American frontier,

German immigrants had been Thomas Jefferson Republicans. And that, in turn, was consistent because Jefferson (who died in 1826) was a man of the Enlightenment, just as, for example, had been the Mallinckrodts' teachers in Germany. The shared intellectual liberal tradition was that of opposing cruel legal powers and arbitrary government, championing freedom of speech, press, and personal liberty, and knowing of God's plan through science and nature while rejecting organized Christianity. Such Enlightenment teachings offered new understanding of consequences as well as causes; it also challenged people to increase their knowledge and thereby narrow the gap between what they thought and how they lived, in short to be better able to "practice what they preached." Immanuel Kant, for example, had taught Germans to think for themselves, to shake off the bonds of authority in politics and religion ("Dare to know! Have the courage to use your own intelligence!"); Jefferson had gone a step further to put the Enlightenment's lessons into practice and launch the American War of Independence.[107] Perhaps not coincidentally, then, it would be found a century later that absolutely the only page in Conrad's twelve-volume Brockhaus encyclopedia folded for special attention was the page containing the entry "Jefferson, Thomas." That page was folded under a quarter inch along its entire left side, making it easy to locate when thumbing through the book.

Holding such liberal beliefs out of education and experience, Conrad and Julius for years voted that tradition when it was called Democrat. Now they supported the new, basically Northern, party of Lincoln, called Republican. Although later historians would often miss the point, Germans such as the Mallinckrodts had not changed their liberal philosophy; instead it was the party representing American liberalism which had changed its name—Republican (Jefferson), to Democrat (for example, Jackson and Van Buren), back to Republican (Lincoln).

On the conservative side of the political spectrum in 1860, the label changes were also confusing. Some key ideas of Alexander Hamilton and his Federalists, who had so ardently opposed Thomas Jefferson after the War of Independence, evolved by the 1830s into concepts of the conservative Whig party.[108] When it split in 1832 over sectional interests, some Whigs went over to the Democratic party. And when that party, in turn, divided over slavery in 1860, more liberal members followed the antislavery new Republicans. This frequently was the transition of Missouri Germans.[109]

Others, however, remained with the Democratic party which now, too, was divided North/South. Therefore, it fielded two candidates in 1860—the Northern Democrats ran Stephen A. Douglas, Lincoln's old foe, as a candidate; the Southern Democrats put up their own candidate, Breckenridge of Kentucky. Another middle-of-the road party had formed, the National Constitutional Union, and its candidate was Bell. The people's choice among these politicians, in eighteen free and fifteen slave states, would decide the fate of the Union.

For Julius and Conrad in spring 1860 the middle-of-the-road still seemed preferable, and both were active in the Femme Osage Township Opposition which was allied with the Constitutional Union. Conrad was on a resolutions committee, and Julius was a Township delegate to the county meeting of the group in Cottleville. The resolutions passed there did not mention secession or slavery but instead gave priority to countering the uncertain stand ("sell-out policy") of the "so-called National Democratic Party" on the issue of energetic support for railroad building—"Resolved: that we make the railroad question the primary issue in the next election." Julius, along with Arnold Krekel and others, was chosen to attend the Opposition Party's district convention and to serve as the executive committee.[110] St. Louis meanwhile had two good German-language newspapers reporting and sorting out these developments. Both were radical Republican, that is, pro-Lincoln. In addition to the *Anzeiger*, the *Westliche Post* had been founded in 1857 by Börnstein's former chief editor Carl Dänzer. He wrote in the first issue of 27 September that the paper intended to "represent the principles of freedom and well-being of the people against every form of injustice, oppression, monopoly, and aristocracy." Moreover, the paper said, "We believe that Kansas must be a free state, and we hold it to be the duty of the current generation to free Missouri from slavery as well . . . transforming Missouri into a flourishing *free state*."[111]

During the summer and autumn of 1860 German Missourians were increasingly troubled by the issue of slavery. It had become a primary focus of their newspapers' reporting and so also of their personal discussion. Moreover, America's political parties were becoming specific about their position on the slavery issue, for it surely would be central to the presidential election taking place in November. Gradually, therefore, concerned citizens reexamined their own political positions, and many German Americans chose to actively support the antislavery Republican Party.

Germans for Lincoln

In St. Louis, as elsewhere, the 1860 election campaign was "unusually hot and acrimonious," wrote a Baptist minister who later would compile an unusual account of the border city's travail.[112]

In August the German residents of St. Louis, most of whom had decided to support Lincoln, invited their well-known "forty-eighter" immigrant countryman from Wisconsin to St. Louis to speak. Carl Schurz accepted and on 1 August 1860 spoke about "The Doom of Slavery." Called a "masterful speech" by many who heard it, it was said that Schurz "appealed to the reason and good sense of the slaveholders, some of whom sat before him, and urged them to abandon their position;" in addition, Schurz commended the Republicans of the state for having given encouragement to the North and set an example to the South.[113] The St. Louis Mallinckrodts were most likely in that audience.

Shortly after Schurz's visit, the *Anzeiger des Westens* followed up with an intensive appeal for slaveowners to come over to the Republican side:

In Missouri there now already are more than five hundred slaveowners who at the same time are antislavery people. These are persons who, unlike so many others, do not hold slaves out of arrogance, but rather bought slaves in part to get their field work done. In part they have inherited slaves, and they have been trying to make use of their inheritance. We receive more and more of these people in our ranks every day, for experience has taught them that slave labor is not as productive in Missouri as free labor; all that prevents them from emancipating their slaves is a fear of further losses, the impossibility of finding enough free white workers, and, finally, often a certain piety that hesitates at placing inherited slaves in strange hands or seeing them go to ruin in freedom.[114]

In the rural areas near St. Louis, for instance in St. Charles County, the political mood also was intense. In late August, readers of the *St. Charles Demokrat* were incensed to read that German farmers in neighboring Lincoln County had fled after being harassed because they did not sympathize with the "peculiar institution," that is, slavery.[115] By September sizable crowds came to Republican gatherings in Augusta and other towns to hear Arnold Krekel, now committed to that party, speak in German, as well as Friedrich Münch. One meeting in Augusta, in mid-October, was followed by a parade led by members of the Turner organization and the town's Harmonie-Verein Band.[116]

On 22 October the *Anzeiger* published a report by Friedrich Münch on the Republican rallies in Augusta and elsewhere in Duden country:[117]

The sixth of October was an important day for the beautifully situated, entirely German town of Augusta in St. Charles County. It had been announced that Mr. A. Krekel and the undersigned would speak there in the afternoon, and for that purpose the residents made the most excellent preparations. The roomy hall nevertheless could not hold everyone, so the open doors and windows were filled with listeners. The understanding as well as the emotions of those present were addressed, so that in conclusion they broke into seemingly unending jubilation. Meanwhile night had come, and now the German band (which, under the leadership of Mr. Fuhr, had reached a perfection rare in such a small town), the speakers, the committee, and the listeners were feted; the Turners carried flags, lanterns, and transparencies, and the procession of enthusiastic people wound through all the main streets of the town while eight bonfires lit the sky. Whoever heard the cheering and saw the fires from afar would better have understood Seward's words, "Missouri is Germanizing itself to make itself free."

The guests were treated to a brilliant supper, at which Augusta's Catawba [wine] played a prominent role. Among the toasts, that for Garibaldi [Italian revolutionary] excited the greatest enthusiasm. The great crowd dispersed only after midnight, and everyone probably said to himself: we do not want to and must not give up our German way of life here, for only Germans can enjoy themselves in such a way by putting thought, heart, and hand to a cause they support.

The same orators spoke on the 8th of October at New Melle, a German village in the same county. We spoke to a totally agrarian population there; some had traveled many miles to come, and everyone listened with rapt attention. I believe we succeeded entirely in answering the questions all those present had to ask and that without exception they will go to the next election as Lincoln men.

Since the Hurrah-for-Douglas boys had no opportunity to disrupt festivities, both of these rallies went off without the slightest disturbance.

On the 13th of October the same orators will speak in Dutzow—currently the residence of the undersigned—and then later also in other parts of Warren County.

Friedrich Münch[118]

As the election approached, the St. Louis newspapers became more specific. On 29 October, for instance, the *Anzeiger des Westens* used the words "civil war" after sketching rather dramatically what was coming: "Every day we are told what the South will do or have done if we elect Lincoln as president. They are trying to frighten us with fears of a civil war; they want to make us believe that South Carolina, Mississippi, and Alabama are only waiting for the news that a Republican president has been elected in order to leave the Union."[119] At the same time, however, editorial concepts of blacks as people and what to do with American slavery remained vague.

In the November 1860 voting, Lincoln won—primarily because of the divisions within the political parties rather than his overwhelming popularity. Carrying every free state, he had a large majority of the electoral college votes; in the popular vote, however, Douglas was a close second.

Missouri's performance was not unexpected. With ten percent of its population in slavery, the state's electoral votes did not go to elect Lincoln.[120] He got only 17,028 votes, primarily in three counties (St. Louis, Gasconade, and Cole). Instead the Democrat's northern candidate, Douglas, carried the state (58,801 votes), and the Constitutional Union party candidate Bell was a close second (58,372). Interestingly, the Democrat's southern candidate fared considerably less well (31,317 votes) than one might have expected in a state with so much overt support of the Southern cause.[121] Missourians clearly were moderates, but not St. Louis. Its Republicans carried the city for Lincoln. And in Augusta, Lincoln also won, 85 to 64.[122] And so through the Republicans, supported by both German newspapers, the Forty-eighters entered the mainstream of American politics.[123]

Although St. Louis's election outcome, due largely to its large German population, was no surprise, what happened in some nearby rural areas was. As a historian of the time wrote about the voting in Montgomery County, bordering the Missouri River west of St. Charles and Warren counties,

For the first time in its history Republican votes had been given openly in Montgomery county. It was known that there were a few Republicans here, but the number was not supposed to exceed 10 or 12, and when 45 men walked up to the polls and announced Abraham Lincoln as their choice for President, there was great astonishment, mingled with indignation. The expulsion of this class of voters was demanded by many, and it is said some of them received written notices to leave the county at once. At that date the method of voting was *viva voce*—that is, by word of mouth—and each voter was compelled to announce openly for whom he voted. Therefore all the Republicans were known.[124]

Several weeks after the election, the *St. Charles Demokrat* wrote that, "As doubtful as it may sound, it nevertheless is certain that also in our country the fanaticism of those confessing Southern beliefs has demanded its sacrifice." The incident, the newspaper said, had taken place in Darst Bottom, a part of the county where most residents were slave holders. There two American brothers, named Bill, had tried to vote for Lincoln on 6 November, but were told that "no damn black Republican vote" would be cast there. One brother voted but was beaten up and told to leave the area within three days; the other brother, arriving at the polls somewhat later, said when asked that he would vote for Lincoln and so received the same treatment. Both Bills fled to St. Charles where they told their story, pointing out that rowdies rather than the slave holders themselves had done the beating.[125]

Another election day disturbance involved Germans and Americans from two towns in Duden country. After sorting out many rumors, the St. Charles newspaper reported that on election day a German in New Melle, bearing a club, rode after a mason who had been drinking and brawling. An American followed the German, shooting at him with a revolver. This action, in turn, attracted fifty to sixty Americans in nearby Wentzville to set out with rifles to take revenge against New Melle. Responding to New Melle's call for help, the sheriff was able to dissuade the actions of the Wentzville riders by threatening to enforce the Riot Law against them. Meanwhile the New Melle Germans had also gotten ready for an ambush against the Americans. After order was restored and the case heard, some twelve men were charged with rioting, ten Germans and two Americans.[126]

Such voting reactions made life for Germans especially difficult. As one of them put it, Missouri's Germans "were in a very critical and even precarious position at the time, when the waves of excitement rose higher and higher every day." Since they "were indiscriminately considered to be abolitionists" and Missouri was a slave state, Germans found life much more difficult there than did their countrymen in free states.[127] All of this Emil Mallinckrodt, too, would have loved to describe to his correspondents in Germany. But cousin Gustav had died a year ago, and now, too, the dearly beloved brother Eduard was gone. At age fifty-five, he had died on 26 September 1859, almost a year after the death of Emil's wife Eleanor and like her also after a lifetime of illness. Now Emil had no one to report to regularly, as he had to Gustav and Eduard over the nearly three decades the Mallinckrodts had been in Missouri.

Some of the personal emptiness in Emil's life, as well as the problems of a single father caring for children, had been met, however, by his remarriage, six months after Eleanor's death, to an old Dortmund friend, Emile Vollmann. When he wrote asking her to marry him, she agreed.[128] "I have become very happy in this new relationship," Emil wrote Gustav II, "especially because of the children who sincerely return the open love of the second mother. So we are living happily and contentedly in our rural surrounding." Son Gustav III was now in his third year with the wholesale drug company, "Eddy" (Eduard) and Otto attended Webster College six miles away, while Minna and "Mimmichen" (probably the youngest child Adele) were at home.[129]

All was quiet in St. Louis after the 1860 election of Lincoln, and the German community was especially pleased with its performance. Throughout the state German immigrants obviously had not all voted for Lincoln, but most had.[130] The German stand on the Union was clear. At the same time, movements were underway that would characterize Missouri politics for years—clandestine groups preparing for armed conflict.[131] In the countryside, too, secret meetings were held by both Union men and secessionists, each getting ready for what was to come but still hoping it would not. For instance, emissaries from Missouri Governor-elect Jackson and other leaders in the central portion of the state encouraged secessionists and "promised them plenty of arms if the time should come to use them, and plenty of powder when the time should come to burn it."[132]

Outside pressure of course was also focused on the politically important border state, although it represented less than 3 percent of America's slave population.[133] In December 1860 the Governor of Alabama sent commissioners to Missouri inviting and urging it to secede from the Union. The secessionist states could go out of the Union together, they argued, and then organize a separate Confederacy of the Southern States of America. Missouri's departing governor, R. M. Stewart, listened to the Alabama delegation unsympathetically. While he earlier may have believed in slavery, a proposed law to expel all free blacks from the state had so appalled him that he killed the legislation through a pocket veto. There was, however, a new Governor-elect, C. F. Jackson, in the wings, and he was enthusiastic about Alabama's proposal.[134]

All the years of debate and talk about secession became a shocking reality on 20 December 1860—South Carolina declared itself free of the Union! Now as the year ended people held their breath, wondering what would happen next. In St. Louis, meanwhile, a New Year's Day event reminded the city of its dreadful position between antislavery and proslavery pressures. It was customary on the first day of the new year to sell at auction, from the granite steps of the city's courthouse, chattel slaves kept in the county jail until they could be sold. Part of the property settlement of estates, seven were scheduled for sale on the first day of 1861. Their auction had been widely advertised, and about two thousand young men had secretly banded together to stop the sale and if possible end "this annual disgrace."[135] (They were said to be the Wide-Awakes, young Germans who had banded together during the recent campaign to protect Republican Congressman Frank Blair. Their rivals were a secessionist paramilitary group called the Minute Men.)[136]

When the auctioneer opened the bidding, the freemen, as they were called, for twenty minutes or more yelled, "Three dollars, three dollars!" Pausing, the auctioneer tried again but was drowned out by the chant of "Four dollars, four dollars!" Finally able to be heard, the auctioneer berated the young men for their conduct and was answered with yet another chorus, this time "Five dollars, five dollars!" At the end of two hours—and a last bid of $8.00—the auctioneer led the blacks back to jail. No public auction of slaves was ever attempted again in St. Louis, Missouri. As the observer wrote, "in the cries and counter cries of the auctioneer and the throng of freemen could be felt the pulsations of the coming conflict. We had before us in concrete form Lincoln's doctrine, that the nation cannot exist half slave and half free."[137]

Secession in the South

One after another in the first days of 1861 secession ordinances were passed in Southern states. In fact, seven states of the lower South withdrew from their affiliation with the United States of America—South Carolina, Mississippi, Florida, Alabama, Georgia, Louisiana, and Texas; four more states in the upper South (Virginia, Arkansas, Tennessee, and North Carolina) warned that they would oppose any federal attempts to coerce a state.[138] It was the old and basic controversy of a federative form of government—states' rights versus federal rights.

Preparing to turn over the presidency to Abraham Lincoln, President Buchanan lamely said that the federal government could not use force to prevent such secession. President-elect Lincoln, however, let it be known that he disagreed. Therewith the handwriting on the wall once again was underlined.

The generally feared violence also came relatively quickly. Earlier, when South Carolina had asked President Buchanan to get the U.S. troops out of Charleston harbor and turn the forts over to the state, he had refused; South Carolina's troops then seized the federal arsenal at Charleston on 30 December. From the Southern point of view, such installations no longer belonged to the government in Washington but to the states. Buchanan, ordering U.S. federal troops to fall back to Ft. Sumter, sent them an unarmed ship with reinforcements and provisions. As the federal ship approached the federal fort on 9 January it was repulsed by the state of South Carolina and forced to withdraw.[139]

Very few in St. Louis, it was said, had anticipated such early, radical, revolutionary action. Some knew that in Washington, the capital of the former unified nation, men were plotting to overthrow the government. It was said, for instance, that to help the South prepare for the coming battles President Buchanan's secretary of war had removed large quantities of arms and ammunition from northern to southern arsenals.[140] As St. Louis watched the sweep of events, its leaders wondered how to prevent the state from being drawn into the whirlpool of secession.[141] As Emil Mallinckrodt later conceded, "In this world one ought to reckon with *every possibility*. I did not do that" and "what I, along with millions of informed people considered impossible—*civil war*—became fact."[142]

The scenario became even clearer on 4 February 1861. The seceding southern states met in Montgomery, Alabama, framed a constitution, and set up a provisional government. They called it the Confederate States of America. A so-called North-South "peace convention" to try to save the union failed. On 9 February, therefore, Jefferson Davis was elected provisional President of the Confederacy, with regular elections set for November. What the German immigrants had most feared had happened—America was now in fact a divided nation. As Emil Mallinckrodt later saw it, the problem had its roots in the very founding of the country:

> The founders of the Union were not statesmen; they did not build up the new constitution in the unitarian manner of an unqualified union. If in the year 1781 the first Congress had possessed the capacity to form an unitarian state, so it would have had to come into the world under the name the Republic of North America, and not as the United States. That title . . . [contained] the seed of internal disunion and civil wars.[143]

In this context they anxiously waited news of Abraham Lincoln's inauguration on 4 March 1861, under a cloud of open conflict at Ft. Sumter, as well as rumors of plots against his life and assassination intentions. The new President's message to the divided nation was simple but grave: "In *your* hands, my dissatisfied fellow countrymen, and not *in mine*, is the momentous issue of civil war. The government will not assail *you*. You can have no conflict, without being yourselves the aggressors. *You* have no oath registered in Heaven to destroy the government, while *I* shall have the most solemn one 'to preserve, protect, and defend' it."[144]

Missouri Stays with the Union

Before long it was Missouri's turn as a slave state to stand up and be counted—to secede with the South and go into the Confederacy or to stay in the Union. There was no way to avoid the choice. Union and disunion forces angrily faced each other across all Missouri's borders, in its major city of St. Louis, and in the towns and villages throughout the state. As a historian with a century of hindsight would write, "No part of the United States would know greater bitterness or misery. Here was a state still close to the frontier, where men were predisposed to violence and where half a decade of dispute over the slavery issue had created many enmities, the lines of hatred running from farm to farm and from neighbor to neighbor. Altogether, it was a bad state in which to ignite a civil war."[145]

The story of how Missouri made its choice between North and South surely belongs in the annals of political astuteness—with the role of St. Louis and its German residents highlighted. Their drama, as later reconstructed, began in early 1861.[146]

Missouri's pro-secession Governor Jackson and the state's equally secessionist legislature passed an act calling for election of delegates to a State Convention that would take up the question of secession. There they, of course, hoped for a pro-Confederacy vote. The legislation establishing that convention had two especially important provisions: (1) if the convention would call for severing relations with the Union, the ordinance had to be ratified by the majority of the people; (2) the convention would end when it adjourned itself. Fearing the intentions of Missouri's pro-Southern governor, Congressman Frank Blair reorganized his Wide-Awakes and members of the German physical education organization, the *Turnverein*, into an armed Home Guard unit, which practiced drilling. He also set up a Committee of Safety, including St. Louis leaders, and kept President Lincoln informed.[147]

On 21 January 1861, the act calling for the convention on secession was approved in the state capital. To the dismay, however, of Governor Jackson, a unionist slate of delegates to that convention was elected by Missouri voters on 18 February; on 28 February they then met in Jefferson City. Not only would the third president of the United States, Jefferson, have been horrified at what was going on in the capital named after him, but the convention delegates, too, were displeased with the so-called city itself. Since the state legislature was in session and using its own meeting halls, the convention members had no equally large place in all of Jefferson City to meet. In addition, they had no desks or libraries, not to mention adequate hotel rooms. As an observer wrote, "There was at the time hardly any considerable town in Missouri more intellectually stagnant than its capital."[148]

In this situation, pro-Union delegates from St. Louis saw an opportunity—if they could only move the convention to their city, the cause of secession would have fewer friends. Maybe they could still save Missouri for the Union. Secretly, then, they began to maneuver behind the scenes. First the St. Louisans found some delegates willing to make the motion that the convention adjourn to meet "in the Mercantile Library Hall of St. Louis." After some discussion, that motion passed, especially when the convention was told that the meeting halls in St. Louis were free (an arrangement obviously previously made by the public-relations-conscious St. Louisans!). Then when, in addition, railroad fare was provided, the Convention was ready to move.[149]

St. Louis's beautiful meeting halls, desks, pages, library facilities, and daily dinner invitations with "very important people" (also secretly arranged) softened deep-seated prejudices among the many lawyers, farmers, merchants, professionals, and craftsmen who were delegates. Feelings were strong, however, for some eighty-two of the ninety-nine members had been born in the South. Although most were proslavery, they were divided on the question of secession—about half were Unconditional Unionists (like the Germans and their St. Louis allies) and half were Conditional Unionists (for preserving the Union if the federal government would not coerce the seceded states).[150]

H. R. Gamble, now sixty-two and still the forceful moderate, dominated the convention.[151] During its long discussions and endless resolutions, several reasons against secession from the Union gained support. If Missouri seceded,

1. its slaves would flee north, east, and west to free territory and could not be brought back;

2. immigration of free white population to Missouri would nearly cease and that was worth more to the state economically than the 112,000 slaves;

3. loss of its border state position might destroy Missouri's ability to influence compromise;

4. it would be acting like the impulsive Southerners who had not even consulted with Missouri before secession was undertaken.

The delegates gradually "came to see that secession antagonized all the commercial, educational, and moral interests of the State; that it was, in short, a suicidal policy."[152]

Finally, on the sixteenth day of the convention, the vote was taken. Missouri would stay in the Union! And that, in turn, meant sister border states Kentucky, the western part of Virginia [which became West Virginia], Delaware, and Maryland stayed in as well. Lincoln was cheered and strengthened. If war would come, more than one hundred thousand Missouri men could be counted on for the Union army (including eight thousand blacks), and pro-Union Home Guards were found in most towns of the state. A St. Louisan later would write with pride, "when some future historian impartially surveys the whole field, he may be constrained to affirm that a band of patriotic men, most of them unknown to fame, in a border city, on the western bank of the Mississippi River, confronted with apparently insurmountable obstacles, by prudent, decisive action, not only saved their State from the madness of secession, but the whole Union from irretrievable disruption."[153]

Of great significance, of course, was the Germans' contribution to Missouri's historic decision. First the German immigrants had been pro-Union Democrats—carrying, for example, St. Charles County into that column.[154] Then, when the parties split, they had switched their important support over to the antislavery party, the new Republicans of Lincoln. And over the recent years they had staunchly and unwaveringly voted their support for politicians favoring the Union cause, sometimes at the price of harassments by anti-Unionists, as noted earlier. Additional public support for the Union was found in the influential German-language newspapers. Both the *Anzeiger des Westens* and *Westliche Post* in St. Louis and Arnold Krekel's *St. Charles Demokrat* supported the Union cause. As historians of the time wrote about Krekel,

> Just preceding the war he was unquestionably one of the foremost Democrats, if not in fact the Democratic leader, of this [St. Charles] county. But when it came to the question of breaking up the Union and destroying the government, he left the Democratic party and identified himself with the loyal element of the State. Indeed, he had never had any sympathy with the proslavery tendencies and anteced- ents of his party, and on that account would undoubtedly have left it, if for no other cause. During the early years of the war he was one of the most prominent and valuable supporters of the Union in Northeast Missouri.[155]

About Missouri's Germans in general it was said,

> When they were finally placed before the alternative to decide, whether they would be unconditional Union men or would consent to a disintegration of the Union, their conscientiousness, by which they resolved and remained true to their oath of [citizenship] allegiance, overbalanced all other considerations and thus the great mass of Germans did not perjure themselves but stood up in defence of the banner of the country.[156]

Not celebrating long his own election victory or Missouri's decision, President Lincoln carefully considered what to do about Ft. Sumter. Probably he especially asked his new attorney general, Edward Bates of St. Louis, for legal advice. After a time, then, Lincoln decided to try again to provision the federal garrison and informed South Carolina that an expedition to do solely that was under way. South Carolina's response was shots—shore batteries of the state opened fire on the fort where the federal troops were stationed.

Firing on Ft. Sumter

With that shot, at 4:30 on the morning of 12 April 1861, the American Civil War began. In the North, the shot was considered treason; the South had aggressed against the federal government. On 15 April, President Lincoln declared that "insurrection" existed but did not formally proclaim hostilities. He did, however, call for 75,000 volunteers for three months.[157]

In the South, Lincoln's call for troops was seen as an invasion of states' rights, just as the sending of the ship to Ft. Sumter had been "coercion of a state." Seen that way, Virginia now, too, left the Union, as it had threatened. It was followed by Arkansas, North Carolina, and then Tennessee, making eleven Confederate states. They seized federal U.S. military arsenals, barracks, arms, custom houses, lighthouses, and so on, in their state territories.

That caused great anxiety in the border state of Missouri for in St. Louis a U.S. arsenal was located on the south side of the city, near the river. It had nearly thirty thousand muskets plus other rifles, and a large quantity of ammunition. The fear was that St. Louisans wanting to force Missouri out of the Union now would follow the example of the seceded states and seize the federal arsenal.

To thwart such a plan, Capt. Nathaniel Lyon, serving as commander of pro-Union volunteer troops at St. Louis, spirited most of the arms out of the arsenal. Among Lyon's armed and drilled volunteers were already many of St. Louis's German citizens—Congressman Blair's Home Guards, sworn into federal military service as "Missouri Volunteers."[158] The city felt more secure, for the moment.

So did leaders in Augusta, in the countryside, for on 1 April the Board of Trustees passed "an ordinance prohibiting the carrying of concealed weapons within the limits of the town." Interestingly, at the next meeting, upon the motion of newly elected Board Chairman L. Bennefeld, it was resolved not to publish the resolution and thereby inform the public.[159]

Everyone, however, sensed what lay ahead for a border state in a civil war. Such a conflict naturally was never a clear-cut "us against them," or in this case North versus South. Rather, out of conviction, some men from the Northern states would go into the Confederate army and vice versa. Such divisions in families, towns, and the state now would cost lives. As Emil Mallinckrodt would later put it, "What child's play a foreign war is, in contrast to a civil war."[160] At its core would be President Lincoln's firm position that

> my paramount object in this struggle is to save the Union, and is not either to save or to destroy slavery. If I could save the Union without freeing any slave, I would do it, and if I could save it by freeing all the slaves, I would do it; and if I could save it by freeing some and leaving others alone, I would also do that. What I do about slavery, and the colored race, I do because I believe it helps to save the Union; and what I forbear, I forbear because I do not believe it would help save the Union.[161]

Mallinckrodts as Soldiers?

There were the Mallinckrodt children, too, and their futures to worry about. Julius had, as one said, two "war age" sons—Conrad Theodor, twenty-six, and Hermann Adolf, twenty-three. The other children were less threatened. In fact, continuing the sad story of disease and death on the frontier, two daughters were already dead. Mathilde, who had married Theodor Wilkens in 1848, died in 1854, leaving a son Jean Paul; Caroline Dorothea, who had married Heinrich Nahm in 1853, died in August 1857, leaving three-year-old daughter Emma Mathilda. The young widow Emilie Mallinckrodt Wachs, who had lived at home caring for her four-year-old daughter Frederika, married Heinrich Nahm (her widowed brother-in-law) on 14 September 1857, providing a new family for her Frederika and his Emma Mathilda.[162] (As justice of the peace, Emilie's uncle, Conrad Mallinckrodt, solemnized the marriage.[163]) That left at home with Julius and Mary their daughters Luise, twenty-one, and Lydia, eighteen, and of course their two younger children, Christian Albert, now eleven, and Wilhelmina, eight.

At Conrad's there were now two boys, born after his fifty-first birthday, but they were still children. In January 1859, Conrad wrote in his notebook, "On January 17, 1859, at quarter after 2 o'clock in the afternoon, my dear wife gave birth to my first born (*Erstling*). He shall be named Theodor."[164] In fact, the baby was named Theodor Feldmann—for the deeply mourned father Conrad had lost as a teenager and for mother Dorothea Feldmann Mallinckrodt. Using a mother's family name as a middle name was most unusual in the German tradition at that time. But it was a way to honor a mother whose first name obviously could not be given a boy; furthermore, including Feldmann in his first son's name would commemorate in the New World the century-long family tie which had marked the Mallinckrodt's history in Dortmund. Similarly, Conrad named his second son Albert Feldmann, probably for his brother remaining in Dortmund and again for his mother. If the third child on the way would be a girl, Conrad and Wilhelmina planned to give her her mother's and grandmother Mallinckrodt's first names. (So it was, in December 1861, when the new daughter was named Wilhelmina Dorothea.)

In St. Louis, Emil's Gustav, twenty-one, was also military age. Eduard was only sixteen and Otto fourteen. In addition, of course, there were Minna, nineteen, Adele, ten, and the new baby Emil junior born of the second marriage with Emilie. At Hermann and Luise's, nineteen-year-old James Ferdinand was his parents' major concern, for Cecilia was seventeen, John Friedrich only fourteen, and Delia ten. In fact, John Friedrich was still in high school. A mechanically inclined youngster, he was constantly inventing something. The family in Germany had offered him a technical education in Switzerland, but Hermann and Luise did not think he should leave home. (Later when John Friedrich learned of the offer, he apparently was resentful of the missed opportunity.)[165] Hermann had finally gotten a job as "collector," but was not yet doing very well financially.[166]

Had the Mallinckrodt men sat together and contemplated the safety of their children, they might have added a sentence or so about the price of their frontier lives, that is, the price to their women. Here they were, Julius and Emil both fifty-five, each with two sets of children to worry about—the older set from a first marriage and the younger set from a second. Had they only, like Hermann and Luise, not lost their wives through disease and ill health—and constant child-bearing! Conrad's fathering young children in his early fifties was, of course, the consequence of his delayed remarriage after the turbulent divorce from Sophie.

24

1861–1864:
Guerrilla Missouri

Missouri's divided soul was clearly visible in the days after President Lincoln called for volunteers to protect the threatened Union. Following South Carolina's 12 April 1861 firing on federal soldiers at Ft. Sumter, the Secretary of War in Washington telegraphed troop quotas to loyal states. The 17 April answer from Missouri's Governor Jackson, said to be a secret secessionist, was terse and insolent:

> Sir: Your dispatch of the 15th inst., making a call on Missouri for four regiments of men for immediate service, has been received. There can be, I apprehend, no doubt but these men are intended to form a part of the President's army to make war upon the people of the seceded States. Your requisition, in my judgment, is illegal, unconstitutional, and can not be complied with. Not one man will the State of Missouri furnish to carry on such an unholy war.[1]

Not only did Missouri's Governor make his bristling defiance of the Union unmistakably clear, but so did its legislature. It quickly authorized takeover of railroad and telegraph lines in the state and organization of new anti-Union militia because the existing Home Guard units would stay loyal to the North. Companies for that pro-Confederate Missouri State Guard were immediately recruited, for example, also in St. Charles County where the Mallinckrodts lived.[2] A training camp for the new Guard units was then set up near St. Louis. Called "Camp Jackson," in honor of the Governor, the military base was put under the command of Gen. Daniel M. Frost and furnished arms by the Confederacy (taken from the federal arsenal at Baton Rouge, Louisiana).[3] That signaled civil war within a state that had voted to stay in the Union. The long, arduous test of loyalty for Missouri's Germans—and other immigrants—now had officially begun.

The Union forces obviously had to gain the upper hand and quickly. In St.

Louis the loyal Missouri Home Guard units, under the command of U.S. military officer General Lyon, would protect the vitally important U.S. Arsenal with its storehouse of military equipment. But more men were needed and the governor of course had refused to supply the federal government with the four regiments (one thousand men each) which President Lincoln demanded. At the moment, therefore, the Union could only get the troops it needed through volunteers and so it advertised for them in newspapers.

German Volunteers

The response to the call for three months of service was astonishing. According to St. Louis editor Heinrich Börnstein at the *Anzeiger des Westens*, the first two companies of 120 men each formed within three days. Then during the week of 22–29 April "newly formed German volunteer companies and their elected officers streamed to the Arsenal from all parts of the city."[4] By the end of April, St. Louis had 4,200 men ready, or more than the requested four Missouri regiments. "With few exceptions almost all were from the German population," Börnstein reported.[5] Some of the three-month volunteers had been drawn from the Wide-Awake clubs earlier organized to protect Republican Party speakers at political rallies, or from the Turner societies, German physical education and gymnastic groups.[6] James Ferdinand Mallinckrodt, nineteen, was among these volunteers.[7]

Since such companies and regiments chose their own officers, the German units arriving at the Arsenal reported in under the command of "Schaefer," "Sigel," and "Börnstein." There they trained tirelessly, Börnstein wrote, singing German soldier songs and talking about the challenge they had taken on. "They knew very well," he said, "that we lived in a slave state where slave-holders were the majority, and that no support or help could be expected from the center of the state."[8]

The German soldiers also knew that they were unpopular with some groups in St. Louis itself. Not only anti-Union secessionists disliked them but the "nativists," too, and often, in fact, these were the same people. The moral fundamentalists among the nativists, for example, especially objected to German ways of observing the Sabbath. In 1859, an unsuccessful effort had been made to forbid the sale of beer on Sunday; in 1861 the protest was against theatrical performances, as at the St. Louis Opernhaus, which drew big German crowds on "the day of rest." Börnstein, the Opernhaus's founder, canceled the 14 April performance to avoid a riot and closed the theater the next week to preclude more trouble.[9]

In the rural areas of Missouri, Germans supported President Lincoln's military cause as strongly as did their countrymen in St. Louis. Julius's son Adolph (Hermann Adolph), for example, promptly went to St. Louis to volunteer and was mustered in at the Arsenal on 16 May for three months' duty. He was placed in a company of the Third Regiment Missouri Infantry, commanded by Colonel Franz Sigel.[10]

By early May, local units of Home Guard were organized in the rural towns of St. Charles County. Conrad Mallinckrodt was on the committee which formulated guide lines for Augusta units: mutual cooperation, self-defense, political neutrality. Subordinated to the county's regular peace-keeping forces, the Guard members were to practice the use of arms each week in groups of twelve to twenty-three, and four to seven of such sections would equal a company. Overseeing the Guard's operations was a standing committee, of which Julius Mallinckrodt was a member.[11] Beginning in June, both Conrad and Julius were on the Home Guard payroll for a month.[12]

In July the supporters of the Union in St. Charles County numbered fifteen companies of Home Guard and so enough men to form a County Regiment. Composed almost exclusively of Germans, it was organized by Gustav Bruere, editor of the *Demokrat*, and commanded by the newspaper's owner Arnold Krekel (later a U.S. District Court judge). Reorganized in August into six companies, the men were known as Krekel's Battalion, U.S.R.C. (Reserve Corps) Mo., or "Krekel's Dutch." He would later write that "on the 6th of August [1861] we came together 1800 strong as a regiment in Cottleville."[13] Some of the volunteers went to St. Louis to join General Lyon.[14]

Elsewhere, however, prosecession feelings ran high, and almost daily, as the *St. Charles Demokrat* wrote, "there are reports of expulsion and mistreatment of Union supporters in the center of the state." Often they were Germans. In neighboring Warren County, for instance, a mob dragged Franz Schifferle into the woods, painted him black, and chased him away. In Wright City, Henrich Mersch, held in a room above a bar, was saved from hanging by the bartender who gained time for his rescue by plying the would-be lynchers with drinks.[15]

Union Troops/St. Louis Germans Take Camp Jackson

In St. Louis the stage, too, was set for the first armed confrontation between Missouri's secessionist and its pro-Union German-Americans. Having refused a communiqué from pro-Confederate General Frost at Camp Jackson, General Lyon instead gave him fair warning that trouble was coming.[16] On 10 May 1861 Lyon wrote General Frost:

> Sir: Your command is regarded as evidently hostile toward the Government of the United States.
>
> It is, for the most part, made up of those Secessionists who have openly avowed their hostility to the General Government, and have been plotting at the seizure

of its property and the overthrow of its authority. You are openly in communication with the so-called Southern Confederacy, which is now at war with the United States, and you are receiving at your camp, from the said Confederacy and under its flag, large supplies of the material of war, most of which is known to be the property of the United States. These extraordinary preparations plainly indicate none other than the well-known purpose of the Governor of this State, under whose orders you are acting . . . having in direct view hostilities to the General Government and co-operation with its enemies.

In view of these considerations . . . I do hereby demand of you an immediate surrender of your command, with no other conditions than that all persons surrendering under this command shall be humanely and kindly treated.[17]

After dispatching that letter, General Lyon moved quickly, storming Camp Jackson on the afternoon of the same day with seven thousand to eight thousand men, including four regiments of Missouri volunteers.[18] His offer to release prisoners, if they would swear to support the Constitution of the United States, was refused. The captured anti-Unionist militiamen were then marched out of the camp between two lines of Union soldiers—scornfully called "the Dutch" because they were mostly St. Louis Germans.[19] Many three-month volunteers, including James Ferdinand, were under the banner of the Third U.S.R.C. Missouri Infantry or with the Third Regiment of Missouri Volunteers, which Adolph would join in a few days.[20]

Raw and undisciplined as the German volunteers were, they responded with violence to heckling yells of "Damn the Dutch!" and attacks by stones and guns.[21] In the shooting and general tumult that broke out, about twenty-five persons were killed or wounded. After the soldiers and their prisoners arrived at the arsenal in south St. Louis, a half-hour march from Camp Jackson, unrest spread:[22]

At different places in the city men were speaking to impromptu audiences, in which some were cheering while others were yelling defiance, to bring them if possible to calmness and reason. In different directions a shot could now and then be heard. As soon as it was dark, from fear of riot, the saloons and restaurants were closed and their doors were bolted and barred. The windows of many private houses were also shut and securely fastened. The theatres and all places of public amusement were empty.[23]

Rioting groups of angry men indeed filled the streets. Not surprisingly they headed for the *Anzeiger des Westens* building, but there the mob was blocked by the police.[24] The bitterness of Southern sympathizers in St. Louis against the Germans, who so openly and stoutly supported the Union, was extreme. The Germans were feared, as well. An observer reported that "those who favored the Southern Confederacy seldom if ever called them Germans, but usually denominated them, 'the Dutch.' The intense contempt which, by the tone of their voices, they injected into that simple phrase, 'the Dutch,' was marvellous."[25]

And yet the German volunteers were satisfied with their contribution. They felt that with their actions "not only was the St. Louis arsenal and its great supplies secured but the state of Missouri was also saved for the Union, the arming of the free western states supplied, and a big step taken to preserve the Union."[26]

The days of fear and panic which followed were troubling to the two St. Louis Mallinckrodt families, Emil and Emilie, Hermann and Luise. Gradually it became clear, however, that the capture of Camp Jackson and control of the arsenal had brought St. Louis under federal rule (as well as nearby St. Charles County).[27] U.S. authorities, for instance, seized St. Louis's notorious slave pen for children and immediately turned it into a U.S. military prison. As a St. Louisan movingly wrote, "No little colored boy or girl was ever again to be sold there." Equally infamous, "Lynch's Slave Pen" for adult blacks was taken over, as well. There for years "men and women, handcuffed and chained together, in a long two-by-two column," had been driven into its earth-floored room "under the crack of the driver's whip, as though they were so many colts or calves . . . to be sold to the good people of St. Louis and of the surrounding towns and country districts; and those not thus disposed of were bought by slave-dealers for the New Orleans market."[28]

By Boat to Secure Jefferson City

With St. Louis, Missouri's major city, secured, the Union's next priority was the capital, Jefferson City, 130 miles up the Missouri River. Already headed there was Governor Jackson's new commander of the state's pro-Confederacy Missouri State Guard, the former Governor and Mexican War hero, General Sterling Price. On the way he burned the major Pacific Railroad bridges from St. Louis westward, hoping to cut off Lyon's pursuit.

General Lyon, however, used another way to get to the center of the state. He loaded his two thousand troops, mostly Germans, on steamboats and moved them up the Missouri River.[29] Once again Conrad and Julius Mallinckrodt saw the currents of the time not far from their doorstep—as slaves had been shipped downstream to the "safety" of the south, now German-speaking soldiers were transported upstream to secure Missouri's capital for the North.

When Lyon's men arrived at Jefferson City's boat landing on 15 June, they took the town quietly. There was no "government" to capture since Governor Jackson had abandoned the capital for safer ground farther south and the legislature apparently had scattered. A few days later the federal soldiers caught up with and overpowered a small unit of the rebel army at nearby Boonville. Union patrols then took over the major Missouri River crossings and ferries from St. Charles all the way up to Kansas City on the Kansas border.[30]

Within several months, thus, General Lyon's Union forces had scored important gains—overthrow of Camp Jackson, suppression of open disloyalty in St. Louis and nearby counties, capture of the state capital, and clearance of hostile forces from the crucial Missouri River waterway.[31] At the same time continuous clashes in Warren County and elsewhere between Germans supporting the Union and Anglo-American citizens favoring the South signaled Missouri's future.[32]

James Ferdinand and Adolph's duty during this time was typical for Missouri's three-month volunteers. After the Camp Jackson action, James's company marched to Wentzville, transported arms to Hermann, and traveled via the Pacific Railroad south to Rolla; returning to St. Louis, Company F undertook an expedition to Callaway County and near Fulton "engaged with the enemy." Adolph, meanwhile, had marched into southwest Missouri, fought at Carthage, and was heading for Springfield.[33]

Such actions throughout rural Missouri would set the Mallinckrodts' pattern of life for the four coming years of the Civil War. Emil and Hermann's St. Louis was relatively secure, and Julius and Conrad's county, St. Charles, was largely stabilized because of its proximity to St. Louis. Equally as important, the Missouri River was safely under federal control. The Mallinckrodts, however, were uneasy, but they believed deeply in the Union cause and, with their long view of history, sensed it would triumph. They had come so far to find their freedom and had already experienced how very hard and sometimes cruel frontier life could be, with death often seemingly just around the corner. War now worsened the odds greatly, and their sons were involved.

Probably speaking for them all, Emil wrote,

> The South hopes for its so-called independence just as certainly as the North does to force a continued union. The latter is a *matter of life and death* (*Lebensfrage*) because there surely can be no doubt that a peace based on separation would be seen only as a cease fire. Indeed, I would go still further and say that such a peace would mean inaugurating eternal warfare between both parts (on a territory without geographical divisions). If our government [the North] understands this situation—which I do not doubt—then even if the war should last 10 years, it can and may not conclude a peace which even long-range would allow the possibility of separation.[34]

St. Charles and Neighboring Counties

In addition to the older Mallinckrodt sons, it was the neighboring counties that caused Julius and Conrad especially great concern. Time and time again pro-Confederate guerrilla bands would strike very close to Augusta, especially in the western counties of Warren and Montgomery. They were a constant target in the civil struggle because the state's important railroad lines crossed their territory—

the North Missouri Railroad, from St. Louis along the Boone's Lick Trail to Macon, and there the connecting Hannibal-to-St. Joseph line tying the two sides of the state together (figure 24-1).

The government in Washington had to control these two crucial east-west rail arteries if it wanted to hold northern Missouri for the Union, as well as move its troops, supplies, and munitions rapidly from one side of the state to the other. And so, of course, the guerrillas' goal was precisely the disruption of that transportation.

In July, for instance, General Price's Southern partisans hit north central Missouri, burning the Salt River bridge on the Hannibal and St. Joseph railroad and destroying culverts near Centralia on the North Missouri line. A historian's totaling up of the consequences of those attacks underlined the essentiality of Missouri's railroads: "Traffic on both lines was stopped for a time, and when it was resumed, the transportation of troops by rail became hazardous as the cars were shot into. . . . On September 3 the Platte River bridge on the Hannibal and St. Joe line collapsed under a train . . . the sabotage was so well done the *St. Louis Republican* stated that St. Louis was almost cut off from the rest of Missouri. Bridges were out on all of the major rail lines."[35]

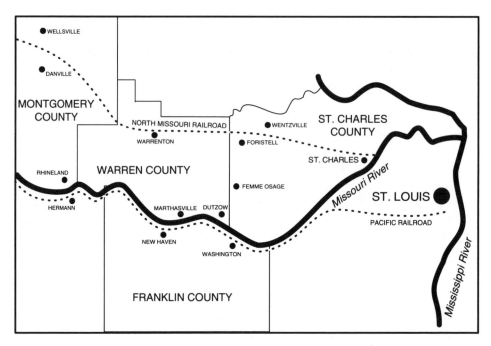

Figure 24-1. In the Civil War, the Duden country area of St. Charles, Warren, and Franklin counties (near Gottfried Duden's original settlement at Dutzow) was endangered because Missouri's three major railroads, crucial to the Union, subjected the area to guerrilla attacks. The Pacific Railroad ran south of the Missouri River, the North Missouri Railroad from St. Charles along the Boone's Lick Trail, and about forty miles farther north of Wellsville was the Hannibal-St. Joseph line (not shown) connecting those two cities and both sides of the state. (*Map by Shelly Price McCaskill.*)

Also obviously vital was Missouri's third and more southern line, the Pacific Railroad. Built south of the Missouri River westward from St. Louis, it was on the other side of the stream from the Mallinckrodts. Perhaps on a clear day, with the wind blowing from the south, they could even hear its whistle or see its puffs of smoke off in the distance. Anti-Union forces had already shown, as noted above, how destruction of railroad bridges on that route to Jefferson City and beyond could slow Union advances.

At the same time, St. Charles County was relatively safe and even Augusta had taken steps to protect itself. By August 1861, for instance it had a Home Guard unit and town guard room for which the Trustees appropriated $1.15 for "a lamp and lard [oil]." Apparently the men were practicing, too, for the Trustees had to remind the captain of the unit that "target shooting within the limits of the town" was prohibited. And like so many, the Town Board's clerk, B. Hoffmann, had gone to take "an active part in the defense of our adopted country."[36]

Julius and Conrad nevertheless continued to be very troubled by the military consequences of guerrilla attacks taking place so close by. They sometimes, indeed, thought they were back in the 1400s when William von Mallinckrodt, their knight ancestor, was racing around the countryside destroying "enemy" property for his employer and taking hostages. Knight William, however, had not killed people, as best Julius and Conrad could recall, while Missouri's guerrillas were doing precisely that. As a later observer summarized, "guerrilla war approaches total war, the war of all against all."[37]

And Germans seemed to be a special target. A historian found, for example, that early in the war a Confederate commander reported a charge by his armed men into a German town. "Scattering the Dutch in all directions," the Confederates killed and wounded the Germans "as they ran through the fields, although unarmed." In the historian's view, "It was somewhat bizarre that Thompson [the commander] would brag about shooting unarmed men on his hunt, but he justified this by saying that they were Federal militia, and his men had done fine by being so quick to fire. And after all, they were only Dutchmen."[38]

The Mallinckrodts were therefore worried about their friends and acquaintances among fellow immigrants who had settled in Montgomery and Warren counties (figure 24-1). By 1860, in fact, more than a sixth of the Germans in rural Missouri lived in St. Charles and Warren County. Many immigrants from one place in the old country had often located in a given settlement in the new where compatriots had already located. For example, this so-called chain migration brought Germans from Melle and Westerkappeln near Osnabrück, Westphalia, to New Melle and nearby Cappeln in St. Charles County.[39]

Now loyal Unionists, those Germans often were harassed by rebels in towns which were largely anti-Union. And as early as 16 May 1861 St. Louis's *Anzeiger* had reported that rural houses owned by Germans were being burned down, and that Germans were oppressed and driven out of Warren County.[40] It was, in short, not so easy to be a German in Missouri's guerrilla areas. Personal respect or rejection because of one's economic status had been as routine in class-conscious old Germany as was acceptance or loathing in slaveholding Missouri because of one's appearance, that is, skin color. But new to many in Duden country was antipathy based on one's sound, that is, English spoken with a German accent!

Union military leaders, too, were concerned about the troublesome but essential counties north of the Missouri River. With his opponent General Price out of the way in Arkansas, busily urging the Confederate Army to invade Missouri, General Lyon could shift his attention to the state's railroads. As early as 5 July, for instance, volunteer Union regiments set out for points along the North Missouri line. According to accounts, when news of their approach reached Warren County, the Confederate units there decided to attack the train. "When the train reached a point just west of Foristell, in St. Charles County, a murderous fire was opened upon it, and this mode of attack continued for several miles." The result, described by county historians, was dramatic:

> This open declaration of war, of course, had the effect to arouse the Union men of the vicinity, who now began to perfect organizations for their own protection. It became necessary to arm and thoroughly equip troops for constant service, and the enlistment of Union men began in earnest. These organized companies were in a short time ready for field service, and their readiness served to repress the daring acts of the Confederates, which at one time threatened to engulf the county in a bloody war.[41]

Several weeks thereafter President Lincoln's national military leaders took an important step to help guerrilla-plagued Missouri. In mid-July, General John C. Frémont, hero of the Germans as Republican Party leader and initially popular commander of the Union's Western Department, ordered General Pope to take command in north Missouri with three regiments.[42] From his St. Charles headquarters, Pope, in turn, issued a 20 July 1861 proclamation to the people along the line of the North Missouri Railroad. It was—and remained—a very controversial "notice" because it held all Missourians, whether Union or secessionist, responsible for the organized guerrilla actions going on around them.[43]

In a follow-up "General Order," distributed up and down the railroad and in the county, General Pope specifically named the problem that would bloody Missouri for years—"It is demonstrated by sufficient testimony, and by experience of the past two weeks, that the disturbances in Northern Missouri have been by small parties of *lawless marauders* [emphasis added]."[44] This time, then, the Union general called for formation of "committees of public safety" in the towns, a strange idea since such groups were to include both Union and Confederate supporters.

What was not discussed in General Pope's 1861 orders to the Missourians was their reluctance to cooperate with the federal government because Union troops had frequently and seriously mistreated them. Accounts of arrests and revenge killings, for instance, were often recorded by Missouri's county historians of the time.[45] Later histories, written with much longer hindsight and research, even contended that "the murder of civilians by Union soldiers was so common that the victims are listed by the dozens in almost every history of central and western Missouri."[46]

Two Governments

At this time Missouri, of course, was not only a military arena, but a political one, as well. Its chief executive, in open rebellion against the government of the United States, called for the state's secession although its people had officially voted to stay in the Union. And then, as noted before, that governor, C. F. Jackson, had fled the state capital ahead of its occupation by Union forces. The governor's office in Jefferson City, on the banks of the Missouri River, was empty.

After two months, steps were taken to fill the vacuum. In late July 1861 the St. Louis Convention, which had voted to keep Missouri in the Union, reconvened itself to deal with the emergency.[47] It could call itself back into business—in one of those strange but lucky quirks of history—because it had previously adjourned temporarily rather than ultimately. This time the convention unanimously elected Hamilton R. Gamble, of St. Louis, as governor for the time being. President Lincoln at once recognized Missouri's Provisional Government as the state's legal governing body, undoubtedly with the enthusiastic support of Edward Bates who not only was Lincoln's attorney general but also Gamble's brother-in-law.

Recognized by the North and damned by the South, the new institution in Jefferson City was unique throughout the entire Civil War. Established by convention, Missouri's Provisional Government was neither duly elected nor militarily appointed. The border state's wartime political arrangements were strange for other reasons, as well. For instance, with its coffers empty and taxes hard to collect in a guerrilla war situation, Missouri was dependent on the Lincoln Administration and had its blessings; on the other hand, it was Lincoln's local military commanders, as well as the state's homegrown secessionists and radical Unionists, who challenged the authority of the Jefferson City government.[48]

The major problem facing "provisional" Governor Gamble was of course the rebellious Missourians who sought revenge against the Union through guerrilla actions or heated agitation about slavery's future. To pacify their underlying hate, Gamble felt moderation and reconciliation were needed. One such step was to remain the state's "provisional" executive, rather than flaunting his replacement of former Governor Jackson. Another accommodating measure was Gamble's offer of amnesty to penitent pro-Southern followers of Jackson and General Price. Not surprisingly, the governor's moderate practices often clashed with the sterner views of Missouri's military leader, General Frémont.

The slave state of Missouri thus had two governments—Gamble's moderate pro-Union administration in Jefferson City and Jackson's problematic pro-Confederate holdovers "in exile," so to speak, first in Arkansas and then Texas. In addition, a remnant general assembly, or so-called legislature, also said it existed outside the capital, specifically at the little mining town of Neosho in the southwest corner of Missouri near Confederate Arkansas. From there some former legislators continued to stir up trouble in the state, ignoring completely the declarations that had deposed them and their former assembly when the new provisional government was created.

Two Armies

Not only did the pro-Union, western border state have these two governments, but it also had two armies. Over the years, 60 percent of all Missouri men would fight in the Civil War, nearly three-fourths of them in the blue uniforms of the Union Army.[49] That was about one hundred nine thousand troops. At the same time, some thirty thousand would serve the South, wearing gray.[50]

And then within Missouri's big force of Union troops there also was an important division—between foreign-born and American-born soldiers. Of the 10,730 Union volunteers recruited during the first year of the war (1861), four-fifths were German immigrants; among the total 85,400 volunteers raised in Missouri during the entire war, there were 30,899 Germans.[51] The proportion of German volunteers remained high because many of the first short-term soldiers subsequently signed up for longer stints.[52] Again the Mallinckrodts were representative. James Ferdinand, for instance, after three months' duty within the state was mustered out of the Third Regiment of Missouri infantry volunteers in August 1861 and at once joined the Seventeenth Missouri Infantry. Organized at the time by General Frémont, the Seventeenth would have a long and illustrious record throughout the Civil War.[53] Entering its Company D as a corporal, James was transferred within several months to the noncommissioned staff as master sergeant.[54]

Adolph Mallinckrodt's three months' duty with the Third Regiment Missouri Infantry also was over in August 1861. Within a week, at age twenty-three, he was mustered into Company E of Krekel's Battalion, U.S. Reserve Corps, Missouri Infantry, as a sergeant. This was the unit of Krekel's men who had been taken into regular service to keep order in the county. Now under the authority of the Union government and paid by it to do primarily local duty, these units guarded railroad bridges and prevented raids into the county. At various times Adolph's Company occupied Missouri towns such as Warrenton, Wellsburgh, Mexico, Hudson, and Fulton.[55]

Historians would later record that in St. Charles County alone, Krekel "was instrumental in enlisting between 1,200 and 1,500 men for the Union service. His prompt action and activity saved all this region of the State north of the Missouri to the Union."[56] Krekel's motivation may have come in part from his family history: paternal grandparents who were Huguenots (a religiously persecuted French Protestant minority group) and four uncles lost in the Napoleonic Wars. Krekel's own son Alfred was permitted "in his fifteenth year [to] go to war."[57]

And as Hermann and Julius Mallinckrodt had each sent a son to protect the Union—indeed, in a way as witness to their own political beliefs—so would Emil. His elder son Gustav would do two years' service.[58] Although Gustav's military records have not been located, it seems that he, too, at once volunteered for three months' duty, subsequently joined a "regular" military unit in the St. Louis area, and from there was recruited as an aide-de-camp to General Frémont.[59]

The general's twenty-eight-man staff, working to organize the Western Department of the Union's war effort, was headquartered in the seventeen-room Brant House at 8th and Chouteau Avenue, St. Louis. It was a bustling undertaking. Basement rooms were used as printing and telegraphic offices, as well as an emergency arsenal. On the first floor lower-ranking officers interviewed the many visitors who came to see the general; on the second floor Gustav Mallinckrodt may have performed his duty, for that is where General Frémont's fifteen aides-de-camp, military secretaries and other staff personnel, had their offices.[60] Also seen around Brant House were members of a special cavalry of some two hundred men known as Frémont's Bodyguard, commanded by the colorful Hungarian Major Zagonyi.[61]

While the North naturally welcomed the many foreign-born troops, their presence in Union ranks did not always help Missouri's efforts to pacify rebels within its borders. In truth, rebel Missourians often hated "foreigners" as much as they did Lincoln's "Yankees," and when both "enemies" were inside a single blue uniform, hate flourished. Stories, adorned by epithets, therefore made the rounds about Germans recruited not out of patriotism but rather through enlistment bounties or hopes for rapid citizenship. Moreover, native-born Union soldiers who were prejudiced against immigrants often spread unfavorable stories about Germans being involved in actions actually committed by non-German Union troops themselves.[62]

In addition to Missouri's loyal Union troops, foreign- or American-born, its second army was of course the thirty thousand men who fought for the South during the Civil War.[63] In addition to those soldiers active in Confederate military units on the battlefields, other Missourians also were "in the service of the South." Working through pro-Confederate groups, they plotted to overthrow the Gamble government, harbored rebel spies, and contributed monies to the Confederates.

Two Kinds of War

Finally and most destructively, because of its two governments and its two military forces, Missouri also had two kinds of war—regular encounters between Union and Confederate troops and irregular, unending guerrilla actions. It was the latter hit-and-run conflict that made the Civil War in Missouri so extraordinarily brutal: "of all regions it [Missouri] produced the most widespread, longest-lived, and most destructive guerrilla war in the Civil War."[64] "Bushwhackers" marauded across the countryside, burning villages, devastating counties, and killing wherever they struck. Remembering his history and the tales his father had told, Emil Mallinckrodt wrote that the war in Missouri "has become a *general* guerilla war, carried out more scandalously than ever was the case in the great French Revolution."[65]

As a later historian of the irregular warfare in Missouri would summarize, the state provided "a horrendous example of the nature of guerrilla war in the American heartland. There, far behind Union lines, the behavior of pro-southern settlers was truly out of Confederate control, and there a guerrilla war raged for four years. . . . Little remained under control, little remained forbidden."[66]

Another general view of the warfare was that

the guerrillas, most of them only boys, fought a total war. West of the Mississippi they plunged a fairly stable, congenial, and conservative society into intense partisan conflict that was felt by every man, woman and child. This was not a war of great armies and captains, this was bloody local insurrection, a war between friends and neighbors—a civil war in the precise definition of that term. Here organized bands of men killed each other and the civil population hundreds of miles behind the recognized battlefronts. Here there was ambush, arson, execution and murder; warfare without rules, law or quarter. . . .

The attack threat of the guerrillas, combined with their unorthodox but highly successful tactics, kept the Union military forces of the border, who overwhelmingly outnumbered them, mobilized, harassed and not available for utilization in other theatres where they were needed badly. Vicious guerrilla activity directed against the civilian population created such fear and disorganization that in many areas normal society collapsed entirely.[67]

These frightful actions alone cost 27,000 Missourians their lives.

The sad total of both kinds of war fought on the soil of the border state—regular and irregular—would exceed one thousand battles and skirmishes, according to some historians.[68] That would be more than in any state other than Virginia or Tennessee.[69] A high price, many thought, to pay for the state's geographic and political divisions.

And it was an especially high price, others thought, for the state's Union-loyal Germans who often were victims of the guerrilla attacks, having been "singled out" as enemy Unionists: "Most southern-born Missourians coupled natavism to politics, targeting Germans, the largest immigrant groups, as the greatest foe. This had been true at least since the mid-1850s when the Know-Nothing party had made strong inroads among Missouri voters, riding on widespread anti-German feelings."[70]

1861

The first six months following President Lincoln's recognition of Missouri's pro-Union Provisional Government were a grim preview of the four years of Civil War to come. With memories of Europe during the Napoleonic Wars, German settlers such as Julius and Conrad Mallinckrodt did not have to imagine the future. They could see its shape in the events going on around them at the moment. And Germans again were attacked, this time as newcomers loyal to an adopted land.

Far from the battlefield, for example, there were repeated acts of organized violence and retaliation in otherwise peaceful communities that Julius and Conrad knew well. After the taking of Jefferson City in May, the *Westliche Post*, for instance, had reported from there that

> at least most of the troops are withdrawing today, to the great relief of the residents. Only yesterday a German citizen of this town was attacked by two secessionists from Clay County and badly cut up by knives. He had given no cause for the dispute, nor any other provocation other than the fact that he was German . . . [In Sedalia a secessionist gang] ripped apart an inn managed by a German named Tisch, and did the same in the "Südwest-Saloon", where the innkeeper is also German. One has *no reasons for these abuses other than that the victims were Germans.* (Emphasis added.)[71]

The Duden country Mallinckrodts also heard of attacks closer to Augusta (figure 24-1), some also reflecting specifically anti-German sentiment. On 15 June the first invasion of their part of Missouri (St. Charles County) occurred when Federal troops, sent out to guard the railroad, "took complete possession of the town" of Wentzville, twenty miles from Augusta. They searched houses, took a number of citizens prisoner, and "also found a secession flag hid away in a hay loft."[72]

On 16 July an attack on a North Missouri train at Foristell, just eighteen miles north of Augusta, brought the first regiment of Federal troops to Montgomery County.[73] "The first Federal soldier that died or was buried in the county" was laid to rest with salutes and flowers.[74]

On 18 July a German Union officer, Lt. Yager [Jäger], was shot near Wellsville in Montgomery County and badly wounded by a one-armed bushwhacker named Alvin Cobb; demanding "that d——d Dutchman" from a woman trying to help the wounded lieutenant, Cobb then shot him dead.[75] An "ardent secessionist" of the area reportedly said about the incident, "as for the Dutchman, he *ought* to have been killed."[76]

In retaliation, Union forces killed two anti-Union colleagues of Cobb at the town of Danville and "found another victim," a secessionist, near Montgomery City.[77]

At the settlement of Rhineland, thirty-five miles upriver from Augusta, federal militia men took the horse of a man named Joe Cole who was going around saying that his principal business during the war would be to "raise h-ll with the Dutch."[78] Losing his horse set Cole "on a war path," and "with only half a dozen men the bold bushwhacker raided the Germans at will."[79]

In addition to Conrad and Julius's vision of enduring guerrilla war, early battles fought by regular troops in Missouri were also signals—or European flashbacks—of the bloodletting to come, especially in the South and East. Pro-Union Missourians were shocked, for instance, when "their side" lost the first and most important battle in their state and the Union commander was killed.[80] That was the six-hour battle of Wilson's Creek on August 10 in which Julius's son Hermann Adolph may have taken part with the Third Missouri Infantry Regiment, commanded by Colonel Franz Sigel.[81]

Fought in the southern part of the state, near Springfield, the Wilson's Creek battle pitted the pro-Southern forces of General Price against General Lyon who had defended the St. Louis arsenal for the Union. The Union forces were divided into two columns, one under Lyon's command, the other under Sigel's. Lyon was killed, giving the Union its first martyr. Then in all the confusion of troop movements, Sigel's soldiers mistook Confederate troops for Lyon's men—their clothing was neither uniform nor distinct—and chaos followed.[82] As Sigel reported, "It is impossible for me to describe the consternation and frightful confusion which was occasioned by this unfortunate event" that led to his order for "the retreat of the army from Springfield."[83]

While many blamed the Wilson's Creek defeat on General Frémont, who had not reinforced Lyon adequately, others criticized Colonel Sigel, the German, who had retreated rather than rallying his troops.[84] Later historians, however, would see the battle lost not only through individual actions but primarily because of the disorganization of initial Union military efforts—lack of experienced officers, trained troops, and adequate supplies, as well as tactical coordination. As Sigel reported, within his two regiments alone that had meant 292 dead, missing, or wounded.

Meanwhile, in central Missouri the violence accelerated so that by 4 September 1861 the *Anzeiger des Westens* called for martial law for the entire state. Speaking of human misery and people fleeing southwestern and western Missouri to Illinois and Iowa, the newspaper said a formal declaration of martial law would avoid the need to station a garrison at every location and on every bridge. "Let us have martial law throughout the state!"[85]

Martial Law in Missouri

Encouraged by the initial Union defeat at Wilson's Creek, pro-Confederate guerrillas continued their strikes in northern Missouri. Hard-pressed, General Frémont retaliated with an extraordinary step—he declared martial, or military, law throughout the state. That, too, was not unfamiliar to Europeans such as the Mallinckrodts from Westphalia. It was an especially frightening signal of what civil war would do to the spirit, as well as letter, of American democracy. People were alarmed, including the civil rights advocate Edward Bates, Lincoln's attorney general.

Frémont's 30 August proclamation meant that persons would be tried by military court for taking up arms against the union and shot if found guilty. That, of course, was customary under martial law. Under Frémont's decree for Missouri, however, the property of citizens found guilty would also be confiscated, including their slaves, who then would be freed. To many supporters of slavery, it seemed like the feared beginning of the end. Even President Lincoln objected to the prematurity of Frémont's move toward emancipation and ordered it modified.[86]

After a month of martial law, Emil Mallinckrodt's cynical reaction may have been typical of what many thought: "The destruction of our railroads and bridges, firing on defenseless trains, scorching, burning, assassination are daily occurrences—although we are under martial law. According to Frémont's proclamation, every rebel encountered with a weapon in his hand is to be shot—until today, however, *not one case* is known where the threat was carried out."[87]

Otherwise, life for Emil's family in the countryside was quiet at the time. As he put it, "evil elements" could no longer surface in their area for "no one can leave the city or county without a pass."[88] While his son Gustav was in the army and Eduard and Otto in German schools in St. Louis, the other children were at home—including a second son, Oskar, born to Emil and his second wife in late 1861.[89]

The arguments over General Frémont's martial law (as indeed over most aspects of the American Civil War) never ended. It was and is contended, for instance, that martial law "had its abuses, to be sure, but conditions in Missouri rendered it imperative."[90] On the other hand, martial law was criticized because rather than being used to police the military establishment, it was extended to Missouri's entire population.[91] Another view was that the proclamation fortunately still allowed civil law and rule by the Provisional Government wherever possible; the decree was not total. Few disagreed with the contention that Missourians paid a high civil liberty price for Frémont's law-and-order measure. It was said, for instance, that "many cruel and tyrannical acts were to be commited against the people" by the authority of martial law:[92] "Literally thousands of men were arrested and imprisoned, charged with believing in rebellion, expressing disloyal sentiments, communicating with and aiding the enemy, or violating the numerous Union orders issued under martial law. Sentences ranged from fines and confiscation of property to banishment, long-term imprisonment, and death. Many women, also, were arrested and jailed."[93]

Test Oath

In October 1861 another highly controversial control measure—a loyalty oath—was adopted at a special state convention called by Governor Gamble to deal with political and fiscal problems. The new regulation required every civil officer in the state to take an oath to support both the U.S. and Missouri constitutions, not to take up arms against either government, and not to aid their enemies. If an official did not take this oath of loyalty, he would forfeit his position and the governor could appoint replacements. The measure did not find much approval—by mid-December the offices of many state officials were empty, for they had refused to swear to the test oath within the allowed sixty days.[94] Moreover, this requirement would be the center of bitter controversy for years to come.

The troubled border state's festering internal divisions and two-government anomaly became even more clear on 28 October when its rebel "assembly" met "in exile" in Neosho. Although lacking quorums in both houses, the so-called Jackson Legislature nevertheless declared the state seceded from the Union.[95] On that basis, Missouri was accepted by the South as its twelfth state of the Confederacy.[96] "And so Missourians then and afterwards in arms against the Federal flag became entitled to the name of *Confederates*," explained chroniclers of the time, rather than "State Guards," "secessionists," or "southern troops."[97]

With General Pope's retaliatory measures in place against the civilian population of northern Missouri and martial law hanging over everyone, chaos increased throughout the state. When Pope, for instance, tried to enforce his demand that citizens pay for damages with goods, the region "was soon in a state near anarchy." As a railroad official there reported to Washington, as well as to General Frémont, such tactics might work in foreign countries but in Missouri they were only alienating friends and making enemies more bitter.[98]

Much of the blame for worsening conditions was heaped on General Frémont. While his leadership in the Republican Party made him a hero to some, including the Germans, others saw Frémont as an irresponsible military leader. (Surely his early antislavery stand also was held against him.) Those opponents pressed their case until President Lincoln reluctantly but finally removed the general from his command, effective 4 November 1861—in fact, on the eve of Frémont's planned attack near Springfield. His troops talked of resignation, and many St. Louisans were not only disappointed but angry about the decision.[99] Both German newspapers—the *Anzeiger* and *Westliche Post*—had opposed his removal.[100] As a non-German of the city wrote, "Frémont returned to St. Louis. The loyal Germans, to whom we and the whole country owed so much, received him with unshaken confidence, and with the warmest expressions of affection. All true Unionists of St. Louis," the historian added, were glad "that these spontaneous and hearty demonstrations of the loyal Germans came to cheer the heart of Frémont in what evidently was to him a dark and bitter day."[101]

Emil Mallinckrodt's bitterness about the affair seemed clear in his report to Köln, although he conceded that camp life had improved Gustav's health, for he suffered from a chest condition: "As aide-de-camp on Frémont's staff, Gustav made the march to Springfield and back. He was dismissed, along with all other officers appointed by Frémont but not confirmed by the President. He can again immediately enter the regular service, at $130 a month. That is his wish but not mine."[102]

The dismissal of Frémont's staff was harsh, indeed. Union commander McClellan ordered Maj. Gen. H. W. Halleck, new commander of the Department of Missouri, to deal harshly with Frémont's entire operation:

> You will find in your department many general and staff officers holding illegal commissions and appointments not recognized or approved by the President or Secretary of War. You will please at once inform these gentlemen of the nullity of their appointment, and see that no pay or allowances are issued to them until such time as commissions may be authorized by the President or Secretary of War.
>
> If any of them give the slightest trouble you will at once arrest them and send them, under guard, out of the limits of your department, informing them that if they return they will be placed in close confinement. You will please examine into the legality of the organization of the troops serving in the department. When you find any illegal, unusual, or improper organizations you will give to the officers and men an opportunity to enter the legal military establishment.[103]

The volatility of feelings among St. Louis's Germans over the Frémont affair but also the Civil War situation generally was reflected in Emil's account to Gustav II in Köln about a businessman in St. Louis whom they both knew:

> Last summer Alexander Kayser almost become a victim of his countrymen's public wrath. He had appeared before them everywhere as a frenzied secessionist, and they attacked him in the First Ward, namely, women brought ropes with which to hang him. Seriously injured and bloody, he was rescued by several Home Guards. It served him right. He had appeared everywhere as a supporter of the traitors who already had caused German blood to flow in the city's streets three times.[104]

St. Louis's Hard Times

Before the year ended yet another measure of military control hit St. Louis hard. On 10 December 1861 the Union placed the entire river commerce of the city under military control and surveillance. Trade was almost paralyzed by a strict system of permits for steamboats, freight, and passengers. As earlier feared, with the South's blockade of the lower Mississippi and St. Louis' rigorous local controls, trade headed for the northwest logically began to avoid the Gateway to the West and go to Chicago instead. On the positive side, as the Union army's western base of supplies, St. Louis had large government orders to fill.[105]

As Emil Mallinckrodt described the city's situation to his Köln relatives in fall 1861,

St. Louis is fortified with earth entrenchments at 16 sites, and 20,000 men are encamped here. From the mouth of the Ohio upstream our ship travel is unhindered, but below that it is completely closed.

You would not recognize St. Louis again. Thousands of houses are empty, and rental prices are minimal. House owners who have to live from rents will be ruined; therefore, land ownership has only nominal value or rather is completely unsalable. In almost the last year and a half I have not sold one foot—and the notes due are not being paid.

Fortunately, the government is spending an incredible amount here for provisions, horses, transportation, workers, and soldiers, and for the most part the population of the city and surrounding area lives from that! Almost all other businesses and liquidation [bankruptcy receivership] is suspended, and legally there is almost no way to collect a debt. Recently a farm near Carondalet, worth $30,000 last year, was sold by law for $1,350.[106]

By the end of the year, Emil estimated, one hundred thousand people had emigrated to other states, especially Illinois. St. Louis "has perhaps lost 25,000 residents. . . . The wharf is desolate."[107]

Lack of Military Progress

Clearly, the Union's military situation in Missouri was unfavorable. To improve it, Governor Gamble made some organizational changes. He obtained the War Department's authorization to organize, arm, clothe, sustain, and pay the Missouri State Militia (MSM) for duty within the state.[108] In addition, the Military District of Missouri was made a separate command, headed by General Schofield, with five subdistricts under their own commanders.[109]

As the first year of Civil War, 1861, thus struggled to an end, the North had not made much progress toward its goal of conquering the challenging South and so restoring the Union of American States. With the war in the East centered around the rival capitals of federal Washington and Confederate Richmond, the Battle of Bull Run had been noteworthy. At that clash in Virginia the Union Army was routed but, on the other hand, its blockade of the southern coast was relatively successful. Emil Mallinckrodt put it succinctly: "Until now Virginia and Missouri have remained the battlefields of this gruesome war." In less than a year, the war had "taken on dimensions which were beyond all human calculations."[110]

In Missouri, the patterns of guerrilla warfare were unchanged. Almost as the year ended, on 20 December for instance, another railroad bridge was burned, this one over Boone's Lick Road west of Warrenton, thirty miles from Augusta.[111] Even more worrisome than the unending attacks was an emerging trend—the number of guerrillas was growing. That increase came at the same time that the three-month volunteer duty in Confederate units expired. One explanation, therefore, for the gain in guerrilla ranks was that many ex-Confederate soldiers, just mustered out of active duty, were restless and angry enough to join vigilante gangs.[112] One such band was led by William Quantrill whose very name would paralyze western Missouri in the coming months.

Probably like most people, Emil Mallinckrodt alternated between optimism and pessimism. In autumn 1861 he thought the end of the war could possibly come by spring: "The South has no fleet, no merchant marine, and has the self-destructive institution in its lap. In addition, its resources and situation are easily exhausted, whereas those of the North are almost inexhaustible. If only England and France will not play us a trick [that is, declare war] because of the blockade, then even with great sacrifice we will force the South to permanent unity, which is our salvation from this endless chaos." As a businessman, Emil added, "I am not giving up hope for better times." But he also readily admitted, "If I had foreseen the present chaos, I today would not own a foot of land in Missouri. The enormous war costs and municipal indebtedness will terribly repress land ownership in the cities. It may be years before I can again sell [real estate]."[113]

By the end of 1861, however, Emil was less optimistic about the war coming to an end soon. Perhaps his mood was affected by a visit with his nephew James Ferdinand; home from Rolla, Missouri, on a short leave before his Regiment headed south into Confederate territory, James undoubtedly reported personally on the war's slow progress.[114] Emil was increasingly bitter about the North's leadership, including President Lincoln:

> This unholy war until now is led so miserably and unworthily that every reasonable person and the whole army is demoralized. The Cabinet in Washington, as well as all Generals until now, have proved to be completely incompetent. . . .
>
> No state has suffered like Missouri. Its territory is ravaged—some of its railroads and bridges for the tenth time and now again along 100 miles of the North Missouri line. Guerrilla bands of murdering arsonists sweep through the country, and still that sleepyhead (*Schlafmütze*) Lincoln says, "Missouri is comparatively pacified"! . . . In contrast, above the Mississippi the state of Illinois is in deep peace. That is the curse of slavery which hits us in Missouri and destroys our prosperity for the next decade! . . .
>
> The best that we can yet hope for is a revolution in the army which with *one* violent move would drive out the incompetent Cabinet in Washington and the devil slavery.[115]

Emil's view was probably representative for many Germans. Whereas General Frémont had been seen as a man of commitment, Lincoln was perceived as weak and an old Whig (conservative), who "never excited more than luke-warm enthusiasm as a candidate among Germans. They doubted until his death his commitment to the abolition of slavery and to the destruction of the retrograde society of the old South."[116]

The prospects of a long war may have been a factor, then, in Adolph Mallinckrodt's autumn 1862 decision whether and how to continue his service to the Union. By that time, like his cousins James Ferdinand and Gustav, Adolph had already served about a year, that is, the initial three-month volunteer stint in spring and summer of 1861 followed by another commitment for a year or more. James, for instance, was signed up for three years with a Missouri volunteer regiment going outside the state as part of the Army of the Tennessee; Gustav was performing a year of U.S. Army staff duty in St. Louis after the Frémont assignment was terminated. With expiration of three months' service in Krekel's Battalion in January 1862, Adolph had two choices for continuing his service—he could transfer to the First Missouri State Military (MSM) Infantry, formed in part out of former Krekel Companies, for three years of service within Missouri; or he could join the Enrolled Missouri Militia (EMM) for a shorter duration. After several months respite, he decided on the latter and in April 1862 signed up with the EMM for a one-and-a-half-year tour of duty.[117]

Slavery as an issue in the conflict was gradually becoming more central to many. Explaining it to cousin Gustav II in Köln, in the broader political context of the Union's military maneuvering, Emil wrote,

> Our government, as well as the South, attempts to maintain slavery for the decadent old ante-bellum history. Thus we are fighting for the same thing the South fights for—why, then, this senseless war? We have only the alternative of making a foul, disgraceful peace with the rebellious South, which cannot last long, or making an open, honest break with the divine institution of slavery and thereby finding permanent deliverance. . . . A permanent restoration of the Union is no longer possible other than through the total and final abolition of slavery. Whether the people are ready for such a rash, difficult measure, time will soon tell.

In an adamant postscript, Emil added, "But the *basic evil remains the institution of slavery* which the scoundrels (*Halunken*) still justify with the Bible![118]

The first year of the American Civil War, indeed, had been evil for Missouri, the tormented border state. According to history's later compilations, not only was the fourth encounter of the war carried out early on Missouri soil—Camp Jackson—but nearly half of the continuing battles or skirmishes of 1861, that is, around sixty-three of the total of 156.[119]

1862

On 8 January, a new General Order from the Office of the Provost Marshal in St. Louis, or military police, must have left Julius and Conrad wondering with some resignation about the repetitions of history. As in their Uncle Arnold Mallinckrodt's day under Napoleon and later the Prussians, Missouri newspapers now were ordered to submit for "inspection" a copy of each published edition.[120] Not much fantasy was needed to imagine what could happen to subsequent issues if an already published one met with disapproval.

Also early in the year there was another provost marshal regulation concerning transportation and travel. This one greatly bothered the Mallinckrodts because they shipped and traveled on the Missouri River. Under the new decree, the Union military would license boats operating on the river and issue passes for people traveling within the state, while quartermaster and customs officials would authorize permits for all cargos and travelers' baggage.[121] These were many restrictions on the private lives and businesses of people. Some seemed unnecessary and exaggerated, but to that complaint the answer always was, "But it's wartime!" And there were more regulations to come.

Loyalty Oath Broadened

By February the most troublesome restriction thus far was making itself felt— the test oath for public officials passed by the St. Louis convention was extended by military law into a general loyalty oath. First General Halleck ordered the arrest of all St. Louis city officials who did not take the oath, then of University of Missouri personnel, licensed attorneys and counselors, jurors on state courts, presidents and directors of railroad companies, and so on. Finally, in early March, it also was ordered that "at all future elections the voters would be required to take the oath," and teachers and preachers were included, as well.[122]

When the order for the oath was posted, some district military commanders added, for example, the following:

> Every citizen who fails to obey the above order will be deprived of the ordinary privileges of loyal citizenship. He shall neither hold any office nor be permitted to vote. He shall not be allowed to serve as a juror or appear as a witness. . . . He shall not be permitted to pass at will on the public highway, but as a punishment for the apparent aid and countenance which he extends to the marauders who are preying upon the country he is declared to be a prisoner within the limits of his own premises.[123]

Some districts also tacked on the requirement of posting a $1,000 bond to guarantee the pledge.

Sometimes there were mass arrests, especially in central and western Missouri, including women. Not surprisingly, jails were full, including the former infamous "Lynch's slave pen" in St. Louis. Banishment of people and confiscation of property from the "disloyal," mentioned above, became routine.[124]

While the severest conditions of martial law did not prevail in Union-loyal Augusta, its records nevertheless reveal problems which must have been typical for many small settlements. Town Board minutes before April 1862, for instance,

335

noted that the judges of the pending election were to be instructed "that an oath of allegiance has to be taken from any voter, according to one of the orders of General Halleck."[125] At the April election, then, there apparently were no problems. When those newly elected trustees were sworn in at the next meeting, it was duly noted by the justice of the peace that they had sworn to "support the Constitution of the United States and of the State of Missouri, that we will not take up arms against the government of the United States, nor the provisional government of the State of Missouri, nor give aid and comfort to the enemies of either during the present civil war; so help us God."[126]

At the April town board election the next year, however, there was trouble in Augusta. In 1863 no notarization of oaths appear in clerk Bennefeld's records, only that the Augusta trustees took the pledge "according to the prescriptions of the late legislation."[127] G. W. Mindrup, elected trustee, however, apparently saw something wrong with the procedure and refused to serve.[128] New elections were then held in November, and this time the records said town trustees had taken the oath "as prescribed by the law of the convention" and "filed for record with the county clerk." Mindrup returned to the board, as chairman, presumably satisfied that now all was legal![129]

Although Mindrup obviously insisted on strict observance of the law, others in German settlements such as Augusta may have had serious misgivings about the loyalty oath per se, as well as other martial law restrictions on civil liberties. Unfortunately that question apparently was not widely pursued by historians. Logic and a few bits of circumstantial evidence, however, suggest that there may have been some opposition in Duden country.

Civil libertarian immigrants, with backgrounds like that of Julius and Conrad Mallinckrodt, for instance, might have had trouble accepting the extent of the restrictions. It had been the family tradition, for instance, of uncle Arnold Mallinckrodt, to loyally serve the homeland of Westphalia, even under the foreign occupation of Napoleon, but to vigorously oppose curbs on civil liberties from one's own rulers, the Prussians. Such restrictions led the Mallinckrodt immigrants to leave Prussia; to then find equally if not more harsh conditions imposed not by foreigners but "one's own" Union military and Missouri civilian leaders may have struck them as unjust. The oath of public officials was one thing; radical curbs on civilian leaders and on the people's precious voting right, for instance, may have been quite another matter.

Several bits of circumstantial evidence raise questions about what may have been the dilemma of Duden country's pro-Union German liberals: Prior to the Civil War, the Augusta Town Board records frequently showed Conrad Mallinckrodt swearing in and notarizing the Trustees' oaths of office. In 1859 he performed this service as justice of the peace; for the 1860 elections it was a different notary public; in 1861 the notarization was not recorded; for 1862 it again was by a different justice of the peace, and so it continued.[130]

In short, Conrad Mallinckrodt's name did not appear in the Augusta Town Record books as notary or justice of the peace during all the years of the test, or loyalty, oath—under the 1861–62 wartime laws and the postwar constitutional taboos of 1865–1870s—that is, until the bans on civil liberties were gradually lifted. He disappears from the town's public service, although in autumn of 1865 the county newspaper noted that Conrad had taken the oath as justice of the peace.

It is of course possible that clerk Bennefeld overlooked recording Conrad's name since not all notarizations for town elections held in the 1862–1872 period were noted in the book of minutes. Then, too, Conrad may have had a personal disagreement with the town fathers during those years, especially concerning how they dealt with the loyalty oaths required of voters.

By his own records, moreover, Conrad also did not perform marriages as justice of the peace during the period 1860–1867. (The August 1865 marriage of his nephew, Hermann Adolph, was a striking exception; it was performed about the time the county reported Conrad's oath.[131])

After the war, beginning around 1868, German settlers in Missouri became so adamant about getting rid of the loyalty oath that one might presume they had long concealed very deep opposition to it. As will be seen, such stored-up resentment in fact, plus some simple confusion, may have been behind Augusta's cancellation of its 1870 election because "no candidates had taken the oath."[132]

Despite its striking coincidence of some dates and events, the Augusta Town Record book and personal records alone obviously are not evidence for concluding that Conrad Mallinckrodt or anyone else, out of principle, at any time registered protest against the loyalty oath by ceasing to act in an official capacity. The record only raises questions.[133] Detailed case studies which could shed light on possible German protest in the countryside against Missouri's loyalty oaths are not available.

Meanwhile, as the second year of America's Civil War began, Missourians were a bit cheered; the war now seemed to be moving more quickly toward Union goals. President Lincoln, in War Order Number One, set a date for launching a general Union offensive, and General Ulysses S. Grant began a sweep southward in late January.[134] If the Union could cut off the Confederacy's western areas— Kentucky, Tennessee, Mississippi—from its eastern strongholds, then the western rivers on which St. Louis depended for trade would also be freed from Southern control. St. Louis urgently needed that, for business was lagging.[135]

In fact, St. Louis's damaged economy was evident every day—when people wanted to ride the horse-drawn street cars, they simply had no coins to pay the fare. When the federal government began to issue paper money (greenbacks), silver and gold coins had just disappeared. St. Louisans therefore paid their horsecar fare in postage stamps! Those got very sticky, however, during the city's hot and humid summer months. In March 1862 the government then issued tiny notes of green paper called "postage currency" which, as an observer wrote, "were now doing the usual work of the silver coins that had gone into hiding." Although they "became worn, tattered, almost illegible, and unspeakably nasty," at least they did not stick.[136]

Inside Missouri the Union continued reorganizing its military to more effectively pursue the guerrilla bands keeping the state in chaos. Early in the year, for instance, units of the St. Charles County U.S. Reserve Corps became four companies of the First Battalion of the Missouri State Militia. Numbering about four hundred men, they were still under the command of Arnold Krekel, now a lieutenant colonel. Three of the St. Charles County companies were cavalry—A, C, and D led by Captains Henry Windmuller, George Muller, and Frederick Heign [Hein], respectively. Infantry Company B, under Adolph Hufschmidt, was ordered to St. Louis. It served there for three years, carrying out primarily guard duties.[137]

Quantrill Strikes

There was no let-up in guerrilla activities, which continued close to Augusta where the Mallinckrodts lived. Marthasville, for instance, just thirteen miles away, was hit on 20 March.[138] Throughout northern and western Missouri, in spring 1862,

> the time was ripe for insurrection and guerrilla activity. Adult pro-Southern men unable to join the Confederate armies in Arkansas, men who desired to remain neutral in the war, very young boys not considered of real military age, men who had served the Southern cause and been paroled, and those who had suffered wrongs at the hands of the Union military were to swarm into the brush as guerrillas. . . . Joined by unstable and lawless border elements, they were to become formidable enemies. Behind them and around them was a large sympathetic population of relatives and friends who would eagerly and secretly maintain and support them.[139]

William Quantrill was one of those "formidable enemies," with a keen sense of where to strike so it really hurt the Union cause. In April 1862, for instance, his men attacked Union communications in western Missouri, ambushing and killing mail carriers or Union troops escorting the mail. The effect of that strike, as a Kansas City newspaper on the western side of the state said, was that "we have had no mail from St. Louis for three weeks."[140]

The endangered mail situation in the state may, in fact, have prompted the government to allocate Augusta a post office of its own. Initially a contracted post rider had gotten Augusta's mail by ferrying across the river to the town of Bowles (Boles) and then Labadie, where the mail was brought from St. Louis by the Missouri Pacific Railroad. The post rider also took the knapsacks marked Femme Osage and Schluersburg by horseback to their destinations. In 1862, then, the settlement was allotted its own post office, set up in the riverfront store of the new postmaster, Frederick Wencker, probably a younger cousin of the Mallinckrodt's late immigrant friend, Carl Wencker.[141] Perhaps the state of Missouri recognized the town's general growth, but possibly, too, its pro-Union stability in an area of unrest was significant to the Union's need for reliable mail routes.

Many Missourians at the time of course were outraged with the state government because it could not bring the guerrillas under control. It was this situation that threatened daily life. The question, therefore, of the guerrillas' weapons was an unending topic of discussion, especially in St. Charles County when, for instance, a newspaper reported that an expedition against secessionists in Darst Bottom had captured numerous weapons there.[142] Later historians studying the guerrilla war concluded indeed that one reason for the success of groups such as Quantrill's raiders was their weapons:

> The real secret of their success in combat against their more numerous Union enemy, aside from their guerrilla tactics, lay in their superior weapon, the Colt revolving pistol. The revolver was the primary weapon of Quantrill's men, and there is abundant evidence that they were deadly with this frontier weapon. It became customary for the guerrillas to carry from two to eight revolvers in their belts and on their saddles. These rapid-firing, five- and six-shot weapons, in addition to the customary Sharps carbine, gave them a tremendous volume of fire power. As the majority of the Union cavalry on the border in 1862 was armed only with single-shot muzzle-loading carbines or muskets and sabers, Federal officers complained continually of their weapons and begged for revolvers for their men.[143]

The other side of the discussion in St. Charles County and elsewhere obviously concerned the Union's weapons, and many people thought the officers' complaints were reasonable. After all, the Colt revolver, with a reach of some fifty yards and therefore effective in the close-range hit-and-run guerrilla war, was not new. It had been invented by Samuel Colt in 1836 and had already been used by the United States some twenty years earlier in the Mexican War.[144] Moreover, the Colt was being manufactured in good supply.[145] If the weapon then was not widely available to Union soldiers trying to curb the guerrillas in Missouri and elsewhere, the shortage seemingly was a matter of short-sighted military procurement.

Another part of the problem was distribution. In fact, there was serious public criticism of the Union's ordinance bureau for having been bureaucratically tardy in making breech-loading, rather than musket, rifles generally available.[146] The modern rifles were only gradually "reaching select bodies of troops," that is, "first in the cavalry and later the infantry."[147] Where the manufactured Colt revolvers went was another and serious question, for during 1862 alone the North reportedly had bought one hundred twenty thousand pistols.[148] Thus, the Colts the Union soldiers so desperately wanted may have been simply another of the "too little too late" actions which were embittering so many people toward the political and military leadership of the Union.

Not only were Missouri's Union soldiers and their supporters troubled by the guerrillas' effective weapons, but also by the considerable moral support they had gained: guerrilla activities now seemed more officially encouraged by the Confederacy. Although the South's president, Jefferson Davis, did not really believe in irregular forms of warfare, by April 1862 he nevertheless had authorized partisan rangers. The Confederacy commander in Arkansas thus sent out orders to men like Quantrill, giving some legality to their guerrilla gangs.[149] Such developments clearly would prolong the guerrilla war in Missouri.

The Union's General Schofield meanwhile was trying harsher measures to weaken the guerrilla movement. In May he declared that "the time is passed when insurrection and rebellion in Missouri can cloak itself under the guise of honorable warfare." All marauders "caught in arms" would be shot on the spot, he said. By June he also ordered stiff compensation from all "rebels and rebel sympathizers" responsible for guerrilla damage—among other sums, they would pay five thousand dollars for every soldier or Union citizen killed and from one thousand dollars to five thousand dollars for every one wounded.

In addition to such efforts against the guerrillas, Schofield needed to strengthen his own military forces, as well. In July 1862, therefore, he ordered an all-out draft of every able-bodied man for the state militia. He had in mind not only the MSM but also the new supplementary force, the Enrolled Missouri Militia (EMM). As always, there was the old problem of how to pay the soldiers. But there was new dissatisfaction, too—men willing to do service to protect Missouri did not necessarily want to be drafted to fight outside its borders.[150] This may have been important in Adolph Mallinckrodt's decision to continue his service in the EMM.

The critical military situation in Missouri—for soldiers such as Adolph as well as the state's residents—was made clear in August 1862 in an urgent order from General Schofield at army headquarters in St. Louis to Lieutenant Colonel Arnold Krekel at St. Charles:

> Colonel: The condition of the northeastern part of Missouri demands the united efforts of all loyal men to put down the rebel bands which infest that part of the State.
>
> I desire you to rally as quickly as possible as large a force as you can raise in Saint Charles, Warren, and Lincoln Counties and take the field at once. You will of course leave sufficient force, either of your own battalion or of the Enrolled Militia, to take care of the railroad now guarded by you.
>
> You have full power to call out all the men subject to military duty in the counties named. . . . Let the men come in with their horses and arms and whatever else they may require for active campaigning and can carry without incumbrance. Let them not wait for organization or muster into service, but organize as they march.

Inform me from day to day what arms and ammunition you require and I will forward them by rail to such points as you may designate. Make the men use the arms to be found in the country as far as practicable. . . .

You will take from the secessionists whatever you may need for the accomplishment of this end. Do not encumber yourself with the transportation of supplies, but live upon the country as you go.[151]

Missourians may indeed have been moved to sign up with forces such as Krekel's when on August 11 the feared bandit Quantrill struck again. Out of nowhere, as it were, he and his guerrilla force swept down on the western Missouri border town of Independence to destroy a major Union post; by 6 September, Quantrill's guerrillas captured and looted the Union's Olathe, Kansas, garrison.[152]

Once again martial law provisions were applied with a vengeance. Especially harsh was the banishment of wives and families suspected of Southern loyalties, obviously including the guerrillas' family members. In the past, either imprisoned or exiled to some Northern states, such families now were also to be sent south. Allowed to take some cash with them, the rest of their property was confiscated.[153] Prisons were filled, and seeds of raging hate sown.

Meanwhile, the regular Missouri Union troops, where James Ferdinand Mallinckrodt served in the Seventeenth Infantry Regiment, had quickened their pace. After the battle of Pea Ridge in Arkansas in March 1862, James was commissioned second lieutenant and replaced the previously killed company H commander; by July the regiment was moving to Alabama; by December, under the command of Major General Grant, the Army of the Tennessee was moving down the Mississippi toward Vicksburg.[154]

Emancipation

In addition to the unending problem of how to deal with the state's irregular warfare, emancipation, too, was becoming an ever-hotter issue in Missouri. Abolitionists were encouraged when the U.S. Congress in June carried out a Republican pledge to abolish slavery in the nation's capital, the District of Columbia.[155] On the other hand, the Missouri Assembly passed an ordinance on 1 July, freeing the state's slaves but not until 4 July 1870.[156] The postponed date greatly angered Missouri's radicals, who demanded immediate emancipation.

At the same time, Provisional Governor Gamble's position remained modest. Since the Missouri Constitution recognized the legal existence of slavery, he had vigorously opposed General Frémont's premature emancipation proclamation in August 1861 and was encouraged when President Lincoln then rescinded it.[157]

The St. Louis *Anzeiger*, however, pursued the goal. On 3 March 1862, it wrote, "The emancipation movement cannot come to Missouri quickly enough. . . . But for us Germans, emancipation is a matter of life and death. If Missouri remains a slave state, then we will not remain here any longer. No one is fooled about that. We will always be seen as a dangerous, incendiary element [because of the Germans' radical antislavery stand] . . . and it would then be best for us to leave."[158] Later in the month, as city council elections approached, the newspaper again wrote, "who is not for us is against us, in toto. Germans can only continue to have a homeland in a Missouri that is committed to freedom."[159] About a month later Duden country's Friedrich Münch, often the moral voice of that area's liberal German-American community, published a long and poignant reflection of its view on slavery. Entitled "To the Germans of the State of Missouri," the article appeared in the *St. Charles Demokrat* and was republished in the *Anzeiger des Westens* on 23 April 1862. In it Münch wrote that in the 1830s,

> we who then traveled to Missouri knew that we were going to a *slave state*, but we did not attribute very great importance to that fact. As long as slavery existed in areas of the United States—we figured—it made no great difference whether we had blacks as close neighbors or only as distant ones; we afterall—so it seemed— were guaranteed by federal law and by the liberal Constitution of the State of Missouri all the rights we could ever wish for. The thought of personally concerning one's self with slavery certainly was entertained by only very few among us; we were sorry that there were slaves here, but we could not do anything about it; we ourselves wanted nothing to do with slavery, but also expected that we would not be particularly burdened by it.
>
> I readily confess, as will thousands of others, that we deceived ourselves in this last expectation. The first few years, when there was no tumult concerning slavery, certainly went by very quietly for us, but gradually it became increasingly clear that slavery and true freedom could not exist side by side. No law really can take away the freedom of thought, and so far as one or another thing is not specifically prohibited, the freedom of writing and speech or of action are totally guaranteed to us by the law of the land. But in reality we were compelled to live in a state of perpetual and incresing guardianship at the hands of slaveowners. Not everyone was equally sensitive to this, because they were not restricted in their ordinary daily lives and were bothered little by other things. But no one can deny the shameful fact that we were not free people in this so-called *free* country, rather had to adapt to the slaveowners' whims.
>
> Were we allowed to tell the owners of human beings what we thought of black serfdom? Were we allowed to tell the slaves, or even indicate to them through silent conduct, that we regarded them as *human beings* and that they had human rights, too? Yet even if we said nothing whatsoever and did nothing at all, were not those grand gentlemen nevertheless suspicious of our convictions and suspected our inner thoughts because we seldom stood out as public *praisers* of the institution, and since we did not participate actively in trading and breeding human beings?
>
> Yet not very long ago in the area where I live, a respected German who simply commented that blacks were *people*, too, was presumptously visited by a group of those gentlemen, cross-examined, and intensively grilled. It also happens that less

than a year ago, also in this region, a so-called vigilance committee was formed to observe our deeds and speech, and meetings were held and resolutions drafted that designated Germans as a group as thieves of Negroes, law breakers, disturbers of the peace, and cursed them in other ways as well. We were placed under the secret surveillance of men we regarded as far beneath us, who in part had never been anything but contemptible good-for-nothings and soon thereafter proved to be public traitors and rebel vagabonds worthy of death on the gallows.

By what right did those people condemn us? Could anyone show that precisely we Germans had done anything illegal, disturbed the general peace, injured the rights of anyone, even the rights of slaveowners? Has really anyone among our countrymen ever actually seized a slave, or enticed him away or stolen him? Nothing of the sort! One cannot accuse us for any of our deeds, but they want to abandon us to general revenge for having superior and more humane convictions; they believe they can read a sentiment in our hearts that is outraged by the daily inhumanity. Our crime is our refusal to agree with the orthodox doctrine that a portion of humankind exists to be driven, whipped, worked to death, or under certain circumstances even to be burned to death. When we were few, our dissenting convictions received little attention; since then, not only has the number of Germans increased—especially in certain parts of the state—but also their importance and prosperity. In part, after having started with little, in many aspects the Germans have overshadowed the slaveholders. They observe us with greater suspicion and would most like to make even us into a sort of slave who would have nothing to say, but who would simply work and be silent.

They have injured our inner feelings no less by the hardness and viciousness with which the preservation of slavery seems naturally to be bound. Many of us have had hungry slaves come to our doors; others have been robbed because great numbers of slaves were famished, or because they had been raised in savagery. We have seen others walking around in rags and tatters and barefoot in harsh weather; finally the screams of those being whipped—not only children being disciplined, but men, women, mothers being beaten—often came to our ears; or we were eyewitnesses to the sale of souls, that dreadful show where parents, children, and married couples were pulled apart in the midst of the raw jesting of traders in human flesh. Could the feelings of any individual among us be so hardened that he no longer was moved by such things? Inwardly outraged? Even if such things did not happen every day, they occurred often enough to convince every good person that all these crudities once had to be ended, and as quickly as possible.

In fact, if slavery were to stay forever in Missouri, Germans would no longer settle in this state, since there also is plenty of room for us in the western free states where we could avoid so much that offends us here. Or those of us who are able must make every effort to save from perdition this state we have chosen as our new homeland. In that case we would be accomplishing as great and important a work as history has to offer. If Germans had never come to Missouri, then slavery here would become increasingly more dominant, and the state would now be in that same dreadful condition into which all the slave states are gradually sinking.

If we reconcile ourselves to the notion of our own free labor continuing to exist alongside slave labor, so we, too, will be guilty of holding our state back from the progress of the free states, and we shall never win true and full freedom for ourselves or our descendants.

Fr[iedrich] M[ünch][160]

President Lincoln's thinking had changed, as well. Lincoln increasingly saw slavery as a millstone around the neck of the United States and resolved to free the slaves in the South (leaving the border states alone for the moment). The time was right, Lincoln thought, after the Union's victory at Antietam, Maryland, in September 1862. The Preliminary Emancipation Proclamation, which Lincoln issued on 22 September, said that all slaves in areas still in rebellion against the United States would be freed on 1 January 1863.[161]

Along with many other Missourians, Emil Mallinckrodt saw moral as well as economic benefits in the promised Proclamation: "Never again can freedom and slavery exist *next to each other* without eternal strife on this continent. *One* principle *must* fall, and with God's help it shall be slavery!" Prompt abolition, he felt, was possible if the government were to "put the colored people under legal protection and pay them for their work. Then the fall in production would be minimal. Indeed, production probably would increase and again give the land well-being, security, and peace."[162]

Although not applying directly to Missouri, Lincoln's Proclamation had a profound effect on its fall 1862 elections of state legislators. The declaration strengthened the demands of Missouri's radical Republicans for immediate emancipation in the border state. Many Missourians, however, were not interested in the election. There was so much unrest in the state that a real campaign was not possible. The bottom had fallen out of economics—poverty, unemployment, inflation, and shortages marked the autumn of 1862. In addition, many people could not vote because they had refused to take the Loyalty Oath. The result among those who did vote was a clear mandate for some form of emancipation.[163]

While waiting for that to come, Missouri's Germans had more immediate concerns. In November, the bushwhacker Joe Cole, who had made war on German settlers, was killed by Union troops.[164] While that undoubtedly brought some sense of relief to Duden country—"One less!"—the summing up there for the year 1862 was not entirely positive. More than sixty thousand soldiers had been on duty in the state to fight some three thousand to four thousand guerrillas, siphoning off money and troops that should have been available elsewhere. In addition, ugly patterns of military behavior and government had been established, which would bear bitter fruit.[165]

Family news from the countryside, meanwhile, was quite positive. Augusta, in fact, was known for the Mallinckrodt orchards, as well as George Münch's Mount Pleasant vineyards, which had been planted about 1861.[166] And in the new year Julius's eldest son and partner, Conrad Theodor, now twenty-eight, would move the Mallinckrodt nursery business to St. Charles and continue it on his own. It was to be located about a half-mile south of the city on fifty-three acres.[167] At the same time, Julius concentrated on his orchards and he and Mary planned soon to deed their "back forty" acres to their son Hermann Adolph when his life settled down after the war.[168] He, too, was following the family tradition of horticulture.[169]

The Augusta Mallinckrodts were also pleased with the improvement in education, despite the war. The town school was still the earlier one-room building on the block Harold had given the settlement but, according to local recollections, it was in 1862 that the school hired a principal, German-educated Professor John Gütlich. Perhaps, typical of rural schools in the German communities at that time, less than an hour a day was devoted to English instruction.[170]

Untypically, however, Professor Gütlich ran a ten-month school.[171]

Emil's Retrospective

In St. Louis, Emil Mallinckrodt, looking back over the second year of civil war, had personal reasons to be grateful: "We have been lucky enough to not yet have suffered any direct losses or disturbances of our family happiness. The nearness of the city has protected us. In contrast, the state of Missouri is in part devastated."

Emil's son Gustav was out of the fighting. After dismissal in November 1861 as a staff officer for General Frémont, Gustav stayed with the Union army despite his father's opposition. His new assignment was at the St. Louis headquarters of the Department of Missouri, in the paymaster's office. Ironically, that office was headed by Lieutenant Colonel T. P. Andrews, the same paymaster who earlier had refused to honor General Frémont's commissions (said to number two hundred) and to pay his officers, including Gustav Mallinckrodt.[172]

In autumn 1862, when U.S. Army troops were sent to St. Paul, Minnesota, to counter an Indian uprising, Gustav was also assigned there as paymaster clerk at the Union headquarters of the Department of the Northwest.[173] As one of the biggest staff departments of the army, the paymaster-general's office sent its civilian clerks, who were not liable to the field duty of a soldier, to wherever the national forces were assigned.[174]

While Emil was grateful for his family's safety, he was horrified at the loss of life around them, recalling perhaps the stories and paintings of Europe's frontal infantry and cavalry conflicts: "The people of the U.S. have drunk so deeply from the chalice of unhappiness that one could almost believe it were empty. No mortal can summarize the measure of our misfortune with all its far-reaching consequences. . . . The loss of human life, healthy limbs, and destroyed family happiness is the most horrifying of all! Almost half a million people are already killed, crippled, or destroyed by illness."

The leadership of the war continued to outrage Emil, motivating descriptive words such as "rashness," "treacherousness," and "incompetence." At the same time, he wrote, both the Northern and Southern armies had been brave, and "even Napoleon the Great could not have wished for better stock." The primary problem, Emil felt, was the president: "In Lincoln we unfortunately have the most miserable President possible in these agitated times. He is a weakling in intelligence and energy. He wants to do right by all parties and every individual and thereby ruins everything. He selected his Cabinet from among similar people."

The nature of slavery apparently had become clearer to Emil over the years, as it had to others. "State sovereignty was the mother of secession," he explained to his cousin Gustav II, "and the damnable institution of slavery the basic cause of all evil, the key to all disgraces." Continuing, he wrote, "Gen. Butler, perhaps the most competent man in the U.S., said 'This war is a war of 350,000 slave owners against the people.' Only the general lack of knowledge of the poor white classes in the South and their prejudices against the black race explain how they—who have no interest in slavery but rather are disadvantaged by the institution a thousand times over—sacrifice themselves for the interests of the slave barons."

Equally as troubling to Emil, and surely many like him, was the future of the country. Passionately and with near-desperation, after two years of war, he occasionally wrote that it would be better to have "a powerful monarchy then this unbelievable division" or, referring to Napoleon, "in vain we wait with increasing tension for such a Messiah."[175] At another time, however, Emil, believing "no people has ever been able to ignore its geographic situation without paying a price," coolly analyzed the geopolitical situation of possible partition:

> One already speaks of four parts: (1) the New England states, (2) the middle states, (3) the slave states, and (4) the Pacific states. Does one think that the last two would take over a *single* dollar of the Washington government's debts?
>
> From his own self-interest, every citizen is already tied to a single government. If there ever should be a partition through the power of the situation, it could only be geographic: (1) the states of the Atlantic coast, (2) the Mississippi Valley from the back of the Alleghenies to the Rocky Mountains, and (3) from the Rocky Mountains westward.[176]

In summary, Emil felt that "no end to our chaos is in sight, our future is dark and unendingly difficult." His city's economics troubled him greatly: "St. Louis has lost tremendously through the loss of its trade to the South. On the other hand, it has regained a bit through deliveries to the government. Property is still unsalable although all buildings, especially houses, are again full, and rents are increasing. Many people are shy of accepting Greenbacks as payment although the Congress declared it legal tender." But, he concluded, "Greenbacks are 60 per cent beneath gold and continue to fall. How and where shall it all end?"[177]

1863

The new year, of course, began with Lincoln's Emancipation Proclamation which went into effect on 1 January. Historians later would write, "This proclamation, more revolutionary in human relationships than any event in American history since 1776, lifted the Civil War to the dignity of a crusade. Yet it actually freed not one slave, since it applied only to rebel states where it could not be enforced."[178]

In Duden country the proclamation brought an almost immediate change of spirit among the German immigrants. The *St. Charles Demokrat* headlined its report "All Honor to the President" and within days used the term *Negro* rather than "slave." Following another proclamation by President Lincoln regarding military deserters and congressional passage of a law forbidding the use of U.S. troops in the recapture of runaway slaves, Augusta's liberal citizens acted on their new mood.[179]

They "rescued" runaway slaves who had been returned forcibly to a notorious master and then at a public meeting read their fellow German-American out of the community for dishonorable conduct disgracing his German name by betraying the slave's whereabouts.[180]

Further clarification of the March law came in the 29 July General Order No. 75 from the Adjutant General's Office for the Missouri military department. It made clear that the congressional legislation applied to all Missouri troops, including active militia, and that they were forbidden from helping civil servants in arresting and turning over runaway slaves.[181]

This, in turn, may have prompted another "rescue" of a slave in October 1863, one who had been apprehended by a justice of the peace. This time a public meeting of Augusta's Radical Liberal party members dismissed the fellow immigrant from all his public offices for betraying the slave. Then with fifty armed men on horseback, the protesters rode out and brought the Negro back from his master to freedom.[182]

Meanwhile, as a border slave state exempt from the national Proclamation, Missouri had followed up on 1 July with gubernatorial approval of its own emancipation ordinance for 1870. The postponed date still displeased many.[183] But as Emil Mallinckrodt wrote, "The certainty that at least in our state slavery will fall is worth all sacrifice; only because of that was the rapid [economic] boom possible."[184]

In July St. Louisans had special reason to celebrate—for the first time since the beginning of the war a steamship from the South arrived in the city. "There was great rejoicing," it was said, because "the Father of Waters was now completely under Federal control. This event was hailed as freeing St. Louis not only from the throes of rebellion, but also from the commercial bondage which it had suffered through the closing of the Lower Mississippi."[185]

Personally, the St. Louis Mallinckrodts also had cause to drink several toasts— Hermann and Luise's officer son James Ferdinand (Ferdy) had survived "numerous bloody battles," especially in spring 1863 with General Grant's Army of the Tennessee at Vicksburg (key to control of the Mississippi River) and Arkansas Post. Emil reported to Germany that "in both battles men next to him [James Ferdinand] fell."[186]

But while the young officer had indeed survived, his health was irreparably damaged—the thunder of the bombardments at Vicksburg so damaged his hearing that some years later he would be totally deaf and receive a "severly disabled" pension. Fellow soldiers testified that after Vicksburg "I noticed for the first time that [his] hearing was much damaged, while at Sedalia, tenting together it was good," and that "there were many hardships on this tour from southwest Missouri through Arkansas in 1861–62, malaria, bad water, much sickness; after the 47-day siege [of Vicksburg] ending on July 4, 1863 I distinctly recollect his becoming very hard of hearing."[187]

Vicksburg was a wrenching experience for many Missourians. The border state was represented on the siege line by twenty-seven organizations, including James's Seventeenth Missouri Infantry Regiment, commanded by Colonel Hassenduebel. By 19 May 1863, when the Confederates had fallen back toward Vicksburg, the Missourians' brigade commander Colonel Charles R. Woods began moving his troops forward for the massive general assault planned by General Grant on the Confederate's Mississippi River stronghold. Separated from the enemy by a deep valley, Woods reported that his troops "found the enemy strongly posted, with from 12 to 17 siege guns in position, covered by strong earthworks, and commanding our position." To strengthen his own emplacement, Woods on 21 May had to send his men across open ground to reach the site from where the general charge would begin, and "fifty or sixty men and officers were killed and wounded in gaining our position."

According to official descriptions of the battle, the general assault then began on 22 May. In addition to infantry, there was an artillery battalion reinforced by two naval forty-two-pound rifled guns furnished by gunboats of the U.S. Navy river squadron.[188] In vain. A Union engineering report put it succinctly: "the fire both of artillery and musketry from the enemy's line was so heavy, and the loss in moving over the rough and obstructed ground so severe, that the assault failed at all points."[189]

The failed Union assault was especially well described and officially recorded by one of James Ferdinand's "enemies" on the other side, the Confederate commander of a regiment of volunteer Texas infantrymen, Colonel Ashbel Smith. During the three days before the assault, Smith wrote about the bombardments around James Ferdinand, which were to damage his hearing. First, the Union "opened on us with cannon and rifled musketry, which increased hour by hour with their augmenting numbers, until the uproar and rattle was almost incessant and very grand." Then, "at an early hour of the morning of Friday, May 22, the enemy opened a most furious cannonade and fire of musketry, which were continued with occasionally varying intensity till 10 a.m." Finally, in Smith's words, "the Second Texas was ready" for the enemy which "fought from 10'clock in the morning till dark, within from 20 to 400 paces of the muzzles of our rifles."

The price of that historic assault was great. Seen from the Confederate point of view, but typical of many shocking Civil War battles,

> the loss of the enemy, considering the numbers engaged on either side, was enormous. The ground in our front and along the road, and either side of the road for several hundred yards way to the right, was thickly strewn with their dead. In numbers of instances two and three dead bodies were piled on each other. Along the road for more than 200 yards the bodies lay so thick that one might have walked the whole distance on them without touching the ground. . . . On the 25th, there was a truce for burying the Yankee dead which had not been removed.[190]

James Ferdinand's commander, Colonel Hassenduebel, killed at Vicksburg, may have been one of those bodies.

Conceding the Union assault's failure—"with much loss on our side in killed and wounded"—General Grant reported that he had then "determined on a regular siege."[191] In other words, he would starve the Confederate stronghold at Vicksburg into submission. The shooting, of course, would continue. From the beginning of the siege, according to the Confederate commander of the Texans, "there was a fierce cannonade once, twice, thrice, or even oftener in the twenty-four hours, with occasional shots at irregular intervals; an incessant stream of Minies swept just above the upper slope of our parapet, increasing in strength day after day, as rifle-pit after rifle-pit was constructed."[192]

The intensity of that cannonade was reflected in the report of a single unit of the Union's light artillery batteries—it alone had fired 13,498 rounds of ammunition from 19 May until the siege ended on 4 July when Vicksburg and the thirty-thousand-man army, which had been defending it, surrendered.[193]

Thus the changing nature of infantry and artillery warfare was gradually being sensed, especially by the many Missouri immigrants who had experienced military training in their European homelands. Instead of massed troops marching frontally toward each other's lines, as was traditional, it now was better tactics to have dug-in troops in protective trenches. From the defensive Confederate point of view, Colonel Smith, for example, wrote, "A fact already perhaps sufficiently established was illustrated—the power of earthen embankments to resist artillery, and the ability of true soldiers, protected by a parapet and ditch, to resist for a long period numbers which would be otherwise overwhelming. . . . The spade is a military weapon."

On the other hand, much of the Civil War infantryman's life, which Colonel Smith graphically described, was not changing. The Southerners' soldiering conditions were what James Ferdinand, on the Union side, also had known and would for yet another long year:

> Up to the last moment of the siege, the men bore with unrepining cheerfulness and undauanted spirit the fatigues of almost continual position under arms, of frequent working parties by night and day, the broiling of the midday sun in summer with no shelter, the chilling night dews, the cramped inaction at all times in the trenches, short rations, at times drenched with rain and bivouacking in the mud, together with the discomforts inseparable from having no change of clothing and an insufficient supply of water for cleanliness, tired, ragged, dirty, barefoot, hungry, covered with vermin, with a scanty supply of ammunition, almost hand to hand with the enemy, and beleaguered on every side, with no prospect and little hope of relief.[194]

After the Vicksburg siege was over, James in August applied for and was granted home leave, having not been away from his unit for two years. Perhaps thus he was able to share his family's celebration of the marriage of his oldest sister Cecilia to William Kueffner. Following his respite in St. Louis, James returned to Major General William T. Sherman's famous Army of the Tennessee battling its way through the south; there James served as C Company commander in his Seventeenth Missouri Infantry Regiment and was promoted to first lieutenant by 1864.[195]

Emil and Emilie Mallinckrodt, too, had cause for happiness amidst all the sorrow of war—a new son, Oscar, was born to them in December 1862. Preparations were also underway to leave for Europe in May with Minna and the three youngest children. "My wife is homesick to once again see her old mother," Emil explained. There were other reasons, as well, why Emil had to return to his old home town, now a city of around twenty-five thousand:[196] "My sister-in-law in Dortmund wishes to have Minna with her, and since the death of my brother I have promised to help her order her affairs. I cannot postpone it any longer. I must make the sacrifice and tear myself loose, but return within a year." Their son Eduard, then eighteen, would stay in St. Louis to keep an eye on the family home and land, and Otto would remain in school in St. Louis, boarding with Hermann and Luise.[197]

The countryside Mallinckrodts, on the other hand, were as troubled as ever. An especially disturbing raid on Missouri's German communities took place on 26 May 1863. The small settlement of Rhineland, thirty-five miles from Augusta, was hit hard by a band of fifteen bushwhackers. The town's founder, Andrew Richeval [Richewohl], who ran a store, was killed, his money was taken, and his goods were stolen. Although the Rhinelanders quickly went across the river to Hermann for soldiers, the bandits were not captured.[198]

Quantrill's Raid on Lawrence, Kansas

Quantrill and his men, too, were back in western Missouri—robbing the mails, tearing up miles of telegraph wire between Union posts, ambushing federal patrols, burning bridges, and attacking steamboats on the Missouri.[199] Then on 14 August the guerrillas got news which would drive them into wrathful madness—the brick building in Kansas City used as a Union prison for women members of guerrilla families collapsed, killing many. The guerrillas were convinced that Union officers had deliberately caused the collapse and the deaths of their relatives.

There was a certain town, the guerrillas vowed, that would pay for the dead wives and sisters. It was Lawrence, Kansas! Quantrill and his men for some time had planned to raid it, and now "like a roaring tide, the guerrilla column poured into Lawrence" at dawn on 20 August. By nine o'clock, it was reported, "the blood bath ended." Some one hundred fifty men were gunned down, leaving eighty widows and two hundred fifty orphans. Property damage totaled more than $2 million. Only one guerrilla lost his life, and "not one Lawrence woman was injured or physically violated."[200]

The massacre at Lawrence shocked the nation. Even Augusta, Missouri, reacted. Its Town Board called a special meeting and issued a proclamation:

> In consideration of the atrocities committed by a gang of robbers and murderers on the city of Lawrence and in consideration of the well known fact that returned rebel soldiers who would perhaps lawfully [*sic*] prepare a similar fate to our town . . . and our neighborhood, be it ordained by the Board of Trustees of the town of Augusta as follows:
>
> > 1. that all male inhabitants of the town of Augusta from the ages of 16 to 60 years have to arm themselves to participate in the nightwatchers and patrols which are established for the safety of the town . . .
> > 2. that all those who neglect to comply with the above order will be subject to a fine of two dollars for each and every such negligence,
> > 3. that we invite all those living close to the limits of the town as well as the neighboring farmers to unite with us for their own safety to the protection of their and our homes.
> > 4. that we hereby openly declare to all whom it may concern that we will hold responsible the well known southern sympathizers living within our reach for all crimes committed in this neighborhood in consequence of this civil war.[201]

At the next regular meeting the Board resolved that anyone not able to serve as nightwatchers when ordered to do so had to arrange for a substitute. A Mr. Roberts apparently refused to serve, and the Town Board ordered the constable to collect the $2 fine from him.[202] The protest spread, and at the following meeting Fr. Wencker and B. Follenius were also cited with a fine for their refusals. At the same time the Board resolved "to cease at present the nightwatchers in consequence of the opposition the measure has found, until events will [have] convinced the citizens of their necessity."[203] Moreover, seeking legal advice in St. Charles, the county seat, the Board was informed that indeed it had no right to force citizens to perform this duty, that is, without compensation. The constable thus was instructed to drop his charge against Wencker and Follenius and refund Roberts.[204]

Regardless of proclamation or nightwatchers, the people in Duden country remained restless throughout the fall of 1863. And not without reason, for in September another nearby settlement was hit. But this attack was different—the village of Wright City was partially burned down not by guerrillas but by Union militia forces who were avenging the killing of a member of their company.[205] Lieutenant Adolph Mallinckrodt led that action.

The guerrilla situation was serious everywhere, "even in the St. Louis *neighborhood*," Emil visiting in Germany wrote. His son had reported from Missouri that "robberies on the highways, as well as murders, etc. perpetrated by demons in the garb of soldiers are of frequent occurence in the vicinity of St. Louis. Several instances of the kind we have but recently heard of. Farmers going to town from the neighborhood now generally carry arms. Edward always manages to get home early from town whenever he goes in."[206]

After Quantrill's bloody raid on Lawrence, Governor Gamble, already long criticized for being more concerned about reconciliation than punishment, came under intense fire.[207] Completely out of patience, Missouri's Radical Republicans convened in Jefferson City on 1 September. St. Louis sent 106 delegates, most of whom were Germans.[208] The convention denounced Gamble's military commander Schofield and the militia. They also naturally demanded immediate emancipation. With the political dissatisfaction and social unrest so intense by autumn 1863, the Mallinckrodts were especially relieved when Hermann Adolph was mustered out of the EMM on 24 September after a total of two years' military service in Missouri.[209]

Tactics and Casualties

Elsewhere in the East and South, Civil War battles, which would preoccupy historians and military strategists for generations to come, were being fought. Often the loss in human life was enormous.[210]

Many persons shocked by the huge numbers of wounded knew that they resulted to a large extent from the improved weapons of the time on the one hand, used with outdated tactics on the other. In the largely infantry-fought U.S. Civil War, the musket rifle, for instance, was the standard small arms weapon on both sides. Its rifled barrel grooved on the inside to rotate the bullet and give it greater accuracy, projected the so-called Minie bullet about a half mile. That bullet, twice as deadly as those used in the Mexican War, slaughtered and stopped attacks at 200 to 250 yards.[211] Many rural and frontier people knew that.

At the same time, however, the military tactics being ordered for the men carrying this gun were fatally outdated, as many of European background knew and others were learning. It was tradition, as during Europe's Napoleonic Wars, for massed lines of soldiers to march toward each other, shooting when they got close enough and finally hacking away with swords; they could not kill each other from great distances because their smoothbore muskets reached only one hundred yards or so. Now, although the rifled muskets reached greater distances and the bullets were more explosive, the soldiers still marched in the old formations. They then literally mowed each other down, leaving horrible wounds when firing the modern arms into closely massed lines of human beings. Entrenchment sometimes was the only effective defense, as at Vicksburg. Large twelve-pound artillery shells from cannon also took their toll in wounded bodies.[212] It all reminded the Missouri Mallinckrodts of the Napoleonic Wars that had marked their childhood—lines and lines of men and dashing horses, the battles Mother and Father had talked about.

Contemplating the carnage of the American Civil War from Germany where he was vacationing, Emil Mallinckrodt apparently expressed revulsion in letters to his son Gustav, stationed in Minnesota. Responding to such a letter, Gustav wrote his disillusioned immigrant father in July 1863 that

> from your last letter I infer you must have suddenly found out that we are all barbarians yet in this *blessed* country. I cannot exactly agree with you on this point. . . . At the present time, comparing our unfortunate state of affairs with those of the peaceful quiet there, I think is unjust . . . we are ridiculed as a general thing by Europeans. They do not consider what we have done within the past two years, what an immense army, such as the world has never seen, has been equipped and put into the field . . . 70,000 prisoners taken within one week by the armies of the union who are still on their triumphal march to glory and victory is a feat not before recorded in the annuals of history.[213]

At the same time that Gustav defended his country in this way, he was no admirer of the Union's military tactics or leadership. "I think this whole Indian war a humbug," he wrote; not much can be accomplished because of "the great immobility of the army, having to haul all their supplies."[214] Several weeks later, in fact, Gustav wrote father Emil,

> the Indian expedition under Sibly ("the great humbug") has just returned. The results are simply that they, a body of over 3000 men, met a body of about 2000 indians near the Missouri after a march of near 500 miles, had three *great* and *decisive* battles with them in which 2 of our soldiers were killed and 33 indians. Just think—an army of that magnitude with all the modern appliances of warfare— canon and with rifles double the range of the firearms and arrows of the indians,

after 3 separate engagements on different days kill *33* indians and let the balance cross the Missouri River in peace. At this rate, each indian in Minnesota and Dakotah has cost the government about ¼ million dollars. This indian war has been an expensive piece of business to Uncle Sam and proved a very lucrative gold mine to the poor Minnesotians.

And about the guerrilla war Gustav reported to his father that "Missouri as a matter of course under [General] Schofield's policy is overrun with guerrilla bands. A delegation has been sent to Washington to ask his removal, consisting of some seventy of Missouri's most prominent radicals."[215]

While chastising his father for greatly misjudging and doing injustice to President Lincoln, Gustav Mallinckrodt, nevertheless, had serious reservations about the Union's military leadership and his own active role in the war:

> Altogether I am thoroughly disgusted with the manner in which the war is carried on and through the imbecility of our leaders that I have little inclination to shoulder the musket for Uncle Sam. Altho' under severe circumstance, would the people of the North show more patriotism and self-devotion to their country and not have only their own pockets in view, I would be one of the first to give my services, if need be sacrifice my life, for the benefit of my country. But under the present circumstances I decline to risk my services, if need be sacrifice my life, for the benefit of my country. But under the circumstances I decline to risk my bones to no purpose.[216]

1864

In the first month of the new year Missouri lost its provisional Governor H. R. Gamble, who died on 31 January. Most historians then and since agreed that he had worked very hard to maintain sanity in his troubled border state. His successor, Willard P. Hall, said of Gamble "he discharged his difficult and arduous duties with an eye single to the best interests of the country."[217]

Spring 1864 was relatively quiet in Missouri, for a change. Still stationed in Minnesota, Gustav Mallinckrodt wrote his father vacationing in Germany that after a period of intense unrest in the St. Louis area quiet had been restored. But more importantly, Gustav had great plans for his younger brothers and their future. First he proposed to his father Emil that brother Edd (Eduard, nineteen) be permitted to go to Europe to perfect himself in chemistry. To make that possible, Gustav said he would give up his job with the Army to return to St. Louis and watch over the family farm.[218] Second, Gustav felt that Otto, seventeen, should go with Edd, "completing himself in a like manner in chemistry or some branch of the same in which he could be of great advantage to Edd and I in our proposed business."[219]

Regarding education, traditionally important to the Mallinckrodts, Gustav now wrote his father,

> I so much feel the want of such a methodical education myself that I cannot refrain from endeavoring to have both Edd and Otto cultivated superior in mind and intellect and have a treasure which they never can lose. I do not mean hereby to insinuate that my education has been slighted, but I am so firmly convinced now that were I to commence my studies again, that I should have improved my time quite differently and more to my satisfaction and edification. Yet it is idle to mourn over that which should have been done and I am endeavoring to make up for that time which I consider lost (that is, to a certain extent). Excuse my thoughts; you probably differ![220]

By May 1864, Edd and Otto Mallinckrodt were off on a steamer from New York to Bremen, to attend the wedding of their sister Minna, who would marry Karl Wisskott of Dortmund on 27 May, as well as to study.[221] "I hope you will spare no means to give them that education which is the object of this visit to Germany," Gustav wrote his father about the boys, adding, "Every branch of manufacture should be closely studied by them . . . which will be of immense benefit to us."[222]

In Wiesbaden they would be students for about two years in the laboratory of Professor Karl Remigus Fresenius, "the father of analytical chemistry," and then serve as apprentices, Otto in Oeynhausen and Edward in the de Haen chemical works near Hanover.[223] And in St. Louis, in addition to managing his father's affairs, Gustav went back to work at Richardson, his old chemical company employer, to gain additional experience useful for the business enterprise he planned to establish with his brothers.[224] Although Gustav earnestly advised his father not yet to return to St. Louis, Emil wished to do so by autumn because of ill-health and discomfort in the German climate.

At Hermann and Luise's there also was happiness and great relief in spring 1864: James Ferdinand was out of danger for a while. On detached duty from his regiment still in Georgia, he was now assigned to Benton Barracks in St. Louis as a recruiting officer.[225] July 20, therefore, was a very special occasion, for James Ferdinand could celebrate his twenty-second birthday at home. Sister Cecelia composed a long poem in his honor, which noted that "Three times, Dear Ferdy, came the Festal Day, While from our home you lingered far away." Other references to his Civil War duty and record were reflected in the poem's words "want and hardship," "modest in merit," and "Soldier brave and strong."[226]

In the countryside, after the horror of summer and fall 1863, the people of Kansas and the few remaining residents of western Missouri hoped for a breather. The ravished counties of Jackson, Cass, and Bates now were "a wilderness."[227] In Duden country, the founding of a new German Evangelical church at Marthasville and the plan for one the next year at Warrenton was somehow taken by some to be a good sign amid the carnage.[228] And among the Mallinckrodts, Hermann Adolph's marriage to Melina Münch was an event to celebrate.

Nevertheless, there were constant rumors that "Quantrill is coming" and pleas for troop reinforcement. And come back he did, in May, cutting telegraph wires at Warrensburg and then, together with his cohort Bill Anderson, attacking steamboats. "By the end of June, transportation had become so hazardous on the Missouri that it was difficult to find pilots and crews who were willing to sign on boats that had become floating shooting galleries."[229]

Again Rhineland,
Again the Germans

The "good sign" for German settlers along the Missouri did not last long. They could hardly believe the news that the little village of Rhineland was hit, for the second time, on 8 July. Now Henry Groteveil (Grotewohl) and his son were wounded before the raiders turned to the Richeval store where they had killed before. This time they chased Richeval's widow and son. Next, horses were stolen from Rudolph Schultener, and then Henry Bresser was killed. As historians recorded the death of Bresser, "He could speak and understand but a few words of English. Him they also shot and he died in a few seconds. Bresser was a harmless, inoffensive man, an alien who had not taken up arms at all, and who had not been long in America. He seemed devoted to his motherless children and they to him, and when a party of rescuers went down to his home after the murder they were sitting by his lifeless body, caring for it."[230]

Rhineland's settlers now took action to protect themselves. They organized a new company of the EMM from among the German-Americans in the neighborhood, and "a number of men were kept on duty all the time. The quarters was a log building formidable enough for a fort."[231] Surely the Rhinelanders especially rejoiced when during the summer the news came that a bushwhacker, a so-called Colonel Brewer, was killed in the area. It was he who had murdered Andrew Richeval in Rhineland the year before.[232] "One less!" the Rhinelanders must have thought.

But there were more. In fact, all Missouri River traffic was stopped around July because of guerrilla attacks. Bushwhacker Anderson and his gang, for instance, crossed the Missouri River into Carroll County and, disguised as Union officers, killed nine men in one day. One victim, pleading that he was loyal to the South, was shot by Anderson who reportedly first said, "Oh, string him up; God damn his little soul, he's a Dutchman anyway." As Anderson slashed across central Missouri, the whole area was said to be terrified. Elsewhere toward the end of August other guerrilla bands attacked "all men of German ancestry."[233] A historian later describing a guerrilla's "special pleasure in killing local Germans," said the guerrilla saw Germans as his "worst enemies . . . we hung them and went our way rejoicing."[234]

"Bloody Bill" Anderson himself was by then operating around Rocheport on the Missouri. There in early September he ambushed the steamboat *Yellowstone*, perhaps the same grand vessel that Julius and Emil had often seen since they first came to Duden country. With the guerrillas now shooting into her again and again, the boat retreated to Jefferson City. Thereafter, "all traffic on the Missouri was stopped," even on the section of the river near the Mallinckrodts' property.[235] In Gustav Mallinckrodt's words in mid-August, "little is being done to quieten our troubles here in Missouri. Towns in the interior are being robbed every day and men murdered for their loyalty. Rebel boat burners have again made their appearance in the city; six boats were burned a few days ago. The Olive Street hotel has also been burned. Fires occur every day."[236]

On 27 September, Anderson and his men again struck close by, at Centralia, northeast of Wellsville. There they robbed the mid-morning stage from Columbia, as well as the noon North Missouri train from St. Charles. Set on fire, the train was then sent off down the track on a westward ghost run, without engineer or passengers. The president of the rail line, writing to the Union's military command, said, "Sir: Since the murdering of the unarmed soldiers on our train on Tuesday a week ago and the burning of our cars we have not felt that we could with any safety go beyond St. Charles with our trains, and the destruction of trains on the Hannibal and St. Joseph Railroad confirms us in the propriety of not attempting to run trains until the road is guarded by a sufficient military force."[237] When Wentzville also was hit, St. Charles men were sent out to guard railroad approaches from there.[238]

After all this, the sentiments of central Missourians toward "Bloody Bill" Anderson were probably not exaggerated in these sentences written by Montgomery County historians of the time: "He is known by his deeds, and all of his deeds were evil. Of all the foul, black and bloody monsters the Civil War produced, Bill Anderson stands out preeminently the foulest, the blackest, and the bloodiest." The only redeeming or palliating feature in his character was his suspected insanity by those who knew him best. To make matters worse, it was widely believed that General Sterling Price, still in Confederate service, had authorized Anderson to operate against the North Missouri Railroad.[239]

General Price Attacks
Central Missouri

It was now General Price himself who planned to make one more stab at central Missouri. He was headed for Franklin County, across from Augusta, on the south side of the Missouri River. That area, as well as the northern side of the river in

St. Charles County, had been relatively peaceful because of the federal control of the river and of the Pacific Railroad that ran along its banks. But now telegraphed warnings came to military leaders in the town of Washington, Missouri, saying on 28 September that advance brigades of Price's cavalry were underway. Word was relayed from town to town by men on horseback, and Washington began to prepare. Unable, however, to defend the settlement adequately, its leaders ordered Washington's soldiers and people to flee across the Missouri River since they perhaps would be safe on the other side:

> People frantically prepared for the raid. Some treasured things were buried, some carried with them. There was some scattering and hiding, but almost all soldiers and many civilians went to the north side of the river by ferry or skiff. The mounted troops of Price's Army came so fast all the people that wanted to cross could hardly be handled by the two steamboats and available skiffs. The last loads left in the early hours of the morning [before] the raiders came into town . . . Many women and children stayed in their homes . . . Some of the older civilian men dared to stay in town.

One of the ferry boats located at Washington during the Civil War was the *Bright Star*. On 2 October it was ordered to take its load of soldiers, civilians, and government property down to St. Charles to get beyond the reach of the Price Raiders.[240]

During this time Augusta, too, was on alert. The October meeting of the Town Board did not attract a quorum, probably because most men of the village were on guard duty.[241] (At a later meeting the Board voted to refund general storekeeper Fr. Wenker $7.50 "for buckshot and gunpowder furnished to the Committee of Safety during the troubles of last [1864] fall."[242]) But they did not have to serve long, for Price's troops quickly moved on.

The Confederate cavalrymen stayed in abandoned Washington and plundered for less than a day. New Haven and Hermann were the next towns on their list of targets. And at Hermann they indeed had an adventure. According to local historians, a "loose conglomerate of men, 25,000 in number, known popularly as Price's army," approached the town of Hermann.

> Most of the able-bodied men of the town were enlisted in the service of the nation. Only a few old men and the women and children remained. When the reckless cohort approached, a half dozen of the old resolute men who had seen service in the German army could not resist the temptation to play a trick on the invaders despite the probable consequences.
>
> They took a small cannon which the town owned [probably the one fired at the 1848 Wine Festival], mounted it on one of the many hills that overlook the town and when the vanguard of Price's army appeared in sight, they discharged a well directed shot at them and then beat a hasty retreat, tugging their cannon with them. The troops halted and opened fire on the unseen foe. After a short time the

attack came from a second hill and soon from a third one. The troops were unmistakably bewildered. They believed that unexpectedly a strong enemy had been encountered. Detachments of troops were detailed to reconnoiter. They ascended the three hills successively and on the last hill found the old cannon alone, and spiked.

Angered at this prank the old cannon was rolled down the bluff and into the muddy Missouri. In later years the citizens extracted it from the river bed and it is now mounted in front of the court house in Hermann. The troops seeing that they had only been played with, passed on without molesting the town.[243]

Shortly thereafter, on 11 October, General Price met in Boonville with some of his "distinguished partisan leaders," including Bill Anderson and William Quantrill. Given new assignments, they once again raided Danville, New Florence, and High Hill.[244] But time was running out. On 26 October 1864, Anderson was killed by the Missouri State Militia with General Price's orders on his body.[245] "One less!" people again said. But there was still Quantrill.

The last effort of the Confederates to win Missouri was General Price's short, racing invasion across the state. It cost Missouri a great deal, for Price reached the Missouri River and among other things burned all the bridges on the western end of the Pacific Railroad.[246] A St. Louisan summarized the cost of Price's raids: "He killed and wounded very many of our troops. During this campaign, though it lasted only a few days, there were more than 40 skirmishes and about 15 battles . . . Price, in his report of this campaign, claims that he destroyed full ten million dollars worth of property. Perhaps that is an exaggeration; but he marched by a circuitous route from one end of our State to the other, devastating a strip of territory about twenty miles wide."[247] Price had failed, however, to rally the state politically to his cause. Instead, defeated at Westport, Price and his army in October reentered the northwest corner of Arkansas from whence it had come; historians would write that the Confederates "had failed completely" to win Missouri.[248]

The guerrilla war, however, had psychologically scarred many people deeply and permanently. It often seemed, in fact, that was especially true for Missouri's German immigrants, who had come from so far with such high hopes of finding a better life. Union Commander Pike, for instance, reported from Washington, Missouri, in autumn 1864 that his troops were "made up largely of Germans, and it has been very hard to restrain them from depredations on people known as Southern sympathizers, from the fact that their countrymen living in the district through which we have passed have been so badly used by the rebel raiders."[249]

Emil Mallinckrodt, too, was one of the immigrants who lost much of his belief in the American Dream because of the Civil War, with its indescribable brutality and, in his view, stupidity. His son Gustav, through correspondence with Emil while he was still vacationing in Europe, frequently tried to make his father see that worrying about America's future was not good for his health. In mid-1864 the tone of that advice became sharper than it had been:

> I am afraid, dear father, that you picture our condition here vastly worse than it really is . . . why give yourself so much anxiety and burden your mind with all that which is not as it should be; give due credit for the right and forget the unpleasant! I do believe I could not find your equal anywhere here in troubling himself about that which he cannot advert or correct in our national struggle in the manner you do. . . . Let me beg you, dear father, not to take unfavorable political news so much to heart. Hope, as we all do here not for the worst but for best, and do not grieve yourself about that which you cannot alter. The country must ere long after this war become as prosperous as heretofore.[250]

Indeed, the war seemed to be winding down across the country. The Union's General Sherman had invaded Georgia and captured Atlanta. On his march to Savannah on the coast, he left a trail of scorched earth behind him, perhaps in fact another Civil War "first." The price for the progress, however, was many human lives. Therefore, James Ferdinand's regimental commander cited a "shortage of company commanders" in the field as reason to request that Lieutenant Mallinckrodt return from duty as recruiting officer in St. Louis to the southern battlefield; there he should take over the leadership of Company K of the Seventeenth Missouri Infantry in August 1864, although the infantrist's three-year term of duty would expire the next month, on 27 September.[251]

Lincoln Reelected

Meanwhile, it was November of an even-numbered year and time for Americans once again to vote. For Missourians, the 1864 presidential election was the first opportunity since the start of the Civil War to choose a full slate of state officials.[252] Many however could not vote because they had not taken the oath of loyalty. Not surprisingly, Lincoln won, with 71,676 votes (versus McClellan's 31,626).[253] St. Louis celebrated, primarily for the end of conservative rule in Missouri:

> The entire radical ticket for State officers was chosen, and the legislature was heavily radical in both its branches. . . . In eighty of one hundred and fourteen counties of the State the radical ticket prevailed. The loyal of our city celebrated this triumph of unconditional Unionism with unbounded joy. They rang the bells; kindled bonfires; marched with torches to martial music; sang patriotic songs; and almost split their throats and the welkin with their huzzas. Well they might do all this. Every plot against the Union had been thwarted; they held at last firmly within their grasp the prize for which they had so long and patiently struggled.[254]

As scholars later would observe, "The Conservatives had held the line throughout the war. But the nation and Missouri were entering a new era with new problems, especially new for a state previously committed to slavery."[255] Radical Republicans would dominate, bringing a great deal of progress but often doing so with vindictiveness born of the Civil War years.[256] Some wanted revenge against disloyal Missourians while others wanted to recreate the state through tolerance.

1865

The "new era" began on 2 January with the inauguration of a duly elected governor, T. C. Fletcher. Thus, the Provisional Government of Missouri officially ended. Then in March, martial law ceased, by joint proclamation of the governor and General Pope.[257] And on 6 January, a new state convention met in St. Louis to propose a postwar constitution and to consider steps for emancipating the state's slaves (that is, earlier than the 1870 date already agreed on). Three-fourths of the delegates were Radical Unionists.

At the convention's second session, Arnold Krekel of St. Charles was elected president of the body. And on the fifth day of the convention, 11 January 1865, emancipation in Missouri was passed, with only four negative votes to sixty. It was said that "more than a hundred thousand slaves were in a moment made freemen and the greatest obstacle to the progress of Missouri was swept away."[258] Missouri thereby was the first slave state to put an end to black bondage.[259] And it did so voluntarily, a month before its General Assembly ratified the Thirteenth Amendment to the United States Constitution, abolishing slavery nationally.[260] St. Louis celebrated with a sixty-gun salute and fireworks.[261]

Tolerance and Punishment: Missouri's New Constitution

In addition to its emancipatory spirit, Missouri's tormented side, however, was also reflected in the acts of its radical Constitutional Convention. One would later describe it as "the high-water mark of hatred and fear in Missouri's public affairs."[262] For instance, with martial law ended, along with its provision for a militarily enforced loyalty oath, convention delegates felt it should be replaced by a new civil law for voting and holding office. Led by Charles Drake, the delegates thus formulated a harsh postwar "Oath of Loyalty," or "Test Oath" as people called it, to punish the South's former supporters.[263]

The new civil oath, sometimes called the "Iron-Clad Oath," included, for instance, eighty-six separate deeds that were reasons to deny Missourians the right to vote[264]—including not only bearing arms for the South but also expressing sympathy for the enemy, advising people to enter enemy service, giving information to the enemy, and so on.[265] In addition there was an oath for public officials, teachers, trustees, attorneys, jurors, and church ministers.[266] Many people were appalled at this turn of events, and the debate inside and outside the convention meeting rooms was fierce. Those who perhaps had hated the oaths during the height of the war but kept quiet now had their say. German voices were loud: the oath disenfranchised loyal persons as well as rebels; it deprived some people of their livelihood; the 1862 oath was adequate while this was revenge.[267]

Another hot issue at the convention that especially upset Germans was the question of suffrage—the most radical delegates did not want noncitizens to vote; Germans wanted that right in order to encourage immigration of their countrymen. In a compromise, it was decided that aliens might vote a year after their declaration of citizenship intention had been filed.[268] And finally there was the resolution to reorganize the judiciary, that is, to declare all jobs vacant by 1 May and then have the governor appoint new judges and clerks to all courts, circuit attorneys and assistants, county recorders, and sheriffs, a total of eight hundred officials. Sizable minorities protested the sense and scope of this measure.[269]

Edward Bates opposed the proposed Constitution, as did many Germans who saw it as a reactionary and unjust law such as they had known in Europe. Especially outspoken among the Germans was Carl Schurz, now co-owner of the St. Louis daily German newspaper, the *Westliche Post*. Throughout the convention Schurz and especially Arnold Krekel were voices of Republican liberal moderation, rather than radical Republicanism.[270] Nevertheless, after weeks of turmoil, by 8 April the new Constitution was passed, including the stern "Oath of Loyalty."[271] Since the electorate now had to accept or reject the constitution in a June referendum, opposition to it could continue as a campaign against its adoption.

Surrender at Appomattox

The convention was still meeting when the telegraphed news came that so many had awaited so long. The day before, 9 April 1865, the Confederacy's General Robert E. Lee had surrendered to the Union's General Ulysses S. Grant at Appomattox, Virginia, just three days short of four years after the capture of Ft. Sumter.[272] The war was all but over! At Missouri's Constitutional Convention and in St. Louis the news was electrifying: "That 10th of April was memorable not only for the whole nation, but also especially for St. Louis. A border city, which, for four long years, had been a bone of contention, fought over and snarled over by the dogs of war, had perhaps a keener appreciation of the surrender of the illustrious Lee, than could be found in any city far to the north of Mason and Dixon's line."[273]

Not only St. Louisans but many others throughout the state felt that by having kept Missouri in the Union they had indeed played a key role in the final Union victory. And that the German settlers had been essential to that role was remembered, too. The cost of their loyalty, however, was apparently not calculated very often, among other things the harassment of their settlements and deliberate killings of the "Dutch."

Lincoln Shot

Despite the celebrations in St. Louis and elsewhere, the rabid dogs of war made one last attack. Five days after Lee's surrender, all the joy was over. There was only stunned grief—President Lincoln was dead! He had been assassinated on the night of 14 April, while attending the Ford Theater in Washington, and died the next morning. St. Louis was silent. All flags were at half-mast. Vice President Andrew Johnson was president. A St. Louisan of the time felt that many who initially had called Abraham Lincoln a clown had come to respect "his clearness of conception, fairness in administration, unflinching advocacy of the rights of all, patience and persistence in duty, and large-heartedness."[274] One more death thus was added to the horrendous costs of the American Civil War.

Those deaths were difficult to calculate accurately, especially Southern losses. Since the 1890 census, for instance, reported 1,466,093 surviving veterans (Union 1,034,073; Confederate 432,020) and casualty estimates were 992,703 (634,703 Union; 358,000 Confederate), that meant some 2.5 million men had been involved and 40 percent had been victims.[275] There was confusion and distress, too, about how to rebuild and heal. Few public officials, or even teachers or ministers, could carry out their professions without swearing the oath required by the Constitutional Convention.[276] While ultimately courts might declare that provision unconstitutional or legislatures eliminate it, until then political life in Missouri would be difficult and divisive.

In addition, the campaign to ratify the new state Constitution would be as bitter as the process of drawing it up had been. In St. Louis, German Radicals, but also moderates and conservatives, opposed its narrow partisanship and punishing tone, as well as the oath requirement itself.

Two events, then, wrote the real finale to Missouri's Civil War chapter:

• On 6 June 1865 the people of the state narrowly approved their new Constitution by referendum.
• The same day, as history and poetic justice would have it, William Quantrill died of wounds in a Kentucky hospital.[277]

"One less," the people thought, "and hopefully the last!"

25

1865: After the Civil War

Peace is expected when a war ends and shooting stops. But it comes gradually, one step at a time. In spring 1865 President Andrew Johnson tried to take some of the first steps Abraham Lincoln had planned to reconstruct the American South after the Civil War. One measure granted amnesty to Confederates taking an oath of allegiance to the reborn American union. Another appointed provisional governors for the defeated southern states until they passed new constitutions abolishing slavery and were readmitted to the U.S. Congress.

The President, however, faced a formidable task. Andrew Johnson had run with Lincoln in 1864 on a wartime National Union ticket. Lincoln was the Republican, and Vice President Johnson, the former governor of Tennessee, represented Democrats accepting the Union, the so-called War Democrats. After Lincoln's assassination, Johnson therefore was bitterly opposed by some members of the Lincoln-appointed cabinet and by the Republican-dominated Congress. From their point of view, the new president's policy of reconciliation was wrong; the South should be punished. Proclaiming the Thirteenth Amendment abolishing slavery (18 December 1865), Congress began its fierce quarrel with the president over who—the legislature or executive—should guide reconstruction and how harsh it was to be.[1]

1865 in Missouri

In Missouri in the spring and summer of 1865 the mood was much the same. There had been too much hate in the border state for forgiveness to come easily. Returning "rebels" were not always welcomed, and distrust stalked the little towns of the state scarred by four years of war. More seriously, guerrillas and bushwhackers still roamed about, terrorizing people.

Notwithstanding the war was over there were a great many acts of lawlessness perpetrated in this [Montgomery] county in the spring and summer of this year [1865]. The war had demoralized people until those of them who were depraved by nature became inexpressibly bad. The same was true of other parts of Missouri. Bands of men combined for the sole purpose of plunder and robbery, and in the defenseless condition of many of the people—their arms having been seized by the military authorities—there was a fine field for their operations.[2]

State politics, too, were anything but soothing or settled in 1865. With elections for the Missouri state legislature coming up in 1866, the thorny problem of who might vote had to be solved. Many citizens, of course, had been made ineligible under the loyalty oaths just written into Missouri's new postwar constitution. In fact, when the referendum on the basic law was held in June, only 85,478 votes were cast in the whole state.[3] Now local registration officials, often under intimidation, took voters' names for next year's polling; a board of revision would make final decisions and certify official voter lists after hearing individual complaints.[4] As local historians reported, "Certain individuals, incensed at being disfranchised, threatened the registrars with violence, and sometimes trouble was feared."[5] No one was certain that the 1866 election would be peaceful.

Exactly how the voting registration was carried out in the little town of Augusta is not clear. According to the 12 July 1866 *St. Charles Demokrat*, Julius Mallinckrodt was the registration official for the eleventh election district, including Augusta, and it was his task to certify his fellow voters. Town records faithfully mentioned that after each board of trustees election from 3 March 1862 onward, the chosen officials, too, had taken the required oath.

While trying to deal with the touchy problem of voting rights, Radical Republicans who dominated state politics proposed other postwar measures to move Missouri forward. Two plans were especially interesting to German settlers. One was an intense campaign by Missouri to increase immigration to its territory, in part to make up for wartime losses in population. (Many Missourians had been killed and others had moved away to safer areas.) The Missouri State Board of Immigration was therefore created in February 1865, with recruiting agents to interest people in coming to Missouri from the eastern states and Europe. Reduced rates on railroads and at hotels were negotiated, promotional material published in newspapers and pamphlets, and public lands made available. Germans were especially sought, and the German Emigrant Aid Society, for example, was unusually active.[6]

Another effort pointing Missouri toward the future was the founding of the Equal Rights League to achieve suffrage for the state's African-Americans. Many Germans favored this postwar move since they had tried a year earlier without success to have voting right for blacks included in the new state constitution. Although the turbulent St. Louis convention had not been able to agree on that issue, it now had to be resolved. There could be no social peace or economic progress until something was done to help Missouri's former slaves. Integrating America's freed slaves into society was, after all, the goal of postwar reconstruction.

Soon there would be a national black-suffrage amendment to the U.S. Constitution, but individual states could and did act more quickly to update their own laws. In Missouri, for instance, prominent black spokesmen and other suffrage advocates lectured across the state to create support. The speakers and meetings were generally well received, and approval for Negroes' right to vote grew steadily throughout 1866. By the next year both houses of the Missouri legislature agreed on a state suffrage amendment to be put to the people at the general election in 1868. If approved, the proposed amendment would strike the word "white" as a constitutional qualification for voting in Missouri.[7]

Other progressive measures in the state cheered the Mallinckrodts, as well, in both city and countryside. Since they made their living from the soil, steps taken in 1865 to stimulate farming were welcome. A State Board of Agriculture, for instance, was created to educate farmers to the advantages of new scientific and mechanized techniques.[8] In Duden country and near St. Louis, the Mallinckrodts wondered if the new board might be helpful to their orchard and vineyard businesses.

Education, Railroads, Bridges

As strong supporters of education, the Mallinckrodts, were encouraged, too, by the attention this aspect of Missouri life received. Help for the schools was in fact critical, for they had been neglected during the Civil War and many had been closed a good part of the time. It had been found, for example, that in 1861–62 "hardly a county had an open school."[9] It was said that 12.5 percent of Missouri's white population was illiterate; there was only one public high school in the state (in St. Louis); and the University of Missouri at Columbia was receiving no appropriations from Jefferson City.[10]

No wonder, then, that Missouri's German settlers applauded the 1865 state convention requirement for education—the General Assembly was to maintain free public schools for all Missourians (that is, blacks, too) between the ages of five and twenty-one; new schools had to be built, teachers trained, and uniform textbooks adopted. Most importantly, legislation should establish a base of sufficient tax support. In short, privately supported schools were inadequate to the state's postwar needs. By April 1866, it was reported that colored children were already participating in the public school, and the teacher said they were doing well. In the opinion of the newspaper editor, "In truly humanistic matters, Augusta is always in the lead with good examples."[11]

Missouri's railroads, so hard hit by the guerrillas, were also given a new boost after the Civil War. By September 1865, the important Pacific Railroad on the south side of the Missouri River, across from the Mallinckrodts and Augusta, was completed to Kansas City, on the state's western border. The people in Duden country read with pleasure that the first passenger train making the run over that line left Kansas City in the early morning hours of 19 September and arrived in St. Louis the next afternoon.[12] There the trip of about fourteen hours—without accident—was greeted with fanfare. That it had taken the state fourteen years to build those 283 miles was almost forgotten.[13]

It was time, too, many people thought, to do something about bridges over Missouri's river lifelines. St. Louis urgently needed a railroad bridge across the Mississippi to Illinois. During the war, when river traffic southward was limited, the Gateway to the West learned the bitter dollars-and-cents cost of being cut off from eastern railroads.[14] And St. Charles, too, needed to connect itself to the growing St. Louis area by a bridge spanning the Missouri River, rather than by slow ferry boat.

Also in Missouri's little towns—at least if they were not located in bushwhackers' territory—people were again looking ahead. In Augusta, for instance, the town board in June 1865 voted to create a public square "intended to be used as a market place in some future time." Donated by C. Knoernschild, it would give the settlement a focus for its public activities.[15]

Another sign of changing times was a new ordinance for peddlers. Apparently they were in business again after the war, and with new conveyances. In July 1865 the trustees resolved that the peddler needed a six-month license which now would cost twenty dollars (the fee in 1858 had been ten dollars for ten days).[16] If they did not have a permit, the fines now were graduated—"if a foot peddler, the sum of $10, on one or more beasts of burden, $25 dollars, and a cart or other land carriages, $50."[17] (After this effort to raise money, the board of trustees must have been preoccupied with unusually serious matters, for they were unable to assemble a quorum of their members for the next three months, August through October 1865.) In September, however, the town celebrated an unusually spirited *Volksfest* attended by Missouri Governor Fletcher who came to thank the townspeople for their loyal support of the Union during the war.[18]

Returning to normal town affairs in 1866, the Board of Trustees faced not only its usual problems of street and cemetery maintenance but apparently also postwar economic hard times. In the March 1866 Amendment of the Town's Act of Incorporation, it added the possibility of issuing bonds to finance town improvements, as well as striking the restrictions on "meetings of slaves" and a poll tax on "free males." In September, then, the trustees decided to issue $1,000 of bonds to raise money.[19] The county said that was possible, if the town had an official seal. Resolved: "a bunch of grapes with the inscription 'Town of Augusta' was selected for the weapon" (surely the clerk was thinking in German, *Wappen*, that is, coat of arms or seal, but it went into his notes as *Waffen* and then came out incorrectly translated English as *weapon*!).[20] By 1867 the town also petitioned the state and received permission to boost its tax rate.[21]

Family life, disrupted for many by the war, also resumed its usual routine of social gatherings and celebrations, especially of marriages. There were two in the Mallinckrodt family in 1865—Julius's second oldest son, war veteran Hermann Adolph, to Auguste Koch in August (his first brief 1864 marriage to Melina Münch had ended when his wife died within a year), and in December the wedding of Julius's daughter Luise to Joseph Guggenmoos of Warrenton, who also had served in the Warren County volunteers.[22]

Bushwhackers

While such peace was possible within individual families in Duden country, in other areas there was continuing chaos. Bushwhackers were still carrying on in western Missouri. One robbery followed another, and it seemed "the era of the desperado had been ushered in." Not illogically, in turn, voluntary groups of "regulators" began to spring up, taking the law into their own hands to deal out "justice" as they saw fit.[23] The accounts of such clashes were echoes of wartime guerrilla days—gangs, gang leaders who had been guerrillas and survived, daylight bank robberies, deaths of civilians, and so on.

In February 1866, Governor Fletcher called for federal help because state units were made up of volunteers who were so partisan that they might not be best suited to put down disorder. Some steps had to be taken since there was an election coming up in November, and without troops it might not be peaceful. At last it was decided, in Washington, D.C., that Missouri's governor would disarm his partisan militia forces and rely instead on a combination of civil authorities and federal troops to keep the election peace.[24] Therefore, to the astonishment of many, by October 1866 federal troops were back in Missouri.[25]

1866 Elections

In the nation's capital, too, there was continuing turmoil about how to get on with "peace" throughout the country. In early 1866 the U.S. Congress had set up the Freedmen's Bureau to care for freed slaves and abandoned lands of the South. It also had passed the Fourteenth Amendment, giving blacks citizenship, and made its acceptance a condition for restoration of the southern states to the Union. Clearly the amendment's path to ratification via state legislatures would be turbulent, for the South flatly rejected it. There was not a suggestion of compromise in the air of Washington, D.C., as politicians prepared for bitter autumn congressional elections in which reconstruction would be a major issue.

In Missouri, in some respects and in some places, there was a somewhat more balanced view toward the South, or at least toward its individuals. For instance, a Southern Aid Society would be formed around Montgomery City to "aid the indigent in the stricken Southern districts." A county fair was even held to raise funds, and some nine hundred dollars gathered.[26]

On the other hand, citizens such as Emil Mallinckrodt continued to be very disturbed about the political issue of states' rights. As he wrote in the *Westliche Post*, "The contention of state rights brought the misfortune of the 60s onto the land and, nevertheless, did not disappear. Rather, state rights prevail in all states, more boldly than ever."[27]

Furthermore, the June 1865 constitutionally required loyalty oath continued to upset many Missourians although it was difficult to enforce against professionals and thus frequently ignored. In October 1865, a Catholic priest, Cummings, had asked the Missouri Supreme Court to set the requirement aside, but he had lost his case and was appealing it to the U.S. Supreme Court.[28]

There were also deep feelings about the pending election. In St. Louis, for example, the Radical Republicans launched their campaign with Chinese lanterns decorating the courthouse and "large transparencies hung suspended between the pillars on the eastern portico" proclaiming, "Loyal men shall rule, not rebels." Thus the Radicals' special appeal to ex-soldiers drew support from the Germans who had been the core of Missouri's volunteers in the Union's cause. A great reunion rally, for instance, was held in August at the Germans' Turner Hall in St. Louis on the fifth anniversary of the Battle of Wilson's Creek.[29] Possibly Union veteran Hermann Adolph Mallinckrodt and his father Julius rode in from Augusta to attend it, along with James Ferdinand and his father Hermann.

At Radical Republican meetings throughout Duden country Julius often was on committees or served as a delegate. Other early immigrants were active as well. In October 1866 Radical party supporters in Femme Osage Township who gathered in Augusta to organize committed support for the coming election included Follenius, Wencker, Münch, Schroer, Nadler, Dammann, and Mindrup.[30]

Despite all the intense feeling, the fall election was held largely without violence, perhaps because of the presence of federal troops. There was, of course, much grumbling and charges of unfairness about the voter registration process. In fact, in one county the state militia had to stop a fight between two groups claiming control of the courthouse.[31] Missouri's Radical Union ticket (Republicans) nevertheless won out over the Conservative Union slate (Democrats) by overwhelming majorities in both houses of the state legislature.[32] The results were much the same across the nation. As the *St. Charles Demokrat* wrote, "St. Charles County is saved once again and stands with honor in the ranks of Missouri's Union counties."[33]

Those 1866 election results strengthened the hard-line view toward the South, for Republicans gained majorities in both houses of the U.S. Congress. That gave them effective control of the country's so-called Reconstruction program that clearly still excluded reconciliation. The turmoil and resentment in the South was therefore great and growing. One consequence was seen in fall 1867 when a violent secret white racist organization, calling itself the Ku Klux Klan, was founded to mete out its own "justice" against blacks.[34]

That Missouri still needed troops, election or not, was reflected in a new state act put on the books in December. To deal with the continuing problem of the bushwhacker-robbers, the law required all men over eighteen years of age to register for possible call-up into the Missouri State Militia.[35] By the end of the year, twenty-four militia cavalry companies and ten infantry companies were on duty, stationed especially in western Lafayette and Jackson counties. For many people the war was still going on, only in a slightly different way.

Schools and Libraries

Elections, such as the one just held, were rarely ignored by Missouri's German settlers. They knew from experience that their everyday life, as well as who went to Washington, D.C. to represent them, was influenced by elections and politics. By 1866, for instance, the changes the Mallinckrodts and others had long wanted in the state's education system were already noticeable, because of the progressive postwar politics in Missouri. It was a time of "rapid development of the public school system throughout the state."[36]

Although teacher Conrad and school pioneer Julius had always been concerned about the future of education, now they had more personal reasons than ever—there were a lot of little, next-generation, American-born Mallinckrodts who needed better schools. For instance, around Augusta there were Conrad and Wilhelmina's little Theodor Feldmann and Albert Feldmann, seven and six years old, and Dorothea, age five.

When they ran across the brow of the hill to Uncle Julius and Aunt Mary they hoped the grandchildren would be there for them to play with because their cousins (Julius's own children) were already grown-ups. Conrad's youngsters often were not disappointed, for Julius's married daughters all had children who came to visit. Soon, too, there would be more playmates around—Julius's first grandson bearing the family name (Bertold, at Hermann Adolph and Auguste's) had been born in May 1866, and Julius's first American-born son, Conrad Theodor, married to Emilie Fuhr in October, would also be contributing more little members to the clan.

In St. Louis, Emil and Hermann, too, were pleased by the progress and reform in schools, for they shared the traditional family emphasis on education. Although neither St. Louis Mallinckrodt had grandchildren who would benefit, at Emil and Emilie's there were their little boys—Emil junior, age six, and Oscar, age four. St. Louis, in fact, was looking forward to rapid school growth and was very proud to already have three public schools for blacks by fall 1866.[37]

Undoubtedly the book-loving Mallinckrodts in city and countryside were also glad that attention was being paid to developing Missouri's public libraries. In a few years most of the larger towns in the state were to have some kind of subscription library, including newspapers and journals, as well as books.[38] Little Augusta would probably not realize this grand plan in his lifetime, Conrad must have thought. But the family bookworm nevertheless savored the idea of more books and more education for people, as he had since his student days in Munich.

Conrad's own library, meanwhile, remained his personal oasis. There were the Bulwer, Shakespeare, and Cooper volumes he often reread for pleasure—surely smiling over the discrepancy between James Fenimore's images of the frontier and those Conrad himself had by now experienced. The Missouri State Statutes, too, were well-thumbed because he often sought clarity in them for his justice of the peace work (and thus, in a sense, fulfilled his father's wish that he go into law). And then the weighty but precious Brockhaus Encyclopedias—how fortunate that he had brought them from Dortmund! Out of his respect for books, Conrad almost never dog-eared the corners of their pages. Yet when using the encyclopedias he occasionally had underlined important entries or marginally marked, commented, or question-marked their ideas.[39] Stimulated during quiet hours of intense inner dialogue with the encyclopedia writers, those comments concerned four major subject matter areas:

Philosophy
  Schelling, Friedrich [Vol. 9]
  Jefferson, Thomas [Vol. 5]

Law
  Saxony/Ancient History/Law [Vol. 9]
  England/Constitution/Parliament [Vol. 3]
  Practice/Juridical [Vol. 8]
  Administrative Law [Vol. 9]

Religion
  Luther [Vol. 6]
  Catholicism [Vol. 6], *Pope* [Vol. 8]
  Festivals/Catholic [Vol. 4]
  Religious Instruction [Vol. 9]
  Mythology [Vol. 7]
  Revelation [Vol. 8])

Science
   Nature [Vol. 7]
   Organ/Organization [Vol. 8]
   Day and Night Life [Vol. 11]

1867: Reconstruction

Libraries, schools, agriculture, railroads—when Missourians looked ahead to such positive developments they were doubly glad their state had not left the Union. They were not now part of the wrenching program of Reconstruction of the South. Although it was a term that seemingly would be argued over forever— for some, a period when northern opportunists ruthlessly exploited the South; for others, years of great legal and social reform—its momentary consequences were distressingly clear at the time.

By March 1867, for example, the U.S. Congress divided the South into five districts to be ruled by martial, or military, law rather than civilian administration. For that purpose President Johnson sent twenty thousand troops south, including Negro militia, which aroused Southern resentments even more. In this period, then, Duden country Germans and others learned two new American-English political terms—scalawags (southern whites cooperating with northern white radicals) and carpetbaggers, (northerners going south with a traveling bag made of carpet cloth to participate in Reconstruction).[40]

In Missouri, a clear sign of the postwar period was given when in 1867 the Supreme Court in Washington, D.C. (Cummings versus Missouri), struck down the state's 1865 requirement for a loyalty oath from lawyers, ministers, and teachers (but not for voters and jurors).[41] Justices of the peace may have been included, for as of autumn 1868 Conrad Mallinckrodt's records again show this service continuing without interruption. Interestingly, in that year and the next Conrad married two "colored" couples, for former slaves now had the right to legalize their partnerships.[42] Also in 1869, as "one of the justices of the peace within and for the County of St. Charles in and for Femme Osage township," he was indicted, charged, and acquitted by the Circuit Court with "wilful misconduct in office [charging illegal fees]."[43]

Reconstruction in Missouri had come to mean primarily recovery from the social and economic stagnation of the Civil War years. The mood was thus quite positive in 1867—it reminded the Mallinckrodts and other German immigrants of their fathers' hopes after the end of the Napoleonic War.

Work on the Mississippi River bridge at St. Louis, for instance, had begun. It was to be called Eads Bridge, in honor of its chief engineer, James Buchanan Eads. People thought he was right for the job because he knew the Mississippi so well. For years he had salvaged wrecked ships from the stream and during the

Civil War had advised President Lincoln on military operations on the river. In addition, Eads had invented a diving bell and built a fleet of ironclad ships for the Union. Now his construction at St. Louis would be an engineering feat in its time, a "first"—the first important bridge to use steel truss construction (three arches) rather than wrought iron.[44] With its two levels, Eads's bridge would carry vital rail traffic, as well as vehicles, across the Father of Waters at the Gateway to the West.[45]

Augusta and Its "German Spirit"

Out in the countryside there were interesting developments, too. For instance, Augusta's Harmonie-Verein, a musical organization that had existed for a dozen years without a charter (possibly because of opposition to its fondness for combining the spirit of the grape with that of music), could now incorporate itself under Missouri law. It was a prosperous organization, including as members "all the leading German residents of the vicinity" who enjoyed its musical performances and dances, as well as a library that would soon number some three thousand volumes. In 1867, then, the Verein incorporated and made plans to build a hall and a bandstand in the village for musical performances. County historians of the time reported that the hall was built in 1869, at a cost of two thousand dollars.[46] (Later chroniclers spoke of an earlier and temporary bandstand before the permanent one was built in 1890.[47])

And the little town was preparing to expand its limits again. It had begun with the forty blocks surveyed by Conrad Mallinckrodt in 1855. Despite sketchy town records, another major expansion seems to have been considered in late 1860. Because of local dissent the next year, and probably because of the advent of the Civil War, the plan did not go forward until late 1867.[48] The ordinance of incorporation for Blocks 42–53 on the edges of the town was then passed on 6 July 1868 (figure 25-1).[49] It included Block 50, a long rectangular piece of land on the north side of Augusta belonging to Conrad Mallinckrodt's wife, Wilhelmina, which he had petitioned for inclusion.[50]

The little village was naturally always pleased when prominent German-Americans periodically came to town to enjoy its culture and *gemütlichkeit* and especially to praise its musical offerings. The political leader Carl Schurz, for example, came to call in July 1867. Respected for his pro-Union efforts among German-Americans in St. Louis, Schurz now was working there at the *Westliche Post*, in partnership with its owner Emil Pretorius. On Sundays it was their custom to visit the German communities in and around St. Louis. (Schurz felt at home among them, saying the Germans in Missouri were "really a fine breed."[51]) About his visit to Duden country, Schurz wrote his wife a long letter that was destined to become one of the most quoted descriptions of life in Augusta after the Civil War:

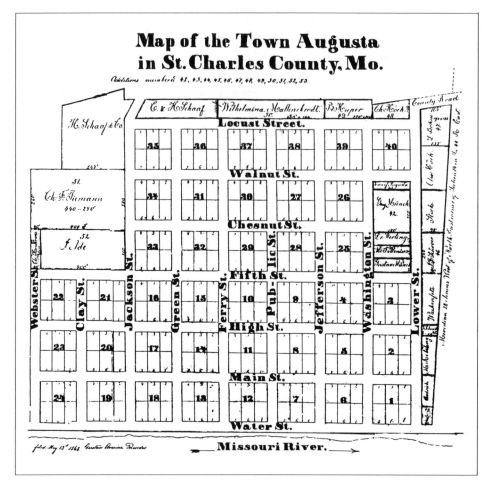

Figure 25-1. In 1868, Augusta, Missouri, "hometown" to the area's growing Mallinckrodt family, was expanded to include fifty-three blocks. (*Courtesy St. Charles County Recorder of Deeds.*)

Morning brought us to Augusta, a little place some fifty miles above the mouth of the Missouri . . . several educated immigrants of the thirties had settled there, who were conserving in that neighborhood, in their own way, the best features of German life. Augusta is a small town of not more than three hundred inhabitants, built upon hills which fall away steeply toward the Mississippi [Missouri].

We were received by an old Mr. Münch from Darmstadt, a sometime theologian and professor who has been in Missouri for thirty-four years [Georg senior]. He is a brother of the well known "Far West," Frederick Münch, who has developed such a useful literary activity in the German press. Our host, after an enthusiastic greeting, took us to his house, which of course lay on one of the many hills, and from which one has a view across the vineyards for many miles along the Missouri. These old German patriarchs do not live elegantly, but cleanly, neatly, and if one does not demand too much, comfortably. There are no carpets, but beautifully scoured floors; no upholstered furniture, but tables spread with fresh white covers, with books upon them. . . .

After breakfast we were of course hustled around over the other hills and joyfully introduced to all friends and acquaintances; and nowhere must we omit to taste the wine which every family produces on its own hill and presses in its own cellar. So it went, from house to house, until finally through the sheer weariness of friendship we were glad to take our return journey to home and dinner table. Meantime our honored friend "Far West," who knew about our visit, arrived on horse-back the same morning fom his eight or nine miles' distant farm to fraternize with us. Our host brought him to us with the words: "Here comes the old Münch; I am the young Münch." The old Münch is nearly seventy years old and the young one some two years younger. Dinner went off with lively and loud philosophical discussion.

After dinner, however, came the great event. Our arrival had become well known in the town; and the population of Augusta, old and young, male and female, gathered together in a small grove to welcome us. They brought along their band, which was made up wholly of amateur musicians, but not at all bad. There was plenty of Augusta wine. Quite naturally speeches had to be made. First I had to talk to the men, then to the women, then to both. Following this, Preetorius came on; then the old Münch; until we all declared it was enough of a good thing. Of course all the speeches were in German, for in Augusta there are no Americans except the shoemaker's apprentice, who has recently arrived and who is learning German, and several negro families, among whom the children can already speak German. An evening meal at the home of a German doctor concluded the delightful affair. About eleven o'clock we went up and down the hills until we reached the home of the sixty-eight-year-old "young" Münch, that offered us a welcome bed. . . .

The little German colony in Augusta certainly gives the impression of prosperity. The old people have preserved the tradition of the German spirit and German training, but they are unable to bequeath this tradition to their children. It is an observation which I have made almost everywhere, that here in America, perhaps with the exception of individual cases in the great cities, the children of educated Germans contrast strikingly with their elders. The German spirit fades away. If the training remains wholly Geman and all contact with Americanism is avoided, a stupid Pennsylvanian Germanism results. Where that is not the case, the waves of Americanism soon overwhelm the second and third generations. "The mission of Germanism" in America, about which some speak so loudly, can consist in nothing other than a modification of the American spirit, through the German, while the nationalities melt into one. In a few years the old patriarchs in pleasant little Augusta will be dead and their successors must be carried away by the universal movement.[52]

Unfortunately Schurz did not define specifically "the German spirit" which he felt was fading away. A lessening of the German drive for education could hardly have been his concern, for the settlers worked hard for improved schools. Obviously, too, knowledge of the German language was not a major reason for Schurz's misgivings; he was right about the use of German, for in 1869 someone found only one English-speaking, that is, American, family in Augusta, the pharmacist Farris.[53] On the other hand, it was clear that there would be increased use of English in the community when the school taught more classes in that language.

Perhaps Schurz's concerns were about more fundamental intellectual values of the German spirit, for instance, the politically liberal, innovative, and risk-taking attitudes of the German immigrants that had brought them to America. Schurz may have been thinking about the evolution of older U.S. immigrant settlements he had seen, where the values of the original immigrants indeed "faded" in the third generation. Using the basis their pioneer fathers had sweated to create, first-generation sons struggled and adjusted to the society around them; grandsons beginning to "make it," so to speak, became intent on conserving the gains rather than taking new risks.

On the other hand, it also was widely understood at the time that it was usually the third generation of America's immigrant families that was able to again achieve (or surpass) the educational level of the first. The initial difficulties of immigrant life and the absence of schools temporarily braked a family's educational achievements, that is, among immigrant sons. For Germans generally, and especially the well-educated followers of Duden who had come to Augusta, that then might have been an answer to Schurz's misgiving—they could regain their traditional family standards in the next generation.

A continued emphasis on education, combined with shadows of the old German values of innovation and risk-taking, might motivate frontier youngsters to try to acquire an education despite their lack of money. And education, in turn, could help maintain other initial German values such as social liberalism. The spread of liberal German-oriented churches also might help keep alive dimensions of the German spirit, including social justice and responsibility. Finally Schurz, with his keen understanding of economics, surely had seen that recurring hard times in Missouri's rural areas kept German thrift and industriousness alive. Survival was also part of the German spirit.

On the humorous side, if Schurz had visited Augusta several years later he would have heard interesting evidence of the continuing German spirit there—the Board of Trustees resolved that "every member of the Board who arrives for the regular meeting later than at 8 o clock p.m. according to the clock in the meeting room, shall forfeit one bottle of wine." Moreover, in the next year, Augusta's grape growers organized the Augusta Wine Company and built the town's Wine Hall to centralize their wine production and sales. Both Julius's and Adolph Mallinckrodt's grapes contributed to Augusta's growing reputation as St. Charles County's wine center, which reported twenty-five thousand gallons in 1869.[54]

Mallinckrodt Chemical Company Begins

While the country Mallinckrodts were pleased with their school and culture and developing their farming, Emil's family in St. Louis was taking a new step that would move them from agriculture into industry.

Sons Eduard and Otto were back from Germany with their education in chemistry, and so in 1867, along with their older brother Gustav, started the pioneer chemical business they had long planned. Beginning with ten thousand dollars' capital, they called their undertaking G. Mallinckrodt & Co.[55] The "G" was Gustav, who would be general administrator and manager of the Mallinckrodt brothers' new operation, using his nearly ten years of experience in the wholesale drug industry where he had risen to divisional manager.[56]

Edward supervised the construction of the first buildings, according to fact or legend, on what had been Emil's potato field.[57] There in a one-story stone structure and several wooden sheds the brothers would produce agricultural chemicals. Historians later recalled, "The attitude of the established fine chemical houses of the time toward this newcomer was one of amusement and condecension . . . there wasn't a wholesale druggist between St. Louis and California. It was obvious, that if the firm of G. Mallinckrodt and Company was to prosper, it had to obtain a fair share of business from the East, in direct competition with companies whose reputations were well-founded and of long duration."

And so they began, purifying commercial grade chemicals and preparing a few uncomplicated organic compounds: "Mallinckrodt was one of the first manufacturers of bromides in the United States, importing the bromine from the famous salt works at Stassfurt, Germany. The manufacture of iodides was also begun during this period."[58]

Edward was in charge of the factory, while Otto was analyst, purchasing agent, and shipping clerk, and Gustav was general administrator and sales manager. As later historians reported,

> Not owning wagon or truck, they used Richardson Drug Company's [where Gustav had worked] two-wheeled dray to haul freight—it often got stuck in the mud of Mallinckrodt Street. The brothers worked day and night. Many evenings Gustav fell asleep over the records. One time Edward was temporarily blinded by an explosion in the laboratory. . . .
>
> With very little capital (and that borrowed by the father) the firm was often in jeopardy and once on the verge of bankruptcy. But slowly and steadily it began to prosper.[59]

As life always seemed to go on the frontier, a gain was followed by a loss— Emil and Emilie lost their one-year-old daughter Elmira the same year that the older sons founded the chemical company on the family property. This would be their last child.

The following fall another loss struck the family—Hermann, Conrad, and

Julius's ninety-two-year-old mother Dorothea died in Dortmund on 29 October 1868. Frail for many years, Mother Dorothea had been cared for by her daughter Dorchen (Dorothea) who had married economist and businessman Karl Metzmacher in 1845. With mother Dorothea's death, the Mallinckrodt ownership of the Rehfuß house at Westenhellweg 451, in the family since 1694, ended.[60] As far as is known, after emigrating to America, Dorothea's sons had not been able to visit their mother. Nephew Emil, on the other hand, had.

1868 Election: Suffrage

In 1868 Missouri's Germans once again were preoccupied with an election. It was an important one, their first opportunity to vote for a president since the Civil War. Many Missourians who had been Southern sympathizers were, however, still disfranchised through the loyalty oath.

In general, the election campaign would be intense, for the political mood of the country was very strained. In spring the U.S. Congress, dominated by radical Republicans, had tried to impeach the Democratic President Andrew Johnson. They almost succeeded, the vote in the Senate being one short of the necessary two-thirds. Historians would see the impeachment procedure as "one of the most disgraceful episodes" in American history.[61] That over with, leaving more bitterness than ever, additional political tension was created when the Fourteenth Amendment was ratified on 28 July. Giving blacks the citizenship denied them in the original Constitution, the amendment also provided for proportional reductions in representation of states denying black suffrage.[62] In addition, the proposed Fifteenth Amendment for outright Negro suffrage (that is, for males) was making its way through the legal process of state ratifications.

The question of suffrage thus was a major and heated campaign issue throughout the country. The Fifteenth Amendment and its supporters were denounced in the campaign by Democrats who saw a glaring discrepancy between giving freed slaves the right to vote while still denying it to thousands of whites, as in Missouri, through the loyalty oath. The Republicans, on the other hand, supported the amendment on the national level, just as they did in Missouri, as part of their policy of radical reconstruction. In Missouri the old problem of voter registration therefore again raised preelection temperatures. Many Democrats in fact considered the situation worse than in the past because the state Assembly had pushed through a measure making county superintendents of election registration appointees of the governor, rather than electees of the people. This measure "gave its sponsors a virtual strangle hold over the electorate," wrote a historian.[63]

Missourians played an important role at the nominating conventions of the national political parties. The Republicans named General Ulysses Grant as their candidate, and St. Louis's Carl Schurz was made temporary chairman of the convention, as well as keynote speaker.[64]

Throughout the late summer and early fall 1868, Missouri politicians then stumped the state for their candidates. "As Radical and Democratic speakers criss-crossed the state," it was said, "rally followed rally until it seemed that no one had an interest in anything but politics." Since most of the German voters in Duden country, St. Louis, and elsewhere were Republican liberals, they came out in crowds to hear Schurz. One of his major themes was the justice of giving Negroes the right to vote, for Missourians now had to approve or disapprove of the affirmative suffrage statute their legislature had earlier passed.[65] For Democrats, on the other hand, voter registration was the key issue.

The November election came and the outcome was as predicted—General Grant won, carrying twenty-six of the thirty-four states. In Missouri, the Republicans had a twenty thousand vote margin. The election was decided for the Republican candidate, it was said, by the vote of freed African-American males who could already go to the polls in many states.[66] That 1868 election, a specialist would write, "brought the Radicals to the zenith of their political power in Missouri."[67]

Prejudice

On the other hand, the election took a strange and somewhat unexpected turn, an illiberal one—Missourians voted down the constitutional amendment that would have given their state's blacks the right to vote. Historians later wrote that race prejudice overcame party loyalty on this issue, and that would have meant the Germans, too. In fact, Carl Schurz, a moderate Republican and surely a German leader, was accused by his party's radicals of responsibility for the amendment's defeat.[68]

If racial prejudice was indeed a factor in the Germans' vote in Missouri, it was an unfortunate black mark on their overall and consistently liberal political record in the state. On the other hand, their action was perhaps understandable at the time, even if later questioned and condemned. Seen politically, for instance, latent prejudice and discriminatory racial attitudes may have surfaced among German immigrants after their overriding political goal of maintaining the American union of states was achieved. For that objective, the Emancipation Proclamation ending slavery had been supported, too, even though perhaps not in all cases with genuine enthusiasm. But then after the war, the real and everyday consequences of the end of slavery may have become quite a different, more personal and emotional, issue for many Germans.

Economic considerations might have brought latent prejudice to the surface. The postwar campaign to encourage fellow Germans to emigrate to Missouri may suddenly have been seen as potentially threatened through job competition from a flood of blacks coming to Missouri if it were a liberal state with voting rights. Such freed ex-slaves—many of whom were skilled workers—then would be serious contenders at the bottom of the economic ladder where immigrants often found themselves when they first arrived.

Psychologically and philosophically, too, German immigrants had had little preparation for practical, day-by-day racial equality and tolerance. Neither had been part of their experience or teaching in the old country. The concept "racism" was not an entry in Conrad Mallinckrodt's intellectually advanced encyclopedias representing post-Napoleonic European liberalism. (There was, however, a long thirteen-page entry on "Slave Trade/Slavery/ White Slavery" that took up the laws about and history of slavery in great detail and clearly condemning tone.[69])

Yet most of Missouri's Germans, to their credit, had not been slave owners— it was somehow almost instinctively immoral to own a human being as one did a horse or oxen. The few Germans who did own slaves rationalized their ownership by saying that, since there was a shortage of labor to hire on the frontier, to help secure their own economic existence, they were justified in buying the laborer in a state that permitted slavery:

Julius Mallinckrodt (1832): "Negroes, which one has to buy because one cannot work a farm alone, cost money."

Hermann Mallinckrodt (1845): "I intend to buy a Negro woman since one apparently never has the possibility of hiring good household help. . . . Furthermore, the wages are so enormously expensive that one hardly can get the money together; 5 to 6 years of wages almost pay for a Negro woman."

Emil Mallinckrodt (1847): Wife at last has "excellent help in the house since I bought a good Negro woman for $450."[70]

Even if morally opposing slavery, Missouri's Germans nevertheless had lived for many years in the state's slave-holding climate. Its public outdoor slave markets, stinking slave pens, frenetic armed manhunts for fugitive slaves, and all the other degrading manifestations of a people in bondage were familiar to anyone with eyes and ears. Unconsciously, over time, Germans, intellectually horrified by the practice of slavery, nevertheless may have assimilated its racist psychological underpinning—that is, the belief that Negroes were inherently inferior beings ("deceptive, lazy, thieving"). Through daily conditioning by Missouri's events, sights, and sounds, the Germans' earlier distinction between cause (the institution of slavery) and effect (behavior of slaves and slave owners) was dulled. Precisely that, in fact, was held by abolitionists to be a primary evil of America's slavery; its poisonous immorality seeped into the total society, as racism historically always had done. It is not illogical then to presume that Germans in Missouri who cheered President Lincoln's Emancipation Proclamation could also nod their heads affirmatively when in reply the president of the Confederacy called America's Negroes "human beings of an inferior race."[71]

The German liberals of the late 1860s also generally lacked philosophical guidelines to help them avoid their racial prejudice and discrimination. Until then liberalism's magic words "freedom" and "liberty" had been defined in Germany as in the United States in primarily negative terms, that is, freedom from interference by government and others. The other positive side of the philosophical coin had not been accepted widely, that is, freedom to resources needed for achieving and progressing on the basis of individual choices. In 1868, therefore, giving slaves freedom from bondage and noncitizen status was favored; giving them freedom to vote, to be equal at the polls was problematic.[72]

Around this time Emil Mallinckrodt, perhaps speaking for many German immigrants, began publishing his troubled views of race relations in America. For example, in a *Westliche Post* commentary entitled "The Dark Continent and Its Residents," Emil traced some of the history of slavery. He contended that in their fatherland, Africans over centuries had sold one another into bondage; thus their emancipation in the United States was to be recognized as a "happy deliverance" which they "never have achieved, either among themselves nor under any other people on earth." Nevertheless, Emil wrote, solving the problems of social relations between the colored and white races remained difficult because of the vast physical and intellectual racial differences. Apparently what he feared most was "race mixing":

Viewed entirely without prejudice, an amalgamation would be a misfortune for the white, or caucasian, element. There are only two human races on earth whose complete amalgamation disparages neither, rather may have good results through their mixing—that is, the Germanic and Semitic tie. Their intelligence and progressive development has conquered the world—Mongolians, Malayan, Indians, and Negroes, even under the most favorable relations, will never lift themselves to such intellectual greatness.

Legal freedom and equality is forever guaranteed the colored in the United States, as was just. But social equalization, which could lead to physical mixing and creation of a mixed race, would be a national misfortune. Even in the present southern states, in which the number of whites and blacks are equal, they will never lift themselves to the intellectual heights of the northern states where the number of colored is negligibly small. Where the white race does not give the stimulus, Negroes, left to themselves, will make little or no progress in civilization.[73]

The years in America obviously had made clear to German immigrants that while perhaps "all men are created equal," that equality remained more a goal than a reality. Humans who were white and male were America's superior beings in the first half of the nineteenth century. Blacks existed in inhumane slavery, deliberately excluded by the founding fathers from citizenship in the socioeconomic system their work sustained. Women, too, were lesser creatures. They also had no right to vote and even now were being omitted, as well, from the Fifteenth Amendment that would grant that right of self-government to black men. Both the Fourteenth and Fifteenth Amendments clearly said that states could not deny suffrage to males over twenty-one "on account of race, color, or previous condition of servitude." True, American women suffrage associations were forming; the territory of Wyoming was pushing to be the first legislature to grant its female citizens the right to vote; and England's John Stuart Mill was writing his famous book *Subjection of Women*, the first philosophical examination of the issue. But all that was still pending.

Thus, when Missouri's Germans went to vote in 1868 on black male suffrage in their state, there were few models in everyday life to whom they could look for guidance about "freedom" and "liberty" for others. They were left rather with their abstract concepts of those blessings for white males, that is, for themselves. It would be at least a century before such attitudes began to change. The revered leader who had made a small dent in them, Abraham Lincoln, had died too soon. He perhaps could have helped Missouri's Germans, and many like them, to move away from racism to freedom and equality that was more than six-gun salutes, hurrahs, and flag-waving. Now they had to learn without him, and their learning would be slow.

Most German newspapers in Missouri supported black suffrage. In late October, the *St. Charles Demokrat*, for instance, rhetorically asked its readers whether it was "right that colored who fought and suffered loyally for the Union should be placed in a lower legal status than those who had fought against it and are still at enmity with it?" Making the challenge very personal, the newspaper concluded, "Think that over before you vote."[74]

In the week before the election the appeal of the newspaper became even more intense. On 2 November the *Demokrat* asked, "Is that justice? The rebels only used their reason to plunge the country into misery, while the Negroes loyally helped to save the Union." Again following its question with a warning, the newspaper said that its readers at any rate should not let it be said that the Germans of Missouri, whose name was so distinguished in the history of the country, had stood in the way of such a reasonable reform.[75] And several days before the election, the paper reminded that "Right continues to be right, whether or not it wins in the first round."[76]

Thus, on election day, 8 November, the *Demokrat* was pleased to report sizable majorities in the county and state for Radical Republican candidates. "St. Charles County is saved again," wrote the paper, "and takes its honorable place in the column of Missouri's Union counties."[77] Subsequently the newspaper reported that the Republican candidate for President, General Grant, had won at seven of eleven polling sites in St. Charles County (St. Charles, Cottleville, St. Peters, New Melle, Femme Osage, Schluersburg, Augusta). In fact, among the Mallinckrodts and their neighbors at Augusta, the Republican win for General Grant was one hundred forty-six to sixty votes.[78]

In almost the same proportion, one hundred thirty-five to sixty-five, voters at Augusta also said "Yes" to black suffrage, and at Femme Osage it was sixty-six "Yes" to twenty-three "No." Astonishingly, these were the only two voting locations within the county that gave black suffrage a majority vote. In Warren County, too, the majority voted *against* Negro voting rights but *for* General Grant.[79]

Despite Radical accusations that he and the Germans had caused the defeat of the Negro suffrage amendment, Schurz was nominated and elected to fill the U.S. Senate seat for Missouri—a political "first" for America's German immigrants. In his acceptance speech, after a raucous session in the state capitol, Schurz said he saw his victory as "evidence of the liberal and progressive spirit moving the people of Missouri." His was to be a campaign for reconciliation, he suggested, within the badly split Republican party of which he would represent the developing liberal, rather than fading radical, wing.[80]

It was seen by some as fitting that Schurz sat in the U.S. Congress in February 1869 when it passed the Fifteenth Amendment granting black suffrage and sent it on to the states for ratification. In Missouri the legislature then was able to do what the voters had not done—quickly rush a resolution of ratification through both houses. Negro suffrage on a national scale, that is, by constitutional amendment, it was said, was a way to "alleviate local fears that Missouri might attract a large colored immigration if it acted alone."[81]

The cause of women's suffrage, too, was making some progress. Wyoming had granted women suffrage; J. S. Mill had published his book. Missouri's Lieutenant Governor Stanard met with a delegation of the Women's Suffrage Association of Missouri in 1869, and by autumn St. Louis hosted the annual national convention of the women's movement.[82]

Emil Mallinckrodt, however, saw these developments from a negative—indeed, reactionary—perspective. Bitterly criticizing the shortcomings of current politics, he gave voice to his elitist views in the *Westliche Post*:

> But what can be expected as long as the great mass of voters among the people are coarse, ignorant, indifferent, or even bribeable. The unqualified, general right to vote has turned out poorly in the United States. That not being enough, during the war some 700,000 colored votes also suddenly tumbled into the voting boxes; all that is now missing to carry out the greatest of all farces at the polls are enfranchised women, black and white, among them the genderless who do not want to be women and cannot be men.
>
> And who then should really govern the people? Who other than their most intelligent, patriotic, honest, sacrificial men filled with a holy fervor for truth, justice, the common weal. Praise God there is no shortage of such men in this nation.[83]

Repealing the Loyalty Oath

In addition to black suffrage, the other old controversy of reenfranchising Missouri's whites was also on its way to resolution. Schurz supported their right to vote, as did his St. Louis paper, the *Westliche Post*.[84] The settling of that issue which had divided Missouri so long—that is, repeal of the state's test oath for voters—would, however, require one more election and another shift in the political landscape. It came in 1870.

Registration went more smoothly this time, with 199,297 voters qualified, contrasted to 154,080 in the 1868 election. About 18,000 to 20,000 of the increase were new Negro voters (enfranchised by proclamation of the Fifteenth Amendment to the U.S. Constitution in March 1870) and some were new immigrants. Election day 1870 would bring out 160,000 voters in Missouri.[85]

At their state convention in late summer, Schurz's liberals broke away from the mainline Republican Party to organize their own convention and support elimination of Missouri's voting and officeholding proscriptions.[86] It was those Liberal Republicans who swept the state's seats in the U.S. Congress. The Democrats, however, did quite well on the local level, gaining seats in the Missouri state legislature and county government.[87]

The Radicals were out, although the black vote had gone to them. In 1871, then, that newly elected Democratic state legislature eliminated the proscription on voting and some on officeholding.[88] Therewith, "the Radical reconstruction of Missouri could be considered officially at an end."[89]

Despite the period's vindictiveness, there also had been much progress from which the Germans in Missouri had benefited and to which they contributed: "The state advanced economically and socially, and the foundations of a modern education system were laid. Having freed the slaves from bondage, the Radical leadership did not abandon the Negro to fend for himself; rather, they sponsored a comprehensive package of civil rights and education for the freedmen while trying to move the white population toward a gradual acceptance of the idea of Negro suffrage."[90]

Yet some problems and confusion apparently remained. In Augusta, for instance, where trustees had taken the loyalty oath from 1862 on, in 1870 there suddenly were no candidates who had done so. The old members therefore served on.[91] Perhaps candidates had thought Missouri's pending repeal of the oath for voters and some officials was already in effect and so did not properly apply; possibly the board initially also thought new state laws already were applicable (therefore in February authorizing purchase of the new statute book with its appendixes).[92] If that was the understanding, it was premature—the oath restriction on voters was not lifted until 1871 and was not removed entirely from all officials until around 1875.[93]

If Conrad Mallinckrodt's hiatus from public service since 1861 had been motivated by principles related to the loyalty oath requirements, he now could gradually return to public duty. In the 1870 county elections, he was elected justice of the peace, and prominent in his preserved papers was an 1871 recertification as notary public.[94] If Conrad had "taken himself out of action," as it were, during the period of the war and postwar loyalty oaths or the town fathers for some reason had chosen to ignore his service, that ostracism was clearly over. Town board clerk C. Tiemann, successor to L. Bennefeld (who died in 1872 after having held that position since 1861), recorded on 7 July 1873 that "Mr. Conrad Mallinckrodt's Bill of $2.00 for swearing 5 Trustees for 2 years in succession was paid by check No. 266."[95] Conrad was once again busy with town affairs.

At the county seat, too, politics apparently were again animated. Augusta's young Carl Wencker (son of Frederick and probably a second cousin of the Mallinckrodt's immigrant friend Carl I), living there as a student and bank clerk, recorded in his diary on 4 July 1872, "The 96th of the declaration of Independence, was woken up by a cannon salute at 5 o'clock a.m. out of a fine sleep. The St. Charles Band played some fine national airs. Strolled about town in the morning, the bank being closed. Read the St. Charles papers—the *Demokrat* had some slanders against Theo Bruere and the *Wahre Fortschritt*."[96]

The holiday was not entirely peaceful, however—the following day young Wencker noted in his diary that "in the afternoon at about 5 p.m. Mr. Theo Bruere gave editor Brukk a cowhide thrashing at which job Mr. Rübeling, one of the police, stopped him."

On 6 August 1872, Carl Wencker again reported a political event in the seat of St. Charles County, somewhat cynically, it seemed, probably from his liberal [Republican] point of view. Regarding the anniversary of Arnold Krekel's organization of German immigrants to fight for the Union, young Wencker wrote: "The renowned 6th, 'Camp Krekel,' was awakened by a band of music at 6.10 a.m., looked out [and] saw the 'Arsenal Band' in full trim marching up Main Street ready to go to Camp Krekel and make music for the Rebels, Democrats, soreheads or the so-called Liberals."[97]

The politics of the Civil War in Missouri had passed from father to son.

26

1870s: Augusta and
Again Its River

The new decade was promising for the Missouri countryside. By 1870, after four years of its immigration campaign, the state's overall population was up 50 percent, to around 1.5 million.[1] Many of the new Missourians settled in the rural areas where land was available, but great numbers also stayed in and around St. Louis (where the population gain from 1860 to 1870 was an incredible 93.4 percent).

Missouri was a state of foreign-born people, and that population had increased 38 percent over the decade. The Germans were prominent, as from the earliest years—by the 1870s they accounted for more than 50 percent of all Missouri's immigrants.[2] Many had done well financially; according to the 1870 census, Julius Mallinckrodt's real estate value, for instance, had increased from $7,000 in 1860 to $18,000 and Conrad's from $6,750 to $10,000.[3]

German settlements, too, had grown. St. Charles County, for example, had only about 16,500 residents in 1860; by 1870 the county topped 21,000, and Femme Osage Township, in which Augusta was located, reported 2,401 people.[4] There the Mallinckrodts and others were pleased that around the turn of the decade their village offered them a flour mill, sawmill, doctor, druggist, tannery, brickyard, carpenter, stonemason, shoemaker, tailor, harness maker, blacksmith/wagonmaker, cooper, saloons, general merchandise stores, and a butcher shop.[5] The business center of the town was no longer just along the riverfront.

The businessmen over the years included the general storekeepers Hermann Damann, Friedrich Wencker, Charles Thiemann, and Joseph Wiedener/Dietrich Baare; hotel keepers Limberg and Arensburg; blacksmith (since 1859) H. Osthoff; shoemaker John Fuhr; steam mill operator Henry Schaaf; butchers Dieckhaus and Tiemann; and lumberman William Koch. In addition, old-timers especially liked to recount their saloonkeepers: Anton Heller, Adam Heller, Herman Limberg, G. H. Mindrup, H. W. Kessler, H. H. Haferkamp, and George Grumpke, among others.[6]

Schools

As planned by Missouri's post–Civil War government, education in the state had improved significantly. In Augusta, Professor Gütlich was still principal, and in 1873 teacher Matilda Damann had begun what would be a quarter-century of instruction.[7] According to later recollections, the language of teaching had by this time changed considerably—during the week, three days were taught in English and two in German.[8] The one-room school now had a kind of annex, a brick building below the hill, where classes also were held.

With few teachers and many children, a split-shift system was used—grades seven and eight met in the morning and five and six in the afternoon in the main school with Professor Gütlich, while in the brick building grades three and four gathered in the morning with Miss Damann and grades one and two in the afternoon.[9] Children were admitted twice a year, and every time a new class came in, the other classes were pushed up a notch. The upper class of beginners then went to the main school building to Professor Gütlich.

That schoolhouse was typical of the times:

> A large woodburning stove was standing in the middle of the aisle and on both sides, a row of homemade benches with desks attached. . . . One side of the aisle was for the boys and the other for the girls. The room had a door on each end. The front door was for the teacher and the girls, the rear door for the boys to enter. The teacher sat in front of the boys' benches. On the girls' side, there were hooks and nails on the wall for them to hang their schoolbags and wraps. The boys had hooks and nails on the wall behind their seats. The front wall was covered with a large map of the United States and the world, and a homemade blackboard. . . .
>
> Occasionally attendance to classes was very irregular. A high percentage of the children lived on a farm up to two miles from town. . . . The roads were all dirt and after a rain or deep snow which would freeze at night and thaw at daytime, they sometimes were almost impassable.[10]

Augusta nevertheless had come a long way—from the 1840s of tutors (such as Conrad Mallinckrodt and Theodore Bruere)[11] and the first simple schools in Augusta and in the woods, to the 1862 hiring of a principal and the beginning of what was called a "school system," with classes taught largely in the German language, and then by 1873 to two teachers, an annex room, and more English-language classes.

Perhaps not surprisingly, then, the handwriting of the town fathers in this period reflected how many years Augusta had had its school. Beginning with the clerkship of F. Tiemann (then twenty years old[12]) in May 1873, model English-language penmanship with its rounded letters replaced the strongly perpendicular German writing, with its distinct *d*, *t*, and *s* of the earlier records written by the first immigrants.[13] Tiemann's style resembled somewhat that of the school principal Gütlich who had been teaching reading and writing in the village for a decade and who was clerk on the town board himself for a while in 1873.[14]

Second-Generation Family Trees

The increasing number of children in the Augusta and outlying schools was visible evidence, too, of how many years had already passed since the first German immigrants arrived in Duden country. First-generation Americans—the children born on U.S. soil, to the 1830s immigrants, for example—were married and, in turn, having second-generation American children who crowded the schools. At the same time, because of the high mortality rate on the frontier, the first immigrants often lost spouses, contracted a second marriage, and thus had a second set of first-generation children along with second-generation grandchildren.

Such changes on the Mallinckrodt family tree in the early 1870s were typical. Julius had built a wine cellar (plate 14) on the northwest corner of the former Dortmund property in 1869[15] and was already teaching winemaking to a grandson (Alfred Nahm, son of his first-marriage daughter Emilie).[16]

About the same time, the family celebrated the March 1870 marriage of Julius's youngest second-marriage daughter Lydia Anna to Rudolf W. Mueller. And in 1871 grandfather Julius was especially pleased, too, when his oldest son, Conrad Theodor, and wife Emilie had their first son in July and named him Robert McClenny Mallinckrodt. Julius thought using the name of the child's grandmother as a middle name (as his brother Conrad had first done with his sons Theodor Feldmann and Albert Feldmann) was a fine way to honor a good woman, Julius's first wife Mary McClenny. But as so often was the pattern of life for Duden country immigrants, a celebrated birth was followed by a mourned death—for Julius and his second wife Mary it was their first son, Christian Albert, dead in November, 1872, at age twenty-two. He was the first Mallinckrodt to be buried in the town of Augusta's public cemetery.

In St. Louis the pattern of life was much the same for Emil Mallinckrodt. On the one hand, he mourned deeply the 1870 death of his first daughter, the happy little Minna he so often wrote about. She died at age twenty-eight in Dortmund, where she had lived with her husband, Karl Wisskott, and three children. The next year Emil and Emilie celebrated the wedding of his first-marriage daughter Adele, born in Italy, to A. Schulenberg, the son of Emil's long-time St. Louis friend. The first grandchild (1872) in this family would be named Eleanor, honoring her grandmother, Emil's first wife Eleanor Luckey.

Hermann and Luise, almost uniquely spared the spousal-death trauma of the frontier, nevertheless mourned the loss of their daughter Cecilia; married about ten years to William Kueffner, she died in 1872 before her thirtieth birthday. On the other hand, Hermann now had a better job selling fire insurance, and the family lived in north St. Louis rather than in the heart of the city. Delia was still at home,[17] and James Ferdinand had a promising future, following the family tradition of surveying—perhaps motivated by his Uncle Conrad at Augusta with whom he maintained contact. John Friederich, having completed his apprenticeship as a machinist, was working on the East Coast: in New York making models and experimental machines for the Scientific American patent agency, in Boston at a sewing machine company, and in Pittsburgh doing lathe work in a locomotive shop.[18]

Bridges and Floods

As the Mallinckrodts and other German settlers in countryside and city lived for their children and their schools, so they lived too with their rivers—those lifelines that were central to their economic activities and that needed improvement after the Civil War.

St. Charles County celebrated, therefore, when almost on schedule, in May 1871, the bridge across the Missouri River at St. Charles was opened to traffic.[19] That would mean better connections to the markets and goods of St. Louis, especially for St. Charles County farmers and businessmen. Understandably, county historians were enthusiastic:

> It is the longest iron bridge in the country. . . . The seven river spans vary in length from 305 to 321 feet. There were eight river foundations—most of them presenting new and extraordinary difficulties in construction—varying from 54 to 76 feet in depth, the caissons for which had to be carried down through alternate strata of quicksand, large boulders, and tangled masses of drift logs. Add to these submarine difficulties the facts that at the bridge site the Missouri river rises and falls 40 feet; that its flood speed is 9½ miles per hour . . . an adequate idea may be formed of the character of the work. . . .
>
> The cost of the entire structure is understood to have been about $1,750,000, and stands as a monument of engineering skill, and we hope will so stand for ages to come.[20]

In St. Louis there was similar jubilation in 1874 when construction of Eads Bridge across the Mississippi River was completed, connecting the city (now a population of about 350,000[21]) and its commerce more closely to the East. Perhaps

Emil and Hermann Mallinckrodt and their families were at the gigantic 4 July celebration when the bridge was officially opened.[22] "Bunting-draped engines parading across the new marvel and cheering crowds," it was reported, were seen by President Grant along with other politicians and financiers attending the festivities.[23]

But while the bridge builders may have felt that they had in part "conquered" the Mississippi and the Missouri, farmers along the streams knew better. Not having forgotten either the lesson of the great flood of 1844 or the years since, they had learned instead to live with the idea of more future channel changes.

Periodic floods, for instance, always seemed to bring some alteration. The sandbars that Julius and Conrad could see from their hilltops got a bit higher, and as they filled in more of the central channel, the displaced water had to go somewhere else. When Julius and Conrad looked out from their hills across the stream to the limestone bluffs on the southern side, the river seemed to be seeking space there.[24] To make a new channel for itself, the Missouri was slowly washing away the rich bottom lands on the south side of the valley—which Emil and Julius on their original sketch had called plantations.

1872: Course Change

While such shifts in the river's course had been gradual over the past decades, some who knew its history also sensed that the stream's changes could be radical. And they were—beginning in 1872. That was the big change, local history says, the one people had somehow known would eventually come and dramatically change the life of the people who lived along the river.[25]

When high waters receded that summer, the Missouri River had decisively moved its course away from the northern bluffs at Augusta, over to the south side of the valley where for a long time it had been trying gradually to cut out a deeper channel for itself. The old northern channel, in fact, was closed up in front of Conrad and Julius's property, as well as in front of Augusta, leaving land where there had once been water. The nearest point where one now could get to the river was some miles out from Augusta, and over time that landing, too, would probably move even farther away.

The clerk of the Augusta Town Board at that time did not leave many written clues about the 1872 changes. (Over the years each clerk showed varying priorities, some concentrating on money matters and others on the detailed discussions of the trustees.) It was, however, recorded in spring 1872 that major street repairs were carried out for $269.30, and the board did not meet in either June or July, which may have been the time of the high water.[26] Moreover, in the next year major road repairs were undertaken along the bluff (where the river would have reached), and payment was made for rocks hauled.[27]

Perhaps the most significant indication of the big change was that some time later the board voted to "pay balance of the money necessary to finish the River Road to the Ferry Landing."[28] There previously had been no mention or map showing a thoroughfare by this name. "*To* the ferry landing" suggested that the landing no longer was at the foot of the town. By 1874 the river was tearing away embankments and land on the south side of the stream and creating accretion land on the north side near Augusta.[29] Big floods in August 1875 and July 1876[30] accelerated this action and it was clear that "the river seeks new channels."[31] Trying to explain the numerous changes in the Missouri River, a Mallinckrodt descendant years later roughly sketched (figure 26-1) how the river had changed its point of contact with its northern limestone bluffs—above the Mallinckrodt property from 1817 through the 1830s and 1840s, and from then on gradually farther east until it had moved to below the Augusta waterfront.[32] (Still other changes came around 1910.)

Looking down from their hills and seeing not water but land, Conrad and Julius were reminded of the story their father had told them about the change of course of the Ruhr River along the Haus Mallinckrodt property in the early 1600s. There was, however, a major difference—the Mallinckrodts had lost land to the Ruhr River in Germany; in Missouri they now gained. Lawyers and geologists called it accretion—that is, the formation of land by the withdrawal or recession, of bodies of water.

The law said accretion land belonged to the owners of contiguous property,

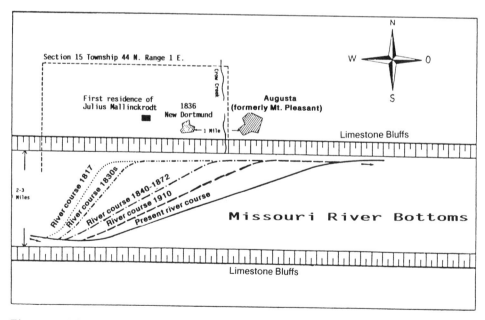

Figure 26-1. The Missouri River's changing course was sketched in 1955 by Hubert William Mallinckrodt (Conrad Mallinckrodt's grandson) who lived in the river bottom directly south of new Dortmund from 1915 to 1951 (when there was another flood higher than that of 1844) and farmed there until the 1960s.

391

that is, the Mallinckrodts owned the land formed south of and touching their original property lines which had run "to the river." The former bed of the Missouri now was a very rich stretch of agriculturally valuable river bottom land. Later plats would show that Julius and Conrad and their heirs ultimately gained about eight hundred additional acres through the river's vagaries. The town of Augusta, being incorporated, had the same right as an individual to accretion land and thus became owner of so-called town land where its waterfront previously was located.

As Julius's new Dortmund had died without a waterfront, Augusta thrived while it had one directly at the foot of the settlement—until 1872 when the Missouri River took it, as well. Augusta, nevertheless, remained connected to its surrounding area by the river. The 1872 diary, for instance, of young Carl Wencker, then working and studying in nearby St. Charles, provided an interesting account of transportation between the county seat and his home town of Augusta.

On 18 May, a Saturday, Wencker reported that he "started for home to go to the May picnic." Apparently wanting to spend some time first in the big city or because of time schedules, Wencker wrote that he first "went to St. Louis on a freight train [cost, one dollar], in the evening on the steamer *Alice* [cost, three dollars]. Got to Augusta . . . went to the ball and had a few dances." On his return, Wencker seems to have crossed the Missouri River to the rail line on its south side "crossing river ferryman 20c," took the train to St. Louis (three dollars) and then to St. Charles (one dollar and fifty cents). (His expense account for the trip also showed the purchase of a newspaper for five cents, a cigar ten cents, necktie fifty cents, and fifty cents for a "treat at the Augusta Wine Hall.") Wencker's diary referred, as well, to the steamboat *St. Luke*, which regularly brought Augusta's wine and people to St. Charles.[33]

By 1877, however, Gert Göbel, a prominent observer of Duden country affairs, wrote skeptically about Augusta's future:

> Unhappily in recent years the previously good [river] landing has been totally ruined by a big sandbank which has formed precisely in front of the little town. For this reason the bottom farmers above and below Augusta bring their surplus either to Washington or to St. Charles or ship their products directly to St. Louis from various landings along the Missouri. Until now Augusta, dependent on itself and on not very expandable surroundings, is nothing more than a trade center for the vicinity.[34]

Indeed, by August 1880, the Augusta columnist wrote for the *St. Charles Demokrat* that the relocation of the town's landing a mile below town "is very disadvantageous" and the two-mile distance by 1882 "makes it extraordinarily hard to ship freight."[35]

The history of the great river changes was recorded some years after the events this way: "Up to 1872 Augusta had a very fine landing under the hills that front the Missouri, but during that year the river changed its current, filled in the main channel opposite the town, and the place became practically shut off from the stream, so that the channel is now on the opposite extreme of the bottom land, on the Franklin county side. The landing is now [1885] twelve miles down the river, from which point all supplies are hauled by wagon."[36] In short, the Missouri River, which for years had "used the space between the bluffs as a playground," as an old-timer put it, "jumping from one side to the other at will," had decided to stick to the south side.[37]

27

1875: Eventide

Many of even the most doubtful, or resentful, Missourians might have concluded by the mid-1870s that the state's deepest Civil War scars were healed. The former president of the Confederacy, Jefferson Davis, visited the former border and slave state in 1875 and his trip went well. As justice would have it, at the very same time that Davis was in St. Louis, his old Civil War enemy Ulysses S. Grant was there, too, now as president of the United States. As a historian later observed, "The two old foes did not meet in what would surely have been a spectacular demonstration of Missouri's triumphant reconciliation."[1] Or as another historian summed up the mood, "The old spirit of vindictiveness had been slowly ebbing in the minds and hearts of many Missourians for some time. As the postwar years had lengthened, Missourians of both political faiths and of differing wartime loyalties found common economic, cultural and social ties."[2] At the same time, some of the state's German immigrants, with memories of Europe's long-enduring enmities, may have been a bit more skeptical.

A new state constitution passed in 1875 also seemed symbolic of Missouri's resettled politics—it "represented moderate reforms of a somewhat conservative nature, and it remained the state's organic law for the next seventy years." Then, too, Carl Schurz, of the breakaway Republican faction, the Liberals, was replaced in the U.S. Senate in 1875 by a Democrat, in fact an ex-Confederate general, who would serve for the coming thirty years.[3] Missouri was clearly moving back from radicalism to its tradition of moderate progress as a new generation of politicians went to the state capital. And they included sons of the German-American community that had become increasingly integrated into society through its participation in the Civil War.[4]

First-Generation Family Politicians

Sometimes the old Mallinckrodt family patriarch, Julius, could hardly believe that immigrant sons now held public office in Jefferson City. Yet his oldest son was addressed as the Honorable Conrad Theodor Mallinckrodt because he had served in the state legislature for two years, and his son-in-law (Lydia Anne's husband) was addressed as the Honorable Rudolph Müller for having served several terms.

Described as a "staunch Republican," Conrad Theodor represented the St. Charles area where he had his orchard and nursery.[5] In such German-settled Missouri River counties the Republican party, to which the immigrants had switched their loyalty because of the Civil War and Lincoln, was especially strong. It was not, however, the radical Republican party of the immediate post–Civil War period (that wing had disappeared) or the liberal Republican Party led by Carl Schurz (whose followers had returned to the main fold). Rather, Missouri's Republicans of the mid-1870s were back to a moderate orientation, enriched by former radical factions that no longer dominated.[6]

It was probably around the time of his legislative duty that Conrad Theodor had the photo made that pleased his father so much (plate 15).[7] Grandfather Julius was also pleased when Conrad Theodor's children came from St. Charles to spend time with him and Mary on their hilltop. Sometimes they and their mother visited for several weeks, and then the house was full of sound and excitement.[8]

Conrad's Quiet Hours

At Conrad's, where the children were all teenagers, life was more quiet and contemplative. Conrad spent a lot of time in his study preparing the work for numerous justice of the peace cases which came his way, especially in the years from 1873 to 1876.[9] He also needed to do homework when the Augusta Town Board asked for legal advice. In 1876, for instance, there was the matter of a resident's refusal to pay the town a debt. H. Limberg had been instructed to clean out the street gutters he had clogged up; when he failed to do so within forty-eight hours, the town street inspector did the work and charged Limberg $1.25, which he refused to pay.[10] Unfortunately, what Conrad advised was not recorded, nor was the outcome of the case; however, since the matter was not mentioned again, good advice and successful collection might be presumed.

Conrad loved his quiet study, with its view east toward Julius's house and south over the river valley. He had designed it very well, he thought. Off to one end of the house, away from the kitchen, it had been adjoined to the larger central and western wings but was elevated above them. That separated it from the noise of family life. The orderly shelves of books, working table, comfortable rocking chair, and efficient writing desk created as pleasant an intellectual atmosphere as he had known in his study in Dortmund. And, of course, his books from there were old friends, as was the treasured but now unused stamp for making wax seals with the family coat of arms.[11]

On the other hand, there were also the tools of his new, American trade— land surveying. Neatly in their place were the surveying instruments, compass and chain, and drawing apparatus. The telescope and barometer were there, too, for all they told him about Missouri's countryside and weather. He had even acquired alchemy scales and dabbled a bit with chemicals.

Satisfied with his life and somewhat at peace with himself, Conrad around 1877 may have been persuaded by his children and their mother to have his image "recorded for posterity," as it were (plate 16). That was possible right there in Augusta, since the Town Board in November 1876 had granted a request from G. L. Collier to put up a "photographic gallery" on the public square for a five dollar fee and later renewed the license for a second year.[12] Perhaps Collier did artistic sketching in addition to, or instead of, what is currently understood as "photography." According to an assessment made much later, the quality art sketch of Conrad was done with carbon pencil on cardboard, while Wilhelmina's was on paper pasted onto cloth stretched over wood.[13] Considerable evidence suggests that the sketch, though undated, was made in 1877, that is, when Conrad was sixty-nine years old.[14]

After Wilhelmina's death in September 1877, Conrad was again alone. Until they married, Conrad probably shared his home with his three teenage children: Theodor eighteen, Albert seventeen, Minna Dorothea (Dorchen) sixteen. As life went for women at that time, Dorchen in all likelihood was expected to keep house for her father and brothers with help, if she needed it, from Aunt Mary on the nearby hill. Whether Theodor worked away from home is not known, but Albert did surveying work with his father, as their field survey notebooks show.[15]

Sorting Out Life and Politics

It is not illogical to assume that Conrad and Julius spent considerable time with each other in these years. The two graying immigrants, sitting on their hilltops surveying the world, had a long life to sort out together. And like most politically aware people looking back over some seven decades of life, they could have concluded that humankind indeed had taken many steps forward but at a considerable price in suffering. Having lived through both the Napoleonic Wars of their childhood and the devastating American Civil War of their adulthood, they probably no longer were very astonished at news reports from a political world they understood all too well.

As for their personal lives, what should they yet say? They had ofttimes reprimanded one another for faults and likewise encouraged one another after failures. At least they usually had had the good sense also to see the roots of problems in the society or system around them rather than only in themselves or other individuals. One day historians would describe the immigrant condition as a severe and continuing trauma, "a history of alienation and its consequences."[16] So it had been, especially for those who came alone or in family groups. As Conrad repeatedly said, "If it were not as it is, ten mules should not hold me in this state of Missouri."[17] Hopefully, the brothers Mallinckrodt could have concluded, the price they had paid would humble those who praised their achievements.

They had reason, nevertheless, also to chuckle. While some people took daily events so seriously, stories they heard about life in their nearby village were often gently humorous. The running argument about where to locate the town's fire ladders, for instance, continued because it was a question of prestige for some and responsibility for others.[18] A new problem, however, was what to do with animals dying within the town's limits.[19]

Property and streets were a constant concern. George Münch was the latest resident to be reminded to get his debris (wood and lumber) off the street, while Mr. Quickert was told again to repair his chimney before it fell across the street.[20] On the other hand, Mr. Grumpke, the town's popular and influential saloonkeeper, was quite provoked with the Town Board—the rock road in front of his business had not been constructed as far as he requested.[21] Then, too, there were the arguments over fences on neighboring land, unpaid taxes, and the unrepaired cemetery fence.[22]

Thank goodness, life in and around a small town was made up of small concerns, Julius and Conrad may have thought as they sat together under their summer shade trees at day's end. For them, as for many country people, it was that magic, restorative time in Missouri when the summer sun drew down to the horizon and the countryside grew quiet. Birds ceased chattering, and it was too early for the frogs. Sounds of the work world faded as weary men left the fields for the house. One could sit then and rest a while before the animals in the barn became restless about their evening feed. It was a good time to figure out what got done today and what was left for tomorrow and the day after.

Not all contemplation in those days of the late 1870s, however, was that peaceful. One thing people uneasily wondered about, for instance, was how long it would be before the state's hard-riding robber gangs were stopped. It was a scandal that Missouri was known between 1875 and 1882 as the "robber state" or "outlaw state." And folks in other parts of the country did not always understand how that, too, was part of the Midwest's Civil War inheritance which would be passed on to the "wild west," as well.

Outlaws like the brothers Jesse and Frank James, claiming the plundered area of western Missouri as their territory, competed with at least three other gangs. Town banks in Liberty, Lexington, Richmond, and Gallatin were hit, as well as a Missouri Pacific train.[23] Historians later calculated that "Jesse's gang succeeded in at least fourteen bank robberies, the holdup of the Kansas City Fair, and in train robberies too numerous to count. Murder was a familiar feature of these crimes."[24] Another earlier historian added stagecoaches to the list of targets, as well as the comment that "there was more than one rumor about political connections with higher-ups, old wartime friendships, and understanding of whom to let alone and why."[25]

Emil Mallinckrodt was especially upset by the public's attitudes toward the bandits who "attain complete sympathy, with trivialization of their misdeeds, especially in the rural part of the country where they have carried on their destruction and terror since the Civil War."[26] Another related fact incensed Emil just as much—the widespread possession of revolvers. As he wrote in the *Westliche Post*,

> Worse yet than all the mentioned evil are the country's bloody deaths, a practice becoming increasingly more frequent. Colt's unholy invention has contributed much to this. His revolvers are cowardly, assassination murder weapons, entirely suited to the present barbaric inclination and customs. Thus they also brought their inventor millions and much honor. Unsuited to hunting and other useful purposes, they put the formerly serviceable Bowie knife in the shade. All coats and pants of the garment trade [now] being sold naturally have sewn-in revolver-pockets, as one can see for himself everywhere.[27]

In the early and mid-1870s, unsavory events characterized politics elsewhere in the Mallinckrodts' America. The Ku Klux Klan was brutally active in the South; a stock market scandal touched the federal government; a panic in 1873, resulting from economic overexpansion, brought bank failures and agricultural hard times. In St. Louis a conspiracy of revenue officials, called the "Whiskey Ring," was uncovered among distillers defrauding the government of revenue taxes. In Washington, President Grant's secretary of war was nearly impeached when it was found he had taken bribes for the sale of trading posts in the Indian Territory.[28]

Under President Grant, in fact, industrialists had gained so much influence and there was so much corruption that Julius and Conrad thought they might have to switch political parties again. If the Republicans continued to represent America's conservative and wealthier classes, that was not exactly the Mallinckrodt brothers' glass of wine. For his part, Emil wrote that "such slovenly wasteful administration as that of the United States [under Grant] would have to ruin every European nation at once."[29]

In fact, by this time Emil was so deeply disillusioned with U.S. politics that he published a six and one-half-inch long list of complaints in the *Westliche Post*, under the title "Anomalies." It was, he wrote, a republic

- where monopolies constitute the ruling power
- where the ignorance of the voters delivers the majorities
- where one cannot use the honest and capable people as lawmakers and administrators

• where the people is the common packass, ruled and exploited by the drudgery of rings and cliques

• where so-called legislatures meet to avoid law and right, or to set them aside to the advantage of individuals and corporations

• where the head of government carries on nepotism and economic favoritism

• where one sends diplomats abroad who disgrace the republic

• where the little thief is punished and the millionaire robber comes off respected and unpunished

• where money and property is the standard for nobility and privileges

• where, flying in the face of whatever legality is left, presidents and governors exercising power consider themselves justified to pardon villains and murderers, to turn them loose again on the poor honest people

• where churches and monasteries obtain tax freedom and may hold immense amortized wealth

• where expelled clerics of all countries come and are happily accepted

• where the affluence of the churches and their servants undermine morality and further dumbness and fanaticism

• where one looks down with obligatory arrogance on all other cultural nations, expecting salvation from the dead letters of so-called republican institutions, without knowing their nature, in the belief that their form is sufficient

• [where there is] a bureaucracy from which no preparatory knowledge is required and one is hired and fired according to the capriciousness of the President and the then-existent parties, with honesty and ability seldom an issue

• where patriotism goes as far as one's hope to cheat state treasuries

• where, increasingly, sinecures are endowed frequently and abundantly

• [where] efforts [are under way] to proclaim a Judeo-Christian Lord God as the basis for national legislation and thereby to declare so-called infidels illegal—to recognize free churches in free (!) states, etc.[30]

Another side of America's political life that was disturbing to many concerned Reconstruction. Strongly opposed by white Southerners who saw it as harsh and even tyrannical rule, Reconstruction ended in April 1877 when federal troops were withdrawn from South Carolina and Louisiana. Throughout the South, however, laws then were rewritten to "reinforce planters' control over their labor force" and to "protect property owned by whites." For blacks in the new South much was again the old South. The goals of free labor and egalitarianism had not been achieved; within that context Reconstruction was a failure.[31] At the same time, nearly every Southern state had a constitution that made free, but separate, public schools available for whites and for Negroes.[32] In St. Louis, too, by 1875 there was a well-established Negro public school system, including primary schools in most areas and even a high school for blacks.[33]

In these years when Julius and Conrad sat together, assessing the pluses and minuses of the politics that so interested them, they (like Cousin Emil) also had a lot to say about their old homeland. Sometimes they thought that German liberalism had become a diaspora, primarily of the "Thirty-er" and "Forty-eighter" immigrants in America.

In Prussia, for instance, liberalism had been weakened by years of war and authoritarian rule under King William I. The fragmented German states finally had been persuaded to rally around the most powerful one among them, namely, Prussia, and in 1871, after Prussia's victory in the Franco-Prussian War, the German states were officially unified. William I now was emperor of Prussia, and Otto von Bismarck was chancellor. Under their rule, liberalism in Prussia also did not advance. Often called the "Iron Chancellor," Bismarck's long cultural struggle (called the *Kulturkampf*) with the Roman Catholic church was fierce and iron-fisted. Mallinckrodts involved in that struggle paid a heavy price for their principles.[34] Bismarck's campaign against the growing workers' movement led by Socialists was equally as ruthless.

Emil's Losses, Julius's Will

Conrad's and Julius's discussions, as always, centered also on events within the big Mallinckrodt family. And they often were sad occurrences. In St. Louis, for instance, Emil had had news that his deceased brother Eduard's widow Dorothea died in 1874—the last Mallinckrodt to be listed in Dortmund's directory of residences and businesses.[35]

In fact, Emil seemed increasingly pessimistic. In 1874, he published a strong critique of the Emancipation Proclamation and its consequences. To this commentary, the editors of the *Westliche Post* appended the footnote, "From a highly respected hand whose articulations we nevertheless cannot always underwrite." Under the title, "The Emancipation of 1863," Emil wrote,

> Only through the greatest emergency—the danger of the Union's dissolution—could President Lincoln find himself so hard-pressed and authorized to suddenly declare 4 million slaves free by proclamation. But to unconditionally guarantee this liberation, therein lay a second great danger. As a firm basis for a newly ordered public good, the leap was too large and risky. Increasingly the conviction grows that through the rashness a terrible mistake was made which now scarcely can be changed or improved. Lincoln had to attach emancipation to prerequisites which Congress, as the rule-making body then in session, should have determined—for example, separation and mass emigration of the entire slave population to a bordering and seized territory, and total freedom related only to their permanent immigration there. And as if nature had foreseen this situation, there lay the Florida peninsula, very fruitful with an almost tropical climate, much more suitable to Blacks than to Whites for the planting and growing of appropriate products such as rice, sugar and cotton—big and fruitful enough to well feed 15 million people. Had the Congress transferred to the slaves this piece of earth, as justified compensa-

tion for their long servitude and unpaid work, to own and inherit when few white settlers were there, so by making Florida into a pure Negro state the government would have completely compensated them for giving up their rights. . . .

Where they are almost equal in number, the black and caucasian races will never be able to develop themselves naturally. Each will be harmed and inhibited by the other, but especially the whites who will sink from their higher cultural and psychological level, as well as intellectual abilities. In constant contact with a lower population, they will fall back in intelligence and moral development, as well as material achievement, especially when compared to the northern states populated by Caucasian races.

Also criticizing the proposed Civil Rights Bill in Congress as inadequate to protect Negroes, Emil called it an "absurdity" and said Congress would have done better to create a really responsible "Freedmans Saving Bank" to help freed slaves being exploited by whites. "They would have been better off in slavery," he contended, "because it was at least in the interest of their masters to protect them."[36]

Emil's unhappiness with the political situation in America went much further than the race question. On 4 July 1876, he wrote a deeply disturbed commentary that contrasted sharply with the joy he had felt on his first Fourth of July in America:

The worst consequences of our first separation from the mother land [the American War of Independence against England] was the criminal slave war from 1861 to 1865! What destruction of human life, family happiness, property, and almost unpayable debts we mad white people brought upon ourselves. The unity of patriotic togetherness was disturbed and the well-being of the entire country undermined for the length of a generation. Have we not also since our so-called liberation carried out innumerable Indian wars which still continue? Most of them were and still are caused by the lack of justice and land-hunger of white invaders and their government, assuring the pending elimination of the natives in thanks for the rich inheritance of which they were robbed. . . .

Despite our rich resources, are we not nevertheless extraordinarily in debt? Are not our elections bought through bribery and deception? Do not the people permit clever lawyers, party hacks and political tricksters to lead them around by the nose? Are competent and honest candidates sought? Would they until now have been hired as civil servants if they had not first been party servants? Has not bloody death through acts of violence with revolver and knife, through murder and assassination, become more and more common? Are robberies of public funds, serial robberies, and mass murder on railroads rare? Are criminals firmly punished or more frequently pardoned? Are not our bloody deaths a shame to the 19th century, as well as the prevalent dishonesty of our entire public administration and system of law? Is life and property holy here and secured? Are not all the bankruptcy laws partial to the debtors and slanted against the property of the creditor? Is not the entire land overrun with predation?[37]

Emil's unhappiness would grow even deeper, indeed become tragic. In December 1876, the St. Louis family carried its promising chemist son and brother Otto to the Bellefontaine Cemetery to be buried in the family plot. As his brother Gustav, in Switzerland for a health cure, wrote their cousin Gustav II in Köln,

> My dear brother Otto (the youngest of we three in the business) died on 30 December, 5 days after a cold developed into serious pneumonia. He was the favorite, as well as pride, of the family, a naturally very talented and very active person in his field. My attachment to him was extraordinary, and, therefore, I am doubly sad that I was not there at the time. For our good, old father, the loss will be never-endingly painful because the blessed one [Otto] was the friend of his [Emil's] old age. He was in the 30th year of life.[38]

Now sons Eduard (thirty-one) and Gustav (thirty-six) were left to continue the chemical business and Emil junior (sixteen) and Oscar (fourteen) to be groomed for it. In June 1875, Emil's son Eduard had married Jennie Anderson in a much-celebrated wedding, and Emil dared to hope that that son and the others now would be well.

Less than six months after Otto's death, however, Emil mourned again. Now he himself wrote Gustav II in Köln of the second death in the family—that of his first-born son Gustav (III), at the age of thirty-seven. Sometimes Emil almost thought his children had been "hexed"—so many so full of promise gone so soon.

Apparently Gustav already had been very ill in Switzerland when he wrote Köln of his brother Otto's death. As father Emil reported, Gustav's "strong will to again reach his homeland sustained him up until he got there—but then he completely broke down on his brother's fresh grave. . . . After such a long, painful separation, we had the joy of having him with us only 14 days."

Then on 31 May, taking along his brother Emil, Gustav left St. Louis by train for Denver, since his "last hope was healing in the high altitudes of Colorado." "I shared his hope," wrote father Emil, "that he would be preserved for us yet longer. I could not comprehend the idea of losing him." As Emil recalled his son Gustav's departure, "No complaint about his long suffering ever crossed his lips. On the evening he left us, he exhausted himself with loving words for our happiness and told his sister how hard it was for him to leave us again so soon. But he must become well in order to be able to help Eddy [with the business]."

Gustav, ill and suffering from weak lungs possibly inherited from his mother, arrived in Denver two days later, "exhausted from his 900-mile trip." A friend there had prepared everything for his arrival, but within days Gustav Mallinckrodt III was dead, on 5 June 1876. "The dear tired wanderer now came to rest," his father wrote, and "in death as in life rests at his brother's [Otto] side."

As for himself, Emil could only add, "We lost the same happiness with my Otto as with Gustav. We enjoyed Heaven's greatest blessing in these children. I am now 71 years old and what still maintains me is the love for my remaining dear ones." Emil meant especially Edward, then 32: "The entire burden of a big business, which the three loyal brothers had carried together, now lies with my mature Eduard. They had finally worked their way through a difficult enterprise, and so we all are struck by a gruesome fate. My two youngest boys of 15 and 16 [Oscar and Emil, Jr., respectively] can give Eddy only a bit of help."[39]

All of this personal sadness may have affected Emil's public outlook. His position on race relations, for instance, had hardened. When he again took up the issue in an 1876 *Westliche Post* article, he continued to base his diagnosis and prognosis on the problematic presumption of racial superiority/inferiority:

> If one thought that the elimination of slavery and legal equality for those freed solved the Black question, so one was fundamentally wrong. . . . The race question, which has much more serious consequences and complications, has replaced the former question of slavery. It is a Pandora's Box containing all kinds of disruptions and acts of violence, to the unhappiness of both races and the entire Union caught up in joint suffering at every step.
>
> In fact, the racial differences between the Caucasian and Negro tribes are too far apart, further than all other races on earth. They are too crass to ever be bridged or erased by legal decisions and efforts at equality. Racial differences are a stamp and impression which Nature indelibly imprints. . . . The Caucasian is and remains master, wherever he comes together with other races. His impulsive intellectual and physical characteristics are significantly different. Nature indeed does not create an organism according to a stereotype. But despite all individual differences within the races, they are always separated by their clearly recognizable, given character. . . .
>
> Under these relationships as they now exist, Negroes in the southern states will forever remain a subordinated, separated caste, a foreign element, the pariahs among the whites, a mixture which is inassimilable. Nothing, however, could have more corrupting consequences than blood relationships with the colored, against which the whites may maintain a natural self-respect! We see the hopeless results of general race-mixing in Mexico, the West Indian islands, and South America as a visible warning example.
>
> One thought the sudden, unconditional freeing and legalized equality of the former slaves and their masters was a wartime measure justified by the emergency. But it was nothing less than a violent, highly dangerous experiment, as was also just seen in the presidential election.

In answering his own question of whether nothing could be done to modify the situation, Emil answered, "Separation!" This time Texas was his choice location, followed by northern U.S. and European immigration to fill up the empty spaces where blacks formerly lived: "We have, after all, the historical example of the Israelites leaving Egypt, where they possessed no land and were kept as slaves and were robbed of all hope for equality with the Egyptians. There the white Moses chose the only possible salvation from servitude for his people through the well-known exodus which saved his nation and its religion from destruction."[40]

At the Hermann Mallinckrodts, meanwhile, there was a more positive mood. Their son John Friedrich, heeding the advice of the American publisher/politician Horace Greeley to "Go West, young man," had done just that around 1873. Finding no work for machinists in Denver, he went to the mills and mines in the mountains. Living in a log cabin at the edge of the silver town, Bonanza Mine, he saved a few hundred dollars, built a little cabin, and after two years married Josephine Weigel.

Life in the West was not easy, however, especially for the working class. At the mine there were troubles with strikers, and John Friedrich reported that he was almost lynched. When Bonanza went broke, he and Josephine moved to another mining camp where he supervised machinery at the Silver Quartz Mill. There he invented an absorption and filtration system to purify the air of the mill in the interest of the workers' health, but the company would not install it. The story was the same at other smelters, increasing John Friederich's disillusionment with business owners and managers.[41]

Moving to the foothills of the Rockies, he had another of his inspirations— while working on a Pullman railroad coach in the machine department of a corporation, he conceived of an air brake for railroad cars. "It was an entirely new principle in railroading," he would write. After successful testing and praise from engineers, John Friedrich founded the Mallinckrodt Brake Company, got some cash and stock, and thought he was on the way to being well off. His sales brochure, listing St. Louis as the company's home address and a Colonel Had as president, included drawings of his invention, as well as detailed descriptions of its operating principles and advantages.[42] However, another existing safety appliance company killed his fortunes through economic maneuvers, sending him back to the machine shop.[43]

In the late 1870s, Hermann and Luise were interested in moving west to join John Friedrich. But James Ferdinand still lived in St. Louis and Delia, as well.

From Germany came news in 1876 that saddened all the American Mallinc-krodts—their cousin Hermann, the famous retired Catholic politician who had done battle with Bismarck in the so-called Kulturkampf (cultural struggle) over principles of religious freedom, had died in Berlin in May.[44] Like Uncle Arnold the publicist, Hermann, too, had made the Mallinckrodt name a symbol for principled political struggle. As a member of Parliament and a leader of the Center Party that fought for freedom of religion and church organizations, Hermann had challenged the Iron Chancellor at many turns of the road.[45]

Hermann's sister, Sister Pauline, meanwhile was strengthening and expanding her religious order. She had even made a successful trip to the United States in 1873 and was working on plans to found and headquarter an American branch of the Sisters of Christian Charity in Philadelphia.[46] By 1877 in the United States, "the Sisters of Christian Charity now had twenty houses there; eleven in Pennsylvania, two in New Jersey, one in Michigan, four in Minnesota, and two in Louisiana. Besides these, a motherhouse where the provincial and her assistants could reside, where young women could enter the postulancy and the novitiate and make their vows, and where, as young Sisters, they could be trained as teachers, was being built in Pennsylvania!"[47]

With all the recent deaths in the family, it was not surprising that Julius wrote his will in 1877, making his son Hermann Adolf, who lived nearby, his executor.[48] (Julius had already bought cemetery plot 34 around 1860.[49]) It would have been understandable, then, if there was a sigh and the comment "Bruder, wir sind nicht mehr jung" ("Brother, we are no longer young") when Julius and Conrad shared their annual birthday *Kaffee und Kuchen* hours in spring 1879 (3 May for Julius, 2 June for Conrad).

Missouri's Outlaws
in the 1880s

If the post–Civil War reconstruction period ended in the late 1870s, then the next decade, so said forward-looking citizens, should be one of technological and economic growth. And it was, in part. It started off, however, with a reminder that the end to some old chapters had not yet been written.

There were still the Missouri outlaws, for instance, especially the notorious James gang. Determined to stop them once and for all, Missouri's Governor Crittenden took a controversial step—he offered a reward for their capture. Since state statutes limited public reward money to three hundred dollars, the Governor in 1881 turned to the railroads.[50] They gladly offered a large reward of fifty thousand dollars since they had been the victims of the outlaws often enough. Crittenden then proclaimed a five thousand dollar reward for Jesse James's arrest and another five thousand dollars for his conviction; identical rewards were put out for Jesse's brother Frank.

The public reaction was interesting. While Missourians had had enough of the bandits, the railroads were bitterly unpopular, too. They were seen as robbers of a different kind, and not everyone was enthusiastic about railroad "bounty" money. Nevertheless, the concentrated search was on. Since many of the outlaws had already been killed or imprisoned, for the "James boys," too, it was only a matter of time.[51]

Emil Mallinckrodt was but one of many Missourians deeply troubled by the atmosphere of lawlessness in the state. Writing in the *Westliche Post*, he criticized Governor Crittenden, adding

the scoundrel (*Hallunken*) brothers Ford travel about the country with loaded revolvers in their hands. For money they present their crimes against banks to the frightened citizenry which idolizes their heroic courage, a model for American youth already beginning with dangerous toy pistols and later extending that to [sitting on] school benches with six-shooters in their pockets. No wonder then that murder and robbery on the railroad is again reported—after all, Mr. James junior recently was acquitted by an enlightened jury to the jubilation of the people present! . . .

After our sad experience, no policeman, executive employee, teacher who disciplines a boy in his school, editor who exposes rascality, not even the President of the country himself is sure of his life. Almost every controversy is settled with murder weapons, according to the pattern of Middle Ages barbarians known as "family feuds."[52]

Colt's invention of the revolver is and remains a curse on the land but, along with the "lynch law," arose out of the necessities of the American situation for self-protection where state protection failed.[53]

While the hunt for the James brothers went on in Missouri in the early 1880s, another violent event marked the times—the assassination of yet another U.S. president. James Garfield was shot in July of 1881 at the railroad station in the nation's capital by a mentally unstable and disappointed office-seeker. The president had been in office for only about a year. Once again, as in the case of Lincoln, the killing was political dissent turned violent—President Garfield and his assassin belonged to different wings of the Republican Party.[54] Not a few people wondered if the Civil War's legacy of violence would ever end. And some, along with Emil Mallinckrodt, asked whether "through the enmity and incitement against the sincere President, do not the presumptuous demagogues of the country then share responsibility with the miserable criminal?"[55]

Sometimes technology—from which so many people expected so much in the post-war period—failed and also brought death. In December 1881, for example, newspapers delivered to the Mallinckrodts in Missouri's countryside told of a disaster at the county's bridge over the Missouri River at St. Charles. It was the second disaster in about a year, for in November 1879 a whole span of the bridge had given way; a freight train with seventeen cars of livestock fell into the river and at least nine people lost their lives. Now in December 1881, a heavy freight train of thirty-one cars went down the same way, killing the engineer and injuring the fireman and brakeman.[56]

Such "streaks of bad luck"—misfortunes people felt they were powerless to influence—were interrupted sooner or later. Missouri's outlaw affair, for instance, finally ended in 1882. Jesse James was killed in April, and his brother Frank surrendered in autumn. The governor's reward, mostly railroad money, had motivated two members of Jesse's own gang to plot against him and kill him. As a local historian of the time, telling the story of the Ford boys "who had been tutored as juvenile robbers by the skillful Jesse," bitterly wrote, "The Fords went there [Jesse's home in St. Joseph], and when the robber's back was turned, Robert shot him dead in the back of the head! . . . the "Terror of Missouri" was effectually and finally "removed," and people were glad he was dead. Robert Ford, the pupil of the dead Jesse, had been selected, and of all was the most fit tool to use in the extermination of his preceptor in crime."[57]

While the killing would never have made the governor "many enemies among the better class of citizens of this State," wrote the historian, what happened next was another matter.[58] The assassins pleaded guilty to murder, were convicted and sentenced to hang for the killing, and then were pardoned by the governor! That brought "an uproar because of the suspicion that the governor had contracted with criminals to slay Jesse James."[59] Clearly twenty thousand dollars had been paid as reward money, but the problem was that Governor Crittenden did not say to whom. That, according to Duden country historians, was "the worst feature of the case . . . the lack of explanation, or the setting forth of sufficient reasons, as is customary in issuing pardons."[60]

In that atmosphere of political suspicion, James's banditry was forgotten but his betrayal was not. Legends and song about it went into Missouri folklore as a statement suggesting that during the Civil War violence, indeed, had become as American as apple pie and that loyalty remained a cardinal frontier principal. Not long after Jesse James's death, Emil Mallinckrodt wrote accusingly about that public mood:

> And even in our St. Louis it presently becomes astonishingly clear what tender attention one gives to western banditry. Just now it was reported that the mourning widow of Jesse James, accompanied by a pretty young woman, arrived at the Southern Hotel and was surrounded by reporters. A few, the favored who were admitted, declare that the widow was a lady of education and talent who told them that her blessed husband had been a tender husband and father. She had come here on business, to publish the biography of her husband and his brother, in cooperation with the mother of these heroes. From the sale of the book she would have an income permitting her to rear her children. This book, after all, will sell quickly as appropriate reading material for instruction and imitation by enterprising American youth![61]

The St. Louis Family

In St. Louis, on the other side of the state and far from the shootouts and robberies, the fortunes of the Mallinckrodt family were a mixed picture. By spring 1879, Emil wrote his cousin Gustav II in Köln, "You cannot imagine the six-year-long decline of *all* values, especially real estate. At the same time, taxes have increased. That unholy Civil War with all its ruinous consequences! Since the beginning of the year a reaction has set in which permits us to be hopeful."

The upswing, however, had not yet personally benefited Emil, who for some years already apparently was depending primarily on real estate transactions for his income: "I have not been in a position for the last 15 years to sell a *single* foot of ground—a depressing situation! . . . All our friends here, have lost steadily for ten years and many are poor, especially those who owned a lot of real estate property. And yet St. Louis has constantly grown, and businesses, especially factories, have multiplied greatly."

Within the family, however, they would be happy, Emil wrote, if the loss of two sons (Otto and Gustav) did not weigh so heavily on them: "The more time that passes since their loss, the more difficult it is." On the other hand, he reported,

> Through touching sacrifice and all love, my loyal Eduard does all he can to substitute for his brothers. He has good success in the business the three brothers founded and is happily married with a healthy son [Eduard Theodor, Jr.]. My good daughter Adele is also content with a fine husband and three children. My two youngest boys are both grown [Emil junior nineteen, Oskar eighteen] and are studying chemistry to be able to help their brother. He already employs 50 persons, and the business constantly grows larger.[62]

About a year later, however, Emil again had sad health news to report to Köln—another case of lung illness among his children. The youngest son of his second marriage, Oskar (also spelled "Oscar"), was afflicted, perhaps infected by his late brothers. "It is the heavy hand of fate, constantly weighing on us, that brings us here," Emil said, writing from North Carolina:

> My youngest, Oskar, now 19 years old, has suffered from consumption for 1½ years, although he had become as strong as a tree. Already since early December, we parents now have been traveling around, trying to support his cure. We spent the winter in South Carolina and, following the climate, then came to this high mountainous area [Hendersonville, N.C.], and are ready with the temperatures to go south to Georgia.
>
> Oskar's brother Emil left again this morning for the 1000-mile trip back to St. Louis after we enjoyed his monthly visit. He is working with his brother Eduard, whose business has made good progress.

As for himself, Emil wrote sadly, "I am now 74 years old and deeply depressed [*niedergebeugt*] with incurable heartaches and new sorrows."[63]

Not long thereafter, in fall 1881, Emil junior went to Wiesbaden to do additional study in the laboratory of Professor Fresenius, where his older brothers also had learned their chemistry. But he was under time pressure, for as his father wrote, "It is important that Emil returns next year to support his brother . . . Eduard's business flourishes and grows constantly. It is *too much for one* to manage alone." As for youngest son Oskar, Emil reported that he had spent two years in the southern states and for the past several months was "in the high altitudes of Mexico (7,800 feet elevation) with hopeful prospects of being cured." Pessimistic, as usual, about his own health, Emil said, "my days, too, are numbered, for I already have 76 years full of worry and distress behind me." He and his wife still lived at their rural home ten miles west of St. Louis, "alone and lonely," as he put it.[64]

In 1882, Eduard incorporated the Mallinckrodt Chemical Company, which he and his late brothers had founded in 1867 under the name G. Mallinckrodt Company. Eduard would be president of the renamed company, helped by twenty-two-year-old Emil junior, who had returned to St. Louis from his studies in Germany in late 1883.[65] They were the brothers Eduard and Emil Mallinckrodt of St. Louis, just as their father and uncle had been the brothers Eduard and Emil of Dortmund.

By 1883 they began to manufacture photographic materials and in 1884 opened a sales office and warehouse in New York.[66] As Emil senior said, his son's business was then "the largest west of New York and Philadelphia." But father Emil worried that Eduard would work too much and damage his health. He hoped that Emil junior would now ease the burden, since help from youngest brother Oskar was not forthcoming. He could not tolerate the St. Louis climate and was instead "far away in southern New Mexico and Texas and then on the way to old Mexico because of his health and work. He is 6 feet tall, strongly built, with a vigorous appearance."[67]

By early 1885, Oskar was indeed in Chihuahua, Mexico, where he found the climate good but had not yet really settled in.[68] Eduard's business was constantly growing, and a plant was planned in New Jersey (it opened in 1887).[69] By 1889, the company had extended into offices in New York and New Jersey.[70] Thus, Mallinckrodt Chemical was directly taking on the eastern competition that had laughed at its beginnings. Although Eduard's administrative work was too strenuous for one person alone, he could not expect assistance from his brother Emil junior, who was busily working in the company's chemical department.[71]

Emil senior, of course, was too old to help with the business. Instead, he read and wrote a great deal and continued to be as amazed by St. Louis's growth as he had been over the decades. By 1885, he reported, the population had reached nearly five hundred thousand. At the same time, he admitted that St. Louis had been outstripped by Chicago, as predicted.[72]

Looking back over his own long life in St. Louis, Emil saw past personal mistakes that he regretted. As he wrote Gustav II,

> My heart has always told me to also admit to you, son of your dear father, how deeply I regret that I acted ungratefully against him who was my best friend—although not on purpose, but rather through failure to recognize and judge correctly my relationship and my obligations to one who was my second father. I am deeply sorry that I did not confess my regret while he lived—unfortunately the insight came too late—that I alone and entirely bore the guilt which I cannot make good. In many respects I am depressed by fates which weigh heavily and trouble my old age—I am already 78.[73]

In another letter, Emil also mentioned empathetically his other cousins in America. He wrote Gustav II in Köln, "Your uncles Julius, Conrad, and Hermann are still living and, like I, nearly 80. Three Mallinckrodt women are also in the same age."[74] Almost as a generational and immigrant's lament, Emil added, "All of us have experienced sad fates; may you and yours be spared that."[75] Nevertheless, through sons, the Mallinckrodt name from Dortmund would continue in the New World, even if old Haus Mallinckrodt on the Ruhr (plate 17) had passed out of the family about 1881, and in Dortmund itself the name no longer gave honor and prestige to public service.

As the end of his life neared, Emil intensively carried out a family tradition, namely, writing for the public about politics as his father had. For years the family scribe, sharing observations of American life with Germany through his letters, Emil wanted to write more for Americans, for readers of the *Westliche Post* of St. Louis. One subject he discussed again and again was the nature of the U.S. political system. Emil had come to oppose its voting practices, as well as the federative form of sharing power between national and state governments. Indeed, at one point he advocated a constitutional monarchy. In short, Emil Mallinckrodt supported an elitist theory of government.

Emil's view of the American political system was expressed in a lengthy editorial entitled "Who Shall Govern?" At the end of it, the *Westliche Post* editors added a note: "Although once more not entirely agreeing with our respected colleague, we nevertheless present his thoughtful article to our readers with welcome, reserving the right to comment at our convenience":

> A democracy where everyone can vote and naked numbers decide is a form of government which cannot lead to good. Indeed, if votes could be measured and weighed according to their value and only so many counted, then it would have meaning. But the votes of the most enlightened statesmen and patriots do not count more and are nullified through the worst demagogs or dumb majority. . . .
>
> According to an ideal, the best would be a unitarian, simple, permanent government which knew how to attract talent, that included a strict sense of justice and humanity, which would be placed at the head of the legal and administrative system. This picture would perhaps be most like a constitutional, hereditary monarchy, although even it, like every human institution, would have its weaknesses. No form of government protects against the misfortune which people everywhere prepare for themselves through their ignorance and wickedness. . . .
>
> Whatever peoples have won in regards to progress was thanks to their few great thinkers, statesmen and clever leaders with ideals and practical goodness, the men of science as well as of genius who created the most important discoveries. Nature manifests itself very aristocratically in the rarity of great minds. Lies therein not a suggestion about who should rule the human race?[76]

Emil Mallinckrodt also continued his attacks on voting rights for blacks. As late as 1888—two decades after the Civil War—he wrote: "The sudden granting of the voting right to the just freed slaves has shown itself to have been a dangerous gift to them. It deeply offended the entire white population and inflamed envy, hate, and violent behavior. In addition, it gave possession of their votes to demagogues and wire-pullers. If the blacks had been smart, they would never have made use of their right to vote. Twenty-five years after their emancipation, that would have been better for them."[77]

The Family in the Countryside

Around Augusta, family news concerned primarily the younger generation, for Julius and Conrad surely were becoming the "old-timers." In April 1884 Conrad's sons were married—Theodor Feldmann to Carolina Sehrt and Albert Feldmann a week later to Carolina's sister Elisa. (The Sehrts were immigrants from Elze in the Kingdom of Hanover.[78]) The family tradition Julius and Conrad had started when they both found second marriage partners in the sisters Böhmer was thus continued. Conrad's younger daughter, Dorchen, also married a Sehrt, Hermann Heinrich, in late 1885. Whether the young couple lived with widowed father Conrad is not clear, although it is probable that they did.

It is known, however, that Albert and Elisa did live close by, just to the west of the big brick family home on the hill, in a log-house structure in the valley. (A frame house was built next to it in 1889 before Albert and Elisa's first son was born.) Albert worked some of his father's land, as did son-in-law Hermann Sehrt who rented Conrad's flourishing orchards as well.[79] Theodor, on the other hand, seems to have left the home place after his marriage to Carolina in the Femme Osage church; they moved across the Missouri River to the settlement of Boles where Theodor's mother had lived. There they farmed and their first child was born.

At Julius's, life also was slowing down. His orchards and vineyards were doing well, and son Hermann Adolf, living nearby, probably did a good part of the work. Augusta, in fact, seemed to have a promising future with these crops. The wine hall in the village was doing a good business, and George Muench had opened the Mount Pleasant winery and cellars in 1881.[80] In St. Charles, the nursery of Julius's son Conrad Theodor was prospering.

In his last years, Julius was especially pleased by a photo of his first American-born son, Conrad Theodor (plate 15). Photography, Julius thought when they gave him the picture, was another of those wonderful developments, recalling the daguerreotype brother Hermann had had made of his family in Milwaukee in 1849 (plate 11), the pencil sketches done of brother Conrad (plate 16) and Wilhelmina a decade ago, and the colored drawing of himself (plate 13).

There was an especial joy, too, in these years for Julius and Conrad—people compiling the history of St. Charles County came out to Augusta to talk to the old immigrants. Encouraged to tell about their achievements during a half-century of difficult life on the American frontier, they did so enthusiastically. They wanted to share some facts and highlights about pioneer efforts in education and horticulture, for they believed history was a precious and reliable guide for the future. They feared, moreover, that here in a new land, unlike in their Dortmund home, the valuable past would be neglected in the race toward so-called progress, which worshipped only that which was new.[81]

Conrad had not forgotten the words his favorite author James Fenimore Cooper had put into the mouth of Hawkeye, the white guide in *The Last of the Mohicans*. Contrasting the knowledge of youth and the wisdom of age in the white and Indian cultures, the guide had said, "Your young white, who gathers his learning from books and can measure what he knows by the page, may conceit that his knowledge, like his legs, outruns that of his father; but where experience is the master, the scholar is made to know the value of years, and respects them accordingly."[82]

The experience Julius especially wanted to tell the historians about concerned how the Missouri River ended his dream of a new Dortmund. The river was still playing tricks, and people should understand that it always would. For instance, there had been heavy rains and flooding in spring 1880 and Augusta had to spend money repairing damages to streets and dikes; again in 1881 there was the work of cleaning debris from the bluff road leading to Hancock Bottoms.[83] After each flood the river changed again. By the time Augusta signed its agreement with the railroad, it would have to ask for crossings over the tracks out to where the boat landings were.[84] If the trend continued, one day there would be a strip of land between the town's southernmost street and the river, whereas the street once had fronted the water.[85]

When the county history was published, the Mallinckrodt brothers must have been pleased that their views were on record. On the other hand, they may have grumbled over errors in dates,[86] even of their own immigration—"Should have been 1831/1832 for Julius and 1836 for Conrad." And they probably also wondered very loudly why local folks had not yet learned to read properly the German letters in *Heßen* as H-e-s-s-e-n and instead wrote "Hespers"![87]

The old farmers chuckled, though, when they read the biography the historians had written for their Augusta friend, wine grower and musician John Fuhr. For some years now (beginning in 1884), farmers had been having a hard time of it again, and their agriculture organizations were targeting causes such as eastern moneyed interests, middlemen, railroads, industrial monopolies, and gold standard advocates.[88] About all of that, and John Fuhr, the county historians had written,

> Formerly Mr. Fuhr carried on the manufacture of boots and shoes quite extensively, and worked from ten to fifteen men. Now, however, the protective tariff upheld by Republican rule has had the effect to place the boot and shoe manufacturing industry, as almost every other industry has been placed, in the hands of a few

large manufacturing capitalists, who have crowded all men of limited means out of the different manufacturing industries, and forced them to go to work at daily labor in large factories, or to engage in other pursuits. Mr. F. makes a few boots and shoes yet, but does nothing in this line at all to what he formerly did. He has a good vineyard, which the protective tariff, and the men made rich by it can't crowd him out of. He makes about 2,800 barrels of excellent wine every year.[89]

"Wahrheit im Wein" (truth in wine), Julius and Conrad probably thought, recalling a favorite German saying. Fuhr's solution was eminently reasonable—stick with vineyards!

Fuhr's economic observations, moreover, reflected precisely the view of many in Duden country. Missouri's Germans were disgusted with the Republican Party and its protective tariffs favoring industry, just as Fuhr had said. In 1884, in fact, Carl Schurz and others formed a Reform Republican group to protest especially corruption and to support the Democratic candidate Grover Cleveland. Other liberal Germans in Missouri favored the growing Populist movement representing farmers, and still others supported splinter parties such as the National Greenback Labor Party. (There was not much German support for the Prohibition Party.) The election of Cleveland, the first Democratic president since Buchanan left office in 1861, signaled a turning of the tide and not only in farm states. Labor, too, felt itself under pressure and was increasingly organizing (merging some twenty-five different groups in the American Federation of Labor in 1886), and demands to regulate the railroads were loud in the land. In short, Democratic leadership was moving toward liberalism, while the Republicans were becoming more openly conservative.[90]

Julius and Conrad may have foreseen that before long Germans in Duden country would join a progressive effort (for example, the 1908 Progressive, or Bull Moose, Party of Theodore Roosevelt) to break away from Republican conservatism. Should that fail, it is almost certain that Julius and Conrad hoped the next generation of their countrymen would do as they themselves had done in 1861 and switch parties (this time to the Democrats) rather than abandon the liberal philosophy and politics that had brought the settlers to and so far in their adopted homeland.

Political forecasts aside, more realistic in the mid-1880s—and exciting to the Mallinckrodt old-timers with their saddles and buggies in the barns—was talk about the coming railroad. The Central Missouri Railway Company had requested a right-of-way at the foot of the bluffs where the line was to be built.[91] Of course the town of Augusta would grant it, and Conrad and Julius, too. (According to his estate settlement, Julius seemingly did so without even a legal deed.)[92]

That, they thought, was at least real progress. They could almost imagine the whistle of a train passing below the very hills where they now sat enjoying their Missouri eventide.

28

1880–1890s:
Their Stories End

The Mallinckrodt brothers at Augusta, though excited about the coming railroad line along their property, wondered whether they would live to see it. They had been eight Mallinckrodt immigrants from Dortmund in the 1830s, and now they were six, all three-score-and-ten.

Uncle Christoph's widow Aunt Helene had been the first to die, in 1840, and her daughter Sophie, once briefly married to Conrad, had remarried in the area. Uncle Detmar's son August had died in St. Louis, and Uncle Arnold's son Emil still lived there. Of Johann Friedrich Theodor Mallinckrodt's children only daughter Dorothea was still alive at home as were the three sons in America—Hermann (and his wife Luise), Julius, Conrad; their brothers in Germany (Gustav, Albert, Leopold) were already deceased.

Conrad

Conrad would be the first of them to pass away. Although the nature of his illness is not on record, he had had periods of sickness since about 1882. Augusta's German-educated physician, Dr. Gustavus Wieland, who had served his time in the Civil War and come to Augusta in 1881, attended Conrad, and pharmacist Dr. Louis Gerling provided him with medicine.[1] Their bills suggest that considerable medical care was available in a rural area of Missouri in the 1880s.[2] When Conrad died on 19 January 1887, at the age of about seventy-nine years and six months, he was buried in Julius's family plot in the Augusta Public Cemetery, next to his wife Wilhelmina (plate 18).[3] A lengthy citation added to his grave marker became illegible over the years.

Unlike his brothers and cousin Emil, Conrad fortunately had not lost his children in early deaths. All three born during his second marriage were alive, with established families, when he died. Since his wife had preceded him in death, Conrad's estate went to the children, Theodor F., Albert F., and Dorothea. The many records available about the settlement of that estate tell much about how Duden country immigrants lived and died in late nineteenth-century Missouri.[4]

In his will Conrad had named his eldest stepson C. A. Meinershagen as administrator. After Conrad's death, however, his children Albert F. and Dorchen (Dorothea) Mallinckrodt Sehrt, petitioned the court to replace Meinershagen, who could not put up bond, with Carl Wencker as administrator of their father's estate. (Son Theodor F., who did not live at Augusta but across the river at Boles, did not sign the request.) Conrad probably would have approved of his children's request, for thirty-five-year-old Carl Wencker was a relative of the earlier and deceased Carl Wencker who had been Conrad's travel companion of 1836. The younger Carl was the town's assessor and treasurer, as well as postmaster.[5]

The court granted the request and on 23 February named Augusta city fathers Fritz Tiemann and George Muench (also sons of Duden country's first immigrants) to accompany administrator Carl Wencker in examining Conrad's property and papers.[6] The inventory and appraisal they made showed $774.00 in U.S. bonds, forty-one acres of unbequeathed land, orchard rent of $21.25 owed by son-in-law Henry Sehrt, household possessions valued at $502.75, and "cash on hand $6.80."

In March and May the required newspaper notices of final estate settlement were published in the *St. Charles Cosmos*, and the deceased's outstanding bills began coming to administrator Wencker. There were wages owed son Albert F. and son-in-law Henry for farm work carried out in autumn 1886 (at $3.00 day), accounts with pharmacist Gerling, doctors Wieland and Clay, general store owners Wencker and Tiemann, vintner Henry Nahm, and lumber mill owner Feldmann. Taxes of $17.80 were due on 161 acres of land and one Augusta city block that Conrad and Wilhelmina had owned.

The promissory notes found among Conrad's papers showed that he had owed Helene Struckhoff $100.00 since late 1883 and Theodor Kahlkoff $742.56 since just the previous autumn, 1886. Since both Struckhoff and Kahlkoff were neighbors of Conrad (figure 22-3), the sums very probably were for land purchases. Written in an already quite shaky handwriting, Conrad's signature on the notes was underwritten by "Attest. Albert F. Mallinckrodt."

Prominent among Conrad's obligations were the promissory notes he had cosigned mostly for his children. They were all debts to Henry Meinershagen, Conrad's youngest stepson. The list of Conrad's cosigned notes prepared by the inventory takers read:

- Note of Theo. Mallinckrodt, dated Nov. 17, 1882, to Henry Meinershagen and by him endorsed. Balance of principle $100, 6 percent interest due thereon $7.75.
- Note of Albert F. Mallinckrodt, dated October 14 1881, to Henry Meinershagen and by him endorsed. $200, 6 percent interest due thereon $16.50.

• Note of Theo. Mallinckrodt and Caroline Mallinckrodt to Henry Meinershagen and by him endorsed. Date of note March 5, 1885. $100, 6 percent interest due thereon $6.00.

• Note of Fritz Kemner and Christine Kemner to Henry Meinershagen and by him endorsed, date of note June 20, 1884. Balance of principal $141.00, interest 5 percent due thereon $7.85.

To settle Conrad's estate, administrator Wencker next had some thirty sale posters printed (four dollars) and hired H. H. Buenemann to cry an auction (ten dollars) and George Muench to clerk it (two dollars fifty cents). With their help then, Conrad Mallinckrodt's worldly goods were put up for public sale on 7 April 1887.

Conrad's various roles in life—farmer, family head, intellectual, surveyor/scientist—were all reflected in the possessions offered the public. And, as characteristic of rural auctions, who bought what of those goods was another mirroring of how people lived and lived together in a community. They bought Conrad's goods not only out of need but also out of sentimental attachment to the deceased, wanting to remember him through some especially meaningful object. For such reasons, some thirty persons—family, neighbors, friends, acquaintances—bought goods that had once belonged to Conrad Mallinckrodt.

Interestingly, however, brother Julius was not recorded among the purchasers. In all probability, because of the close ties between the families, Conrad already had given to the Julius Mallinckrodts items of remembrance, or prior to the sale Julius had arranged with administrator Wencker to acquire certain things. On the other hand, at eighty-two, Julius may have been unable to attend because of illness; as early as 1869 Julius's signature already had shown evidence of palsy and he would die just a year after Conrad.[7] Thus it seems likely that Julius was represented at the sale of Conrad's belongings by a grandson (Alfred Nahm, who bought some of Conrad's books) and a son-in-law (Adam Rübeling, who bought farm produce).

The categories of goods sold and some of their purchasers included:

Farm Equipment and Produce. Men of the community generally bought these items—colter, plow, saw, wagon, buggy, chickens, corn, oats, lumber. Conrad's sons also bought some of the equipment that their father and they had used: Theodor bought a hoe, chain, mower, and scraper, and Albert bought a lot of garden tools, two bundles of barbed wire, two lots of lumber, ten sacks of wheat, and so on.

Household Furnishings. Daughter Dorchen and her husband Henry Sehrt (married only about one and a half years and still in the process of furnishing their home) purchased many pieces of furniture their father had lived with and utensils his household had used—iron kettle, lamp, bureau, chairs, stove, apple barrels, table, wash wringer and tub. His son Albert bought some furniture, too—a cupboard, five chairs, three beds. Family friend Carl Wencker acquired Conrad's rocking chair and a table.

Books. What had been inventoried as two shelves of library (assessed at $55.00) and books in drawers ($2.00) were sold in six separate lots divided by authors:

The *Laws of Missouri* were divided among eight different people, including son Theodor and friend Wencker, bringing a total of $6.75.

Shakespeare volumes went to son Albert, for $4.75.

James Fenimore Cooper volumes separated among four book-loving people, including son Albert, Julius's grandson Alfred Nahm, and friend Wencker, for a total of $5.75.

Bulwer volumes spread among seven different bidders, many going to son Albert, for a total of $15.25.

Volumes by Reuter were sold to two persons, son Albert and friend Wencker, for $1.30.

Latin books, going to son Albert, brought $3.00.

The total received for Conrad's books was $36.80, whereas they had been appraised for $57. His Brockhaus encyclopedias were neither inventoried nor put on sale, apparently having been bequeathed to his son Albert earlier. (Son Theodor later would write his cousin James Ferdinand that all the books were sold on public sale and that "brother Albert and I bought the books of foreign languages and sent them to St. Louis to a book merchant who sold them for us to students of those languages."[8])

Surveying/Science. With few exceptions Conrad's surveying and other scientific equipment brought more at the public sale than the items' appraised value.:

Compass/chain—Son Albert bought for $20.00 (appraised at $5.00).

Drawing apparatus—Son Albert bought for $1.35 (not listed in appraisal).

2 sets of surveying equipment—Inventoried but apparently bequeathed and/or sold to son Albert before the sale[9]

Barometer—Wencker bought for $4.00 (appraised at $2.50).

Telescope—Son Theodor bought for $5.25 (appraised at $3.00).[10]

Lot of chemicals—Son Theodor bought for $.50 (appraised at $1.00).

Alchemy scales—George Muench bought for $.50 (not inventoried).

Music. An organ, appraised at $20.00, was sold to Conrad's son Theodor for $15.00.

Miscellaneous. Other interesting possessions belonging to Conrad Mallinckrodt and sold at his public estate sale included two old guns (son Theodor bought the rifle, son Albert the shotgun); the gold ring and silver watch listed on the inventory were not available at the public sale and neither were the "2 sets of survey outfits."

Coming close to the inventoried value of $502.75, the public sale of Conrad's belongings brought $551.20. According to one document, in May 1889, two years after Conrad's death, each of his children received one-third—or $144.27 and two-thirds cents—of an inheritable balance. (Additional settlements may also have been made at other times.)

The legacy of Conrad's children was greater than that document indicated. Although Conrad's original will has not been located, it left his land to his three children: The "home place," Conrad's big brick house centrally located on the original "3 hills and two valleys" of the Mallinckrodts, went to eldest son Theodor. (He lived there all his life, using the family organ he bought at his father's sale to practice for his service as church organist, but leaving father Conrad's study securely locked as a family "holy of holies.") The valley west of the "home place" was bequeathed to son Albert, who had been living there since his marriage; the land farthest west was inherited by Dorchen (figure 20-1).

Following Conrad's death, the *St. Charles Demokrat* initially published a very brief notice of his passing, and a delayed, somewhat longer notice a week later referring to "the old Prof." The newspaper reported, "Despite the terribly bad roads, very many relatives and friends came to show the deceased the last honor. M. was among the oldest citizens of this region."[11] If there was a formal obituary, it might have mentioned what probably was Conrad Mallinckrodt's greatest, though nonmaterial, achievement—intellectual stimulation, direct or indirect.

His tutorial and teaching work was known. Perhaps he also gave supplementary tutorial instruction to his and Julius's children; clearly, part of Conrad's legacy to that generation was reflected in the purchase of his library by his sons, especially Albert. Unfortunately, though, Conrad's grandchildren would not know him. Theodor's first son, named well within the family tradition (Theodor Conrad), would be born a month after his grandfather's death; Albert's first child, daughter Elfrieda, was not quite two; Dorchen as yet had no children. Yet especially Albert, in turn, apparently passed on Conrad's love of books and learning—under very difficult circumstances, two of Albert's eight children and eleven of his fifteen grandchildren acquired higher education.

Julius

Across the hill from the brick house, Julius missed Conrad. How often they had stood together at family graves, and now he, the older brother, was left to mourn the younger. And how much time did he still have? He did not feel very well and had written his will several years earlier, adding a codicil on 21 March 1888 to deal with his U.S. bonds. Wanting to provide equally for everyone, he remembered wryly his early observation that frontier families having many children leave only piecemeal inheritances. His solution was to bequeath each (plus the children of his daughter Mathilde Wilkins, Paul J. and Annie) "free gifts or presents to establish themselves in life" and to request that "my real estate shall be sold in partition in public sale . . . the proceeds therefore shall be divided in even shares."[12]

Of the eleven children Julius had fathered—eight in his first marriage and three in the second—only six were alive: his sons Conrad Theodor (wife Emilie Fuhr) and Hermann Adolph (wife Auguste Koch), as well as four daughters Emilie (Wachs) Nahm, Anna Mueller, Louise Guggenmoos, and Wilhelmina (Meinershagen) Ruebling.[13] (They and grandson Paul J. Wilkins thus would each inherit one-seventh of the estate.)

Julius's children had married into Duden country's "first [immigrant] families," leaving him with many grandchildren.[14] Five boys would pass on the Mallinckrodt name—Conrad Theodor's sons Robert McClenny and Julius, and Hermann Adolph's sons Bertold, Otto, and William.

And so Julius Mallinckrodt died on his blufftop home—known in the family as "the Bluff"—near Augusta on 25 April 1888, a week short of his eighty-second birthday. He was buried, again with the Reverend G. von Luternau officiating, near brother Conrad in the Augusta town cemetery (plate 18). There Conrad's tombstone proudly read "born in Dortmund, Westphalen" and Julius's would say "born Dortmund, Prussia." Once again—and for the last time—the brothers Mallinckrodt were politically precise. Dortmund was part of Prussia when Julius was born in 1806 and within the Kingdom of Westphalia when Conrad had come into the world in 1808. They now rested together, probably in the shade of Mallinckrodt trees—ornamental trees Julius's son Conrad T. had given to the cemetery some years ago.[15]

The St. Charles newspaper, which Julius had so faithfully read, published the following obituary about a week after his death:

Mr. Julius Mallinckrodt, father of local nursery owner C. T. Mallinckrodt, died on 25 April on his farm near Augusta at the age of nearly 82. The following about the life of the deceased was shared with us by a member of the deceased's family:

Mr. Julius Mallinckrodt emigrated here at the end of 1831 and immediately settled on the farm at Augusta where he lived until now. With a great deal of effort and work he wrested land from the forest which within a few years rewarded his efforts and persistence with a beautiful home, where he founded a happy family.

In 1835 the deceased founded the nursery which later led to his renown. In 1861 he transferred it to his son Conrad Theodor who moved the business to St. Charles in 1863 where he continues it. In addition to the nursery, Mr. M. constantly developed his farm. He devoted special attention to the production of fruit for marketing and soon was successful, especially with apples. Planting the first larger orchards in the county exclusively for market production, he deserves the honor of having been the "Nestor" [wise old counselor] of orchard production in St. Charles County.

Mr. M. always took an active part in the political events of the state without ever striving for or having held a public office, other than director of the public grade school. He involved all his energy and strength for the school at the time the federal government gave the state an area of forest for the purpose of establishing a first school [probably early 1840s] which the citizens would then improve in honor of and to the benefit of the state. It gave the old man pleasant satisfaction to see the work in which he had so actively participated constantly being developed and perfected.

The United States and especially Missouri had become home to him from the moment he arrived and he thereafter acknowledged them as his home-land. He did not, nevertheless, ever lose interest in the land of his origin. The writer remembers not [sic?] with what attention and suspense the deceased followed the events in Europe during 1848–1871 and later and with what enthusiasm he greeted the final reconstitution of the German Empire. When Mr. M. chose America as his place of residence, he became an American. He devoted his entire heart and mind to his new fatherland, that of his descendants. But that could not extinguish his love and interest for his land of origin, and both feelings, undiminished, accompanied him until the end of his life.

In June 1832 Mr. M. married Mary E. McClenny and lived with her in happy marriage until September 1844 when his precious wife was taken from him through death, leaving him with 7 helpless children, among whom the oldest was 12 years and the youngest 9 months. In 1849 he married his surviving and sorrowful widow, then widow Rothert born Böhmer. In addition to his widow, Mr. M. leaves 6 adult and married children—2 sons and 4 daughters—in addition to 29 grandchildren and 2 great-grandchildren. Peace to his ashes and honor to his memory! (*Friede seiner Asche und Ehre seinem Andenken!*)[16]

Emil

The next of the old Mallinckrodt pioneers to die was Emil in 1892, on 9 May, at the age of eighty-six. Emil, who had worried so about his health and been ill so long, outlived his cousins Gustav, Conrad, and Julius, as well as his brother Eduard. Emil was buried in the Mallinckrodt family plot at Bellefontaine Cemetery in north St. Louis (plate 18).[17]

Like Julius, Emil left a second wife, Emilie Vollmann Mallinckrodt, to mourn him. Also like Julius, Emil had fathered many children. Four died in infancy and five more were born during his first marriage to Eleanor Luckie and then three in his second marriage to Emilie. Only four, however, were still alive at the time of Emil's death—Eduard Theodor (wife Jennie Anderson), Adele Mallinckrodt Schulenberg, and unmarried Emil junior (thirty-two) and Oskar (thirty).

At the end of his long and adventuresome life in St. Louis, Emil's obituary appeared in the *Westliche Post*, for which he had often written:

Emil Mallinckrodt

Yesterday at the very advanced age of 85 years one of our German pioneers, Mr. Emil Mallinckrodt, died at his country house at Centralia, St. Louis County. During two generations he lived and worked among us and his memory will be greatly honored in broad circles.

A born Westphalian, he combined with the firm character of his people a broad education which enabled him as counselor to have a well-deserved influence on his countrypeople. For a number of years he occasionally wrote interesting, educational articles for the *Westliche Post* which—they were usually famous through the initials E. M.—our readers will remember with pleasure.

The well-known and loved family of the deceased is certain of general sympathy. For some years the sons have carried on a chemical business here with great success, while a daughter is married to our old fellow citizen Mr. Aug. Schulenberg.

Countless friends mourn with the family the passing of an honorable old man. May the earth rest gently on him! [*Sei ihm die Erde leicht!*][18]

At some point a four-foot obelisk with Emil senior's name on it was placed in the center of the modest plot, with all the small family gravestones appropriately facing the early pioneer and founder of their St. Louis branch. With additional family members added, their tombstones today form a *U* around Emil's marker.

Hermann and Luise

Hermann and Luise, who perhaps had fewer serious illnesses than the other first Mallinckrodt immigrants to Missouri, did not lose each other through early death and lived to reach eighty-five and eighty, respectively. They had moved to Colorado, probably in the 1870s, to join their son John Frederick; daughter Delia had gone, too, to become a Denver high school teacher of German. Hermann and Luise had lived with Delia until 1893 and then moved to Boulder with son John.[19] There Hermann died in 1895 and Louise two years later, in 1897. Of the six children born during their frontier marriage, three had survived—two sons, James Ferdinand and John Friedrich, and daughter Delia.

A week after Hermann's death and burial in Columbia Public Cemetery in Boulder, his son John—the writer and inventor—wrote a tribute to his father in the Boulder newspaper. Although it is short on facts (for example, Hermann's work after he gave up farming) and sometimes long on son John's own philosophy, rather than father Hermann's (for instance, Hermann's initial attitude toward Prussian military service), the essay nevertheless is a spirited characterization of the family's early 1830s immigrants:

Herman Mallinckrodt
(A Study of Character)

In these day of almost Roman corruption, in which almost every man has his price and personal morality is looked upon as a lack of intellect, it is fitting to hold up to view the life of a man whose every act through all the vicissitudes of a long career exemplified courage, perseverance and the love of home.

In the death of Herman Mallinckrodt a strong character left our midst. His ancestors for centuries were among the strongest families of the German nobility; his immediate ancestors, recognizing that true nobility could only be based on nobility of character, threw to the dogs their titles and their coat of arms as fit only for a brood which true men nowadays stigmatize as Goulds and Vanderbilts and Rockefellers. Born of wealthy parents, their money bought off six years of the compulsory military service under the German monarch, but the one year of service, from which there is no escape, made him an American even while he served in that tyrant's army.[20] While beholding the spectacle of an army of able bodied men, unfortunately poor in purse, wasting by compulsion seven of the best years of their lives in playing soldier for a tyrant, preparatory to being made food for cannon— the mere caprice and selfishness of any of the crowned heads of Europe being able to precipitate death and destruction in an ignoble war—this roused Herman Mallinckrodt to take an oath that he would never rear soldiers for a tyrant. True to his oath, his wedding tour consisted in emigrating to America, there to raise a family of freemen. This was about 60 years ago.

"To the west, to the west, to the land of
    the free,
Where the mighty Missouri rolls down to the sea;
Where a man is a man if he's willing to toil,
And the humblest may gather the fruits of the
    soil."

Sixty years ago these words of our poet were strictly true—anyone willing to toil could be a man. Sixty years ago the railroad extended but a few miles west of Philadelphia. Ohio was the "west" and Missouri the "far west." After weeks of tedious travel by stage, canal and river, our hero with his bride reached Missouri. Out of the primeval forest, although raised in luxury, he hewed his farm. Here, free and unrestrained, in direct communion with nature his family grew. In every blade of grass, in every tree, he saw God, the unfathomable; with Thomas Paine, the World was his church, to do good his religion; and later when the agitation against slavery commenced, he was an ardent abolitionist. The civil war found him giving his quota of soldiers for the preservation of the union and the eradication of slavery. By word and deed he was an American. He was an American by choice, and enlightened native Americans are beginning to see that an American by choice is just as creditable a citizen as one who is born into American citizenship without any choice or effort on his part. Everyone acquainted with the history of Missouri knows that the "foreigners," especially the "Dutch," as ignorant people call the Germans, saved the state.

Herman Mallinckrodt wielded a powerful pen with an ease that was born of genius and strength, and in speaking he was truly eloquent when animated by his subject. His thoughts, whether expressed in English or German, were not subject to misinterpretation; his word picturing was so vivid that even the dull could see the great truths he was teaching. His illustrations and story telling were often so bright and comical that amid showers of tears of laughter the blind were made to see. Herman Mallinckrodt at 86 calmly died an unbeliever—an unbeliever in churchianity. An "infidel" is what men would call him, but I who have known him almost half a century, know that by self-conquest he achieved all the attributes ascribed to Jesus. He was a manly man from head to foot. He reached the highest form of immortality for he lives in the hearts of those who knew him. If christianity signifies true manhood then he was truly a christian. J.F.M.[21]

With Johann Friederich and Delia in Colorado, and James Ferdinand moving from St. Louis in 1917 to live with nieces and nephews in Salt Lake City, the western branch of the Mallinckrodt family was established.

August

The last detailed evidence of the life of Luise's brother August was his association with Friedrich Münch in Augusta in 1847–1850 and his presence there at the 1852 death of cousin Julius's son-in-law. In all likelihood, August soon thereafter moved from the Augusta area to St. Louis, to his sisters and brothers-in-law (Sophie and Wilhelm Amend, Lina and Louis Reutz, and Luise and Hermann Mallinckrodt). Whether August and Hermann worked together is unclear, as is the cause of August's death on 29 March 1859 at the age of fifty-one. Along with other members of his family, August was initially buried in Holy Ghost Cemetery in south St. Louis. In 1906, their remains were exhumed and cremated (plate 18).[22]

Sophie

Among the original Mallinckrodt immigrants from Dortmund, Sophie also became hard to trace. Following her divorce from Conrad and remarriage to Christian Koch, there were few reports of her whereabouts: A letter from Emil to his brother Eduard in 1847 said Sophie and Christian Koch had one child.[23] According to the 1850 census, the child was a girl named Clara, and by 1860 there also were two boys, Wilhelm nine and Moritz four.[24]

During the Civil War period there again was some mention of Sophie—Albert Mallinckrodt of Germany wrote his Missouri brother Hermann in 1865 that he had seen letters from Sophie Koch while visiting their sister Dorchen Metzmacher in Dortmund and that he, Albert, had been surprised to read of Sophie's opposition to President Lincoln's wartime tactics.[25]

Other clues to Sophie's family life are found in the 1870s. Possibly by then she was a grandmother, for in reporting on the whereabouts and events of immigrants in Missouri, Friedrich Münch wrote for a German-language periodical in Cincinnati that "Christian Koch and his brother Dr. Koch from Churhessen—the former still lives on his farm land near Augusta as farmer, beer brewer, and grape grower . . . both with children and grandchildren."[26] (On the county plat for the 1870s [figure 22-3], one of the blocks north of Augusta designated "40" seems indeed to be the C. Koch property referred to in the above report.) The 1870 census lists the Koch family with the three children at the family residence, but by 1876 Moritz, who would have been twenty-five years old, either was working away from home or was deceased.[27]

The final evidence of Sophie's family is the 1882 death notice of her husband, Christian Koch. The area's English-language newspaper described him as "an old and respected citizen," while Sophie herself in a signed letter to the German newspaper thanked all who had helped her and her children through the tormented weeks of her husband's dying.[28] No record of his burial or Sophie's can be found.[29] By the early 1900s, when a new plat was published, the name "C. Koch" no longer appears.

Helene

No evidence was found for the burial place of Sophie's mother Helene. Although German records indicate she died in St. Louis, there is no gravestone for her in St. Louis's Bellefontaine Cemetery where Emil and members of his family rest. While it is possible, then, that Helene was buried at Augusta on the tiny Mallinck-rodt plot behind Conrad's home, her gravestone must have deteriorated over the years, for there is none now.

The Property Legacy

After the deaths in the United States of the Mallinckrodt pioneers from Dortmund in the late 1880s and 1890s, much of their redistributed property remained within the family and does to the present time.

Augusta

The first redistribution of the Mallinckrodts' "three hills and two valleys" came in the years after Conrad and Julius's deaths (figure 28-1).

When contrasted to the earlier plat (figure 22-3), it is clear that Mallinckrodt land at the turn of the century included river bottom acreage formed through accretion (Section 22). The railroad, opened through the area in 1891 (figure 28-1), marked the former northern banks of the Missouri River.[30]

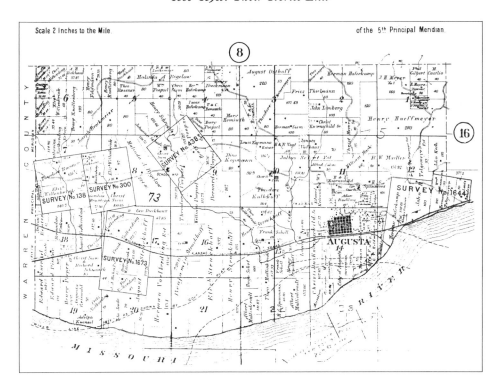

Figure 28-1. The second generation of Mallinckrodt property ownership along the Missouri River was shown in the St. Charles County atlas of 1903. (St. Charles County Atlas, *1903*.)

• The central one-third of the original Mallinckrodt property, including Conrad's brick house on the central hill where Julius and Emil had initially lived, was inherited by his son Theodor (Block 15). Today Conrad's "home place" (including the remains of his house) is owned by Earl G. Mallinckrodt, Theodor's grandson, who also retains some of Conrad's river bottom accretion land.

• The western one-third of the Mallinckrodt's original property was bequeathed by Conrad to son Albert. Today Hubert E. Mallinckrodt owns his grandfather Albert's "home place" house, as well as some of the bottom land accruing to Julius through accretion.

• Julius's eastern hill and Dortmund property passed from family ownership when it was sold at public auction in 1902 by his heirs after the death of Julius's widow Mary. The Schell family purchasers demolished Julius's buildings but preserved old family papers found in his house. A portion of the Dortmund field returned to Mallinckrodt ownership, that is, to the author, Julius's great niece, in the early 1990s.

St. Louis

Emil Mallinckrodt's property, which became the Mallinckrodt Chemical Company, remained in the family through his sons Eduard Theodor (1845–1928) and

Emil junior (1860–1929). (Oskar died in 1900.) By 1928 the company's worth was estimated at some 17 million dollars, and it had helped build the chemical laboratory bearing its name at Harvard University.[31]

This new prominence was reflected in the Bellefontaine Cemetery. When his wife Jenny died in 1913, Eduard had a family mausoleum built in sight of his father's tall marker on the old plot. In 1928 Edward, too, was interred in the tomb where the name Mallinckrodt is engraved above the door, along with a quote from the Twenty-third Psalm. Later historians would characterize him as a "wise businessman, warm family man, good friend" and say that he was "a liberal born and bred."[32]

Under the guidance of Eduard's Harvard-educated grandson Edward junior (1878–1967), the company went on to gain an international reputation for the purity of its chemicals. In 1942, Mallinckrodt became involved in the atomic age when Edward agreed to try to purify uranium in large amounts for the top secret Manhattan Project (which worked to produce the atomic bomb). Within three months, the company was producing a ton of pure uranium daily, called "a technological and industrial miracle" by Arthur Holly Compton, renowned physicist working on the University of Chicago project.

One key to that Mallinckrodt success was the company's traditional good relations with its workers. In the 1940s they were paid above-average wages and "became a family"; in the emerging atomic age, Edward junior from the beginning "insisted that employees wear respirators and go to Barnes Hospital for tests. Most other nuclear plants didn't take such precautions until four years later." Under the old Atomic Energy Commission, the Mallinckrodt Chemical Company later began "the first industrial hygiene and safety program in the uranium-processing industry."[33]

But like his grandfather Emil, Edward junior also had tragically lost sons who could carry on the name and business. Edward III died in 1932 in an airplane crash; a heart ailment took the life of Henry Elliott in 1945; in 1968, a year after father Edward junior's death, his last son George also was killed in the crash of a private plane.[34] All three sons are buried with their parents Edward junior and Elisabeth Elliott, in the family mausoleum, along with their grandparents. Mallinckrodt Chemical then passed out of the family but retains the famous name.

Plate 17. Haus Mallinckrodt on the Ruhr, in 1903, after it passed from family ownership, as depicted by Wilhelm L. F. Riefstahl. (*From* Bilder aus Westfalen von W. Riefstahl *[Elberfeld, 1859]. Courtesy Dortmund Museum of Art and Cultural History, Inv. Nr. C 5161.*)

Plate 18. Graves of six of the eight Mallinckrodt immigrants from Dortmund to Missouri
in 1831 and 1838 are extant. *Top*: The graves of
Conrad (front row) and Julius Mallinckrodt
(second row) and their wives Wilhelmina and
Marie, respectively, are among the oldest in
the Augusta, Missouri, Public Cemetery (*courtesy Richard Goldmann*). *Middle*: The obelisk
honoring Emil Mallinckrodt in the Bellefontaine Cemetery in St. Louis is surrounded by
smaller graves of family members (*courtesy Roland Mallinckrodt*). *Bottom*: August Mallinckrodt's ashes were preserved with those of
other family members, but the location of the
urn is unknown (*courtesy Philip A. Mallinckrodt*). The gravestone of Hermann and Luise
Mallinckrodt at their burial site in the Boulder, Colorado, Public Cemetery has not been
located.

Epilogue

The old pioneers did not live to read the ironic footnote to their family's history written in 1903: in Germany the Prussian government recognized the old nobility and Mallinckrodts were again "vons." In Missouri, on the other hand, the first eight 1830s Mallinckrodt immigrants from Dortmund—Emil, Julius, Conrad, Sophie, Helene, Hermann, Luise, and August—had wrenched their own nobility from frontier soil, forests, and books. While that would not be recorded on genealogical tables, it was a rich legacy for descendants and communities who knew not only how but for what the pioneers had lived.

Friede ihrer Asche und Ehre ihrem Andenken!
(Peace to their ashes and honor to their memories!)

Appendixes

Notes

Bibliography

Index

Appendix A

Index to the Letter Collection
Die Auswanderer der Familie Mallinckrodt
(Ed. Kurt von Mallinckrodt)

Note: Abbreviations have been spelled out in full as an aid to the reader. An additional column of content highlights (*Stichwort*) has been deleted from the original.

Nr. (No.)	Datum (Date)	von–an (From–To)	Quelle (Source)
001	1796–1820	Theodor (Dortmund)	Dtm. Stadtarch./333
002	07.11.1809	Arnold I (Dortmund) an Wilhelm (Dortmund)	Hist. Archiv Köln/ Carton 94
003	06.06.1813	Arnold I (Dortmund) an Wilhelm (wo?)	Missouri Hist. Soc.
004	24.11.1820	Arnold/Wilhelmine (Schwefe) an Eduard/Emil (Soest)	Missouri Hist. Soc.
005	18.02.1821	Gustav (Petersburg) an Familie (Dortmund)	Hist. Archiv Köln/100
006	10.05.1821	Gustav (Petersburg) an Familie (Dortmund)	Hist. Archiv Köln/100
007	08.10.1822	Feldmann (Dortmund) an Gustav/Julius (Petersburg)	Hist. Archiv Köln/93
008	17.10.1822a	Gustav (Petersburg) an Meininghaus (Dortmund)	Hist. Archiv Köln/93
009	17.10.1822b	Meininghaus (Dortmund) an Gustav (Petersburg)	Hist. Archiv Köln/93
010	17.11.1822a	Meininghaus (Dortmund) an Gustav (Petersburg)	Hist. Archiv Köln/93
011	17.11.1822b	Leopold (Dortmund) an Gustav/Julius (Petersburg)	Hist. Archiv Köln/93
012	—.11.1822	Mutter (Dortmund) an Gustav/Julius (Petersburg)	Hist. Archiv Köln/93
013	03.05.1825	Arnold I (Schwefe) an Gustav (Crombach)	Hist. Archiv Köln/93
014	11.05.1825	Gustav (Hagen) an Arnold I (Schwefe)	Hist. Archiv Köln/93
015	14.05.1825	Arnold I (Schwefe) an Gustav (Crombach)	Hist. Archiv Köln/93
016	—06.1825	Julius (en route) an Mutter (Dortmund)	Hist. Archiv Köln/93
017	05.06.1825	Julius (Cronstadt) an Gustav (Crombach)	Hist. Archiv Köln/93
018	13.07.1825	Leopold (Dortmund) an Vollmann-Gustav (Drolsaagen-Crombach)	Hist. Archiv Köln/21
019	1825 and 1827	Arnold und Wilhelmine Grabsteine (Schwefe)	Friedhof in Schwefe
020	30.09.1825	Leopold/Julius (Dortmund) an Gustav (Crombach)	Hist. Archiv Köln/21

Nr. (No.)	Datum (Date)	von–an (From–To)	Quelle (Source)
021	25.10.1825	Julius (Münster) an Mutter (Dortmund)	Hist. Archiv Köln/21
022	26.01.1826	Arnold II (Elberfeld) an Gustav (Crombach)	Hist. Archiv Köln/21
023	27.05.1826	Arnold II (Elberfeld) an Gustav (Crombach)	Hist. Archiv Köln/21
024	10.07.1826	Royal Prussian Provincial and City Court (Dortmund)	Hist. Archiv Köln/21
025	20.07.1826	Arnold II (Elberfeld) an Gustav (Crombach)	Hist. Archiv Köln/21
026	07.08.1826	Julius (Münster) an Gustav (Crombach)	Hist. Archiv Köln/93
027	17.10.1826	Gustav (Crombach) an Julius (Dortmund)	Hist. Archiv Köln/93
028	14.11.1826	Julius (Crombach) an Gustav (Dortmund)	Hist. Archiv Köln/93
029	04.12.1826	Gustav (Iserlohn) an Meininghaus (Dortmund)	Hist. Archiv Köln/93
030	01.01.1827	Hermann (Antwerpen) an Gustav (Crombach)	Hist. Archiv Köln/99
031	07.07.1827	Julius (Dortmund) an Gustav (Iserlohn)	Hist. Archiv Köln/93
032	20.07.1827	Julius (Dortmund) an Gustav (Iserlohn)	Hist. Archiv Köln/93
033	12.03.1828	Julius (Dortmund) an Gustav (Crombach)	Hist. Archiv Köln/93
034	26.04.1828	Julius (Crombach) an Gustav (Dortmund)	Hist. Arch. Köln/93
035	29.04.1828	Julius (Crombach) an Gustav (Dortmund)	Hist. Archiv Köln/93
036	20.07.1828	Julius (Dortmund) an Gustav (Crombach)	Hist. Archiv Köln/93
037	29.09.1828	Arnold II (Elberfeld) an Gustav (Crombach)	Hist. Archiv Köln/21
038	22.10.1828	Eduard (Herdecke) an Gustav (Crombach)	Hist. Archiv Köln/21
039	19.12.1828	Arnold II (Elberfeld) an Gustav (Crombach)	Hist. Archiv Köln/21
040	23.03.1829	Conrad (München) an Meininghaus (Dortmund)	Hist. Archiv Köln/63
041	02.02.1830	Emil (Schwefe) an Gustav (Crombach)	Hist. Archiv Köln/93
042	05.05.1830	Conrad (München) an Gustav (Crombach)	Hist. Archiv Köln/93
043	01.06.1830	Emil (Schwefe) an Gustav (Crombach)	Hist. Archiv Köln/93
044	21.06.1830	Emil (Schwefe) an Gustav (Crombach)	Hist. Archiv Köln/93
045	03.07.1830	Julius (Antwerpen) an Meininghaus (Dortmund)	Hist. Archiv Köln/63
046	without date, 1830	Albert (Antwerpen) an Meininghaus (Dortmund)	Hist. Archiv Köln/63
047	29.10.1830	Emil (Schwefe) an Gustav (Crombach)	Hist. Archiv Köln/93
048	13.11.1830	Emil (Schwefe) an Gustav (Crombach)	Hist. Archiv Köln/21
049	23.11.1830	Hermann (Dortmund) an Gustav (Crombach)	Hist. Archiv Köln/21
050	08.09.1831	Emil (Schwefe) an Frau Strohn (Wehringhausen)	Hist. Archiv Köln/94
051	22.10.1831	Emil/Julius (Le Havre) an Gustav (Crombach)	Hist. Archiv Köln/21
052	23.10.1831	Emil (Le Havre) an Eduard (Dortmund)	Missouri Hist. Soc.

Index to Die Auswanderer der Familie Mallinckrodt

Nr. (No.)	Datum (Date)	von–an (From–To)	Quelle (Source)
053	26.12.1831	Emil (New Orleans) an Gustav (Crombach)	Hist. Archiv Köln/21
054	07.01.1832	Leopold (Dortmund) an Gustav (Crombach)	Hist. Archiv Köln/21
055	12.02.1832	Julius (St. Louis) an Gustav (Crombach)	Hist. Archiv. Köln/21
056	24.03.1832	Emil/Julius (St. Charles Co.) an Gustav (Crombach)	Hist. Archiv Köln/21
057	—.—.1832	Gustav (Crombach) an Meininghaus (Dortmund)	Hist. Archiv Köln/21
058	06.04.1832	Hermann (Elberfeld) an Gustav (Crombach)	Hist. Archiv Köln/21
059	08.04.1832	Gustav (Crombach) an Hermann (Dortmund)	Hist. Archiv Köln/21
060	09.04.1832	Gustav (Crombach) an Hermann (Dortmund)	Hist. Archiv Köln/21
061	14.05.1832	Albert (Antwerpen) an Gustav (Crombach)	Hist. Archiv Köln/21
062	22.07.1832	Emil (St. Charles Co.) an Gustav (Crombach)	Hist. Archiv Köln/21
063	08.08.1832	Albert (Antwerpen) an Gustav (Crombach)	Hist. Archiv Köln/21
064	06.11.1832	Albert (Antwerpen) an Gustav (Crombach)	Hist. Archiv Köln/21
065	16.11.1832	Albert (Antwerpen) an Gustav (Crombach)	Hist. Archiv Köln/21
066	22.11.1832	Hermann (Dortmund) an Gustav (Crombach)	Hist. Archiv Köln/21
067	24.11.1832	Hermann (Dortmund) an Gustav (Crombach)	Hist. Archiv Köln/21
068	27.11.1832	Albert (Antwerpen) an Gustav (Crombach)	Hist. Archiv Köln/21
069	30.11.1832	Albert (Antwerpen) an Gustav (Crombach)	Hist. Archiv Köln/21
070	02.12.1832	Leopold (Dortmund) an Gustav (Crombach)	Hist. Archiv Köln/21
071	—.12.1832	Dorothea (Dortmund) an Gustav (Crombach)	Hist. Archiv Köln/21
072	11.12.1832	Gustav (Crombach) an Hermann (Dortmund)	Hist. Archiv Köln/21
073	12.12.1832	Hermann (Dortmund) an Gustav (Crombach)	Hist. Archiv Köln/21
074	13.12.1832	Albert (Brüssel) an Gustav (Crombach)	Hist. Archiv Köln/21
075	18.12.1832	Meininghaus (Dortmund) an Gustav (Crombach)	Hist. Archiv Köln/21
076	20.12.1832	Hermann (Dortmund) an Gustav (Crombach)	Hist. Archiv Köln/21
077	23.12.1832	Albert (Brüssel) an Gustav (Crombach)	Hist. Archiv Köln/21
078	26.12.1832	Albert (Brüssel) an Gustav (Crombach)	Hist. Archiv Köln/21
079	28.12.1832a	Julius (St. Charles Co.) an Gustav (Crombach)	Hist. Archiv Köln/21
080	28.12.1832b	Emil (St. Charles Co.) an Gustav (Crombach)	Hist. Archiv Köln/21
081	01.03.1833	Emil/Julius (St. Charles Co.) an Gustav (Crombach)	Hist. Archiv Köln/21
082	13.08.1834a	Emil (St. Charles Co.) an Eduard (Dortmund)	Hist. Archiv Köln/21
083	13.08.1834b	Emil (St. Charles Co.) an Gustav (Crombach)	Hist. Archiv Köln/21
084	12.10.1834	Eduard (Dortmund) an Gustav (Crombach)	Hist. Archiv Köln/21
085	20.12.1834	Frau Strohn (Wehringhausen) an Emilie (Crombach)	Hist. Archiv Köln/21

Nr. (No.)	Datum (Date)	von–an (From–To)	Quelle (Source)
086	02.01.1835a	Conrad (Dortmund) mit Gustav (Crombach)	Hist. Archiv Köln/93
087	02.01.1835b	Gustav (Crombach) an Meininghaus (Dortmund)	Hist. Archiv Köln/21
088	13.01.1835	Gustav (Crombach) an Meininghaus (Dortmund)	Hist. Archiv Köln/21
089	21.02.1835	Frau Kuithan (Dortmund) an Gustav (Crombach)	Hist. Archiv Köln/21
090	25.02.1835	Meininghaus (Dortmund) an Gustav (Crombach)	Hist. Archiv Köln/21
091	22.03.1835	Meininghaus (Dortmund) an Gustav (Crombach)	Hist. Archiv Köln/21
092	31.03.1835	Meinberg (Schuren) an Meininghaus (Dortmund)	Hist. Archiv Köln/21
093	28.05.1835	Dorothea (Dortmund) an Gustav (Crombach)	Hist. Archiv Köln/21
094	29.05.1835	Meininghaus (Dortmund) an Gustav (Crombach)	Hist. Archiv Köln/21
095	30.06.1835	Gustav (Marburg) an Meininghaus (Dortmund)	Hist. Archiv Köln/21
096	12.07.1835	Emil (St. Louis Co.) an Gustav (Crombach)	Hist. Archiv Köln/100
097	11.10.1835	Frau Kuithan (Dortmund) an Gustav (Crombach)	Hist. Archiv Köln/21
098	14.10.1835	Frau Kuithan (Dortmund) an Gustav (Crombach)	Hist. Archiv Köln/21
099	16.10.1835	Emil (St. Louis Co.) an Gustav (Crombach)	Hist. Archiv Köln/100
100	15.03.1836	Emil (St. Louis Co.) an Gustav (Crombach)	Hist. Archiv Köln/100
101	18.01.1837	Emil (St. Louis Co.) an Gustav (Crombach)	Hist. Archiv Köln
102	31.01.1837	Gustav (Cöln) an Emil (St. Louis)	Hist. Archiv Köln/100
103	14.05.1837	Emil (Louisiana) an Gustav (Cöln)	Hist. Archiv Köln/100
104	28.08.1837	Conrad (Dortmund) und Gustav (Cöln)	Hist. Archiv Köln/93
105	19.10.1837	Gustav (Cöln) an Emil (Louisiana)	Hist. Archiv Köln/100
106	23.09.1838	Emil (Pike County, Mo.) an Gustav (Cöln)	Hist. Archiv Köln/100
107	14.03.1839	Emil (Pike County, Mo.) an Eduard (Dortmund)	Missouri Hist. Soc.
108	22.07.1839	Emil (Bremerhaven) an Gustav (Cöln)	Hist. Archiv Köln/100
109	23.07.1839	Emil (Bremerhaven) an Eduard (Dortmund)	Missouri Hist. Soc.
110	09.08.1839	Emil (Wangerooge) an Gustav (Cöln)	Hist. Archiv Köln/100
111	10.08.1839	Emil (Wangerooge) an Eduard (Dortmund)	Missouri Hist. Soc.
112	16.09.1839	Emil (Dortmund) an Gustav (Cöln)	Hist. Archiv Köln/100
113	24.10.1839	Emil (Cöln) an Eduard (Dortmund)	Missouri Hist. Soc.
114	17.11.1839	Emil (Dortmund) an Gustav (Cöln)	Hist. Archiv Köln/100
115	23.11.1839	Gustav (Cöln) an Emil (Dortmund)	Hist. Archiv Köln/100
116	16.12.1839	Emil (Dortmund) an Gustasv (Cöln)	Hist. Archiv Köln/100
117	31.12.1839	Emil (Dortmund) an Gustav (Cöln)	Hist. Archiv Köln/100
118	17.02.1840	Emil (bei Arnheim) an Eduard (Dortmund)	Missouri Hist. Soc.

Index to Die Auswanderer der Familie Mallinckrodt

Nr. (No.)	Datum (Date)	von–an (From–To)	Quelle (Source)
119	01.03.1840	Emil (Liverpool) an Eduard (Dortmund)	Missouri Hist. Soc.
120	28.03.1840	Emil (New York) an Eduard (Dortmund)	Missouri Hist. Soc.
121	10.05.1840	Emil (St. Louis) an Eduard (Dortmund)	Missouri Hist. Soc.
122	15.10.1840	Emil (St. Louis) an Eduard (Dortmund)	Missouri Hist. Soc.
123	12.02.1841	Hermann (Pike County) an Gustasv (Cöln)	Hist. Archiv Köln/93
124	29.04.1841	Emil (St. Louis) an Eduard (Dortmund)	Missouri Hist. Soc.
125	30.07.1841	Gustav (Cöln) an Hermann (Pike County, Mo.)	Hist. Archiv Köln/93
126	31.10.1841	Emil (St. Louis) an Eduard (Dortmund)	Missouri Hist. Soc.
127	03.04.1842	Emil (St. Louis) an Eduard (Dortmund)	Missouri Hist. Soc.
128	17.12.1842	Emil (St. Louis) an Eduard (Dortmund)	Missouri Hist. Soc.
129	09.06.1843	Emil (St. Louis) an Eduard (Dortmund)	Missouri Hist. Soc.
130	25.01.1844	Emil (St. Louis) an Eduard (Dortmund)	Missouri Hist. Soc.
131	28.05.1844	Emil (St. Louis) an Eduard (Dortmund)	Missouri Hist. Soc.
132	23.08.1844	Emil (St. Louis) an Eduard (Dortmund)	Missouri Hist. Soc.
133	11.01.1845	Emil (St. Louis) an Gustav (Cöln)	Hist. Archiv Köln/100
134	01.05.1845	Hermann (Pike County) an Gustav (Cöln)	Hist. Archiv Köln/93
135	14.06.1845	Emil (St. Louis) an Gustav (Cöln)	Hist. Archiv Köln/100
136	04.10.1845	Emil (St. Louis) an Eduard (Dortmund)	Missouri Hist. Soc.
137	30.11.1845	Emil (St. Louis) an Gustav (Cöln)	Hist. Archiv Köln/100
138	22.12.1845	Hermann (Pike County) an Gustav (Coeln)	Hist. Archiv Köln/93
139	30.08.1846	Emil (St. Louis) an Eduard (Dortmund)	Missouri Hist. Soc.
140	19.12.1846	Gustav (Coeln) an Sophie (Dortmund)	Hist. Archiv Köln/93
141	04.01.1847	Hermann (Pike County) an Gustav (Cöln)	Hist. Archiv Köln/93
142	05.01.1847	Sophie (Dortmund) an Gustav (Cöln)	Hist. Archiv Köln/93
143	21.01.1847	Emil (St. Louis) an Eduard (Dortmund)	Missouri Hist. Soc.
144	25.02.1847	Gustav (Cöln) an Hermann (Pike County/Mo.)	Hist. Archiv Köln/93
145	04.05.1847	Sophie (Dortmund) an Gustav (Cöln)	Hist. Archiv Köln/93
146	04.07.1847	Emil (St. Louis) an Eduard (Dortmund)	Missouri Hist. Soc.
147	12.12.1847	Emil (St. Louis) an Eduard (Dortmund)	Missouri Hist. Soc.
148	26.04.1848	Emil (St. Louis) an Eduard (Dortmund)	Missouri Hist. Soc.
149	24.08.1848	Sophie (Dortmund) an Gustav (Cöln)	Hist. Archiv Köln/93
150	29.12.1848	Emil (St. Louis) an Eduard (Dortmund)	Missouri Hist. Soc.
151	05.07.1849	Emil (St. Louis) an Eduard (Dortmund)	Missouri Hist. Soc.

Appendix A

Nr. (No.)	Datum (Date)	von–an (From–To)	Quelle (Source)
152	03.09.1849	Emil (St. Louis) an Eduard (Dortmund)	Missouri Hist. Soc.
153	20.11.1849	Emil (St. Louis) an Eduard (Dortmund)	Missouri Hist. Soc.
154	11.04.1850	Sophie (Dortmund) an Gustav (Cöln)	Hist. Archiv Köln/93
155	28.01.1851	Emil (Nizza) an Gustav II (Cöln)	Hist. Archiv Köln/99
156	22.04.1851	Emil (Rolandseck) an H. Kayser (St. Louis)	Missouri Hist. Soc.
157	16.06.1851	Emil (Hallwyll) an Eduard (Dortmund)	Missouri Hist. Soc.
158	17.07.1851	Hermann (Milwaukee) an Emil/Gustav (Cöln)	Hist. Archiv Köln/93
159	19.08.1851	Emil (Nizza) an Eduard (Dortmund)	Missouri Hist. Soc.
160	11.09.1851	Emil (Nizza) an Schulenburg (St. Louis)	Missouri Hist. Soc.
161	04.10.1851	Emil (Nizza) an Eduard (Dortmund)	Missouri Hist. Soc.
162	07.12.1851	Emil (Nizza) an Eduard (Dortmund)	Missouri Hist. Soc.
163	03.02.1852	Emil (Nizza) an Eduard (Dortmund)	Missouri Hist. Soc.
164	16.02.1852	Hermann (St. Louis) an Emil/Gustav (Cöln)	Hist. Archiv Köln/93
165	10.03.1852	Hermann (St. Louis) an Emil/Gustav (Cöln)	Hist. Archiv Köln/93
166	18.03.1852	Emil (Nizza) an Eduard (Dortmund)	Missouri Hist. Soc.
167	27.03.1852	Gustav (Cöln) an Hermann (St. Louis)	Hist. Archiv Köln/93
168	12.05.1852	Emil (Cöln) an Eduard (Dortmund)	Missouri Hist. Soc.
169	15.05.1852	Emil (Cöln) an Eduard (Dortmund)	Missouri Hist. Soc.
170	06.12.1852	Emil's Sohn Gustav (Dortmund) an Gustav (Cöln)	Hist. Archiv Köln/93
171	16.11.18??	Dorothea (Dortmund) an Emil (wo?)	Missouri Hist. Soc.
172	21.02.1853	Gustav II (Havanna) an Gustav (Coeln)	Hist. Archiv Köln/95
173	09.03.1853	Gustav II (N. Orleans) an Gustav (Coeln)	Hist. Archiv Köln/95
174	01.04.1853	Gustav II (St. Louis) an Gustav (Coeln)	Hist. Archiv Köln/95
175	19.04.1853	Gustav II (New York) an Gustav (Coeln)	Hist. Archiv Köln/95
176	28.09.1854	Sophie (St. Louis) an Gustav (Coeln)	Hist. Archiv Köln/93
177	04.02.1855	Emil (Dortmund) an Gustav (Coeln)	Hist. Archiv Köln/93
178	07.03.1855	Emil (Dortmund) an Gustav (Coeln)	Hist. Archiv Köln/93
179	04.09.1855	Emil (Dortmund) an Gustav (Coeln)	Hist. Archiv Köln/93
180	03.12.1855	Sophie (St. Louis) an Gustav (Coeln)	Hist. Archiv Köln/93
181	28.02.1856	Dorothea (Dortmund) an Gustav (Coeln)	Hist. Archiv Köln/93
182	12.04.1856	Gustav (Cöln) an Emil (bei St. Louis)	Hist. Archiv Köln/93
183	07.06.1856	Emil (near St. Louis) an Gustav (Coeln)	Hist. Archiv Köln/93
184	29.03.1857	Emil (St. Louis) an Gustav II (Coeln)	Hist. Archiv Köln/95

Index to Die Auswanderer der Familie Mallinckrodt

Nr. (No.)	Datum (Date)	von–an (From–To)	Quelle (Source)
185	10.06.1858	Emil (St. Louis) an Gustav II (Coeln)	Hist. Archiv Köln/95
186	20.10.1858	Emil (St. Louis) an Gustav II (Coeln)	Hist. Archiv Köln/95
187	24.10.1859	Emil (St. Louis) an Gustav II (Coeln)	Hist. Archiv Köln/95
188	27.09.1861	Emil (St. Louis) an Gustav II (Coeln)	Hist. Archiv Köln/95
189	27.12.1861	Emil (St. Louis) an Gustav II (Coeln)	Hist. Archiv Köln/95
190	04.02.1863	Emil (St. Louis) an Gustav II (Coeln)	Hist. Archiv Köln/22
191	03.07.1863	Emil (Anholt) an Gustav II (Coeln)	Hist. Archiv Köln/95
192	20.08.1863	Emil (Anholt) an Gustav II (Coeln)	Hist. Archiv Köln/95
193	31.08.1863	Emil (Anholt) an Gustav II (Coeln)	Hist. Archiv Köln/95
194	08.09.1863	Emil (Anholt) an Gustav II (Coeln)	Hist. Archiv Köln/95
195	16.11.1863	Emil (Anholt) an Gustav II (Coeln)	Hist. Archiv Köln/95
196	06.12.1863	Emil (Anholt) an Gustav II (Coeln)	Hist. Archiv Köln/95
197	22.12.1863	Emil (Anholt) an Gustav II (Coeln)	Hist. Archiv Köln/95
198	10.11.1874	Conrad Theodor (St. Charles) an Delia (wo ?)	Hist. Archiv Köln/?
199	07.02.1877	Gustav III (Davos) an Gustav II (Coeln)	Hist. Archiv Köln/93
200	17.06.1877	Emil (St. Louis) an Gustav II (Coeln)	Hist. Archiv Köln/95
201	04.06.1879	Emil (St. Louis County) an Gustav II (Coeln)	Hist. Archiv Köln/95
202	12.10.1880	Emil (North Carolina) an Gustav II (Coeln)	Hist. Archiv Köln/95
203	10.09.1882	Emil (St. Louis County) an Gustav II (Coeln)	Hist. Archiv Köln/95
204	06.12.1882	Emil II (Bonn) an Gustav II (Coeln)	Hist. Archiv Köln/93
205	14.01.1884	Emil (St. Louis County) an Gustasv II (Coeln)	Hist. Archiv Köln/95
206	27.03.1885	Emil (St. Louis County) an Gustav II (Coeln)	Hist. Archiv Köln/95
207	27.06.1900	Dorothea (Köln) an Gustav IV (Köln)	Hist. Archiv Köln/100
208	02.07.1900	Dorothea (Köln) an Gustav IV (Köln)	Hist. Archiv Köln/100

Appendix B

The Mallinckrodt Family Tree
from the Fifteenth Through the Nineteenth Generations

(The names of immigrants to America are within dotted lines)

338
345
347

299	300	301	302
Wilh. Andr. 1727–87 ⚭ Soelling Anna Elis. Huyssen Kath. Soph. Th.	Katharina SOPHIA Sibilla 1729–66 ⚭ Krupp Ernst	Theodore Katharina Gertrud 1732–48	J. D. Fried. II 1734–1814 ⚭ 298 Mallinckrodt Chr. Marg. Dorothea

346	348	349		353	350	355	351	352
Heinrich LUDWIG 1778–1834 ⚭ Feldmann ELISABETH Dor. Wilh.	Joh. ARNOLD Theodor 1764–1849 ⚭ Engels Wilhelmine (Elberfeld)	Kath. HELENE Friederike 1787–1840 ⚭ 355 Mallinckrodt Joh. CHRIST.		ARNOLD And. Fried. 1768–1825 ⚭ 359 Mallinckrodt WILHELMINE	Johann Friedrich 1762–1800 ⚭ v. Steinen Johanna Kath. Soph.	Johann CHRISTIAN 1772–1815 ⚭ 349 Kath. HELENE Friederike	Sibilla KATHARINA Dorothea 1764–1809 ⚭ Wiskott Joh. Ernst	GERTRUD Katharina Sophia 1766–67

419–428   1429 – 435   436–442

431	447	444	445	446	443
HERMANN Theodor 1819–72	Emil I 1806–92 ⚭ ⚭ Didier Lucky Eleonore Vollmann Emilie	Eduard 1797–98	Wilhelmine * ? †'gleich'	Eduard 1804–59 ⚭ Heine Dorothea	Wilhelm Theodor Friedrich 1795–1817

(1st Marriage) ···· (2d Marriage)

448	449	450	451	452	454	455
Ernst 1808–34	SOPHIA H. 1814–? ⚭ ⚭ 458 Mallinckrodt Conrad Koch Christian	FERDINAND Bernhard Karl 1812–12	BERNHARD Arnold Ferdinand 1813–13	'Sohn' 'gleich gestorben'	FERDINAND Heinrich 1801–12	Sophia Dorothea 1803–11

(1st Marriage)   (2d Marriage)

524	525	526	527	528	529	530	531	532
Emma 1834–34	Gustav III 1840–77	Wilhelmina (Minna) 1842–70 ⚭ Wisskott Karl	Eduard Theodor 1845–1928 ⚭ Andersen Jennie	Otto 1847–76	Adele 1851–1937 ⚭ Schulenburg August	Emil II 1860–1925 ⚭ Armstrong Mar. Louise	Oscar 1861–1900	Elmira 1866–67

(1st Marriage)   ↓630   631–632 ↓

543	544	545	546	547	548	549	550	551
Mathilde 1833–54 ⚭ Wilkins Theodor	Caroline Dorothea ⚭ Nahm Heinrich	CONRAD Theodore ⚭ Fuhr Emilie	Emilie 1837–90 ⚭ ⚭ Wachs Friedrich Nahm Heinrich	Her. ADOLPH 1838–1905 ⚭ ⚭ Muench Malinda Koch Auguste	Luise 1840–? ⚭ Guggemoos Joseph	George Washington 1842–43	Lydia Anna 1843–90 ⚭ Mueller Rudolf W.	Cristian Albert 1850–72

↓ 656–662   ↓ 663–667

I
e

16th Generation

304	305	307	306
Christine Wilhelmine 1746–1805 ∞ Barop Joh. Kasp.	'Sohn' ca. 1742 'gleich gestorben'	Anna DOROTHEA 1747–93 ∞ Feldmann Fried. Zach.	ARNOLD Gerhard Friedrich 1744–? ∞ Gerstmann Jul. Wil. Ch.

17th Generation

359 ◆ → 368

356	357	358	362
Johann Dietrich 1772–79	Joh. Fried. THEODOR 1774–1822 ∞∞ Fabricius Sophia / Feldmann Dorothea	DOROTHEA Judith Friederika ∞∞ Huelsemann Chr. Dietr. / Meininghaus Herm. Adam	DETMAR Franz Fr. 1777–1841 ∞ 436 Mallinckrodt Christine

464	465	466	467	468	469	470
Joh. Fried. AUGUST 1808–59	DETMAR Ludwig 1809–09	SOPHIA Christine 1814–84 ∞ Amend Wilh.	Moritz 1812–? ∞ Heider Elise	Fr. Hen. The. Louise 1817–97 ∞ 459 Mallinckrodt Hermann	Soph. Wilh. KAROLINE 1819–55 ∞ Ruitz Louis	Kar. Liset. Christine AUGUSTE 1826–27

18th Generation

(1st Marriage)　(2d Marriage)

456	453	460	461	458	459	462	463
Arnold LEOPOLD 1804–69 ∞ Wagener Auguste	Gustav I 1799–1856 ∞∞ Strohn Henriette / Strohn Emilie	Albert 1812–71	Mar. Henr. DOROTHEA 1814–1900 ∞ Metzmacher Karl	Conrad 1808–87 ∞∞ 449 Mallinckrodt Sophie / Meinershagen Wilh. Carol	Hermann 1810–95 ∞ 468 Mallinckrodt Louise 1818–97	Auguste 1816–22	Sophie 1820–20

537–542 ↓

19th Generation

533	534	535	536		559	560	561	562
'Sohn' * ? †'gleich'	Gustav II 1829–1904 ∞ Deichmann Bertha	Henriette 1828–? ∞∞ Heymann Heinrich / Hammacher Wilhelm	Felix 1834–80 ∞ Peill Anna		Delia 1841–41	James Ferdinand 1842–1921	Caecilia Henriette 1844–72	John Friedrich 1847–1919 ∞ Weigel Josephine

633–638 ↓　(2d Marriage)　639–641 ↓　684–686 ↓

553	554	555	556	557	558	563	564	565
Wilhelmina 1853–1938 ∞ Meinershagen Wilhelm / Ruebling Adam	Ellen 1839–39	THEODOR Feldmann 1859–1938 ∞ Sehrt Annemarie Caroline	ALBERT Feldmann 1860–1933 ∞ Sehrt Elisa (Elise)	Wilhelmina DOROTHEA 1861–1923 ∞ Sehrt Herm. Hein.	Maria Wilhelmine 1866–67	Delia Louise 1850–?	Hermann Theodor 1854–54	Franz Albert 1856–56

668–674 ↓　675–683 ↓

Notes

1. Early Times

1. Luise von Winterfeld, "Die Enstehung der Stadt Dortmund," 8–12; Norbert Reimann, *Königshof-Pfalz-Reichsstadt*, 5–8.

2. A. Voelske and R. H. Tenbrock, *Urzeit-Mittemeerkulturen und werdenes Abendland*, 164–66.

3. James Laver, *The Concise History of Costume and Fashion*, 50–52.

4. Reimann, *Königshof-Pfalz-Reichsstadt*, 3–9.

5. Werner Conze and Volker Hentschel, eds., *Ploetz Deutsche Geschichte*, 28.

6. Carlton J. H. Hayes, Marshall Whithed Baldwin, Charles Woolsey Cole, *History of Europe*, 146–54.

7. *Conversations-Lexikon*, vol. 3, s.v. "Dortmund"; Reimann, *Königshof-Pfalz-Reichsstadt*, 9.

8. Conze and Hentschel, *Ploetz Deutsche Geschichte*, 30.

9. *Encyclopedia Americana*, 1989, s.v. "Feudalism."

10. Veit Valentin, *The German People*, 19–25; Reimann, *Königshof-Pfalz-Reichsstadt*, 13.

11. H. Jellinghaus, "Der Name Dortmund," 119–20; Winterfeld, "Die Enstehung," 7, 43.

12. Joachim Bumke, *Höfische Kultur* 2:403.

13. Bumke, *Höfische Kultur* 1:39.

14. Bumke, *Höfische Kultur* 1:42.

15. Bumke, *Höfische Kultur* 1:97–100.

2. 1100

1. Dietrich von Mallinckrodt, "Das Rittergut Mallinckrodt und die Grundherrschaft der von Mallinckrodt," 5.

2. Dietrich von Mallinckrodt, "Die Burgmannen von Meskenwerke und Mallingrode zu Volmestein und Wetter an der Ruhr," 11.

3. Bumke, *Höfische Kultur* 1:165.

4. Dietrich von Mallinckrodt, "Das Rittergut," 5, 28.

5. Bumke, *Höfische Kultur* 1:137.

6. Horst Wientzek, *Wetter-Stadt an der Ruhr*, 18.

7. George Savage, *A Concise History of Interior Decoration*, 62.

8. Bumke, *Höfische Kultur* 1:9; Edith Ennen, *Frauen im Mittelalter*, 35.

9. Laver, *Concise History of Costume*, 62.

10. Bumke, *Höfische Kultur* 2:534.

11. Dietrich von Mallinckrodt, "Die Burgmannen," 11.

12. Dietrich von Mallinckrodt, "Das Rittergut," 31–32.

13. *Encyclopedia Americana*, 1989, s.v. "Feudalism"; Dietrich von Mallinckrodt, "Die Burgmannen," 11.

14. Dietrich von Mallinckrodt, "Das Rittergut," 66.

15. *Encyclopedia Americana*, 1989, s.v. "Feudalism."

16. Dietrich von Mallinckrodt, "Die Burgmannen," 11, 24.

17. *Encyclopedia Americana*, 1989, s.v. "Feudalism."

18. Bumke, *Höfische Kultur* 1:10, 224.

19. Bumke, *Höfische Kultur* 1:213.

20. Laver, *Concise History of Costume*, 58–60.

21. Bumke, *Höfische Kultur* 1:53.

22. Anne Fremantle, *Age of Faith*, 74, 82.

23. Luise von Winterfeld, "Die Dortmunder Wandschneider-Gesellschaft," 42.

24. Bumke, *Höfische Kultur* 1:181.

25. Winterfeld, "Die Dortmunder Wandschneider-Gesellschaft," 2, 67; August Meininghaus, "Der soziale Aufsteig der Dortmunder Mallinckrodt," 396.

26. Bumke, *Höfische Kultur* 1:58; Winterfeld, "Die Dortmunder Wandschneider-Gesellschaft," 6–7.

27. Winterfeld, "Die Enstehung," 74; Reimann, *Königshof-Pfalz-Reichsstadt*, 24.

28. Dore Bolege-Vieweg, *Straßen erzählen Stadtgeschichte*, 15. The Order of Teutonic Knights was originally founded in Acre in the Holy Land as a medical fraternity to tend people wounded there during the Third Crusade; however, the healers soon were turned into a spiritual order of knights and officially recognized by the pope. Increasingly involved in fighting the "heathens," the Teutonic Order was then given privileges and property by both the emperor and pope.

29. Laver, *Concise History of Costume*, 60–62,

30. Ennen, *Frauen im Mittelalter*, 94–108.

3. 1200–1300

1. Dietrich von Mallinckrodt, "Die Burgmannen," 10; Bumke, *Höfische Kultur* 1:47.

2. Dietrich von Mallinckrodt, "Das Rittergut," 12–15, 32.

3. Dietrich von Mallinckrodt, "Die Burgmannen," 18–19.

4. Later historians would suggest that as early as 890 a fortress already existed there, surrounded by moats (Friedrich Thörner, "Viele Geschichten um Schloß Mallinckrodt [I]").

5. Dietrich von Mallinckrodt, "Die Burgmannen," 19–20, 26.

6. Quoted in Bumke, *Höfische Kultur* 1:138.

7. Dietrich von Mallinckrodt, "Das Rittergut," 22.

8. Bumke, *Höfische Kultur* 1:47, 137.

9. Dietrich von Mallinckrodt, "Die Burgmannen," 12–13.

10. Dietrich von Mallinckrodt, "Das Rittergut," 17–20.

11. Dietrich von Mallinckrodt, "Die Burgmannen," 18.

12. Dietrich von Mallinckrodt, "Die von Mallinckrodt zu Steinberg und ihre Nachkommen in Dortmund und Paderborn."

13. Dietrich von Mallinckrodt, "Die Burgmannen," 21–23.

14. Bumke, *Höfische Kultur* 1:48; Dietrich von Mallinckrodt, "Die Burgmannen," 12.

15. Bumke, *Höfische Kultur* 1:214.

16. Bumke, *Höfische Kultur* 1:219–221.

17. Fremantle, *Age of Faith*, 154.

18. Winterfeld, "Die Entstehung," 28, 76.

19. Winterfeld, "Die Enstehung," 30; Bolege-Vieweg, *Straßen*, 30; Winterfeld, "Die Entstehung," 43, 48.

20. Robert von den Berken, *Dortmunder Häuserbuch von 1700 bis 1850*, 79, 72.

21. Bolege-Vieweg, *Straßen*, 6.

22. Winterfeld, "Die Entstehung," 43.

23. Bumke, *Höfische Kultur* 1:52–53.

24. Karl Rübel, "Die Bürgerlisten der Frei- und Reichsstadt Dortmund," 3.

25. Winterfeld, "Die Entstehung," 36, 44–45.

26. Berken, *Dortmunder Häuserbuch*, 115; Bolege-Vieweg, *Straßen*, 31.

27. Traute Preuss, *Starkes schwaches Geschlecht*, 69–70, 98–115; Ennen, *Frauen*, 145–50.

28. Hayes, Baldwin, and Cole, *History of Europe*, 245–50.

29. Bumke, *Höfische Kultur* 1:57.

30. Bolege-Vieweg, *Straßen*, 3.

31. Meininghaus, "Der soziale Aufsteig," 409.

32. Winterfeld, "Die Dortmunder Wandschneider-Gesellschaft," 331–32.

33. Winterfeld, "Die Enstehung," 27.

34. Albrecht Brinkmann, *Geschichte der Dortmunder Volksschulen*, 7.

35. Reimann, *Königshof-Pfalz-Reichsstadt*, 37; Dietrich von Mallinckrodt, "Die Burgmannen," 27.

36. Hans Georg Kirchoff, "Die Dortmunder Große Fehde 1388/89," 109–24.

37. Dietrich von Mallinckrodt, "Die Burgmannen," 27.

38. Kirchoff, "Die Dortmunder Große Fehde," 126.

39. Fremantle, *Age of Faith*, 89.

40. Fremantle, *Age of Faith*, 125.

4. *1400*

1. Dietrich von Mallinckrodt, "Das Rittergut," 22, 23; Dietrich von Mallinckrodt, "Die Burgmannen," 29.

2. Dietrich von Mallinckrodt, "Das Rittergut," 24.

3. Bumke, *Höfische Kultur* 1:143.

4. Friedrich Thörner, "Brände und Verwüstungen gehörten zur Geschichte der 'Burg Mallinckrodt.'"

5. Bumke, *Höfische Kultur* 1:144, 149.

6. Bolege-Vieweg, *Straßen*, 25.

7. *Conversations-Lexikon*, vol. 4, s.v. "Femgerichte."

8. Wientzek, *Wetter*, 31.

9. *Conversations-Lexikon*, vol. 4, s.v. "Femgerichte."

10. Wientzek, *Wetter*, 33.

11. *Conversations-Lexikon*, vol. 4, s.v. "Femgerichte."

12. Gerrit Haren, "Rittergut Mallinckrodt und seine Besitzer. (Ergänzung S. 30)."

13. Haren, "Rittergut Mallinckrodt."

14. Wientzek, *Wetter*, 34.

15. Wientzek, *Wetter*, 34–36.

16. Wientzek, *Wetter*, 36.

17. "Hermann von Mallinckrodt vor dem Femegericht, 1450."

18. Bumke, *Höfische Kultur* 1:214.

19. Haren, "Rittergut Mallinckrodt."

20. "Hermann von Mallinckrodt."

21. Dietrich von Mallinckrodt, "Die Burgmannen," 29.

22. Gustav von Mallinckrodt, *Urkundenbuch der Familie von Mallinckrodt* 1:205–39, nos. 466, 470, 474–86, 491–93, 499, 501–2 (hereafter *Urkundenbuch*).

23. Heinz Hartmann, " 'Auf Jahr und Tag' in Dortmund (1480)."

24. Ferdinand Schmidt, "Wilhelm von Mallinckrodt, ein Kriegsmann des Herzogs von Geldern-Egmont."

25. At this time, ownership of salt sources and trade in the precious commodity was a lucrative monopoly controlled, for instance, by the Archbishop of Köln and/or the ruling prince.

26. *Urkundenbuch* 1:224–37, nos. 468, 469, 472, 473, 488–89, 495–97.

s. 1500

1. Dietrich von Mallinckrodt, "Die von Mallinckrodt," 52; Berken, *Dortmunder Häuserbuch*, 107.

2. This line of descent was long a controversy between branches of the family. Based on information available at the time, some declared themselves "direct" descendants and said others were not. However, the new documentation uncovered by Dietrich von Mallinckrodt, and published posthumously in 1987, has established the direct lineage. It seems, then, that throughout history the von Mallinckrodts have been one family, and all members now living are descendants of the Dortmunders. See Dietrich von Mallinckrodt, "Die von Mallinckrodt," 33–37.

3. Bumke, *Höfische Kultur* 1:53.

4. Rübel, "Die Bürgerlisten," 33–36, 63.

5. *Conversations-Lexikon*, vol. 3, s.v. "Dortmund."

6. Bernd Kersting, "Die Grabplatten in der Ev. St. Marienkirche zu Dortmund," 45.

7. Brinkmann, *Geschichte der Dortmunder Volksschulen*, 12.

8. *Conversations-Lexikon*, vol. 3, "Dortmund."

9. Winterfeld, "Die Dortmunder Wandschneider-Gesellschaft," 50.

10. Savage, *Concise History of Interior Decoration*, 79, 104–5, 110.

11. Herman Schmitz, ed., *The Encyclopedia of Furniture*, 23–29; Savage, *Concise History of Interior Decoration*, 66, 75–93.

12. Meininghaus, "Der soziale Aufsteig," 409.

13. Winterfeld, "Die Dortmunder Wandschneider-Gesellschaft," 13.

14. Laver, *Concise History of Costume*, 71, 85.

15. *Urkundenbuch* 1:365, no. 751.

16. Through the marriage of Hermann and Elsa, Haus Küchen had come into the Mallinckrodt family around 1517.

17. *Urkundenbuch* 2:401–3, no. 781a.

18. *Urkundenbuch* 1:407, no. 840.

19. Karl Rübel, "Die Dortmunder Morgensprache," 31.

20. *Urkundenbuch* 1:418, no. 860.

21. Winterfeld, "Die Dortmunder Wandschneider-Gesellschaft," 15, 37–39.

22. *Urkundenbuch* 2:51, no. 85.

23. Later generations, seeing prestige differently, would resume the "von," even going to court to restore it.

24. Laver, *Concise History of Costume*, 86.

25. Horst-Gerhard von Mallinckrodt, "Die Reformation in Dortmund."

26. Rübel, "Die Bürgerlisten," 34, 67–68, 143.

27. Brinkmann, *Geschichte der Dortmunder Volksschulen*, 5.

28. Horst-Gerhard von Mallinckrodt, "Die Reformation."

29. From the 1200s on, the church was known as St. Mary of Indulgences (*Ablaß*) because of the central role it played in Palm Sunday festivities. On that day the Archbishop of Köln started a festive procession of believers from the great cathedral (*Dom*) near the Rhine River. (The cathedral's foundation was laid in 1248, its enormous western façade begun in the early 1300s, and the uncompleted main naves roofed over for religious services in 1560.) The procession's first stop was at Saint Gereon's church near the city wall. (Originally a fourth-century Roman building, by the mid 1050s Saint Gereon had become a dramatic decagon structure with ten ribs rising up from the church's main vault to merge nearly a hundred feet above the floor.) Continuing on, the Palm Sunday procession reached Saint Maria Ablaß, where the archbishop granted believers their Palm Sunday indulgences. It, too, was a large church, complete with cemetery and courtyard. Built with three naves, it was known for a venerated fresco of Mary and Child painted in the early 1400s in a recessed, roofed niche on one of its outside walls. In the period 1431–1467, a side chapel called the Liebfrauen Kapelle (Chapel of Our Lady) was built around the fresco.

30. *Urkundenbuch* 1:474, no. 970.

31. *Urkundenbuch* 2:169, no. 417.

32. Paul Clemen, *Die Kunstdenkmäler der Stadt Köln,* 857–68; Heinz Firmenich, "St. Maria-Ablaß-Kappelle," 28.

33. By this time, gunpowder had been imported from Egypt (Bumke, *Höfische Kultur* 1:57) and muzzle-loading guns were being manufactured.

34. *Urkundenbuch* 2:82, no. 137.

35. Dietrich von Mallinckrodt, "Das Rittergut," 69–72.

36. Kurt von Mallinckrodt, "Transcription of Notary Public Testimony in *Urkundenbuch der Familie von Mallinckrodt*, vol. 2, 83ff. (No. 139)."

37. Dietrich von Mallinckrodt, "Das Rittergut," 44–45, 71.

38. *Urkundenbuch* 2:32–33, no. 58.

6. 1600–1750

1. Dietrich von Mallinckrodt, "Das Rittergut," 116–19. (Modern maps refer to the location as "Elbsche at Wengern.")

2. *Urkundenbuch* 1:473–74.

3. Dietrich von Mallinckrodt, "Das Rittergut," 119–22.

4. Dietrich von Mallinckrodt, "Das Rittergut," 25.

5. Carl Schulze Henne, *Haus Küchen*, 68.

6. *Urkundenbuch* 1:458, no. 934.

7. Henne, *Haus Küchen*, 69; *Urkundenbuch* 2:170, no. 421; *Urkundenbuch* 2:193, no. 486.

8. *Urkundenbuch* 2:193, no. 490.

9. Winterfeld, "Die Dortmunder Wandschneider-Gesellschaft," 17, 56–57, 281–84.

10. Winterfeld, "Die Dortmunder Wandschneider-Gesellschaft," 10–11.

11. Laver, *Concise History of Costume*, 99, 124.

12. Winterfeld, "Die Dortmunder Wandschneider-Gesellschaft," 24.

13. Winterfeld, "Die Dortmunder Wandschneider-Gesellschaft," 74; Meininghaus, "Der soziale Aufsteig," 409.

14. Wilhelm Feldmann, *Die Dortmunder Feldmanns*, 16–40.

15. Wilhelm Garg, "Zeichen der unendlichen Liebe Gottes." (Created in the midst of the Thirty Years' War by the well-known sculptor Adam Stenelt of Osnabrück, the monument—18½ feet tall and nearly 8 feet wide—was damaged in World War II.)

16. Henne, *Haus Küchen*, 68–74; Wilhelm Schulte, *Westfälische Köpfe*, 189; "Mallinckrodt," in *Allgemeine Deutsche Biographie*, 143; "Mallinckrodt," in *Neue Deutsche Biographie*, 731–32.

17. Feldmann, *Die Dortmunder Feldmanns*, 19.

18. Henne, *Haus Küchen*, 64.

19. Horst-Gerhard von Mallinckrodt, "Reformation"; Valentin, *The German People*, 214.

20. Conze and Hentschel, eds., *Ploetz Deutsche Geschichte*, 131.

21. Conze and Hentschel, eds., *Ploetz Deutsche Geschichte*, 153–54.

22. Conze and Hentschel, eds., *Ploetz Deutsche Geschichte*, 154.

23. Winterfeld, "Die Dortmunder Wandschneider-Gesellschaft," 26; Winterfeld, "Die Enstehung," 68.

24. Meininghaus, "Der soziale Aufstieg," 411.

25. August Meininghaus, "Das Haus 'zum Rehfuß' am Westenhellweg"; August Meininghaus, "Das Wein- und Gasthaus 'Der Rehfuß' am Westenhellweg zu Dortmund"; Berken, *Dortmunder Häuserbuch*, 116. (Rehfuß remained in the Mallinckrodt family for 150 years, until 1868.)

26. Berken, *Dortmunder Häuserbuch*, 97.

27. Bolege-Vieweg, *Straßen*, 20.

28. Berken, *Dortmunder Häuserbuch*, 10.

29. Heinrich Scholle, *Dortmund im Jahre 1610*, 215.

30. Berken, *Dortmunder Häuserbuch*, 71–72.

31. Berken, *Dortmunder Häuserbuch*, 139–40.

32. Although the houses referred to no longer exist, the Dortmund streets where the Mallinckrodt homes were located do remain.

33. Laver, *Concise History of Costume*, 124–30, 139.

34. Schmitz, *Encyclopedia of Furniture*, 30–49; Savage, *Concise History of Interior Decoration*, 136, 140–45.

35. Winterfeld, "Die Dortmunder Wandschneider-Gesellschaft," 23–24.

36. Meininghaus, "Der soziale Aufsteig," 410.

37. Bernd Kersting, "Grabplatten ehrten verdiente Dortmunder," 17.

38. Gustav von Mallinckrodt, "Die Dortmunder Rathslinie seit dem Jahre 1500."

39. Meininghaus, "Der soziale Aufsteig," 396; Winterfeld, "Die Dortmunder Wandschneider-Gesellschaft," 281–84.

40. Gustav von Mallinckrodt, "Die Dortmunder Rathslinie"; August Meininghaus, "Die Dortmunder Magistratslinie von 1803 bis 1918"; Winterfeld, "Die Dortmunder Wandschneider-Gesellschaft"; Berken, *Dortmunder Häuserbuch*.

7. 1750–1810

1. *Ploetz Deutsche Geschichte*, 148.

2. Anita M. Mallinckrodt, *Why They Left: German Immigration from Prussia to Missouri*, 3–4.

3. *Ploetz Deutsche Geschichte*, 154, 156.

4. Anita M. Mallinckrodt, *Why They Left*, 5.

5. Brinkmann, *Geschichte der Dortmunder Volksschulen*, 20–22.

6. Dietrich von Mallinckrodt, "Die von Mallinckrodt," 54–58.

7. Dietrich von Mallinckrodt, "Die von Mallinckrodt," 58.

8. Gustav Luntowski, "Arnold Mallinckrodt (1768–1825), ein Vertreter des frühen Liberalismus in Westfalen," 287; "Mallinckrodt," in *Allgemeine Deutsche Biographie*, 141–42; "Mallinckrodt," *Neue Deutsche Biographie*, 732–33.

9. Luntowski, "Arnold Mallinckrodt," 294.

10. Luntowski, "Arnold Mallinckrodt," 295.

11. Diary of Sophie Fabricius, 1796, in von Mallinckrodt Nachlaß, Bestand 1068, Kasten 94.

12. Not only did Sophie's father have to give her permission to marry, but he also had the responsibility of negotiating for her with the groom and groom's father a marriage contract appropriate to the new couple's upper-class status and their families' wealth.

13. Valentin, *German People*, 314, 326–27.

14. Ernst Maurmann, "Dr. Arnold Mallinckrodt (1768–1825)," 5.

15. Luntowski, "Arnold Mallinckrodt," 295.

16. Luntowski, "Arnold Mallinckrodt," 295.

17. Helmut Esser, "Das Dortmunder Gymnasium in den ersten Jahrzehnten des 19. Jahrhunderts," 21.

18. Luntowski, "Arnold Mallinckrodt," 297.

19. Johann Friedrich Theodor Mallinckrodt, "Für mich und die meinigen Merkwürdigen Nachrichten."

20. Johann Friedrich Theodor Mallinckrodt, "Merkwürdigen Nachrichten."

21. Valentin, *German People*, 316–17.

22. Luntowski, "Arnold Mallinckrodt," 288; Dietrich von Mallinckrodt, "Die von Mallinckrodt," 58.

23. Dietrich von Mallinckrodt, "Die von Mallinckrodt," 61.

24. Berken, *Dortmunder Häuserbuch*, 97.

25. Berken, *Dortmunder Häuserbuch*, 18; Meininghaus, "Die Dortmunder Magistratslinie," 44.

26. Winterfeld, "Die Dortmunder Wandschneider-Gesellschaft," 28.

27. Valentin, *German People*, 322.

28. *Politische Journal*, August 1803, 755. Founded around 1780 and published in Hamburg by a "society of scholars," the *Journal*'s goal was "to present a complete summary of political news, as well as an over-view of diplomatic, statistical, and other historical occurrences." Following the signing of the Louisiana Purchase treaty in late April 1803, the *Journal* in its July issue promptly reported on the size of the territory and in succeeding numbers published detailed information about Louisiana's trade, geography, demography, economics, customs, land prices, etc. The index to the twelve numbers of the *Journal* published in 1803 listed thirty-five entries for "America, (Nord-) Republik" and some eight entries for "Louisiana."

29. Anita M. Mallinckrodt, *How They Came*, 2.

30. Esser, "Das Dortmunder Gymnasium," 31–36.

31. Laver, *Concise History of Costume*, 151–52.

32. Savage, *Concise History of Interior Decorating*, 189–234.

33. Valentin, *German People*, 327.

34. Johann Friedrich Theodor Mallinckrodt, "Merkwürdigen Nachrichten."

35. Friedrich Zunkel, "Gustav Mallinckrodt (1799–1856)," 97.

36. Luntowski, "Arnold Mallinckrodt," 298.

37. Letter dated 7 November 1809, Mallinckrodt Family Papers, St. Louis.

38. Winterfeld, "Die Dortmunder Wandschneider-Gesellschaft," 29.

8. 1815–1819

1. Valentin, *German People*, 344–47.

2. Conze and Hentschel, *Ploetz Deutsche Geschichte*, 171, 183.

3. Valentin, *German People*, 350.

4. Dietrich von Mallinckrodt, "Die von Mallinckrodt," 63–64.

5. Johann Friedrich Theodor Mallinckrodt, "Merkwürdigen Nachrichten."

6. Letter of 6 June 1813, Mallinckrodt Family Papers, St. Louis.

7. Luntowski, "Arnold Mallinckrodt," 297.

8. Luntowski, "Arnold Mallinckrodt," 297.

9. *Preußen-Ploetz*, 62–64; Valentin, *German People*, 344.

10. Esser, "Das Dortmunder Gymnasium," 55, 113.

11. Berken, *Dortmunder Häuserbuch*, 86.

12. Bolege-Vieweg, *Straßen*, 4.

13. Maurmann, "Dr. Arnold Mallinckrodt," 11.

9. 1820–1825

1. Dietrich von Mallinckrodt, "Die von Mallinckrodt," 67–68.

2. Zunkel, "Gustav Mallinckrodt," 97.

3. *Westfälischer Anzeiger* 28 (March ?) 1817.

4. Maurmann, "Dr. Arnold Mallinckrodt," 8–9.

5. Luntowski, "Arnold Mallinckrodt," 298.

6. Friedrich Eulenstein, "Die siedlungsgeographische Entwicklung Dortmunds," 116.

7. Schulte, "Arnold Mallinckrodt."

8. Berken, *Dortmunder Häuserbuch*, 81; Maurmann, "Arnold Mallinckrodt," 53.

9. Luntowski, "Arnold Mallinckrodt," 299.

10. Maurmann, "Arnold Mallinckrodt," 50, 126–34.

11. Letter dated 24 November 1820, Mallinckrodt Family Papers, St. Louis.

12. Letter dated 24 November 1820, Mallinckrodt Family Papers, St. Louis.

13. Zunkel, "Gustav Mallinckrodt," 97–98.

14. Appendix A, no. 11.

15. Appendix A, no. 12.

16. Appendix A, no. 10.

17. Information on Klöpper from Brinkmann, *Geschichte der Dortmunder Volksschulen*, 40.

18. Appendix A, no. 10.

19. Appendix A, no. 11.

20. Appendix A, no. 12.

21. Appendix A, no. 8.

22. Appendix A, no. 7.

23. Appendix A, no. 8.

24. "Tutorium," 10 July 1826, Mallinckrodt Nachlaß, Kasten 21.

25. Appendix A, nos. 15, 14.

26. Appendix A, no. 13.

27. Appendix A, no. 14.

28. Appendix A, no. 13.

29. Appendix A, no. 14.

30. Appendix A, no. 17.

31. Appendix A, no. 16.

32. Appendix A, no. 18.

33. Appendix A, no. 18.

34. Maurmann, "Dr. Arnold Mallinckrodt," 12.

35. Berken, *Dortmunder Häuserbuch*, 50, 54; Meininghaus, "Der Dortmunder Magistratslinie," 61; Bolege-Vieweg, *Straßen*, 18.

36. Appendix A, no. 18.

37. Appendix A, no. 20.

38. Appendix A, no. 21.

39. Esser, "Das Dortmunder Gymnasium," 37, 68–72.

10. 1826–1830: New Roles

1. Zunkel, "Gustav Mallinckrodt," 99–100; *Neue Deutsche Biographie*, s.v. "Mallinckrodt."

2. Appendix A, nos. 27, 28, 29, 31–36.

3. Appendix A, no. 47.

4. Appendix A, nos. 46, 49.

5. Esser, "Das Dortmunder Gymnasium," 128.

6. Appendix A, no. 40.

7. Appendix A, no. 45.

8. Appendix A, no. 46.

9. Appendix A, no. 49.

10. Appendix A, no. 41.

11. Appendix A, no. 43.

12. Appendix A, no. 43.

13. Appendix A, no. 44.

14. Appendix A, no. 47.

15. Zunkel, "Gustav Mallinckrodt," 106.

11. *1831: Taking the Risk*

1. Appendix A, no. 96.

2. Gottfried Duden, *Bericht über eine Reise nach den westlichen Staaten Nordamerika's und einen mehrjährigen Aufenthalt am Missouri (in den Jahren 1824, 25, 26 und 1827) . . . in Bezug auf Auswanderung und Übervölkerung.*

3. James Goodrich, "Editor's Introduction," in *Report on a Journey to the Western States of North America . . .* , by Gottfried Duden, vii–xxiv.

4. Duden, *Report*, 178, 183.

5. Agnes Bretting, "Deutschsprachige Auswandererliteratur im 19. Jahrhundert: Information oder Spiegel der Träuma?"

6. Paul C. Nagel, *Missouri: A Bicentennial History*, 30–35.

7. Nagel, *Missouri*, 30.

8. *History of St. Charles, Montgomery, and Warren Counties, Missouri*, 29.

9. Harrison Anthony Trexler, *Slavery in Missouri 1804–1865*, 103.

10. Nagel, *Missouri*, 43, 86–87.

11. Appendix A, no. 79.

12. Kathleen Neils Conzen, "Germans," 406–10.

13. Berthold A. Haase-Faulenorth, "Der Traum von New Dortmund," 222–23.

14. Anita M. Mallinckrodt, *How They Came*, 14–15.

15. Anita M. Mallinckrodt, *How They Came*, 5–11.

16. Appendix A, nos. 79, 80.

17. Appendix A, no. 82.

18. Appendix A, no. 51.

19. Appendix A, no. 82.

20. Appendix A, no. 51.

21. *Bolivar* Passenger Manifest, 27 December 1831.

22. Appendix A, no. 148.

23. Julius and Emil also mentioned a report they had heard that "recently eighty whites in Louisiana were murdered by Negroes." This may have been the August 1831 slave revolt led by Nat Turner in eastern Virginia.

24. Appendix A, no. 153.

25. William G. Bek, trans., "Gottfried Duden's 'Report,' 1824–1827," *Missouri Historical Review*, 21 October 1917.

26. Appendix A, nos. 53, 55.

27. *Auswanderung Bremen-USA*, 59.

28. Fred Gustorf, *The Uncorrupted Heart*, 18–19.

29. Mark Wyman, *Immigrants in the Valley*, 6.

30. Appendix A, no. 56. The ten-to-one ratio of black and white residents in Louisiana

and Mississippi reported in this letter was not correct: In 1830 Louisiana had 126,000 Negro and 89,000 white residents; in Mississippi in 1830 there were 70,000 white and 66,000 Negro residents (*Historical Statistics of the United States,* 28, 30).

31. Wyatt Winton Belcher, *The Economic Rivalry Between St. Louis and Chicago 1850–1880,* 28.

32. Belcher, *Economic Rivalry,* 29.

33. *History of St. Charles,* 556.

34. Appendix A, no. 146.

35. Appendix A, no. 55.

36. Appendix A, no. 55.

37. Gustorf, *Uncorrupted Heart,* 82.

38. Nagel, *Missouri,* 87.

39. Nagel, *Missouri,* 88.

40. William G. Bek, "The Followers of Duden," *Missouri Historical Review,* vol. 16, no. 4 (July 1922): 538–41.

41. *History of St. Charles,* 105.

42. *History of St. Charles,* 7.

43. Joseph Schafer, ed. and trans., *Intimate Letters of Carl Schurz 1841–1869,* 134.

44. *History of St. Charles,* 1029.

45. Gustorf, *Uncorrupted Heart,* 121–22.

46. Gustorf, *Uncorrupted Heart,* 86.

47. *History of St. Charles,* 94–95, 309.

48. *History of St. Charles,* 142.

49. *History of St. Charles,* 127.

50. Lori Breslow, *Small Town,* 198–99.

51. *History of St. Charles,* 141.

52. Michael Edward Shapiro et al., *George Caleb Bingham,* 83, 88, 133–39.

53. *Daniel Boone Region of Missouri,* 1–2.

54. *History of St. Charles,* 142–43, 573–74.

12. 1832: *Putting Down Roots in Missouri*

1. Appendix A, no. 56.

2. *History of St. Charles,* 104.

3. *History of St. Charles,* 231–36.

4. Bek, "Followers of Duden," *Missouri Historical Review,* vol. 17, no. 1 (October 1922): 36.

5. Appendix A, no. 156. The private land was bought from Louis Eversmann, Duden's companion (Recorder of Deeds [b]).

6. Appendix A, no. 117.

7. *History of St. Charles,* 563.

8. Friedrich Münch, *Gesammelte Schriften,* 113–20.

9. Appendix A, no. 62.

10. *History of St. Charles,* 109–10.

11. Appendix A, no. 56.

12. Appendix A, no. 56.

13. Appendix A, nos. 48, 72, 71, 59, 76.

14. Appendix A, nos. 58, 66, 73.

15. Appendix A, no. 76.

16. Appendix A, no. 73.

17. Appendix A, no. 60.

18. Appendix A, no. 72.

19. Appendix A, no. 62.

20. Duden, *Report*, 68.

21. Duden, *Report*, 68.

22. Bek, "Followers of Duden," *Missouri Historical Review*, vol. 15, no. 4 (July 1921): 674.

23. Appendix A, no. 62.

24. Appendix A, no. 62.

25. Donald Jackson, *Voyages of the Steamboat "Yellow Stone,"* 14, 24, 28, 163, 166.

26. When Duden and Eversmann arrived in 1824, three Haun brothers, living as "backwoodsmen," were reportedly the only other Germans in the area. (Charles van Ravenswaay, *The Arts and Architecture of German Settlements in Missouri*, 22.) Duden returned to Germany in 1827. The 1830 census for Femme Osage Township showed only the well-known Anglo-American families of the time—Leonard Harold, Charles M. Farris, Micajah McClenny, Moses Bigelow, Nathan Boone, Squire Boone, plus the Howell and Callaway families (1830 Census, Missouri, 268)—before the Mallinckrodts arrived in early 1832. Thus, it is possible that the "six Germans" at the Fourth of July celebration in 1832 were Eversmann and the three Hauns from Lake Creek and the two Mallinckrodts from near Mount Pleasant.

27. Appendix A, no. 62.

28. Appendix A, no. 62. The marriage was performed by Moses Bigelow, Femme Osage Township justice of the peace. (Recorder, St. Charles County, Marriage Book II, 1826–1844, 55.)

29. Appendix A, no. 63.

30. Bek, "Followers of Duden," *Missouri Historical Review*, vol. 16, no. 4 (July 1922): 529.

31. Gustorf, *Uncorrupted Heart*, 82.

32. Bek, "Followers of Duden," *Missouri Historical Review*, vol. 16, no. 2 (January 1922): 305–6.

33. Bek, "Followers of Duden," *Missouri Historical Review*, vol. 15, no. 4 (July 1921): 674.

34. Francis Lieber, "Die Frauen," 9–11.

35. Duden, *Report*, 72.

36. Heinrich von Martels, *Briefe über die westlichen Theile der Vereinigten Staaten von Nordamerika*, 37.

37. Adolf E. Schroeder and Carla Schulz-Geisberg, eds., *Hold Dear, as Always*, 1.

38. This 1988 book, *Hold Dear, as Always*, is the story of Henrietta Bruns, called Jette, who emigrated from Westphalia, Germany, with her physician husband to Westphalia, Missouri, in 1836.

39. Martels, *Briefe*, 36.

40. Probably other family members had already written Emil and Julius about the important political event of 27 May 1832—the first mass demonstration of German demo-

crats, at Castle Hambach in the Palatinate. The demonstration had failed, however, to bring any change in Germany's autocratic political rule.

41. Appendix A, nos. 61, 63.

42. Appendix A, nos. 79, 80.

43. Appendix A, no. 80.

44. Trexler, *Slavery in Missouri*, 10, 12, 18.

45. *History of St. Charles*, 576; Nagel, *Missouri*, 90; Trexler, *Slavery in Missouri*, 38.

46. Trexler, *Slavery in Missouri*, 27, 63–68, 179; Nagel, *Missouri*, 92.

47. Trexler, *Slavery in Missouri*, 174–75, 184; Nagel, *Missouri*, 91.

48. *History of St. Charles*, 970.

49. Trexler, *Slavery in Missouri*, 127.

50. Gert Göbel, *Länger als ein Menschenleben in Missouri*, 6.

51. Bek, "Followers of Duden," *Missouri Historical Review*, vol. 15, no. 4 (July 1921), 661.

52. Ottilie Assig, "Die Deutschen in Missouri," 313.

53. Appendix A, no. 81. The marriage was performed by Micajah McClenny, judge of the St. Charles County Court (Recorder, St. Charles County, Marriage Book II, 60).

54. Appendix A, no. 96.

55. Appendix A, no. 99.

56. Appendix A, no. 81.

57. Appendix A, no. 81.

58. Appendix A, no. 83.

59. Appendix A, no. 83.

60. Appendix A, no. 83.

61. Appendix A, no. 96.

62. James Neal Primm, Introduction, 3.

63. Appendix A, no. 83.

64. Appendix A, no. 83.

65. *History of St. Charles*, 106.

66. Bek, "Followers of Duden," *Missouri Historical Review*, vol. 18, no. 1 (October 1923): 36–38; Gerd Alfred Petermann, "Friends of Light (*Lichtfreunde*)," 135 n. 12.

67. Petermann, "Friends of Light," 135 n. 12.

13. *1834: Emil to St. Louis*

1. Appendix A, nos. 100, 96.

2. Appendix A, no. 96.

3. Appendix A, no. 96.

4. Appendix A, no. 96.

5. Appendix A, no. 79.

6. Appendix A, no. 96.

7. Appendix A, no. 100.

8. Appendix A, no. 96.

9. Appendix A, no. 106.

10. Bek, "Followers of Duden," *Missouri Historical Review*, vol. 15, no. 3 (April 1921): 542.

11. Appendix A, no. 96.

12. Appendix A, no. 99.
13. Wyman, *Immigrants in the Valley*, 94.
14. Dan Elbert Clark, *The Middle West in American History*, 214.
15. Wyman, *Immigrants in the Valley*, 94.
16. Jackson, *Voyages*, 100–101.
17. Bek, "Followers of Duden," *Missouri Historical Review*, vol. 15, no. 23 (April 1921): 527–28.
18. Jackson, *Voyages*, 100–101.
19. Gustorf, *Uncorrupted Heart*, 50.
20. Apppendix A, no. 100.

14. *1835: Julius's Dream—New Dortmund*

1. Citizenship archives, St. Charles, Missouri.
2. Appendix A, nos. 79, 80.
3. Bek, "Followers of Duden," *Missouri Historical Review*, vol. 16, no. 3 (April 1922): 368.
4. Bek, "Followers of Duden," *Missouri Historical Review*, vol. 18, no. 1 (October 1923): 36–38.
5. Bek, "Followers of Duden," *Missouri Historical Review*, vol. 14, no. 3–4 (April–July 1920): 446, 457.
6. Appendix A, no. 83.
7. Bek, "Followers of Duden," *Missouri Historical Review*, vol. 18, no. 4 (July 1924): 575–76. For details of these immigration societies, see Adolf E. Schroeder, "To Missouri, Where the Sun of Freedom Shines," and Helbich, Kamphoefner, and Sommer, *Briefe aus Amerika*, 15.
8. Helbich, Kamphoefner, and Sommer, *Briefe aus Amerika*, 15.
9. Petermann, "Friends of Light," 110.
10. Appendix A, no. 96.
11. Recorder of Deeds, St. Charles County, Book K, 218 (b).
12. Appendix A, no. 99.
13. Appendix A, no. 62.
14. Appendix A, no. 100.
15. Appendix A, no. 99.
16. Recorder of Deeds, St. Charles County, Plat Book K, 224, and Township Plats 2 (d).
17. Recorder of Deeds, St. Charles County (g).
18. Recorder of Deeds, St. Charles County (e).
19. Appendix A, no. 101.
20. Gustorf, *Uncorrupted Heart*, 124–28.
21. St. Charles Papers, Julius Mallinckrodt.
22. Recorder of Deeds, St. Charles County (f).

15. *1836: Conrad's Visit*

1. Author's notes from a no-longer-extant 1851 letter to Conrad from his mother.
2. Helmut Esser, "Die Lehrer am Stadtgymnasium."

3. Berthold A. Haase-Faulenorth, "Der Traum von New Dortmund," 228. The director was probably Dr. Bernhardt Thiersch, who assumed that position in 1833 (Esser, "Das Dortmunder Gymnasium," 95, 97).

4. Anita M. Mallinckrodt, *How They Came*, 8–9.

5. Anita M. Mallinckrodt, *How They Came*, 12.

6. Schroeder and Schulz-Geisberg, *Hold Dear*, 59–61.

7. Earl Mallinckrodt, family memorabilia.

8. Schroeder and Schulz-Geisberg, *Hold Dear*, 62.

9. *Hafengeld-Ausgehende Schiffe*, 1836.

10. *Dortmunder Wochenblatt*, 23 July 1836.

11. Schroeder and Schulz-Geisberg, *Hold Dear*, 67–68.

12. Brig *Ulysses* passenger manifest.

13. Schroeder and Schulz-Geisberg, *Hold Dear*, 68.

14. Robert C. Keith, *Baltimore Harbor*, 126.

15. T. Courtney J. Whedbee, *The Port of Baltimore in the Making 1828–1878*, 22.

16. Keith, *Baltimore Harbor*, 126.

17. Whedbee, *Port of Baltimore*, 33–34.

18. Gail F. Stern, *Freedom's Door*, 35–36.

19. Frederic L. Paxson, *History of the American Frontier*, 414; Gustorf, *Uncorrupted Heart*, 62–64; Clark, *Middle West*, 123, 150.

20. Anita M. Mallinckrodt, *How They Came*, 33–34.

21. Bek, "Followers of Duden," *Missouri Historical Review*, vol. 15, no. 3 (April 1921): 528–533.

22. Archer Butler Hulbert, *The Cumberland Road*, 144.

23. Hulbert, *Cumberland Road*, 174, 179, 185.

24. Hulbert, *Cumberland Road*, 123, 144.

25. Hulbert, *Cumberland Road*, 102–8, 141.

26. Hulbert, *Cumberland Road*, 119–20.

27. Hulbert, *Cumberland Road*, 132, 138.

28. Hulbert, *Cumberland Road*, 127–29.

29. Hulbert, *Cumberland Road*, 128, 131, 164.

30. Hulbert, *Cumberland Road*, 157, 171.

31. Schroeder and Schulz-Geisberg, *Hold Dear*, 68–69.

32. Schroeder and Schulz-Geisberg, *Hold Dear*, 69

33. Schroeder and Schulz-Geisberg, *Hold Dear*, 69; Appendix A, no. 101.

34. Nagel, *Missouri*, 77.

35. Belcher, *Economic Rivalry*, 30.

36. Nagel, *Missouri*, 64–65.

37. Belcher, *Economic Rivalry*, 97–99.

38. *History of St. Charles*, 583–584.

39. Trexler, *Slavery in Missouri*, 51, 224.

40. Dietrich von Mallinckrodt, "Die von Mallinckrodt zu Steinberg," 65, 70.

41. Delphine Wedmore, S.C.C., *The Woman Who Couldn't Be Stopped*, 38, 62.

42. Bek, "Followers of Duden," *Missouri Historical Review*, vol. 17, no. 3 (April 1923): 334.

43. Bek, "Followers of Duden," *Missouri Historical Review*, vol. 18, no. 4 (July 1924): 571.

44. Bek, "Followers of Duden," *Missouri Historical Review*, vol. 15, no. 4 (July 1921): 681.

45. Bek, "Followers of Duden," *Missouri Historical Review*, vol. 15, no. 4 (July 1921): 681.

46. Steven Rowan, "German Language Newspapers in St. Louis, 1835–1974," 45, 48.

47. Petermann, "Friends of Light," 134 n. 7.

48. Petermann, "Friends of Light," 121.

49. Petermann, "Friends of Light," 123.

50. Petermann, "Friends of Light," 135 n. 19.

51. *History of St. Charles*, 314; Bek, "Followers of Duden," *Missouri Historical Review*, vol. 16, no. 1 (October 1921): 119.

52. Bek, "Followers of Duden," *Missouri Historical Review*, vol. 16, no. 1 (October 1921): 119–120.

53. Bek, "Followers of Duden," *Missouri Historical Review*, vol. 15, no. 4 (July 1921): 688.

54. *St. Charles Demokrat*, 3 May 1888.

55. Appendix A, no. 101.

56. Schroeder and Schulz-Geisberg, *Hold Dear*, 78, 87.

57. Bek, "Followers of Duden," *Missouri Historical Review*, vol. 16, no. 3 (April 1922): 382.

58. Appendix A, no. 101; Primm, Introduction, 4.

59. Appendix A, nos. 101, 68.

60. Appendix A, no. 103.

61. Haase-Faulenorth, "Der Traum von New Dortmund," 231.

62. Haase-Faulenorth, "Der Traum von New Dortmund," 228.

63. Berken, *Dortmunder Häuserbuch*, 10.

64. Berken, *Dortmunder Häuserbuch*, 86.

65. Ingeborg Weber-Kellermann, *Frauenleben im 19. Jahrhundert*, 21, 25, 34.

66. F. Erdbrink and F. Barich, "Verzeichnis der Lehrer und Leherinen an den evangelischen Volksschulen zu Dortmund 1570–1, Juli 1913"; Dortmund Stadtarchiv correspondence with the author, 6 November 1989.

67. Esser, "Das Dortmunder Gymnasium," 127.

68. Appendix A, no. 86.

69. Appendix A, no. 79.

70. Appendix A, no. 106.

71. Apppendix A, no. 103.

72. Appendix A, no. 105.

73. Appendix A, no. 104.

74. Appendix A, no. 104.

75. Appendix A, no. 96.

76. Appendix A, no. 106.

77. Appendix A, no. 104.

78. The exchanges of correspondence with Conrad in 1835 and 1837 must have been so irritating to Gustav, or seen as so typical of Conrad's behavior, that Gustav kept these letters, although few others from Conrad are preserved in his files.

79. Appendix A, no. 105.

16. 1837: Emil to Pike County

1. Appendix A, no. 101.

2. Appendix A, no. 106.

3. Appendix A, no. 102.

4. Appendix A, no. 103.

5. Appendix A, no. 105.

17. *1838: Second Emigrant Contingent*

1. Appendix A, nos. 103, 106.

2. Laver, *Concise History of Costume*, 161–68.

3. Dortmund Stadtarchiv correspondence with the author, 15 November 1989.

4. Esser, "Das Dortmunder Gymnasium," 92, 98.

5. Bates Papers, 1840. (Sophie's reference may have been to a private school she operated.)

6. Esser, "Das Dortmunder Gymnasium," 32, 36 n. 83, 38.

7. Wilhelm Knörich, *Mitteilungen über die städtische höhere Mädchenschule zu Dortmund—zu Feier des 25. jährigen Bestehens (1867–1892)*," 5–7.

8. Esser, "Das Dortmunder Gymnasium," 102–4.

9. Bek, "Followers of Duden," *Missouri Historical Review*, vol. 15, no. 4 (July 1921): 694.

10. The Bulwer and Cooper books, along with the Latin and Shakespeare volumes, were listed on the bill of sale prepared at the public auction of Conrad's possessions after his death in 1877 (Probate Office, St. Charles County Circuit Court). Since Conrad's son Albert Feldmann purchased many of the lots of his father's books at the sale, and apparently had directly inherited others, the Cooper, Bulwer, Brockhaus, and three Campe volumes (1797, 1804, 1806) were handed down through the family to the author, Conrad's great-granddaughter. The Latin and Shakespeare volumes, however, are missing. (Anita M. Mallinckrodt, family memorabilia.)

11. Johann Friedrich Theodor Mallinckrodt, "Für mich."

12. During the period of Napoleonic influence, civil marriage was possible (*Conversations-Lexikon* 3:443, s.v. "Ehe").

13. Laver, *Concise History of Costume*, 160–61.

14. *Dortmunder Wochenblatt*, 18 April 1838.

15. "Hafengeld—Ausgehende Schiffe" (1838).

16. Bremen Stadtarchiv Bild Archiv, Beschreibung Bild Nr. 525.

17. *Copernicus* passenger manifest.

18. Kirchenbuch der St. Reinoldi-Gemeinde, no. 7, 1838, no. 8, 1838.

19. Departure, 17 May 1838 ("Hafengeld," 1838, 58); arrival, 28 June 1838 (*Copernicus* passenger manifest).

20. Appendix A, no. 106.

21. Appendix A, no. 115.

22. Appendix A, no. 106.

23. Appendix A, no. 107.

24. Appendix A, no. 108.

25. Appendix A, no. 109.

26. Gustorf, *Uncorrupted Heart*, 77.

27. Bates Papers.

28. Schroeder and Schulz-Geisberg, *Hold Dear*, 93.

29. Schroeder and Schulz-Geisberg, *Hold Dear*, 95.

18. 1839: Mallinckrodts in Missouri Courts

1. Appendix A, no. 127.
2. Bates Papers.
3. Bates Papers.
4. Bates Papers.
5. Bates Papers.
6. Circuit Court, St. Charles County (c).
7. Circuit Court, St. Charles County (a).
8. *History of St. Charles*, 212–13.
9. William Francis English, *The Pioneer Lawyer and Jurist in Missouri*, 68.
10. *History of St. Charles*, 126–27.
11. *St. Charles Demokrat*, 10 December 1857. (The newspaper also warned its German readers that not all justices of the peace were as well educated as one might expect: "Too frequently the men who hold this office are too little or not at all acquainted with the laws whose application are entrusted to them . . . in cases where bad character combines with ignorance, the office is not rarely used as a means of repression and legal distortion.")
12. English, *Pioneer Lawyer*, 15–16.
13. *St. Charles Demokrat*, 10, 17, 24 December 1857.
14. *History of St. Charles*, 206.
15. English, *Pioneer Lawyer*, 13, 113.
16. Mrs. Ted Rauch, "Seventieth Birthday for County Court House."
17. Nelson Manfred Blake, *The Road to Reno*, 52–57.
18. Missouri, *The Revised Statutes of the State of Missouri (1834–1835)*, 225.
19. Blake, *Road to Reno*, 56.
20. English, *Pioneer Lawyer*, 69.
21. Blake, *Road to Reno*, 52–57.
22. Circuit Court, St. Charles County (a).
23. Circuit Court, St. Charles County (c).
24. Bates Papers.
25. Appendix A, no. 107.
26. Appendix A, no. 114.
27. Appendix A, no. 115.
28. Circuit Court, St. Charles County (a).
29. *History of St. Charles*, 211.
30. *History of St. Charles*, 195.
31. William Van Ness Bey, *The Bench and Bar of Missouri*, 92–94.
32. *History of St. Charles*, 196.
33. Circuit Court, St. Charles County (a).
34. Rauch, "Seventieth Birthday."
35. Appendix A, no. 116.
36. Appendix A, no. 117.
37. Appendix A, no. 113.
38. Appendix A, no. 112.
39. Wedmore, *Woman Who Couldn't Be Stopped*, 90ff.
40. Appendix A, no. 120.
41. Appendix A, no. 120.

42. Appendix A, no. 121. (Mr. Angelrodt was German consul in St. Louis.)

43. Bates Papers.

44. Appendix A, no. 122.

45. Bates Papers.

46. Circuit Court, St. Charles County (e).

47. Circuit Court, St. Charles County (a).

48. Frederic A. Culmer, *A History of Missouri for High Schools*, 75.

49. Clarence H. McClure, *History of Missouri*, 78, 121–22; Claude Anderson Phillips, *A History of Education in Missouri*, 2–3.

50. *History of St. Charles*, 65.

51. Phillips, *History of Education*, 2–4, 10.

52. Earl Mallinckrodt, family memorabilia.

53. Bates Papers.

54. Mallinckrodt Genealogy, Table 9.

55. Circuit Court, St. Charles County (b).

56. Bates Paper.

57. Circuit Court, St. Charles County (c).

58. Circuit Court, St. Charles County (c).

59. Circuit Court, St. Charles County (c).

60. Circuit Court, St. Charles County (d).

61. Bey, *Bench and Bar of Missouri*, 468.

62. *History of St. Charles*, 194, 207.

63. Bates Papers.

64. *History of St. Charles*, 340, 983.

65. Bates Papers.

66. Bates Papers.

67. Bates Papers.

68. Appendix A, no. 122.

69. Appendix A, no. 79.

70. Circuit Court, St. Charles County (d).

71. *Conversations-Lexikon*, vol. 3, s.v. "Diffamation."

72. Martin L. Newell, *The Law of Defamation, Libel, and Slander*, 651.

73. Azel F. Hatch, *Statutes and Constitutional Provisions Regarding Libel and Slander*, 58–59.

74. Franklin Fiske Heard, *A Treatise on the Law of Libel and Slander*, 2, 6, 41.

75. Circuit Court, St. Charles County (d); 1840–1844 Records, Book E, 62.

76. Circuit Court, St. Charles County (c); 1840–1844 Records, Book E, 60.

77. *History of St. Charles*, 199, 107; Arnold Krekel Papers.

78. *History of St. Charles*, 237.

79. Circuit Court, St. Charles County (d)

80. Circuit Court, St. Charles County (d); 1840–1844 Records, Book E, 82, 83, 84, 87, 91.

81. William E. Parrish, *Turbulent Partnership*, 42.

82. English, *Pioneer Lawyer*, 119.

83. Gamble Papers, "Emil Mallinckrodt."

84. Gamble Papers.

85. Appendix A, no. 127.

86. Mallinckrodt Nachlaß, Kasten 100.

87. Gamble Papers.

88. Circuit Court, St. Charles County (e).

89. Bey, *Bench and Bar of Missouri,* 468.

90. Circuit Court, St. Charles County (e).

91. Circuit Court, St. Charles County (e).

92. Circuit Court, St. Charles County (e); 1840–1844 Records, Book E, 150, 168, 174.

93. Circuit Court, St. Charles County (d); 1840–1844 Records, Book E, 156.

94. Gamble Papers.

95. Appendix A, no. 131.

96. Warren County, Missouri, Circuit Court Marriage Records, 14 February 1842.

97. Circuit Court, St. Charles County, 1840–1844 Records, Book E, 37.

98. Appendix A, no. 126.

99. Gamble Papers.

100. Warren County Marriage Records, 14 February 1842.

101. Circuit Court, St. Charles County (d); 1840–1844 Records, Book E, 191.

102. Circuit Court, St. Charles County (e); 1840–1844 Records, Book E, 209.

103. Circuit Court, St. Charles County (f); 1840–1844 Records, Book E, 239, 248.

104. Circuit Court, St. Charles County (e); 1840–1844 Records, Book E, 248.

105. Circuit Court, St. Charles County (e).

106. Circuit Court, St. Charles County (e).

107. Circuit Court, St. Charles County (e); 1840–1844 Records, Book E, 312, 315, 320.

108. Circuit Court, St. Charles County (e).

109. Circuit Court, St. Charles County (e); 1840–1844 Records, Book E, 335.

110. Circuit Court, St. Charles County (e); 1840–1844 Records, Book E, 373.

111. Appendix A, no. 127.

112. Appendix A, no. 133.

113. Appendix A, no. 135.

114. Appendix A, no. 135.

115. Appendix A, no. 181.

116. Appendix A, no. 152.

19. *1840: Emil's New Beginning*

1. Appendix A, no. 117.

2. Appendix A, no. 117.

3. Appendix A, no. 117.

4. Appendix A, no. 118.

5. Appendix A, no. 119.

6. Appendix A, no. 120.

7. Appendix A, no. 121.

8. Appendix A, no. 121.

9. Galusha Anderson, *The Story of a Border City During the Civil War,* 2.

10. Appendix A, no. 122.

11. Appendix A, nos. 122, 124.

12. Appendix A, no. 127.

13. Appendix A, no. 124.

14. Appendix A, no. 127.

15. Appendix A, nos. 118, 122.

16. Appendix A, no. 123.

17. Appendix A, nos. 126, 127; Citizenship Archives, St. Charles, 15 May 1840.

18. Appendix A, no. 126.

19. *History of St. Charles*, 587.

20. Samuel Eliot Morison, *The Oxford History of the American People*, 456.

21. "Scandinavian in Origin."

22. Bek, "Followers of Duden," *Missouri Historical Review*, vol. 15, no. 4 (July 1921): 692.

23. Morison, *Oxford History*, 458; *History of St. Charles*, 588.

24. Bek, "Followers of Duden," *Missouri Historical Review*, vol. 17, no. 3 (April 1923): 334–35.

25. Morison, *Oxford History*, 520; Barbara Chase-Riboud, *Echo of Lions*.

26. Primm, Introduction, 4.

27. Culmer, *History of Missouri*, 127.

28. Primm, Introduction, 4.

29. Appendix A, no. 124.

30. Belcher, *Economic Rivalry*, 52.

31. Appendix A, no. 121.

32. Appendix A, no. 122.

33. Appendix A, no. 126.

34. Appendix A, no. 127.

35. Anita M. Mallinckrodt, *Why They Left*, 22–23.

36. Zunkel, "Gustav Mallinckrodt," 105; David McLellan, *Karl Marx*, 43–61.

37. McLellan, *Karl Marx*, 45–61.

38. Zunkel, "Gustav Mallinckrodt," 106.

39. Zunkel, "Gustav Mallinckrodt," 106, 110.

40. Appendix A, no. 126.

41. Appendix A, no. 127.

42. Appendix A, no. 128.

43. Appendix A, no. 127.

44. Appendix A, no. 128.

45. Appendix A, nos. 128, 133.

46. Appendix A, no. 135.

47. Appendix A, no. 128.

48. *History of St. Charles*, 588.

49. Appendix A, no. 124.

50. Appendix A, no. 124.

20. *1844: Flood, Disease, Death*

1. Recorder of Deeds, St. Charles County, Direct Index 1804–1852, Book N (f).

2. *History of St. Charles,* 237.

3. Appendix A, no. 130; *Laws of the State of Missouri, Passed at the First Session of the Twelfth General Assembly* (City of Jefferson: Allen Hammond, 1843), 166; J. W. Schiermeier,

"Cracker Barrel News," *Washington Missourian*. Legends about the choice are endless, and some are ludicrous: For example, "Augusta," the English spelling of the female German name "Auguste," was not the name of Leonard Harold's wife, nor the first name of German town fathers (the masculine would have been something like Augustusburg, Augustville, etc.), or a town in Prussia, Hesse, or Hanover from where they came. (Augsburg was in Bavaria.) Rather, the name Augusta may simply have been copied from non-German settlements in other parts of America: Georgia (1735), Kentucky (1792), Maine (1797), Arkansas (1846). Or, seen historically, there could have been a touch of political irony in the German settlers' choice. Since Emperor Friedrich Wilhelm IV's crushing of the 1848 revolution had disappointed many who wanted reform in their old homeland, they hoped the next Prussian ruler, Prince William I, would be a better ruler. He had spent the year 1848 in England, and, especially important, his wife, Auguste, the next empress, was believed to be a very intelligent woman, indeed, more clever than her husband! A princess of Weimar "with a strong feeling for peace and liberty," Auguste represented the Germany of culture (Valentin, *The German People*, 450–51). To the politically conscious Mount Pleasant settlers, she may have symbolized both their hopes for the political future of the old homeland as well as the new hometown on the Missouri.

4. McClure, *History of Missouri*, 123.

5. Culmer, *History of Missouri*, 138.

6. Bek, "Followers of Duden," *Missouri Historical Review*, vol. 18, no. 1 (October 1923): 36–42.

7. Femme Osage Church Records; Bek, "Followers of Duden," *Missouri Historical Review*, vol. 18, no. 1 (October 1923): 43; *Ebenezer 1851–1951*.

8. Bek, "Followers of Duden," *Missouri Historical Review*, vol. 18, no. 1 (October 1923): 47; Petermann, "Friends of Light," 124.

9. Bek, "Followers of Duden," *Missouri Historical Review*, vol. 18, no. 2 (January 1924): 231.

10. *History of St. Charles*, 1010.

11. Petermann, "Friends of Light," 124. The pro-Kirchenverein point of view is found in Carl E. Schneider, *The German Church on the American Frontier*.

12. Petermann, "Friends of Light," 136 n. 20.

13. Petermann, "Friends of Light," 125, 136 n. 25.

14. *Anzeiger des Westens*, 21 January 1843.

15. Petermann, "Friends of Light," 125–26. See also Bek, *Hermann*, 256–65.

16. *Licht-Freund*, 1 May 1844. (Mühl died of cholera on 7 July 1854 [*Anzeiger des Westens*, 21 July 1854, 29 July 1854].)

17. *History of St. Charles*, 237, 200.

18. *History of St. Charles*, 237.

19. Appendix A, no. 128.

20. *History of St. Charles*, 225.

21. *Washington Missourian*, 16 June 1955. Harold received only one dollar for this block of land.

22. *St. Charles Demokrat*, 3 May 1888.

23. *History of St. Charles*, 225.

24. *History of St. Charles*, 69.

25. Hubert E. Mallinckrodt, family memorabilia.

26. Hubert E. Mallinckrodt, family memorabila; U.S. Bureau of Census, Microfilm M432 (1850), roll 413, p. 65.

27. The quotation is based on the author's 1950s notes of no-longer-extant family documents, including a June 1851 letter from seventy-four-year-old Dorothea Mallinckrodt, in Dortmund, to her son Conrad.

28. *History of St. Charles*, 199–200.

29. *History of St. Charles*, 107.

30. Arnold Krekel Papers.

31. *History of St. Charles*, 211.

32. Circuit Court, St. Charles County (e).

33. Citizenship Archives, St. Charles County. (See also Circuit Court, St. Charles County, Book D, 489, for August's declaration of citizenship intent, as well as Book E, 453, for naturalization.) It is interesting to note that in their declarations of intent neither Conrad nor August Mallinckrodt reported their date of arrival from Germany in Baltimore correctly or, indeed, even gave the same date although they were on the same ship. Conrad's declaration states an arrival date of 15 September 1836, although that was the year of his first visit to America, when the ship *Ulysses* arrived in Baltimore on 19 September. August lists his 1838 arrival as 12 June, although Baltimore's harbor records say the *Copernicus* anchored on 28 June.

34. Trexler, *Slavery in Missouri*, 213–14.

35. Morison, *Oxford History*, 523.

36. Appendix A, no. 129.

37. Appendix A, no. 130.

38. Appendix A, no. 131.

39. *History of St. Charles*, 592.

40. Appendix A, no. 132.

41. Rufus Terral, *The Missouri Valley*, 89–91.

42. Terral, *Missouri Valley*, 85.

43. Bek, "Followers of Duden," *Missouri Historical Review*, vol. 17, no. 1 (October 1922): 43–44.

44. *Washington Missourian*, "Missouri River High Stages," 11–12 October 1986.

45. Appendix A, no. 132.

46. Bek, "Followers of Duden," *Missouri Historical Review*, vol. 17, no. 4 (July 1923): 489.

47. Bek, "Followers of Duden," *Missouri Historical Review*, vol. 17, no. 4 (July 1923): 489.

48. Terral, *Missouri Valley*, 10.

49. Appendix A, no. 133.

50. Appendix A, no. 135.

51. Appendix A, no. 133.

52. Appendix A, no. 135.

53. Appendix A, no. 133.

54. Bek, "Followers of Duden," *Missouri Historical Review*, vol. 16, no. 3 (April 1922): 348–49.

21. *1845: Boom Times for the Nation and Cities*

1. Appendix A, no. 130.

2. Appendix A, no. 135.

3. John S. D. Eisenhower, *So Far from God*.

4. *History of St. Charles*, 57.

5. Trexler, *Slavery in Missouri*, 140.

6. Bek, "Followers of Duden," *Missouri Historical Review*, vol. 17, no. 4 (July 1923): 494.

7. *History of St. Charles*, 173–75.

8. Appendix A, no. 136.

9. Appendix A, no. 137.

10. Appendix A, no. 135.

11. Appendix A, no. 136.

12. Appendix A, no. 139.

13. Appendix A, no. 133.

14. Appendix A, nos. 135, 139.

15. Appendix A, no. 137.

16. Mallinckrodt Nachlaß, Kasten 100.

17. Appendix A, no. 150.

18. Appendix A, nos. 135, 139.

19. Appendix A, nos. 131, 135, 130, 146.

20. Appendix A, no. 148.

21. Appendix A, no. 146.

22. Appendix A, no. 148.

23. Appendix A, no. 150.

24. Belcher, *Economic Rivalry*, 15.

25. Appendix A, no. 150.

26. Appendix A, no. 146.

27. Appendix A, no. 137; Belcher, *Economic Rivalry*, 14.

28. Appendix A, no. 135.

29. Belcher, *Economic Rivalry*, 26, 112.

30. Shapiro et al., *George Caleb Bingham*, 141–74.

31. Belcher, *Economic Rivalry*, 47.

32. Appendix A, no. 137.

33. Belcher, *Economic Rivalry*, 15, 75, 95 (quote), 115.

34. Belcher, *Economic Rivalry*, 102–3.

35. Belcher, *Economic Rivalry*, 11, 28, 96.

36. Belcher, *Economic Rivalry*, 74, 75.

37. Belcher, *Economic Rivalry*, 68–71, 78–91.

38. Culmer, *History of Missouri*, 135.

39. Appendix A, no. 146.

40. Walter O. Forster, *Zion on the Mississippi: The Settlement of the Saxon Lutherans in Missouri 1839–1841*, 252–53.

41. Forster, *Zion on the Mississippi*, 271.

42. David W. Detjen, *The Germans in Missouri, 1900–1918*, 8.

43. Forster, *Zion on the Mississippi*, 273–75.

44. Appendix A, nos. 147, 146.

45. Appendix A, no. 135.

46. Appendix A, no. 135.

47. Appendix A, no. 129.

48. Appendix A, nos. 147, 148.
49. Appendix A, no. 135.
50. *History of St. Charles*, 340.
51. Appendix A, no. 135.
52. Appendix A, no. 134.
53. Appendix A, no. 138.
54. Appendix A, no. 141.
55. Appendix A, no. 144.
56. Appendix A, no. 145.
57. Appendix A, no. 150.
58. Appendix A, no. 147.
59. Appendix A, no. 148.
60. Bek, "Followers of Duden," *Missouri Historical Review*, vol. 17, no. 4 (July 1923): 493.
61. Appendix A, no. 148.
62. Bek, "Followers of Duden," *Missouri Historical Review*, vol. 17, no. 4 (July 1923): 493.
63. Appendix A, no. 137.
64. Zunkel, "Gustav Mallinckrodt," 111–12.
65. Zunkel, "Gustav Mallinckrodt," 112–13.
66. Wedmore, *The Woman Who Couldn't Be Stopped*, 110–11, 156, 169, 176.
67. Schroeder and Schulz-Geisberg, *Hold Dear*, 72n.
68. Richard B. Morris, ed., *Encyclopedia of American History*, 207.
69. *History of St. Charles*, 1023.
70. *History of St. Charles*, 592.
71. *Columbia Encyclopedia*, s.v. "John Augustus Sutter."
72. Trexler, *Slavery in Missouri*, 83.
73. Nagel, *Missouri*, 92–93.
74. Bek, "Followers of Duden," *Missouri Historical Review*, vol. 17, no. 3 (April 1923): 336.
75. Bek, "Followers of Duden," *Missouri Historical Review*, vol. 17, no. 3 (April 1923): 337.
76. Wyman, *Immigrants in the Valley*, 63.
77. Morris, *Encyclopedia of American History*, 213.
78. Trexler, *Slavery in Missouri*, 224.
79. Appendix A, no. 150. Previously, Emil had said that he "hired" Negro help. Appendix A, nos. 96, 100.
80. Appendix A, no. 150.
81. Appendix A, no. 151.
82. Appendix A, no. 152.
83. Bek, "Followers of Duden," *Missouri Historical Review*, vol. 17, no. 4 (July 1923): 489.
84. Appendix A, nos. 153, 152.
85. Appendix A, no. 152.
86. Appendix A, no. 153.
87. Appendix A, no. 150.
88. Appendix A, no. 151.

89. Appendix A, no. 154.

90. U.S. Bureau of Census, Microfilm M432 (1850), roll 413, p. 61.

91. Berken, *Dortmunder Häuserbuch*, 119.

92. Eulenstein, "Die siedlungsgeographische Entwicklung."

93. Appendix A, no. 160.

94. Appendix A, no. 155.

95. Appendix A, no. 160.

96. Appendix A, nos. 161, 160.

97. Appendix A, no. 161.

98. Appendix A, no. 158.

99. Appendix A, no. 164.

100. Appendix A, nos. 163, 165.

101. Appendix A, nos. 164, 165.

102. Appendix A, no. 167.

103. Appendix A, no. 171.

104. Appendix A, no. 170.

105. Appendix A, no. 172.

106. Appendix A, nos. 172, 173.

107. Appendix A, no. 174.

108. Appendix A, no. 175.

22. *1845: Growth in the Countryside*

1. *History of St. Charles*, 141–42.

2. Petermann, "Friends of Light," 128–29.

3. Bek, "Followers of Duden," *Missouri Historical Review*, vol. 18, no. 2 (January 1924): 243–44.

4. *History of St. Charles*, 138.

5. Samuel F. Harrison, *History of Hermann, Missouri*, 138.

6. Harrison, *Hermann*, 239–40.

7. Bek, "Followers of Duden," *Missouri Historical Review*, vol. 17, no. 3 (April 1923): 332–33.

8. *History of St. Charles*, 237.

9. *History of St. Charles*, 106.

10. Although not officially documented but supported by family records, the 18 June birth resulted in twins; one of the infants, named Christina, died the same day. The baptism was noted in the Femme Osage Church Records. Also see *Washington Missourian*, 24 August 1950, for the church's history.

11. Missouri State Case Records, *Philipp Wachs v. Gustavus Schäfer* (1852).

12. *St. Charles Demokrat*, 17 December 1857.

13. Circuit Court, 1851–1855 Records, Book G, 137.

14. Missouri State Case Records.

15. Circuit Court, 1851–1855 Records, Book G, 141.

16. Missouri State Case Records.

17. Circuit Court, 1851–1855 Records, Book G, 236.

18. Some eighteen years later Friedrich Münch, translator of the initial witness testimony

in the Wachs murder case, offered an account of the affair perhaps colored by the years that had passed. According to Münch, Wachs had been a well-educated immigrant whom Julius Mallinckrodt had been glad to have as a son-in-law and for whom he had built a house on his property.

The murder, in Münch's opinion, resulted from Wachs's drinking too much and irritating Schäfer. Interestingly, Münch reported that Schäfer's sentence had been pardoned by the governor and that Wachs's brother, Philipp, who brought the charge against Schäfer, died only several weeks later and that the brothers were buried side-by-side. No evidence of Philipp Wachs's grave, has been found, however (Friedrich Münch, "Noch ein gräßlicher Auftritt").

19. Recorder of Deeds, St. Charles County (i).

20. *History of St. Charles*, 138.

21. St. Charles County, *St. Charles County Atlas*, 1875.

22. Recorder of Deeds, St. Charles County (h).

23. After his 1840 marriage, celebrated at Emil's in St. Louis, and the birth of children, Carl Wencker apparently continued to live at Mount Pleasant (Appendix A, nos. 122, 124, 126). Then he and his wife moved to Quincy, Illinois, in 1849, where they died of cholera. A younger cousin, Frederick, carried on the cigar making business where August Mallinckrodt worked (Appendix A, nos. 151, 152). He and his descendants, who became leaders in the Augusta community (*History of St. Charles*, 259) maintained close relations with the Mallinckrodts. The ties extended into the next generation, when Conrad Mallinckrodt's children asked Friedrich Wencker's son, Carl, to administer Conrad's estate.

24. U.S. Bureau of Census, Microfilm M704 (1840), roll 230, p. 24; M432 (1850), roll 413, p. 65.

25. *History of St. Charles*, 237.

26. W. M. Gillespie, *Treatise on Land-Surveying*. Anita M. Mallinckrodt, family memorabilia.

27. Hubert E. Mallinckrodt, family memorabilia (Conrad Mallinckrodt's surveying equipment, field note books, and original surveys of Townships 45 and 46 [1847], the Dortmund Road [1851], Augusta [1855], and Holstein [c. 1863]).

28. The meeting declared its general support for the party's fundamentals "adopted 1840, 1844 and 1848 which had been taught by Thomas Jefferson and Andrew Jackson" and specific support for an "independent treasury system—the import customs law of 1846 in contrast to that of the Whigs of 1842—and opposition to a national bank" (*St. Charles Demokrat*, 13 March 1852).

29. *St. Charles Demokrat*, 6 November 1852.

30. *St. Charles Demokrat*, 1852–1856.

31. *St. Charles Demokrat*, 18 December 1852.

32. *St. Charles Demokrat*, 11 June 1853.

33. Münch, Friedrich, Account Books—August Mallinckrodt, 1847–1848.

34. *Ebenezer 1851–1951*.

35. Petermann, "Friends of Light," 132. Even 150 years later, when the anniversary of the Evangelical Synod was celebrated in "Duden country," the German Rationalists' beliefs and history were not reported with balance, that is, within the context of early 1800 distrust of clergy and authoritarian church organizations ("150 Years Anniversary of Evangelical Synod Marked," *Washington Missourian*, 10 October 1990).

36. *Augusta Town Record Book* (3 March 1855), 1.

37. *Augusta Town Record Book* (3 March 1855), 2.
38. *Augusta Town Record Book* (17 November 1855), 6.
39. *Augusta Town Record Book* (8 April 1856), 14.
40. Recorder of Deeds, St. Charles County (g).
41. Recorder of Deeds, St. Charles County (j).
42. *Augusta Town Record Book* (17 November 1855), 6–7.
43. *Augusta Town Record Book* (January–October 1856), 10–20.
44. *Augusta Town Record Book* (24 July 1856), 17.
45. *Augusta Town Record Book* (27 December 1855; 24 January 1856), 9–10.
46. *Augusta Town Record Book* (15 May 1856), 15.
47. *Augusta Town Record Book* (13 September 1859), 61.
48. *Augusta Town Record Book* (24 August 1858), 50.
49. *Augusta Town Record Book* (4 October 1858), 51.
50. *Augusta Town Record Book* (19 April 1858), 35.
51. Conrad Mallinckrodt, "Register of Marriages."
52. *History of St. Charles*, 237.
53. Göbel, *Ein Menschenleben in Missouri*, 136.
54. *History of St. Charles*, 200, 222.
55. Culmer, *History of Missouri*, 138.
56. Phillips, *History of Education*, 10–11.
57. Belcher, *The Economic Rivalry*, 79–82, 91.
58. Paxson, *History of the American Frontier*, 413.
59. Railroads Collection.
60. *St. Charles Demokrat*, 3 November 1855.
61. Appendix A, no. 181.
62. St. Charles County Missouri, *Atlas 1875*.

23. *1850: A State and Nation Divided*

1. *History of St. Charles*, 176–77.
2. Helbich, Kamphoefner, and Sommer, *Briefe aus Amerika*, 13.
3. Rowan, "German Language Newspapers," 46, 50–51.
4. Primm, Introduction, 6.
5. Culmer, *History of Missouri*, 136.
6. Trexler, *Slavery in Missouri*, 147f, 163, 231.
7. Trexler, *Slavery in Missouri*, 117–18, 231.
8. Emil Mallinckrodt would later publicly call it "infamous" and see its provisions as "finally leading to the disastrous, bloody civil war" (Emil Mallinckrodt's Scrapbook, "Staaten im Staate," 81).
9. *Columbia Encyclopedia*, s.v. "Harriet Beecher Stowe"; Morris, *Encyclopedia of American History*, 215.
10. Morison, *Oxford History*, 518, 523.
11. Trexler, *Slavery in Missouri*, 203–4.
12. Morison, *Oxford History*, 598.
13. Morison, *Oxford History*, 598–99.
14. Chase-Riboud, *Echo of Lions*, 48–49.

15. Morison, *Oxford History*, 597–98.

16. Trexler, *Slavery in Missouri*, 173–74.

17. Nagel, *Missouri*, 125.

18. Trexler, *Slavery in Missouri*, 166, 226.

19. Anderson, *Border City*, 1, 12–13.

20. Nagel, *Missouri*, 98. In 1850 the city of St. Louis had a population of 77,860, of whom about half (38,397, or 49.3 percent) were foreign-born. The "Germans" and "Prussians" among them numbered 23,541, or 30.2 percent of the city's total population and 61 percent of all its foreign-born (*Seventh Census 1850: Statistical View, Compendium*, 380, 399). By 1860, St. Louis's population had grown to 160,773 (to 188,561 if St. Louis County was included), of whom more than half were foreign-born. The German-born, then numbering 50,510, were still about a third of the city's total population, that is, 31.4 percent. Within the United States, by 1860 there were 1.3 million Germans. In the state of Missouri they had increased by around 88,000 in the decade of the 1850s, to represent some 55 percent of the state's foreign-born residents (*Eighth Census 1860, Population*, xxix, xxxi–xxxii, 297, 300).

21. Trexler, *Slavery in Missouri*, 166.

22. Primm, Introduction, 6.

23. Anderson, *Border City*, 9.

24. Clark, *Middle West*, 135.

25. McClure, *History of Missouri*, 120.

26. Trexler, *Slavery in Missouri*, 117.

27. Chase-Riboud, *Echo of Lions*, 297.

28. Detjen, *Germans in Missouri*, 8.

29. Detjen, *Germans in Missouri*, 8.

30. *History of St. Charles*, 594.

31. *History of St. Charles*, 594–95; Morris, *Encyclopedia of American History*, 218.

32. Morison, *Oxford History*, 590; Morris, *Encyclopedia of American History*, 218.

33. Morris, *Encyclopedia of American History*, 218.

34. Albin Böhme, "Temperanz," 291.

35. Emil Mallinckrodt's Scrapbook, "Staats- und Regierungsformen" (November 1874), 16.

36. Culmer, *History of Missouri*, 136.

37. Conzen, "Germans," 421.

38. *St. Charles Demokrat*, 24 April 1854.

39. Morison, *Oxford History*, 589.

40. *Anzeiger des Westens*, 29 July 1854.

41. Morris, *Encyclopedia of American History*, 217–18.

42. Morris, *Encyclopedia of American History*, 217.

43. Morison, *Oxford History*, 591.

44. Morison, *Oxford History*, 591; Culmer, *A History of Missouri*, 136.

45. Morris, *Encyclopedia of American History*, 219.

46. Shapiro, *George Caleb Bingham*, 52, 81, 84–85. (For other Bingham paintings of Missouri election scenes, see also *County Politicians* [p. 68], *Canvassing for a Vote* [pp. 69, 148], *Stump Speaking* [pp. 72, 76–77], and *The County Election 2* [p. 73].)

47. Nagel, *Missouri*, 125–26.

48. Morris, *Encyclopedia of American History*, 219.

49. Trexler, *Slavery in Missouri*, 200–202.

50. Richard S. Brownlee, *Gray Ghosts of the Confederacy. Guerrilla Warfare in the West, 1861–1865*, 8.

51. *St. Charles Demokrat*, 3 November 1855.

52. Morris, *Encyclopedia of American History*, 218.

53. *St. Charles Demokrat*, 29 March 1856.

54. Nagel, *Missouri*, 126.

55. Morison, *Oxford History*, 592.

56. *History of St. Charles*, 595; Samuel E. Morison and Henry S. Commager, *The Growth of the American Republic*, 625.

57. Trexler, *Slavery in Missouri*, 217; Parrish, *Turbulent Partnership*, 43.

58. Trexler, *Slavery in Missouri*, 205.

59. *St. Charles Demokrat*, 6 August 1857.

60. *St. Charles Demokrat*, 13 August 1857.

61. *Augusta Town Record Book* (4 August 1857), 28.

62. *Augusta Town Record Book* (19 April 1858), 33–34.

63. *Augusta Town Record Book* (19 April 1858), 36–37.

64. *Augusta Town Record Book* (22 April 1858), 45–46.

65. *St. Charles Demokrat*, 9 August 1856, 25 July 1853.

66. *St. Charles Demokrat*, 10 September 1857.

67. *Augusta Town Record Book* (2 September 1856), 18; (13 December 1859), 53.

68. Apparently, Wilhelmina's first husband, Heinrich Adolph Meinershagn, a Warren County farmer, died around 1854, for Warrenton, Missouri, church records show her marriage on 2 July of that year to Adolph Kleineberg. The Augusta church records show that Rev. L. Knauhs married Conrad Mallinckrodt to Wilhelmina Caroline *Kleineberg* in 1858. (Ebenezer UCC church records, Augusta, Missouri; Friedens UCC church records, Warrenton, Missouri.)

69. U.S. Bureau of the Census, Microfilm M653 (1860), roll 644, p. 612.

70. The two floor levels were necessitated by the construction problems of joining two additional wings to the initial eastern one with its high, heavy rock foundation.

71. *St. Charles Demokrat*, 8 July 1858.

72. U.S. Bureau of the Census, Microfilm M653 (1860), roll 644, p. 612.

73. *History of St. Charles*, 236–37.

74. *History of St. Charles*, 588.

75. Anita Mallinckrodt, family memorabilia ("Certified Copy of Trust Deed and Release from Julius Mallinckrodt and wife to Charles V. Spankern"); Recorder of Deeds, St. Charles County (p), Books Nff.

76. Recorder of Deeds, St. Charles County (l).

77. Münch, "Die Duden'sche Niederlassungen in Missouri," *Der Deutsche Pioneer*, 230–31. (That Münch's reporting was not always accurate is seen in Petermann's study, "Friends of Light," nn. 6 and 7, cited in ch. 15.)

78. Recorder of Deeds, St. Charles County (l). One explanation for some of the "irregularities" is that Julius had not yet fully paid Louis Eversmann for the entire land purchase of 1834 on which Dortmund was located and platted. With Eversmann thus continuing to hold the deed to at least eighteen acres of that purchase—the site of new Dortmund—and not paying the taxes on it for several years, Julius was able to purchase that precise area for $4.25 at a tax sale in 1865 (Recorder of Deeds [k]). Possibly the two old settlers had "arranged" the transaction.

79. *St. Charles Demokrat*, 6 January 1853.

80. Morris, *Encyclopedia of American History*, 537.

81. W. S. Bryan Papers, Bill of Sale from Julius Mallinckrodt.

82. *History of St. Charles*, 138; "Conrad T. Mallinckrodt," 335.

83. Emil Mallinckrodt Papers, St. Louis.

84. Friedrich Münch, *Der Staat Missouri*, 204.

85. Appendix A, no. 178.

86. Appendix A, no. 179.

87. Appendix A, no. 183. The dates of these deaths in St. Louis are taken from the photograph of a family cremation urn—Reutz, Amend, Mallinckrodt—inscribed, "Here repose the mingled ashes of Eight Persons . . . Exhumed from Holy Ghost Cemetery and incinerated November 12, 1906" (Philip A. Mallinckrodt, family memorabilia). Church and mortuary records do not shed light on illegible dates on the urn or show who in the family arranged the cremation and received the ashes.

88. Appendix A. no. 176.

89. Appendix A, no. 181.

90. Appendix A, nos. 181, 183.

91. Appendix A, no. 183–84.

92. Appendix A, no. 183.

93. Appendix A, no. 183.

94. Appendix A, no. 182.

95. Zunkel, "Gustav Mallinckrodt," 117.

96. Appendix A, nos. 187, 184.

97. Appendix A, no. 185.

98. Appendix A, no. 185; A. C. Meyer, "Mallinckrodt Chemical Works," 72.

99. Appendix A, no. 184. Minna's sensitive brother Gustavus later would recall this period as his sister's "formerly monotonous life" (Gustavus Mallinckrodt, "Letters from St. Paul," 23 August 1863).

100. Appendix A, no. 186.

101. Appendix A, no. 184–85.

102. Morison, *Oxford History*, 595.

103. Morris, *Encyclopedia of American History*, 224.

104. Morison, *Oxford History*, 601–2, 605.

105. Political labels such as "liberal" and "conservative" over time obviously represent changing positions on current issues, as well as enduring, basic philosophical concepts. Here the terms reflect Missourians' understanding of their positions in the 1800s, not designations that might be applied with twentieth-century hindsight or standards.

106. These Jeffersonian concepts included support for agrarian democracy, individual rights, and limitations on federal government power, as well as opposition to a national banking system and high tariffs.

107. Peter Gay, *The Enlightenment*, 3; Dumas Malone, *Jefferson the Virginian*, 101f.

108. Federalist concepts included support for a strong centralized government, as well as the interests of industry and large property owners.

109. In St. Louis, the Republican party evolved primarily from the Democratic Party (William L. Burton, *Melting Pot Soldiers*, 39).

110. *St. Charles Demokrat*, 21 April 1860; 26 April 1860.

111. *Westliche Post*, 27 September 1857.

112. Anderson, *Border City*, 15.

113. Anderson, *Border City*, 16–18.

114. *Anzeiger des Westens*, 16 August 1860.

115. *St. Charles Demokrat*, 23 August 1860.

116. *St. Charles Demokrat*, 27 September 1860; 18 October 1860.

117. In the same issue the newspaper, on its twenty-fifth anniversary, commented that it had "to this hour loyally supported the antislavery party, since this party had principles and perceptions that coincide most closely with those which both German emigrations [probably Thirty-ers and Forty-eighters] already strove and fought for in the old homeland" (*Anzeiger des Westens*, 22 October 1860).

118. *Anzeiger des Westens*, 22 October 1860.

119. *Anzeiger des Westens*, 29 October 1860.

120. Nagel, *Missouri*, 91.

121. *History of St. Charles*, 598.

122. *St. Charles Demokrat*, 8 November 1860.

123. Primm, Introduction, 12–13; Rowan, *Germans for a Free Missouri*, 27, 41.

124. *History of St. Charles*, 599.

125. *St. Charles Demokrat*, 29 November 1860.

126. *St. Charles Demokrat*, 29 February 1861; 4 April 1861.

127. Bek, "Followers of Duden," *Missouri Historical Review*, vol. 17, no. 3 (April 1923): 338–39.

128. Haase-Faulenorth, "Der Traum von New Dortmund," 225.

129. Appendix A, no. 187.

130. A long controversy among historians concerned the extent of immigrant-group voting influence on the outcome of the election. Although Germans obviously did not constitute a solid ethnic voting bloc—differing instead for economic, religious, regional reasons—their influence was considered very significant, even if not determining (Frederick C. Luebke, *Ethnic Voters and the Election of Lincoln*; Paul Kleppner, *The Cross of Culture*.)

131. Anderson, *Border City*, 19.

132. *History of St. Charles*, 606.

133. Nagel, *Missouri*, 91.

134. Anderson, *Border City*, 23.

135. Anderson, *Border City*, 30.

136. Primm, Introduction, 13.

137. Anderson, *Border City*, 28–31.

138. Morris, *Encyclopedia of American History*, 228.

139. Morris, *Encyclopedia of American History*, 228–29.

140. Anderson, *Border City*, 34.

141. St. Louis's leadership reflected its history as well as pragmatic interests—unlike the rural areas of the state originally settled by Southerners, St. Louis's native white population had come "largely from New York, Pennsylvania, Ohio, and Illinois" (Burton, *Melting Pot Soldiers*, 39).

142. Appendix A, no. 188.

143. Emil Mallinckrodt's Scrapbook, "Der nationale Einheitsstaat," 20.

144. Anderson, *Border City*, 37.

145. Bruce Catton, *The Coming Fury*, 381.

146. Anderson, *Border City*, 40f.

147. Primm, Introduction, 15.

148. Anderson, *Border City*, 43.

149. Anderson, *Border City*, 44–45.

150. Parrish, *Turbulent Partnership*, 8–9.

151. Parrish, *Turbulent Partnership*, 11.

152. Anderson, *Border City*, 60.

153. Anderson, *Border City*, 62.

154. *History of St. Charles*, 193.

155. *History of St. Charles*, 200.

156. William G. Bek, "Followers of Duden," *Missouri Historical Review*, vol. 17, no. 3 (April 1923): 339.

157. Morison, *Oxford History*, 611.

158. Anderson, *Border City*, 81; Primm, Introduction, 16.

159. *Augusta Town Record Book* (1 April, 19 April 1861), 78–79.

160. Appendix A, no. 188.

161. Morison and Commager, *Growth of the American Republic*, 688.

162. Schiermeier, *Cracker Barrel Country*, 130–31.

163. Conrad Mallinckrodt, "Register of Marriages."

164. Earl Mallinckrodt, family memorabilia.

165. John Strongwil, *Your Sister's Keeper*, 7.

166. U.S. Bureau of the Census, Microfilm M653, roll 649, p. 215.

24. *1861–1864: Guerrilla Missouri*

1. *History of St. Charles*, 43–44.

2. *History of St. Charles*, 179.

3. *History of St. Charles*, 45; Parrish, *Turbulent Partnership*, 22.

4. Heinrich Börnstein, "Apriltage in Missouri," 258, 264.

5. Börnstein, "Apriltage in Missouri," 261; Trexler, *Slavery in Missouri*, 167.

6. Detjen, *Germans in Missouri*, 9. Missouri had five three-month German units, called "ethnic regiments" by later historians (Burton, *Melting Pot Soldiers*, 104).

7. James F. Mallinckrodt, Compiled service records, roll 402.

8. Börnstein, "Apriltage in Missouri," 261–65.

9. Detjen, *Germans in Missouri*, 8.

10. Adolph Mallinckrodt, Compiled service records, roll 413.

11. *St. Charles Demokrat*, 16 May 1861.

12. Conrad Mallinckrodt, Compiled service records, roll 714. (Paid $24.75 for one month fifteen days service, 15 June–30 July 1861.) Julius Mallinckrodt, Compiled service records, roll 714. (Paid $13.05 for twenty-seven days service, 15 June–12 July 1861.)

13. Arnold Krekel Papers.

14. *History of St. Charles*, 181–83.

15. *St. Charles Demokrat*, 23 May 1860.

16. Parrish, *Turbulent Partnership*, 23.

17. *History of St. Charles*, 46–47.

18. Primm, Introduction, 18.

19. Anderson, *Border City*, 96–97.

20. Missouri, *Annual Report of the Adjutant General of Missouri, for the Year Ending December 31, 1865*, 63, 75.

21. Parrish, *Turbulent Partnership*, 24.

22. Brownlee, *Gray Ghosts*, 13.

23. Anderson, *Border City*, 101.

24. Parrish, *Turbulent Partnership*, 24.

25. Anderson, *Border City*, 160.

26. Börnstein, "Apriltage in Missouri," 262.

27. *History of St. Charles*, 180.

28. Anderson, *Border City*, 182f.

29. Parrish, *Turbulent Partnership*, 32.

30. Brownlee, *Gray Ghosts*, 16.

31. Anderson, *Border City*, 202–3.

32. *St. Charles Demokrat*, 23 May 1861.

33. James F. Mallinckrodt, Compiled service record; Adolph Mallinckrodt, Compiled service record.

34. Appendix A, no. 188.

35. Brownlee, *Gray Ghosts*, 24.

36. *Augusta Town Record Book* (12 August, 2 September, 2 October 1861), 81.

37. Michael Fellman, *Inside War*, v.

38. Fellman, *Inside War*, 181.

39. Walter D. Kamphoefner, *The Westfalians*, 85f.

40. *Anzeiger des Westens*, 16 May 1861.

41. *History of St. Charles*, 992.

42. *History of St. Charles*, 620.

43. In that proclamation General Pope made reference to "wanton destruction of bridges and culverts" and openly reprimanded inhabitants of the villages and stations along the railroad for not having offered resistance. "It is very certain," he declared, that the people living along the rail line "can very easily protect it from destruction." Cryptically he added, "It is my purpose to give them strong inducement to do so," that is, in the future individual communities would be held responsible and funds would be collected from them to cover damages not *prevented* by their residents (*History of St. Charles*, 621).

44. *History of St. Charles*, 623.

45. *History of St. Charles*.

46. Brownlee, *Gray Ghosts*, 173.

47. Parrish, *Turbulent Partnership*, 33–47.

48. Parrish, *Turbulent Partnership*, 47, 197–99.

49. Nagel, *Missouri*, 129.

50. Morris, *Encyclopedia of American History*, 231.

51. Trexler, *Slavery in Missouri*, 167, n. 114.

52. Although their first three months' service often was with an ethnic, that is, German regiment, most Germans then served in nonethnic units throughout the war (Burton, *Melting Pot Soldiers*, 110).

53. Unlike the Twelfth and Fifteenth Missouri Infantry regiments, the Seventeenth was not considered a German unit (Burton, *Melting Pot Soldiers*, 105).

54. James F. Mallinckrodt, Compiled service records, roll 402, 513; Missouri, *Annual Report of the Adjutant General, 1865*, 173.

55. Adolph Mallinckrodt, Compiled service records, roll 413, 702.

56. *History of St. Charles*, 200.

57. Arnold Krekel Papers.

58. Emil Mallinckrodt Papers (*Harvard Alumni Bulletin*, c. 1923, 956), St. Louis Historical Society.

59. Evidence of Gustav's prior service is suggested by his father Emil Mallinckrodt's late 1861 letter saying Gustav had been an "aide-de-camp on Fremont's staff," an "officer appointed by Fremont," who after that service "can *again enter* regular service" (Appendix A, no. 189, emphasis added). Gustav's military rank is suggested by an eye-witness account of Frémont's "15 aides-de-camp with military rank from colonels down to captains" (*Memoirs of Gustave Koerner 1809–1868*, 172).

60. Allan Nevins, *Frémont*, 494; Stone, *Immortal Wife*, 360; Koerner, *Memoirs*, 172; Howard, *Remembrance of Things Past*, 138–75.

61. Jessie Benton Fremont, *The Story of the Guard*.

62. Fellman, *Inside War*, 202.

63. Morris, *Encyclopedia of American History*, 231.

64. Fellman, *Inside War*, v. See also Jim Denny, "The War Within the State," 14–19.

65. Appendix A, no. 188.

66. Fellman, *Inside War*, vi.

67. Brownlee, *Gray Ghosts*, 4–5.

68. Nagel, *Missouri*, 129, 133.

69. Phistere, *The Army in the Civil War*, 219.

70. Fellman, *Inside War*, 39–40.

71. *Westliche Post*, 29 May 1861.

72. *History of St. Charles*, 608.

73. *History of St. Charles*, 611, 992.

74. *History of St. Charles*, 612.

75. *History of St. Charles*, 613–20.

76. *History of St. Charles*, 618.

77. *History of St. Charles*, 617, 619.

78. *History of St. Charles*, 637.

79. *History of St. Charles*, 637.

80. Anderson, *Border City*, 211.

81. It is not absolutely clear from Adolph's military records that he was with the Third Regiment on 10 August 1861, at Wilson's Creek. Adolph's record says he was mustered out on 27 August (Adolph Mallinckrodt, Compiled service records, roll 413), which would have put him at the battle site. The postbattle date, however, may have been the Regiment's expiration date (*Annual Report of the Adjutant General, 1865*, 63), and Adolph might have left the unit earlier, as Colonel Sigel noted many men had done—"The Third Regiment, of which 400 three-months' men had been dismissed, was composed for the greatest part of recruits, who had not seen the enemy before and were only insufficiently drilled. . . . About two-thirds of our officers had left us. Some companies had no officers at all; a great pity, but the consequence of the system of the three-months' service" (*War of the Rebellion*, series I, 3, 88).

82. William Mackey Wherry, *The Campaign in Missouri and the Battle of Wilson's Creek, 1861*, 14.

83. *War of the Rebellion*, series I, 3, 87–88.

84. Parrish, *Turbulent Partnership*, 52; *War of the Rebellion*, series I, 3, 85–98; Hokombe and Adams, *An Account of the Battle at Wilson's Creek*.

85. *Anzeiger des Westens*, 4 September 1861.

86. Parrish, *Turbulent Partnership*, 60–63.

87. Appendix A, no. 188.

88. Appendix A, no. 188.

89. Appendix A, no. 189.

90. Parrish, *Turbulent Partnership*, 63.

91. Brownlee, *Gray Ghosts*, 151.

92. Brownlee, *Gray Ghosts*, 146.

93. Brownlee, *Gray Ghosts*, 150.

94. Parrish, *Turbulent Partnership*, 78–79, 86.

95. Brownlee, *Gray Ghosts*, 18.

96. Parrish, *Turbulent Partnership*, 34, 41; Brownlee, *Gray Ghosts*, 18.

97. *History of St. Charles*, 629.

98. Brownlee, *Gray Ghosts*, 35–36.

99. Nevins, *Fremont*, 540–41.

100. Rowan, "German Language Newspapers," 52.

101. Anderson, *Border City*, 224–25.

102. Appendix A, nos. 188, 189. This failure of the Union to recognize Frémont's appointment of officers, staff, etc., and refusing them pay or pension, has made tracing Gustav's military record nearly impossible, for he does not appear in the national records of Compiled Service.

103. Fremont, *The Story of the Guard*, 208–9; *War of the Rebellion*, series I, 3, 568.

104. Appendix A, no. 189.

105. Belcher, *Economic Rivalry*, 140, 158.

106. Appendix A, no. 188.

107. Appendix A, no. 189.

108. *History of St. Charles*, 633.

109. Parrish, *Turbulent Partnership*, 90.

110. Appendix A, no. 188.

111. *History of St. Charles*, 630.

112. Brownlee, *Gray Ghosts*, 30–31.

113. Appendix A, no. 188.

114. James F. Mallinckrodt, Compiled service records.

115. Appendix A, no. 189.

116. Rowan, *Germans for a Free Missouri*, 29.

117. *History of St. Charles*, 182–83; Adolph Mallinckrodt, Compiled service record, roll 702; Adolph Mallinckrodt, Case files of approved pension applications.

118. Appendix A, no. 189.

119. Phistere, *The Army in the Civil War*, 83–92.

120. *History of St. Charles*, 49.

121. Brownlee, *Gray Ghosts*, 173.

122. Parrish, *Turbulent Partnership*, 89; Thomas S. Barclay, *The Liberal Republican Movement in Missouri*, 15.

123. Brownlee, *Gray Ghosts*, 158.

124. Brownlee, *Gray Ghosts*, 159–79.

125. *Augusta Town Record Book* (3 March 1862), 84.

126. *Augusta Town Record Book* (15 April 1862), 85. The pre–Civil War oath had simply said the Trustees "make oath that we will support the constitution of the United States and of this state and that we will faithfully demean ourselves in office" (*Augusta Town Record Book* [19 April 1858], 81). The new oath then was published in English by the German-language *Demokrat* on 16 October 1862, i.e., prior to the November elections at which Conrad Mallinckrodt served as election judge (*St. Charles Demokrat*, 16 October 1862, 23 October 1862).

127. *Augusta Town Record Book* (April [no date] 1863), 93.

128. A special election was held to fill Mindrup's seat, but legal counsel from the county said that the 1862 officers still held office because their "successors" had not been qualified (*Augusta Town Record Book* [14 May, 3 August, 26 October 1863], 94, 95, 98).

129. *Augusta Town Record Book* (7 December 1863), 99. Even allowing for possible imprecision in the clerk's recording, obviously the nature of the oath was confusing. If the town used the words "late legislation" and the county changed that to "law of the convention," it may have been because strictly speaking the St. Louis convention resolution was not "legislation."

130. *Augusta Town Record Book* (11 April 1859), 57; (11 April 1860), 65; *Augusta Town Record Book* (1 April 1861), 77; *Augusta Town Record Book* (19 April 1862), 85; *St. Charles Demokrat*, 14 September 1865, 2 November 1865.

131. Conrad Mallinckrodt, "Register of Marriages," *St. Charles Demokrat*, 14 September 1865.

132. *Augusta Town Record Book* (20 April 1870), 136.

133. Unfortunately Conrad Mallinckrodt's more complete Justice of the Peace records, which were preserved, could not be located in county archives.

134. Morris, *Encyclopedia of American History*, 235.

135. Anderson, *Border City*, 244, 251.

136. Anderson, *Border City*, 268–70.

137. *History of St. Charles*, 182–83.

138. *History of St. Charles*, 993.

139. Brownlee, *Gray Ghosts*, 52.

140. Brownlee, *Gray Ghosts*, 69.

141. *Washington Missourian*, 16 June 1955; *History of St. Charles*, 259. After Frederick's death in 1879, his son Carl [II] became postmaster.

142. *St. Charles Demokrat*, 5 June 1862.

143. Brownlee, *Gray Ghosts*, 104.

144. *Columbia Encyclopedia*, s.v. "Samuel Colt."

145. At his Hartford, Connecticut, armory, Samuel Colt "devoted his entire energy and skill to the production for Union forces of pistols and a new rifle musket" (*Colliers Encyclopedia*, s.v. "Samuel Colt").

146. Morison, *Oxford History*, 622; Allan Nevins, *The War for the Union*, 469.

147. Nevins, *War for the Union*, 469–70.

148. Nevins, *War for the Union*, 469.

149. Brownlee, *Gray Ghosts*, 77–78.

150. Parrish, *Turbulent Partnership*, 91f.

151. *War of the Rebellion*, series I, 13, 550–51.

152. Parrish, *Turbulent Partnership*, 98; Brownlee, *Gray Ghosts*, 94–101.

153. Parrish, *Turbulent Partnership*, 110.

154. James F. Mallinckrodt, Compiled service records, roll 513.

155. Morison, *Oxford History*, 653.

156. Trexler, *Slavery in Missouri*, 236.

157. Parrish, *Turbulent Partnership*, 123.

158. *Anzeiger des Westens*, 3 March 1862.

159. *Anzeiger des Westens*, 26 March 1862.

160. *Anzeiger des Westens*, 23 April 1862.

161. Morris and Commager, *Encyclopedia of American History*, 237–38. See also Foner and Mahoney, *A House Divided*.

162. Appendix A, no. 190.

163. Parrish, *Turbulent Partnership*, 135.

164. *History of St. Charles*, 638.

165. Brownlee, *Gray Ghosts*, 108. Enraged by martial law and how it was implemented, the "Missouri artist" George Caleb Bingham created a large painting, about five by six feet, entitled *Order No. 11*. In it he depicted the results of the August 1863 order calling for evacuation of four western Missouri counties—despotic military power leading to burning crops, fleeing people, frightened blacks, dead and injured civilians, and kneeling women pleading with military officers for mercy (Shapiro, *George Caleb Bingham*, 42–45, 89). The Loyalty Oath similarly incensed Bingham. In 1866 he would paint a small 14–1/2 inch by 14–1/2 inch oil over photograph on paper, entitled *Man in Jail*. It depicted a Baptist minister imprisoned because he preached before taking the Loyalty Oath. Seated parallel to a barred window, the minister reads from a book (probably the Bible), while the *Baptist Journal* newspaper lies on the floor next to a blanket and uncovered mattress. Dressed as if ready to be about his business, in a suit and tie with his hat nearby on the floor, the Reverend Mr. Dean obviously appears out of place in the jail cell (Shapiro, *George Caleb Bingham*, 88–90).

166. *History of St. Charles*, 255; *St. Charles Demokrat*, 10 September 1857.

167. "Conrad T. Mallinckrodt," *Portrait*, 335.

168. Recorder of Deeds, St. Charles County (1).

169. *History of St. Charles*, 138.

170. William E. Parrish, *Missouri under Radical Rule*, 152.

171. *History of St. Charles*, 248.

172. Frémont's aide-de-camp Gustave Körner at that time had written directly to President Lincoln that, "Deputy Paymaster-General Lieutenant Colonel Andrews refuses to honor Frémont's commissions, which have heretofore invariably been accepted by him" (*War of the Rebellion*, series I, 3, 541).

173. Gustavus Mallinckrodt, "Letters from St. Paul (Minn.)," Folder 90 (1 September 1863; 27 September 1863).

174. *War of the Rebellion*, series I, 13, 590–91; series III, 3, 66, 620; series III, 4, 869–70.

175. Appendix A, no. 190.

176. Appendix A, no. 194.

177. Appendix A, no. 190.

178. Morison, *Oxford History*, 654.

179. *St. Charles Demokrat*, 5 January, 6 August 1863.

180. *St. Charles Demokrat*, 26 March, 9 April, 23 April, 7 May 1863.

181. *St. Charles Demokrat,* 6 August 1863.

182. *St. Charles Demokrat,* 8 October, 15 October 1863.

183. Trexler, *Slavery in Missouri,* 236–37.

184. Appendix A, no. 190.

185. Belcher, *Economic Rivalry,* 142.

186. Appendix A, no. 190.

187. James F. Mallinckrodt, case files of approved pensions.

188. *War of the Rebellion,* series I, 24, pp. 152, 250f, 618; Missouri Commission to Locate the Missouri Troops at Vicksburg, "Report."

189. *War of the Rebellion,* series I, 24, part II reports, 170.

190. *War of the Rebellion,* series I, 24, part II reports, 389.

191. *War of the Rebellion,* series I, 24, part I reports 55–59. (Grant's report listed 545 killed at Vicksburg, 3,688 wounded, and 303 missing.)

192. *War of the Rebellion,* series I, 24, part II reports, 387–90.

193. *War of the Rebellion,* series I, 24, part II reports, 292–93.

194. *War of the Rebellion,* series I, 24, part II reports, 392–93.

195. James F. Mallinckrodt, Compiled service records, roll 513.

196. Eulenstein, "Die siedlungsgeographische Entwicklung."

197. Appendix A, no. 190; Gustavus Mallinckrodt, "Letters," Folder 90 (21 October 1863).

198. *History of St. Charles,* 639.

199. Brownlee, *Gray Ghosts,* 113.

200. Parrish, *Turbulent Partnership,* 157; Brownlee, *Gray Ghosts,* 113–18, 124–25.

201. *Augusta Town Record Book* (26 August 1863), 96.

202. *Augusta Town Record Book* (8 September 1863), 96–97.

203. *Augusta Town Record Book* (12 September 1863), 97.

204. *Augusta Town Record Book* (20 September 1863), 97.

205. *History of St. Charles,* 991, *St. Charles Demokrat,* 17 September 1863.

206. Appendix A, no. 195.

207. Nagel, *Missouri,* 134.

208. Trexler, *Slavery in Missouri,* 237–38.

209. Parrish, *Turbulent Partnership,* 162; Adolph Mallinckrodt, case files of approved pension applications.

210. The following Civil War battles experienced unusually high losses: Chancellorsville, Virginia (2–4 May 1862), the South's costliest victory, with 1,665 Confederate casualties; siege of Vicksburg, Mississippi (22 May–4 July 1863), a Union victory (9,000 Union and 10,000 Confederate casualties); Gettysburg, Pennsylvania (27 June–4 July 1863), Union victory (3,155 Union deaths and 20,000 wounded and missing; 3,903 Confederate dead and 24,000 wounded and missing—on 19 November that bloody battlefield was dedicated with Lincoln's brief Gettysburg Address remarks, the most memorable of all American addresses); Chickamauga, Georgia (19–20 September), a Confederate victory (Union casualties—1,657 killed, almost 15,000 wounded and missing; Confederate losses—2,312 dead and about 16,000 wounded and missing); Lookout Mountain, Tennessee (23–25 November 1863), Union victory (casualties: Union, 735 killed, 5,000 wounded and missing; Confederate, 361 dead, 6,000 wounded and missing) (Morris, *Encyclopedia of American History,* 241–42).

211. Morison, *Oxford History,* 630.

212. Morison, *Oxford History*, 629–30; *Columbia Encyclopedia*, s.v. "Small Arms."

213. Gustavus Mallinckrodt, "Letters," Folder 90 (21 July 1863). (Gustav's reaction to the brutality of the war perhaps is reflected in the fact that he cites only statistics about prisoners, not the dead or wounded.)

214. Gustavus Mallinckrodt, "Letters," Folder 90, (? June 1863; 19 July 1863).

215. Gustavus Mallinckrodt, "Letters," Folder 90 (27 September 1863).

216. Gustavus Mallinckrodt, "Letters," Folder 90 (7 December 1863).

217. Parrish, *Turbulent Partnership*, 179.

218. Gustavus Mallinckrodt, "Letters," Folder 91 (5 January 1864).

219. Gustavus Mallinckrodt, "Letters," Folder 91 (1 March 1864).

220. Gustavus Mallinckrodt, "Letters," Folder 91 (21 March 1864).

221. Gustavus Mallinckrodt, "Letters," Folder 91 (15 May 1864).

222. Gustavus Mallinckrodt, "Letters," Folder 91 (5 June 1864).

223. *Mallinckrodt Magazine*, 1967, 7; Edward A. McCreary and Wilbur Cross, "The Story of Mallinckrodt," 6; Mallinckrodt Papers, St. Louis (*Harvard Alumni Bulletin*, 956).

224. Gustavus Mallinckrodt, "Letters," Folder 91 (5 June 1864).

225. James F. Mallinckrodt, Compiled service records, roll 513.

226. Philip A. Mallinckrodt, family memorabilia.

227. Brownlee, *Gray Ghosts*, 182.

228. *History of St. Charles*, 1011–12.

229. Brownlee, *Gray Ghosts*, 180f, 190.

230. *History of St. Charles*, 645.

231. *History of St. Charles*, 645–46.

232. *History of St. Charles*, 641–42.

233. Brownlee, *Gray Ghosts*, 196–98, 203–6.

234. Fellman, *Inside War*, 252.

235. Brownlee, *Gray Ghosts*, 212. (Some accounts of the steamboat refer to its name as *Yellow Stone*, rather than *Yellowstone*.)

236. Gustavus Mallinckrodt, "Letters," Folder 91 (13 August 1864).

237. Brownlee, *Gray Ghosts*, 217–18, 220–21.

238. *St. Charles Demokrat*, 6 October 1864.

239. *History of St. Charles*, 646.

240. *Washington Missourian*, 24 May 1989.

241. *Augusta Town Record Book* (October 1864), 104.

242. *Augusta Town Record Book* (6 March 1865), 106.

243. *Hermann*, 208–9.

244. Brownlee, *Gray Ghosts*, 223–25.

245. *History of St. Charles*, 646; Brownlee, *Gray Ghosts*, 228–29.

246. Parrish, *Radical Rule*, 194.

247. Anderson, *Border City*, 330–31; *St. Charles Demokrat*, 6 October, 13 October, 20 October 1864.

248. Parrish, *Turbulent Partnership*, 194.

249. *War of the Rebellion*, series I, 41, part 4, 133.

250. Gustavus Mallinckrodt, "Letters," Folder 91 (13 August 1864).

251. James F. Mallinckrodt, Compiled service records, roll 513.

252. Parrish, *Turbulent Partnership*, 182.

253. *History of St. Charles*, 641.

254. Anderson, *Border City*, 341.

255. Parrish, *Turbulent Partnership*, 195.

256. Parrish, *Radical Rule*, vii–viii.

257. Parrish, *Turbulent Partnership*, 199; Brownlee, *Gray Ghosts*, 233.

258. Anderson, *Border City*, 344–45.

259. Nagel, *Missouri*, 137.

260. Trexler, *Slavery in Missouri*, 239–40.

261. Parrish, *Radical Rule*, 19.

262. Nagel, *Missouri*, 137.

263. Anderson, *Border City*, 353.

264. Nagel, *Missouri*, 138; Parrish, *Turbulent Partnership*, 202–3.

265. Parrish, *Radical Rule*, 27. In St. Charles County, the newspaper published lists of teachers, preachers, lawyers, and justices of the peace who had taken the oath (*St. Charles Demokrat*, 14 September 1865).

266. Barclay, *Liberal Republican Movement*, 16.

267. Barclay, *Liberal Republican Movement*, 25–26.

268. Parrish, *Radical Rule*, 30.

269. Barclay, *Liberal Republican Movement*, 22–23. (Notary publics were exempted from this reorganization but justices of the peace apparently were included, thus still affecting Conrad Mallinckrodt's professional activities. In fact, the county newspaper published a separate listing of justices of the peace who had taken the oath—Conrad Mallinckrodt's name was on that list [*St. Charles Demokrat*, 11 November 1865].)

270. The history of radical Republicanism in Missouri is admirably documented in William E. Parrish's *Missouri under Radical Rule 1861–1865* and extensively cited in the following pages.

271. Trexler, *Slavery in Missouri*, 239; Anderson, *Border City*, 357; Parrish, *Turbulent Partnership*, 202f.

272. *History of St. Charles*, 656.

273. Anderson, *Border City*, 361.

274. Anderson, *Border City*, 362f.

275. Morison and Commager, *Growth of the American Republic*, 653. Of the 992,703 casualties, 62 percent were deaths (359,528 Union; 258,000 Confederacy). The dead were often the victims of disease, rather than bullets. While the killing power of the American Civil War was great, medical science was incredibly bad, and many men perished in hospitals. Of the total casualties, another 38 percent were the wounded (275,175 Union; 100,000 Confederacy) (Morris, *Encyclopedia of American History*, 245).

276. Anderson, *Border City*, 357.

277. Brownlee, *Gray Ghosts*, 54.

25. 1865: After the Civil War

1. Morris, *Encyclopedia of American History*, 246.

2. *History of St. Charles*, 657.

3. *History of St. Charles*, 662.

4. Parrish, *Radical Rule*, 97.

5. *History of St. Charles*, 666.

6. Parrish, *Radical Rule*, 181f.

7. Parrish, *Radical Rule*, 133.

8. Parrish, *Radical Rule*, 186.

9. Culmer, *History of Missouri*, 236.

10. Parrish, *Radical Rule*, 140–41.

11. Parrish, *Radical Rule*, 140f; *St. Charles Demokrat*, 26 April 1866.

12. Belcher, *Economic Rivalry*, 162.

13. Belcher, *Economic Rivalry*, 80.

14. Belcher, *Economic Rivalry*, 146.

15. *Augusta Town Record Book* (19 June 1865), 110.

16. *Augusta Town Record Book* (22 April 1858), 44.

17. *Augusta Town Record Book* (31 July 1865), 110.

18. *Augusta Town Record Book*, 111. One possible cause for such disruption in the usual affairs of the town was a periodic flooding of the Missouri River. (*St. Charles Demokrat*, 28 September 1865.)

19. Missouri Department of State, Cornelius Roach, Secretary of State. "An Act to amend Section 4 of an Act entitled, 'An Act to Incorporate the town of Augusta, in St. Charles County, Missouri, approved March 3, 1855,' approved March 13, 1866." Jefferson City, Mo.: 22 September 1915. *Augusta Town Record Book* (3 September 1866), 114.

20. *Augusta Town Record Book* (15 October 1866), 115.

21. *Augusta Town Record Book* (21 February 1867), 117; (8 April 1867), 119.

22. This marriage of nephew Hermann Adolph was the only one solemnized by justice of the peace Conrad Mallinckrodt during the 1860–1867 period of loyalty oaths for public officials. Since Conrad had not performed his nephew's first marriage the previous year, perhaps he did so the second time because one could take advantage of a quasi-grace period after the June 1865 acceptance of the new constitution (Barclay, *Liberal Republican Movement*, 58) before again abiding by the oath. Meline's death resulted in an interesting legal controversy. Her father, George Münch, and father-in-law, Julius Mallinckrodt, had both contributed to giving Meline and Adolph a good financial start in their marriage— each five hundred dollars for land and the bride's father gave his daughter household and kitchen furniture. There was no marriage contract, such as was customary in Germany in earlier centuries regarding disposition of assets the bride brought to the marriage in case of her death and apparently no applicable Missouri civil law. Thus, George Münch wanted the money he had given his daughter for land returned and took back the furniture. The Court granted Adolph's request for an injunction against Münch, staying their execution of a deed of trust they held over the land provided Adolph and Meline (St. Charles County Circuit Court [g]). *History of St. Charles*, 994.

23. Parrish, *Radical Rule*, 90–91.

24. Parrish, *Radical Rule*, 91f.

25. Brownlee, *Gray Ghosts*, 241.

26. *History of St. Charles*, 662–63.

27. "Emil Mallinckrodt's Scrapbook" ("Der nationale Einheitsstaat"), 20.

28. Barclay, *Liberal Republican Movement*, 59–65.

29. Parrish, *Radical Rule*, 83, 86–87.

30. *St. Charles Demokrat*, 25 August 1864, 9 September 1864, 8 November 1866.

31. Parrish, *Radical Rule*, 100.

32. *History of St. Charles*, 663.

33. *St. Charles Demokrat*, 8 November 1866.

34. Morison, *Oxford History*, 722.

35. Brownlee, *Gray Ghosts*, 241–42.

36. Parrish, *Radical Rule*, 141f.

37. Parrish, *Radical Rule*, 126.

38. Parrish, *Radical Rule*, 175.

39. Anita M. Mallinckrodt, family memorabilia.

40. Morris, *Encyclopedia of American History*, 248.

41. Foner, *Reconstruction*, 272; Morris, *Encyclopedia of American History*, 249, 492; Barclay, *Liberal Republican Movement*, 269.

42. Conrad Mallinckrodt, "Register of Marriages."

43. Circuit Court, St. Charles County (h).

44. *Columbia Encyclopedia*, s.v. "James Buchanan Eads."

45. Parrish, *Radical Rule*, 203.

46. *History of St. Charles*, 238.

47. Washington *Missourian*, 6 September 1989. Old Augusta documents show that Julius Mallinckrodt's son, Hermann Adolf, was president of the Augusta Harmonie-Verein in 1891 (Betty Boffa, town of Augusta memorabilia).

48. *Augusta Town Record Book* (3 December 1860), 74; (4 February 1861), 75; (? November 1867), 121–22.

49. *Augusta Town Record Book* (6 July 1868), 126–27.

50. Unanswered but interesting is the question whether this "intown" property of Wilhelmina Mallinckrodt gave her husband, Conrad, any rights within the village that he had not had all the years he owned land only outside the town limits.

51. Joseph Schafer, ed., *Intimate Letters of Carl Schurz 1841–1869*, 387.

52. Schaefer, *Intimate Letters of Carl Schurz*, 380–83.

53. *Washington Missourian*, 24 August 1950; Schiermeier, "Touring."

54. *Augusta Town Record Book* (3 May 1869), 132. *St. Charles Demokrat*, 5 March 1868, 26 March 1868, 23 July 1868, 7 July 1868, 21 October 1869.

55. Curt Matthews, "Chain Reaction at Mallinckrodt."

56. A. C. Meyer, "Mallinckrodt Chemical Works," 72.

57. Carolyn Bower, Louis J. Rose, and Theresa Tighe, "Atomic Waste in One Legacy of a St. Louis Firm's Patriotic Work."

58. Meyer, "Mallinckrodt Chemical Works," 72–73.

59. *Mallinckrodt Magazine*, 8.

60. Meininghaus, "Der soziale Aufsteig," 411.

61. Morison, *Oxford History*, 721.

62. Morris, *Encyclopedia of American History*, 247.

63. Parrish, *Radical Rule*, 239, 241–42.

64. The Democrats for their part put up Horatio Seymour, former New York governor, with the Missouri politician Frank Blair as his vice-presidential candidate. Blair was popular with many Democrats in Missouri because of his fight to eliminate the loyalty oath as a prerequisite for voting and holding office.

65. Parrish, *Radical Rule*, 250–51.

66. Morris, *Encyclopedia of American History*, 249.

67. Parrish, *Radical Rule*, 257–58.

68. Parrish, *Radical Rule*, 258, 264.

69. *Conversations-Lexikon*, vol. 10, 296–310.

70. When economic conditions changed, so did slave ownership, probably when Emil spent years in Europe and when Hermann moved from the farm to the city. Evidence suggests that Julius, too, did not long keep the slave last referred to in 1836. The 1840 U.S. census, for instance, does not list any slave belonging to Julius's household, although there was space on the form for such information and it was included for other residents of the area. Also in 1850 and 1860, when more detailed and separate slave schedules were prepared by the census takers, on the forms for Femme Osage Township no slave was listed as belonging to Julius Mallinckrodt (U.S. Bureau of the Census, Microfilm M704 [1840], roll 230, p. 24; M432 [1850], roll 424; M653 [1860], roll 664).

71. Morison, *Oxford History*, 505.

72. Peter Gay, *The Enlightenment*, II, 410–23.

73. Emil Mallinckrodt's Scrapbook ("The Dark Continent und seine Bewohner"), 18.

74. *St. Charles Demokrat*, 29 October 1868.

75. *St. Charles Demokrat*, 2 November 1868.

76. *St. Charles Demokrat*, 5 November 1868.

77. *St. Charles Demokrat*, 8 November 1868.

78. *St. Charles Demokrat*, 8 November 1868. Not only those published election results reminded people in St. Charles County of the Civil War's continuing effect on their lives— for instance, according to the newspaper, the night before the election the town of Augusta experienced the kind of lawlessness increasingly occurring in the postwar period, the theft of goods from businesses. "A great quantity of goods," said the newspaper, was taken from Koch and Jeude's Store, as also had been done ten days earlier at Henecke's Store in New Melle. Another sign of the post–Civil War times was the new game, called baseball, the newspaper said now was being practiced on the drill ground of the former Home Guard of St. Charles. Finally, county newspapers also frequently carried "Stray Notices" about mules branded "U.S." (obviously formerly belonging to Union Army troops) that were wandering unclaimed about the countryside until they were caught, appraised, and offered for sale.

79. *St. Charles Demokrat*, 19 November 1868.

80. Parrish, *Radical Rule*, 267.

81. Parrish, *Radical Rule*, 272.

82. Parrish, *Radical Rule*, 274–77.

83. Emil Mallinckrodt's Scrapbook ("Amerikanisches Parteiwesen"), 72.

84. Parrish, *Radical Rule*, 278.

85. Parrish, *Radical Rule*, 307–9.

86. *History of St. Charles*, 667–68.

87. Parrish, *Radical Rule*, 309–10.

88. Parrish, *Radical Rule*, 27.

89. Parrish, *Radical Rule*, 319.

90. Parrish, *Radical Rule*, viii.

91. *Augusta Town Record Book* (20 February 1870), 136.

92. Nagel, *Missouri*, 141; *Augusta Town Record Book* (7 February 1870), 134.

93. Parrish, *Radical Rule*, 27.

94. Earl Mallinckrodt, family memorabilia; *St Charles Demokrat*, 10 November 1870.

95. *Augusta Town Record Book* (7 July 1873), 155.

96. The controversy reflected partisan postwar disputes. Breure, city attorney at the

time, was Republican, as was the short-lived *Wahre Fortschritt*; the *Demokrat*, formerly owned by Breure and liberal, had passed into ownership reflecting conservative Democratic Party politics (*History of St. Charles*, 222–23, 313, 367).

97. Carl Wencker, "Day Book."

26. *1870s: Augusta and Again Its River*

1. *History of St. Charles*, 12.
2. Parrish, *Radical Rule*, 185–86.
3. U.S. Bureau of the Census, M653 (1860), roll 644, p. 612; M593 (1870), roll 806, p. 24.
4. *History of St. Charles*, 142.
5. *Washington Missourian*, 24 August 1967.
6. *Washington Missourian*, 24 August 1950.
7. *Washington Missourian*, 16 June 1955.
8. *Washington Missourian*, 7 September 1967.
9. *Washington Missourian*, 16 June 1955.
10. *Washington Missourian*, 7 September 1967.
11. *Washington Missourian*, 16 June 1955.
12. *History of St. Charles*, 257.
13. *Augusta Town Record Book*, 153f.
14. *Augusta Town Record Book*, 150–52.
15. It was said to have been one of the first brick structures in the area and that Julius Mallinckrodt specialized in apple wine.
16. *Washington Missourian*, 24 August 1950.
17. U.S. Bureau of the Census, M593 (1870), roll 822, p. 866.
18. Strongwil, *Your Sister's Keeper*, 7–10.
19. Parrish, *Radical Rule*, 197.
20. *History of St. Charles*, 328–29.
21. *History of St. Charles*, 12.
22. Parrish, *Radical Rule*, 203.
23. Nagel, *Missouri*, 70.
24. See *Washington Missourian*, 31 August 1967, for recollections of the Missouri River's behavior at Augusta.
25. Despite many oral history accounts referring to a big 1872 flood, the *St. Charles Demokrat* reports "high water" in June and July but no major flood (*St. Charles Demokrat*, 13 June–15 August 1872).
26. *Augusta Town Record Book* (1 April 1872), 144, 146–47.
27. *Augusta Town Record Book* (4 August, 1 September 1873), 155–56.
28. *Augusta Town Record Book* (7 December 1874), 165.
29. *St. Charles Demokrat*, 25 June 1874, 13 May 1875.
30. *St. Charles Demokrat*, July–September 1875, June–July 1876.
31. *St. Charles Demokrat*, 13 July 1876.
32. The original sketch was refined for publication in a German journal (*Beiträge*, 54, 1958) and readapted here.
33. Carl Wencker, "Day Book."

34. Göbel, *Länger als ein Menschenleben in Missouri*, 135.

35. *St. Charles Demokrat*, 26 August 1880, 7 September 1882.

36. *History of St. Charles*, 236.

37. *Washington Missourian*, 31 August 1967.

27. 1875: Eventide

1. Nagel, *Missouri*, 143.

2. Parrish, *Radical Rule*, 319.

3. Parrish, *Radical Rule*, 323–24.

4. Helbich, Kamphoefner, and Sommer, *Briefe aus Amerika*, 23.

5. "Conrad T. Mallinckrodt," *Portrait*, 336.

6. Parrish, *Radical Rule*, 323f.

7. The photo was preserved by Conrad Theodor's son Julius Walter and family, of Elsberry, Missouri.

8. Appendix A, no. 198.

9. *Augusta Town Record Book*, 155, 167, 169, 181.

10. *Augusta Town Record Book* (6 December 1875; 7 February 1876), 175–77.

11. Earl Mallinckrodt, family memorabilia.

12. *Augusta Town Record Book* (6 November 1876), 187; (6 May 1878), 203.

13. Anita M. Mallinckrodt, family memorabilia.

14. One clue to the date is the existence of Collier's gallery in Augusta by November 1876. Another is the existence of a similar, but seemingly slightly later, pose of Conrad designated as "In 1878" when it was used on Conrad's school plan which his nephew James Ferdinand reprinted in 1909. A final clue is Wilhelmina's death date, September 1877. If it can be presumed that Conrad's earlier portrait, above, and that of his wife were done locally at about the same time, they would then probably have been completed in the first half of 1877—that is, before Wilhelmina's death and before the older, second pose was made (which James Ferdinand out of first-hand information dated as 1878).

15. Hubert E. Mallinckrodt, family memorabilia.

16. Oscar Handlin, *The Uprooted*, 4.

17. Philip A. Mallinckrodt, family memorabilia (16 January 1903, letter from Theodor Mallinckrodt to James Ferdinand Mallinckrodt).

18. *Augusta Town Record Book* (5 November 1877), 198.

19. *Augusta Town Record Book* (3 June 1878), 204.

20. *Augusta Town Record Book* (20 May 1873), 154; (2 September 1878), 207.

21. *Augusta Town Record Book* (29 July 1876), 183.

22. *Augusta Town Record Book* (3 August 1874), 163; (3 May 1875), 169; (5 February 1877), 188; (29 May 1876), 182.

23. Brownlee, *Gray Ghosts*, 243–44.

24. Nagel, *Missouri*, 12.

25. Culmer, *History of Missouri*, 237.

26. Emil Mallinckrodt's Scrapbook ("Krankhafte Gemüthsstimmung in Sympathien mit Verbrechen und Verbrecher"), 32.

27. Emil Mallinckrodt's Scrapbook ("Unbeliebsame Vergleiche"), 76.

28. Morris, *Encyclopedia of American History*, 250–52. (Regarding the impact of the 1873 Panic on Reconstruction, see Erich Foner's *Reconstruction*.)

29. Emil Mallinckrodt's Scrapbook ("Der Distrikt von Columbia"), 84.

30. Emil Mallinckrodt's Scrapbook ("Anomalien"), 32.

31. Foner, *Reconstruction*, 593–94, 603–12.

32. Morris, *Encyclopedia of American History*, 253.

33. Parrish, *Radical Rule*, 127.

34. Hermann von Mallinckrodt, as a member of the "Zentrum," a conservative Christian faction in the Reichstag, led the resistance to efforts by Bismarck to have state authority prevail over that of the church in matters of welfare, education, marriage, etc. (*Neue Deutsche Biographie*, s.v. "Mallinckrodt," 731.)

35. Meininghaus, "Der soziale Aufsteig," 397.

36. Emil Mallinckrodt's Scrapbook ("Die Emancipation von 1863," November 1874), 98–99.

37. Emil Mallinckrodt's Scrapbook ("Gedanken bei der Feier des vierten Juli," *Westliche Post*, 4 July 1876), 70.

38. Appendix A, no. 199.

39. Appendix A, no. 200.

40. Emil Mallinckrodt's Scrapbook ("Wenn mann geglaubt hat," 1876), 108.

41. Strongwil, *Your Sister's Keeper*, 16–31.

42. John F. Mallinckrodt, "Automatic Car Brake of the Mallinckrodt Brake Co. of St. Louis."

43. Strongwil, *Your Sister's Keeper*, 36–40.

44. Wedmore, *The Woman*, 335–37.

45. Wedmore, *The Woman*, 301f.

46. Wedmore, *The Woman*, 316f.

47. Wedmore, *The Woman*, 378; *Neue Deutsche Biographie*, s.v. "Mallinckrodt."

48. Recorder of Deeds, St. Charles County (1).

49. *Augusta Town Record Book* (November/December 1860), 73.

50. *History of St. Charles*, 83; Culmer, *History of Missouri*, 237.

51. Nagel, *Missouri*, 12–13; Brownlee, *Gray Ghosts*, 244.

52. Perhaps Emil was recalling the fatal family feud between the Mallinckrodt brothers, Dietrich VIII and Hermann III, in 1594.

53. Emil Mallinckrodt's Scrapbook ("Worauf beruht Freiheit, Wohlfahrt und Frieden der Völker?"), 48.

54. Morris, *Encyclopedia of American History*, 256.

55. Emil Mallinckrodt's Scrapbook ("Grant, Arthur, Conkling und Consorten"), 78.

56. *History of St. Charles*, 329–30.

57. *History of St. Charles*, 84–85.

58. *History of St. Charles*, 85.

59. Nagel, *Missouri*, 13.

60. *History of St. Charles*, 85.

61. Emil Mallinckrodt's Scrapbook ("Krankhafte Gemüthsstimmung in Sympathien mit Verbrechen und Verbrecher"), 33.

62. Appendix A, no. 201.

63. Appendix A, no. 202.

64. Appendix A, no. 203.

65. Appendix A, no. 205.
66. Meyer, "Mallinckrodt Chemical Works," 73.
67. Appendix A, no. 205.
68. Appendix A, no. 206.
69. Meyer, "Mallinckrodt Chemical Works," 73.
70. Edward Mallinckrodt, Jr., Papers.
71. Appendix A, no. 206.
72. Appendix A, nos. 205, 206.
73. Appendix A, no. 205.
74. Appendix A, no. 206. (Emil surely meant Luise in Colorado and possibly her sister Sophie Mallinckrodt Amend in St. Louis, although other records say Sophie had died in 1884. Perhaps Emil meant Conrad's former wife, Sophie Mallinckrodt Koch, or cousin Dorothea Mallinckrodt Metzmacher, of Dortmund.)
75. Appendix A, no. 206.
76. Emil Mallinckrodt's Scrapbook ("Wer soll regieren?," July 1874), 52.
77. Emil Mallinckrodt's Scrapbook ("Der gegenwärtige Exodus der Farbigen," 1888), 59.
78. Earl Mallinckrodt, family memorabilia.
79. Probate Office, St. Charles County Circuit Court, Conrad Mallinckrodt Estate, 1887.
80. J. W. (Bill) Schiermeier, "Touring Nineteenth Century Augusta."
81. *History of St. Charles*, 236.
82. James Fenimore Cooper, *The Last of the Mohicans*, 256.
83. *Augusta Town Record Book* (5 July 1880), 225; (5 December 1881), 236.
84. *Augusta Town Record Book* (7 October 1886), 274–75.
85. *Augusta Town Record Book* (8 August 1892), 331.
86. *History of St. Charles*, 236, 105.
87. *History of St. Charles*, 104.
88. Morris, *Encyclopedia of American History*, 257.
89. *History of St. Charles*, 245.
90. *Columbia Encyclopedia*, s.v. "Democratic party," "Republican party."
91. *Augusta Town Record Book* (7 October 1886), 274. (The Central Missouri went bankrupt [*Washington Missourian*, 31 August 1967] after it opened its line past Augusta in 1891 [*Washington Missourian*, 16 June 1955], and by 1892 it was the Missouri Kansas and Eastern Railway Company with which the town negotiated. [*Augusta Town Record Book*, 331].)
92. Recorder of Deeds, St. Charles County (1).

28. 1880–1890s: Their Stories End

1. *History of St. Charles*, 259–60.
2. The doctor's bills indicated frequent medical visits in summer 1882 to Conrad's home about two miles outside of Augusta. In addition, there was "surgical attendance" in autumn, another period of illness in spring 1883, and again in January and June 1884 (including night visits). An apparently serious bout occurred in June/July 1885, and there were periodic problems throughout 1886. In January 1887, the medical care was intensive during the days before Conrad's death on Tuesday the nineteenth. On the twelfth and thirteenth, as well

as the day of his death, for instance, he was visited both morning and evening by Dr. Wieland, as well as on two days (date illegible) by Dr. H. S. Clay ("visit, medicine, consultation"); the pharmacist supplied medicine on both the eighteenth and nineteenth (Probate Office, St. Charles County Circuit Court).

3. The Reverend G. von Luternau of the Ebenezer Evangelical Church in Augusta officiated (Ebenezer United Church of Christ records, Augusta, Missouri) "at the grave" (*St. Charles Cosmos Monitor*, 2 February 1887).

4. Probate Office, St. Charles County Circuit Court.

5. *Augusta Town Record Book* (3 May 1866), 270; *History of St. Charles*, 259.

6. In this generation the old family name Münch usually was being spelled Muench.

7. The signature appears with that of Julius's son Conrad T. as underwriting bond for Conrad in his "wilful misconduct in office" court case. In autumn 1882, it had been reported in the Augusta newspaper column that Julius was ill and not expected to live (*St. Charles Demokrat*, 14 September 1882).

8. Philip A. Mallinckrodt, family memorabilia.

9. Hubert E. Mallinckrodt, family memorabilia.

10. Earl Mallinckrodt, family memorabilia.

11. *St. Charles Demokrat*, 27 January 1887, 3 February 1887.

12. Recorder of Deeds, St. Charles County (l).

13. Hermann Adolph himself was very ill and would not live to be as old as his father had been. Apparently the Civil War, in which Adolph had served so long, had taken its toll on his health, as it had with his now-deaf cousin James Ferdinand. As the latter had done in 1885, Adolph applied to the U.S. Army for an invalid's pension in 1890. Medical certificates testified to diseases of lungs and heart, which reduced by half his capacity to perform normal manual labor, as well as partial deafness, chronic rheumatism, and a massive scrotal tumor. After several rejections, the application was granted, and Adolph was granted a small partial-disability pension. When he died with great suffering (Wencker family memorabilia, 13 January 1906, letter) on 22 December 1905, his wife was granted a widow's pension, as well (Adolph Mallinckrodt, case files of approved pension applications). Adolph was a charter member of the Grand Army of the Republic group founded in Augusta (*Washington Missourian*, 16 June 1955).

14. *History of St. Charles*, 104–5.

15. *Augusta Town Record Book* (13 April 1882), 239.

16. *St. Charles Demokrat*, 3 May 1888. An English-language obituary appeared in the *St. Charles Cosmos Monitor*, 9 May 1888.

17. A space had been reserved for Emil's grave between Eleanor's corner gravesite (1858) and those of their sons Otto (1876) and Gustav (1877). In 1868, when the first daughter of his second marriage died, Emil had begun a second row of graves, forming a right angle with the original row, thus separating his two families, as it were. In that second row (or the foot of the L) were the first buried year-old daughter Emilie (Elmira ?) (1868), later her mother and Emil's second wife Emilie Vollmann (1896), and finally their two sons, Oskar (1900) and Emil junior (1929).

18. *Westliche Post*, 11 May 1892.

19. The Denver City Directory for 1894 listed both Hermann and Delia Mallinckrodt as residents at 2523 Stout Street; the *Boulder Daily Camera*'s 18 December 1895 death notice for Herman Mallinckrodt "at his son's residence, South Ninth Street," said Herman had been a resident of Boulder "the past two years."

20. After the Military Service Reform of 1814, military service was two years plus two years reserve duty.

21. *Boulder Daily Camera*, 24 December 1895.

22. Hermann and Luise's son James Ferdinand, then still living in St. Louis, may have arranged the 1906 cremation of his aunts and uncles because there were plans to discontinue the Holy Ghost Cemetery, which indeed was closed in 1917.

23. Appendix A, no. 146.

24. U.S. Bureau of the Census, 1850, p. 66; 1860, p. 602.

25. Philip A. Mallinckrodt, family memorabilia.

26. Münch, "Die Duden'sche Niedelaßung in Missouri," 231.

27. U.S. Census 1870, Femme Osage Township; St. Charles County, Missouri, 1876 Census, Femme Osage Township, p. 230.

28. *St. Charles Cosmos*, 8 March 1882. *St. Charles Demokrat*, 16 March 1882.

29. Augusta church records contain no evidence of the Christian Koch family, nor do the church, public, and family cemeteries and burying grounds in the area (*Cemeteries of St. Charles Co., Mo.*).

30. In 1896, the Missouri Kansas & Texas Railroad, known as the MK&T, or "The Katy," had taken over the line (V. V. Masterson, *The Katy Railroad and the Last Frontier*, 249).

31. "Edward Mallinckrodt Jr. Dies; Industrialist and Civic Leader," *St. Louis Post-Dispatch*, 19 January 1967.

32. *Mallinckrodt Magazine*, 7.

33. Bower, Rose, and Tighe, "Atomic Waste," "Some Feared for Health of Ore Handlers." *St. Louis Post-Dispatch*, 13 and 14 February 1989.

34. "Edward Mallinckrodt Jr. Dies," *St. Louis Post-Dispatch*, 19 January 1967. Mallinckrodt, Inc., letter to Richard Goldmann (Dortmund), 13 July 1981.

Bibliography

Papers, Letters, Archives, Documents

Augusta Town Record Book, 1855–1903. Town Board of Trustees. Augusta, Missouri.

Bates Papers. "Report of Mistress Sophie Mallinckrodt, 1840." Missouri Historical Society Archives, St. Louis.

Boffa, Betty. Town of Augusta memorabilia. Augusta, Missouri.

Bolivar passenger manifest, 27 December 1831. Passenger and crew lists of vessels arriving at New Orleans 1820–1902. National Archives Microfilm Publication M259, roll 10, Record Group 85. Washington, D.C.

Brig *Ulysses* passenger manifest, 19 September 1836. Passenger and crew lists of vessels arriving at Baltimore 1820–1891. National Archives Microfilm Publication M255, roll 1, Record Group 85. Washington, D.C.

Bryan, W. S. Papers. Bill of sale from Julius Mallinckrodt, 1857. Missouri Historical Society Archives, St. Louis.

Circuit Court, St. Charles County. St. Charles, Missouri.

   (a) *Sophie Mallinckrodt v. Conrad Mallinckrodt* (divorce). September 1839–November 1840. St. Charles County Historical Society, box 141, file 5872.

   (b) Helene Mallinckrodt Estate. July 1840. St. Charles County Historical Society Archives.

   (c) *William Koch v. Conrad Mallinckrodt* (unpaid debts). September–December 1840. St. Charles County Historical Society Archives; St. Charles Circuit Court 1840–1844 Records, Book E, 60.

   (d) *Sophie Mallinckrodt v. Julius Mallinckrodt* (slander). September 1840–March 1842. St. Charles County Historical Society, box 141, file 5873; St. Charles Circuit Court 1840–1844 Records, Book E, 62, 82, 83, 84, 87, 91, 156, 191.

   (e) *William Koch v. Julius Mallinckrodt* (slander). July 1841–November 1843. St. Charles County Historical Society, box 127, file 5279; St. Charles Circuit Court 1840–1844 Records, Book E, 150, 168, 174, 209, 248, 312, 315, 320, 335, 373.

   (f) *State of Missouri v. Julius Mallinckrodt* (assault and battery). July–August 1842. St. Charles Circuit Court 1840–1844 Records, Book E, 239, 248.

   (g) *Adolph Mallinckrodt v. Albert Munch, George Munch.* November 1868. St. Charles County Historical Society Archives, box 141, file 5875; Court Docket 12 November 1866–22 January 1869.

   (h) *State of Missouri v. Conrad Mallinckrodt* (willful misconduct in office). May 1869. St. Charles Circuit Court; St. Charles County Historical Society Archives, box 259, file 1669.

———. 1840–1844 Records, Book E. St. Charles County Circuit Court.

————. 1851–1855 Records, Book G. St. Charles County Circuit Court.

————. Judgement Book 1851–, St. Charles County Circuit Court. St. Charles County Historical Society.

Circuit Court, Warren County, Missouri. Marriage Records. 14 February 1842.

Citizenship Archives. St. Charles County Historical Society, St. Charles, Missouri.

"Copernicus." Beschreibung-Bild Nr. 525. Bremen Stadtarchiv Bild Archiv, Bremen, Germany.

Copernicus passenger manifest, 28 June 1838. Passenger and crew lists of vessels arriving at Baltimore 1820–1891. National Archives Microfilm Publication M255, roll 2, Record Group 85. Washington, D.C.

"Diary of Sophie Fabricius, 1796." Von Mallinckrodt Nachlaß (closed archive), Bestand 1068, Kasten 94. Historisches Archiv, Köln, Germany.

Ebenezer Church Records. Ebenezer United Church of Christ, Augusta, Missouri.

Ebenezer 1851–1951. Ebenezer United Church of Christ, 1951, Augusta, Missouri.

Esser, Helmut. "Die Lehrer am Stadtgymnasium." Manuscript. Stadtarchiv, Bestand 204/02-57, Dortmund, Germany.

Feldmann, Wilhelm. *Die Dortmunder Feldmanns*. Istanbul, Turkey: privately published, 1932. [Historischer Verein für Dortmund und die Grafschaft Mark Library, Dortmund, Germany.]

Femme Osage Church Records. St. Charles County Historical Society, St. Charles, Missouri.

Frémont's Body Guard, Missouri Cavalry. Compiled records showing service of military units in volunteer Union organizations—Missouri. National Archives Microfilm Publication 594, roll 95, Record Group 94. Washington, D.C.

Gamble, Hamilton R. Papers. "Emil Mallinckrodt." Missouri Historical Society Archives, St. Louis.

"Hafengeld–Ausgehende Schiffe." Bremen Stadt Archiv, Hauptbuch 2 (1836, 1838). Bremen, Germany.

Haren, Gerrit. "Rittergut Mallinckrodt und seine Besitzer. (Ergänzung S. 30)." Historisches Archiv, Von Mallinckrodt Nachlaß, Abt. 1068, Kasten 15. Köln, Germany.

"Hermann von Mallinckrodt vor dem Femegericht, 1450." Wetter: Information Sheet, Stadt Wetter am Ruhr, Germany.

History of St. Charles, Montgomery, & Warren Counties, Missouri. St. Louis: National Historical Co., 1885. Reprint, St. Louis: Paul V. Cochrane, 1969.

Kirchenbuch der St. Reinoldi-Gemeinde. Nr. 7, 1838; Nr. 8, 1838. Kirchenkreis Dortmund-Mitte. Kreiskirchen Amt. Dortmund, Germany.

Knörich, Wilhelm. *Mitteilungen über die städtische höhere Mädchenschule zu Dortmund—zur Feier des 25 jährigen Bestehens (1867–1892)*. Dortmund: Hermann Meyer, 1892.

Krekel, Arnold. Papers. St. Charles County Historical Society Archives, St. Charles, Missouri.

Mallinckrodt, Adolph, Corporal, Co. L & I, 3rd Regiment Missouri Infantry. Compiled service records of volunteer Union soldiers who served in organizations from the state of Missouri. National Archives Microfilm Publication 405, roll 413, Record Group 94. Washington, D.C.

————, Sgt., Co. E, Krekel's Battn. U.S. Res. Corps, Missouri Infantry. Compiled service records of volunteer Union soldiers who served in organizations from the state of Missouri. National Archives Microfilm Publication 405, roll 702, Record Group 94. Washington, D.C.

————, 2nd Lt., Soldier's Certificate No. 610, 950, Co. F., 1 Prov. En. Mo. Mil. Case files of approved pension applications of veterans who served in the Army and Navy mainly in the Civil War and the War with Spain, 1861–1934. National Archives, Record Group 15. Washington, D.C.

Mallinckrodt, Anita. Mallinckrodt family memorabilia. Augusta, Missouri.

Mallinckrodt, Conrad, Corp., Capt. New's Co. (A), Home Guard Regiment, Missouri Home Guard. Compiled service records of volunteer Union soldiers who served in organizations from the state of Missouri. National Archives Microfilm Publication 405, roll 714, Record Group 94. Washington, D.C.

————. "Deutsche Knaben- und Mädchen-Erziehungs-Anstalt, am Missouri, zu Dortmund, St. Charles Co." *Anzeiger des Westens*, 15 September 1838.

————. "Field Notes, 1847." Hubert E. Mallinckrodt, Mallinckrodt family memorabilia. Augusta, Missouri.

————. "Register of Marriages Solemnized before Conrad Mallinckrodt as Justice of the Peace for and within the County of St. Charles, Missouri." Earl Mallinckrodt, Mallinckrodt family memorabilia. Augusta, Missouri.

Mallinckrodt, Earl. Mallinckrodt family memorabilia. Augusta, Missouri.

Mallinckrodt, Edward, Jr. Papers. Western Historical Manuscript Collection No. 452. University of Missouri, St. Louis.

Mallinckrodt, Emil. Papers. Missouri Historical Society Archives, St. Louis.

————. Scrapbook (Collection of *Westliche Post* articles). Accompanying index, "Emil Mallinckrodt im Spiegel seiner Zeitungs-Veröffentlichungen," edited by Kurt Müller von Blumencron, Hamburg, 1951. Mallinckrodt Family Papers, Missouri Historical Society Archives, St. Louis.

Mallinckrodt Family Papers 1809–1852 (original letters, transcriptions, translations). Missouri Historical Society Archives, St. Louis. (Transcriptions also in Kurt von Mallinckrodt's monograph, *Die Auswanderer der Familie Mallinckrodt*, Historisches Archiv, Köln, Germany.)

Mallinckrodt Genealogy, Tables I–XI. Stadtarchiv, Dortmund, Germany.

von Mallinckrodt, Gustav, ed. *Urkundenbuch der Familie von Mallinckrodt*. 2 vols. Bonn: Carl Georgi Universitäts-Buchdruckerei u. Verlag, 1911.

Mallinckrodt, Gustavus. Letters from St. Paul (Minn.). Western Historical Manuscript Collection No. 452 (Edward Mallinckrodt, Jr., Papers), Folder 90 (1863), Folder 91 (1864). University of Missouri, St. Louis.

von Mallinckrodt, Horst-Gerhard. "Die Reformation in Dortmund und unsere Familie." Typescript. Hamburg 1977; revised 1988.

Mallinckrodt, Hubert E. Mallinckrodt family memorabilia. Augusta, Missouri.

Mallinckrodt, James F. Company F, 3d U.S.R.C. Missouri Inf. Compiled service records of volunteer Union soldiers who served in organizations from the state of Missouri. National Archives Microfilm Publication 405, roll 402, Record Group 94. Washington, D.C.

————. Company D, 17th Mo. Infantry. Compiled service records of volunteer Union soldiers who served in organizations from the state of Missouri. National Archives Microfilm Publication 405, roll 513, Record Group 94. Washington, D.C.

————, 2 Lt., Soldier's Certificate No. 468441; Co. H, 17th Mo. Vol. Inf. Case files of approved pension applications of veterans who served in the Army and Navy mainly in the Civil War and the War with Spain 1861–1934. National Archives, Record Group 15. Washington, D.C.

Mallinckrodt, Johann Friedrich Theodor. "Für mich und die meinigen Merkwürdigen Nachrichten—Rechnungsbuch des Kaufmanns Johann Friedrich Mallinckrodt, jun. In Anhang." Stadtarchiv, Bestand 333 (Familie Mallinckrodt). Dortmund, Germany.

Mallinckrodt, John F. "Automatic Car Brake of the Mallinckrodt Brake Co. of St. Louis." Earl Mallinckrodt, Mallinckrodt family memorabilia. Augusta, Missouri.

Mallinckrodt, Julius, Private, Capt. New's Co. (A), Home Guard Regiment, Missouri Home Guard. Compiled service records of volunteer Union soldiers who served in organizations from the state of Missouri. National Archives Microfilm Publication 405, roll 714, Record Group 94. Washington, D.C.

von Mallinckrodt, Kurt. *Die Auswanderer der Familie Mallinckrodt*. Monograph. Hünxe/ Krudenburg, Germany, 1990. Historisches Archiv, von Mallinckrodt Nachlaß (closed archive). Köln, Germany.

———. *Sippendatei derer von Mallinckrodt*. Monograph. Hünxe/Krudenburg, Germany, 1989. Historisches Archiv, Köln, Germany; St. Louis Historical Society, St. Louis.

———. "Transcription of Notary Public Testimony in *Urkundenbuch der Familie von Mallinckrodt*, Vol. 2, 83ff. (No. 139)." Typescript. Hünxe/Krudenburg, Germany, 1987.

Mallinckrodt, Philip A. Mallinckrodt family memorabilia. Salt Lake City, Utah.

von Mallinckrodt Nachlaß. Closed archives, Historisches Archiv, Abt. 1068. Köln, Germany.

Meyer, A. C. "Mallinckrodt Chemical Works." In *The Earlier Years of the Drug and Allied Trades in the Mississippi Valley*. St. Louis, 1948, 71–74. (Privately printed; available in Missouri Historical Society Archives, St. Louis.)

Münch, Friedrich. Account Books—August Mallinckrodt, 1847–1848. Missouri Historical Society Archives, St. Louis.

Probate Office, St. Charles County Circuit Court, St. Charles Missouri. Conrad Mallinckrodt Estate, 1887, box 89, file 2124.

Railroads Collection. *The St. Louis Evening News*, 2 November 1855; Passenger Letter, 2 November 1855. Missouri Historical Society Archives, St. Louis.

Recorder of Deeds, St. Charles County. St. Charles, Missouri.

(a) Emil and Julius Mallinckrodt 1832 Land Purchase (41.34 acres in Southern fractional half of Section 15, Township 44 North, Range 1) from United States. Land Patent No. 3211. Filed 9 September 1835, Book V, no. 2, 235.

(b) Julius Mallinckrodt 1832 Land Purchase (151.32 acres) from Louis Eversmann. U.S. Land Patent No. 2593 of 11 February 1832, Book 76, 31. Filed 10 March 1834, Book K, 218.

(c) Emil Mallinckrodt Land Sale to Julius Mallinckrodt. Filed 1836, Book K, 217.

(d) Town of Dortmund. Township Plats Book 2 (28 May 1836). Book K, 223–24 (7 June 1836).

(e) Town of Dortmund Revision. Book D, 27 (1 July 1836).

(f) Dortmund Lot Sales. Direct Index 1804–1852, Books K–S.

(g) Mount Pleasant. Township Plats Book 2 (27 April 1836). Book K, 200 (17 September 1836).

(h) Julius Mallinckrodt Land Sale to Conrad Mallinckrodt (8 June 1850). Book B, no. 2, 330.

(i) Conrad Mallinckrodt's Land Purchases. Inverted Index, 1804–70. Book U, 224, 1848–1849; Direct Index, 1804–1852. Book B–2, 330–31, 1853–1854.

(j) Town of Augusta. St. Charles County Township Plats Book 2, 4, 7.

(k) Julius Mallinckrodt Purchase of Eversmann Land (18 acres) at Tax Sale. Book V, no. 2, 237.

(l) Julius Mallinckrodt's Deeds/Will. No. 4288 Abstract of Title to Part East 1/2 Section 22. Township 44 North, Range 1 East, St. Charles County, Missouri.

(m) Sale of Land by Dorchen and Henry Sehrt to Albert F. Mallinckrodt, 20 June 1890. Book 43, 361.

(n) Sale of Land by Hermann Adolf Mallinckrodt to Albert F. Mallinckrodt, 1903. Book 83, 548.

(o) Sale of Land by Julius Mallinckrodt Heirs to Albert F. Mallinckrodt, 8 May 1903. Book 83, 548.

(p) Direct Index 1804–1852, Books K–S.

(q) Inverted Index 1804–1870, Book U.

(r) Marriage Book II, 1826–1844.

St. Charles County, Missouri. *Atlas 1875.*

St. Charles County, Missouri. *Atlas 1903.*

St. Charles County, Missouri. 1876 Census. St. Charles County Historical Society Archives, St. Charles, Missouri.

St. Charles Papers. Julius Mallinckrodt. Missouri Historical Society Archives, St. Louis.

U.S. Bureau of the Census. State of Missouri, County of St. Charles, Township of Femme Osage. National Archives, Record Group 29. Washington, D.C.

(a) *Fifth Census of the United States, 1830.* National Archives Microfilm Publication M19, roll 268, Record Group 29. Washington, D.C.

(b) *Sixth Census of the United States, 1840.* National Archives Microfilm Publication M704, roll 230, Record Group 29.

(c) *Seventh Census of the United States, 1850.* National Archives Microfilm Publication M432, roll 413, Record Group 29; slave schedules, roll 424, Record Group 29.

(d) *Eighth Census of the United States, 1860.* National Archives Microfilm Publication M653, roll 644, Record Group 29; slave schedules, roll 664, Record Group 29.

(e) *Ninth Census of the United States, 1870.* National Archives Microfilm Publication M593, roll 806, Record Group 29.

———. State of Missouri, St. Louis City. National Archives, Record Group 29. Washington, D.C.

(a) *Eighth Census of the United States, 1860.* Microfilm Publication M653, roll 649, 4th Ward, Record Group 29.

(b) *Ninth Census of the United States, 1870.* Microfilm Publication M593, roll 822, 12th Ward, Record Group 29.

———. *Seventh Census 1850: Statistical View, Compendium.* Washington, D.C.: Beverly Tucker, Senate Printer, 1854.

———. *Eighth Census 1860: Population of the United States in 1860.* Washington, D.C.: GPO, 1864.

———. *Historical Statistics of the United States, Colonial Times to 1970.* Bicentennial edition, part 1. Washington, D.C.: GPO, 1975.

War of the Rebellion. Official Records of the Union and Confederate Armies. Series 1–4. Washington, D.C.: GPO, 1880–1900.

Wencker, Carl. "Day Book" (1872). Betty Boffa, town of Augusta memorabilia. Augusta, Missouri.

Bibliography

Newspaper Files, Newspaper Reports

Anzeiger des Westens (St. Louis), 1839–1869. State Historical Society of Missouri, Columbia.

Boulder Daily Camera (Boulder, Colorado), 1895. Denver Public Library.

Bower, Carolyn, Louis J. Rose, and Theresa Tighe. "Atomic Waste Is One Legacy of a St. Louis Firm's Patriotic Work." *St. Louis Post-Dispatch*, 13 February 1989.

———. "Some Feared for Health of Ore Handlers." *St. Louis Post-Dispatch*, 14 February 1989.

Dortmunder Wochenblatt. Institut für Zeitungsforschung, Dortmund.

"Edward Mallinckrodt Jr. Dies; Industrialist and Civic Leader." *St. Louis Post-Dispatch*, 19 January 1967.

Garg, Wilhelm. "Zeichen der unendlichen Liebe Gottes." *Mindener-Tageblatt* (Minden, Westphalia), 1–2 April 1988.

Licht-Freund (Hermann, Missouri), 1843–1845. State Historical Society of Missouri, Columbia.

Matthews, Curt. "Chain Reaction at Mallinckrodt." *St. Louis Post-Dispatch*, 2 July 1967.

Maurmann, Ernst. "Dr. Arnold Mallinckrodt (1768–1825)." *Tremonia* (Dortmund, Germany), 27 June–4 July 1913.

Mississippi Blätter (St. Louis), 1858. Missouri Historical Society, St. Louis.

Rauch, Mrs. Ted. "Seventieth Birthday for County Court House." *St. Charles (Missouri) Journal*, 31 December 1973.

St. Charles (Missouri) Cosmos, 1882. St. Charles County Historical Society Archives.

St. Charles (Missouri) Demokrat, 1852–1888. State Historical Society of Missouri Microfilms.

"Scandinavian in Origin." *Washington Post*, 23 March 1989.

Schiermeier, J. W. (Bill). "Cracker Barrel News." *Washington Missourian*, 18 January 1989.

———. "Touring Nineteenth Century Augusta." *Wentzville (Missouri) Messenger-Tribune*, 26 September 1979.

Thörner, Friedrich. "Brände und Verwüstungen gehörten zur Geschichte der 'Burg Mallinckrodt.' " *Westfälischer Rundschau*, 4 January 1979.

———. "Viele Geschichten um Schloß Mallinckrodt (I)." *Westfälische Rundschau*, 11 March 1988.

———. "Über Schloß Mallinckrodt (II)." *Westfälischer Rundschau*, 17 March 1988.

Washington Missourian. "Augusta Remembered—By Its Oldest Living Resident." 24 August, 31 August, 7 September 1967.

———. "Augusta's Centennial Celebration Begins Friday." 16 June 1955.

———. "A Book Played Vital Part in Augusta's History." 24 August 1950.

———. "Missouri River High Stages." 11–12 October 1986.

———. "150 Years Anniversary of Evangelical Synod Marked." 10 October 1990.

———. "Price's Rebels Hit City in October, 1864." 24 May 1989.

———. "Restored Gazebo Reflects Bygone Era." 6 September 1989.

Westliche Post (St. Louis), 1857–1892. Missouri Historical Society, St. Louis.

Books and Articles

Anderson, Galusha. *The Story of a Border City During the Civil War*. Boston: Little, Brown, 1908.

Assig, Ottilie. "Die Deutschen in Missouri." In *Was die Deutschen aus Amerika berichteten 1828–1865*, ed. Maria Wagner, 312–15. Stuttgart: Verlag Hans-Dieter Heinz Akademischer Verlag, 1985.

Auswanderung Bremen—USA. Bremerhaven, Germany: Deutsches Schiffarhtsmuseum, 1976.

Barclay, Thomas S. *The Liberal Republican Movement in Missouri 1865–1871*. Columbia: State Historical Society of Missouri, 1926.

Bek, William G. "The Followers of Duden." *Missouri Historical Review*, October 1919–July 1924.

———. *The German Settlement Society of Philadelphia and Its Colony Hermann, Missouri*. Ph.D. diss., University of Pennsylvania, 1905–1907. Reprint, Hermann, Missouri: Historic Hermann, Inc., 1984. Trans. Elmer Danuser. Ed. Dorothy Heckmann Shrader.

Belcher, Wyatt Winton. *The Economic Rivalry Between St. Louis and Chicago 1850–1880*. Studies in History, Economics, and Public Law No. 529. New York: Columbia University Press, 1947.

von den Berken, Robert. *Dortmunder Häuserbuch von 1700 bis 1850*. Wattenscheid, Germany: Karl Busch Verlag, 1927.

Bey, William Van Ness. *The Bench and Bar of Missouri*. St. Louis: Thomas & Co., 1878.

Blair, Francis Preston. *Frémont's Hundred Days in Missouri, Speech of Hon. F. P. Blair, Jr., of Missouri, on Frémont's Defense; Delivered in the House of Representatives, March 7, 1862*. Washington: Congressional Globe Office, 1862.

Blake, Nelson Manfred. *The Road to Reno: A History of Divorce in the United States*. New York: Macmillan, 1962.

Böhme, Albin. "Temperanz." In *Was die Deutschen aus Amerika berichteten 1828–1865*, ed. Maria Wagner, 288–92. Stuttgart: Verlag Hans-Dieter Heinz Akademischer Verlag, 1985.

Bolege-Vieweg, Dore. *Straßen erzählen Stadtgeschichte*. Dortmund: Dortmund in Wort & Bild, [1985].

Börnstein, Heinrich. "Apriltage in Missouri." In *Land Ohne Nachtigall—Deutsche Emigranten in Amerika 1777–1886*, ed. Rolf Weber, 258–72. Berlin: Buchverlag Der Morgen, 1981.

Breslow, Lori. *Small Town*. St. Charles, Missouri: John J. Buse Historical Museum, 1977.

Bretting, Agnes. "Deutschsprachige Auswandererliteratur im 19. Jahrhundert: Information oder Spiegel der Träuma?" In *Einwandererland USA-Gastarbeiterland BRD*, ed. Dirk Hoerder and Diethelm Knauf, 63–71. Berlin and Hamburg: Argument Verlag, Argument Sonderband AS 163, 1988.

Brinkmann, Albrecht. *Geschichte der Dortmunder Volksschulen*. Dortmund: Verlag von Fr. Wilh. Ruhfus, 1951.

Brownlee, Richard S. *Gray Ghosts of the Confederacy: Guerrilla Warfare in the West, 1861–1865*. Baton Rouge: Louisiana State University Press, 1958.

Bumke, Joachim. *Höfische Kultur. Literatur und Gesellschaft im hohen Mittelalter*. 4th ed. 2 vols. Munich: Deutscher Taschenbuch Verlag GmbH KG, 1987.

Burton, William L. *Melting Pot Soldiers*. Ames: Iowa State University Press, 1988.

Catton, Bruce. *The Coming Fury*. Vol. 1 of *The Centennial History of the Civil War*. Garden City, N.Y.: Doubleday, 1961.

Chase-Riboud, Barbara. *Echo of Lions*. New York: William Morrow, 1989.

Clark, Dan Elbert. *The Middle West in American History*. New York: Thomas Y. Crowell, 1937.

Clemen, Paul, ed. *Die Kunstdenkmäler der Stadt Köln.* Vol. 2. Düsseldorf: Verlag von L. Schwann, 1934.

Collier's Encyclopedia. New York: P. F. Collier, 1984.

Columbia Encyclopedia. 3d ed. New York: Columbia University Press, 1963.

"Conrad T. Mallinckrodt." In *Portrait and Biographical Record of St. Charles, Lincoln, and Warren Counties, Missouri,* 335–36. Chicago: Chapman Publishing, 1895.

Conversations-Lexikon. Allgemeine deutsche Real-Encyklopädie für die gebildeten Stände. 7th ed. Leipzig: F. U. Brockhaus, 1830.

Conze, Werner, and Volker Hentschel, eds. *Ploetz Deutsche Geschichte. Epochen und Daten.* 4th ed. Freiburg/Würzburg: Verlag Ploetz, 1988.

Conzen, Kathleen Neils. "Germans." In *Harvard Encyclopedia of American Ethnic Groups,* ed. Stephan Thernstrom, 405–25. Cambridge: Harvard University Press, 1980.

Cooper, James Fenimore. *The Last of the Mohicans.* New York: Dodd, Mead, 1951.

Culmer, Frederic A. *A History of Missouri for High Schools.* Mexico, Missouri: McIntyre Publishing, 1939.

Daniel Boone Region of Missouri. Jefferson City: Missouri State Division of Resources and Development, [early 1950s].

Denny, Jim. "The War Within the State." *Missouri Resource Review,* 10, no. 2 (summer 1993):14–19.

Detjen, David W. *The Germans in Missouri, 1900–1918: Prohibition, Neutrality, and Assimilation.* Columbia: University of Missouri Press, 1985.

Duden, Gottfried. *Bericht über eine Reise nach den westlichen Staaten Nordamerika's und einen mehrjährigen Aufenthalt am Missouri (in den Jahren 1824, 25, 26 und 1827) in Bezug auf Auswanderung und Übervölkerung.* Elberfeld: Sam Lucas, 1829.

———. "Gottfried Duden's 'Report,' 1824–1827." Trans. William G. Bek. *Missouri Historical Review,* 12, no. 1 (October 1917): 1–21; no. 2 (January 1918): 81–89; no. 3 (April 1918): 163–79; no. 4 (July 1918): 258–70.

———. *Report on a Journey to the Western States of North America—and a Stay of Several Years along the Missouri (During the Years 1824, 25, 26, and 1827).* Trans. James W. Goodrich, general editor, et al. Columbia: University of Missouri Press, 1980.

Eisenhower, John S. D. *So Far from God: The U.S. War with Mexico, 1846–1848.* New York: Random, 1989.

Encyclopedia Americana. International ed. Danbury, Conn.: Grolier, 1989.

English, William Francis. *The Pioneer Lawyer and Jurist in Missouri.* University of Missouri Studies 21, no. 2. Columbia, 1947.

Ennen, Edith. *Frauen im Mittelalter.* 3d ed. Munich: C. H. Beck Verlag, 1987.

Erdbrink, F., and F. Barich. "Verzeichnis der Lehrer und Leherinnen an die evangelischen Volksschulen zu Dortmund 1570–1 Juli 1913." In *Beiträge zur Geschichte Dortmunds und der Grafschaft Mark* (Dortmund, Germany), 23 (1914): 170ff.

Esser, Helmut. "Das Dortmunder Gymnasium in den ersten Jahrzehnten des 19. Jahrhunderts." In *Beiträge zur Geschichte Dortmunds und der Grafschaft Mark* (Dortmund, Germany), 73 (1981): 9–138.

Eulenstein, Friedrich. "Die siedlungsgeographische Entwicklung Dortmunds." In *Beiträge zur Geschichte Dortmunds und der Grafschaft Mark* (Dortmund, Germany), 55 (1958): 115ff.

Fellman, Michael. *Inside War: The Guerrilla Conflict in Missouri During the American Civil War.* New York: Oxford University Press, 1989.

Firmenich, Heinz. "St. Maria-Ablaß-Kapelle." In *Rheinische Kunststätten*, 1969–72 ed. Köln/Deutz: Rheinischer Verein für Denkmalpflege und Heimatschutz, nos. 7–9 (1970): 26–30.

Foley, William E. *The Genesis of Missouri: From Wilderness Outpost to Statehood*. Columbia: University of Missouri Press, 1989.

Foner, Eric. *Reconstruction: America's Unfinished Revolution, 1863–1877*. New York: Harper and Row, 1988.

Foner, Eric, and Olivia Mahoney. *A House Divided: America in the Age of Lincoln*. New York: Norton, 1990.

Forster, Walter O. *Zion on the Mississippi: The Settlement of the Saxon Lutherans in Missouri, 1839–1841*. St. Louis: Concordia Publishing, 1953.

Fremantle, Anne. *Age of Faith*. Great Ages of Man series. New York: Time-Life Books, 1965.

Fremont, Jessie Benton. *The Story of the Guard: A Chronicle of the War*. Boston: Ticknor and Fields, 1863.

Gay, Peter. *Age of Enlightenment*. Great Ages of Man series. New York: Time-Life Books, 1966.

———. *The Enlightenment: An Interpretation*. 2 vols. New York: Alfred A. Knopf, 1966, 1969.

Gillespie, W. M. *Treatise on Land-Surveying*. New York: D. Appleton, 1855.

Göbel, Gert. *Länger als ein Menschenleben in Missouri*. St. Louis: Witter's Buchhandlung, 1877.

Gustorf, Fred. *The Uncorrupted Heart: Journal and Letters of Frederick Julius Gustorf 1800–1845*. Columbia: University of Missouri Press, 1969.

Haase-Faulenorth, Berthold A. "Der Traum von New Dortmund." In *Beiträge zur Geschichte Dortmunds und der Grafschaft Mark* (Dortmund, Germany), 54 (1958): 219–34.

Handlin, Oscar. *The Uprooted*. New York: Grosset & Dunlap, 1951.

Harrison, Samuel F. *History of Hermann, Missouri*. Hermann: Historic Hermann, Inc., 1966.

Hartmann, Heinz. " 'Auf Jahr und Tag' in Dortmund (1480)." West German Radio/Schulfunk (Köln), 7 July 1964.

Hatch, Azel F. *Statutes and Constitutional Provisions Regarding Libel and Slander*. Brooklyn: Press and Eagle, 1895.

Hayes, Carlton J. H., Marshall Whithed Baldwin, and Charles Woolsey Cole. *History of Europe*. New York: Macmillan, 1950.

Heard, Franklin Fiske. *A Treatise on the Law of Libel and Slander*. Lowell, Mass.: Fischer A. Hildreth, 1860.

Helbich, W., W. D. Kamphoefner, and U. Sommer. *Briefe aus Amerika. Deutsche Auswanderer schreiben aus der Neuen Welt 1830–1930*. Munich: Verlag C. H. Beck, 1988.

Helbich, Wolfgang J. *"Alle Menschen sind dort gleich . . ." Die deutsch Amerika-Auswanderung im 19. und 20. Jahrhundert*. Düsseldorf: Pädagogischer Verlag Schwann-Bagel GmbH, 1988.

Henne, Carl Schulze. *Haus Küchen*. Ahlen, Germany: Everhard Sommer KG, 1979.

Hokombe and Adams. *An Account of the Battle of Wilson's Creek*. Springfield, Missouri: Springfield Public Library/Green County Historical Society, 1961.

Howard, John Raymond. *Remembrance of Things Past*. New York: Thomas Y. Crowell, 1925.

Hulbert, Archer Butler. *The Cumberland Road*. Vol. 10 of *Historic Highways of America*. New York: AMS Press, 1971.

Jackson, Donald. *Voyages of the Steamboat "Yellow Stone."* New York: Ticknor & Fields, 1985.

Jellinghaus, H. "Der Name Dortmund." In *Beiträge zur Geschichte Dortmunds und der Grafschaft Mark* (Dortmund, Germany), 26 (1919): 119–27.

Kamphoefner, Walter D. *The Westfalians: From Germany to Missouri*. Princeton: Princeton University Press, 1987.

Keith, Robert C. *Baltimore Harbor: A Picture History*. Baltimore: Ocean World Publishing, 1982.

Kersting, Bernd. "Grabplatten ehrten verdiente Dortmunder." *Heimat Dortmund* (1986): 16–19.

———. "Die Grabplatten in der Ev. St. Marienkirche zu Dortmund." In *Roland zu Dortmund* 7, no. 3 (1986): 42–46.

Kirchoff, Hans Georg. "Die Dortmunder Große Fehde 1388/89." In *Dortmund 1100 Jahre Stadtgeschichte*, ed. Gustav Luntowski and Norbert Reimann, 107–28. Dortmund: Verlag Fr. Wilh. Ruhfus, 1982.

Kleppner, Paul. *The Cross of Culture: A Social Analysis of Midwestern Politics 1850–1900*. New York: Free Press, 1970.

Laver, James. *The Concise History of Costume and Fashion*. New York: Abrams, 1969.

Lieber, Francis. "Die Frauen." In *Was die Deutschen aus Amerika berichteten 1828–1865*, ed. Maria Wagner, 9–15. Stuttgart: Verlag Hans-Dieter Heinz Akademischer Verlag, 1985.

Luebke, Frederick C., ed. *Ethnic Voters and the Election of Lincoln*. Lincoln: University of Nebraska Press, 1971.

Luntowski, Gustav. "Arnold Mallinckrodt." In vol. 15 of *Westfälische Lebensbilder*, ed. Robert Stupperich, 91–107. Münster: Aschendorff Verlag, 1990.

———. "Arnold Mallinckrodt (1768–1825), ein Vertreter des frühen Liberalismus in Westfalen." In *Beiträge zur Geschichte Dortmunds und der Grafschaft Mark* (Dortmund, Germany), 73 (1981): 283–99.

McClure, Clarence H. *History of Missouri*. Chicago and New York: A. S. Barnes, 1920.

McCormack, Thomas J., ed. *Memoirs of Gustave Koerner, 1809–1896*. Vol. 2. Cedar Rapids: Torch Press, 1909.

McCreary, Edward, and Wilbur Cross. *The Story of Mallinckrodt: Company in Transition 1867–1967*. St. Louis: Mallinckrodt, Inc., 1967.

McLellan, David. *Karl Marx: His Life and Thought*. New York: Harper and Row, 1973.

"Mallinckrodt." In *Allgemeine Deutsche Biographie* 20:141–45. Leipzig: Verlag von Duncker & Humblot, 1884.

"Mallinckrodt." In *Neue Deutsche Biographie* 15:730–36. Berlin: Duncker & Humblot, 1987.

Mallinckrodt, Anita M. *How They Came: German Immigration from Prussia to Missouri*. Washington, D.C.: Mallinckrodt Communications Research, 1989.

———. *Why They Left: German Immigration from Prussia to Missouri*. 2d rev. ed. Washington, D.C.: Mallinckrodt Communications Research, 1989.

von Mallinckrodt, Dietrich. "Die Burgmannen von Mesekenwerke und Mallingrode zu Volmestein und Wetter an der Ruhr. Ursprung und älteste Geschichte der von Mallinckrodt." In *Jahrbuch des Vereins für Orts- und Heimatkunde, in der Grafschaft Mark, mit dem Sitz in Witten an der Ruhr* (Witten-Ruhr, Germany) 65 (1966): 9–34.

———. "Das Rittergut Mallinckrodt und die Grundherrschaft der von Mallinckrodt." In

Jahrbuch des Vereins für Orts- und Heimatkunde, in der Graftschaft Mark, mit dem Sitz in Witten an der Ruhr (Witten-Ruhr, Germany) 71 (1973): 1–125.

———. "Die von Mallinckrodt zu Steinberg und ihre Nachkommen in Dortmund und Paderborn." In *Beiträge zur Geschichte Dortmunds und der Grafschaft Mark* (Dortmund, Germany), 78 (1987): 31–73.

von Mallinckrodt, Gustav. "Die Dortmunder Rathslinie seit dem Jahre 1500." In *Beiträge zur Geschichte Dortmunds und der Grafschaft Mark* (Dortmund, Germany), 6 (1895): v–147.

Mallinckrodt Chemical Co. *Mallinckrodt Magazine: 1867–1967, 100th Anniversary*, 12, nos. 10–11. St. Louis: Mallinckrodt Chemical Co., 1967.

Malone, Dumas. *Jefferson the Virginian*. Boston: Little, Brown, 1948.

Marshall, Howard Wight, and James W. Goodrich, eds. *The German-American Experience in Missouri*. Columbia: University of Missouri–Columbia Extension Division, 1986.

von Martels, Heinrich. *Briefe über die westlichen Theile der Vereinigten Staaten von Nordamerika*. Osnabruck, Germany, 1834.

Masterson, V. V. *The Katy Railroad and the Last Frontier*. Norman: University of Oklahoma Press, 1952.

Maurmann, Ernst. "Arnold Mallinckrodt: Sein Leben und Wirken (1768–1825)." Ph.D. diss. University of Münster, 1921. (Dortmund Stadtarchiv Library, Department of Handwritten Materials.)

Meininghaus, August. "Die Dortmunder Magistratslinie von 1803 bis 1918." In *Beiträge zur Geschichte Dortmunds und der Grafschaft Mark* (Dortmund, Germany), 26 (1919): 1–60.

———. "Das Haus 'zum Rehfuß' am Westenhellweg." In *Die Heimat, Beilage zur Zeitung Tremonia* (Dortmund, Germany), 22 November 1925.

———. "Der soziale Aufsteig der Dortmunder Mallinckrodt." In *Beiträge zur Geschichte Dortmunds und der Grafschaft Mark* (Dortmund, Germany), 44 (1938): 373–417.

———. "Das Wein- und Gasthaus 'Der Rehfuß' am Westenhellweg zu Dortmund." In *Tremonia* (Dortmund, Germany), 2 July 1933.

Meyer, Duane. *The Heritage of Missouri*. 3d ed. St. Louis: River City Publishers, Ltd., 1982.

Morison, Samuel Eliot. *The Oxford History of the American People*. New York: Oxford University Press, 1965.

Morison, Samuel E., and Henry S. Commager. *The Growth of the American Republic*. Vol. 1. New York: Oxford University Press, 1956.

Morris, Richard B., ed. *Encyclopedia of American History*. Rev. ed. New York: Harper and Brothers, 1961.

Münch, Friedrich. "Die Duden'sche Niederlaßungen in Missouri." *Der Deutsche Pionier* (Cincinnati) 2 (September 1870): 197–202.

———. *Gesammelte Schriften*. St. Louis: Verlag C. Witter, 1902.

———. "Noch ein gräßlicher Auftritt." In *Der Deutsche Pionier* (Cincinnati) 1 (January 1870): 341–42.

———. *Der Staat Missouri*. St. Louis: Ed. Bühler & Co., 1859.

Nagel, Paul C. *Missouri: A Bicentennial History*. The States and the Nation series. New York: Norton, 1977.

Nevins, Allan. *Frémont, Pathmaker of the West*. New York: Longmans, Green, 1955.

———. *The War for the Union*. Vol. 2. New York: Scribner's, 1960.

Newell, Martin L. *The Law of Defamation, Libel, and Slander*. Chicago: Callaghan, 1890.

Parrish, William E. *Missouri under Radical Rule 1865–1870*. Columbia: University of Missouri Press, 1965.

———. *Turbulent Partnership: Missouri and the Union 1861–1865*. Columbia: University of Missouri Press, 1963.

Paxson, Frederic L. *History of the American Frontier*. Cambridge: Houghton Mifflin, 1924.

Petermann, Gerd Alfred. "Friends of Light (Lichtfreunde): Friedrich Münch, Paul Follenius, and the Rise of German-American Rationalism on the Missouri Frontier." In *Yearbook of German-American Studies* 23 (1988): 110–39. Lawrence, Kansas: Society for German-American Studies.

Phillips, Claude Anderson. *A History of Education in Missouri*. Jefferson City, Missouri: Hugh Stephens Printing, 1911.

Phistere, Frederick. *The Army in the Civil War: Statistical Record of the Armies of the United States*. Vol. 13. New York: Charles Scribner's Sons, 1882.

Politische Journal. Vol. 20. Hamburg: Hoffman Buchhandlung, 1803.

Preuss, Traute. *Starkes schwaches Geschlecht. Weg und Leistung der Frau*. Hamm, Germany: G. Grote, 1956.

Primm, James Neal. Introduction to *Germans for a Free Missouri*, ed. Steven Rowan. Columbia: University of Missouri Press, 1983.

van Ravenswaay, Charles. *The Arts and Architecture of German Settlements in Missouri: A Survey of a Vanishing Culture*. Columbia: University of Missouri Press, 1977.

Reimann, Norbert. *Königshof-Pfalz-Reichsstadt: Bilder und Text zur Entstehung der Stadt Dortmund*. Dortmund: Stadtarchiv Dortmund, no. 7, 1984.

Rowan, Steven, "German Language Newspapers in St. Louis, 1835–1974." In *The German-American Experience in Missouri*, ed. Howard Wight Marshall and James W. Goodrich, 45–60. Columbia: University of Missouri–Columbia Extension Division, 1986.

———, ed. *Germans for a Free Missouri: Translations from the St. Louis Radical Press, 1857–1862*. Columbia: University of Missouri Press, 1983.

Rübel, Karl. "Die Bürgerlisten der Frei- und Reichstadt Dortmund." In *Beiträge zur Geschichte Dortmunds und der Grafschaft Mark* (Dortmund, Germany), 12 (1903): 33–210.

———. "Die Dortmunder Morgensprachen." In *Beiträge zur Geschichte Dortmunds und der Grafschaft Mark* (Dortmund, Germany), 9 (1900): 1–40.

Savage, George. *A Concise History of Interior Decoration*. New York: Grosset and Dunlap, 1966.

Schafer, Joseph, ed. and trans. *Intimate Letters of Carl Schurz 1841–1869*. New York: Da Capo, 1970.

Schiermeier, J. W. (Bill). "The Nahms and Augusta Wine." In *Cracker Barrel Country* (New Melle, Missouri) 3: 130–33.

Schlenke, Manfred, ed. *Preußen-Ploetz*. Freiburg/Würzburg: Verlag Ploetz, 1983.

Schmidt, Ferdinand. "Wilhelm von Mallinckrodt, ein Kriegsmann des Herzogs von Geldern-Egmont." *Beiträge zur Geschichte der Familie von Mallinckrodt*, no. 2. Arnheim, Holland: S. Gouda Quint Publishers, 1913.

Schmitz, Herman, ed. *The Encyclopedia of Furniture*. New York: Frederick A. Praeger, 1957.

Schneider, Carl E. *The German Church on the American Frontier*. St. Louis: Eden Publishing, 1939.

Scholle, Heinrich. *Dortmund im Jahre 1610. Maßstäblich Rekonstruktion des Stadtbildes*. Dortmund: Verlag des Historischen Vereins Dortmund, 1987.

Schroeder, Adolf E. "To Missouri, Where the Sun of Freedom Shines: Dream and Reality on the Western Frontier." In *The German-American Experience in Missouri*, ed. Howard Wight Marshall and James W. Goodrich, 1–24. Columbia: University of Missouri–Columbia Extension Division, 1986.

Schroeder, Adolf E., and Carla Schulz-Geisberg, eds. *Hold Dear, as Always: Jette, A German Immigrant Life in Letters*. Columbia: University of Missouri Press, 1988.

Schulte, Wilhelm. "Arnold Mallinckrodt." *Soester Heimatkalender* (1968): 56–57.

———. "Die Mallinckrodt." *Westfälische Köpfe. 300 Lebensbilder bedeutender Westfalen.* Münster, 1963, 189–92.

Shapiro, Michael Edward, et al. *George Caleb Bingham*. St. Louis: St. Louis Art Museum, 1990.

Stern, Gail F., ed. *Freedom's Doors: Immigrant Ports of Entry to the United States*. Philadelphia: The Balach Institute for Ethnic Studies, 1986.

Stone, Irving. *Immortal Wife: The Biographical Novel of Jessie Benton Fremont*. Garden City, N.Y.: Doubleday, Doran, 1944.

Strongwil, John [John F. Mallinckrodt]. *Your Sister's Keeper*. Salt Lake City: Equity Publishing, 1912.

Terral, Rufus. *The Missouri Valley*. New Haven: Yale University Press, 1947.

Trexler, Harrison Anthony. *Slavery in Missouri 1804–1865*. Johns Hopkins University Studies in Historical and Political Science, series 32, no. 2. Baltimore: Johns Hopkins Press, 1914.

Valentin, Veit. *The German People: Their History and Civilization from the Holy Roman Empire to the Third Reich*. New York: Alfred A. Knopf, 1946.

Voelske, A., and R. H. Tenbrock. *Urzeit-Mittelmeerkulturen und werdenes Abendland*. Paderborn/Hanover: Schönigh. Schroedel, 1970.

Weber-Kellermann, Ingeborg. *Frauenleben im 19. Jahrhundert*. Munich: Verlag C. H. Beck, 1983.

Wedmore, Delphine, S. C. C. *The Woman Who Couldn't Be Stopped*. N.p.: Sisters of Christian Charity, 1986.

Whedbee, T. Courtney J. *The Port of Baltimore in the Making, 1828–1878*. Baltimore: F. Bowie Smith & Sons, 1953.

Wherry, William Mackey. *The Campaign in Missouri and the Battle of Wilson's Creek, 1861*. Publications of the Missouri Historical Society, St. Louis, no. 1, 1880.

Wientzek, Horst. *Wetter—Stadt an der Ruhr. Eine Dokumentation in Schrift und Bild.* Wetter, Germany, n.d.

von Winterfeld, Luise. "Die Dortmunder Wandschneider-Gesellschaft. Quellen zur Geschichte des Tuchhandels in Dortmund." In *Beiträge zur Geschichte Dortmunds und der Grafschaft Mark* (Dortmund, Germany), 29–30 (1922): 1–337.

———. "Die Enstehung der Stadt Dortmund." In *Beiträge zur Geschichte Dortmunds und der Grafschaft Mark* (Dortmund, Germany), 48 (1950): 5–77.

Wittenborn Wiechens, Lucille, and Carrol Geerling. *Cemeteries of St. Charles County, Missouri*. Vol. 4. Bridgeton, Missouri: Lineage Press, 1988.

Wyman, Mark. *Immigrants in the Valley: Irish, Germans, and Americans in the Upper Mississippi Country 1830–1860*. Chicago: Nelson-Hale, 1984.

Zunkel, Friedrich. "Gustav Mallinckrodt (1799–1856)." In *Rheinisch Westfälische Wirtschaftsbiographien*, vol. 12, *Kölner Unternehmer im 18., 19. und 20. Jahrhundert*, 94–120. Münster: Aschendorffsche Verlagsbuchhandlung, 1986.

Index

Anita M. Mallinckrodt graduated from the University of Missouri with a bachelor of journalism degree and from The George Washington University (Washington, D.C.) with a masters degree in international affairs and a doctorate in political science. After working as a journalist at the U.S. Department of State and the U.S. Information Agency, she taught political science in Washington, D.C., retiring in 1992 as an adjunct professor from The American University. Beginning in the 1970s, she resided primarily in Cologne, Germany, working as a freelance radio journalist, as well as researching and publishing numerous articles and seven books about the German Democratic Republic. Her published works also include regional Missouri history brochures about German immigration, currently an intensified writing focus since she returned to the Midwest, to her residence Haus Dortmund near her hometown, Augusta.